Apple Pro Training Series

macOS Support Essentials 11

Supporting and Troubleshooting macOS Big Sur

Arek Dreyer and Adam Karneboge

Apple
Certified

macOS Support Essentials 11: Supporting and Troubleshooting macOS Big Sur – Apple Pro Training Series
Arek Dreyer and Adam Karneboge
Copyright © 2021 by Peachpit Press. All Rights Reserved.

Peachpit Press
www.peachpit.com
Peachpit Press is an imprint of Pearson Education, Inc.
To report errors, please send a note to errata@peachpit.com

Apple Series Editor: Laura Norman
Development Editor: Victor Gavenda
Senior Production Editor: Tracey Croom
Production Coordinator: Maureen Forys, Happenstance Type-O-Rama
Technical Editor: Steve Leebove
Apple Program Manager—Training and Certification: Drew Winkelman
Copy Editor: Elizabeth Welch
Proofreader: Scout Festa
Compositor: Cody Gates, Happenstance Type-O-Rama
Indexer: Valerie Perry
Cover Illustration: Von Glitschka
Cover Production: Cody Gates, Happenstance Type-O-Rama

IMPORTANT: Some of the exercises contained in this guide can be temporarily disruptive, and some exercises, if performed incorrectly, could result in data loss or damage to system files. As such, it's recommended that you perform these exercises on a Mac computer that is not critical to your daily productivity.

ISBN 13: 978-0-13-734595-3
ISBN 10: 0-13-734595-X

1 2021

Thanks to Heather Jagman for her love, support, and encouragement.

—*Arek Dreyer*

This book is dedicated to my father, who gave me the greatest gift anyone could give another person. He believed in me.

—*Adam Karneboge*

Acknowledgments Thank you, dear reader, for staying on top of what's new, while keeping your users' needs as the root of what you do.

Thanks to Tim Cook and everyone at Apple for always innovating.

Thank you to Kevin White, Gordon Davisson, and Susan Najour for all their foundational work.

Thank you to Steve Leebove for insightful technical editing and for going above and beyond.

Thank you to Craig Cohen for technical assistance.

Thank you to Schoun Regan, who reviewed this book at the request of Apple Training. His tenacity for accuracy is unmatched and you have a better guide because of that.

Thank you to the amazingly capable Laura Norman and Victor Gavenda for gently making sure these materials made it into your hands, and to Liz Welch, Scout Festa, and Maureen Forys and her team at Happenstance Type-O-Rama for working their editorial and production magic.

Thank you to the readers who sent corrections.

Thank you to the many contributors to the macadmins.org Slack instance for asking questions and answering questions.

Thanks to the people who generously provided feedback and assistance, including:

Mike Boylan	Rich Goon	Keith Mitnick
Tom Bridge	Steve Hayman	Ryan Pasch
Mark Buffington	Christopher Holmes	Timothy Perfitt
Craig Cohen	Kennedy Soo Hong	Vernon Rooze
Chris Dawe	Andre LaBranche	Sam Valencia
Charles Edge	Steve Leebove	Joan Work
Nat Fellows	Ben Levy	David Yoon
John Filardo	Michael Lynn	

Contents at a Glance

Apps and Processes

Network Configuration

Network Services

System Management

Table of Contents

Network Services

System Management

About This Guide

Audience

Whether you're an experienced system administrator or you just want to dig deeper into macOS, you'll learn to update, upgrade, reinstall, configure, maintain, diagnose, and troubleshoot macOS Big Sur.

You should be comfortable using a Mac before you read this guide. If you're not sure about basic Mac use, see "Mac Support" at support.apple.com/explore/new-to-mac.

How to Use the Guide

Use the reference sections to get familiar with macOS Big Sur. Then, use the exercises to practice what you've learned. After you've completed the guide, you should be able to:

- ▶ Explain how macOS Big Sur works
- ▶ Explain the best practices for updating, upgrading, reinstalling, configuring, and using macOS Big Sur
- ▶ Explain macOS Big Sur troubleshooting and repair procedures
- ▶ Use appropriate tools and techniques in macOS Big Sur to diagnose and resolve issues

Accessing the Web Edition and Lesson Files

Unless otherwise specified, references to macOS in this guide refer to macOS Big Sur 11.1. When you buy this guide from Peachpit (in any format), you automatically get access to its Web Edition.

If you bought an ebook from peachpit.com, your Web Edition will appear under the Digital Purchases tab on your Account page. If you bought an ebook from a different vendor or you bought a print book, you must register your purchase on peachpit.com to access the online content:

1   Go to www.peachpit.com/apts.macosBigSur.
2   Sign in or create a new account.
3   Enter ISBN: **9780137345953**.

4   Click Submit.

5   Answer the question as proof of purchase.

6   The lesson files can be accessed from the Registered Products tab on your Account page. Click the Access Bonus Content link below the title of your product to proceed to the download page. Click the lesson file link(s) to download them to your computer.

The Web Edition can be accessed from the Digital Purchases tab on your Account page. Click the Launch link to access the product.

Exercises

The exercises in this guide are designed for independent learners and require a dedicated Mac. If you use a Mac that is also used for daily productivity, the exercises will not work as expected and they might disrupt your Mac. To complete the exercises, ensure that you have the following:

▶   An Intel-based Mac that meets the requirements to install macOS Big Sur

▶   macOS Big Sur (see Exercise 2.3, "Erase a Mac and Install macOS Big Sur")

▶   A high-speed internet connection

▶   Lesson files (see "Accessing the Web Edition and Lesson Files," earlier)

▶   An Apple ID dedicated to your independent learning (you don't need to provide credit card information to get free apps from the App Store)

The following items are not required, but they can be helpful:

▶   An iCloud account associated with the Apple ID you use for your independent learning

▶   An erasable external storage disk with a capacity of at least 12 GB for Exercise 5.2, "Create a macOS Install Disk"

▶   At least two Wi-Fi networks (one should be visible)

▶   A Mac with all-flash storage

Additional Materials

Apple Support

The Apple Support website (support.apple.com) includes the latest free online Apple Support articles.

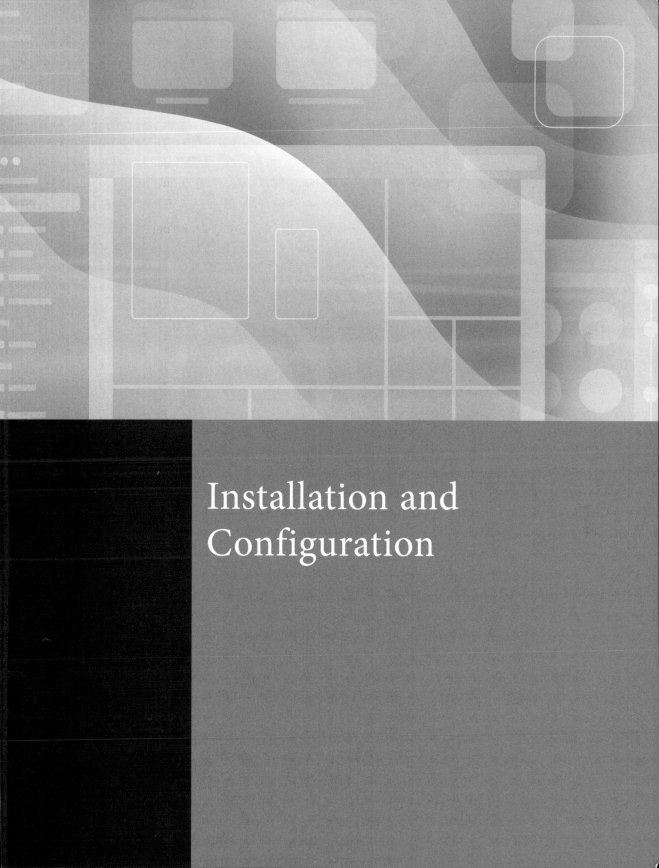

Installation and Configuration

Lesson 1
Introduction to macOS

Since its introduction in 2001, macOS (formerly known as Mac OS X or OS X) comes preinstalled on Mac computers. It offers the ease of use that the iPhone, iPad, Apple Watch, and Apple TV are famous for. macOS also provides an exceptional software development platform, with the result that a large selection of high-quality third-party software is available for macOS.

Reference 1.1
macOS Big Sur 11

macOS Big Sur 11 is the latest version of macOS. macOS combines a powerful open source UNIX foundation with a state-of-the-art user interface.

Integration Through Standards

Much of the success of macOS can be attributed to Apple embracing industry-standard formats and open source software. Adoption of common standards saves engineering time and allows for much smoother integration with other platforms. When Apple developers engineer a technology for a new feature, Apple often releases the technical specifications to the developer community. This fosters a new standard. An example of this is Bonjour network discovery, which Apple pioneered and has maintained as an industry-standard protocol commonly known as Multicast DNS (mDNS) for others to develop and use.

Another example is the Swift programming language for macOS, iOS, iPadOS, tvOS, watchOS, and beyond. After Apple unveiled Swift, it quickly became one of the fastest-growing languages in history. Swift makes it easy to write software that is incredibly fast and safe by design.

Here are some examples of common standards supported by macOS:

▶ Connectivity standards—Universal Serial Bus (USB), including USB-C, Thunderbolt, Bluetooth wireless, and the IEEE 802 family of Ethernet and Wi-Fi standards.

▶ File-system standards—A file system determines how information, usually in the form of a file, is stored on and retrieved from a storage device. macOS supports file-system standards such as File Allocation Table (FAT), New Technology File System (NTFS), ISO 9660 optical disc standard, and the Universal Disk Format (UDF).

▶ Network standards—Dynamic Host Configuration Protocol (DHCP), Domain Name System (DNS), Secure Hypertext Transfer Protocol (HTTPS), Internet Message Access Protocol (IMAP), Simple Mail Transfer Protocol (SMTP), File Transfer Protocol (FTP), Web Distributed Access and Versioning (WebDAV), and Server Message Block/Common Internet File System (SMB/CIFS), including SMB3.

▶ Document standards—ZIP file archives, Rich Text Format (RTF), Portable Document Format (PDF), Tagged Image File Format (TIFF), Joint Photographic Expert Group (JPEG), Portable Network Graphics (PNG), Advanced Audio Coding (AAC), the Moving Picture Experts Group (MPEG) family of media standards, High Efficiency Video Coding (HEVC, also known as H.265), and High Efficiency Image Format (HEIF, based on HEVC).

Reference 1.2
What's New in macOS Big Sur

macOS Big Sur is the first macOS that runs on Mac computers with Apple silicon. In fact, Mac computers with Apple silicon require macOS Big Sur.

And, of course, macOS Big Sur runs on Intel-based Mac computers as well. As this guide goes to press, there are currently three models of Mac computers with Apple silicon, listed in Apple Support article HT211814, "Mac computers with Apple silicon" at support.apple.com/HT211814:

▶ MacBook Pro (13-inch, M1, 2020)

▶ MacBook Air (M1, 2020)

▶ Mac mini (M1, 2020)

Apart from the vast improvement in performance and battery life, users shouldn't notice a difference between macOS Big Sur on a Mac with Apple silicon or on an Intel-based Mac most of the time. This guide addresses scenarios where behavior is different with a Mac with Apple silicon.

In addition to the features you can find in previous versions of macOS, macOS Big Sur includes hundreds of small improvements and a few significant new features. macOS Big Sur is the 16th major version of the Mac operating system since its initial release in 2001. Each release of the Mac operating system has a version number and associated name. Previously, each release used a version number that started with 10, like macOS Mojave 10.14 and macOS Catalina 10.15. macOS Big Sur is version 11. In this guide, older Mac operating system versions are called out with the version name, such as macOS Catalina.

The macOS Big Sur web page (www.apple.com/macos/big-sur) highlights the new features of macOS Big Sur with colorful interactive animations and demonstrations. Be sure to check it out.

Additionally, you can find an exhaustive list of new features in the article "New features coming with macOS Big Sur," at www.apple.com/macos/big-sur/features.

Throughout, macOS Big Sur includes yet more privacy and security enhancements. Learn more in Lesson 9, "Manage Security and Privacy."

The next several sections highlight some major features and improvements.

New Design for a Refined Experience

macOS Big Sur has a more cohesive look and feel throughout. New symbols are redesigned and common across controls, toolbars, and sidebars. This is true for macOS, built-in apps, and the apps you install. You'll know exactly where to click.

macOS Big Sur helps you focus on your content. Apps are streamlined and more transparent. App sheets don't have borders and bezels. The menu bar (at the top of your screen) is taller and more translucent, making more room for your desktop picture to shine. Menus are larger and have more space, improving legibility.

Windows have more room, making them easier to work with. They are more translucent. Edges are more rounded to match macOS. Sidebars extend to the full height of their windows, making it easier for you to find what you want. Toolbars have been redesigned. macOS Big Sur uses a new set of common symbols throughout macOS and your apps to represent common tasks. You'll see these symbols in controls like toolbars, sidebars, navigation bars, context menus, and widgets. These new symbols add clarity and consistency, and they make it easy for you immediately recognize where to click.

The Dock now floats just above the bottom of your display. App icons are redesigned to feel both familiar and fresh; they have a uniform shape, making it easier for you to recognize at a glance.

System sounds are all new, but they sound familiar because they're based on the originals. And the Mac startup chime is back!

New Control Center for Mac

Click Control Center ⚏ in your menu bar to instantly access the controls you use the most, like Wi-Fi, Bluetooth, and AirDrop. Drag your favorite controls to the top of your menu bar for one-click access. Customize using Dock & Menu Bar preferences in System Preferences.

NOTE ▶ To highlight specific features on the printed page, the reference portion of this guide uses an all-white desktop background for many figures. The exercises use different desktops to help differentiate between different users. We recommend you set your desktop background to an image or color that works great for you on your Mac.

Updated Notification Center

macOS Big Sur combines notifications and widgets in a single dedicated column. Notifications are grouped by app. Redesigned widgets come in three sizes. Just click the date or time to open Notification Center. Click Edit Widgets at the bottom of Notification Center to personalize your experience.

Biggest Safari Update Ever

Safari is vastly improved. There are more options than ever to customize your start page, like the ability to set a background image. At the same time, Safari now performs better and is more power efficient than ever. A new privacy report feature helps you understand just how often Safari prevents cross-site trackers from following you around on the web. Find out more about how Safari protects privacy and security in Lesson 9.

Improved Messages

Pin up to nine of your most important conversations to the top your list. And searching your past messages is easier than ever. Reply inline to a specific message in a conversation.

Redesigned Maps

Create Guides for your favorite places, or discover Guides created by brands you trust. Maps includes improvements for indoor maps, as well as new routes customized for the different needs of cycling and electric vehicles.

New App Store Privacy Information

A completely new section for each app in the App Store is dedicated to that app's privacy practices. See Lesson 18, "Install Apps," for more details on the App Store.

Time Machine Improvements

macOS Big Sur significantly improves Time Machine backup performance when you use a disk that's formatted with Apple File System (APFS). See Lesson 17, "Manage Time Machine," for more details on using Time Machine to back up your content.

Improved Accessibility Features

macOS Big Sur introduces features that make it even easier for everyone to control their Mac. Voice Control is just one example.

Voice Control

macOS Big Sur adds improvements to Voice Control, which was introduced with macOS Catalina. With Voice Control, users who don't use traditional input devices can completely control their Apple devices just with their voice. Become more efficient with improved dictation and text editing features. Open and control almost any app by speaking.

After you enable Voice Control, your Mac completes a one-time download from Apple, and an onscreen microphone appears.

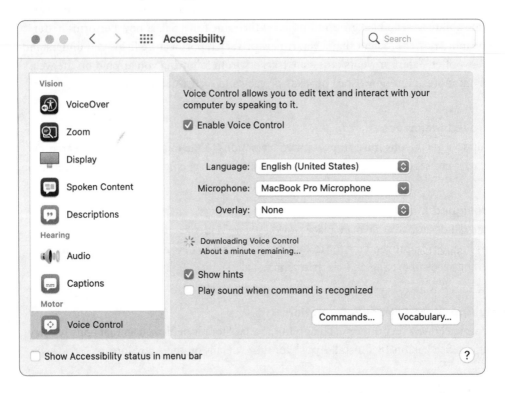

Reference 1.3
Use macOS Help

macOS includes Help, which you can access from the Help menu or by clicking the Help button (it looks like a question mark) in a preference pane or dialog.

In the Finder or an app that has the Help menu, go to the menu bar, click the Help menu, and do one of the following:

▶ Enter a search term in the Search field, then choose from the Menu Items list or move the pointer over a menu item to reveal its location.

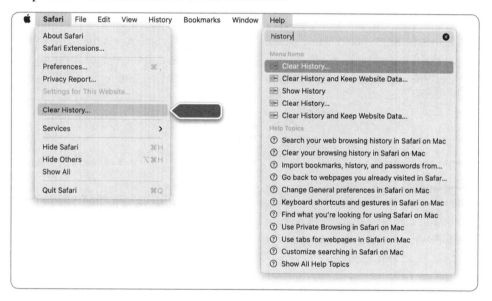

▶ Enter a search term in the Search field, then choose one of the Help Topics in the results.

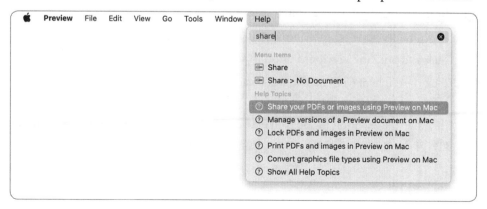

▶   Enter a search term in the Search field, then choose Show All Help Topics.

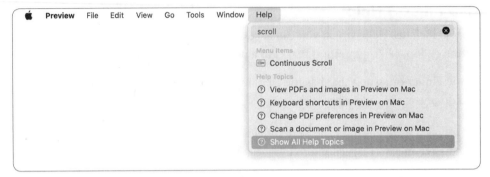

▶   Leave the Search field blank and choose "*app* Help," where *app* is the name of the app in the foreground, to open the User Guide for that app. If the Finder is the app in the foreground, choose macOS Help to open the macOS User Guide.

When you use the macOS User Guide or the User Guide for an app, the window stays visible on top of your desktop and all your other apps so that you can always see its contents. The following list includes some things you can do while using the macOS User Guide or the User Guide for an app:

▶   Drag the title bar to move the entire window.

▶   Drag an edge or corner of the window to resize the window.

▶   Enter a search term in the Search field.

▶   Show the Previous (<) topic or Next (>) topic.

▶   Click and hold the Previous button to see a list of previously viewed topics.

▶   Click the Table of Contents button beside the Next button to show or hide more topics.

▶   Click the Share button (it looks like a box with an arrow pointing up) to open the topic in Safari, print the topic, or choose other options.

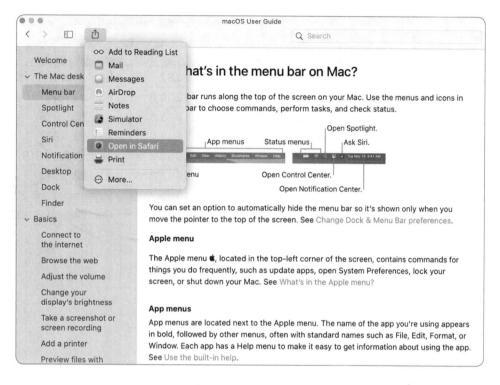

▶ Press Command-Plus (+) or make the text bigger or press Command-Minus (–) to make the text smaller.

▶ Press Command-F, then enter the text you want to find in the current topic.

Most of the app user guides are available at a URL that has the pattern of support.apple.com/guide/*app*, where *app* is the name of the app.

See "Use built-in help on your Mac" at support.apple.com/guide/mac-help/hlpvw003 in the macOS User Guide for more information.

Reference 1.4
Review macOS History

The following table shows Mac operating system versions since OS X Mavericks 10.9, which is the earliest Mac operating system that you can directly upgrade to macOS Big Sur. See Apple Support article HT201260, "Find out which macOS your Mac is using," for more information.

Name and version	Release date	Latest version	Latest date
OS X Mavericks 10.9	October 22, 2013	10.9.5	September 17, 2014
OS X Yosemite 10.10	October 16, 2014	10.10.5	August 13, 2015
OS X El Capitan 10.11	September 30, 2015	10.11.6	July 18, 2016
macOS Sierra 10.12	September 20, 2016	10.12.6	July 19, 2017
macOS High Sierra 10.13	September 25, 2017	10.13.6	August 28, 2018
macOS Mojave 10.14	September 24, 2018	10.14.6	July 22, 2019
macOS Catalina 10.15	October 7, 2019	10.15.7	September 24, 2020
macOS Big Sur 11	November 12, 2020	11.1	December 14, 2020

Lesson 2

Update, Upgrade, or Reinstall macOS

Every new Mac comes with the Mac operating system. To get the latest features and security updates, you will eventually need the latest macOS. If you have a qualifying Mac, you can upgrade at no cost.

> **WARNING ▸** Some exercises in this lesson involve significant changes to your Mac setup. Some of the steps are difficult or impossible to reverse. If you perform the exercises in this lesson, do so on a spare Mac or an external disk that doesn't contain critical data.

Reference 2.1
macOS Installation Methods

Identifying the parts of a Mac operating system name will help you understand the difference between an upgrade and an update. A Mac operating system has a version name and a version number, such as macOS Big Sur 11.

When Apple releases an *update* to macOS Big Sur:

▸ The version name stays the same (Big Sur).

▸ The first part of the version number stays the same (11).

▸ Apple adds additional numbers after 11. For example, the first update for macOS 11.0 was 11.0.1. And the next update released was 11.1.

When Apple releases a major version *upgrade* of the Mac operating system, there is a new version name (for example, Big Sur instead of Catalina).

GOALS

▸ Describe the differences between a macOS update, upgrade, and reinstallation

▸ Describe the macOS installer

▸ Verify system information

▸ Update macOS

▸ Upgrade macOS

▸ Reinstall macOS

▸ Troubleshoot an upgrade or reinstallation

Although all previous versions of macOS have a version number that starts with "10." (for example, macOS 10.0 through macOS 10.15), macOS Big Sur uses "11." to start its version numbers.

This list summarizes the differences between updating, upgrading, reinstalling, and installing a Mac operating system:

▸ Update: Installs an incremental update of the Mac operating system but doesn't upgrade it to the next major version (if one exists).

▸ Upgrade: Installs a next major standalone version of the Mac operating system.

▸ Reinstall: Installs the same major version of macOS on a volume that already has macOS. This overwrites existing system files but leaves apps, user home folders, and other files in place.

▸ Install: Installs macOS on a volume that doesn't have macOS—for instance, a volume you erased.

  NOTE ▸ The terms *disk*, *volume*, and *storage* have similar meanings. Where possible, this guide uses terms that appear in apps on screen. Read Lesson 11, "Manage File Systems and Storage," for more information.

Lesson 6, "Update macOS," describes in more detail updating macOS and keeping macOS automatically updated.

Upgrading, reinstalling, or installing macOS Big Sur requires internet access.

Erase Your Startup Disk

If you want to get a fresh start with macOS and you don't need the existing content on your Mac, erase the startup disk before you install macOS. The macOS installer (an app named Install macOS Big Sur) doesn't erase disks, but you can use Disk Utility to erase a disk before you run the macOS installer:

▸ If you want to erase the system disk your Mac is currently running from, you can erase it if you start up from macOS Recovery, as covered in Lesson 5, "Use macOS Recovery."

▸ If the destination is another disk, such as an external storage device, erase and install from your Mac, as covered in Lesson 11.

Reference 2.2
Prepare to Upgrade or Reinstall macOS

Follow these steps to prepare to start a macOS upgrade:

1   Verify installation requirements.

2   Back up important content.

3   Plug notebook computers into power.

4   Download macOS Big Sur.

Verify Installation Requirements

Verify that both your Mac and its operating system meet the requirements for an upgrade to macOS Big Sur. This includes verifying the hardware and the software.

To upgrade from OS X Mountain Lion 10.8, first upgrade to OS X El Capitan 10.11, then upgrade to macOS Big Sur.

Upgrading to macOS Big Sur has the following requirements:

- OS X Mavericks 10.9 or later
- 4 GB of memory
- 35.5 GB of available storage to upgrade from macOS Sierra 10.12, or 44.5 GB of available storage to upgrade from an earlier release
- Compatible internet service provider (for some features)
- Apple ID (for some features)

macOS Big Sur supports the following Mac models:

- MacBook introduced in 2015 or later
- MacBook Air introduced in 2013 or later
- MacBook Pro introduced in late 2013 or later
- Mac mini introduced in 2014 or later
- iMac introduced in 2014 or later
- iMac Pro
- Mac Pro introduced in 2013 or later

See Apple Support article HT211238, "macOS Big Sur is compatible with these computers" at https://support.apple.com/support.apple.com/HT211238 for more information about requirements for specific features. Some features of macOS Big Sur require specific Mac and iOS or iPadOS device models, such as the following features:

▶ **Continuity Camera**—Use your iPhone, iPad, or iPod touch to scan documents or take a picture of something nearby and it appears instantly on your Mac. Continuity Camera is supported in many apps, including Mail, Messages, the Finder, and more. See Apple Support article HT209037, "Use Continuity Camera on your Mac," for more information.

▶ **Handoff**—With Handoff, you can start work on one device, then switch to another nearby device and pick up where you left off. Use Handoff with any Mac, iPhone, iPad, iPod touch, or Apple Watch that meets the Continuity system requirements. See Apple Support article HT204689, "System requirements for Continuity on Mac, iPhone, iPad, iPod touch, and Apple Watch," for more information.

▶ **Instant Hotspot**—With Instant Hotspot, the Personal Hotspot on your iPhone or iPad (Wi-Fi + Cellular) can provide internet access to a Mac, iPhone, iPad, or iPod touch without requiring you to enter the password on those devices. Use Instant Hotspot with any Mac, iPhone, iPad, or iPod touch that meets the Continuity system requirements. See Apple Support article HT209459, "Use Instant Hotspot to connect to your Personal Hotspot without entering a password," for more information.

▶ **Universal Clipboard**—With Universal Clipboard, you can copy content such as text, images, photos, and videos on one Apple device, then paste the content on another Apple device. Use Universal Clipboard with any Mac, iPhone, iPad, or iPod touch that meets the Continuity system requirements. See Apple Support article HT209460, "Use Universal Clipboard to copy and paste between your Apple devices," for more information.

See Apple Support article SP833, "macOS Big Sur – Technical Specifications" at support.apple.com/kb/SP833 for more information.

Verify System Information

You need to know your Mac computer's specifications when you install new software, upgrade installed software, perform maintenance, or troubleshoot a problem. In this section you learn how to find essential system information with About This Mac and System Information.

You can open the Apple menu and choose About This Mac to gather most of the information necessary to confirm that your Mac supports macOS Big Sur. About This Mac displays information such as the macOS software version, Mac model name, chip (for a Mac with Apple silicon) or processor type and speed (for an Intel-based Mac), total system memory, startup disk, graphics card information (for an Intel-based Mac), and Mac serial number.

> **NOTE ▶** A Mac may not display a serial number if the necessary post-repair procedures were not successfully completed after a logic board replacement.

The Mac in the following figure has 16 GB of RAM and meets the memory requirements to run macOS Big Sur.

A few items are vital to identifying your macOS version and Mac model:

▶ The macOS version number represents the system software version currently installed.

▶ The macOS build number is more specific than the macOS version number alone. In the About this Mac window, click the macOS software version number to find the build number. Apple creates specific build versions of each macOS version as they refine it. A newly released model of Mac may require a specific build of macOS; the specific build may differ from the standard installation versions. For example, the first day the new MacBook Pro (13-inch, 2020, Two Thunderbolt 3 ports) was shipped, one model came with macOS 10.15.4 (19E2265), another model with different options came with macOS 10.15.4 (19E2269), but other Mac computers that were up to date were running macOS 10.15.4 (19E287). For more information, see Apple Support article HT201686, "Use the Mac operating system that came with your Mac, or a compatible newer version."

▶ The Mac computer model name is derived from the product marketing name for the Mac, followed by a relative release date. For example, the previous screenshot was taken on a "MacBook Pro (15-inch, 2018)."

▶ The Mac serial number is located on the Mac case. The serial number is a unique number used to identify a Mac for maintenance and service.

Click the Storage button to review how much disk space is available.

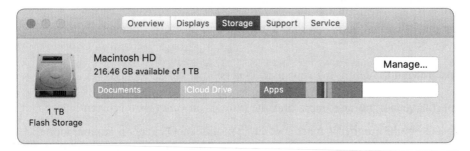

The Mac in this figure meets the available-storage requirements to upgrade to macOS Big Sur.

The Support and Service buttons link directly to specific areas of the Apple Support website. The contents of the links are generated dynamically to show the most up-to-date support information about macOS and your Mac. For example, the Specifications link opens a webpage with the full specifications for your Mac.

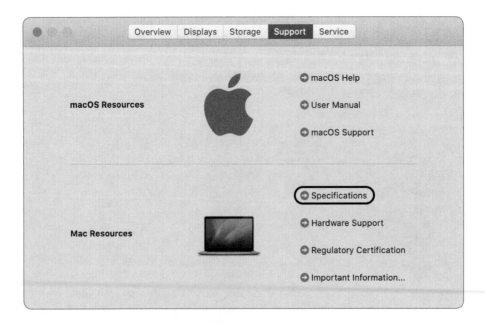

The information in the About This Mac window is a subset of what you can find with System Information. From the Overview window in the About This Mac window, click the System Report button to open System Information. Or you can press and hold the Option key and then choose Apple menu > System Information. Or you can use Spotlight; click the Spotlight icon (which looks like a magnifying glass) in the menu bar in the upper-right corner of your screen, enter **System Information** in the search field, then press Return.

If you have a version of the Mac operating system that shipped with the name OS X (instead of macOS), it includes System Profiler instead of System Information.

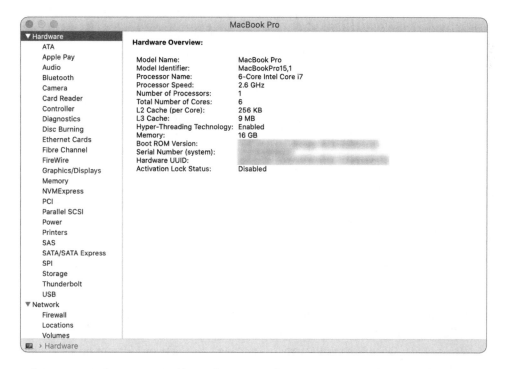

When you need to create a file to document the current state of a Mac, use System Information. Go to the menu bar, then choose File > Save. This creates a System Information–specific file (with the .spx filename extension) that you can open from other Mac computers.

Verify App Compatibility

When you upgrade to macOS Big Sur, your third-party apps might need updates to function properly. You can use System Information to view installed apps. For older

Mac computers with System Profiler instead of System Information, verify that View > Full Profile is selected to reveal the Applications section in the Contents list. Selecting Applications from the Contents list prompts macOS to scan common locations on the local volume for available apps.

You don't have to worry about the apps that came with your Mac, such as Safari, Mail, and Photos. They are automatically upgraded when you install macOS Big Sur. You might have to visit third-party vendor websites to find out if your third-party apps require updates.

Back Up Important Files and Folders

It's always crucial to keep backups of your important files and folders. Having a current backup is even more critical when you make significant changes to a Mac, such as installing a major version upgrade to the Mac operating system. If a new installation or upgrade is done improperly, it could result in complete data loss.

You can't uninstall or revert an update or upgrade. If it turns out that an app you need is not compatible with macOS Big Sur, the only way to install an earlier version of macOS is to erase and restore from backup.

You can use Time Machine to create a backup before you start your installation. Using Time Machine is covered in Lesson 17, "Manage Time Machine."

Document Network Settings

The macOS installer helps ensure that you don't lose previous settings when you upgrade to macOS Big Sur. But some settings are so vital to your Mac that you should document them in case something goes wrong.

In particular, if you have any special network configuration, such as a static IPv4 address, or a specific Domain Name Service (DNS) server to use, document your network settings before you upgrade. Open System Preferences and click the Network icon to observe your current network settings. Avoid missing settings by navigating through the network interface and all the configurations.

You can quickly document your settings by using the Screenshot utility. Just press Shift-Command-5. Press the Space bar to change the pointer to a camera icon; then you can move your pointer to highlight different windows. Click to capture the highlighted window, or use the Screenshot menu to change what's captured, to capture video, to change where you save the file, to set a timer, or to modify several other options. After you finish your screenshot or video capture, its preview appears in the corner of the screen. Drag the preview into a document, click the preview and mark it up, or just leave it and the Screenshot utility will automatically save it to your desktop with a filename of "Screen Shot" followed by the date and time of the capture. Be sure to print or copy your screenshots to another storage device before you install macOS Big Sur.

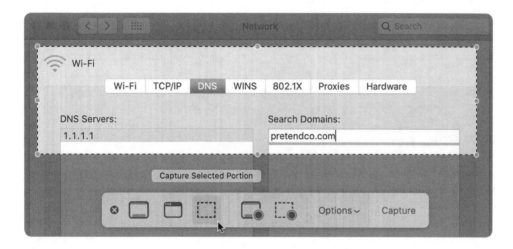

NOTE ▶ When you use Screenshot to capture a window, you can exclude the window's shadow. Just press and hold the Option key when you click. To copy a screenshot to the Clipboard, press and hold the Control key while you take the screenshot. You can then paste the screenshot somewhere else. Or you can use Universal Clipboard to paste it on another Apple device. See Apple Support article HT201361, "Take a screenshot on your Mac," for more information.

Plug Mac Notebooks into Power

Plug your Mac into an AC power outlet during the upgrade to ensure that the upgrade completes successfully.

Download macOS Big Sur

If you're using OS X El Capitan v10.11.5 or later, macOS Big Sur downloads in the background, making it easier to upgrade your Mac. When the download finishes, you receive a notification indicating that macOS Big Sur is ready to be installed. Click Install in the notification to get started.

macOS Big Sur is free and available from Software Update preferences or the App Store.

If you're using macOS Mojave 10.14 or later:

1   Open System Preferences.

2   Open Software Update preferences.

3   Click Upgrade Now.

Or open the macOS Big Sur page in the App Store: "macOS Big Sur" at apps.apple.com/app/macos-big-sur/id1526878132. Then click the Get button.

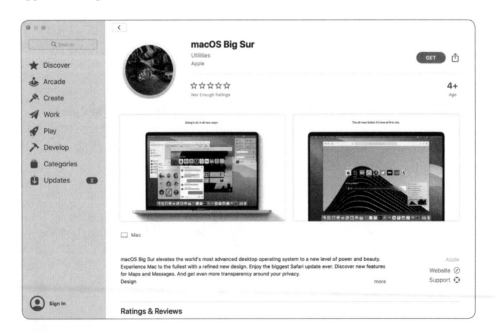

NOTE ▶ In the previous figure, App Store displays the number 2 next to Updates. This is because there are two apps that have updates available, but you can install these updates only after you upgrade to macOS Big Sur.

Reference 2.3
Upgrade or Install macOS

The App Store downloads Install macOS Big Sur and places it in your /Applications folder. After the download is complete, Install macOS Big Sur automatically opens.

Follow these steps to upgrade to macOS Big Sur:

1 Begin installation.

2 Allow installation to complete.

Begin Installation

Be sure you are connected to the internet when you upgrade or install macOS. The macOS installer downloads any available firmware updates specific to your Mac. These firmware updates don't apply to external devices, such as those connected with USB, Thunderbolt, or target disk mode.

You can use these supported tools and methods to upgrade or install macOS:

▶ macOS installer.

▶ Bootable installer, then the macOS installer. Read Exercise 5.2, "Create a macOS Install Disk."

▶ Start up from macOS Recovery and install macOS. Read Lesson 5 to learn more.

▶ Use the startosinstall command, inside the Install macOS Big Sur app, which is outside the scope of this guide. See Apple Support article HT208020, "How to install macOS at your organization," for more information.

▶ Use the "Install OS update" command using your organization's mobile device management (MDM) solution, which is outside the scope of this guide.

Use the Install macOS Big Sur app to install macOS on your startup disk. For details on using macOS Recovery to upgrade, reinstall, or install macOS Big Sur, read Lesson 5.

Select the Installation Destination

During macOS Big Sur installation, the only choice you make is the installation destination—you select the disk where macOS is installed. This can be an internal or external volume, as long as it's properly formatted. The default selection is the current startup disk. The Show All Disks button appears if it is possible for you to select an alternate destination.

If necessary, provide administrator credentials to install a helper tool.

You may not be able to select certain disks or partitions when using the installer (read Reference 11.1, "File Systems," for more information about partitions). This happens when the installer determines that your Mac can't start from those disks or partitions. Possible reasons include the following:

▶ The disk is in target disk mode. Read Reference 11.5, "Troubleshoot File Systems," for more information about target disk mode.

▶ The disk doesn't have the proper partition scheme for your Mac. Mac computers use the GPT (GUID Partition Table) scheme. Use Disk Utility to repartition the disk.

▶   The partition isn't formatted properly. macOS Big Sur requires a partition formatted as Apple File System (APFS). Use Disk Utility to erase an improperly formatted
partition.

▶   The macOS installer doesn't support installing to a volume that's part of a RAID
(Redundant Array of Independent Disks) set.

▶   The macOS installer doesn't support installing to a disk containing Time Machine
backups.

▶   The storage volume isn't from Apple and isn't compatible with macOS Big Sur.

You might need to click Restart to continue the macOS Big Sur installation.

Allow Installation to Complete

During normal installation, the Mac restarts at least once and possibly multiple times. If a
power loss or storage device disconnection occurs, restart the installation.

The macOS installer is designed to never delete nonsystem data from the selected destination. The macOS installer ensures that user data and compatible third-party apps remain
functional after an installation. The macOS installer upgrades your current Mac operating
system or installs macOS to a volume (except a volume connected by target disk mode)
that's attached to your Mac.

If the Install macOS Big Sur app detects incompatible files and settings during an upgrade,
it moves those files to a folder named Relocated Items in the /Users/Shared folder of your
startup volume. See "If you see a Relocated Items folder on your Mac after upgrading
macOS" in the macOS User Guide support.apple.com/guide/mac-help/mchl8ae423a3 for
more information.

Apps that are not compatible with macOS Big Sur are left in place, but macOS displays
a prohibitory symbol as part of the app icon. If you try to open incompatible software,
macOS displays information about why the app cannot be opened.

Reference 2.4
Troubleshoot Installation Issues

The macOS installer can back out of an installation and restore the previous system if an
installation goes wrong. Verify that your Mac meets the requirements for macOS Big Sur
and complete the installation preparation steps as outlined in this lesson to avoid installation problems.

macOS Installer Troubleshooting

Beyond failing to prepare for an installation, the most common installation failures come from internet access and destination volume problems. For example:

▶ The installer has filtered or no access to the internet.

▶ The installer might be unable to verify the selected volume or partition. This indicates serious storage device problems. Refer to the troubleshooting steps in Lesson 11 to resolve this issue.

For more information, see Apple Support article HT204904, "How to reinstall macOS."

Installer Log

You can use the log file to troubleshoot macOS. The Installer log contains progress and error entries for nearly every installation step, including steps not shown in the standard interface.

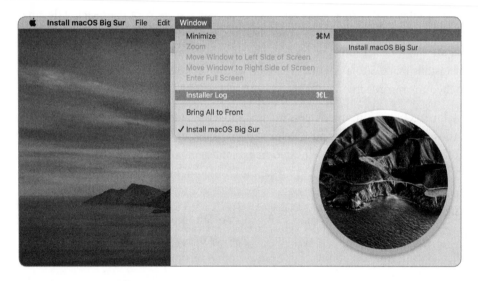

During the initial installation phases, choose Installer Log from the Window menu to access the log. The Installer log helps you pinpoint problems or verify installation.

After the preliminary installation phases, the installer enters the main installation phase and locks the Mac screen. You can only watch the installation progress bar. If the installation fails, the system restarts to the previous version of macOS.

After the Mac resumes normal operation, you can access the full Installer log with Console after you log in.

When you use macOS, error dialogs appear only if an issue is something you can resolve or that requires immediate attention. Otherwise, running processes and apps leave detailed information in log reports throughout macOS.

Console collects log messages and reports that are generated from your Mac and connected devices. Use Console to collect diagnostic information so that you can troubleshoot problems. You can open Console in at least two ways:

▶ Search with Spotlight.

▶ Navigate to /Applications/Utilities/ and double-click Console.

After Console opens, select Log Reports in the left column, then select install.log.

Even during a successful installation, there are warnings and errors. Many of the reported issues are benign, and you should concern yourself with them only if you are trying to isolate a problem that prevents a successful upgrade to macOS Big Sur.

Exercise 2.1
Prepare a Mac for Upgrade

NOTE ▶ This exercise is for independent study only. You don't perform this exercise in a classroom environment. Perform this exercise only if you are upgrading your Mac from an earlier version of macOS.

▶ **Prerequisites**

- ▶ Your Mac must be running OS X Mavericks 10.9 or later.

- ▶ Your Mac must have 4 GB of memory.

- ▶ If your Mac is running macOS Sierra 10.12 or later, it must have 35.5 GB of available storage. If your Mac is running OS X El Capitan 10.11 or earlier, it must have 44.5 GB of available storage.

- ▶ For more information on compatible Mac computers, see Apple Support article HT211238, "macOS Big Sur is compatible with these computers."

In this exercise, you verify that your Mac supports macOS Big Sur. You also check for old software and record important settings.

NOTE ▶ This exercise can't be used to prepare an independent-study Mac for the rest of the course. Independent learners must complete Exercise 2.3, "Erase a Mac and Install macOS Big Sur," to continue to Exercise 3.1, "Configure a Mac for Exercises."

Check Hardware and App Compatibility

1   Log in to your existing administrator account.

2   In the Finder, navigate to the /Applications/Utilities folder.

You can also use the Finder keyboard shortcut Shift-Command-U.

3   Open System Information.

4 If necessary, select the Hardware category in the sidebar.

5 Verify that there is at least 4 GB of memory.

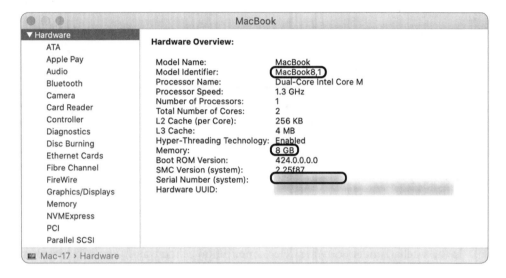

6 Record the Model Identifier and Serial Number entries:

Model Identifier:

Serial Number:

7 Select the Storage category in the Hardware section of the sidebar. If there is no Storage entry, select the entry for the bus your Mac startup disk is attached to. For most models, this is the Serial-ATA bus.

8 Find your startup volume in the list on the right, then verify that it has at least 35.5 GB of available storage.

NOTE ▶ If you are upgrading from OS X El Capitan 10.11 or earlier, you need at least 44.5 GB of available storage.

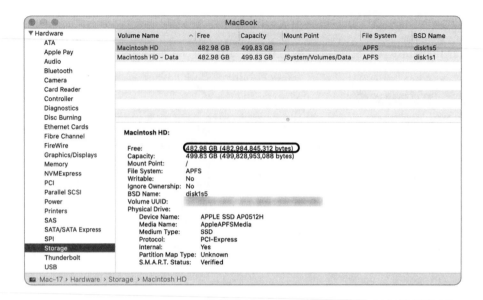

9   In the sidebar, under Software, select Applications, then wait for macOS to gather information on installed apps.

10 Click the heading for the Last Modified column on the right. If the arrow at the top of the column is pointing down, click again so that it points up.

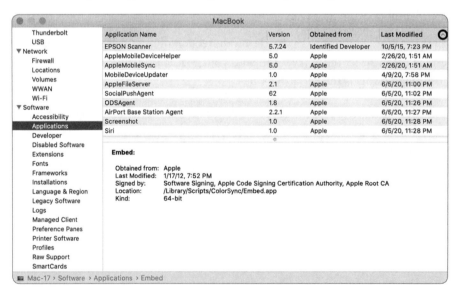

The oldest apps are listed at the top. In general, older apps are more likely to be incompatible with newer versions of macOS. Research older apps to find out if they are compatible with macOS Big Sur or if updates are available. Often, a developer website has information about compatibility and updates. The most likely incompatible app could be an app that is not 64-bit.

11 Quit System Information.

12 Open Safari, then navigate to the Apple Tech Specs website (checkcoverage.apple.com).

13 Enter your Mac computer's serial number (recorded in step 6) in the field, enter the code, then click Continue.

Your Mac computer's model name, along with information about your warranty coverage and links to set up a repair, appears. Verify that the model name is on the list of supported models in Reference 2.2, "Prepare to Upgrade or Reinstall macOS."

14 Do one of the following:

▶ If your Mac is running macOS High Sierra 10.13 or earlier, from the Apple menu choose App Store. If necessary, click the Updates icon in the toolbar and wait while your software is checked for updates.

▶ If you are running macOS Mojave 10.14 or later, open Software Update preferences and verify that no operating system updates are available.

15 If the No Updates Available message is displayed, proceed to the "Document Network Settings" section of this exercise.

16 Depending on your macOS version, if updates are available click the Update buttons for those you want to install. You may find a More option. Clicking More shows a more detailed list of system updates. Click the Update All button to install updates. Follow prompts and instructions to complete the updates.

17 After the updates have finished, repeat starting at step 15 to verify that all updates installed successfully and that no more updates are available.

Document Network Settings

1 From the Apple menu, choose System Preferences.

2   In System Preferences, click Network.

3   Select each of the network services (listed on the left of the preference pane), and record settings assigned to them. Click the Advanced button for each service to display the full settings. An easy way to do this is to take screenshots with the shortcut Shift-Command-5 to give you a record of the information to work from.

4   If your Mac has more than one location defined, repeat this process for each location.

5   Quit System Preferences.

Back Up Your Data

You should always have a current backup copy of the content on your Mac. Third-party backup solutions are available, and macOS includes a backup utility, which is described in Lesson 17, "Manage Time Machine." Whichever solution you choose, after you complete a backup try restoring files to ensure that it works.

Exercise 2.2
Upgrade to macOS Big Sur

NOTE ▶ This exercise is for independent study only. You don't perform this exercise in a classroom environment. Perform this exercise only if you want to upgrade your Mac from an earlier version of macOS. This exercise can't be used to prepare an independent study Mac for the rest of the course. Independent learners must complete Exercise 2.3, "Erase a Mac and Install macOS Big Sur," to continue to Exercise 3.1, "Configure a Mac for Exercises."

▶ **Prerequisite**

   ▶   You must have performed Exercise 2.1, "Prepare a Mac for Upgrade," before you begin this exercise.

In this exercise, you download macOS Big Sur from the App Store and install it, as an upgrade, on your Mac.

If you are upgrading from macOS High Sierra 10.13 or earlier, use the steps in the "Use the App Store to Download the Installer" section. If you are upgrading from macOS Mojave 10.14, use the steps in the "Use Software Update to Download the Installer" section.

Use the App Store to Download the Installer

1   If necessary, log in to your existing administrator account on your Mac.

2   From the Apple menu, choose App Store.

3   In the search field of the App Store window, type **Big Sur**, then press Return.

4   Find macOS Big Sur in the search results, then click the view button under its name (it is labeled either "Download" or "Get").

Search Results for "Big Sur"

macOS Big Sur
Utilities

DOWNLOAD

5   Wait for the Install macOS Big Sur app to download.

When the download is complete, the app opens automatically.

Skip the next section, "Use Software Update to Download the Installer," and continue to the section "Upgrade Your Mac to macOS Big Sur."

> **NOTE ▶** As part of the installation process, the installer app is automatically deleted. If you want to upgrade several Mac computers or create a macOS Big Sur install disk, quit the installer and make a copy of it before you proceed. Find the process for creating an install disk in Exercise 5.2, "Create a macOS Install Disk."

Use Software Update to Download the Installer

1 If necessary, log in to your existing administrator account on your Mac.

2 From the Apple menu, choose System Preferences, then open Software Update preferences.

macOS checks for available updates.

3 Software Update shows macOS Big Sur as an eligible update.

Other updates may be shown as well. For the purposes of this exercise, you will upgrade to macOS Big Sur.

4 Click Upgrade Now, then wait for macOS to finish downloading macOS Big Sur.

When the download is complete, the app opens automatically.

Upgrade Your Mac to macOS Big Sur

1   If necessary, open the Install macOS Big Sur app.

Install macOS Big
Sur

2   At the first screen, click Continue.

3   Read the license agreement, and if its terms are acceptable to you, click Agree.

4   In the confirmation dialog that appears, click Agree.

5   Select the installation destination. The default selection is the current startup volume. If you intend to upgrade a different volume, click the Show All Disks button to select a different destination.

NOTE ▶ The Show All Disks button will appear only if more than one volume is available for installation of macOS Big Sur.

6   Click Install to start the installation. If you're warned about not being connected to a power source, connect your power adapter before you continue.

7   Enter the password of your administrator account to authorize the installation.

To learn installation details, follow the instructions in Exercise 2.4, "Verify That macOS Is Installed Correctly," after the installation starts.

The installation restarts several times and completes automatically.

Exercise 2.3
Erase a Mac and Install macOS Big Sur

NOTE ▶ This exercise is for independent study only. You don't perform this exercise in a classroom environment. Complete this exercise only if you must erase the contents of your Mac before you install macOS Big Sur, as covered in Reference 2.1, "macOS Installation Methods." Perform this exercise to prepare your Mac to continue with Exercise 3.1, "Configure a Mac for Exercises."

▶ **Prerequisite**

> ▶ You need macOS Recovery with macOS Big Sur or a macOS Big Sur install disk (see Lesson 5, "Use macOS Recovery," for details).

WARNING ▶ This exercise erases all of your Mac content. If you want to keep the content, back it up to an external storage device before you start.

Start Up from macOS Recovery or an External Installer

1   Before you proceed with this exercise, back up your data to an external storage device.

2   If your Mac is running, shut it down.

3   If you are using macOS Recovery to replace your current installation of macOS Big Sur:

   a   Press the power button on your Mac to turn it on.

   b   Immediately press and hold Command-R until the Apple icon appears in the middle of the screen.

   c   After the Apple icon appears, release the keys and skip ahead to the next section, "Erase Your Storage Device."

4   If you are using an external macOS Big Sur install volume, connect the storage device to your Mac.

5   Press the power button on your Mac to turn it on, then immediately press and hold the Option key until a row of icons appears on the screen.

6   Click the install disk icon (usually labeled "Install macOS Big Sur").

7   Click the arrow that appears under the icon.

Your Mac starts up into the installer/recovery environment. Lesson 5 has more information about using these startup modes.

Erase Your Storage Device

1   If a language selection screen appears, select your preferred language, then click the right arrow to continue.

2   Open Disk Utility.

▶   If the macOS Utilities window appears, select Disk Utility, then click Continue.

▶   If an installer screen appears, from the menu bar choose Utilities > Disk Utility.

Disk Utility opens. Lesson 11, "Manage File Systems and Storage," has more information about using Disk Utility.

3   From the sidebar, select the storage device or volume that you will erase to install macOS Big Sur.

4   Click the Erase button near the top of the Disk Utility window.

5   Enter a new name for your storage device. The rest of this guide assumes that it is named Macintosh HD.

6   From the Format menu, choose APFS if it is not already selected.

Many volumes may be formatted as Mac OS Extended (Journaled), which is still an option in some cases. If your volume is formatted as Mac OS Extended, the macOS Installer converts your volume to APFS automatically during installation.

7 If the dialog contains a Scheme menu, choose GUID Partition Map.

8 Click Erase.

9 When the process finishes, click Done.

10 From the menu bar, choose Disk Utility > Quit Disk Utility.

Install macOS Big Sur

1 If the macOS Utilities window appears, select Install macOS or Reinstall macOS, and click Continue.

2   In the Install macOS Big Sur window, click Continue.

3   If you are asked to connect to the internet, use the Wi-Fi istatus menu at the right end of the menu bar to choose a Wi-Fi network, or connect using Ethernet.

4   If you are notified that your Mac computer's eligibility will be verified with Apple, click Continue.

5   Read the license agreement, and if its terms are acceptable to you, click Agree.

6   In the confirmation dialog that appears, click Agree.

7   Select your volume, then click Continue.

To learn the details of the installation, follow the instructions in Exercise 2.4, "Verify That macOS Is Installed Correctly," after the installation begins.

The installation restarts several times and completes automatically.

After restart, Setup Assistant opens, as covered in Lesson 3, "Set Up and Configure macOS." Follow the instructions in Exercise 3.1, "Configure a Mac for Exercises," to set up your Mac for the rest of the exercises.

Exercise 2.4
Verify That macOS Is Installed Correctly

> **NOTE ▸** This exercise is for independent study only. You don't perform this exercise in a classroom environment.

▶ Prerequisite

> ▸ You must have started installing macOS Big Sur using the instructions in Exercise 2.2, "Upgrade to macOS Big Sur," or Exercise 2.3, "Erase a Mac and Install macOS Big Sur."

In this exercise, you use the Installer log to view the installation process.

View the Installer Log

During installation, you can bring up the Installer log by following these steps:

1 If the installer is running in full-screen mode, the menu bar is hidden. Move your mouse to the top of the screen and leave it there for a few seconds to reveal the menu bar.

2 From the menu bar, choose Window > Installer Log (or press Command-L).

3   Choose Show All Logs from the Detail Level menu to view the entire contents of the Installer log.

4   Use the Spotlight search field in the toolbar to view entries in the Installer log.

5   To save the Installer log, click the Save button in the toolbar.

The installer restarts the Mac partway through installation. When the Mac restarts for the second phase, the log window doesn't automatically reopen. It isn't available during this part of the installation.

Lesson 3

Set Up and Configure macOS

This lesson covers initial setup and ongoing macOS configuration. You use Setup Assistant to set up a new Mac. Then you use System Preferences and configuration profiles.

Reference 3.1
Configure a Mac with a New Installation of macOS Big Sur

If you're using a new Mac for the first time or you have just completed an upgrade to macOS Big Sur, you'll see Setup Assistant. For new Mac computers or installations of macOS on a previously blank volume, Setup Assistant guides you through the preliminary configuration.

If you just upgraded an existing Mac that was using a previous version of a Mac operating system, you'll still see Setup Assistant but you'll be presented with fewer configuration steps. Most importantly, you will be asked to enter your Apple ID and password to complete iCloud setup. Apple ID and iCloud are covered later in this lesson.

Even if you previously set up iCloud on an existing Mac, when Setup Assistant is running you need to reenter your authentication information to complete the upgrade to macOS Big Sur.

iCloud is optional and free of charge. Many macOS features require iCloud.

After you turn on a new Mac, Setup Assistant starts automatically. It guides you through setting up your Mac by providing step-by-step screens. The screens you see vary based on the features of your Mac and the choices you make while using Setup Assistant. Each screen varies in what you're required to do:

- ▶ Take action or make a selection.
- ▶ Read, then click Continue.
- ▶ Click the option to set up a feature later.

These are some of the screens that require you to agree to something or make a selection or configuration:

- ▶ Region selection
- ▶ Accessibility options
- ▶ Keyboard setup
- ▶ Apple terms and conditions acceptance
- ▶ First account creation

You can use System Preferences to change most of the settings you selected in Setup Assistant.

If your organization uses Apple School Manager or Apple Business Manager, you can use Automated Device Enrollment to automate mobile device management (MDM) enrollment and simplify initial Mac setup. You can use your MDM solution to prevent some or all Setup Assistant screens from appearing. Unless otherwise indicated, this guide describes the Setup Assistant process for a Mac that's not automatically enrolled in an MDM solution using Automated Device Enrollment. For more information about Device Enrollment, see Apple Support articles HT204142, "Use Automated Device Enrollment," at support.apple.com/HT20412, and "Mobile Device Management Settings for IT Administrators" at support.apple.com/guide/mdm/.

During the initial stages of Setup Assistant, you can choose to enable VoiceOver to interact with macOS using only audio cues. After you turn on your Mac, you can press the Esc (Escape) key to learn how to set up your Mac with VoiceOver and show the VoiceOver Quick Start guide. At any point you can use a keyboard shortcut to turn VoiceOver on and off:

▶   Press Command-Option-F5 (you might need to press the Fn [Function] key to access the F5 key).

▶   If your Mac has Touch ID, triple-click Touch ID (in the upper-right corner of the keyboard).

Find out more about assistive technologies from the Apple Accessibility website, www.apple.com/accessibility.

Select Your Country or Region

The "Select Your Country or Region" screen requires that you select your country or region. macOS uses this information to set regional language and keyboard options and to set the appropriate Apple online stores. You can change your region settings later from Language & Region preferences.

> **NOTE** ▶ The first time you turn on a new Mac, the Mac displays a Language Chooser window before it displays the "Select Your Country or Region" screen.

Accessibility

On the Accessibility screen, you can turn on accessibility options that can help you complete Setup Assistant. Click a category (Vision, Motor, Hearing, Cognitive) to configure options related to that category. For example, click Vision, then in the Cursor Size window, select a different-sized cursor (also called the pointer).

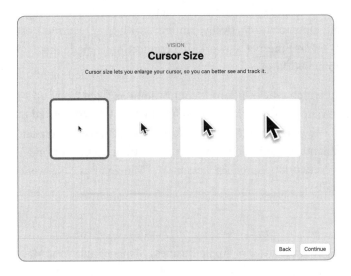

When you complete the screens for a category, Setup Assistant returns you to the Accessibility screen and displays a green checkmark for any category that you have already visited.

You can always use System Preferences later to configure these options.

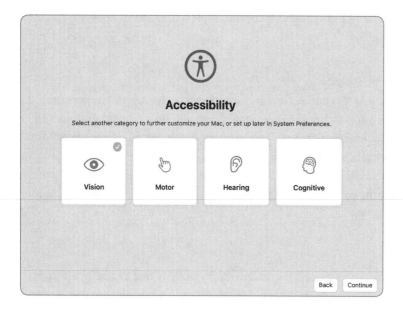

Network Settings

Setup Assistant attempts to establish a connection to the internet by automatically configuring Mac network settings. It attempts to automatically configure with the Dynamic Host Configuration Protocol (DHCP) on an Ethernet network. If a connection is made this way, you won't be asked to set up networking.

Setup Assistant tries to figure out which type of network connection you need to set up and presents you with the appropriate configuration screen. If your Mac isn't connected to Ethernet with an Ethernet cable, you'll see the Wi-Fi network setup screen, where you can select a wireless network and authenticate to it. You can postpone setting up networking at this point and do it later from Network preferences. Lesson 21, "Manage Basic Network Settings," covers this topic in detail.

Remote Management

If your organization uses Apple School Manager or Apple Business Manager and your Mac is assigned to use an MDM solution, then you will see the Remote Management screen.

Sign In with Your Apple ID

New Mac computers and Mac computers that are upgraded to macOS Big Sur may ask you to enter your Apple ID authentication. At the Sign In with Your Apple ID screen, you can:

▶ Enter an existing Apple ID.

▶ Recover a lost Apple ID or password.

▶ Create a new Apple ID.

▶ Use different Apple IDs for iCloud than for Apple media purchases (such as App Store and Music).

▶ Learn more about how data related to your Apple ID is used.

▶ Click Set Up Later to go to the next step.

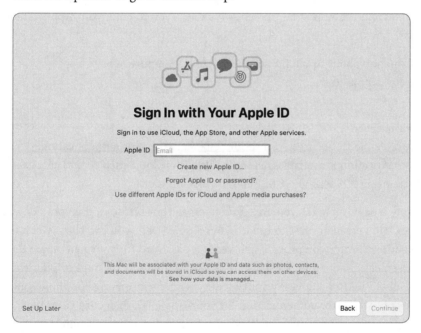

Apple ID

Your Apple ID is the name for your personal account. You use it to access Apple services like the App Store, iCloud, iMessage, FaceTime, and more. It includes the information you use to sign in, as well as all the contact, payment, and security details that you'll use across Apple online stores and services. For more information about Apple ID, see appleid.apple.com.

You can set up an Apple ID at no cost. If you've made online purchases from Apple, you already have an Apple ID.

After you enter or create an Apple ID during Setup Assistant, the account is configured for several services, including Messages, FaceTime, Podcasts, and iCloud. Additionally, if you ever used the Apple ID to buy anything, it's already configured in the App Store, Apple Music, Apple TV, and Apple Books Store. But you must still enter your Apple ID password to buy items. In later Setup Assistant screens, this Apple ID is already entered for you.

If you use one Apple ID for iCloud and a different Apple ID for store purchases, then you can click "Use different Apple IDs for iTunes and iCloud?" You'll first see the "Sign In to iCloud" screen, which asks you to enter your Apple ID for iCloud. Then you'll see the "Sign In to iTunes and the App Store" screen, which asks you to enter your Apple ID for store purchases.

For more information about Apple ID, see the Apple ID Support website, support.apple.com/apple-id.

Two-Factor Authentication

To improve your Apple ID security, you should enable two-factor authentication. Two-factor authentication is available for Apple IDs with iCloud enabled and at least one device that's using iOS 9 or OS X El Capitan 10.11 or later.

If you're creating a new Apple ID, you are asked to enter your birthday, then provide your name and an existing email address to use for your Apple ID, or you can click "Get a free iCloud email address." After you provide and verify a password for your new Apple ID, you're asked to enter a phone number that can be used with a text message or phone call to verify your identity. After you verify your identity with a text message or phone call, your Mac turns on two-factor authentication for your Apple ID, then configures your Apple ID to consider your Mac a trusted device for two-factor authentication.

iCloud

iCloud is a free cloud-storage and communication service that you can set up on current Apple devices. Though not required for completing Setup Assistant, iCloud is the easiest way to share information between macOS, iOS, iPadOS, tvOS, and even non-Apple devices.

If an existing Apple ID was never used for iCloud, entering this account during Setup Assistant enables the Apple ID to include iCloud services. Setup Assistant can configure your Mac to use iCloud for most services.

The following iCloud services are turned on by default in most cases: iCloud Drive, Photos, Contacts, Calendars, Reminders, Safari, Siri, Notes, Find My, News, Stocks, and Home. If the Apple ID you entered has two-factor authentication turned on, iCloud Keychain will be turned on. If the Apple ID you enter belongs to the @mac.com, @me.com, or @icloud.com domain, Mail is also configured.

If you enter an Apple ID that belongs to someone under the age of 13 (made possible with Apple School Manager or Family Sharing), no iCloud services are turned on by default.

> **NOTE ▶** If your school or company created a Managed Apple ID for you, you can enter it in the "Sign In with Your Apple ID" screen, but be aware that you can access more services with your personal Apple ID than you can with your Managed Apple ID. You can learn more in Apple Support article HT205918, "About Managed Apple IDs for education," and Apple Support article HT210737, "About Managed Apple IDs for business."

After setup, you can verify and modify iCloud service settings from iCloud preferences. iCloud is covered throughout this guide, including Lesson 9, "Manage Security and Privacy"; Lesson 18, "Install Apps"; Lesson 19, "Manage Files"; and Lesson 24, "Manage Network Services."

For more information about iCloud, see the iCloud Support website, support.apple.com/icloud.

Terms and Conditions

You must accept the Apple terms and conditions to complete Setup Assistant. When you do, you don't send personal or technical information to Apple. In fact, you can accept terms and conditions even if your Mac is offline and never accesses the internet.

For more information about Apple terms and conditions, see the Apple Legal website, www.apple.com/legal/.

Create a Computer Account

On the Create a Computer Account screen, you must create the initial administrator user account for the Mac. At first, this account is the only administrator user account allowed to modify system settings, including the creation of additional user accounts. Until you create additional administrator user accounts, you must remember the authentication information for this account.

If you previously entered an Apple ID, that information is used to configure services for a new local administrator account. Setup Assistant automatically populates the full name based on your full name associated with your Apple ID. Then Setup Assistant uses the full name to prepopulate the account name, which can be used to create the user's home folder. You can change the full name or account name here.

Create a Computer Account

Fill out the following information to create your computer account.

Full name: Barbara Green

Account name: barbaragreen
This will be the name of your home folder.

Password: new password   verify

Hint: optional

☑ Allow my Apple ID to reset this password

If you didn't enter an Apple ID during Setup Assistant, the name fields won't be prepopulated.

You must provide a new password for the local administrator account. The password you define for this account cannot match the Apple ID password if you entered your Apple ID.

You can define a password hint, which is a clue intended to help you if you forget this account's password. Although you can define more than one word for the password hint, you can't set the password hint to the same text as the password.

By default, the option "Allow my Apple ID to reset this password" is selected if you provided your Apple ID during Setup Assistant. You can deselect this feature, but you might need it later if you forget your password. Read more about using your Apple ID to reset your password in Reference 10.2, "Reset Lost Passwords."

After setup, you can modify local user accounts from Users & Groups preferences, then adjust iCloud settings from the iCloud pane of Apple ID preferences in System Preferences. Additional user account creation and management are detailed in Lesson 7, "Manage User Accounts."

NOTE ▶ Although it's common to use your own Apple ID and your real name, this guide uses the following for the first computer account to illustrate several features of administering a Mac with multiple computer accounts:

Full name: Local Administrator

Account name: ladmin

Apple ID: Not used for the first computer account

Find My

You'll see the Find My screen if you signed in with your iCloud account. You'll also see this screen if Find My was already enabled for your Mac before macOS was reinstalled on your Mac. This screen displays a portion of the iCloud account that Find My uses. You can click the "See how your data is managed" link or click Continue.

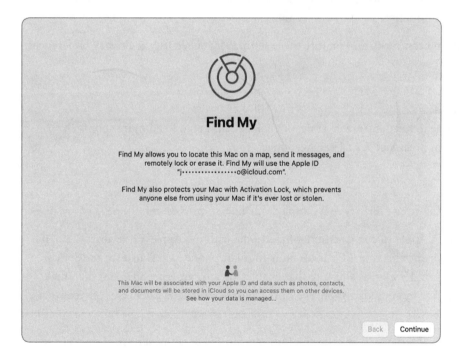

Express Set Up

The Express Set Up screen lets you quickly enable several options at once. If you click Continue, several screens are skipped. It's the same as if you click Customize Settings and then enable each option for each of the screens listed in the Express Set Up screen.

Enable Location Services

If you enable Location Services, you allow macOS and apps to locate your Mac using a Wi-Fi–based geolocation technology. You need Location Services for Find My, which you can enable later during Setup Assistant. You can further adjust Location Services in Security & Privacy preferences. Lesson 9 covers Location Services in greater detail.

If you don't enable Location Services, you see the Select Your Time Zone screen.

After setup, you can verify and modify settings from Date & Time preferences. Regardless of your Location Services choice, macOS sets the date and time using Apple time servers.

Analytics or iCloud Analytics

macOS can send diagnostic and usage information to Apple and third-party developers. If you decide to share this information, you help developers to improve system and app performance. If providing this kind of feedback is a privacy concern for you, you can disable sharing this information.

After setup, you can verify and modify these settings from Security & Privacy preferences, as covered in Lesson 9.

Screen Time

Click Continue to turn on Screen Time, or click Set Up Later. Read more about Screen Time in Reference 7.1, "User Accounts."

Siri

If you don't want to use Siri, leave it disabled during Setup Assistant.

For a Mac with Apple silicon or an Intel-based Mac with the Apple T2 Security Chip, if you enable Ask Siri and your Mac has a built-in microphone, you'll also see the Set Up "Hey Siri" screen. Hey Siri is a feature that enables you to say, "Hey Siri" and then make your request. For more information, see Apple Support article HT209014, "Devices that support 'Hey Siri.'"

If you enable Ask Siri, you'll also see the Improve Siri & Dictation screen. Here you can choose to help Apple improve Siri, Dictation, and other natural language processing functionality. Select Share Audio Recording to share audio recordings of your interactions with Siri, Dictation, and Translate features with Apple.

After setup, you can verify and modify Siri settings from Siri preferences, as covered in Lesson 9.

FileVault Disk Encryption

You can use FileVault to protect your startup disk. You see this screen in new Mac computers and Mac computers you upgrade to macOS Big Sur if the following is true:

▶ Your Mac doesn't already have FileVault turned on.

▶ Your Mac has a single local user account.

▶ You are signed in to iCloud.

▶ Your Mac starts up from a built-in solid-state drive (SSD) or flash storage.

If you select the option to turn on FileVault, you can save a FileVault recovery key to iCloud. If you don't choose to allow iCloud to unlock the disk, you see another screen showing the FileVault recovery key. In this case, you are responsible for remembering the recovery key.

NOTE ▶ macOS sometimes says "iCloud account" instead of "Apple ID." Because you access Apple services, including iCloud, with Apple ID authentication, this guide uses Apple ID when it describes Apple service authentication.

NOTE ▶ If your organization uses an MDM solution to escrow your FileVault recovery key, you may not see your personal recovery key.

A Mac with Apple silicon or an Intel-based Mac with the T2 chip integrates security into software and hardware to provide encrypted-storage capabilities. The built-in storage for a Mac with Apple silicon or an Intel-based Mac with the T2 chip is encrypted. Even so, you should turn on FileVault so that your Mac requires a password to decrypt your data. For more information about FileVault, see Apple Support article HT208344, "About encrypted storage on your new Mac."

If your Intel-based Mac doesn't have the T2 chip and you turn on FileVault, macOS begins to encrypt the system volume contents. Encryption finishes in the background while your Mac is connected to power.

If you don't turn on FileVault, you can do so later from Security & Privacy preferences. Lesson 12, "Manage FileVault," covers this topic in greater detail.

Touch ID

If your Mac has Touch ID, you can use your fingerprint to unlock your Mac and make purchases with Apple Pay. You can use the Touch ID pane of System Preferences to change Touch ID later.

Choose Your Look

You can choose Light Mode, Dark Mode (to help you focus on your work), or Auto Mode, which dynamically adjusts the appearance of buttons, menus, and windows as the day progresses. You can use the General pane of System Preferences to change the look later.

True Tone Display

If your Mac notebook or display is equipped with True Tone, you'll see the True Tone Display screen. True Tone makes images on your display and Touch Bar appear more natural. True Tone technology uses multichannel sensors to adjust the color and intensity of your display and Touch Bar to match the ambient light.

You can turn True Tone on or off in the System Preferences Displays pane. See Apple Support article HT208909, "Use True Tone on your Mac," for more information.

Reference 3.2
Manage System Settings

After you complete Setup Assistant, you can modify macOS and user settings with System Preferences and configuration profiles.

Open System Preferences

macOS gives you at least five ways to open System Preferences:

▶ You can open System Preferences from the Apple menu.

▶ You can open System Preferences from the /Applications folder.

▶ You can open System Preferences from the Dock. The Dock is a convenient place to keep items you use frequently. It's at the bottom of your screen after the first time you log in. If you see a red badge on the System Preferences icon in the Dock, you need to take one or more actions. For example, if you didn't fully set up iCloud, the badge appears on the icon in the Dock. When you click the icon, iCloud preferences opens and you can complete setup. Click and hold System Preferences in the Dock to see the preferences you can configure. With a default installation of macOS, System Preferences is in the Dock, but you can remove it.

▶ Open System Preferences from Launchpad. It's an easy way to find and open apps. Click Launchpad in the Dock, or pinch-close your thumb and three fingers on your trackpad, then click System Preferences.

▶ Open System Preferences from Spotlight.

Use System Preferences

System Preferences organizes options for your Mac into preferences. For example, use Dock preferences to set options for your Dock.

The View menu gives you quick access to preferences. You can organize preferences alphabetically or by category. You can hide some preferences when you choose View > Customize.

If you're not sure which preferences you need, enter a search term in the Search field in the upper-right corner of System Preferences. System Preferences lists the options that match your search term and highlights the preference panes where they're located.

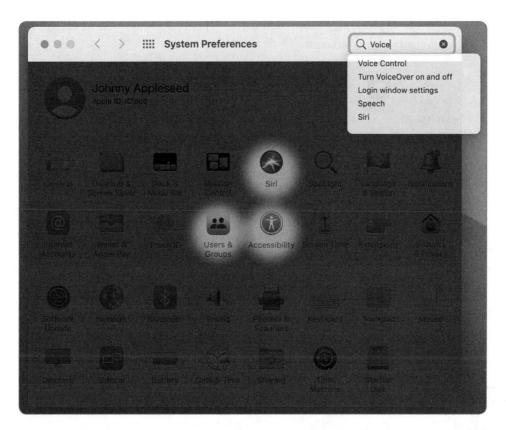

Click a preferences icon to access its settings. Most System Preferences changes are instantaneous and don't require you to click an Apply or OK button. Click the Show All button (a grid of squares) from any of the preference panes to return to the System Preferences pane. Or click and hold the Show All button to view an alphabetical list of all available preferences.

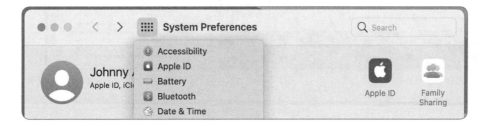

Some preferences have a lock in the lower-left corner. These preferences can be accessed only by an administrator user account.

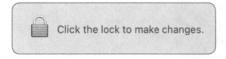

If you are logged in as a non-administrator user, more preferences are locked than if you are logged in as an administrator user. For example, if you are logged in as an administrator user, Time Machine preferences won't show the lock. The lock will show, however, if you're logged in as a non-administrator user.

The lock also appears outside System Preferences. The lock icon is an indication that access to an item requires administrator authentication, often when the item represents a change that affects all users.

Most System Preferences panes include a Help button (question mark) in the lower-right corner for more information about the options.

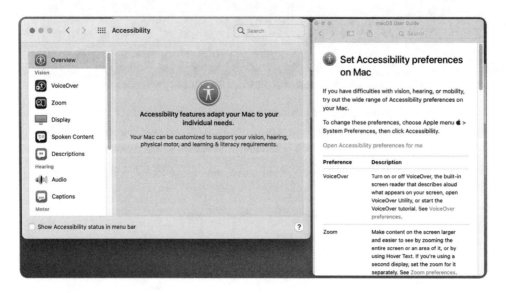

Configure Appearance, Accent, and Highlight Color

Setup Assistant asks you to select Light Mode, Dark Mode, or Auto Mode. You can always use System Preferences to change your selection. In System Preferences, open General preferences.

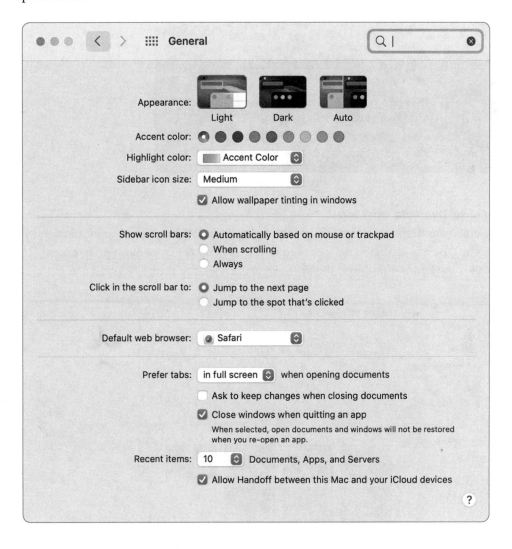

For Appearance, select Light, Dark, or Auto. When you update the Accent color, the Highlight color changes, and you can further adjust the Highlight color. The changes you make happen immediately, and System Preferences updates the look of the graphics in the Appearance preview.

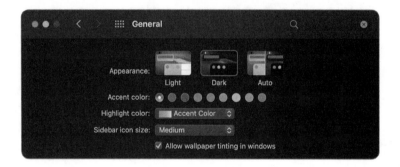

Configure Dynamic Desktop

By default, your desktop picture changes throughout the day, based on your location and time zone. You can configure this behavior in the Desktop & Screen Saver preferences. The following figure shows several built-in Dynamic Desktop themes you can use.

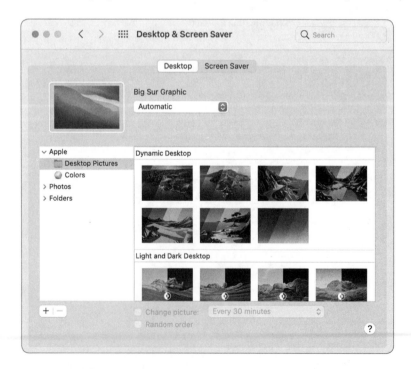

For many of the Dynamic desktops, you can click the menu and choose a desktop that is still (as opposed to Dynamic).

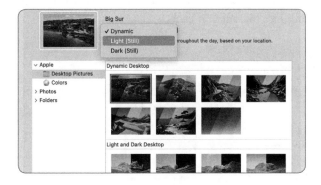

NOTE ▶ After this point, this guide uses a white desktop background for many screenshots to optimize appearance for the printed page.

Configure Dock & Menu Bar

The Dock & Menu Bar preferences pane is new with macOS Big Sur; previous versions of macOS have Dock preferences, but macOS Big Sur adds Menu Bar preferences. You now have the option of automatically hiding the menu bar.

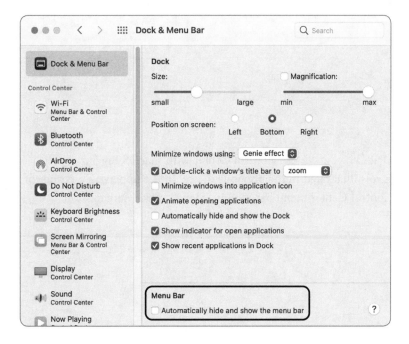

Additionally, many items in the left column offer a checkbox to control whether the item appears in the menu bar. In the following figure, Wi-Fi is listed with Control Center, because the option is turned off to show Wi-Fi in the menu bar. But Screen Mirroring displays Menu Bar & Control Center because it's included in each.

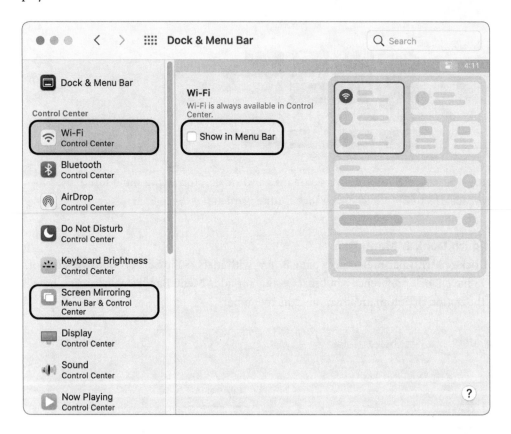

Use Control Center

Just like with iOS and iPadOS, you can use Control Center with macOS Big Sur to instantly access the controls illustrated in the previous figure. In the upper-right corner of your screen, click the Control Center menu bar item to open Control Center.

You can use Dock & Menu Bar preferences to add more items to Control Center. In the following figure, Accessibility Shortcuts and Battery were added to Control Center.

Configure Accessibility

In System Preferences, click Accessibility to configure the settings.

Use the Shortcut pane in Accessibility preferences to toggle accessibility shortcuts that appear in the Accessibility Shortcuts panel, which you can use to quickly turn on or off accessibility options.

The following figure illustrates that when VoiceOver, Zoom, and Increase Contrast are selected in Accessibility shortcuts, these are the shortcuts that appear when you click the Accessibility menu bar item. Furthermore, in the menu bar item, the icon for Zoom is highlighted because an option related to Zoom is currently turned on.

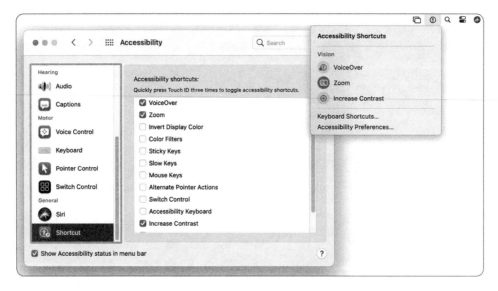

At any point when you are logged in, you can use a keyboard shortcut to open the Accessibility Shortcuts panel:

▸   Press Option-Command-F5.

▸   If your Mac has Touch ID, quickly press Touch ID three times.

Continuing the example, here's how macOS displays the Accessibility Shortcuts panel that displays the Accessibility shortcuts in the middle of the screen. The checkbox is selected for any Accessibility option that is currently turned on.

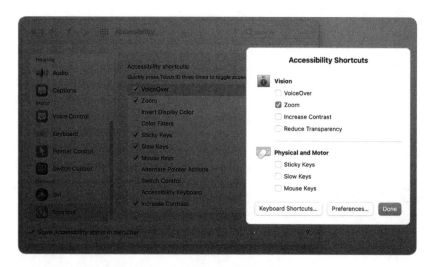

In the Accessibility Shortcuts panel, select accessibility options to turn them on. Or use the Tab key to navigate, then press the Space bar to select an option. Press Return or click Done to close the Accessibility Shortcuts panel.

Here is another example of Accessibility preferences: you can use the Zoom pane to configure how to make the entire screen larger or enlarge just the portion of the screen where you move the pointer.

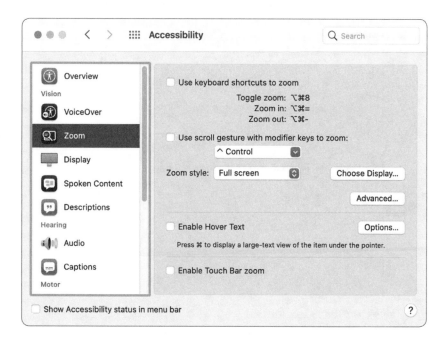

Use the Spoken Content pane of Accessibility preferences to customize the voice that your Mac uses. You can turn on announcements when alerts appear or apps need your attention. You can turn on the option for your Mac to speak the selected text when you press a keyboard shortcut.

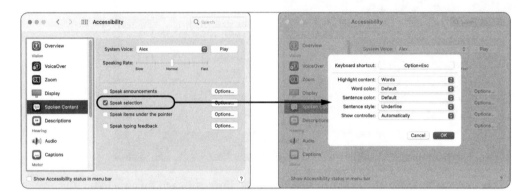

Open the Keyboard pane of Accessibility preferences to turn on Sticky Keys and Slow Keys. With Sticky Keys, you can use modifier keys (like Shift, Fn [Function], Control, Option, and Command) in keyboard shortcuts without holding down modifier keys. When Sticky Keys is turned on, each time you press a modifier key its symbol appears in the upper-right corner of the screen until you use it in a keyboard shortcut.

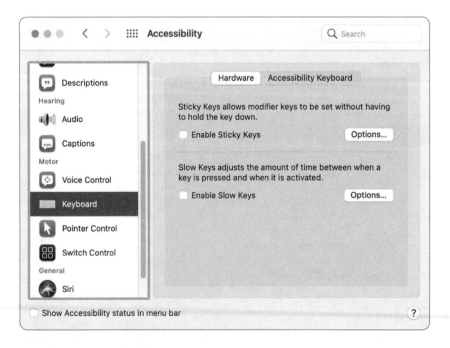

You can use the onscreen Accessibility Keyboard to type and interact with macOS as an alternative to using the hardware keyboard. Click the Accessibility Keyboard tab, then select the checkbox for Enable Accessibility Keyboard.

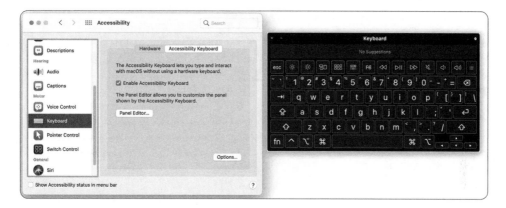

The Switch Control pane enables you to use one or more adaptive devices to enter text, interact with items on your screen, and control your Mac.

When you enable Switch Control, the Switch Control Home panel appears. If you're not an administrator user, you need administrator credentials to enable Switch Control.

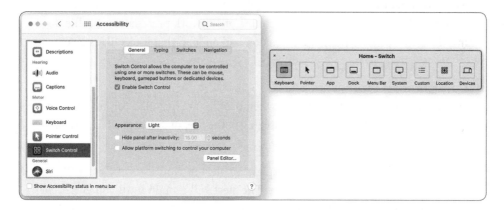

You can use the Panel Editor to add custom panels to the Switch Control or Accessibility Keyboard panel collection.

In Accessibility preferences, select an item in the left column and click the Help button (question mark) to read more about that topic. For example, with Voice Control selected in the Accessibility pane of System Preferences, click Help to read "Change Voice Control preferences for accessibility on Mac."

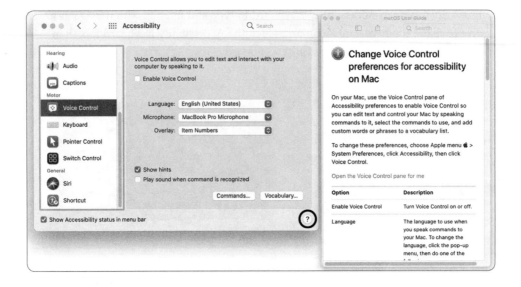

Configuration Profiles

You can use configuration profiles, trust profiles, and enrollment profiles to configure and manage Apple devices.

A profile is a document that includes instructions for settings. For example, configuration profiles may contain settings for internet accounts or Network preferences. Profile documents have the .mobileconfig filename extension and an icon that looks like a gear.

Install Configuration Profiles

The Profiles preferences pane appears only when profiles are installed (or are about to be installed). To manually install a profile, double-click the file, or select the file and choose File > Open.

After you open a profile, macOS Big Sur displays an alert in Notification Center. You need to review the profile before macOS installs it. The alert will remain until you either click the alert or open Profiles preferences, or approximately eight (8) minutes go by without you taking either action.

To continue with the process of manually installing a profile, open the Profiles pane of System Preferences. The Profiles pane displays information about the profile. A profile that has not yet been installed is displayed on the left with an exclamation mark and on the right with Ignore and Install buttons.

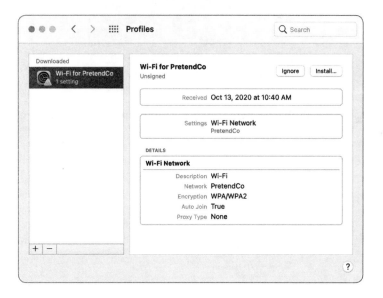

After you click Install, macOS displays a confirmation dialog.

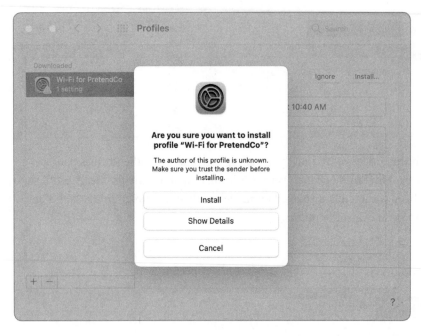

After you've installed the profile, Profiles preferences displays information about the profile.

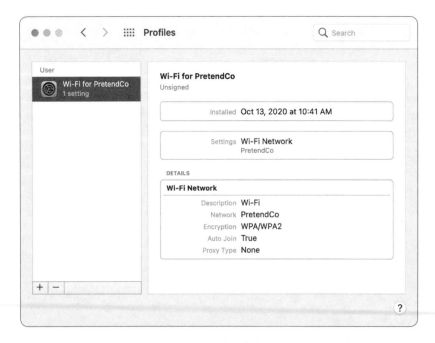

When you install a profile, user and system settings are automatically configured based on the profile's content. You are able to create a configuration profile that contains a variety of settings and share the profile with multiple users. This way, users can install the profile instead of manually configuring settings.

Configuration profiles contain settings that automatically configure certain functions. Trust profiles contain digital certificates, which are used to validate and secure service connections. Enrollment profiles are used to establish a connection to an MDM solution. Apple and third-party developers provide software for creating configuration profiles. Apple offers an MDM solution called Profile Manager, a service of the Server app.

You can share profiles just like you share documents. For example, you can share a profile through email, from a website link, or by using AirDrop (which is covered in Lesson 25, "Manage Host Sharing and Personal Firewall"). You can automatically push profiles to a Mac that's enrolled in an MDM solution like Profile Manager. You can find out more about Profile Manager at support.apple.com/guide/profile-manager/.

You might have to provide administrator authentication to install or remove some profiles. For example, a profile that enrolls your Mac in your organization's MDM solution requires that you authenticate as an administrator. And some profiles that were installed from your organization's MDM solution cannot be removed, not even by an administrator.

> **NOTE ▸** Although it's best practice to use an MDM solution to deploy profiles, this guide focuses on the fundamentals of managing a Mac that isn't enrolled in an MDM solution.

For more information about MDM, see "MDM overview for Apple Devices" in "Mobile Device Management Settings for IT Administrators" at support.apple.com/guide/mdm/mdmbf9e668.

Exercise 3.1
Configure a Mac for Exercises

▶ **Prerequisite**

    ▶   Your Mac must have a default installation of macOS Big Sur. A default installation is the result when you install macOS on an internal storage device that has been erased.

In this exercise, you learn how your initial configuration settings affect macOS. You configure a new macOS installation on a Mac as if you just took it out of the box. You use Setup Assistant to answer some questions and create the initial administrator user account.

Configure macOS with Setup Assistant

1   On the Welcome screen, select the appropriate country or region and click Continue. If the VoiceOver tutorial begins, you can either listen or move forward. VoiceOver is an assistive technology.

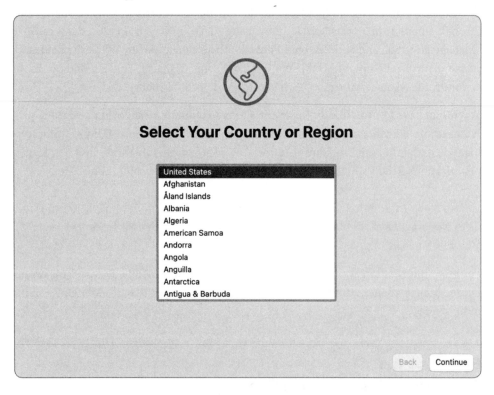

2   At the Accessibility screen, turn on any assistive needs, then click Continue. If you don't want to configure Accessibility at this time, click Not Now.

Setup Assistant evaluates your network environment and tries to determine whether you are connected to the internet. This can take a few moments.

3   If you are asked to select your Wi-Fi network, select an appropriate network, then click Continue. Enter your password or credentials as applicable.

If you don't use Wi-Fi, choose Other Network Options, then select your internet connection type. If you aren't asked about your internet connection, your Mac network settings are already configured using DHCP, and you may move to step 4. After your network connection is configured, click Continue.

4   On the Data & Privacy screen, read Apple's privacy policy, then click Continue.

Click "Learn more" to read further information surrounding Apple's privacy policy.

5   On the Migration Assistant screen, click Not Now, then click Continue.

If you were replacing a Mac, the transfer options would assist you in migrating user data, apps, and system information from the current Mac to the new one.

6   On the Sign In with Your Apple ID screen, click Set Up Later, then click Skip in the confirmation dialog that appears.

You set up an Apple ID account in a later exercise.

7   At the Terms and Conditions screen, read the macOS Software License Agreement, then click Agree.

8   In the confirmation dialog that appears, click Agree.

9   At the Create a Computer Account screen, enter the following, then click Continue:

NOTE ▶ Create this account as specified here. If you don't, future exercises might not work as written. This guide uses **bold text** to indicate text you should enter exactly as shown.

Full name: **Local Administrator**

Account name: **ladmin**

Password: **Apple321!**

Don't provide a password hint.

Change the account picture if you want to do so.

NOTE ▸ On the Mac you use for your daily work, never use a password such as Apple321!. It's easy to guess, so it's not secure.

Create a Computer Account

Fill out the following information to create your computer account.

Full name:	Local Administrator
Account name:	ladmin
	This will be the name of your home folder.
Password:	••••••••• •••••••••
Hint:	optional

10 At the Express Set Up screen, click Continue. Your Mac enables Location Services and Analytics. Analytics shares diagnostics and usage data with Apple and, by proxy, third-party developers.

11 At the Analytics screen, click Continue.

12 At the Screen Time screen, click Set Up Later.

13 If the Siri screen appears, deselect Enable Ask Siri, then click Continue.

14 If you're asked to set up Touch ID, click Continue; click Set Up Touch ID Later, then click Continue in the confirmation dialog. These exercises don't require Touch ID.

15 At the Choose Your Look screen, select the appearance you prefer for your Mac, then click Continue.

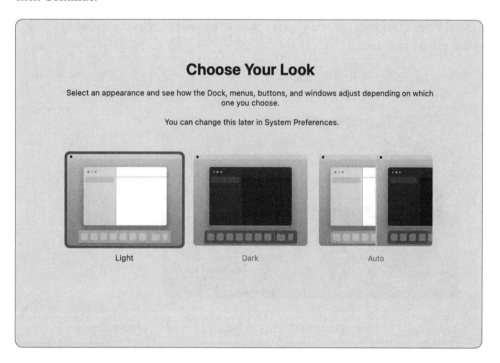

16 If the True Tone Display screen appears, click Continue.

Your Mac is now set up and ready for use.

Exercise 3.2
Configure System Preferences

▶ **Prerequisites**

- ▶ You must have created the Local Administrator account (Exercise 3.1, "Configure a Mac for Exercises").

- ▶ You must pick a student number between 01 and 17.

In this exercise, you configure preference settings to ease navigation and provide a consistent experience. You also configure app and system preferences.

Several types of notifications may appear at any time during these exercises or while you're using your Mac.

▶ If the Updates Available notification appears during this exercise, hover over the lower-right corner, click Options, then choose Remind Me Tomorrow.

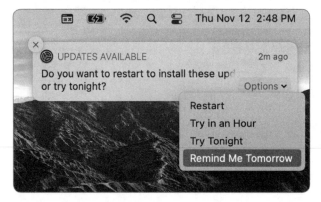

You install software updates in the exercises in Lesson 6, "Update macOS."

▶ If a notification appears with a "Do you want to use the disk *some volume* to back up?" prompt, hover over the lower-right corner, click Options, and then choose "Don't ask me again."

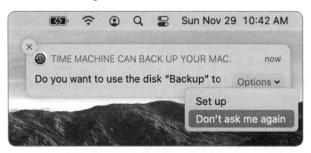

Adjust the Finder Preferences

The default Finder settings make it easy for users to find and work with their files. You can configure the settings so that you can access files outside of a user's home folder.

1   From the menu bar, choose Finder > Preferences. If you prefer, you can use the keyboard shortcut Command-Comma.

2   If necessary, click General in the toolbar, then select "Hard disks" and "Connected servers" to have the Finder display them on your desktop.

3   From the "New Finder windows show" menu, choose your startup volume.

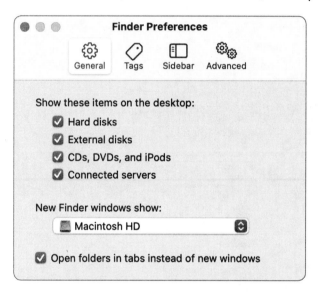

4   In the toolbar of the Finder Preferences window, click the Sidebar button.

5   Select "ladmin" in the Favorites section of the sidebar and "Hard disks" in the
Locations section. "Hard disks" should be fully selected (a checkmark in the checkbox), not partially selected (a dash in the checkbox).

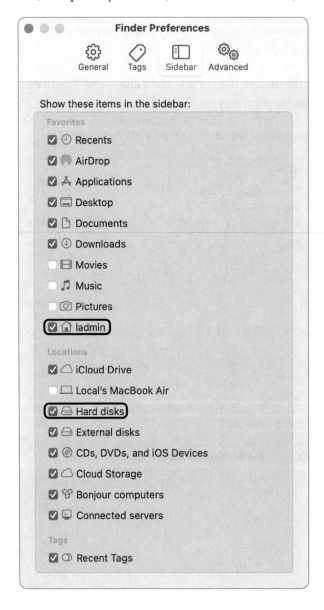

6   Close the Finder Preferences window. You can use the Command-W shortcut if
you wish.

Set the Computer Name

When you're performing the exercises in an in-person classroom setting, your Mac may have the same default name as the other students' Mac computers. It is a good practice to use a unique name.

1 From the Apple menu, choose System Preferences.

2 In System Preferences, click the icon for Sharing preferences.

   If you aren't sure where to find something in System Preferences, enter the text you're looking for into Spotlight in the top right of the window. Spotlight searches for matching or related settings and highlights the preference panes where they are located.

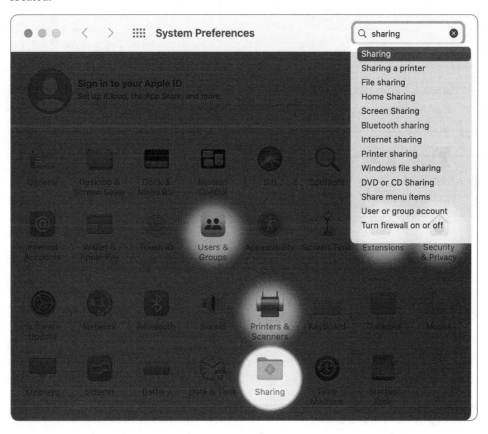

3 Enter a unique name for your Mac in the Computer Name field. This guide follows the convention **Mac-***NN*, where *NN* is your student number that you assigned yourself in the prerequisites.

4 Press Return.

Your local hostname (.local name) displayed under your computer name updates to match your new computer name.

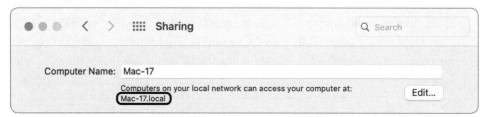

5 From the left sidebar, select the Remote Management checkbox.

In an in-person course, Remote Management allows your trainer to control the keyboard and mouse, gather information, and update your Mac throughout the course, enabling your trainer to help you with steps if necessary.

A dialog asks what you want users to be able to do using Remote Management.

6 Press and hold the Option key while clicking one of the checkboxes to select all options in the dialog.

7   Click OK.

Adjust Your Trackpad and Mouse Preferences

In macOS you can customize the user interface. For example, depending on your personal preferences, you might want to change the default scrolling behavior. Also, you can control how macOS recognizes primary and secondary mouse clicks (analogous to left- and right-clicks in other operating systems).

Since Control-click works as a secondary click, these exercises describe it as Control-click.

1   Click the Show All (grid icon) button in the toolbar.

The Show All button displays all System Preference pane icons and can aid your navigation.

2   If you are using a trackpad, click the Trackpad button to open the Trackpad preference pane.

▶   Adjust the "Tap to click" and "Secondary click" options to your personal preference. A secondary click opens shortcut menus, equivalent to clicking the right mouse button or Control-clicking.

▶   Adjust the "Force Click and haptic feedback" option to your personal preference.

▶   Click Scroll & Zoom and use the "Scroll direction: Natural" option to adjust the scroll direction. The default is that if you move two fingers up, you move the window contents up.

▶   Check the other options under Scroll & Zoom and More Gestures and make appropriate changes based on your personal preferences.

▶   When you have finished using the Trackpad pane, click the Show All button.

3   If you are using a mouse, click the Mouse button.

▶   If your mouse has a scroll wheel or equivalent, use the "Scroll direction: Natural" option to adjust the scroll direction. The default is that if you push the wheel up, you move the window contents up.

▶   If your mouse has multiple buttons, use the menu on the left side of the mouse image to control which button is the primary one. You use this button to select; it's usually the left button. Use the menu on the right side of the mouse image to control which button is the secondary button. You use this button to open shortcut menus; it's usually the right button, or Control-click.

Turn On FileVault

NOTE ▶ If you lose the passwords and the recovery key for a FileVault-encrypted volume, you won't have access to the content stored in it. If you are performing this exercise on your own Mac and have files you don't want to risk losing, back up your Mac before starting this exercise.

In this exercise, you turn on FileVault to encrypt your startup volume. Enabling encryption on your startup volume is a best practice and can be done at any time. You will be able to continue to work on your Mac while the startup volume is being encrypted.

1   Click Show All (grid icon), then open the Security & Privacy pane.

2   Click FileVault.

3   Unlock the preference pane, then authenticate as Local Administrator (password: Apple321!).

4   Click Turn On FileVault.

If a dialog appears saying "A recovery key has been set by your company, school, or institution," it means your Mac was preloaded with an institutional recovery key (described in Apple Support article HT202385, "Set a FileVault recovery key for computers in your organization"). In this case, click Continue and skip to step 9. You will also not be able to perform Exercise 12.2, "Use a FileVault Recovery Key."

If an institutional key wasn't set, a dialog appears giving you the choice between allowing your iCloud account to unlock the disk or creating a recovery key. The dialog will be slightly different if you haven't linked the Local Administrator account to an Apple ID.

5 Select "Create a recovery key and don't use my iCloud account," then click Continue.

Your iCloud account can be used to unlock your disk and reset your password if you forget it.

If you do not want to use an iCloud account, you can create a recovery key and store it in a safe place to reset your password.

- ◯ Set up my iCloud account to reset my password
- ◉ Create a recovery key and do not use my iCloud account

?   Cancel   Back   Continue

6 Record your recovery key. Your recovery key will be different than the key in this example.

The recovery key is a code which can be used to unlock the disk if you forget your password.

Make a copy of this code and store it in a safe place. If you forget your password and lose the recovery key, all the data on your disk will be lost.

JCQT-EJWQ-69R2-PMKR-Z74B-ER6N

?   Cancel   Back   Continue

Recovery key: _____

For these exercises, you must record your recovery key for later use. You could take a screenshot of the recovery key window and use AirDrop to send it to your mobile device. You could also take a picture of the screen with the camera in your mobile device or write it in the area provided.

NOTE ▸ For the purposes of this training, storing the recovery key as an image on your mobile device is acceptable, However, in production you should always store the recorded recovery key in a physically secure location.

7 Click Continue to begin the encryption process.

Encrypting the entire volume might take a while, depending on the speed and type of your Mac, the type of storage device, and the amount of data. You can use your Mac normally during the encryption process.

If you are using a Mac with Apple silicon, or an Intel-based Mac computer with the Apple T2 Security Chip, there is no encryption process or time estimate, because internal storage is encrypted by default.

If your Mac does not have a T2 chip or isn't an Mac with Apple silicon and you are using a portable Mac computer, you must be plugged in to power for encryption to take place.

8   Quit System Preferences.

Because System Preferences is a single-window app, you can either click the close button or open the System Preferences menu and choose Quit System Preferences.

Exercise 3.3
Download Student Materials

▶ **Prerequisite**

   ▶   You must have completed Exercise 3.2, "Configure System Preferences."

In this exercise, you download the student materials (called StudentMaterials) required for the rest of the exercises.

Download the StudentMaterials Folder from the Internet

You need to connect to the Pearson Education website to download the student materials.

1   Open Safari.

2   Navigate to www.peachpit.com/register. Register for a new account or sign in with your existing account.

3   Enter the ISBN number for this guide: 9780137345953.

4   Answer the challenge question(s) as proof of purchase.

5   On your Account page, click the Registered Products tab.

6   Click the Access Bonus Content link below the title of your product to proceed to the download page.

NOTE ▶ If you purchase or redeem a code for the electronic version of this guide directly from Peachpit, the student materials will automatically appear on the Registered Products tab without the need to redeem an additional code.

7   Click the link to download Student Materials.

8   When you are asked to allow downloads on www.peachpit.com, click Allow.

The student materials for these exercises will be downloaded as a ZIP archive and automatically expanded into the StudentMaterials folder.

9   Click the Downloads (down-arrow icon) button near the top right of the window.

10 Click the view (magnifying-glass icon) button next to StudentMaterials.

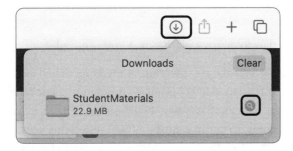

Your Downloads folder opens in the Finder, showing the StudentMaterials folder inside it.

Organize the StudentMaterials Folder on your Mac

1   On your desktop, find the icon for your startup disk (typically Macintosh HD), and double-click it.

This opens a new Finder window showing the contents of the startup disk.

2   Open the Users folder, then open the Shared folder.

3 Drag the StudentMaterials icon from the Downloads folder into the Shared folder.

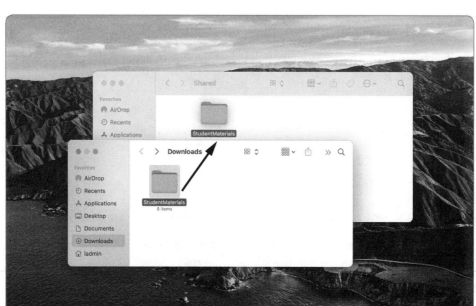

4 Close the Downloads folder.

5 Put your copy of the StudentMaterials folder in a place where you can find it.

▶ Drag the StudentMaterials folder into the right section of the Dock. The Dock is divided into up to three sections. The left side holds apps, and the right side holds folders, documents, and other items such as aliases to network shares. The Dock can also display a middle section that holds up to three apps that you've recently opened and that aren't otherwise in the Dock. Place the StudentMaterials folder in the right section of the Dock, next to other entries—so it is added to the Dock—rather than over another entry, which would move it into that folder.

▶ You can also drag the StudentMaterials folder to the Finder sidebar in the Favorites section. Place it between other entries.

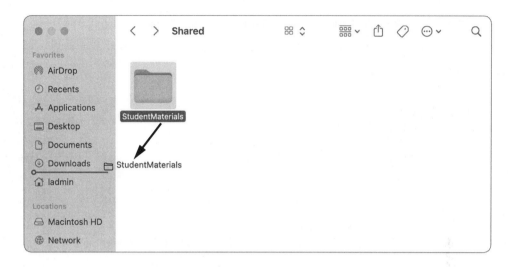

6 Choose Go > Applications or use the shortcut Shift-Command-A.

7 Drag the TextEdit app into the left side of the dividing line in your Dock so that you have an easy way to open it.

Exercise 3.4
Install a Configuration Profile

> **Prerequisite**
>
> ▶ You must have completed Exercise 3.3, "Download Student Materials."

You can manually configure settings in macOS for one Mac. You can also configure one or many Mac computers at one time with configuration profiles.

In this exercise, you manage Dock settings with a configuration profile.

Change Your Dock Settings with a Configuration Profile

1 Locate the Dock at the bottom of your screen and note its configuration. It may differ slightly from the example shown here.

2 Open the StudentMaterials folder. Remember that you placed a shortcut to it in your Dock and the sidebar in Finder windows.

3 Open the Lesson3 folder.

4 Double-click Dock.mobileconfig to begin installation of the profile.

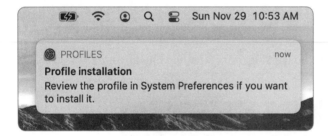

A notification appears telling you to "Review the profile in System Preferences if you want to install it."

5 Open System Preferences, and click Profiles.

6 The details of the profile and its payload (the settings it contains) are displayed. Scroll down to see its full contents.

Confirm that the Dock Orientation has a value of left.

7 Click Install.

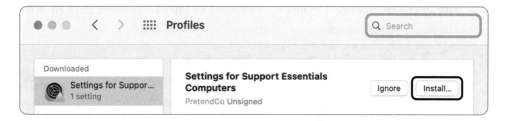

8 In the dialog that appears, click Install.

9 Authenticate as Local Administrator (**Apple321!**) at the prompt.

The Profiles pane lists the Settings for Support Essentials Computers configuration profile as installed.

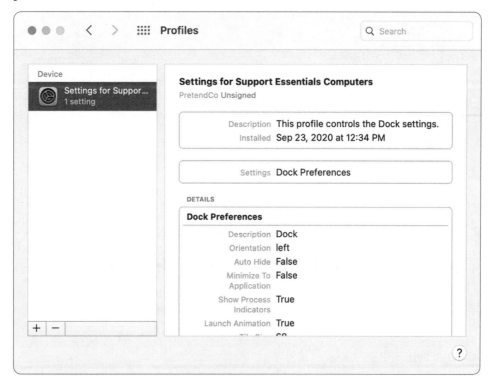

10 Confirm that the Dock is now on the left side of your screen.

Remove a Configuration Profile

1 With the profile Settings for Support Essentials Computers selected, click Remove (–).

2 In the confirmation dialog that appears, click Remove.

3 If necessary, authenticate as Local Administrator (**Apple321!**) at the prompt.

The profile is removed and the dock returns to the bottom of the screen. Because you have no other profiles installed, the Profiles system preference pane will be removed as well.

4 Quit System Preferences.

Exercise 3.5
Examine System Information

> **Prerequisites**
>
> ► You must have created the Local Administrator account (Exercise 3.1, "Configure a Mac for Exercises").
>
> ► You must have turned on FileVault (Exercise 3.2, "Configure System Preferences").

System Information is the primary tool you use to gather macOS configuration information. System Information displays information and options for repair and warranty coverage of your Mac. In this exercise, you explore its features.

Use About This Mac and System Information

1 From the Apple menu, choose About This Mac.

A dialog appears showing basic information about your Mac.

2   Select your serial number and copy it using Command-C.

3   Click the macOS version number (below the large "macOS Big Sur"). The build number (a more specific identifier for the version of macOS you are using) is displayed.

4   Click through the Displays, Storage, and (if it is shown) Memory buttons in the About This Mac window toolbar to view more information about your hardware configuration.

5   At the right end of the toolbar, click Service.

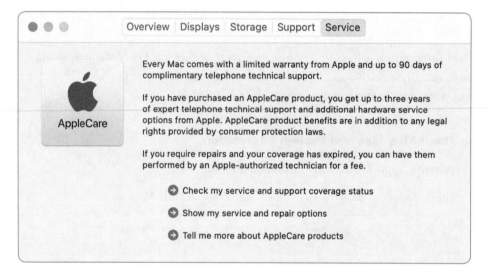

6   Click "Check my service and support coverage status."

7   In the confirmation dialog that appears, click Allow.

Safari opens and displays a coverage check page at apple.com.

8   Paste your serial number, enter the CAPTCHA challenge code, and click Continue.

The coverage page shows your Mac model name and warranty status.

9   Quit Safari.

10   In the About This Mac window, click Overview in the toolbar.

11   Click the System Report button.

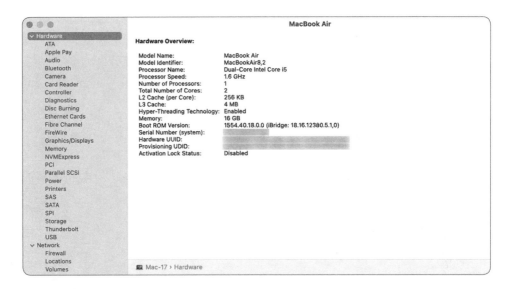

System Information opens and displays a more detailed report about your Mac hardware, network, and software configuration. You can also find System Information in the /Applications/Utilities/ folder or in the Other section of Launchpad. You can directly access System Information from the Apple menu by holding the Option key. This changes the About This Mac menu choice to System Information.

12 Click information categories in the report sidebar to explore the system. Some categories might take a while to load.

13 From the menu bar, choose File > Save, decide on a naming convention that includes the Mac name (or other identifier) and the date, then click Save.

System Information finishes gathering information about your Mac and saves it in a report that documents your Mac computer's current status.

14 Quit System Information.

Lesson 4

Use the Command-Line Interface

Use the command-line interface (CLI) to access additional administrative functionality.

Reference 4.1
CLI Basics

The CLI includes these advantages:

▶ Additional administrative and troubleshooting options are available from the CLI. For example, the following apps have CLI equivalents that include additional options: System Information (system_profiler), Installer (installer), Software Update (softwareupdate), Disk Utility (diskutil), and Spotlight (mdfind). These are just a few instances, as you can accomplish many administrative tasks by using an app or by using a command in Terminal.

▶ From the CLI you have more access to the file system. For example, the Finder hides many files and folders that are visible in the CLI. Also, there are many file-system permissions settings that the Finder doesn't display.

▶ You can remotely log in to a Mac computer's CLI using the Secure Shell (SSH) protocol. The next section contains more information about SSH.

▶ By using the sudo command, any administrator can run commands as the System Administrator user, also known as root. This enables greater administrative flexibility in the CLI. Read Reference 7.1, "User Accounts," for more information about the root account.

▶ If you are comfortable with the CLI syntax, you can apply it to a command-line script. This enables you to automate repetitive tasks.

▶ If you combine CLI instructions with Apple Remote Desktop (ARD), you can remotely administer multiple, even thousands, of Mac computers simultaneously. ARD enables you to remotely send the same command to several Mac computers with one click. You can find out more information about Apple Remote Desktop in the Apple Remote Desktop User Guide, at support.apple.com/guide/remote-desktop/.

Access the CLI

A shell is the first command that runs when you access the CLI. It displays the CLI. You can access the CLI in several ways:

▶ You can use Terminal. It's in /Applications/Utilities/Terminal. Terminal has a customizable interface. It includes a tabbed interface for multiple command-line sessions, multiple split panes for viewing history, support for full-screen mode, and Touch Bar shortcuts.

```
johnny — -zsh — 80×12
— ~ less • man rm          tail -f /var/log/install.log          — ~ -zsh
johnny@Johnnys-MacBook-Pro ~ % ls -l
total 0
drwx------+ 21 johnny  staff    672 Nov 15 17:47 Desktop
drwx------+  4 johnny  staff    128 Nov 15 14:45 Documents
drwx------+  5 johnny  staff    160 Nov 15 14:33 Downloads
drwx------@ 66 johnny  staff   2112 Nov 15 15:06 Library
drwx------   4 johnny  staff    128 Nov 14 21:10 Movies
drwx------+  3 johnny  staff     96 Nov 13 09:35 Music
drwx------+  4 johnny  staff    128 Nov 14 21:12 Pictures
drwxr-xr-x+  4 johnny  staff    128 Nov 13 09:35 Public
johnny@Johnnys-MacBook-Pro ~ % ls -lae
total 56

drwx------+  5 johnny  staff    160 Nov 15 14:33 Downloads
 0: group:everyone deny delete
drwx------@ 66 johnny  staff   2112 Nov 15 15:06 Library
 0: group:everyone deny delete
drwx------   4 johnny  staff    128 Nov 14 21:10 Movies
drwx------+  3 johnny  staff     96 Nov 13 09:35 Music
 0: group:everyone deny delete
drwx------+  4 johnny  staff    128 Nov 14 21:12 Pictures
 0: group:everyone deny delete
drwxr-xr-x+  4 johnny  staff    128 Nov 13 09:35 Public
 0: group:everyone deny delete
johnny@Johnnys-MacBook-Pro ~ %
```

You can customize Terminal window settings, such as typeface, color, background, and other settings. A Terminal profile is a collection of style and behavior settings. Open Terminal preferences, then select Profiles in the toolbar. Select a preexisting profile or create new profiles to match your needs. If you use multiple Terminal windows, you can use different profiles to help you spot the appropriate window at a glance.

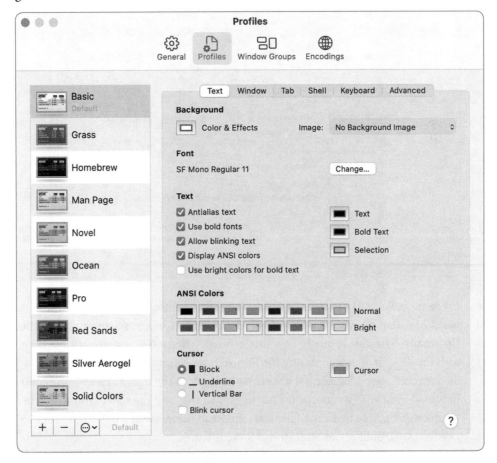

After you modify or create a new profile, click General in the toolbar, click "On startup open," and choose the profile you want. The next time you open a new Terminal window, it will use this profile.

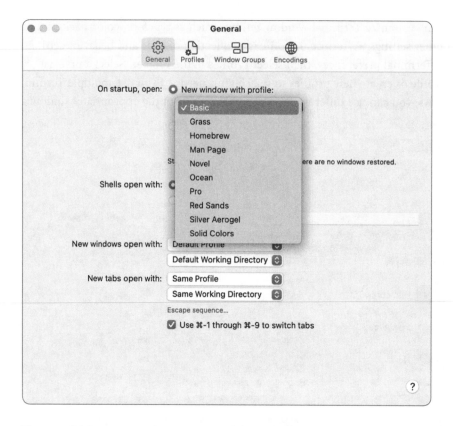

► Use macOS Recovery to open Terminal from the Utilities menu. Or for an Intel-based Mac that does not have the Apple T2 Security Chip, at startup press and hold Command-S to start in single-user mode. Single-user mode is also available for a Mac with the T2 chip if you configure the Secure Boot setting to No Security, which we do not recommend for normal use. This mode starts the minimum system required to provide you with a command-line prompt so that you can enter commands to troubleshoot a Mac that can't fully start up. Read more about single-user mode in Lesson 28, "Troubleshoot Startup and System Issues."

► SSH remote login enables you to securely log in from a remote computer to access your Mac computer's command line. SSH is a common standard, so you can use any operating system that supports SSH to remotely log in to your Mac. This remote access allows administrators to make changes at the command line without alerting the user to their work. Before you can use SSH to connect to your Mac, you have to turn on SSH access.

WARNING ► We recommend that you do not turn on SSH remote login because it lessens the security of your Mac. If you turn on SSH remote login to accomplish a task, turn off SSH remote login after you complete your task.

Work in the Command Line

When you first open Terminal, it may display information about your last login. Then it will display the prompt.

The prompt indicates that you can enter a command. By default, the prompt shows you the following:

► Your current user account name

► The @ symbol

► The name of the Mac you're using

► Your location in the file system

► A special character that provides a hint about which shell you're using

macOS Catalina and macOS Big Sur use the Z shell (zsh) by default, but if you upgraded your Mac from a version earlier than macOS Catalina, you might still be using the bash shell:

► zsh uses % at the end of the prompt.

► bash uses $ at the end of the prompt.

Read Apple Support article HT208050, "Use zsh as the default shell on your Mac" at https://support.apple.com/HT208050, for more information about different shells, including instructions about script compatibility.

Where you are in the computer's file system is called the *working directory*, and it changes as you navigate through the file system.

At the prompt, you enter your command string, often more than one word, and press Return to initiate or execute the command.

An executing command takes over the Terminal window with a text interface, shows the results of the command, and returns to the prompt, or performs some work and returns to the prompt when complete. Many commands display results only if a problem occurs. Read what the command returns to make sure it doesn't indicate a problem.

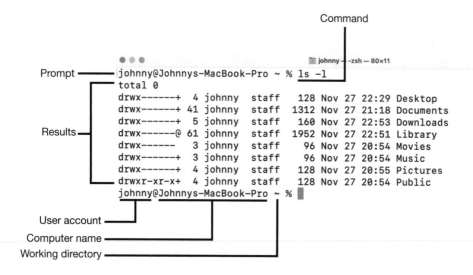

Some commands take time to execute and may not give a progress indication. If a new prompt does not appear, generally assume your last command is still running.

When you use Terminal to access some file and folders on your Mac for the first time, macOS asks for your explicit approval. This includes portions of your home folder and removable volumes.

You'll see the results of your privacy decisions in the Privacy pane of the Security & Privacy preferences in System Preferences.

We recommend that you remove the ability for Terminal to access files and folders after you complete the task that requires access. Read Reference 9.5, "Manage User Privacy," for more information. The following figure illustrates a scenario in which the logged-in user first granted Terminal access to files and folders, and then in Privacy preferences, the user deselected the checkboxes to remove access.

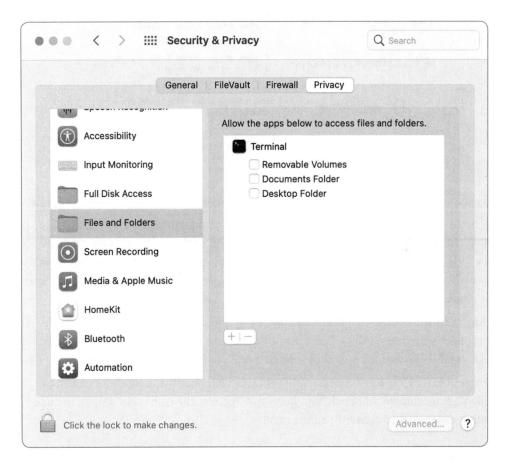

Command String

The command string includes a few parts:

1 **Command Name** In this example the "ls" command displays a list of a folder's contents.

2 **Command Options** Options add conditions, limits, or other modifiers to the command.

3 **Arguments** This is the recipient of the action, often specified as a file or folder path.

4 **Extras** Redirected output, or other commands, as needed. In this example a text file is created from the list output.

▶ Command name (1)—Some commands just need you to enter their name to execute.

▶ Command options (2)—After a command name, you might specify options (or flags) that change a command's default behavior. Options might not be required and can be different for every command. Options start with one or two dashes to distinguish them from arguments. Many commands can include several single-letter options after a single dash. For example, ls -lA is the same as ls -l -A.

▶ Arguments (3)—After the command and its options, you typically specify an argument (or parameter), which is the item or items you want the command to modify. An argument is needed only if the command requires an item to act upon.

▶ Extras (4)—Extras aren't necessary, but they can enhance the capabilities of a command. For example, you could add items that redirect the command output, include other commands, or generate a document.

Command-Line Example

Here is an example in which the user Joan works on a Mac called MyMac and her working directory is her Public folder. She deletes a file called list.txt. Joan presses Return after she enters her command.

```
joan@MyMac Public % rm list.txt

joan@MyMac Public %
```

In this example the command was entered and executed properly, and macOS returns to a new prompt. This is an example of a command that returns information only if it didn't execute properly. The Mac usually lets you know if you entered something incorrectly by returning an error message or help text. macOS won't prevent or warn you from entering a destructive command, such as accidentally deleting files in your home folder. Always double-check your typing.

Use Manual (man) Pages

When you want to learn more about a command, you type **man** followed by the name of the command. Manual (man) pages include detailed information about commands and references to other commands. After you open a man page, use navigation shortcuts to move through it:

▶ Use the Up Arrow and Down Arrow keys to scroll.

▶ Use the Space bar to move down one screen at a time.

▶ Enter a slash (**/**), enter a keyword, then press Return to search through a man page.

▶ Exit the man page by typing **q**.

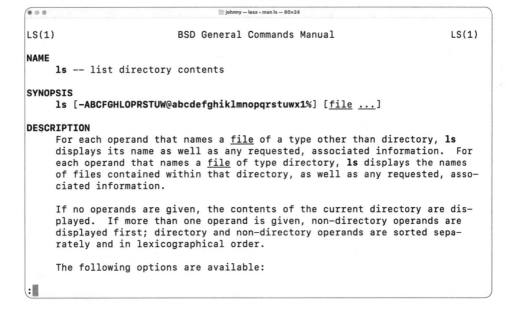

Reference 4.2
CLI Navigation

The command line is case-sensitive and requires that you use full filenames with filename extensions. For example, unless you specify to ignore case, the CLI won't locate the "music" app, but it will locate the "Music.app" app.

A path represents a file or folder's location in the file system. For instance, Disk Utility's file-system path is /Applications/Utilities/Disk Utility.app. In the CLI, you use the pathname to navigate the file system and to identify the location of items.

There are two types of file-system pathnames:

▶ Absolute paths are full descriptions of an item location, starting from the root (or beginning) of the system (startup) volume. An absolute path begins with a forward slash (/) to indicate the beginning of the file system. An example of the absolute path to the user Joan's drop box folder is /Users/joan/Public/Drop Box, which means: Start from the startup volume; go to the Users folder, then the joan subfolder, then the Public subfolder; and select the item named Drop Box.

▶ Relative paths are partial descriptions of an item location. They're based on where you're currently working in the file system. When you first open Terminal, your session starts at your home folder. The relative path from your home folder to your drop box is Public/Drop Box. This means: From where you are now, go into the Public subfolder and select the item named Drop Box.

Navigate with Commands

You use three commands to navigate the file system: pwd, ls, and cd. Short for "print working directory," pwd reports the absolute path of your current working location:

```
joan@MyMac ~ % pwd
/Users/joan
```

Short for "list," ls lists the folder contents of your current working location. Enter a pathname following the ls command to list the contents of the specified item. The ls command has additional options for listing file and folder information that are covered throughout this lesson.

Short for "change directory," cd is the command you use to navigate. Enter a pathname following the cd command to change your current working location to the specified folder. Entering cd without specifying a path returns you to your home folder.

Use Special Characters

You can use special characters at the prompt or in pathnames to save time and to be able to use special characters in filenames and pathnames.

Enter a space between command items to separate the items. If you don't want the space character to separate items, use the backslash (\) before a space character.

> joan@MyMac ~ % **cd Public/Drop\ Box**
>
> joan@MyMac Drop Box % **pwd**
>
> /Users/joan/Public/Drop Box

Another way to enter filenames and paths with spaces is to surround filenames and paths with quotation marks:

> joan@MyMac ~ % **cd "Public/Drop Box"**
>
> joan@MyMac Drop Box % **pwd**
>
> /Users/joan/Public/Drop Box

You can drag and drop items from the Finder to Terminal. When you do this, Terminal enters an item's absolute path with the appropriate backslash characters before spaces in names. Use the Tab key completion feature that's built into the command line to automatically complete filenames and pathnames.

Other special characters include !, $, &, *, ;, |, \, parentheses, quotes, and brackets. The Finder drag-and-drop and Tab key completion parse these characters. In the CLI you can enter a backslash before any special character to treat that special character as regular text rather than as a special character.

Use double periods (..) to indicate a parent folder. For example, if you are in your home folder at /Users/username, type **cd ..** to navigate to the /Users folder.

Use the tilde (~) to indicate the current user home folder in a pathname. For example, say the current user's drop box is in ~/Public/. Use the tilde to specify another user's home folder. For example, **~jill/Public** specifies Jill's Public folder.

Use Tab Key Completion

Use Tab key completion to automatically complete filenames, pathnames, and command names. Tab key completion prevents you from making typos and verifies that the item you're entering exists.

Here's an example of Tab key completion. Start from your home folder by typing **cd**, then **P**, and then press the Tab key. The Terminal window flashes quickly, and you may hear an audible alert, letting you know there is more than one choice for items that begin with "P" in your home folder. Press the Tab key again, and the Mac displays your two choices, Pictures and Public. Now, type **u** after the initial P, and then press the Tab key again, and the Mac automatically finishes Public/ for you. Finally, type **D** and press the Tab key one last time, and the Mac finishes the path with Public/Drop\ Box/.

When completing a folder name, Tab key completion puts a forward slash (/) at the end. It assumes that you want to continue the path. Most commands ignore the trailing slash, but a few behave differently if it's there. If in doubt, you should delete the / at the end of a path.

Tab key completion reads only into folders you have permission to access. You may run into issues trying to use this feature for items that are readable only by the root user.

View Invisible Items

The CLI and the Finder hide many files and folders from view. The hidden items are often created and used by macOS. Leave them alone. In the Finder, these items are set with a hidden file flag. The CLI ignores the hidden file flag and shows most hidden items. If you type the **ls** command, filenames that begin with a period won't appear. To see hidden items in long format at the command line, add the **-a** option to the **-l** option when you enter the **ls** command:

```
joan@MyMac ~ % ls -la /Users

total 0

drwxr-xr-x      8 root      admin      256 Aug 25  13:29 .

drwxr-xr-x     22 root      admin      704 Aug 20  22:57 ..

-rw-r--r--      1 root      wheel        0 Jul 14  15:30 .localized

drwxrwxrwt      6 root      wheel      192 Aug 21  10:59 Shared

drwxr-xr-x+    11 jill      staff      533 Aug 25  13:23 jill

drwxr-xr-x+    11 joan      staff      352 Aug 25  13:29 joan
```

Any item with a period at the beginning of its name is hidden by default in the CLI and the Finder.

Navigate to Other Volumes

The CLI uses a concept called *firm links*, explained in Reference 11.1, "File Systems," to present both the read-only APFS System volume and the read-write APFS Data volume as if they were a single volume, known as the root volume. The root volume is identified by a lone forward slash. Other nonroot volumes appear as part of the main file system in the Volumes folder at the root of the startup disk.

Use Marks and Bookmarks

Add marks and bookmarks as you work, then use them to quickly navigate through lengthy Terminal output.

Select a line in Terminal, then choose Edit > Marks > Mark to add a mark. By default, Edit > Marks > Automatically Mark Prompt Lines is selected, so each prompt line sets a mark. Then you can choose Edit > Select Between Marks or choose Edit > Navigate > Jump to Previous Mark, or just press Command-Up Arrow.

Choose Edit > Marks > Mark as Bookmark to add a bookmark. Then choose Edit > Bookmarks to display a list of bookmarks. Choose a bookmark to jump to that bookmark.

Reference 4.3
Manipulate Files in the CLI

When you manage and edit files in the CLI, you have more options—and more chances to make mistakes.

File-Examination Commands

Use the cat, less, and file commands to examine files. Read the man pages for these commands to find out more about them.

Short for concatenate, the cat command displays the contents of a file sequentially to Terminal. The syntax is cat, followed by the path to the item you want to view. Use the cat command to append to text files using the >> redirect operator. In the following example, Joan uses the cat command to view the content of two text files in her Public folder, TextDocOne.txt and TextDocTwo.txt. Then she uses the cat command with the >> redirect operator to append the second text file to the end of the first text file.

```
joan@MyMac ~ % cat Public/TextDocOne.txt
```

This is the content of the first plain text document.

```
joan@MyMac ~ % cat Public/TextDocTwo.txt
```

This is the content of the second plain text document.

```
joan@MyMac ~ % cat Public/TextDocTwo.txt >> Public/TextDocOne.txt
```

```
joan@MyMac ~ % cat Public/TextDocOne.txt
```

This is the content of the first plain text document.

This is the content of the second plain text document.

Use the less command to view long text files. It enables you to browse and search the text. Type **less**, followed by the path to the item you want to view. The less interface is the same interface you use to view man pages, so the navigation shortcuts are the same.

The file command determines a file type based on its content. This is useful for identifying files that don't have a filename extension. The syntax is file, followed by the path to the file you're trying to identify. In the following example, Joan uses the file command to locate the file type of two documents in her Public folder: PictureDocument and TextDocument:

```
joan@MyMac ~ % file Public/PictureDocument.tiff
```

Public/PictureDocument.tiff: TIFF image data, big-endian

```
joan@MyMac ~ % file Public/TextDocument.txt
```

Public/TextDocument.txt: ASCII English text

To use Spotlight from the command line, enter the mdfind command. The syntax is mdfind, followed by your search criteria. Like Spotlight, mdfind returns only items that the current user has permissions to access. Read Reference 16.2, "Spotlight and Siri," for more information.

Use Wildcard Characters

You can use wildcard characters to define pathname and search criteria. Here are three of the most common wildcards:

▶ Use the asterisk (*) wildcard to match any string of characters. For instance, entering * matches all files, and entering *.tiff matches all files that end in .tiff.

▶ Use the question mark (?) wildcard to match a single character. For example, entering **b?ok** matches book but not brook.

▶ Use square brackets ([ ]) to define a range of characters. For example, **[Dd]ocument** locates items named Document or document, and **doc[1-9]** matches files named doc#, where # is a number between 1 and 9.

You can combine filename wildcards. Consider a collection of five files with the names ReadMe.rtf, ReadMe.txt, read.rtf, read.txt, and It's All About Me.rtf. Using wildcards to specify these files:

▶   *.rtf matches ReadMe.rtf, read.rtf, and It's All About Me.rtf.

▶   ????.* matches read.rtf and read.txt.

▶   [Rr]*.rtf matches ReadMe.rtf and read.rtf.

▶   [A-Z]*.* matches ReadMe.rtf, ReadMe.txt, and It's All About Me.rtf.

Use Recursive Commands

When you direct a command to execute a task on an item, it acts on only the item you specify. If the item you specify is a folder, the command won't navigate inside the folder to execute the command on the enclosed items. If you want a command to execute on a folder and its contents, you must tell the command to run recursively. Recursive means: "Execute the task on every item inside every folder starting from the path I specify." Many commands accept -r or -R as the option to indicate that you want the command to run recursively.

Modify Files and Folders

The mkdir, touch, cp, mv, rm, rmdir, and nano commands enable you to modify files and folders.

Short for "make directory," mkdir is used to create folders. The syntax is mkdir, followed by the paths of the folders you want to create. The -p option tells mkdir to create intermediate folders if they don't already exist in the paths you specify.

Use the touch command to update the modification date of a specified item. The touch command creates an empty file if it doesn't exist.

Use the cp (copy) command to copy items from one place to another. The syntax is cp, followed by the path to the original item, ending with the destination path for the copy. If you specify a destination folder but no filename, cp makes a copy of the file with the same name as the original. If you specify a destination filename but not a destination folder, cp makes a copy in your current working folder. Unlike the Finder, the cp command won't warn you if your copy replaces an existing file. It deletes the existing file and replaces it with the copy you told it to create.

Use the mv (move) command to move items from one place to another. The syntax is mv, followed by the path to the original item, ending with the new destination path for the item. You can also use mv to rename an item. The mv command uses the same destination rules as the cp command.

Use the rm (remove) command to permanently delete items. There is no Trash in the CLI. The rm command removes items forever. The syntax is rm, followed by the paths of the items you wish to delete.

Use rmdir (remove directory) to permanently delete folders. The rmdir command removes folders forever. The syntax is rmdir, followed by the paths of the folders you want to delete. The rmdir command can remove a folder only if it's empty. You can use the rm command with the recursive option, -R, to remove a folder and all its contents.

The text editor nano features a list of commonly used keyboard shortcut commands at the bottom of the screen. There's an illustration of using the nano command in Exercise 4.2, "Manage Files and Folders with Commands."

Reference 4.4
Manage macOS from the CLI

In this section, you look at commands that enable you to access items normally restricted by file-system permissions.

Use the su (substitute user identity or super user) command to switch to another user account. Enter su, followed by the short name of the user you want to switch to, and enter the account password. The password won't display. The command prompt changes, indicating that you have the access privileges of a different user. Type **who -m** to verify your currently logged-in identity. You remain logged in as the substitute user until you quit Terminal or enter the exit command. In the following example, Joan uses the su command to change her shell to Johnny's account, and then she will exit back to her account:

```
joan@MyMac ~ % who -m
joan ttys001 Aug 20 14:06
joan@MyMac ~ % su johnny
Password:
johnny@MyMac ~ % who -m
johnny ttys001 Aug 20 14:06
johnny@MyMac ~ % exit
```

```
exit

joan@MyMac ~ % who -m

joan ttys001 Aug 20 14:06
```

Use sudo

Precede a command with sudo (substitute user do) to tell macOS to run the command using root account access. You must have an administrator user account to use sudo. sudo works even when the root user account is disabled in the graphical interface. Be careful with sudo and limit access to it.

System Integrity Protection (SIP) prevents changes to parts of macOS, even for the root user. Read Reference 15.2, "System Integrity Protection," for more information about the specific resources that are protected.

If, as an administrator user, you need to execute more than one command with root account access, you can temporarily switch the entire command-line shell to have root-level access. Type sudo -s and your password to switch the shell to root access. You remain logged in as the root user until you quit Terminal or enter the exit command.

For more information about the root account, go to Reference 7.1, "User Accounts."

> **NOTE** ▶ Do not enable the root user account for daily use. Its privileges allow you to make changes that you can undo only by reinstalling macOS. If you need to enable the root user account (instead of just using the sudo command), be sure to disable the root user account after you complete your task.

Reference 4.5
Command-Line Tips and Tricks

Here are some command-line tips that help you customize your experience and save time:

▶ Control-click a command and choose "Open man Page" to read more about that command.

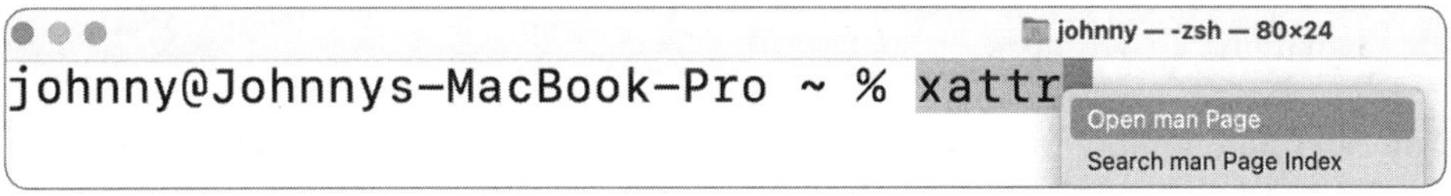

```
● ● ●                                    johnny — -zsh — 80×24
johnny@Johnnys-MacBook-Pro ~ % xattr
                                              Open man Page
                                              Search man Page Index
```

▶ If your Mac has a Touch Bar, type a command and press the button for that command in the Touch Bar to open a new Terminal window that displays the man page for the command. The figure shows the Touch Bar displaying a button for the xattr command man page.

▶ Use Tab key completion when you enter file paths.

▶ Drag and drop files and folders from the Finder to Terminal to automatically enter their locations at the command line.

▶ Type **open** . ("open" followed by a space, followed by a period) at the prompt to open your current command-line location in the Finder.

▶ Explore Terminal preferences (from the menu bar, choose Terminal > Preferences, or press Command-Comma) to customize the look and feel of your command line.

▶ To cancel a command or clear your current command entry, use Control-C.

▶ You can edit commands before submitting. The Left and Right Arrow keys and the Delete key work as you would expect.

▶ At the command prompt, use the Up Arrow and Down Arrow keys to view and reuse your command history. This includes editing old commands before rerunning them. Enter the history command to display your recent command history.

▶ To clear the Terminal screen, enter the clear command or press Control-L.

▶ To move the cursor to the beginning of the current line, press Control-A.

▶ To move the cursor to the end of the current line, press Control-E.

▶ To move the cursor forward one word, press Esc-F.

▶ To move the cursor back one word of the line, press Esc-B.

▶ To move the cursor to a location in a command string, Option-click where you'd like the cursor to be.

▶ Use the inspector to view and manage running processes as well as edit window titles and background colors. To open the inspector, press Command-I. To send a command to a process, select it, click the action menu, then choose a command from the Signal Process Group.

You can find out more information about Terminal in the Terminal User Guide, at support.apple.com/guide/terminal/.

Exercise 4.1
Command-Line Navigation

In this exercise, you use commands in Terminal to navigate the file system, to view items
that aren't visible from the Finder, and to access the manual (man) pages that tell you
about commands.

View Your Home Folder

1   If necessary, log in to your Mac as Local Administrator.

2   Click Launchpad in the Dock.

3   In the Search field at the top of the screen, type **Terminal**.

4   Click Terminal.

    A new Terminal window opens.

```
●  ●  ●                   🖥 ladmin — -zsh — 80×24
Last login: Wed Sep 23 15:31:17 on ttys000
ladmin@Mac-17 ~ %
```

The second line includes your user name and computer name followed by a prompt—
for example:

ladmin@Mac-17 ~ %

In this example, the user named ladmin is logged into a computer named Mac-17. A space separates the computer name from the path to your current working directory, which is ladmin's home folder, indicated by the tilde (~). The path is followed by the prompt, which is %.

5   At the prompt, type **ls** and press Return.

Terminal displays output that looks something like this, followed by another prompt:

Desktop	Downloads	Movies	Pictures
Documents	Library	Music	Public

6   Switch to the Finder. If you don't find an open Finder window, choose File > New Finder Window or press Command-N.

7   Select ladmin's home folder in the Finder sidebar and compare the contents of the home folder in the Finder and Terminal.

With the exception of the Library folder, what you see in Terminal is the same as in the Finder. (User Library folders are hidden in the Finder by default; see Reference 14.1, "Examine Hidden Items.")

8   Switch back to Terminal and type **ls -A** (lowercase LS followed by space, a hyphen, and an uppercase A) at the prompt.

In general, the command-line environment is case-sensitive. For example, ls -a isn't the same as ls -A.

The list includes some additional files that begin with a period. Files beginning with a period are hidden in directory listings unless you ask for them by typing ls -A. The Finder doesn't show files beginning with a period (sometimes called *dot-files*).

Examine and Change Your Current Working Directory

Think of your current working directory as the place where you are in the file system. When you open a new Terminal window, your default working directory is your home folder. Use the cd command to change your current working directory.

1   At the prompt, type **pwd**.

The period (.) ends the sentence and isn't part of the command, so don't type it. This guide tells you if a trailing "." is part of the command. Also, press Return at the end of each step unless otherwise instructed.

Terminal displays:

/Users/ladmin

This is where Local Administrator's home folder exists in the file system. It's the folder you're "in" in this Terminal window.

2   At the prompt, type **cd Library**.

This changes your current working directory to the Library folder inside your home folder.

This command uses a relative path. A relative path means "Start in my current working directory."

Your prompt changes to something like this:

ladmin@Mac-17 Library %

The path component of the prompt indicates the folder you are in, not the entire path.

The **cd** command changed your working directory without providing feedback. A command that completes and doesn't need to provide feedback will exit silently. If you get an error message, you should investigate its cause before continuing.

3   At the prompt, type **pwd**. Terminal displays:

/Users/ladmin/Library

You changed to the Library folder that was inside your previous working directory.

4   Type **ls** to view what files and folders are in this Library folder.

5   At the prompt, type **cd /Library**. Note the **/** that precedes Library this time.

6   At the prompt, type **pwd**. Terminal displays output like this:

/Library

This is a different folder.

A path that starts with a leading **/** is an absolute path. It means "Start at the root folder and navigate from there." A path that doesn't start with a leading **/** is a relative path. It means "Start in your current working directory and navigate from there." (For more information on file system structure, go to Reference 15.1, "macOS File Resources.")

7   Type **ls** to view the files and folders that are in this Library folder.

There is some overlap in the item names in this Library and the one in ladmin's home folder, but the names aren't entirely the same.

8 At the prompt, type **cd** and a space character. Don't press the Return key.

Terminal enables you to drag and drop items from the Finder to Terminal and have the path to the items appear in the command line.

In this part of the exercise, you use the Finder to locate a folder you want to use as your working directory in Terminal.

9 Switch to the Finder.

When you don't know exactly what you are looking for, it's sometimes faster and easier to find a file or folder in the Finder.

10 Open a new Finder window if necessary.

11 Click Macintosh HD in the sidebar.

12 Open the Users folder.

13 Drag and drop the Shared folder to Terminal.

Terminal fills in the path (/Users/Shared). Macintosh HD doesn't appear in the path that Terminal fills in.

The Finder shows you volume names to make locating a particular volume easier. Terminal doesn't show volume names in the same way.

14 Switch to Terminal and press Return.

15 Type **pwd** at the prompt.

You are in the Shared folder.

Read About ls in the Man Pages

In Terminal, you can read the details about commands using the man command. man is short for manual.

1 In Terminal, type clear, then press Return.

The clear command moves all of the text in the command line interface one page up.

2 At the prompt, type **man ls**, then press Return.

This opens the man page for the ls command.

Each man page is divided into various parts. The number in parentheses on the top line indicates in which section of the manual this command is documented. In this case, ls is documented in section 1, which is for general-use commands. Next, Terminal displays the name of the command and a terse summary of what the command does: "list directory contents." The synopsis is supposed to be a formal representation of how to use the command. Anything contained in square brackets is optional. The synopsis isn't always completely accurate. For example, a few options for ls are mutually exclusive of each other, but this synopsis does not indicate that. Options or switches (which change the behavior of a command) immediately follow the command, and arguments (which tell the command what to operate on) follow options or switches. The description, which explains the various uses of the command, follows the synopsis.

3   Type **q** to quit viewing the man page for ls.

4   At the prompt, type **man man**, then press Return.

You can also Control-click a command to open its man page. On a MacBook Pro with Touch Bar, you can tap the icon for a man page to open it.

5   Read about the man command.

6   When you are done, type **q** to exit.

Exercise 4.2
Manage Files and Folders with Commands

▶ **Prerequisites**

▶   You must have created the Local Administrator account (Exercise 3.1, "Configure a Mac for Exercises").

▶   You must have enabled FileVault (Exercise 3.2, "Configure System Preferences").

In this exercise, you learn to copy, move, rename, and delete files and folders with commands.

Create Files

1   If necessary, authenticate as Local Administrator.

2   Open TextEdit.

TextEdit should be in your Dock from when you performed Exercise 3.3, "Download Student Materials." If it isn't in your Dock, you can find it in /Applications.

3   If the file navigation dialog opens, click the New Document button.

4   In the TextEdit menu bar, choose Format > Make Plain Text, or press Shift-Command-T.

5   Add the following names to the yet Untitled (default) TextEdit document:

MacBook Air

MacBook Pro

iMac

iMac Pro

Mac Pro

Mac mini

iPhone

iPad

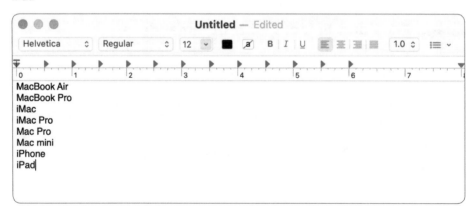

6   From the TextEdit menu bar, choose File > Save and name the document **Comps**.

Leave the document in the Documents folder.

7   Close the Comps document window.

8   Create a new document in TextEdit and change the format to Plain Text.

9   Save and name the new document **Empty**. Leave the document in the Documents folder.

10 Quit TextEdit.

Copy and Move Files and Create a Folder

1   In the Finder, open your Documents folder.

2   If necessary, open Terminal. Select Edit > Clear to Start (command-K) to clear your Terminal window.

Unlike the **clear** command used above, the Clear to Start command is unique to the Terminal app and does not save any output.

3   Arrange the Finder window showing the Documents folder and the Terminal window so that you can see most of both on the screen.

You will observe how commands that you run in Terminal affect the Finder.

4   Type **cd ~/Documents** to change to the Documents folder.

5   Type **ls** to view the files in the Documents folder.

A dialog appears requesting that you allow Terminal to access files in your Documents folder.

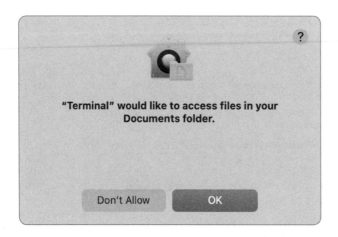

WARNING ▸ To protect your data, macOS has strict privacy preferences that prevent apps from accessing other apps' data (commonly referred to as cross-app data access). Allowing access to your Documents folder lessens the security of your Mac. For the purposes of this exercise, you will allow access and then disallow access at the end. In production, when you see these prompts, understand what you are allowing before you click OK. If the dialog mentioned in step 5 doesn't appear, you'll need to grant Terminal access to your files and folders in the Security & Privacy pane of System Preferences. All of these topics are covered later in Reference 9.5, "Manage User Privacy," and in Exercise 9.2, "Allow Apps to Access your Data."

6   Click OK.

View the output (also called stdout, or standard output) of the **ls** command. When you save a plain-text file from TextEdit, the program adds the filename extension **.txt** to it.

7   Use **cp** to make a copy of Comps.txt and rename it **MacModels.txt**.

ladmin@Mac-17 Documents % **cp Comps.txt MacModels.txt**

Many commands that take a source and a destination list the source first.

8   Type **less** with the complete filename to view each file, then type **q** to exit each file.

MacModels.txt is an exact copy of Comps.txt.

ladmin@Mac-17 Documents % **less MacModels.txt**

9   Type **q** to exit.

10 Enter the same command for the file Comps.txt:

ladmin@Mac-17 Documents % **less Comps.txt**

11 When you are done, type **q** to exit.

Create a Folder and Copy a File to It

1 Create a new folder in the Documents folder:

ladmin@Mac-17 Documents % **mkdir AppleInfo**

Because AppleInfo is a relative path, the folder is created in the Documents folder.

2 Type **cp** to copy MacModels.txt into AppleInfo. You can press the Tab key after typing the first few characters to use Tab key completion to fill in the rest of the filename. This makes entering text in the command-line interface more efficient and accurate:

ladmin@Mac-17 Documents % **cp MacModels.txt AppleInfo**

NOTE ▶ Tab key completion often adds a trailing **/** (forward slash) at the end of a command. This exercise produces the same result whether or not the trailing **/** is present.

3 Type **ls** to view the contents of AppleInfo:

ladmin@Mac-17 Documents % **ls AppleInfo**

Fix a Naming Error

The text list in MacModels.txt includes a couple of items that are not technically Mac computers. Let's rename the file and clean up the extra copies.

1 Remove the Comps.txt file from the Documents folder and the MacModels.txt file from the AppleInfo folder:

ladmin@Mac-17 Documents % **rm Comps.txt AppleInfo/MacModels.txt**

You entered the command once to delete both files. The command line doesn't have an undo function. Any change you make is permanent.

2 Move the MacModels.txt file into the AppleInfo folder using the **mv** command:

ladmin@Mac-17 Documents % **mv MacModels.txt AppleInfo**

3 Type **cd AppleInfo** to change your working directory to AppleInfo.

4   Type **mv** to rename the MacModels.txt file to **AppleHardware.txt**.

ladmin@Mac-17 AppleInfo % **mv MacModels.txt AppleHardware.txt**

Alternatively, you can also move and rename a file in one command:

% **mv MacModels.txt AppleInfo/AppleHardware.txt**

Remove a Folder

1   Change your working directory back to the Documents folder. You can do so in one of three ways:

▶   Use the absolute path /Users/ladmin/Documents.

▶   Use the tilde character to navigate to your home folder ~/Documents.

▶   Use the relative path (..).

The .. notation refers to the parent directory of the current directory. Because your current working directory is /Users/ladmin/Documents/AppleInfo, .. refers to /Users/ladmin/Documents.

Occasionally, you see the .. notation in the middle of a path instead of at the beginning—for example, /Users/ladmin/Documents/../Desktop. It still has the same meaning, so in this example, it refers to Local Administrator's Desktop folder.

Similarly, a single . refers to the current directory or location in the path.

Each directory contains a reference to both itself and its parent. These are visible if you use ls -a (note the lowercase a instead of the uppercase A you used previously).

2   Move the AppleHardware.txt file to Documents and rename it **AppleHardwareInfo.txt**.

Don't press the Return key until you type **AppleHardwareInfo.txt**.

ladmin@Mac-17 Documents % **mv AppleInfo/AppleHardware.txt AppleHardwareInfo.txt**

The path AppleHardwareInfo.txt is relative to your current working directory, so this step moves AppleInfo/AppleHardware.txt to the current working directory (Documents) and renames it AppleHardwareInfo.txt.

3   Type **rmdir** to remove the AppleInfo directory:

ladmin@Mac-17 Documents % **rmdir AppleInfo**

rmdir succeeds because AppleInfo is empty. rmdir removes only folders that are empty. Type **rm -r** to remove a folder that contains files. An example is:

% **rm -r AppleInfo**

Create and Edit a Text File

macOS includes several command-line text editors. In this exercise, you use the nano editor to create and edit a file.

1   Type **nano** to create a new file named fruit.txt:

ladmin@Mac-17 Documents % **nano fruit.txt**

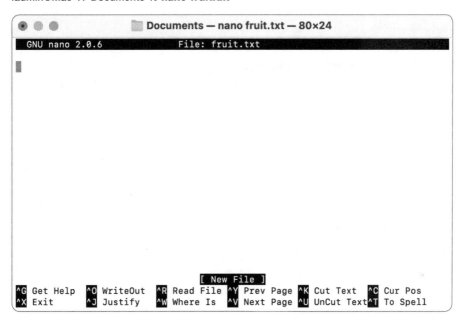

2   Enter the following words in the file on separate lines. Press Return at the end of each line.

apple

pineapple

grapefruit

pear

banana

blueberry

strawberry

3   Press Control-X to quit nano.

You see "Save modified buffer (ANSWERING "No" WILL DESTROY CHANGES)?"

4 Type **Y**.

You see "File Name to Write: fruit.txt."

5 Press Return.

nano saves your file in the Documents folder inside your home folder, or ~/Documents, and exits, returning you to the prompt.

6 Quit Terminal.

Edit and Re-secure Privacy Preferences

Earlier in this exercise, you allowed Terminal to access any files in the Documents folder. For security purposes, you should disallow this access to protect your Mac. Apple provides this setting as a default to protect you from malicious commands.

1 Open System Preferences, then select Security & Privacy.

2 Click Privacy.

3 In the left sidebar, select Files and Folders.

Earlier, you allowed Terminal access to your Documents folder.

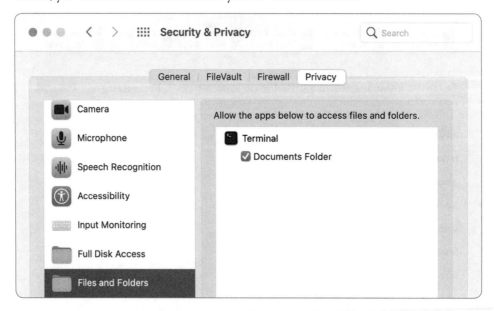

4   Deselect the Documents Folder checkbox.

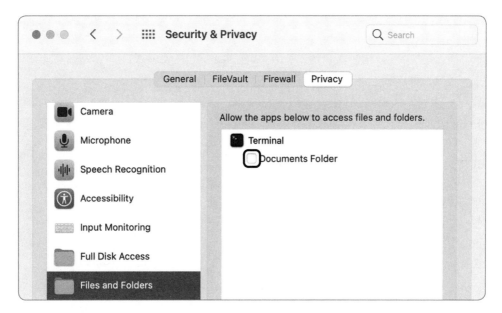

Terminal no longer has access to any files in your Documents folder.

5   Quit System Preferences.

Lesson 5

Use macOS Recovery

One of the most useful macOS features for troubleshooting is macOS Recovery.

You can use macOS Recovery to reinstall macOS as well as to access administration and troubleshooting utilities. macOS Recovery is a hidden volume on your Mac. This gives you easy access to recovery utilities without the need for additional media.

In this lesson, you learn how to access macOS Recovery. You also explore the utilities available from macOS Recovery. You learn how to set the security policy for macOS on Mac computers with Apple silicon. For Intel-based Mac computers, you learn how to set a firmware password. And for Intel-based Mac computers with the Apple T2 Security Chip, you learn how to configure the Secure Boot and external boot options that help secure your Mac against unauthorized access. Finally, you learn how to create an external macOS installer that you can use when local macOS Recovery isn't available.

GOALS

- ▶ Access macOS Recovery

- ▶ Manage the security policy for Mac computers with Apple silicon

- ▶ Set a firmware password to secure macOS startup for Intel-based Mac computers

- ▶ Manage Secure Boot and external boot options for Intel-based Mac computers that have the Apple T2 Security Chip

- ▶ Reinstall macOS from macOS Recovery

- ▶ Create an external storage device that includes macOS Recovery

Reference 5.1
Start Up from macOS Recovery

Mac computers running macOS Big Sur include a hidden macOS Recovery volume. This built-in recovery volume doesn't appear in Disk Utility or in the Finder when a Mac is running macOS. After starting in macOS Recovery, you can install, reinstall, or upgrade macOS and choose from a variety of maintenance apps.

On a Mac with Apple silicon, you can use macOS Recovery to do the following and more:

▶ Repair your internal disk

▶ Reinstall macOS

▶ Restore your files from a Time Machine backup

▶ Set the security policy for different disks

▶ Transfer files between two Mac computers

▶ Start up in safe mode (see Reference 28.4, "Use Startup Shortcuts," for more information about safe mode)

On an Intel-based Mac, you can use macOS Recovery to do the following and more:

▶ Repair your internal disk

▶ Reinstall macOS

▶ Restore your files from a Time Machine backup

▶ Set security options

Start macOS Recovery from the Built-In Recovery System

The way to start up from macOS Recovery varies by the kind of Mac you have:

▶ For a Mac with Apple silicon: If your Mac is turned on, shut down your Mac. Press and hold the power button until you see "Loading startup options." A new screen appears that displays available startup volumes and an Options icon. Use the arrow keys or the mouse or trackpad to select Options, then press Return or click Continue.

▶ For an Intel-based Mac: Restart or turn on your Mac, then immediately press and hold Command-R. Release the keys when your Mac displays anything on the screen.

If your Intel-based Mac has a firmware password, you must provide it before you can access macOS Recovery (see Reference 5.3, "Secure Startup," for more information about firmware password).

If your Mac has FileVault or Activation Lock turned on, Recovery Assistant starts when you try to start in macOS Recovery (see Lesson 12, "Manage FileVault," and Reference 9.7, "Protect Your Mac with Activation Lock," for more information). If Recovery Assistant starts, it displays administrator accounts from your startup volume.

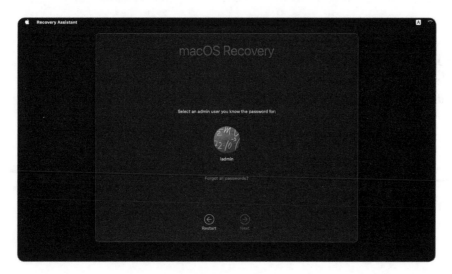

In order to continue and access macOS Recovery, you must select one of the displayed administrator accounts, click Next, enter the administrator account's password, then click Continue.

You know macOS Recovery has successfully started when your screen displays the following:

▶ Next to the Apple menu, the app name, "Recovery"

▶ A window with four utilities

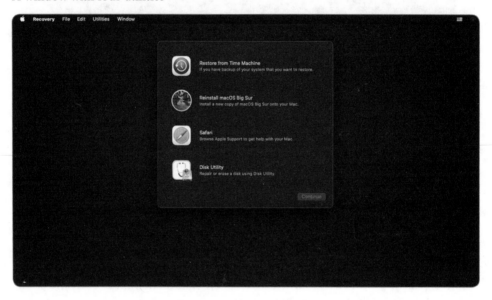

If macOS Recovery doesn't start, the next few sections cover some alternatives for accessing it.

Start macOS Recovery from an External Storage Device

You can use another Mac to create a macOS installer on an external storage device, which includes the hidden macOS Recovery volume. Then you can start from the macOS Recovery volume on the external storage device. Connect the device with the installer to your Mac, then:

▶ For a Mac with Apple silicon: If your Mac is turned on, shut down your Mac. Press and hold the power button until you see "Loading startup options." Use the arrow keys or the mouse or trackpad to select the external storage device, then press Return or click Continue.

▶ For an Intel-based Mac: Start up or restart while you press and hold the Option key. This opens the Mac computer's Startup Manager. If your Mac isn't connected to Ethernet, use the Choose Network menu to connect to a Wi-Fi network. Use the arrow or the mouse or trackpad to select the external storage device, then press Return or click the Up Arrow icon.

See Reference 5.4, "Create a Bootable Installer for macOS," for more information.

Mac computers with Apple silicon have no restrictions for booting from external media. However, the Allowed Boot Media settings for your Intel-based Mac with the T2 chip affects your ability to start from macOS Recovery from an external storage device. The Allowed Boot Media settings are covered in Reference 5.3.

If your Intel-based Mac with the T2 chip:

▶ Has Allowed Boot Media set to "Disallow booting from external or removable media" (the default and highly recommended), your Mac cannot start from macOS Recovery from a macOS installer on an external storage device.

▶ Has Allowed Boot Media set to "Allow booting from external or removable media," your Mac can start from macOS Recovery from a macOS installer on an external storage device.

NOTE ▶ For Mac computers with Apple silicon, each volume has its own independent security settings.

Reinstall macOS Recovery on Mac with Apple Silicon

In rare situations—for example, if you erase the APFS container that holds the macOS Recovery volume—your Mac with Apple silicon automatically uses the System Recovery volume, which is in a separate and hidden APFS container on the internal storage of your Mac. Follow the onscreen directions to open Recovery Utilities, then reinstall macOS Big Sur.

Use Apple Configurator 2 to Revive or Restore Your Mac

Under extremely rare circumstances, such as power loss during a small window of time when you are updating firmware, your Mac may become unresponsive, and you might have to use Apple Configurator 2 to revive or restore your firmware.

This applies only to:

▶ Mac computers with Apple silicon

▶ Intel-based Mac computers with the T2 chip

The revive process updates the firmware, and the restore process updates the firmware and erases the internal flash storage. The details are outside the scope of this guide. See the appropriate article in the Apple Configurator 2 User Guide for more information:

▶ "Revive or restore a Mac with Apple silicon with Apple Configurator 2," at support.apple.com/guide/apple-configurator-2/apdd5f3c75ad

▶ "Revive an Intel-based Mac with Apple Configurator 2," at support.apple.com/guide/apple-configurator-2/apdebea5be51

For Intel-Based Mac Computers, Use Internet recoveryOS

If the local built-in recovery volume is missing, some Intel-based Mac computers automatically attempt to access Internet recoveryOS. You'll know your Mac is attempting to access Internet recoveryOS when you see the spinning globe instead of an Apple logo during startup. This applies to Intel-based Mac computers released in mid-2010 or later with available firmware updates installed.

You can access some Internet recoveryOS options by pressing specific key combinations while starting up. Turn on or restart your Intel-based Mac, and then immediately press and hold one of these combinations:

▶ Command-R—Reinstall the latest macOS that was installed on your Mac (with possible exceptions for situations in which your Mac logic board was replaced, or you erased the entire internal volume, instead of erasing just the startup volume).

▶ Option-Command-R—Upgrade to the latest macOS that is compatible with your Mac.

▶ Shift-Option-Command-R—Reinstall the macOS that came with your Mac, or the version closest to it that is still available.

   NOTE ▶ Internet recoveryOS is available only for Intel-based Mac computers.

See Apple Support article HT204904, "How to reinstall macOS," for more information about the differences in the key combinations.

Reference 5.2
Use macOS Recovery

When you start up from macOS Recovery, you can access several administration and maintenance utilities.

From the main window in macOS Recovery, you can access the following functions:

▶ Restore from Time Machine—Use this option to restore a full Mac
  Time Machine backup from a network Time Machine backup, a locally connected external storage device, or a local snapshot. See Lesson 17, "Manage Time Machine," for more information.

▶ Reinstall macOS Big Sur (or Install macOS Big Sur)—Use this option to open the macOS Installer. You need a wired or wireless network connection before you can install or reinstall macOS.

  NOTE ▶ You might not be able to access the internet in macOS Recovery if the network uses a captive portal or an enterprise network.

▶ Safari—When you use this option, Safari opens to a page about using macOS Recovery. You can also use Safari to go to any site, such as the Apple Support website.

▶ Disk Utility—Use Disk Utility to repair, erase, and manage disks. It's useful when you start up a Mac from macOS Recovery because you can use it to manage a system disk that you can't manage when you use it as a startup disk. You can also use Disk Utility to prepare a disk for a new macOS installation or attempt to repair a disk that fails installation. See Lesson 11, "Manage File Systems and Storage," for more information.

▶ Startup Disk (by choosing Startup Disk from the Apple menu)—Use Startup Disk to select the default macOS startup disk. You can override the default startup using the startup modes discussed in Lesson 28, "Troubleshoot Startup and System Issues."

macOS Recovery has a few extra features in the Utilities menu at the top of the screen:

▶ Startup Security Utility—This utility gives you control over how your Mac starts up. Learn about firmware passwords and Startup Security Utility in Reference 5.3.

▶ Terminal—This is your primary interface to the command-line interface (CLI) of macOS. One command you can enter from here is resetpassword, followed by pressing the Return key. Use Terminal in macOS Recovery to troubleshoot network issues that could prevent the download of macOS installation assets. For more information about using the CLI to investigate network issues, see Lesson 23, "Troubleshoot Network Issues." See Lesson 4, "Use the Command-Line Interface," to learn more about the CLI.

You can use the resetpassword command to reset the password of any local user account on a selected system volume. This includes standard users, administrator users, and the root user. You can run resetpassword only from Recovery Assistant in macOS Recovery. Find out more about Recovery Assistant in Lesson 10, "Manage Password Changes."

▶ Share Disk—This option is available only for Mac computers with Apple silicon. Use it to share files with another Mac that's connected using a USB-C, USB, or Thunderbolt cable. See "Transfer files between a Mac with Apple silicon and another Mac," at support.apple.com/guide/mac-help/mchlb37e8ca7 in the macOS User Guide, for more information.

You can also choose Window > Recovery Log to open a window that displays logging information while you're started in macOS Recovery.

macOS Recovery utilities can be used to compromise the security of Intel-based Mac computers without the T2 chip. Any Mac with a default startup volume that can be overridden by an unauthorized user during startup isn't secure. You can use a firmware password, FileVault, Find My, and Startup Security Utility to help protect your Mac computers. The next section has information about firmware passwords and Startup Security Utility.

Reference 5.3
Secure Startup

In this section you learn about using Startup Security Utility to configure security-related settings for your Mac. Startup Security Utility has different options depending on the kind of Mac you have.

For Apple computers with Apple silicon, use Startup Security Utility to configure the security policy for macOS. Mac computers with Apple silicon maintain a separate security policy for each installation of macOS.

In contrast, security-related settings for Intel-based Mac computers apply to the entire Mac. Use Startup Security Utility to configure the following for Intel-based Mac computers:

▶ Firmware password for all Intel-based Mac computers

▶ Secure Boot and Allowed Boot Media for Intel-based Mac computers that have the T2 chip

Use Startup Security Utility

Use Startup Security Utility to configure features that help secure your Mac. The options available in Startup Security Utility vary for these three different kinds of Mac computers:

▶ Mac computers with Apple silicon

▶ Intel-based Mac computers without the T2 chip

▶ Intel-based Mac computers with the T2 chip

Each of the three scenarios has its own section following this introduction.

> **NOTE** ▶ If your Mac has Apple silicon, or your Intel-based Mac has the T2 chip, you must authenticate as an administrator user before you can use Startup Security Utility. This means that for a new installation of macOS Big Sur, you must use Setup Assistant to configure an administrator account before you can use Startup Security Utility. See Reference 3.1, "Configure a Mac with a New Installation of macOS Big Sur," for more information.

To open Startup Security Utility, start your Mac in macOS Recovery. The Utilities menu for a Mac with Apple silicon displays three commands (Startup Security Utility, Terminal, and Share Disk):

The Utilities menu for an Intel-based Mac displays two commands (Startup Security Utility and Terminal):

From the Utilities menu, choose Startup Security Utility.

If your Mac has FileVault or Activation Lock enabled, you must authenticate as an administrator user from a valid startup volume before you can use Startup Security Utility.

Click "Enter macOS Password," select a user, enter the user's password, then click OK. macOS Recovery then displays Startup Security Utility.

The following three figures illustrate how Startup Security Utility appears for three different kinds of Mac computers.

Identify Startup Security Utility for a Mac with Apple Silicon

The following figure of Startup Security Utility is for a Mac with Apple silicon.

If your Mac has Apple silicon, use Startup Security Utility to set the security policy for each volume that runs macOS on your Mac. See the section "Configure Security Policy for Mac Computers with Apple Silicon," later in this lesson, for more details.

Identify Startup Security Utility for an Intel-Based Mac with the T2 Chip

The following figure of Startup Security Utility is for an Intel-based Mac computer with the T2 chip.

The section "Turn On a Firmware Password," later in this lesson, covers turning on a firmware password for Intel-based Mac computers.

The section "Configure Secure Boot and Allowed Boot Media Settings," later in this lesson, covers the additional options available in Startup Security Utility for Intel-based Mac computers with the T2 chip.

Identify Startup Security Utility for an Intel-Based Mac That Doesn't Have the T2 Chip

If your Intel-based Mac doesn't have the T2 chip, you can use Startup Security Utility only to turn on or off a firmware password.

See "What is the Startup Security Utility on Mac?" at support.apple.com/guide/mac-help/mchlf5346320 in the macOS User Guide for more information.

Configure Security Policy for Mac Computers with Apple Silicon

On your Mac with Apple silicon, when you first open Startup Security Utility, it displays a window with the message "Select the system you want to use to set the security policy." If a volume has FileVault turned on, you must unlock the volume first. Select a volume, then click Security Policy.

After you select a volume, the Security Policy configuration window appears. By default, Full Security is selected. This ensures that only the current operating system (OS) from Apple, or an OS that's currently signed and trusted by Apple, can run. You need a network connection when you install the OS with this setting.

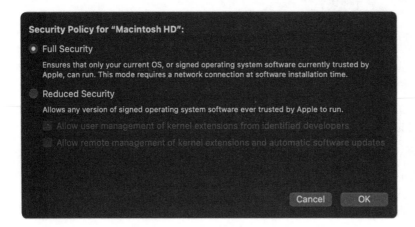

Two other options are outside the scope of this guide, and we do not recommend that you select them:

▶ Reduced Security allows the Mac to run any version of signed OS software that Apple ever trusted. Selecting the Reduced Security option enables two additional options related to legacy system extensions (also called kernel extensions or kexts). Lesson 9, "Manage Security and Privacy," has more information about legacy system extensions.

▶ Permissive Security enforces no requirements on the bootable OS, and we do not recommend it for use except by developers when creating specialized software. The Permissive Security option isn't displayed when System Integrity Protection is enabled.

Turn On a Firmware Password

If you want the most security for your Intel-based Mac, you must set a firmware password.

A firmware password prevents users who don't have the firmware password from modifying firmware settings on a specific Mac. A firmware password prevents anyone with physical access to your Intel-based Mac from accessing the following:

- ▶ macOS Recovery
- ▶ Single-user mode
- ▶ An unauthorized volume
- ▶ Target disk mode

A firmware password also blocks use of most startup key combinations. Startup keyboard shortcuts are covered in Lesson 28.

For example, on an Intel-based Mac with a firmware password enabled, if you start up while you press and hold the Option key, an authentication window appears where you can enter the firmware password.

If you enter the correct firmware password, you can select a different startup disk from Startup Manager.

It's especially important to set a firmware password to reduce the risk of attacks on Intel-based Mac computers without the T2 chip. For example, an unauthorized person with physical access to an Intel-based Mac that doesn't have the T2 chip can boot into macOS Recovery, then disable System Integrity Protection, run the resetpassword command, and use Startup Security Utility to set a firmware password if that Mac:

- ▶ Doesn't have FileVault turned on
- ▶ Doesn't already have a firmware password set

For all Intel-based Mac computers, you set a firmware password with Startup Security Utility. If the firmware password isn't set, click Turn On and enter the password.

Remember this password and store it somewhere safe.

If a firmware password is set, you can change or disable it, but you must know the current firmware password to do so.

You can also use Find My to remotely lock your Mac with a firmware passcode for one-time use. Read Reference 9.4, "Manage Systemwide Security," for more information. Lost Mode works even while you're using a firmware password.

If you can't remember your firmware password or the passcode you used for a remote lock or erase, schedule a service appointment with an Apple Store or Apple Authorized Service Provider. Bring your original receipt or invoice as proof of purchase.

For more about firmware passwords, see Apple Support article HT204455, "Set a firmware password on your Mac."

Even if you don't set a firmware password, you should turn on FileVault to prevent unauthorized access to the startup disk.

> **NOTE ▶** Consult the man page for **firmwarepasswd** for additional options, such as the **--disable-reset-capability** option. Consider using your organization's mobile device management (MDM) solution to manage firmware passwords if your MDM solution supports that feature.

Configure Secure Boot and Allowed Boot Media Settings

If your Intel-based Mac has the T2 chip, Startup Security Utility offers two additional features to help secure your Mac against unauthorized access: Secure Boot and Allowed Boot Media.

Configure Secure Boot

If your Intel-based Mac has the T2 chip, use Secure Boot to ensure that your Mac starts up using only a legitimate and trusted version of an operating system (OS), including macOS or Microsoft Windows.

There are three Secure Boot settings:

▶   Full Security

▶   Medium Security

▶   No Security

Configure Secure Boot for Full Security

Full Security is the default Secure Boot setting and is the highest level of security. This setting ensures that the only operating systems that can boot your Mac are trusted by Apple and are still being signed by Apple. This includes the current macOS as well as Windows if you used Boot Camp Assistant to install Windows.

If you leave Secure Boot at the Full Security setting, during startup your Mac verifies that the OS on your startup disk is trusted by Apple. If the OS is unknown or can't be verified as legitimate, your Mac uses the internet to download updated integrity information from Apple. The integrity information is unique to your Mac.

If FileVault is turned on while your Mac attempts to download updated integrity information, you must first unlock your disk.

If your Mac can't verify that the OS being used during startup is legitimate even after downloading updated integrity information, then the next steps vary, depending on the OS:

▶   macOS: An alert informs you that a software update is required to use this startup disk. Click Update, then reinstall macOS on the startup disk. Or click Startup Disk to use a different startup disk (which your Mac must verify).

▶   Windows: An alert informs you that you must install Windows with Boot Camp Assistant. For more information about Boot Camp Assistant, see Apple Support article HT201468, "Install Windows 10 on your Mac with Boot Camp Assistant."

If your Mac can't verify the OS on your startup disk and can't connect to the internet, then your Mac displays an alert that an internet connection is required. In this case, if you're using Wi-Fi use the Wi-Fi status menu item to make sure you're using an active Wi-Fi network.

If your Mac doesn't have an internet connection and can't verify the integrity of the OS on your startup disk, then you can click Startup Disk and choose another startup disk or use Startup Security Utility to change the security level to Medium Security.

Configure Secure Boot for Medium Security

When Medium Security is turned on, your Mac verifies only the signature of the OS on your startup disk. Apple signs macOS, and Microsoft signs Windows. The Medium Security setting doesn't require an internet connection, and it doesn't use updated integrity information from Apple, so your Mac can still start up from an OS even if Apple or Microsoft no longer signs the OS.

If the OS doesn't pass verification, an alert appears for macOS or Windows just like it does when High Security is turned on.

Configure Secure Boot for No Security

When you select No Security in the Secure Boot section, your Mac doesn't enforce any of the security requirements that Full Security or Medium Security enforces for your startup disk. This setting places your Mac at greater risk and we don't recommend that you use it.

Prepare for Configuration Changes

When you change from Medium Security or No Security to Full Security, you must be connected to the internet.

For more information about Secure Boot, see Apple Support article HT208198, "About Startup Security Utility."

Configure Allowed Boot Media Options

Use Allowed Boot Media to control whether your Intel-based Mac with the T2 chip can start up from an external storage device or other external media.

The default and most secure setting is "Disallow booting from external or removable media." When you select this setting, your Mac can't be made to start up from any external media. If you attempt to start up from external media, the following happens:

- ▶ Startup Disk preferences displays a message that your security settings don't allow this Mac to use an external startup disk.

- ▶ Startup Manager enables you to select an external startup disk, but it will display the message "Security settings do not allow this Mac to use an external startup disk."

You can change this by restarting and pressing and holding Command-R to open macOS Recovery, then choosing Startup Security Utility."

If you select the option "Allow booting from external or removable media," then your Mac can start up from an external storage device.

For more information about the Apple T2 Security Chip, see Apple Platform Security at support.apple.com/guide/security.

Use Recovery Assistant

If Recovery Assistant opens when you try to start in macOS Recovery and you don't remember any administrator password, you can click the "Forgot all passwords" link.

What happens next depends on how your Mac is configured:

▶ If you turned on FileVault and didn't escrow your recovery key with your Apple ID account, you can enter the recovery key.

▶ If you turned on FileVault and escrowed your recovery key with your Apple ID, you can enter your Apple ID credentials.

▶ If you didn't turn on FileVault but you turned on Activation Lock, you can enter the credentials for the Apple ID associated with Activation Lock.

After successfully entering the appropriate credentials, you can reset a password. See Reference 10.2, "Reset Lost Passwords," for more information about the ramifications of resetting a user account password.

If you don't have the recovery key or the Apple ID credentials, you can go to the Recovery Assistant menu and choose Erase Mac.

This opens an Erase Mac screen with information about erasing this Mac.

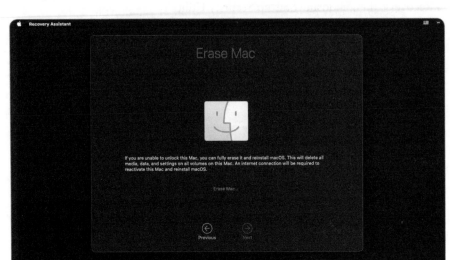

After you click Erase Mac and confirm that you really want to erase your Mac, your Mac automatically restarts. Then you can take the following steps:

1   If your Mac has Activation Lock turned on, enter the Apple ID credentials associated with Activation Lock.

2   Use Disk Utility to erase the internal storage and create a volume named Macintosh HD.

3   Use Install macOS Big Sur to install macOS on the newly erased disk.

Reference 5.4
Create a Bootable Installer for macOS

Sometimes a Mac doesn't have a local built-in recovery volume. For example, if your Mac has had its internal storage replaced, it may not contain any operating system. Also, Mac computers on RAID sets and disks with nonstandard Boot Camp partitioning (available for Intel-based Mac computers) won't have a local built-in recovery volume.

macOS Big Sur includes a command named createinstallmedia, in the macOS Installer (Install macOS Big Sur.app), that converts a standard external storage device into a bootable installer volume. createinstallmedia copies the macOS Recovery volume and the macOS installation assets to an external storage device. To use createinstallmedia, you must have an external storage device with at least 12 GB available, and it must be configured with the GUID partition scheme and formatted as Mac OS Extended (not APFS).

The createinstallmedia command includes the option --downloadassets for download-ing on-demand assets that may be required for installation. If you don't have a copy of Install macOS Big Sur, you can get it from the App Store. When you download macOS Big Sur, you download the latest version of Install macOS Big Sur that's available. Exercise 5.2, "Create a macOS Install Disk," outlines the steps to create this disk type.

See "About macOS Recovery," at support.apple.com/guide/mac-help/mchl46d531d6 in the macOS User Guide, for more information.

Exercise 5.1
Use macOS Recovery

> **Prerequisites**

> ▸ You must have created the Local Administrator account (Exercise 3.1, "Configure a Mac for Exercises").

> ▸ You must have turned on FileVault (Exercise 3.2, "Configure System Preferences").

> ▸ You must have an Intel-based Mac computer..

In this exercise, you start up your Mac from the macOS Recovery volume. The oper-ating system on macOS Recovery is called recoveryOS, just like the operating sys-tem on Macintosh HD is called macOS. You also review the included apps and how macOS Recovery can reinstall macOS.

NOTE ▸ You won't perform an installation, but you'll get an opportunity to look at the steps leading up to the installation.

Start Up Using macOS Recovery
To access the installer and other apps in recoveryOS, start up from macOS Recovery.

1 If your Mac is on, shut it down by choosing Shut Down from the Apple menu.

2 Turn on your Mac and immediately press and hold Command-R until the Apple logo appears on the screen, then release the keys.

When you press and hold Command-R during startup, the Mac attempts to start up using the macOS Recovery volume.

If the macOS Recovery volume isn't available on your Mac, it can start up from Internet recoveryOS automatically. If you know you need Internet recoveryOS, such as in the event of an internal storage device failure, press and hold Option-Command-R or Shift-Option-Command-R to manually start up from Internet recoveryOS.

3   If a language selection screen appears, select your preferred language and click the right arrow.

4   Because you have FileVault enabled, after recoveryOS starts up, your Mac displays the macOS Recovery screen, where you are asked to select a user for whom you know the password.

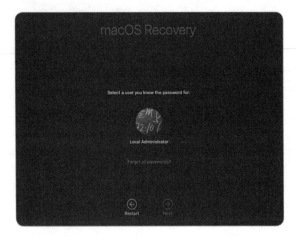

5   Select Local Administrator, click Next, enter the password (**Apple321!**), then click Continue.

6   After you authenticate, the Recovery window opens.

Examine the macOS Recovery Apps

While using recoveryOS, you have access to apps for recovering, repairing, and reinstalling macOS. In this part of the exercise, you get to know some of these apps.

View macOS Recovery Information

Use Safari to view the built-in instructions for macOS Recovery and to browse the web.

1   Verify that you are connected to the internet, either by Ethernet or by observing the Wi-Fi icon in the recoveryOS toolbar in the upper right of your screen.

2   Select Safari, then click Continue.

Safari opens and displays a document with information about how to use macOS Recovery on an Intel-based Mac.

3   Review the document.

This document is stored in macOS Recovery, but as long as you have an internet connection, Safari can access additional online documentation such as Apple Support articles.

4   If Safari displays a message saying "You are not connected to the Internet," join a wireless network by choosing a network from the Wi-Fi status menu near the right end of the menu bar.

5   From the menu bar, choose Safari > Quit Safari (or press Command-Q) to return to the Recovery window.

When you close a window in Safari, you don't quit Safari. To quit a Mac app, choose Quit *App Name* from the app menu (the menu next to the Apple menu, named for the current app). Or you can use Command-Q.

Examine Disk Utility

Disk Utility enables you to repair, image, reformat, or repartition your Mac disk.

1   Select Disk Utility, then click Continue.

macOS Big Sur has several volumes inside an Apple File System (APFS) container, two of which are called *volumename* - Data and *volumename* (where *volumename* is typically Macintosh HD). In your day-to-day use of macOS Big Sur you will experience a unified volume experience, but Disk Utility displays both volumes. For more information, see Lesson 11, "Manage File Systems and Storage."

In the device list on the left, Disk Utility displays both volumes of your startup disk and a Base System disk image. Because your startup disk is encrypted, to perform any functions on it, you must unlock it with Local Administrator's password. If you are in the Show All Devices view, Disk Utility displays the primary entry for each storage device and an indented list of volumes on each device.

2   Select the entry for the system volume of your startup disk. Typically, it is named Macintosh HD.

3   Review the buttons in the Disk Utility toolbar. These buttons represent functions that are discussed in detail in Lesson 11.

With Disk Utility you can use First Aid to verify or repair the startup volume file structure or erase the volume before you reinstall macOS Big Sur.

4   From the menu bar, choose Disk Utility > Quit Disk Utility or press Command-Q.

You are returned to the Recovery window.

Examine the macOS Installer

Here you examine reinstallation, but you don't reinstall macOS. When you complete these steps, you perform the steps leading up to a reinstallation, but you don't then have to wait while macOS is reinstalled on your Mac.

1 Select Reinstall macOS Big Sur, then click Continue.

The Install macOS Big Sur app opens.

2 Click Continue.

3 Review the license agreement, then click Agree.

4 In the license confirmation dialog, click Agree to indicate that you have reviewed and agree to the terms of the software license agreement.

The installer displays a list of volumes where you can install or reinstall macOS.

WARNING ▶ Don't click the Continue or Unlock button. If you do, the installer reinstalls macOS.

5 Quit Install macOS Big Sur.

Examine Startup Security Utility

The options available to you in Startup Security Utility vary depending on the model of your Mac.

1 From the Utilities menu, choose Startup Security Utility.

2 If necessary, authenticate as Local Administrator.

The Startup Security Utility dialog opens.

If you are not using an Intel-based Mac computer with an Apple T2 Security Chip or a Mac with Apple silicon, you only have the option to turn on the Firmware Password.

If your Mac has the T2 chip, or is a Mac with Apple silicon, you have additional options to help secure your Mac against unauthorized access.

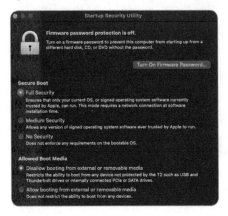

WARNING ► Lowering your secure boot and external boot settings to less secure settings may put your Mac at risk for unauthorized access. If you choose to lower the security, you should consider re-elevating the security before putting the Mac in production. If you have a Mac with Apple silicon, your options will look different. This exercise is intended for Intel-based Mac computers.

3   Examine the features that you have based on the model of your Mac. Don't change boot security options or turn on the firmware password at this time.

Select Your Startup Disk and Restart

Startup Disk enables you to select the volume to start up from. If you encounter problems with your internal storage device during startup, connect a second storage device, with macOS installed, and use Startup Disk to configure your Mac to start up from the new disk.

1   From the Apple menu, choose Startup Disk.

Startup Disk lists all available startup volumes. Options may include external media, depending on the model of your Mac and your Allowed Boot Media settings found in Startup Security Utility.

2   Verify that your normal startup volume (typically named Macintosh HD) is selected. If necessary, select it.

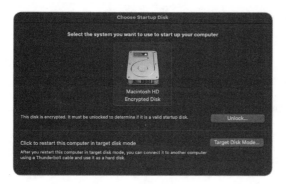

Because you enabled FileVault, you must unlock the disk in order to start up from it.

3   Click Unlock, enter the password for Local Administrator (**Apple321!**), then click Unlock

4   Click Restart.

5   In the confirmation dialog, click Restart.

You could also restart without using Startup Disk by choosing Restart from the Apple menu.

Exercise 5.2
Create a macOS Install Disk

> **Prerequisites**
>
> ▸ You need an erasable external disk with a capacity of at least 12 GB.
>
> ▸ You must have created the Local Administrator account (Exercise 3.1, "Configure a Mac for Exercises").
>
> ▸ You must have enabled FileVault (Exercise 3.2, "Configure System Preferences").

In this exercise, you create a macOS install disk, which includes the macOS Recovery environment, apps, and installation assets. When you create a macOS install disk this way, you can start up from an external storage device to install macOS. Record the version of the macOS installer that you use. If you need to, go to the App Store to get an updated installer.

Get a Copy of the Install macOS Big Sur App

You download the macOS Big Sur installer using the following steps:

1   Log in as Local Administrator (password: **Apple321!**).

2   From the Apple menu, choose App Store. For more about the App Store, see Lesson 18, "Install Apps."

3   In the search field of the App Store window, type **Big Sur**, then press Return.

4   Find macOS Big Sur in the search results, then click the View button next to its name.

5   Click the Get button. Software Update preferences opens and finds the update.

Software Update preferences opens and finds the update.

6   When asked if you are sure you want to download macOS Big Sur, click Download.

When the installer finishes downloading, the Install macOS Big Sur app opens.

7   Quit both Install macOS Big Sur and App Store.

Reformat the External Storage Device

Most new external storage devices come preformatted with the Master Boot Record (MBR) partition scheme. To allow a Mac to start up from external storage devices, reformat the device with the GUID partition scheme. For more information about storage device formats, see Lesson 11.

> **NOTE ▶** This operation erases all content on the external storage device. Don't perform this exercise with a device that contains important content you haven't backed up.

1   Open Disk Utility from /Applications/Utilities.

2   Connect the external storage device to your Mac.

3   If you're asked for a password to unlock the device, click Cancel.

You don't have to unlock the device to erase it.

4   In the toolbar, choose View > Show All Devices.

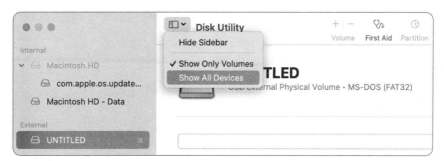

5 Select the external storage device entry in the Disk Utility sidebar. Select the device entry, not the volume entry indented beneath it.

6 Check the partition map listed at the bottom of the window.

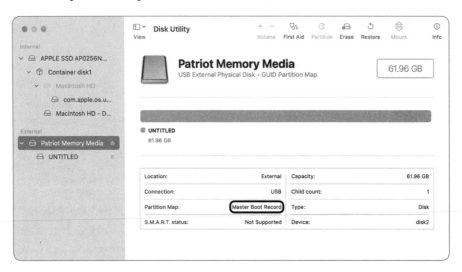

7 Click the Erase button in the toolbar.

8 Give the device a descriptive name, choose GUID Partition Map from the Scheme menu, and choose Mac OS Extended (Journaled) from the Format menu.

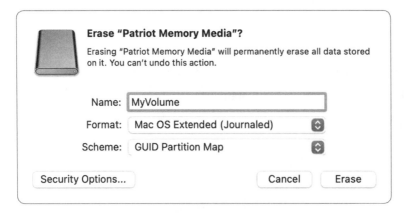

9 Click the Erase button.

10 When the process finishes, click Done to dismiss the erase dialog.

11 Verify that the Partition Map entry is GUID Partition Map.

Location:	External	Capacity:	61.96 GB
Connection:	USB	Child count:	2
Partition Map:	GUID Partition Map	Type:	Disk
S.M.A.R.T. status:	Not Supported	Device:	disk2

12 Quit Disk Utility.

Create a macOS Install Disk

1 Open Terminal.

2 Switch to the Finder, then open the Applications folder.

3 Control-click the Install macOS Big Sur app, then choose Show Package Contents from the shortcut menu.

See Reference 14.2, "Examine Packages," for more information.

4 In the installer package, open the Contents folder, then open the Resources folder.

5 Drag the createinstallmedia file from the Finder into Terminal.

This inserts the full path to createinstallmedia in Terminal.

6 Switch back to Terminal, then press Return.

This executes the createinstallmedia command as a command-line program. It prints a usage summary and explains how to use the command. You observe that the command must be run as root.

7 Type **sudo** followed by a space to start another command, but don't press Return until step 11.

8 Drag createinstallmedia from the Finder to Terminal again.

9 In Terminal, type **--volume** (enter two hyphens before *volume*) followed by a space.

10 Drag the MyVolume (or whatever you named it) volume icon from the desktop to Terminal.

At this point, Terminal displays something like this:

```
● ● ●                          🗔 ladmin — -zsh — 80×24
Last login: Tue Oct  6 13:03:58 on console
[ladmin@Mac-17 ~ % sudo /Applications/Install\ macOS\ Big\ Sur.app/Contents/Resou]
rces/createinstallmedia --volume /Volumes/MyVolume▊
```

11 Switch to Terminal, then press Return.

The following operation requires admin access.

12 Enter the Local Administrator account password (**Apple321!**), then press Return.

This operation erases the device, so you are asked to confirm the operation.

13 Verify that the volume name (listed after /Volumes/) is the one you intend to use, enter **Y,** then press Return.

14 Wait while the install disk is prepared. This may take several minutes, depending on the type and speed of the external device you use.

When the process finishes, Terminal displays several lines, ending with Install media now available at "/Volumes/Install macOS Big Sur".

15 Quit Terminal.

NOTE ► For more information, see Apple Support article HT201372, "How to create a bootable installer for macOS."

Test the macOS Big Sur Install Disk

Test the installer disk, but don't reinstall macOS.

NOTE ► Your ability to do this portion of the exercise will depend on the model of your Mac and your Allowed Boot Media settings. See "Configure Secure Boot and Allowed Boot Media Settings" in Reference 5.3, "Secure Startup."

1 From the Apple menu, choose Restart, then click Restart in the confirmation dialog to restart your Mac.

2 Press and hold the Option key to enter Startup Manager, which will display a row of icons.

3   Click the Install macOS Big Sur icon.

4   Click the arrow that appears under the icon.

The Mac starts up in the installer environment, which is similar to the recoveryOS environment. Explore it, but don't reinstall macOS.

5   If necessary, in Recovery Assistant, authenticate as Local Administrator, then click Continue.

6   When you finish exploring the installer environment, go to the Apple menu and choose Restart to restart your Mac.

Lesson 6

Update macOS

In this lesson, you configure and use macOS and App Store software update technologies, which are automatic ways to keep your Apple-sourced software up to date. You also learn how to install updates manually.

Reference 6.1
Automatic Software Updates

You should keep your Mac software up to date. macOS updates improve the stability, performance, and security of your Mac. They include updates for Safari and other apps that are part of macOS.

macOS includes update methods that automatically check Apple servers, through the internet, to ensure that you're running the latest Apple-sourced software.

You need an internet connection to download update installers for both automatic and manual software updates. Software update methods check only for updates of currently installed Apple-sourced software:

- Updates and upgrades to macOS and software bundled with macOS

- Updates to software you bought from the App Store

You need an administrator account to change Software Update preferences and the preferences in the App Store app.

App Store software updates require appropriate Apple ID authentication, except for apps that were purchased by your organization with Apple School Manager or Apple Business Manager, then assigned directly to your Mac by your organization's MDM solution. You can use Apple School Manager or Apple Business Manager to buy apps (and books) in volume. For apps, you can use your MDM solution to assign them to users or devices, install them on your Mac computers, and update them when updates are available. You can use your MDM solution to assign, install, and update apps even if the App Store is disabled or if those Mac computers don't have a user with an Apple ID signed in to the App Store. See Apple Support article HT207305, "Availability of Apple programs and payment methods for education and business," to find out which Apple programs and payment methods are available in your country or region. See the Apple School Manager User Guide at support.apple.com/guide/apple-school-manager/ or the Apple Business Manager User Guide at support.apple.com/guide/apple-business-manager/ for more information.

> **NOTE ▶** The behavior of apps assigned directly to your Mac by your organization is outside the scope of this guide.

If there is a Mac that provides the Content Caching service on your network, your Mac will automatically use the Content Caching service to help reduce internet data usage and speed up downloading macOS updates and App Store updates. See Reference 25.1, "Turn On Host-Sharing Services," for more information about the Content Caching service.

Automatic Software Update Behavior

macOS uses Notification Center to tell you as soon as new updates are available.

By default, important macOS updates (for example, security updates) are automatically downloaded and installed. By default, other macOS updates are automatically downloaded in the background but not installed.

When macOS updates are ready to be installed, macOS displays an Updates Available notification in an alert (a banner goes away automatically, and an alert stays on screen until you dismiss it) with a Software Update icon.

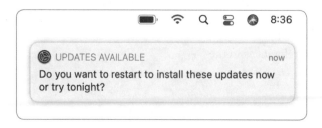

Notification Center shows your alerts in the upper right of your screen, without interrupting what you're doing. You can show and hide Notification Center by clicking the date and time in the menu bar.

Click the alert to open Software Update preferences.

Or hover your pointer over the alert, which makes the word Options appear. Click Options, then click one of the following:

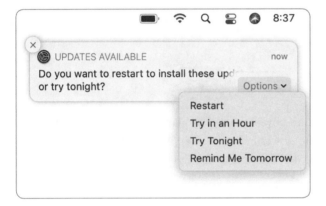

- ▶ Restart—This option is displayed if an update requires a restart. Click Restart for macOS to immediately download any updates not already downloaded, then install available updates. macOS will try to restart.

- ▶ Install—This option is displayed if an update doesn't require a restart. Click Install for macOS to immediately download any updates not already downloaded, then install available updates.

- ▶ "Try in an Hour"—Send an alert again in an hour.

- ▶ "Try Tonight"—Send an alert later tonight.

- ▶ Remind Me Tomorrow—This option doesn't turn on automatic updates.

You can use the "Try in an Hour" or "Try Tonight" option to update the software at a more convenient time. These options are useful because some system updates prevent you from using the Mac while the installation completes, and they might require a restart.

If you click "Try in an Hour" or "Try Tonight," this causes macOS to attempt to change the automatic software update setting for all users of your Mac. If you're not logged in as an administrator, macOS asks you to provide administrator credentials.

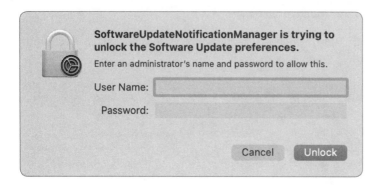

If your Mac notebook isn't connected to power, macOS displays a Not Connected To Power alert. You must be connected to power before you can install software updates. After you connect to power, you can click the alert to dismiss the alert.

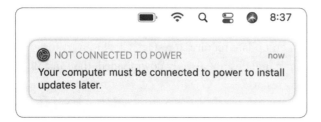

Continuing the scenario of clicking either "Try in an Hour" or "Try Tonight," macOS displays an Automatic Updates Turned On alert.

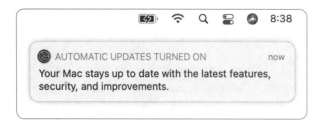

Apple recommends that you keep automatic updates turned on. However, there are some scenarios, such as if you're performing testing on a specific version of macOS, where you might want to turn off automatic updates. To turn off automatic updates, hover the pointer over the alert and click Turn Off.

If you click Turn Off, when you are ready to manually check for new macOS updates, you can use any of the following methods:

▶ Open System Preferences, then open Software Update.

▶ In the About This Mac window, click the Software Update button.

macOS treats macOS updates separately from App Store updates. When an update is available for an app from the App Store that is installed on your Mac, you receive an alert with an App Store icon.

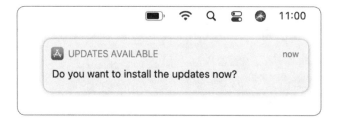

Click the alert to open the App Store.

Or hover the pointer over the alert to reveal Options.

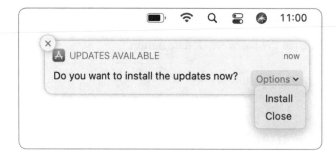

Click Install to open the App Store, or click Close to dismiss the alert.

In addition to the alerts, macOS has other ways to let you know when updates are available.

When macOS software updates are available:

▶ A red badge with the number of available macOS updates appears next to the System Preferences icon in your Dock.

► A red badge with the number of available macOS updates appears next to the Software Update icon in System Preferences.

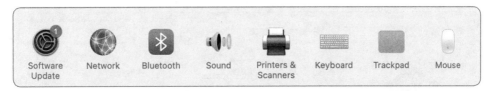

► The number of available macOS updates appears in the Apple menu next to System Preferences.

When App Store software updates are available:

► A red badge with the number of available app updates appears next to the App Store icon in your Dock.

► The number of available app updates appears in the Apple menu next to App Store.

macOS Software Update Preferences Behavior

When you open Software Update preferences, it checks for available macOS updates.

If no updates are available, Software Update preferences displays "Your Mac is up to date," followed by your macOS version. If macOS updates are available, Software Update preferences lists them.

Click Update Now to install all the available macOS updates. Click "More info" to display a list of macOS updates that includes the update name, the version, and a description.

Select an update to get more details about that update. Updates that require a restart include a notice next to the update name in the details section for that update.

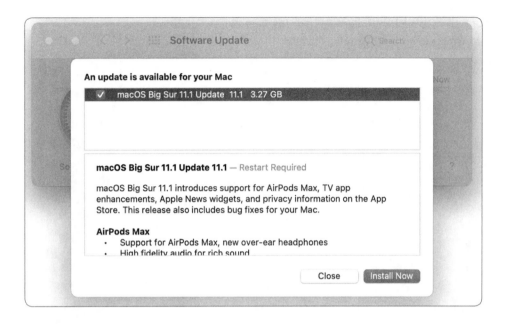

App Store Update Behavior

When you open the App Store, then click Updates in the sidebar, App Store displays the apps that have an update available. The Available section displays each App Store app that has an update available. The Updated Recently section displays apps that were updated recently.

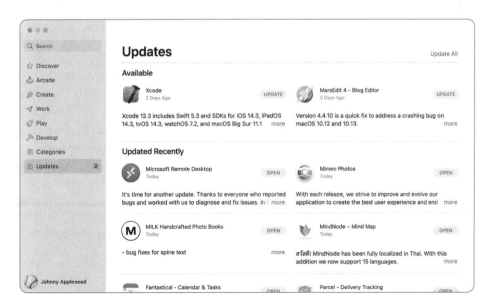

You can refresh available updates by pressing Command-R. Click an app's icon to display more information about the update or click More for an app to get a quick summary of its updates.

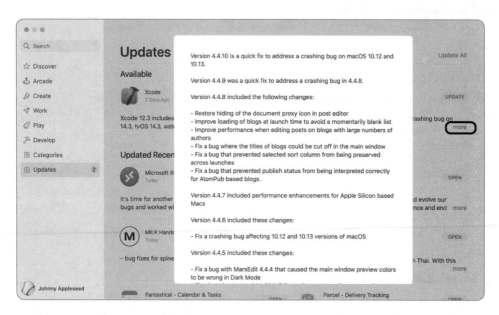

To install a single update, click the corresponding Update button, or click the Update All button to install available updates.

If you aren't signed in to the App Store, macOS asks you to sign in with your Apple ID before you can install updates. If you want to update an App Store item that was installed with a different Apple ID, you must authenticate with the Apple ID used to buy the original item.

Software Update Preferences for Automatic Updates

You can select "Automatically keep my Mac up to date" in Software Update preferences. Changes you make in Software Update preferences apply to all users, so you must have administrator credentials to select or deselect "Automatically keep my Mac up to date" and to select or deselect any of the options in the Advanced pane.

Selecting the option "Automatically keep my Mac up to date" turns on all the options that are available in the Advanced pane. From the Advanced pane in Software Update preferences, you can select or deselect individual options:

▶ Check for updates—This option is selected by default. When it is selected, macOS checks for updates once a day. macOS needs only a small amount of internet bandwidth to determine whether you need updates.

▶ Download new updates when available—This option is selected by default. macOS might need a lot of bandwidth to download macOS system updates.

▶ Install macOS updates—You can select this option; it is unselected by default. After you select it, macOS tells you when macOS updates are automatically installed, as long as they don't require a restart. macOS updates that require a restart notify you, and you can restart immediately or wait until later.

▶ Install app updates from the App Store—You can select this option; it is unselected by default. After you select it, the App Store automatically installs updates to App Store apps. If you select this option, the option Automatic Updates is selected in App Store preferences. Likewise, if you deselect Automatic Updates in App Store preferences, the option "Install app updates from the App Store" is unselected in Software Update preferences.

▶ Install system data files and security updates—This option is selected by default. The best practice is to leave it selected. That way, your Mac checks daily for required security updates and tells you when one is available. If the update doesn't require you to restart your Mac, it's installed automatically. Otherwise, the update is installed the next time you restart your Mac. The security updates include updates to XProtect, the built-in technology for the signature-based detection of malware, and updates to the malware removal tool.

NOTE ▶ To receive the latest updates automatically, select "Check for updates," "Download new updates when available," and "Install system data files and security updates."

App Store Preferences for Automatic Updates

Reference 18.1, "The App Store," has more information about using the App Store app to install apps. This section focuses on using the App Store to automatically keep your App Store apps updated.

When you open the App Store and then open App Store preferences, the following options are available for keeping your App Store apps up to date:

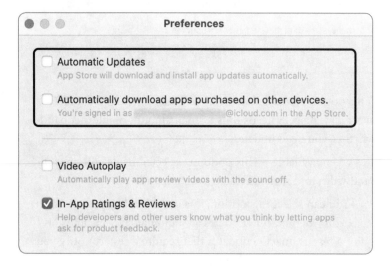

▶ Automatic Updates—You can select this option if you have administrator credentials. Also, if you turn on automatic macOS updates in an Updates Available alert or in Software Update preferences, this option is selected. When you select this option, the App Store downloads and installs app updates automatically.

▶ Automatically download apps purchased on other devices—You can select this option if you are signed in to the App Store. When you sign in to the App Store with the same Apple ID on more than one Mac and you buy an app on a different Mac, that app is installed on any Mac with this option selected.

Reference 6.2
Use MDM to Install macOS Updates

You might be able to use your MDM solution to automatically install all available macOS updates on Mac computers that are enrolled with your MDM solution.

To use MDM to install available macOS updates:

▶ Your Mac must be enrolled in your MDM solution.

▶ Your MDM solution must support the "Install OS update" MDM command.

For more information about using your MDM solution to install macOS updates, visit support.apple.com/guide/mdm.

Reference 6.3
Examine Installation History

Both the update screen in the App Store and Software Update preferences display only recently installed updates. System Information lists Apple and third-party installed software, whether it was installed manually or automatically. To view the System Information list, open System Information and select Installations in the left column. System Information displays the software name, version, software source, and installation date (the Installations section does not display software that you installed by dragging an app to the /Applications folder).

Exercise 6.1
Use Automatic Software Update

▶ **Prerequisite**

▶ You must have created the Local Administrator account (Exercise 3.1, "Configure a Mac for Exercises").

In this exercise, you use the automatic update feature of the Software Update preferences to check for, download, and install updates for macOS. You also learn how to view installed software and updates.

Check Your Software Update Preferences

1   From the Apple menu, choose System Preferences.

2   Click Software Update.

Software Update automatically checks for any available updates and indicates whether your Mac is up to date.

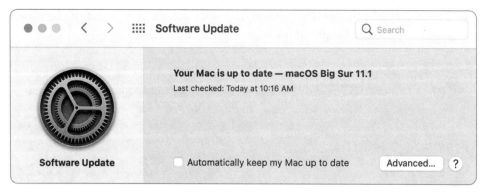

3   Click Advanced.

By default, macOS automatically downloads new updates in the background and notifies you when they are ready to be installed. In production environments, allowing automatic installation of system data files and security updates is recommended.

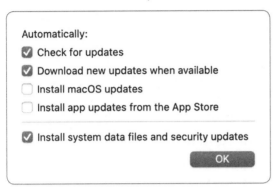

You have the option to enable Software Update to automatically install macOS updates and app updates from the App Store. You can select other preferences if you don't want automatic downloads or updates.

4   Click OK.

5   Select "Automatically keep my Mac up to date."

6   If necessary, authenticate as Local Administrator.

7   Click Advanced.

As a result of selecting "Automatically keep my Mac up to date," all options are selected, and your Mac will install macOS updates and app updates in addition to system data files and security updates automatically.

Update Your Software

1   If necessary, open Software Update preferences and wait while your Mac checks for new software. If no updates are displayed, press Command-R to reload the updates.

2   If your Mac displays the message "Your Mac is up to date," skip the rest of this section and proceed to "Check Installed Updates."

If updates are available, an Update Now button appears, and available updates are listed.

3   Click More Info to get information about the updates.

4   If any of the updates are subject to license agreements, review the agreements, and if they are acceptable to you, continue with this exercise.

5   If more than one update is available, decide which ones you want.

6 Click Install Now for individual updates, or click Update All if you want all updates.

7 If a license agreement appears, read it and if you find the terms acceptable, click Agree.

The macOS update begins to download. After the download is complete, Mac prepares to update, and then if necessary, restarts.

You see a notification for a short period of time telling you that the computer will restart.

8 If the update restarted your Mac, log back in as Local Administrator. If you're asked to sign in with your Apple ID, select "Don't sign in," click Continue, and click Skip in the confirmation dialog.

9 Reopen Software Update and check for additional updates. Some updates must be installed in sequence, so you may have to repeat the update process again.

10 After all updates are installed, quit System Preferences.

Check Installed Updates

1 Press and hold the Option key while you choose System Information from the Apple menu. The System Information menu item appears in place of About This Mac only when you hold down Option.

System Information opens and displays its report.

2 In the Software section of the sidebar, select Installations.

A list of installed software and updates appears, including the updates you just installed. Select specific updates from the list to get more information about them.

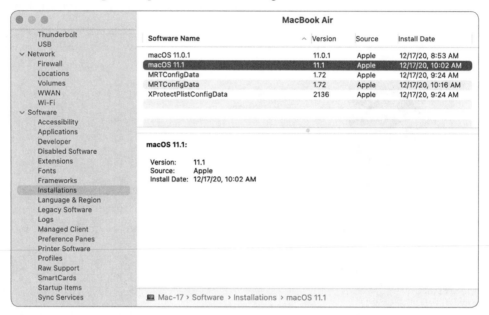

3 Quit System Information.

User Accounts

Manage User Accounts

With a few exceptions, you must log in with a user account to perform any task on a Mac. Even when a Mac starts up and displays the login window (the screen where you log in)—and you haven't yet authenticated—macOS is using system user accounts to maintain background services. Every file and folder on a Mac volume, and every item and process, belong to a user account. This lesson focuses on local user accounts that are available on a single Mac.

Reference 7.1
User Accounts

When you configure your Mac for the first time, Setup Assistant prompts you to create your first administrator account. (If your Mac is enrolled in a mobile device management [MDM] solution, it's possible that the first account you create could be a standard account.)

This administrator account is a local user account, because macOS stores information about that user in the local user database on your Mac. This lesson focuses on local user accounts, but macOS can use other types of user accounts as well, including:

▸ Network user accounts—A network user account is available to multiple Mac computers and is stored on a shared directory server, such as an Active Directory server, that centralizes identification, authentication, and authorization information. The home folder for a network user account is usually stored on a network file server. A Mac must be able to contact both the shared directory server and the home folder server in order to use a network user account.

▶ Mobile user accounts—A mobile user account is a network user account that has been synced with the local user database so that you can use a mobile user account even when your Mac can't contact the shared directory server. The home folder for a mobile user account is usually stored on the startup disk. This is often used with Active Directory and is outside the scope of this guide.

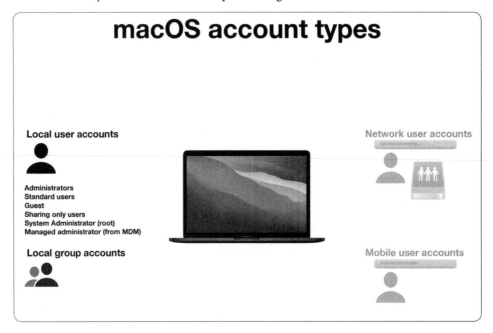

Local User Account Types

If your Mac has multiple users, set up a local account for each person so that users can configure their own settings and options without affecting other users. macOS offers several local account types to provide greater flexibility for managing user access. Because each account type allows different levels of access, be aware of each account type's potential security risk.

There are six local account types on a Mac (five user account types and the group account type):

▶ Administrator

▶ Standard

- Guest

- Sharing Only

- System Administrator (root)

- Group

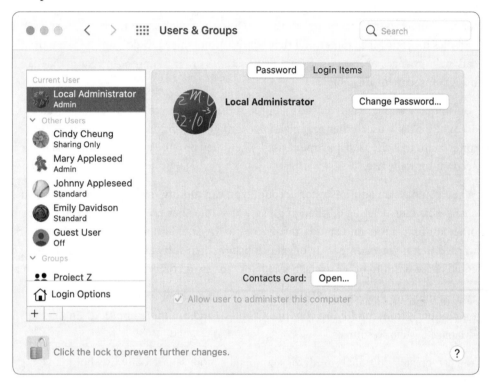

Administrator Accounts

You can use your administrator user account (also called an administrator account) to add and manage other users, install apps, and change settings that affect all users of a Mac. The first new user account you create when you first set up your Mac is an administrator account.

Your Mac can have multiple administrators. Administrator accounts are part of a group called admin.

To keep your Mac secure, don't share administrator names and passwords.

By default, administrator account users don't have access to other users' items except for shared items like their Public folders in the Finder. Administrator account users can also use Terminal to bypass some restrictions that they cannot bypass with the Finder.

Because an administrator account is the initial account type created when you configure your Mac for the first time using Setup Assistant, you may decide to use the administrator account as your primary account type. Doing so enables you to change many settings and files on your Mac (something that administrators need to do). At the same time, you can make changes or install software from sources other than the App Store that can make macOS insecure or unstable.

Some organizations assign a Mac to a user and allow them to use an administrator account for daily use. Other organizations configure each Mac with an administrator account that the IT department uses. Then they provide each user with a standard account for daily use.

When you have an administrator account, you can modify many parts of macOS. Such changes include deleting or changing passwords for other user accounts. You can change other administrators into standard users or change standard users into administrators. Be warned that if you open poorly or maliciously written software as an administrator, you could cause harm to other users' home folder items or compromise the security of macOS.

System Integrity Protection (SIP) prevents all user account types, even administrator accounts, from modifying core macOS files. Find out more about SIP in Lesson 15, "Manage System Resources."

You can create additional standard accounts for more secure daily use, but managing macOS requires access to at least one administrator account.

If you need to help a user but don't want that user to see your user account when they log in, visit Apple Support article HT203998, "Hide a user account in macOS," to learn how to hide a user account in the macOS login window.

macOS privacy controls prevent all user account types from reading certain files without the owner of those files granting permission. Find out more about privacy in Lesson 9, "Manage Security and Privacy."

An MDM solution can modify Setup Assistant to configure an account called a managed administrator user account, or a managed administrator, on a Mac. This is possible only for Mac computers that are enrolled in Apple School Manager or Apple Business Manager *and* enrolled in your organization's MDM solution. You can use your MDM solution to hide the managed administrator and to change their password.

The following figure illustrates that you can use Apple's MDM solution, Profile Manager, to create a managed administrator during Setup Assistant.

> **NOTE** ▸ You can find out more about Apple management technologies by visiting support.apple.com/guide/deployment-reference-macos/, support.apple.com/guide/profile-manager/, and "Options for setting up a local administrator account with MDM for Apple devices" at support.apple.com/guide/mdm/mdmca092ad96/.

Standard Accounts

Standard user accounts are secure if an appropriate password is set. They have read access to most items, preferences, and apps. Users with standard accounts also have full control over their home folder, which allows them to install third-party apps there.

Standard account users are allowed to take advantage of nearly all the resources and features of a Mac, but they generally can't change anything that might affect other users on it with these exceptions:

▸ Standard account users can install apps and app updates from the App Store.

▸ Standard account users can choose when to update software when they receive a notification that macOS software updates are available.

Even though standard account users can download and install some kinds of apps in their own home folder and are allowed full access to the App Store, they aren't allowed to manually modify the systemwide Applications folder (outside of using the App Store app) or use other installation methods that might modify shared parts of macOS. This means that standard account users aren't allowed to install many items that are distributed outside the

App Store. Apple maintains tight control over App Store distribution. As a result of this control, content remains safe for standard account users to install.

> **NOTE ▸** If your organization wants to restrict users from installing apps, system updates, or App Store items, you can create managed accounts or use an MDM solution to configure Mac computers. For example, you can use MDM to configure a Mac to restrict the App Store to display only apps installed by MDM and software updates. For more information see "MDM restrictions for Mac computers" at support.apple.com/guide/mdm/mdmba790e53.

Guest Account

macOS features a special account called the guest user, or the guest account, that anyone with physical access to the Mac can use to log in. In Users & Groups preferences, select Guest User to configure it. The guest account is disabled by default in macOS. Select "Allow guests to log in to this computer" to enable the guest account. When the guest account is enabled, it is similar to a standard user but it doesn't require a password.

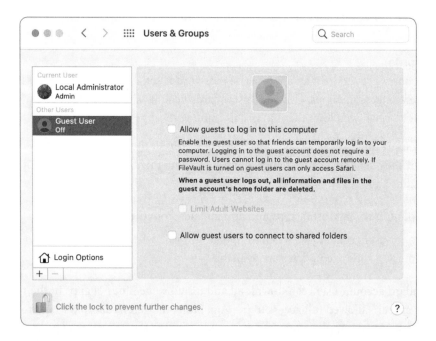

When the guest user logs out, the guest account home folder is deleted, including any home folder items that would normally be saved, such as preference files or web browser history. The next time someone logs in as a guest, a new home folder is created for that user.

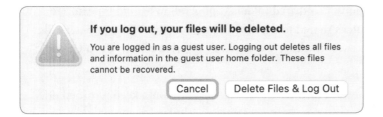

FileVault affects how a guest account operates. If you've enabled FileVault and someone logs in to your Mac with the guest account, your Mac restarts. Safari is the only app the guest user can use. A guest account doesn't have access to the startup disk.

When the user with the guest account quits Safari or restarts the Mac, the guest account home folder is deleted and the Mac restarts.

If you don't enable FileVault, the guest user has access to the /Users/Shared folder and other users' Public folders. Unlike the guest user's home folder, the contents of these other folders remain after the guest logs out. This means that a guest user could fill the disk with unwanted files. Guest users can restart or shut down a Mac, potentially allowing them to attempt to compromise macOS during startup.

You can change the access permissions on shared folders so that a guest user isn't allowed to copy items to the Mac. Changing file and folder permissions is covered in Lesson 13, "Manage Permissions and Sharing."

The "Allow guest users to connect to shared folders" option allows another person to connect to your Mac computer's shared folders if you turn on your Mac computer's file sharing service without a password, which is covered in Reference 25.1, "Turn On Host-Sharing Services."

Unless you have a specific need to turn on Guest access, you should keep it turned off.

Sharing-Only Accounts

When you want to share files with someone on a different computer but you don't want that person to be able to log in to your Mac, create a sharing-only user account. Users of sharing-only accounts have access to shared files and folders only. Sharing-only accounts have no home folder, and those users can't log in to your Mac at the login window or use the Secure Shell protocol (SSH) to log in remotely. Sharing-only accounts are, by default, allowed file sharing access to users' Public and Drop Box folders. Like a guest user, these users could fill internal storage with unwanted files.

You can configure a sharing account to require a password, and you can set file and folder permissions for the account.

Sharing-only accounts are safer than guest user accounts for file sharing.

Root User Account

You can use the root user account (also called the System Administrator account, the root account, or just root) to perform tasks that require more privileges than administrator user accounts have. Although more than one administrator account can exist, there is only *one* root account.

Since many macOS processes are owned by the root account, the root account must exist. macOS wouldn't be able to start up without processes run with root privileges.

The root account can:

▶ Access many files in other users' home folders

▶ Read, write, and delete many nonsystem files

▶ Modify many system settings

The root account can't change items that are protected by SIP. In macOS Big Sur, the root account can't access additional files, including files in other users' home folders that are especially private and sensitive, such as files in each user's ~/Library/Application Support/ folder.

The root account has more access to files than an administrator account has. An administrator account doesn't have access to files in another user's home folder (except Public and Drop Box folders and files stored at the top level of the other users' home folders).

The default macOS configuration doesn't have a password set for the root user account. The term "enabled" for a user refers to the user being for you to use at the login window to log in. So by default in macOS, the root user isn't enabled. Apple recommends that you leave the root user disabled.

Although some tasks require you to use root user account privileges, you can acquire root user privileges to accomplish the task without enabling the root user. Any administrator can use their own password to use the sudo command to run a command with root user account privileges in the command-line interface (CLI).

> **WARNING ▶** Do not enable the root user for daily use. Its privileges allow you to make changes that you can undo only by reinstalling macOS. If you need to enable the root user account (instead of just using the sudo command), be sure to verify you have a reliable backup of your Mac and disable the root user account after you complete your task.

Although it's not recommended, understand that any administrator user can enable the root account or change an existing root account password. Two apps that enable an administrator user to make these changes are Terminal and Directory Utility. Directory Utility is in the /System/Library/CoreServices/Applications/ folder. If someone has enabled the root user on your Mac, you can use Directory Utility to disable the root user: in Directory Utility, click the lock, authenticate with administrator credentials, then choose Edit > Disable Root User.

If your Intel-based Mac does not have the Apple T2 Security Chip, anyone with physical access to your Mac can start your Mac in single-user mode and obtain root access to your Mac, or use macOS Recovery to reset the password for any local account, including the root account. Consider turning on FileVault to restrict access to macOS Recovery. Turning on FileVault is covered in Lesson 12, "Manage FileVault." Consider setting a firmware password to restrict access to single-user mode. Setting a firmware password is covered in Reference 5.3, "Secure Startup." Single-user mode is covered in Lesson 28, "Troubleshoot Startup and System Issues."

Local Group Accounts

A group account is a list of user accounts. Groups give you greater control over file and folder access. macOS has several built-in groups to facilitate secure processes and sharing. For instance, all user accounts are members of the staff group. Administrator user accounts are also members of the admin group. The root account has its own group (called wheel). Using groups to manage sharing is discussed in Lesson 13.

Standard accounts are members of the staff group. Administrator accounts are members of both the staff group and the admin group.

Reference 7.2
Configure User Accounts

In this section, you examine different ways to manage local user accounts.

Users & Groups Preferences

From Users & Groups preferences, local users can manage basic settings for their accounts.

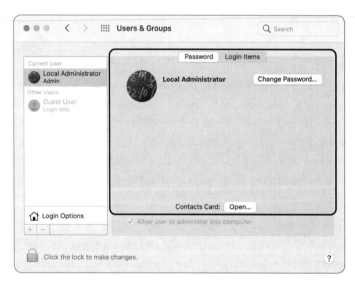

Any administrator account user can unlock Users & Groups preferences and manage attributes for local accounts.

Create and Edit New User Accounts

From Users & Groups preferences, after authenticating as an administrator you can manage any account by selecting it from the list and modifying items to the right. Click Add (+) at the bottom of the Users & Groups list to create a new account. A dialog appears where you can define the basic attributes for a new user account.

The New Account menu at the top of the user creation pane enables you to define the type of local user account being created: Administrator, Standard, or Sharing Only.

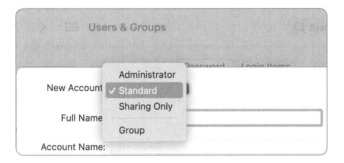

When you create a new local user account, enter a full name. macOS automatically enters an account name based on the full name, but you can change that account name before you click Create User. Enter an initial password for the user. You can also enter an optional password hint.

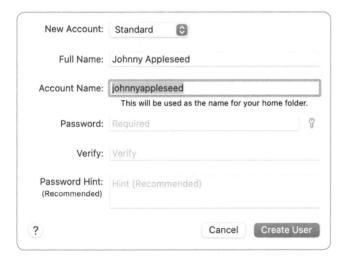

Setup Assistant for Additional Users

After you've completed Setup Assistant for the first time on your Mac, the next time you log in to your Mac with an additional user account you see an abbreviated version of Setup Assistant for that user. Setup Assistant is described in Reference 3.1, "Configure a Mac with a New Installation of macOS Big Sur."

Just as in the initial Setup Assistant process, at some screens you must take action or make a selection; at other screens, you only have to read and then click Continue; and at other screens, you can click the option to set up a feature later.

If Find My is enabled on your Mac, you'll see the Find My screen that gives you a few of the characters in the Apple ID that Find My uses. Reference 9.6, "Use Find My," includes more information about this feature.

Mac computers that are enrolled in an MDM solution might skip screens of the abbreviated Setup Assistant.

User Account Attributes

On a Mac, Open Directory maintains local user account information. Open Directory stores this information in a series of XML-encoded text files in a protected location in the /private/var/db/dslocal/nodes/ folder. The text files contain lists of user account attributes and their associated settings. Only the root user account can read these files.

You can also access many user attributes from Users & Groups preferences. After you unlock Users & Groups preferences, Control-click a user account and choose Advanced Options from the shortcut menu to display the Advanced Options dialog and view the attributes.

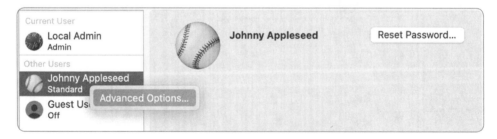

You can edit user account settings. User account settings include:

▶   User ID—A number that identifies an account with file and folder ownership. This number is usually unique to each account on a single Mac, though overlaps are possible. User accounts start at 501, whereas most macOS system accounts are below 400. The User ID is unique from other users' IDs on a local Mac. Other Mac computers use similar ID numbers between Mac computers. For example, the first local user you create on any Mac will have the ID number 501. When you delete a user account, the user's ID becomes available, and the next user you create gets the lowest available ID.

▶ Group—The user's primary group. The default primary group for local users, even administrator accounts, is the staff group. An administrator account is also a member of the admin group.

▶ Account name—Also called the "short name." You use this name to uniquely identify an account and, by default, to name a user's home folder. A user can choose either the full name or the account name, interchangeably, to authenticate. Other accounts in macOS must have a unique name, and the name can't contain special characters or spaces. Special characters not allowed include commas, slashes, colons, semicolons, brackets, quotes, and symbols. Allowed characters include dashes, underscores, and periods.

> **NOTE ▶** A user's account name and home folder name must match. So if you need to change a user's account name, don't just change the account name field here. You must use an administrator account to first change the user's home folder name, then change the user's account name. See Apple Support article HT201548, "Change the name of your macOS user account and home folder" for more information.

▶ Full name—The full name of the user. It can be long and contain nearly any character. Other accounts in macOS must have a unique full name. You can change the full name later.

▶ Login shell—This file path defines the default command-line shell in Terminal by the account. Any user who is allowed to use the command line in Terminal has the path set to /bin/zsh by default for new users. Users who were migrated from earlier versions of macOS may have a different shell, /bin/bash. Both administrator and standard users are given this access.

▶ Home directory—This file path defines the location of the user's home folder. All users except for sharing-only account users, who don't have home folders, have this set to /Users/*name* by default, where *name* is the account name.

▶ Universally Unique ID (UUID)—Sometimes referred to as Generated UID (GUID), this alphanumeric attribute is generated by a Mac during account creation and is unique across space and time. After the attribute is created, no system will create an account with the same UUID. The UUID is used to refer to the user's password and for group membership and file permissions. UUIDs created on one Mac are unique to that Mac.

▶ Aliases—Used to associate a local Mac user account with other service accounts. For example, a user's Apple ID can be associated with a local account. This attribute is optional for macOS, but it is required for integration with Apple internet services like iCloud.

Advanced Options

User: "Johnny Appleseed"

WARNING: Changing these settings might damage this account and prevent the user from logging in. You must restart the computer for the changes to these settings to take effect.

User ID:	502
Group:	staff
Account name:	johnny
Full name:	Johnny Appleseed
Login shell:	/bin/zsh
Home directory:	/Users/johnny Choose...
UUID:	051ED731-D28E-4B0F-9A8D-2EEEB98D972C
Aliases:	

+ | −

Cancel   OK

Local user account passwords are stored as an encrypted attribute to enhance security. Password management is covered in detail in Lesson 10, "Manage Password Changes."

Reference 7.3
Restrict Local User Access with Screen Time

Use Screen Time to do the following:

▶ View daily and weekly charts and get insights about your screen time.

▶ Set a schedule for time away from the screen.

▶ Set daily time limits for app categories and specific apps.

▶ Restrict communications settings (if you're signed in with an iCloud account).

▶ Restrict settings for explicit content, purchases, and downloads.

▶ Restrict settings for privacy.

▶ Set a passcode to secure Screen Time settings and to allow for more time when time limits expire.

▶ Monitor and limit a child's use of Apple devices, when they're logged in to their own account or using a device while logged in to iCloud with Family Sharing enabled.

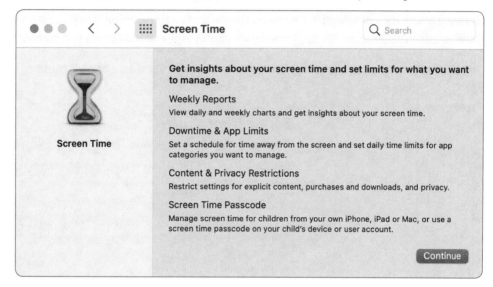

Configure Screen Time

Screen Time preferences are available in System Preferences. If one or more children you are responsible for uses your Mac, you can configure a separate set of limits for each child. You can even set a separate passcode for each child so that they can't change the settings or allow for more time without you or another adult first entering the passcode.

You can log in as each child, then configure Screen Time for that child. Family Sharing makes the process even easier. When you turn on Family Sharing, you can log in with your account, open Screen Time preferences, select a child account, configure Screen Time preferences for that child, and repeat for each child, without logging out.

Family Sharing makes it easy for up to six people in your family, without sharing accounts, to share the following and more:

▶ Apple services like Apple Music, Apple TV+, Apple News+, and Apple Arcade

▶ iTunes, Apple Books, and App Store purchases

▶ iCloud storage plan

▶ Shared family calendars and photo alums

▶ Location with Find My

You can find out more about Family Sharing at www.apple.com/family-sharing.

The first time you log in to your Mac with any user account, Setup Assistant displays the Screen Time screen. If you click Continue, then after you finish Setup Assistant macOS gathers information about the apps you use, websites you visit, and alerts you receive.

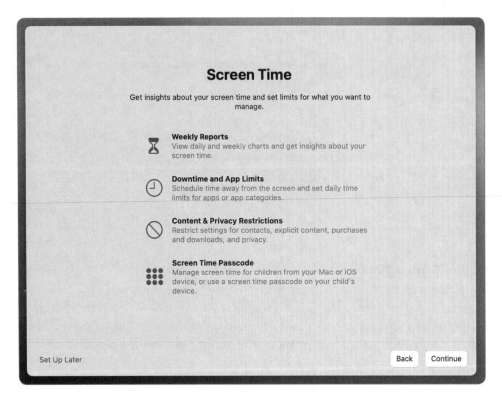

Instead, if you click Set Up Later you have to turn on Screen Time before you can start applying limits with Screen Time preferences. Open System Preferences, open Screen Time preferences, then click Turn On.

If you are signed in with your iCloud account, Screen Time preferences displays two additional items:

► Share across devices

► Communication

When you select "Share across devices," Screen Time reports your combined screen time on any iPhone, iPad, or Mac that you're signed in to with your iCloud account.

The Set Up Family Sharing button appears if you are logged in with your iCloud account and haven't yet set up Family Sharing.

You can use Screen Time for the currently logged-in user. Or if you're logged in with an Apple ID that has Family Sharing with children, click the menu in the upper-left corner to choose and configure Screen Time for a child instead.

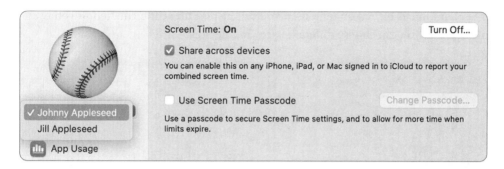

When you configure Screen Time for a child, you can select Include Website Data to enable website data when viewing usage. And you can set a Screen Time passcode to secure the Screen Time settings for the child.

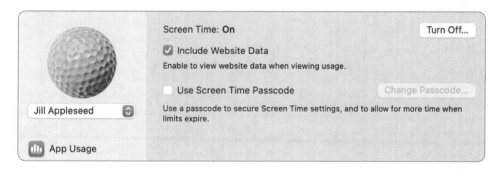

When you set a Screen Time passcode, enter four numbers. The numbers you enter will be obscured, so you'll be asked to verify the passcode after you enter it. Be sure to enter a passcode for a child before they have a chance to enter their own passcode.

After Screen Time is turned on for a user, you can inspect usage information. If you use Family Sharing, you can choose different users and devices.

You can configure the following categories for each user:

▶ Downtime: Schedule time to be away from screens, such as during meals or bedtime.

▶ App Limits: Limit the amount of time allowed for apps and on websites. You can set limits for specific apps, app categories, and websites. And if you use Family Sharing, you can select "Block at end of limit" so that the child can ask the parent or guardian for more time.

▶ Communication: This is a new feature of Screen Time for macOS Big Sur. You can specify who the user of the computer or device is allowed to communicate with.

These limits apply to Phone, FaceTime, Messages, and iCloud contacts. During screen time, you can select the following options: "Contacts Only," "Contacts & Groups with at Least One Contact," or "Everyone." During downtime, you can select specific contacts or select Everyone. Communication to known emergency numbers that your carrier identifies is always allowed.

▶ Always Allowed: Select apps that can be used at any time, even during downtime (for example, FaceTime and Messages to be used in an emergency).

▶ Content & Privacy: Restrict content (web content, Siri & Dictionary, games, Music), purchases, specific apps, and downloads, and choose privacy settings.

If you select Use Screen Time Passcode while modifying settings for an administrator user, then you see a dialog that recommends converting the account to a standard account:

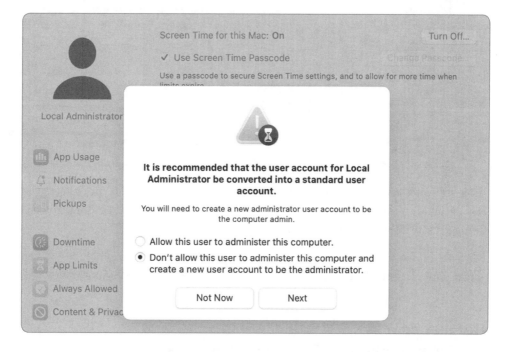

▶ If you click Not Now, you won't create a Screen Time passcode at this time, and macOS returns you to the Screen Time preferences.

▶ If you select "Allow this user to administer this computer," then click Next, you can set a Screen Time passcode for yourself.

▶ The "Don't allow this user to administer this computer and create a new user account to be the administrator" option is appropriate if you provided your child's name when you created your first computer account during Setup Assistant and are currently logged in with your child's account—an administrator account. If you select this option, then click Next, Screen Time preferences displays a dialog that lets you create an administrator account for yourself or another adult.

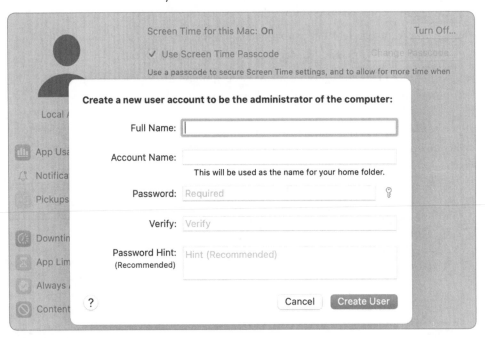

After you enter valid information for this new administrator account, click Create User and the child's administrator account will be converted to a standard account. You'll still be logged in with the child's account.

For more information about Screen Time, see Apple Support article HT210387, "Use Screen Time on your Mac."

Reference 7.4
Configure Login and Fast User Switching

With fast user switching, macOS enables multiple users to be logged in on a single Mac at the same time.

You can manage login window behavior on multiple Mac computers with an MDM solution.

Manage User Login Items

You can adjust items that automatically open during login from the Login Items pane of Users & Groups preferences. The list of items to open applies only to the currently logged-in user.

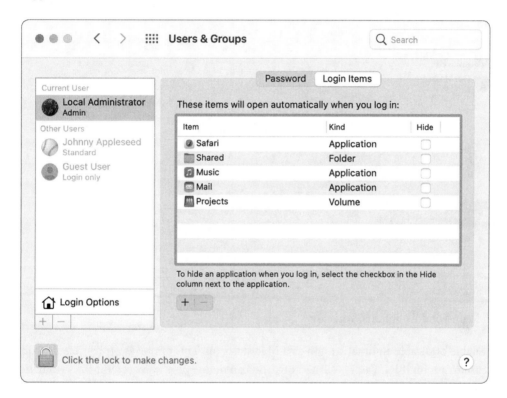

Drag items to the Login Items list or click the Add (+) button and browse for items to add them. Select an item from the list and click the Remove (–) button to remove it. Select the Hide option to make an app open but hide it from view.

Manage System Login Window Options

Authenticate as an administrator user and click Login Options at the bottom of the user accounts list to adjust the systemwide behavior of the login window.

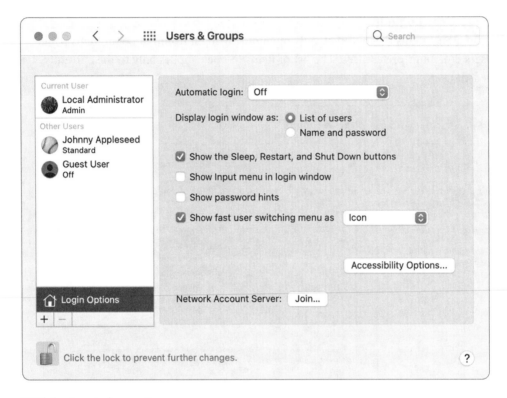

With login window options, you can:

► Enable or disable automatic login as a Mac starts up. This option is off by default. You can turn it on if FileVault is turned off. You can define only one account for automatic login.

   NOTE ► Apple recommends that you not configure automatic login for an administrator. If you do, someone with physical access to your Mac could restart your Mac and gain access with administrator privileges.

► Choose whether the login window shows a list of available users, the default setting, or blank name and password fields. If your Mac displays the list of available users, an unauthorized user can select one and attempt to guess the password to log in. If your Mac doesn't display available users, an unauthorized user must guess both a user name and a password to log in.

▶ Specify the availability of the Restart, Sleep, and Shut Down buttons. Mac computers in environments that require more security shouldn't have these buttons available at the login window.

▶ Specify whether users can use the input menu. This menu gives users access to non-Roman characters, like Cyrillic or Kanji, at the login window.

▶ Determine whether the login window shows password hints after three failed password attempts.

▶ Disable the fast user switching menu or adjust the look of the menu items. The fast user switching menu can appear as the user's full name, the account name, or the generic user icon.

▶ Enable users to use accessibility items at the login window, including VoiceOver audible assistant technology, Voice Control, Zoom, Accessibility Keyboard, Sticky Keys, Slow Keys, and Mouse Keys.

▶ Configure options to allow all, none, or only specified network users to log in at the login window. This option is displayed only if your Mac is bound to a directory service.

▶ Configure a Mac to use network accounts hosted from a shared network directory.

You can configure a three-line message for the login window or when the screen is locked from Security & Privacy preferences, as covered in Lesson 9. If your organization requires a full login banner, configure it with the instructions in Apple Support article HT202277, "How to set up policy banners in macOS."

Fast User Switching

Fast user switching lets a Mac switch between user accounts without users having to log out or quit apps. This enables a user to keep work open in the background while one or more other users are logged in to the Mac. Returning users can resume tasks after they log in.

The fast user switching menu appears after you create additional local user accounts. This menu item appears in the upper-right corner of the screen. By default, the fast user switching menu appears as a silhouette inside a circle. In the following figure, an orange checkmark is displayed next to the currently logged-in user, Local Administrator. If you select the other user, Johnny Appleseed, you'll be prompted to provide Johnny Appleseed's password.

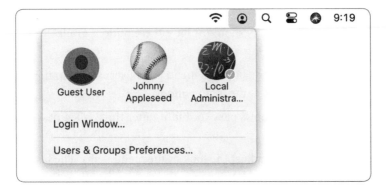

And the following figure shows what happens after you provide Johnny Appleseed's password, then click the Fast User Switching menu bar item:

▶   An orange checkmark is displayed next to the picture for currently logged-in user, Johnny Appleseed.

▶   A gray checkmark is displayed next to the picture for any other user that's also logged in; in this case, Local Administrator is also logged in.

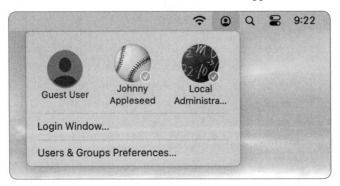

If you don't see this menu item, an administrator can turn it on from the Login Options pane of Users & Groups preferences.

Any user can also configure whether or not to display the Fast User Switching item in Dock & Menu Bar preferences.

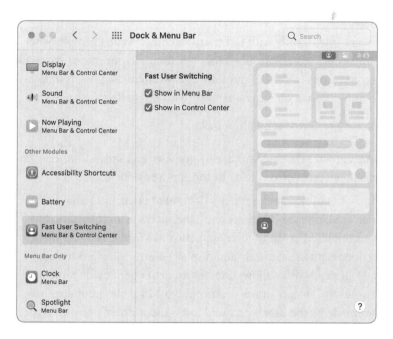

Any user can change the appearance of the Fast User Switching menu item.

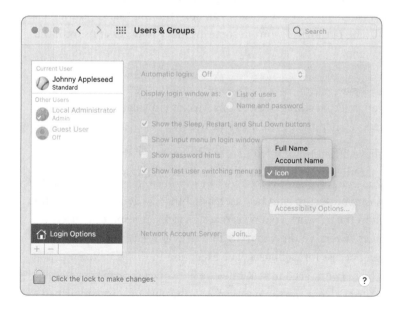

When another user is logged in, select that user's name from the fast user switching menu and have the user enter their password to switch to that user.

Fast User Switching Contention

macOS apps from Apple work intelligently with fast user switching. As an example, when you switch between accounts Music automatically mutes or unmutes your music and Mail continues to check for new messages in the background. In rare circumstances, resource contention may occur when more than one user attempts to access an item.

Examples of fast user switching resource contention include:

▶ App contention—Some apps are designed for use by one user at a time . If other users try to open these apps, they see an error dialog or the app won't open.

▶ Document contention—Sometimes one user has a document open and remains logged in with fast user switching. This can prevent other users from fully accessing the document. As an example, Microsoft Office apps such as Word and Excel allow other users to open a document as read-only and display an error dialog if the user tries to save changes. Other apps don't allow different users to open the document at all. In the worst-case scenario, an app allows two people to edit a file simultaneously but saves only changes made by the user who saved last—and it doesn't give an error message.

▶ Peripheral contention—Some peripherals can be accessed by only one user at a time. Peripheral contention can happen if a user leaves an app running that's communicating with a peripheral. The peripheral won't become available to other apps until the user quits the original app.

Fast User Switching Storage Issues

When one user attaches an external storage device to a Mac, it is available to other users, even if they weren't logged in when the device was attached.

Mounted disk images behave differently. Only the user who mounted the disk image has full read/write access to it. Other users may have read access to the mounted disk image.

Shared network volumes remain secure with fast user switching. By default, only the user who originally connected to the network volume can access it. Even if multiple users attempt to access the same network volume, macOS automatically generates multiple mount points with different access for each user. The exception to this is the network home folder shares used by network accounts. While one network user can successfully log in, additional network users from the same server won't be able to access their network home folders. For this reason, fast user switching doesn't support network accounts.

Resolving Fast User Switching Issues

Because resources and apps act differently, fast user switching issues aren't always consistently reported or readily apparent. If you are experiencing access errors for files, apps, or peripherals, check if other users are logged in. If so, have them log out and try to access the items again.

You can't change a password or manage a user account for a logged-in user. Logged-in user accounts are dimmed, as Johnny's is in the following figure.

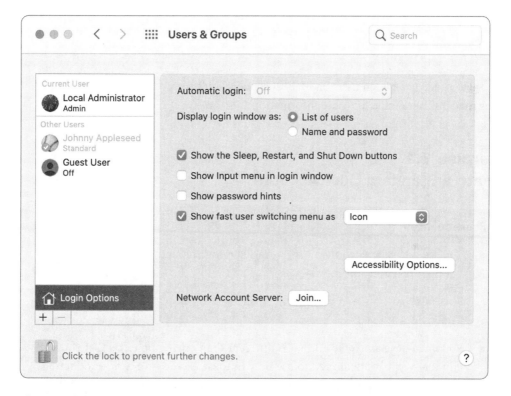

If you can't log out the other users, you can force apps opened by other users to quit or force the other users to log out by restarting the Mac. Forcing an app with open files to quit might result in data loss. You can force an open app to quit, using techniques covered in Lesson 20, "Manage and Troubleshoot Apps."

If you restart a Mac, you may encounter other issues. If other users are logged in, you have to force their open apps to quit before you restart. macOS provides an authenticated restart dialog to enable you to force-quit apps, but you might lose data from open apps.

Restarting may cause other users logged into this computer to lose unsaved changes.

To avoid losing unsaved changes, log out all users before restarting. To continue without saving changes, enter an administrator name and password and then click Restart.

Name: [   ]

Password: [   ]

[Switch User...]   [Cancel]   [Restart]

See "Switch quickly between users on Mac" at support.apple.com/guide/mac-help/mchlp2439 in the macOS User Guide for more information.

Exercise 7.1
Create a Standard User Account

▶ **Prerequisites**

- ▶ You must have created the Local Administrator account (Exercise 3.1, "Configure a Mac for Exercises").

- ▶ You must have turned on FileVault (Exercise 3.2, "Configure System Preferences").

- ▶ You must have an Apple ID that is different than other Apple IDs that you use and that you have dedicated to use only in these exercises (a "non-production Apple ID"). Don't use an Apple ID that you employ on a day-to-day basis for personal use on other Apple devices you own.

NOTE ▶ This exercise is required for most of the remaining exercises.

You created an administrator account when you first configured your Mac. In this exercise, you create an additional account (a standard user account) so that you understand the user experience.

You also associate the new account with an Apple ID so that you can access iCloud services with it. Doing this enables you to complete subsequent exercises that use iCloud.

Create a Standard User Account

1   If necessary, log in as Local Administrator.

2   Open System Preferences, then click Users & Groups.

3   Click the lock and authenticate as the Local Administrator user to access Users & Groups preferences.

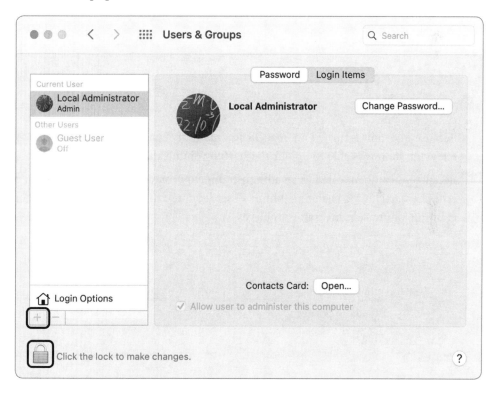

4   Click the Add (+) button below the account list, then enter the following information:

New Account: Standard

Full Name: **Johnny Appleseed**

Account Name: **johnny**

Password: **Apple321!**

It is important to remember the password, because you need to reenter it periodically.

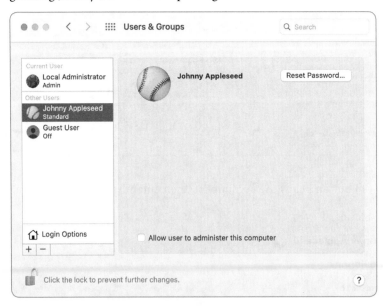

5   Click Create User.

Because FileVault is turned on, macOS automatically enabled Johnny's account to use FileVault; Johnny is able to unlock the startup volume after the Mac restarts.

Because you authenticated as an administrator, you can configure other account properties here, including changing Johnny's user icon, resetting Johnny's password, or granting Johnny administrator privileges.

Log In to the New User Account

In these steps, you log in to Johnny's user account to configure the account further. Ensure that you're connected to the internet before you attempt this exercise.

1   From the Apple menu, choose Log Out Local Administrator.

2   In the dialog that asks if you are sure, click Log Out.

3   In the login window, select Johnny Appleseed, then enter the password.

4   On the Accessibility screen, turn on any assistive needs, then click Continue. If you don't want to configure Accessibility at this time, click Not Now.

5   On the Data & Privacy screen, read and agree to Apple's privacy policy, then click Continue.

6   On the Sign In with Your Apple ID screen, enter your non-production Apple ID, then click Continue.

Because this account isn't associated with an Apple ID, you'll use a non-production Apple ID to connect Johnny's account with the Apple ID. Do not use your personal Apple ID.

You use this Apple ID to set up iCloud on your Mac.

7   Enter the password for your Apple ID, then click Continue.

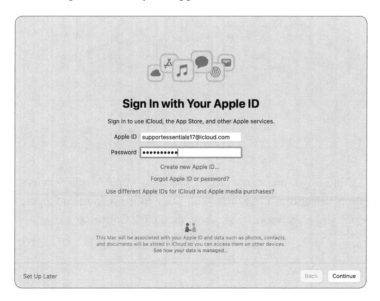

8   If you are prompted to enable two-factor authentication, leave the checkbox "Use two-factor authentication" selected, then follow the prompts. If you don't want to enable two-factor authentication at this time, deselect the checkbox, click Continue, then at the prompt, click Don't Upgrade.

> **NOTE ▶** For any production Apple ID, it is strongly recommended that you enable two-factor authentication to protect your Apple ID.

9   If necessary, verify your identity through one of your devices. Follow the prompts to finish authenticating. If you are not prompted, skip to step 10.

Because your Apple ID is enabled with two-factor authentication, you are asked to verify your identity.

10   If you do not have a trusted device, select "Didn't get a verification code?" and then select "Text code to your trusted phone number." Follow the prompts to finish authenticating.

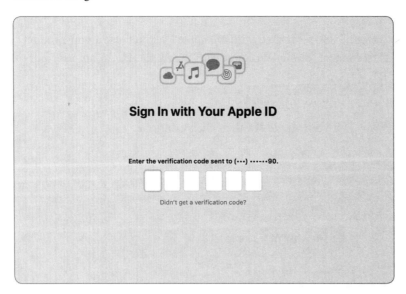

11   On the Terms and Conditions screen, read the iCloud and Apple Media Services Terms and Conditions, select the "I have read and agree to the iCloud and Apple Media Services Terms and Conditions" checkbox, then click Continue.

12 If a confirmation dialog appears, click Agree.

13 If you are asked to set up iCloud Keychain, select Set Up Later, then click Continue.

14 If a Find My screen appears, read the information provided and click Continue.

15 On the Screen Time screen, click Set Up Later.

16 At the iCloud Analytics screen, choose whether you want to allow analytics of usage and data from your iCloud account, then click Continue.

17 If you are asked to set up Siri, deselect Enable Ask Siri, then click Continue.

18 On the "All your files and photos in iCloud" screen, deselect "Store files from Documents and Desktop in iCloud Drive" and "Store photos and videos in iCloud Photos," then click Continue.

19 If you are asked to set up Touch ID, click Set Up Touch ID Later, then click Continue in the confirmation dialog.

20 If you are asked to set up Apple Pay, click Set Up Later.

21 On the Choose Your Look screen, choose your preferred appearance, then click Continue.

22 If the True Tone Display screen appears, click Continue.

Adjust Johnny Appleseed's Preferences

Just as you did with the Local Administrator account, you can adjust Johnny Appleseed's preferences to enable alternative access to content.

1 In the Finder menu bar, choose Finder > Preferences.

2 If necessary, click General in the toolbar, then select "Hard disks" and "Connected servers" to have macOS display them on your desktop.

3 From the "New Finder windows show" menu, choose your startup volume (typically named Macintosh HD).

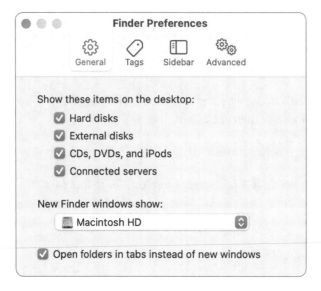

4 In the toolbar of the Finder Preferences window, click Sidebar.

5 Select "johnny" in the Favorites section of the sidebar and "Hard disks" in the Locations section. "Hard disks" should be fully selected (a checkmark in the check-box), not partially selected (a dash in the checkbox).

6 Close the Finder Preferences window.

7 Navigate to the /Applications folder (choose Go > Applications or press Shift-Command-A).

8 Just as you did in the Local Administrator account in Exercise 3.3, "Download Student Materials," drag the TextEdit app to the left side of the dividing line in Johnny's Dock.

9 Navigate to /Users/Shared. Since Johnny's Finder preferences are set to show the hard disks on the desktop, you can open Macintosh HD from the desktop, open Users, and open Shared.

10 Drag the StudentMaterials folder to the right side of the dividing line in Johnny's Dock.

11 Choose Go > Applications, then drag the TextEdit app into the left side of the dividing line in your Dock.

12 Open System Preferences, then click Desktop & Screen Saver preferences.

13 Select a different desktop picture.

14 Adjust Trackpad and/or Mouse preferences, as you did for the Local Administrator account in Exercise 3.2. "Configure System Preferences."

Examine Johnny Appleseed's Account

Use the following steps to confirm that Johnny Appleseed's account, a standard account, does not have as many privileges as an administrator account.

1 If necessary, open System Preferences, then click Users & Groups.

You have different options than you had when you logged in as Local Administrator. For instance, you aren't able to allow yourself to administer the Mac or select any account other than your own. You can, however, configure a Contacts card or add login items for your own account (the login items will open every time you log in).

2 Confirm that you can't select any account other than Johnny Appleseed.

3 In the lower-left corner, click the lock and authenticate as Local Administrator (either the full name Local Administrator or the account name **ladmin**). This unlocks Users & Groups preferences and enables you to make changes to other user and group accounts while you remain logged in as Johnny Appleseed.

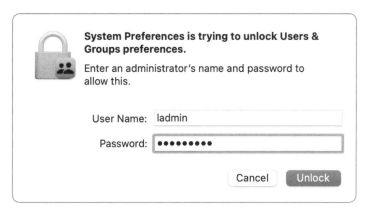

4   Control-click Johnny's account in the account list, then choose Advanced Options
    from the shortcut menu.

    The Advanced Options dialog appears and displays the hidden attributes of the
    Johnny Appleseed account.

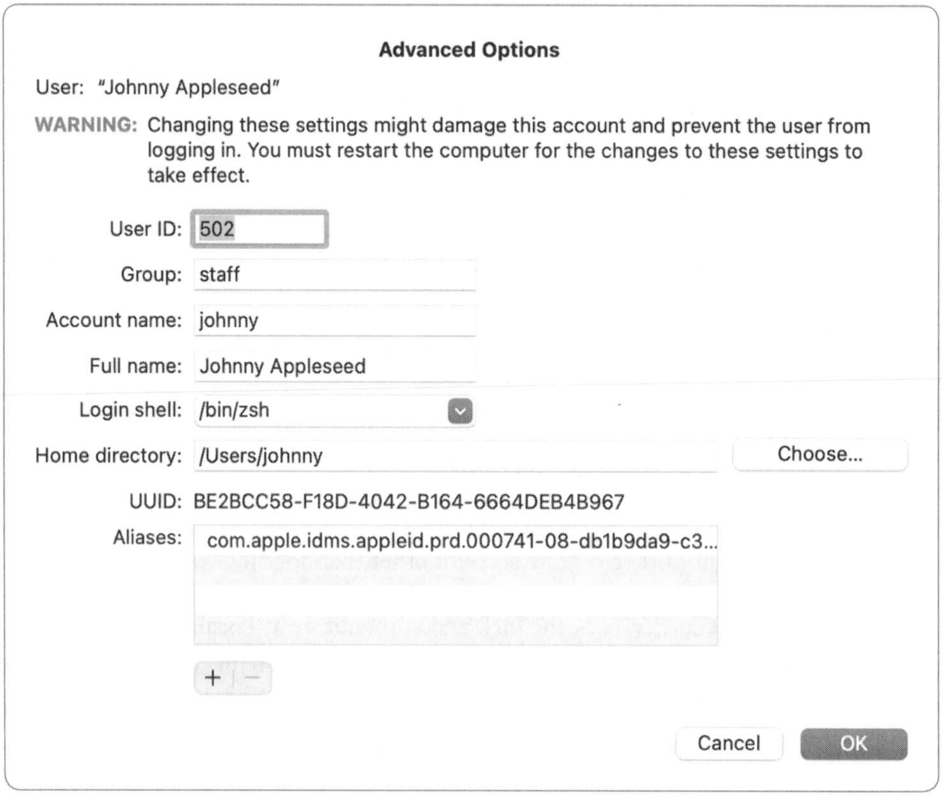

Advanced Options

User: "Johnny Appleseed"

WARNING: Changing these settings might damage this account and prevent the user from
          logging in. You must restart the computer for the changes to these settings to
          take effect.

User ID:	502
Group:	staff
Account name:	johnny
Full name:	Johnny Appleseed
Login shell:	/bin/zsh
Home directory:	/Users/johnny Choose...
UUID:	BE2BCC58-F18D-4042-B164-6664DEB4B967
Aliases:	com.apple.idms.appleid.prd.000741-08-db1b9da9-c3...

+ −

Cancel   OK

    Your attributes list may have entries that relate to your Apple ID.

5   Click Cancel (or press Command-Period) to dismiss the dialog.

6   Leave System Preferences open for the next exercise.

Exercise 7.2
Manage a User Account Using Screen Time

▶ **Prerequisites**

- ▶ You must have created the Local Administrator account (Exercise 3.1, "Configure a Mac for Exercises").

- ▶ You must have turned on FileVault (Exercise 3.2, "Configure System Preferences").

In this exercise, you create a standard account and use Screen Time to set up limitations on the use of the account.

Create an Account

1 If necessary, log in as Johnny Appleseed, open Users & Groups preferences, then click the lock and authenticate as Local Administrator. You can use the account name **ladmin** instead of the full name Local Administrator.

2 Click the Add (+) button below the account list, then enter the following information:

New Account: Standard

Full Name: **Mary Appleseed**

Account Name: **mary**

Password: **Apple321!**

Remember this password. You need it periodically as you complete these exercises. You can provide a hint in the Password Hint field to help you remember it.

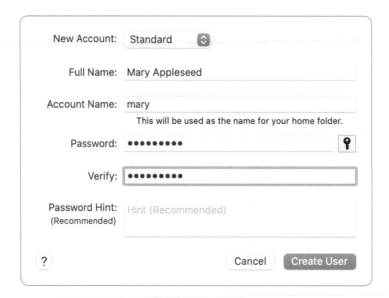

3   Click Create User.

Log In to the New User Account

In these steps you log in to Mary Appleseed's user account to enable and manage it using Screen Time.

1   From the Apple menu, choose Log Out Johnny Appleseed.

2   In the dialog that asks if you are sure, click Log Out.

3   In the login window, select Mary Appleseed and enter the password.

4   On the Accessibility screen, turn on any assistive needs, then click Continue. If you don't want to configure Accessibility at this time, click Not Now.

5   On the Data & Privacy screen, read the Apple privacy policy, then click Continue.

6   On the "Sign in with Your Apple ID" screen, select Set Up Later, then click Skip in the confirmation dialog that appears.

7   On the Screen Time screen, click Continue.

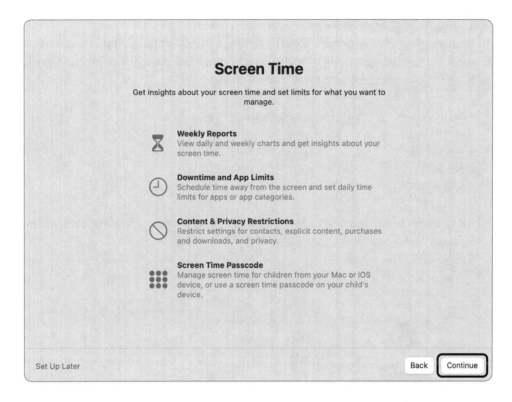

This enables Screen Time for this Mac.

8   If the Siri screen appears, deselect Enable Ask Siri, then click Continue.

9   If you are asked to set up Touch ID, click Continue; click Set Up Touch ID Later, then click Continue in the confirmation dialog.

10 On the Choose Your Look screen, choose your preferred appearance, then click Continue.

11 If the True Tone Display screen appears, click Continue.

Set Up and Test Screen Time

In these steps, you set up Screen Time by setting some Downtime, App Limits, and Content & Privacy restrictions. You also set a Screen Time passcode to protect your selections and allow for exceptions to your management.

1   Open System Preferences, then select Screen Time.

If you have been logged in to Mary Appleseed's account for a few minutes, you may already have some App Usage data.

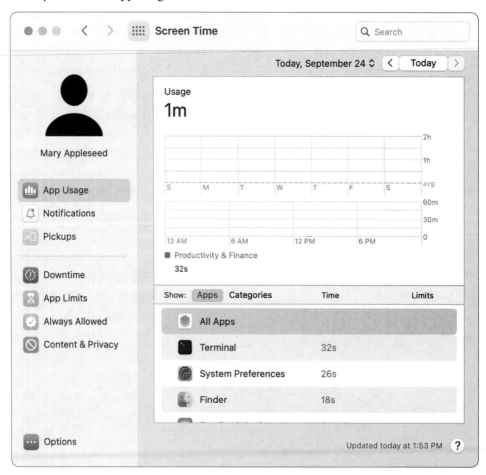

2   Select Options, then select the Use Screen Time Passcode checkbox.

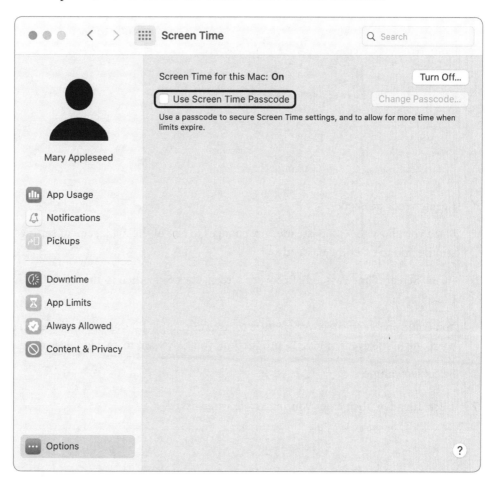

3   Set a passcode of **1234** to secure the management and restrictions you choose to place on Mary.

NOTE ▶ Although 1234 is sufficient for this exercise, in a production environment you should use a passcode that is nonsequential and more secure.

4   Reenter your passcode.

Since you chose to set a passcode, any changes to any of the management settings require you to enter the passcode.

5   At the Screen Time Passcode Recovery screen, click Skip, then in the following dialog, click Skip.

You could enable this recovery feature to use your Apple ID to reset the Screen Time passcode in the event of loss. In production, you may want to enable this feature.

6   Select Downtime.

7   Click Turn On, then enter your passcode when asked.

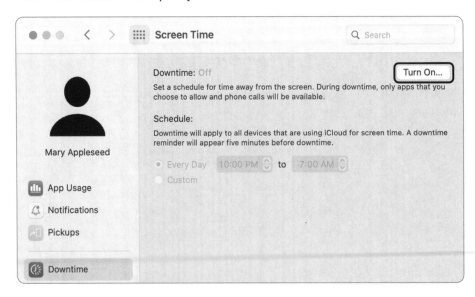

You have the option to set an Every Day time limit or a Custom per day limit.

8 If necessary, select Every Day.

9 Change the start time to be the current time and the end time to be ten minutes from the current time unless instructed otherwise.

10 If prompted, provide the passcode.

Notice the dimmed icons on some of the apps in the Dock. Only apps that you choose to allow under Always Allowed and phone calls will be available during the Downtime period.

11 From the Dock, click Notes. Even though Notes opens, its content remains unavailable until the Downtime period is over unless you ask for more time.

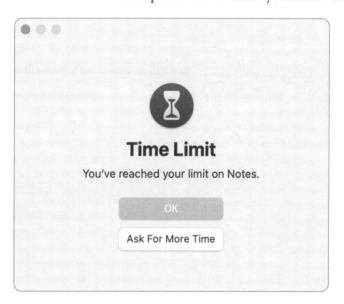

12 Click Ask For More Time, then click One More Minute.

13 If you are prompted to Turn On iCloud, click Cancel.

14 Wait one minute.

When your minute has elapsed, the content of Notes will again become unavailable.

15 Click Ask For More Time, click Enter Screen Time Passcode, then provide the passcode.

As the person with the passcode, you now have the ability to approve different intervals of time.

16 Click Cancel, then choose Notes > Quit Notes.

17 Select Always Allowed from the sidebar, then deselect FaceTime. Notice that it is now dimmed in the Dock.

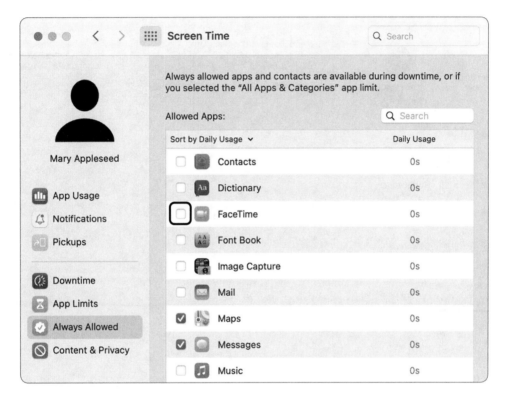

18 Select Content & Privacy, then click Turn On.

19 If necessary, provide your Screen Time passcode.

20 Explore the management options.

You have the ability to restrict Web Content, limit iTunes and App Store purchases, control which apps are allowed, and other privacy restrictions. Notice that these options can apply to other Mac, iOS, and iPadOS devices that have Screen Time enabled and that are signed in with the same Apple ID.

21 When you're finished, select Options from the sidebar, then click Turn Off to disable Screen Time for this Mac. Provide your passcode if prompted.

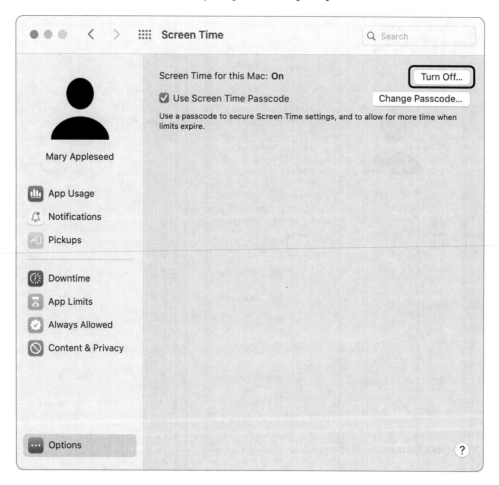

22 At the confirmation dialog, click Turn Off.

23 Quit System Preferences, then log out of the Mary Appleseed account.

Lesson 8

Manage User Home Folders

When you log in to your Mac, you can securely store documents in your home folder. You can store and access documents in other locations, but this lesson focuses on your home folder. In macOS Catalina and macOS Big Sur, your home folder is stored on the read-write APFS Data volume, technically separate from your read-only APFS System volume, but this separation doesn't make a difference in your troubleshooting.

Reference 8.1
User Home Folders

The default location for a locally stored home folder is /Users/*name*, where *name* is the user account name.

Many Mac users don't have much reason to think about files and folders outside of their home folder. But if you're going to share files with other users on your Mac, share files to other devices on your network, or help someone else troubleshoot their Mac, it helps to understand how the Users folder fits into the file system in general.

One way to start is with the Finder. Choose Go > Computer (or press Shift-Command-C). The Finder displays your startup disk, which is named Macintosh HD by default.

> **NOTE** ▸ The Finder might also display other storage devices if they are mounted. Additionally, macOS simplifies how it presents parts of the file system in Terminal and in the Finder; you'll find more details in Lesson 11, "Manage File Systems and Storage."

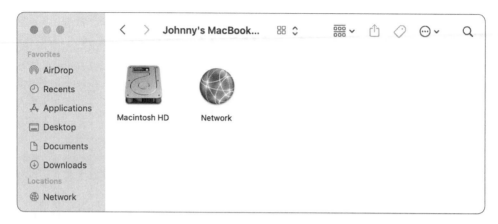

After you open your startup disk, the Finder displays folders, including the Users folder.

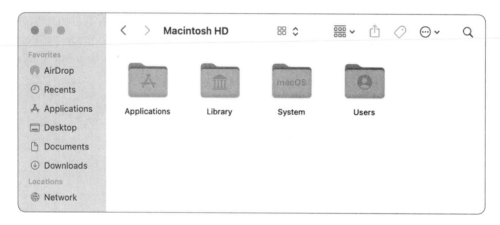

The Users folder contains home folders and the Shared folder. Additionally, if the Guest user was ever turned on, you'll also see the Guest folder. The Finder displays your home folder with an icon of a house. In the following example, edavidson, jane, johnny, and ladmin are user account names.

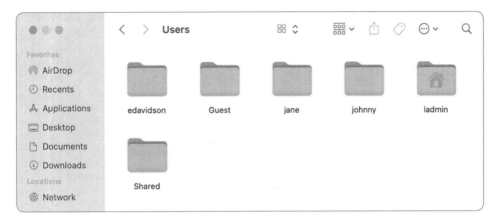

In the Finder window toolbar, click the View As menu (it looks like four boxes with up and down arrows) ⌗, then choose "as Columns" (or choose View > As Columns) to change how the Users folder is presented.

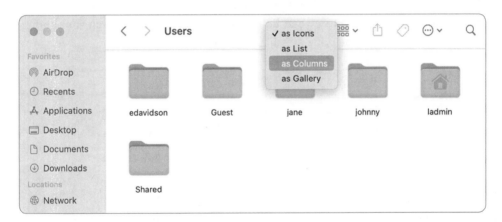

NOTE ▸ By default, the Finder window displays the View As menu, but if your Finder window is wide enough, it displays four icons (Icons, List, Columns, and Gallery) instead of the View As menu.

As the following figure illustrates, the Users folder appears to be contained inside your startup disk and the Users folder contains home folders.

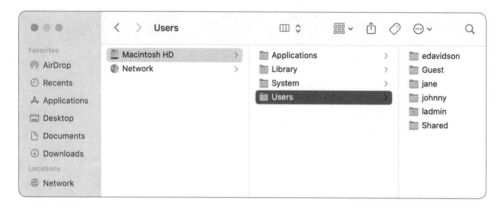

When you create a new user account, macOS generates a home folder for that account. The home folder contains these default visible home folders: Desktop, Documents, Downloads, Movies, Music, Pictures, and Public. In the Finder, you can open your home folder by choosing Go > Home or by pressing Shift-Command-H.

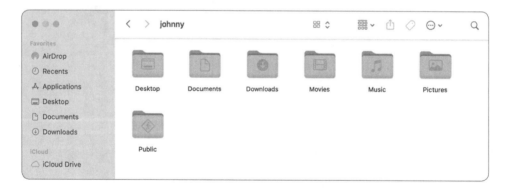

NOTE ▶ If you are signed in with your iCloud account and you have iCloud Drive turned on, with the Desktop & Documents Folders option enabled, then the Finder displays your Desktop and Documents folders only in the Finder window sidebar, in the iCloud section. Reference 19.4, "Store Documents in iCloud," covers this in detail.

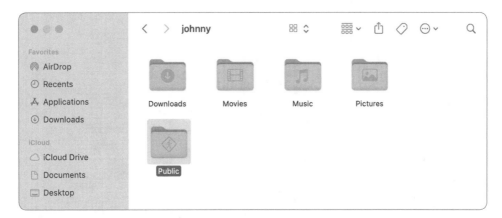

Files you save to your desktop appear on your desktop and in the Desktop folder.

You can use stacks on the desktop to keep files neatly organized in groups. When you save a file to the desktop, it's automatically added to the appropriate stack. This helps you keep your desktop tidy. To turn on Stacks, click the desktop to make the Finder the active app; then from the View menu, choose Use Stacks. Or at any point you can Control-click the desktop and choose Use Stacks.

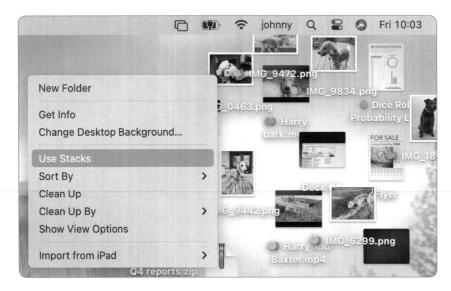

When you download content from the internet, it goes into the Downloads folder by default.

Your home folder also contains a folder called Library that includes user-specific preference files, fonts, contacts, keychains, mailboxes, favorites, screen savers, and other app resources. The Library folder is hidden in the default Finder view.

The Documents, Movies, Music, and Pictures folders are the default locations for document, movie, music, and picture files, respectively.

If you open other users' home folders, you can't see inside their default folders, except for their Public folders.

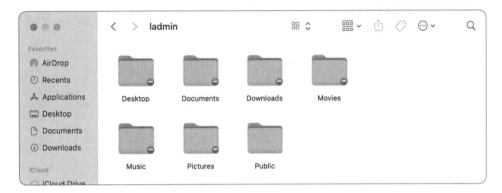

But if someone stores a file at the top level of their home folder—not inside a folder in their home folder—other users can see that file. You'll find more information about changing the permissions for a file in Lesson 13, "Manage Permissions and Sharing." The following figure illustrates that if Johnny stores a file called Confidential in his home folder, another user on that Mac will be able to see and open that file (but not make any changes to it).

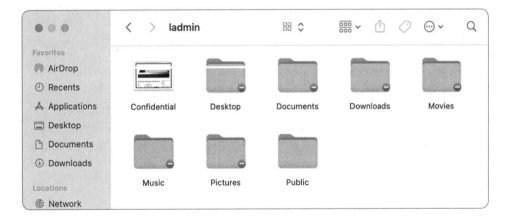

If you want to share items with other users on your Mac, put these items in your Public folder. If you turn on the File Sharing service, users who connect to your Mac can see files here, too. Lesson 25, "Manage Host Sharing and Personal Firewall," has more information about sharing files over the network. The following figure is from the perspective of Johnny Appleseed, for a file named Checklist in Johnny Appleseed's Public folder.

Other users can view the contents of your Public folder, and you can view the contents of any other user's Public folder. Continuing the example from the previous figure, the following figure illustrates how the Finder displays the contents of Johnny Appleseed's home folder, including his Public folder, to other local users.

If you want to give a copy of a file to another user, you can use the other user's Drop Box folder (not to be confused with a third-party service with a similar name). The Drop Box folder is a special folder. Every user has a folder named Drop Box that's inside that user's Public folder. You can put files into another user's Drop Box folder, but you can't remove the files once you put them there. And you can't see what's inside another user's Drop Box folder.

Except for putting items in Drop Box, other users can't add items or make changes to files in your Public folder.

You can change folder permissions as described in Lesson 13.

You might see an Applications folder in your home folder. When you are logged in as a standard user and install some apps, they automatically create an Applications folder in your home folder. For other apps, you can choose to place them there. Only you have access to the contents of your personal Applications folder (though someone with access to an administrator user account can take steps to access your personal Applications folder). See Reference 18.3, "Install Apps Using Software Packages and Drag-and-Drop," for more information.

Reference 8.2
Delete User Accounts and Preserve Their Home Folder Contents

You might have to delete a user account. If you do, you must decide what to do with the user's home folder contents.

To delete a user:

1   Select the user from the list of users in Users & Groups preferences.

2   Click the Remove (–) button at the bottom of the list.

3   Select an option for the user's home folder contents:

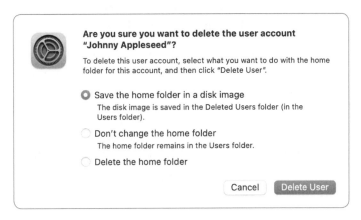

▶ Select "Save the home folder in a disk image" to save a user's home folder as a disk image file. macOS saves the disk image file in the /Users/Deleted Users folder and gives it the user account name. You can copy it to other Mac computers or into another user's home folder. You must have enough local storage space to duplicate the home folder. The process might take several hours depending on how much storage the home folder uses.

▶ Select "Don't change the home folder" to leave a user home folder unchanged. macOS appends "(Deleted)" to the home folder name to signify that the user no longer exists. The deleted user home folder keeps the same access restrictions as a normal user home folder. If you want to access the deleted home folder contents, you must change folder and file ownership and permissions. Read Lesson 13 to find out more.

▶ Select "Delete the home folder" to delete home folder contents. The content won't be stored in the Trash, so you can't easily restore it.

Reference 8.3
Migrate and Restore Home Folders

Migration Assistant enables you to copy settings, user accounts, and content from a Mac or Windows computer to your new Mac.

You can copy content over Wi-Fi, Ethernet, or an appropriate cable. If you have a lot of content, the copy could take several hours. If one or both computers are notebook computers, be sure to plug them into a power source before you start.

You can use a Time Machine backup to copy your content. If you don't have a Time Machine backup of the original Mac content, create one. Connect the external storage device that contains the Time Machine backup to your new Mac.

When you migrate content from another Mac, a Time Machine backup, or a startup disk, Migration Assistant scans the local network for Mac computers that are running Migration Assistant and are ready to transfer content.

Migration Assistant scans locally mounted disks and the local network looking for Time Machine backups. It scans locally mounted disks for a previous system as well. Previous systems include external disks, or Mac computers in target disk mode, that are connected with an appropriate cable or adapter. Using target disk mode is detailed in Lesson 11. See Apple Support article HT204350, "Move your content to a new Mac," for instructions.

When you migrate content from a Windows computer, Migration Assistant scans the local network for Windows computers that are running Windows Migration Assistant and are ready to transfer content. This enables you to migrate content from Windows 7 or later if the Windows computers are running Windows Migration Assistant. You can download Windows Migration Assistant from the Apple Support website. See Apple Support article HT204087, "Move your data from a Windows PC to your Mac," for detailed instructions.

Migration Assistant runs as part of macOS Setup Assistant on new or newly reinstalled Mac computers. You can use Migration Assistant at any time. It's in /Applications/Utilities. You can search for it with Spotlight or Launchpad.

1 Before you use Migration Assistant, check for Apple software updates on the source and destination computers.

   This ensures that you're using the latest copy of Migration Assistant.

2 If any other users are also logged in, log out all other users.

3 Open Migration Assistant.

4 Click Continue to start Migration Assistant.

5 Authenticate as an administrator user.

   Migration Assistant quits running apps and logs out users.

6 Select how you want to transfer information:

   ▶ From a Mac, Time Machine backup, or Startup disk

   ▶ From a Windows PC

   ▶ To another Mac

   If you select "From a Mac, Time Machine backup, or Startup disk" or "From a Windows PC," Migration Assistant scans attached disks and the local network for migration sources. If you select "To another Mac," open Migration Assistant on the destination Mac as well.

   The rest of this list addresses the scenario where you select "From a Mac, Time Machine backup, or Startup disk."

7 Select the source external storage device. When you select a Time Machine backup, you can select a backup from a specific date and time.

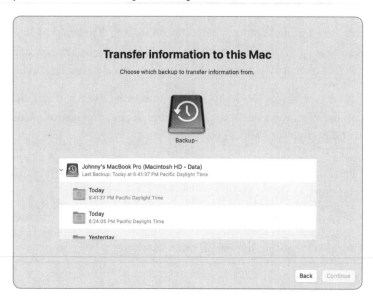

8 After you select a source, Migration Assistant scans the contents and presents you with a list of items you can migrate.

Migration Assistant doesn't create new volumes or partitions on the destination Mac. It creates folders that include the contents of the migrated source.

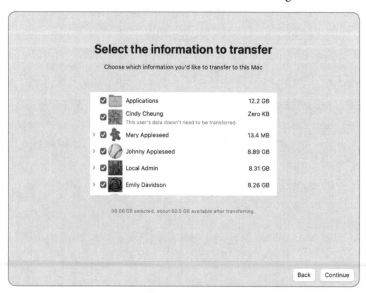

Select the information you want to transfer; this includes user accounts. Then click Continue.

9   After you make selections, record the temporary and random password that Migration Assistant assigns to all standard users that you will migrate. If you don't record the random password, you'll have to reset each user's password, which resets their login Keychain. This is covered in more detail in Reference 10.2, "Reset Lost Passwords." When a user first logs in using the temporary password that you provide them, macOS prompts them to change their password. If they provide their old password, their login Keychain will not be modified.

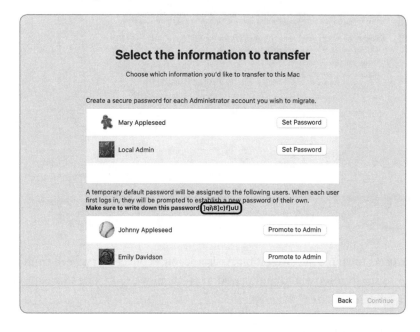

10 Click Set Password for an administrator user account.

11 Enter and verify a password for the administrator account that you're migrating, then click Set Password.

12 Repeat steps 10 and 11 for any additional administrator accounts.

13 If you want to promote a standard user to an administrator user, click "Promote to Admin" next to the user, and then set and verify a new password for that user.

14 Click Continue.

15 If any user account that you selected to restore already exists on your Mac, Migration Assistant displays a prompt for each conflicting user account. You can replace the user account, optionally keeping its home folder, or keep both user accounts by entering a new name and user account name.

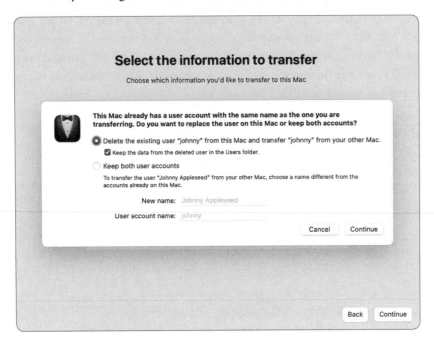

16 To add new users to your Mac, Migration Assistant must collect a password from an existing administrator user who is authorized to create new users. Next to an administrator user, click Authorize.

17 Enter the password for the user you selected, then click OK.

18 Click Continue to begin the transfer. The more content you transfer, the longer it takes.

Manually Restore a User Home Folder

See Exercise 8.1, "Restore a Deleted User Account," to learn how to restore a user's home folder after you delete that user.

Exercise 8.1
Restore a Deleted User Account

▶ **Prerequisite**

▶   You must have created the Local Administrator account (Exercise 3.1,
    "Configure a Mac for Exercises").

In this exercise, you create a user account and create files in the user's home folder. Then, you delete the account, preserving the contents of the home folder. You also create a new account, ensuring that the new user gets the old user's home folder contents and changing the user account name. What you learn in this exercise provides an alternative to Migration Assistant for moving user accounts between Mac computers.

The scenario for this exercise is that Emily Parker changed her name and now has the last name of Davidson. The company she works for uses the account naming convention *first initial, last name*. So, you must change her account name from eparker to edavidson.

Create Emily Parker's Home Folder

1   Log in as Local Administrator.

2   Open Users & Groups preferences.

3   Authenticate as Local Administrator.

4   Click the Add (+) button under the user list.

5   Enter the account information for Emily Parker:

New Account: Standard

Full Name: **Emily Parker**

Account Name: **eparker**

Password: **Apple321!**

Verify: **Apple321!**

Don't provide a password hint.

6 Click Create User.

You can optionally change the account picture.

7 Control-click Emily Parker's account, then choose Advanced Options from the menu.

Take a screenshot of the System Preferences window to record Emily Parker's account attributes for later reference.

8 Press Shift-Command-5, followed by the Space bar.

Your pointer changes to a camera icon, and the region of the screen it is over is highlighted in blue. If you see a crosshair, press the Space bar again.

9 Move the camera pointer over the System Preferences window, then click to record its contents.

This is one of several ways of taking screenshots in macOS. Shift-Command-3 records the entire screen, Shift-Command-4 enables you to select a rectangular region to record or a single window if you hold down the Space bar, and Shift-Command-5 gives you the ability to do timed captures, record the screen, and select destinations for your screenshots. See support.apple.com/guide/mac-help/mh26782/ for more information on taking screenshots or screen recordings on a Mac.

The image is saved to your desktop and named "Screen Shot," followed by the date and time it was taken.

10 In the Advanced Options dialog, click Cancel, or press Command-Period, which is a way to select Cancel in most macOS dialogs.

11 Log out as Local Administrator.

12 Log in as Emily Parker (password: **Apple321!**).

13 On the Accessibility screen, turn on any assistive needs, then click Continue. If you don't want to configure Accessibility at this time, click Not Now.

14 On the Data & Privacy screen, carefully review Apple's privacy policy, then click Continue.

15 On the Sign In with Your Apple ID screen, select Set Up Later, then click Skip in the confirmation dialog.

16 On the Screen Time screen, select Set Up Later.

17 If the Siri screen appears, deselect Enable Ask Siri, then click Continue.

18 If you're asked to set up Touch ID, select Set Up Touch ID Later, then click Continue in the confirmation dialog.

19 At the Choose Your Look screen, choose your preferred appearance, then click Continue.

20 If the True Tone Display screen appears, click Continue.

21 In the Dock, click the Launchpad icon.

22 In Launchpad, begin typing **text**.

TextEdit should become available.

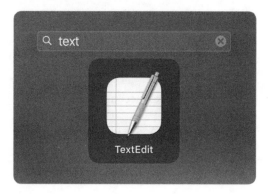

23 Click the TextEdit icon to open TextEdit.

24 In the Untitled document, type the text **This is Emily Parker's project document.**

25 From the menu bar, choose File > Save (or press Command-S) to save the file.

26 Name the file **Project**, then save it to Emily Parker's desktop. You can use the shortcut Command-D to select the desktop.

27 Quit TextEdit.

28 Open System Preferences, then click Desktop & Screen Saver preferences.

29 Select a different desktop picture.

30 Quit System Preferences, then log out of the Emily Parker account.

Delete Emily Parker's Account

Next, you delete Emily Parker's account without removing the files in her home folder.

1 Log in as Local Administrator.

2 Open Users & Groups preferences, then unlock the pane.

3 Select Emily Parker's account name, then click the Remove (–) button to remove her account.

4   In the dialog that appears, make sure "Save the home folder in a disk image" is selected.

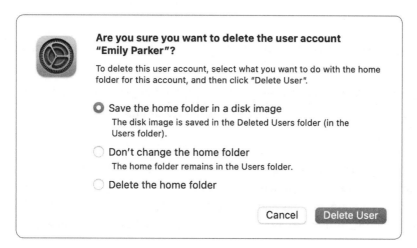

5   Click Delete User.

While Emily Parker's account is being archived, it appears in the Users & Groups list with the text "Deleting Account."

6   Wait until the archiving process is complete and Emily Parker's account is no longer visible in the list, then quit System Preferences.

Restore Emily Parker's Account for Emily Davidson

Emily Parker's files (soon to be Emily Davidson's files) are preserved in a disk image. Now you copy them to Emily Davidson's new home folder so that when you create the new account, she gets the files and settings from her previous account (the Emily Parker account).

Since disk images are portable and easy to store, you can use this technique to re-create the account on another computer at any time. You can also use a disk image as a way to archive a home folder.

1   Open the folder /Users/Deleted Users by choosing Go > Go to Folder or by opening Macintosh HD from your desktop and navigating to the folder.

   If you don't have permission to open the Deleted Users folder, you may be logged in as a standard user. Log out, then log back in as Local Administrator.

2   Open eparker.dmg.

   The disk image opens and displays the contents of the eparker account home folder. As Reference 14.1, "Examine Hidden Items," discusses, a hidden subfolder named Library contains account settings and preferences for the eparker account. To fully restore this account, restore the entire home folder, not just the visible contents.

3   Close the eparker window (but don't eject the disk image).

   The disk icon is visible on your desktop.

4   Select (single-click) the eparker icon on your desktop.

5   Choose File > Duplicate (or use the shortcut Command-D).

6   If you are asked to enter the name and password for an administrator, click Continue, then authenticate as Local Administrator.

   The Finder copies the contents of the image (including the hidden Library folder) to a folder named eparker on your desktop.

7   After the copy finishes, unmount the eparker volume. Click the Eject button next to its entry in the Finder sidebar.

8 Select the new eparker folder on your desktop, then press Return. You may also Control-click the eparker folder, then choose Rename.

This enables you to edit the folder's name.

9 Change the folder name to **edavidson**, then press Return.

10 Navigate back to the /Users folder.

11 Drag the edavidson folder from your desktop to the /Users folder.

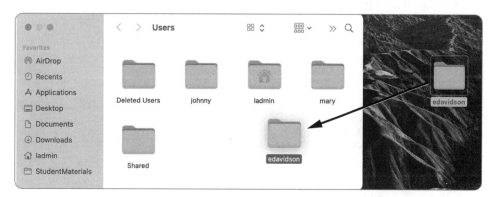

The file permissions for the /Users folder prevent you from adding items to it. The Finder asks you to authenticate as an administrator to override the permissions.

12 Enter the Administrator password (**Apple321!**), then click OK.

13 Open the edavidson folder, then the Desktop folder inside that.

You see Emily Parker's Project document. Because you (Local Administrator) created this copy of Emily Parker's home folder, you own it and have full permission to access it.

Create and Verify Emily Davidson's Account

Create the Emily Davidson user account using the renamed home folder as her new account home folder.

1   Open Users & Groups preferences.

2   Authenticate as Local Administrator.

3   Click the Add (+) button to create another account:

New Account: Standard

Full Name: **Emily Davidson**

Account Name: **edavidson**

Password: **Apple321!**

Don't provide a password hint.

4   Click Create User.

A dialog appears asking whether you want to use the edavidson folder for this account.

5   Click Use Existing Folder.

6   Control-click Emily Davidson's account, then choose Advanced Options from the menu.

7   Open the Screen Shot file on your desktop, then compare the account attributes of Emily Davidson's new account with her original account (Emily Parker).

macOS assigns each account a new UUID (Universally Unique Identifier) when you create it.

8   Quit Preview.

9   In the Advanced Options dialog, click Cancel, then quit System Preferences.

10   Try to reopen the Desktop folder in Emily Davidson's home folder. If your Finder window is still displaying the Desktop folder, click the Back button, then double-click the Desktop folder. You no longer have permission to see the files because they are owned by Emily Davidson's new account.

11   Close the Finder window.

Verify Emily Davidson's Home Folder

Explore Emily Davidson's home folder to confirm the files are available.

1   Log out as Local Administrator, then log in as Emily Davidson.

2   Verify that the Project file is on the desktop and that the desktop picture is the one you chose previously.

3   In the Finder, open Emily Davidson's home folder by choosing Go > Home (or by pressing Shift-Command-H).

4   Make sure you can see the default subfolders: Desktop, Documents, Downloads, Movies, Music, Pictures, and Public.

5   Open the Desktop folder, then verify that you see the Project document.

6   Navigate back to the home folder, then open the Public folder, where you see a Drop Box folder. For more information about these folders, read Lesson 13.

In addition to the visible folders in Emily Davidson's home folder, the folder should contain an invisible Library folder.

7   Press and hold the Option key, then choose Go > Library.

The Library choice is hidden except when you hold the Option key.

Emily Davidson's Library folder contains many subfolders. For more information about this folder and its contents, read Reference 14.1 and Lesson 15, "Manage System Resources."

8   Close the Library folder, then log out as Emily Davidson.

Lesson 9

Manage Security and Privacy

This lesson covers built-in macOS security and privacy features and how to manage and troubleshoot them.

Reference 9.1
Password Security

In macOS, there are several ways to authenticate or to verify your identity:

▶ You can provide your user name and password to authenticate.

▶ If your Mac has Touch ID, you can set up Touch ID and use your fingerprint instead of typing when you're asked for your password as long as you're logged in.

▶ If you have an iPhone and Apple Watch configured as described later in this chapter, you can use your Apple Watch to unlock your screen saver and approve authentication requests from macOS and Apple apps, supported third-party apps, secure notes, and passwords saved in Safari.

For more information about Touch ID, see Apple Support article HT207054, "Use Touch ID on your Mac."

Passwords You Use in macOS

You use several passwords to secure your Mac. You set an account password and resource and keychain passwords. You can also set a firmware password.

GOALS

▶ Describe password types and use

▶ Manage secrets in Keychain

▶ Turn on iCloud Keychain and manage it

▶ Manage systemwide security and user privacy

▶ Approve Legacy System Extensions

▶ Approve System Extensions

▶ Use Find My

▶ Secure your Mac with Activation Lock

▶ Lock your screen

Users might use several password types:

▶ Each local user account has attributes that define the account. Users enter their local account password (an account attribute) to log in to their Mac. For security reasons, a user's local-account password is encrypted and stored in the user account record.

▶ Users might have an Apple ID and password. They use these to authorize Apple services, including iCloud, Apple Music, Apple Podcasts, Apple TV, iMessage, FaceTime, and the App Store.

▶ With the exception of a user account password, macOS protects authentication assets in encrypted keychain files. Each keychain file is encrypted with a keychain password. By default, macOS keeps two default keychain files (covered in the next section) synchronized with your local account password. You can maintain unique keychain passwords separate from an account password too. Maintaining synchronization between a user's keychain password and account password is covered in Lesson 10, "Manage Password Changes."

▶ Resource passwords are required by most macOS services (for example, email, websites, file servers, apps, and encrypted disk images). Many resource passwords are saved for you by Keychain Access.

▶ A firmware password prevents you from starting up an Intel-based Mac from any device other than your designated startup disk. As a result, it also blocks you from using most startup key combinations. For example, if you set a firmware password on an Intel-based Mac, an unauthorized user can't hold down the Option key during startup to select an alternate operating system, bypassing your secure startup disk. Setting a firmware password is covered in Reference 5.3, "Secure Startup."

Keychain

macOS keeps your resource passwords, certificates, keys, website forms, and secure notes in encrypted storage called keychains. When you allow macOS to remember a password or other sensitive items, it saves them to a keychain. Your login password is not saved to a keychain.

macOS encrypts keychain files. They are impenetrable unless you know the keychain password. If you forget a keychain password, the resource user names and passwords stored in that keychain are unrecoverable.

You can use Keychain Access to inspect and modify most keychain items. You can use Launchpad or Spotlight to open Keychain Access, and you can open it directly from /Applications/Utilities. You can also create and delete keychain files and change keychain settings and passwords. You can manage web-specific keychain items from Safari preferences.

Local Keychain Files

Keychain files are stored throughout macOS for different users and resources. Here are some examples:

▶ /Users/username/Library/Keychains/login.keychain-db—When you use Keychain Access, this keychain name is "login." macOS creates every standard or administrator user with a single login keychain. As a default, the password for this keychain matches the user's account password, so this keychain is automatically unlocked and available when the user logs in. If the user's account password doesn't match the keychain password when the user logs in, macOS renames the keychain with a filename that begins with "login_renamed_" followed by a number. For example, the first time the password mismatch happens, the new filename is login_renamed_1.keychain-db. macOS then creates a new login keychain with a password that matches the user's password. This is covered in more detail in Reference 10.2, "Reset Lost Passwords."

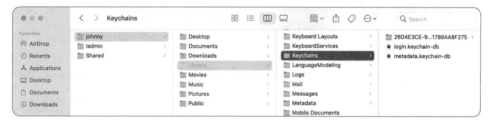

▶ /Users/username/Library/Keychains/others.keychain—You can create more keychains if you want to segregate your authentication assets. For example, you can keep your default login keychain for items that require less security and create a more secure keychain that doesn't automatically unlock for items that require a lot of security.

▶ /Users/username/Library/Keychains/UUID/—This keychain folder is created for every user account and contains the keychain database used by iCloud Keychain. If iCloud Keychain isn't turned on, the database is still created and this keychain folder appears with the name Local Items in Keychain Access. If iCloud Keychain is turned on, this keychain folder appears with the name iCloud in Keychain Access. The folder's universally unique identifier (UUID) doesn't match a user's local account UUID, but the folder is associated with the user because it's in the user's home folder.

▶ /Library/Keychains/System.keychain—This keychain appears with the name System in Keychain Access. This keychain maintains authentication assets that aren't user specific. Items stored here include Wi-Fi wireless network passwords, 802.1X network passwords, self-signed certificates, intermediate and root certificate authorities (CAs) installed by you, and local Kerberos (a network authentication protocol) support items. Although all users benefit from this keychain, only administrator users can make changes to it.

▶ /System/Library/Keychains/—Most of the items in this folder don't appear in Keychain Access by default. The one item you will see in Keychain Access from this folder is System Roots. This keychain stores root certificates Apple provides as part of macOS that are used to identify trusted network services. You can't modify these items.

Apple and third-party developers might create additional keychains for securely storing data. You can find keychain files with seemingly random names throughout macOS. Leave these files alone unless you're instructed by a trusted source to remove or modify them to resolve an issue.

Reference 9.2
Manage Secrets in Keychains

To manage keychain items, including saved passwords, open Keychain Access. In the left side of the Keychain Access window, select a keychain from the list to inspect its contents.

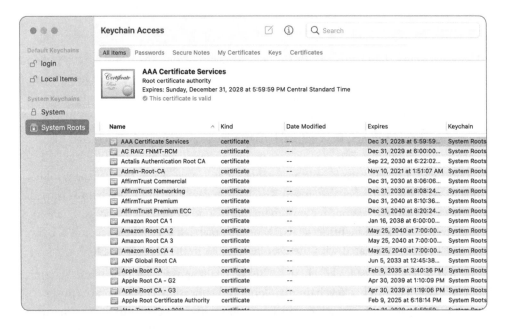

Or search for an item by name or kind with Spotlight in the upper-right corner of the toolbar.

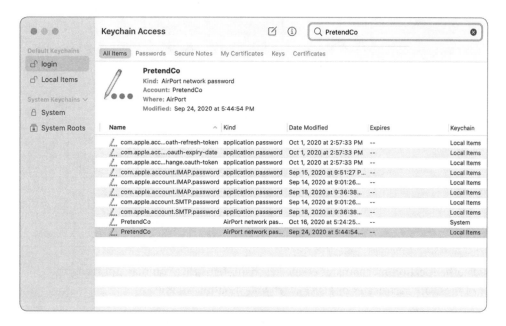

Double-click a keychain item to inspect its attributes. If the item is a password, select "Show password" to see the saved password. You're often asked to provide a keychain password.

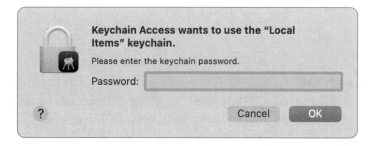

The request for the password ensures that only a keychain owner can access the secret or make changes. After you authenticate, you can change attributes in the keychain item dialog. Click the Access Control button to adjust app access for a selected item.

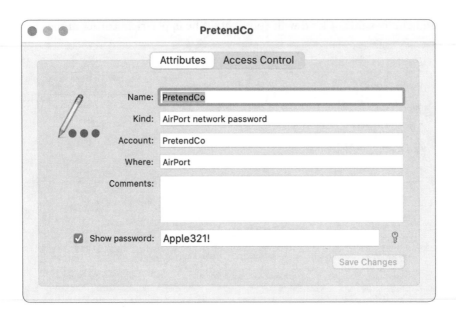

iCloud authentication mechanisms create keychain items that you may not recognize. Many of these are certificates or keys, which you shouldn't modify.

You can store secret text in keychains. In Keychain Access, choose File > New Secure Note Item to create a new secure note. You can open this kind of secure note only with Keychain Access. For additional flexibility, consider using the Notes app to create a note in iCloud and then lock it (this requires upgraded iCloud notes). This way, you can unlock and access the locked note from any Apple device that you're signed in to with your iCloud account. See "Lock your notes on Mac" at support.apple.com/guide/notes/not28c5c54f068 for more information.

Manage Keychain Items with Safari

When you use Safari, you probably interact with keychains. Safari AutoFill prompts you to start saving web-form information and site passwords. It also suggests secure passwords for you to use for websites and asks if you'd like to save credit card information.

If iCloud Keychain isn't turned on (iCloud Keychain is covered in Reference 9.3, "Use iCloud Keychain"), Safari offers to save secret information in your Local Items keychain.

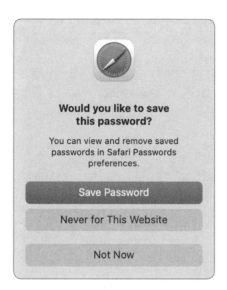

If iCloud Keychain is turned on, Safari offers to save secret information in your iCloud Keychain.

When you revisit a site or navigate to a new site with similar form information, Safari AutoFill automatically fills in information for you, as long as the keychain file is unlocked. If allowed, Safari also pulls information from your contact information.

To manage Safari AutoFill settings, choose Safari > Preferences, then click the AutoFill button.

The settings allow you to specify which items are automatically saved and filled. Edit buttons let you manage items such as website passwords and saved credit card information.

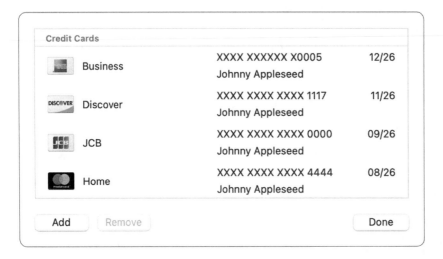

With the exception of your contact information, which is stored in Contacts, Safari AutoFill data is securely stored in your iCloud or Local Items keychain. Click the Help button (question mark) in the AutoFill pane of Safari preferences to learn more about AutoFill items.

In Safari preferences, select Passwords from the toolbar, then authenticate with your login keychain password to inspect, add, and remove the user name and password items that Safari AutoFill can use. These user name and password combinations are stored in your iCloud or Local Items keychain.

By default, the option "Detect passwords compromised by known data leaks" is selected. If you leave that option selected, and you see a yellow attention icon next to a password, you can click it for information about that password.

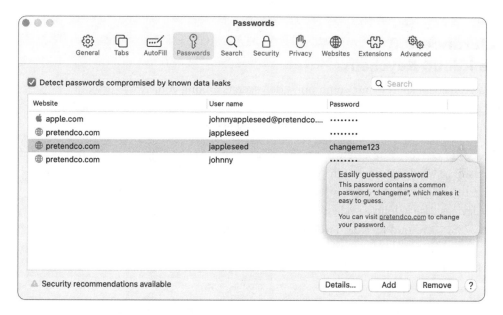

You can also use Keychain Access to inspect and manage items that were saved with Safari.

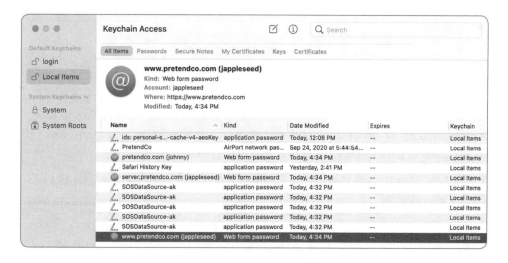

Some websites remember your authentication inside a cookie, so you may not see an entry in a keychain file for every website that automatically remembers your account. See Reference 9.5, "Manage User Privacy," for more information about cookies.

Reference 9.3
Use iCloud Keychain

iCloud Keychain shares your commonly used secrets among your Apple devices through iCloud. iCloud includes strong personal security technology, as detailed in Apple Support article HT202303, "iCloud security overview."

When you need to create a new password for a website, Safari suggests a unique, hard-to-guess password and saves it in your iCloud Keychain. Safari fills it in automatically the next time you need to sign in, so you don't have to remember it or enter it on any of your devices. Use iCloud Keychain to keep information safe. See Apple Support article HT203783, "If iCloud Keychain won't turn on or sync," for more information.

If you turn on iCloud Keychain, the Local Items keychain is renamed iCloud and contents in your iCloud Keychain are also stored on the Apple iCloud servers and pushed to your other configured Apple devices. iCloud Keychain provides a secure way to access your secrets from any of your Apple devices that are connected to the internet.

If you disable it, your iCloud Keychain is renamed Local Items, and you can choose to keep secret items locally.

Use your login keychain password to access your Local Items keychain or your iCloud Keychain. When you change your login keychain password, macOS applies the change to your Local Items keychain or your iCloud Keychain. For this reason, Keychain Access doesn't allow you to change your Local Items keychain or your iCloud Keychain password.

Two-Factor Authentication for Apple ID

With two-factor authentication, your account can be accessed only on devices you trust, like your iPhone, iPad, or Mac. When you sign in to a new device for the first time, you must provide two pieces of information—your Apple ID password and the six-digit verification code that's displayed on one of your trusted devices. When you enter the code, you verify that you trust the new device. For example, if you signed in with your Apple ID on your iPhone and then sign in to your Apple ID account for the first time on a newly purchased Mac, you are asked to enter your Apple ID password and the verification code that's automatically displayed on your iPhone. You can have the verification code sent to additional trusted phone numbers as well.

Because your Apple ID password alone is no longer enough when you sign in to a new Apple device or icloud.com, two-factor authentication dramatically improves the security of your Apple ID and all the personal information you store with Apple.

After you sign in, you won't be asked for a verification code on that device again unless you sign out completely, erase the device, or need to change your password for security reasons. When you sign in on the web at www.icloud.com, you can choose to trust your browser so that you won't be asked for a verification code the next time you sign in. See Apple Support article HT204230, "System requirements for iCloud," for more information.

If you updated your Apple ID from two-step verification to two-factor authentication in iOS 11 and later, or macOS High Sierra and later, and you have a recovery key, you can use the recovery key to help reset your password.

For more information about two-factor authentication, see Apple Support articles HT204915, "Two-factor authentication for Apple ID," HT205075, "Availability of two-factor authentication for Apple ID," and HT207198, "Two-step verification for Apple ID."

If you sign in to another Apple device using an Apple ID with two-factor authentication, iCloud Keychain is automatically turned on. For Apple IDs without two-factor authentication, you can grant access for additional devices with a device authorization mechanism. Any device configured with the iCloud Keychain service is a trusted device. Any trusted device can be used to verify additional devices for iCloud Keychain.

For example, after you set up iCloud Keychain on your Mac, if you switch to a different Mac try to turn it on there, macOS asks if you want to allow this.

After you click Allow, you see a randomly generated six-digit code. Continuing the example, enter this verification code on your second Mac and then click Done.

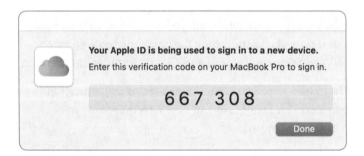

If you don't have two-factor authentication enabled and you set up an iCloud Security Code instead, you can use the iCloud Security Code for verification rather than device-based authorization.

Reference 9.4
Manage Systemwide Security

In addition to account passwords and keychain items, there are macOS-wide security preferences that affect all users on a Mac. Several of these preferences are disabled by default.

Security & Privacy: General Settings

Security & Privacy preferences is a combination of systemwide settings and personal settings that enable you to manage macOS security features. You must be an administrator user to make changes to settings that might affect systemwide security or other users. In Security & Privacy preferences, systemwide security settings are dimmed when the lock is locked. The lock indicates that administrator user authentication is required. Personal security settings are always available.

In addition to using Users & Groups preferences, users can change their login password in the General settings pane.

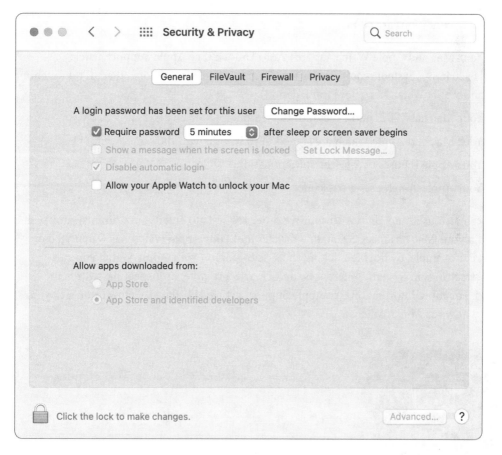

You can choose to require a password to wake a Mac from sleep or screen saver mode and to define a delay before this requirement sets in. Both standard and administrator users can specify this setting for their accounts. If you want to do so for every account from

Security & Privacy preferences, consider using a configuration profile, which was mentioned in Reference 3.2, "Manage System Settings."

Administrators can also configure a custom message that will display in the login window or when the screen is locked. When creating the message, you can press Option-Return to force a new line. You can have up to three lines of text.

If the Mac has more than one account or the Mac is connected to a directory service, administrators can disable automatic login for all accounts (unless FileVault is turned on). If FileVault is turned on, this option won't appear.

The option "Allow your Apple Watch to unlock your apps and your Mac" appears if the following conditions are all met:

▶ Your Mac and Apple Watch support Auto Unlock (See Apple Support article HT204689, "System requirements for Continuity on Mac, iPhone, iPad, iPod touch, and Apple Watch," for more information).

▶ Your Mac has Wi-Fi and Bluetooth turned on.

▶ Your Mac and Apple Watch are signed in to iCloud with the same Apple ID.

▶ Your Apple ID uses two-factor authentication.

▶ Your Apple Watch uses a passcode.

You can also use Auto Unlock to approve other requests to enter your administrator password if your Mac has macOS Catalina or later and your Apple Watch has watchOS 6 or later. For example, by double-clicking the side button on your Apple Watch you can unlock settings in System Preferences, unlock a secure note, or inspect passwords in Safari. For more information, see Apple Support article HT206995, "How to unlock your Mac with your Apple Watch."

macOS enables you to restrict the opening of untrusted apps that are downloaded from the internet. Near the bottom of the General pane, you can configure the sources of apps that macOS allows you to run. Lesson 18, "Install Apps," covers this topic in greater detail.

Security & Privacy: Advanced Settings

To view advanced security settings, unlock Security & Privacy preferences and click the Advanced button in the lower-right corner of the pane.

You can choose to require users to automatically log out of accounts after a certain amount of inactivity and to require an administrator password to access systemwide preferences. The option to log out after a specific period of inactivity may not be available if a user has a file open with unsaved changes because the app may require the user to save those changes.

Security & Privacy: FileVault Settings

This pane is where you enable and configure FileVault. Lesson 12, "Manage FileVault," covers FileVault in greater detail.

Security & Privacy: Firewall Settings

This pane is where you turn on and configure personal network firewall settings. Lesson 25, "Manage Host Sharing and Personal Firewall," covers this topic in greater detail.

Reference 9.5
Manage User Privacy

macOS includes privacy settings that are turned on by default for every user. These settings might prevent functionality that a user would like. You can edit these settings to allow access to private information. macOS uses a privacy database, which stores decisions a user makes about whether apps may access personal data. Use the following section to learn how to edit settings that allow access to private information.

Find out more about Apple's deep commitment to personal privacy at www.apple.com/privacy/.

More information on managing privacy for Siri and Spotlight is in Lesson 16, "Use Metadata, Siri, and Spotlight."

An app must get your consent before it can access the camera or microphone on your Mac or access sensitive data like your location, your Messages history, and your Mail database. Safari limits advertisers' ability to track you by reducing the amount of information that sites can learn about your browser and device. Intelligent Tracking Prevention keeps embedded content such as social media buttons and content from tracking you without your permission. Safari can help you use unique and strong passwords by offering to create and store passwords, then autofill the right password when you visit a website. You can use Safari preferences to update passwords that you've used across more than one website so that you can ensure you have unique and robust passwords for every website that requires one.

Siri enables you to use your voice to request actions. This virtual assistant performs tasks or finds things locally on your Mac and on the internet and uses a microphone to listen to your requests.

Security & Privacy: Privacy Settings

Administrator and standard users can manage service access to personal information in the Privacy pane.

When an administrator specifies a privacy selection (turns it on or off), standard users can't change it. For example, if an administrator turns off the ability for Weather to access Location Services, it remains turned off for all standard users.

When a new app requests access to certain classes of data, macOS asks you for permission. For example, when you make a new event and specify a location for the event, Calendar asks you to allow access to Location Services to provide you with improved location searches and travel time estimates.

"Calendar" would like to use
your current location.

Your location is required to provide you
with improved location searches and
travel time estimates.

Don't Allow   OK

If you click OK, the app or service is added to your privacy database for the appropriate class of data. If you click Don't Allow, the app or service won't have permission to the class of data, and it won't ask for permission again unless you reset the privacy database. For more information about resetting the privacy database, see the man page for tccutil.

> **NOTE ▸** Your organization might be able to use your organization's mobile device management (MDM) solution to apply a Privacy Preferences Policy Control payload to enable or disable app access to classes of data. This topic is outside the scope of this guide.

From the Privacy pane of Security & Privacy preferences, you can review apps or services that have asked for information and choose to allow or disallow further attempts by those apps to collect information. The left column in the Privacy pane displays a list of classes of data related to information that apps and services might request.

Each class of data on the left has a list on the right of apps and services that can access that class of data. Some settings in the Privacy pane apply to all users on your Mac. Other settings—for example, Contacts, Calendars, Reminders, and Photos settings—are limited to the currently logged-in user.

Select a class of data on the left, then deselect an app or service on the right to prevent it from accessing the class of data. For some categories such as Accessibility and Full Disk Access, you can click Add (+) and add an app to the list of apps that can access the category.

▶ Location Services—Location Services allows apps and websites to gather and use information based on the current location of your Mac. Your approximate location is determined using information from local Wi-Fi networks and is collected by Location Services in a way that doesn't personally identify you. Location Services lets apps, such as web browsers, gather and use information based on your location. You can turn off Location Services completely, or you can select which apps can see information about your location. Click About Location Services & Privacy for detailed information. Click Details next to System Services to see or edit the list of services that can determine your location. While Location Services is selected, next to System Services you can click Details to configure the system services that are allowed to access Location Services. You can modify these settings only if Security & Privacy preferences is unlocked. There's also an option to display a location icon in the menu bar when System Services requests your location. The menu item appears as a compass arrow pointing northeast.

Allow System Services to determine your location:

☑ Location-Based Suggestions

◀ ☑ Time Zone & System Customization

◀ ☑ Significant Locations   [Details...]

◀ ☑ Find My Mac

☑ HomeKit

◀ ☑ Wi-Fi Networking

☐ Show location icon in menu bar when System Services request your location

[Done]

▶ Contacts, Calendars, Reminders, and Photos—Shows apps that may gather and use information from your contacts, photos, calendar, or reminders.

▶ Camera, Microphone, and Speech Recognition—Shows apps that have access to the microphone or camera on your Mac.

▶ Accessibility—Shows apps that run scripts and system commands to control your Mac. After you enable them, these assistive apps can control macOS input and modify interface behavior.

▶ Input Monitoring—Shows apps that can access the input from your keyboard.

▶ Full Disk Access—Shows apps that can access your entire disk in order to access sensitive data like Mail, Messages, Safari, Home, and Time Machine backups, or in order to back up your entire disk. If an app requires full disk access, the first time you open that app it may ask you to manually add one or more apps to the Full Disk Access pane. If you've upgraded your Mac from macOS High Sierra to macOS Big Sur, you may have to manually add apps and even helper apps that require full disk access to the Full Disk Access pane in order for those apps to continue to work correctly in macOS Big Sur.

▶ Files and Folders—Shows apps that can access specific files and folders.

▶ Screen Recording—Shows apps that can record the contents of your screen.

▶ Media & Apple Music—Shows apps that can access Apple Music, your music and video activity, and your media library.

▶ HomeKit—Shows apps that have access to home data.

▶ Bluetooth—Shows apps that have access to use Bluetooth.

▶ Automation—Shows apps that can access and control other apps on your Mac. This list can include apps that are created with Automator or Script Editor, which are built into macOS. Automator enables you to automate much of what you do on your Mac. It creates workflows with hundreds of actions that are available in the Automator Library. Script Editor lets you create scripts, tools, and apps that perform repetitive tasks; automate complex workflows; manipulate apps; or even control your Mac. You can use various scripting languages, including AppleScript, JavaScript for Automation, shell scripts, and some third-party scripting languages. For more information about automation, open Automator and choose Help > Automator Help, or see macosxautomation.com.

▶ Apple Advertising—To review what information about your device is used to deliver ads to you in the App Store, Apple News, and Stocks, click View Ad Targeting Information. If you turn off the Personalized Ads option, you limit Apple's ability to deliver relevant ads to you, but you don't reduce the number of ads you receive. To review Apple's Advertising and Privacy policy, click About Apple Advertising & Privacy.

▶ Analytics & Improvements—To help Apple and other developers serve customers better and improve the quality of their products, you can choose to automatically send analytics information to Apple and app developers. If you agree to send Mac Analytics to Apple, such information could include the following: details about app or macOS crashes, freezes, or kernel panics; information about events on your Mac (for example, whether a function such as waking your Mac was successful); and usage information (for example, data about how you use Apple and third-party software, hardware, and services). This information helps Apple and app developers resolve recurring issues. All analytics information is sent to Apple anonymously. Some options require administrator credentials to turn off and on, but each user can choose whether or not to enable the Improve Siri & Dictation option. Click "About Analytics and Privacy" for more information.

Dictation Privacy

Turn on and manage the Dictation feature in the Dictation pane of Keyboard preferences. Dictation supports many languages, including multiple regional dialects.

To use a different language or to help Dictation automatically enter the correct spoken text, click the Language menu, choose Add Language, then select the languages and dialects that the users of your Mac speak. Dictation supports basic text-related spoken commands for formatting and punctuation.

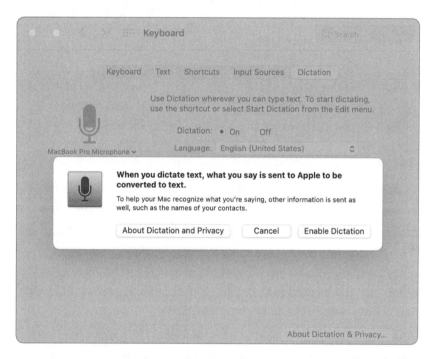

Dictation is turned off by default. After you turn on dictation, when you dictate text what you say is sent to Apple to be converted to text. To help your Mac recognize what you're saying, other information is sent, too, such as the names, nicknames, and relationships (like "Mom") of your contacts.

When you turn off Dictation, you see the message "The information Dictation uses to respond to your requests is also used for Siri and will remain on Apple servers unless Ask Siri is also turned off."

Click About Dictation & Privacy for more details.

See Apple Support article HT202584, "Use Voice Control on your Mac," for more information.

Safari Privacy

Safari can try to block the hidden methods used to gather information about your web use. For example, whenever you use Safari to visit a website Safari presents a simplified version of your system configuration to the site in order to reduce the ability of the site to uniquely identify your Mac.

Find additional privacy settings in the Safari preferences window.

The "Prevent cross-site tracking" option is turned on by default. Some websites use third-party content providers, which can track you across websites to advertise to you. With this option turned on, tracking data is periodically deleted unless you visit the third-party content provider.

The "Block all cookies" option is turned off by default. Cookies are bits of information about your web history that can be used to track your presence on the internet. Turning on this option might prevent some websites from working properly.

Click Manage Website Data to see which websites store cookies and other information on your Mac. You can remove cookies and website data for individual websites or for all of them.

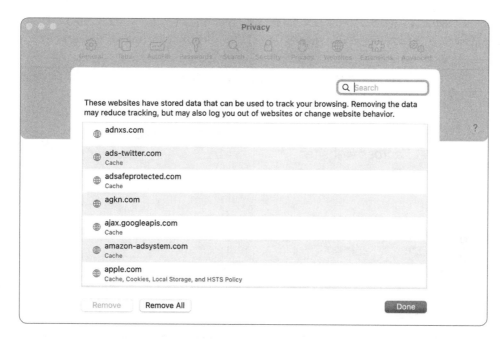

New with Safari 14 (the default web browser for macOS Big Sur, but also available for macOS Catalina) is the privacy report, which displays sites that Safari has blocked from tracking you. For a report on an individual website, open the website, click Privacy Report (the icon looks like a shield) next to the Smart Search field, then click the disclosure triangle to expand the list of trackers.

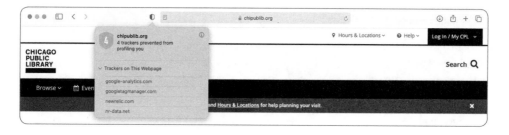

Or choose Safari > Privacy Report to get a report on all the websites you've visited recently.

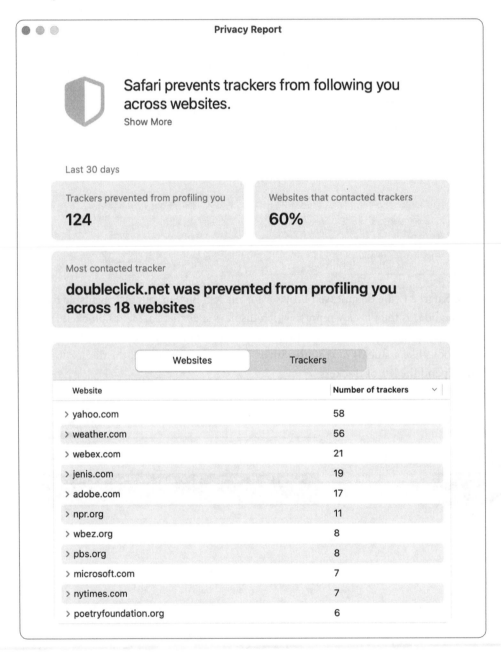

Click Trackers for a list of trackers, who owns the tracker, and how many sites you've visited that use that tracker. On either tab you can click Show More or Show Less to toggle the display of an explanation of cross-site trackers and intelligent tracking prevention.

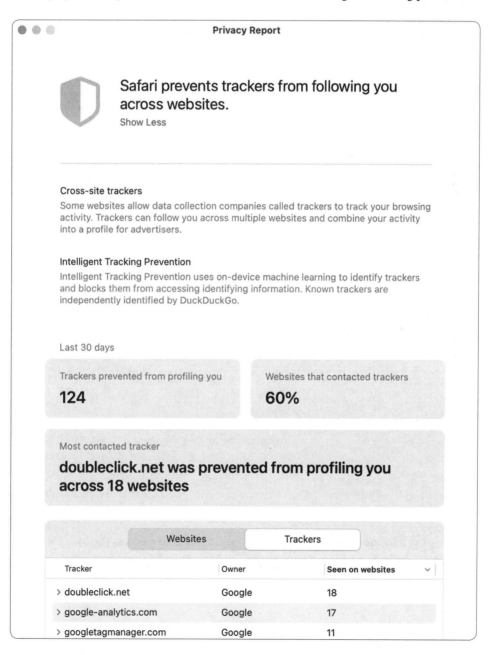

Reference 9.6
Use Find My

Use Find My to:

- ▶ Stay in touch with friends and family members who share their location with you.
- ▶ Locate Apple devices and increase the chance of finding lost Apple devices, even if they aren't connected to the internet.

Find My works with many kinds of Apple devices, but this section focuses on using Find My with Mac.

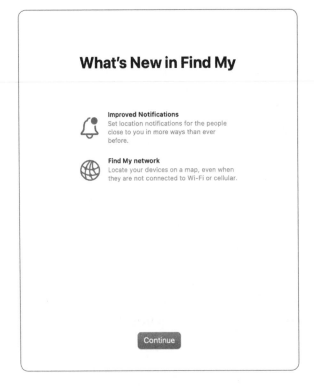

Find My helps you locate a lost Mac by enabling you to remotely access the Mac computer's Location Services. In addition to locating a lost Mac, Find My enables you to remotely lock, erase, and for Intel-based Mac computers, display a message on a Mac.

After you turn on Find My on your Mac, it broadcasts Bluetooth signals with information about its location, even when it's offline or sleeping. Other nearby Apple devices in use relay that information to iCloud so that you can use Find My to locate your missing Mac.

The location information is anonymized and encrypted so that no one, not even Apple, knows the identity of the devices that send their location information. And the location information packets are tiny, so you don't need to worry about transmission of the location information impacting battery life on your Apple devices.

When you open Find My, if you haven't logged in with your iCloud account yet you're asked to sign in. There's a link to System Preferences, which opens Apple ID preferences.

If Find My is not already turned on for Location Services in the Privacy pane of Security & Privacy preferences, Find My asks you to allow Find My to use the location of your Mac.

If you don't give permission, Find My lets you know that you can locate your device if you turn on Find My Mac in the iCloud section of Apple ID preferences.

There are two options that are turned on automatically when you enable Find My Mac:

▶ Find My Mac—This allows you to locate, lock, or erase your Mac and supported accessories.

▶ Find My network—This enables your Mac to send Bluetooth signals with encrypted and anonymized information about its location, even when it's offline and sleeping.

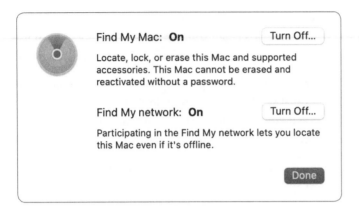

When you turn on Find My for a Mac, the Mac must:

▶ Have an active internet connection.

▶ Have Location Services enabled. If you don't enable Location Services during Setup Assistant or from Security & Privacy preferences, you're asked to when you turn on Find My.

▶ Be configured to use iCloud, with Find My turned on. You can configure or disable Find My any time from iCloud preferences. Although multiple users can sign in to most iCloud services on a single Mac, only one iCloud account per device can be enabled for Find My.

The first time you open Find My, it displays the People pane, but the focus of this guide is the Devices pane.

Click Devices to see a map with the location of your devices that have Find My turned on and that are associated with your iCloud account. If you use Family Sharing and family members share their device location with you, you'll also see their devices that have Family Sharing turned on.

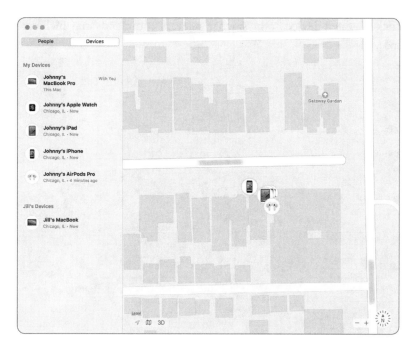

You can control sharing in the Location Sharing pane of Family Sharing preferences.

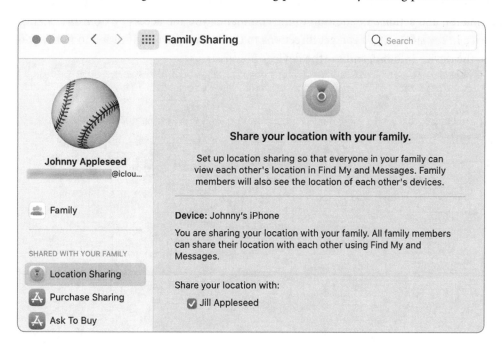

When you Control-click a located device in the sidebar, relevant commands may include:

▶ Play Sound

▶ Directions

▶ Mark as Lost

▶ Erase This Device

▶ Remove This Device

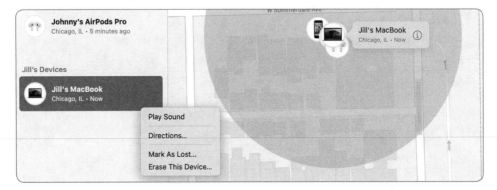

You can also select a located device, then click the information icon (i) to display more information and actions. In addition to the commands you can access by Control-clicking a device in the sidebar, you can get directions to the device, set a notification to notify you when the device is found, and see the device's power status.

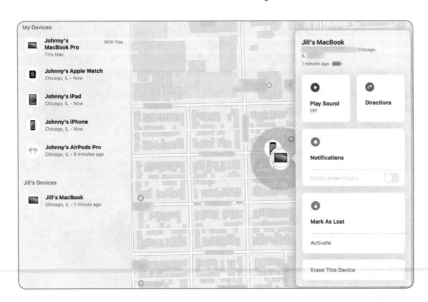

When you take action to mark a Mac as lost (which acts differently for an Intel-based Mac computer than for a Mac computer with Apple silicon) or to erase a Mac, macOS prompts you to confirm the action.

Confirm Mark As Lost

For the Mark As Lost command, the prompt is "Lock this Mac? Are you sure you want to lock this Mac? A locked device cannot be erased." This is because a locked Mac won't be able to receive a command to be erased until the Mac is unlocked again. Before you take action, decide which action is most appropriate. If you think you might not be able to find and retrieve the Mac, it might be best to send the command to erase the Mac instead.

To continue with the remote lock, you must provide a six-digit passcode (also referred to as a PIN), then verify the passcode. This PIN applies only to an Intel-based Mac computer; it's ignored for a Mac with Apple silicon.

After you enter and verify the passcode, you can enter a message that will be displayed on an Intel-based Mac after it has been locked or erased (the message is ignored for a Mac with Apple silicon).

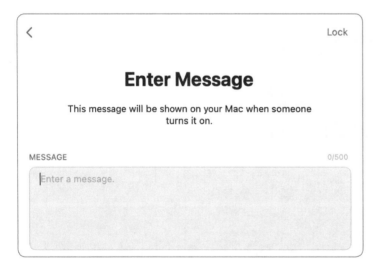

In the upper-right corner, click Lock to send the command.

Confirm Erase This Mac

For the Erase This Mac command to erase a remote Mac, the prompt is "Erase Mac? All your content and settings will be erased when this Mac connects to the internet. An erased Mac cannot be located or tracked any longer."

And you can provide a message that will be shown on an Intel-based Mac after it has been erased (the message is ignored for a Mac with Apple silicon).

In the upper-right corner, click Erase to send the command.

Finally, enter your Apple ID to confirm your identity.

NOTE ▸ MDM solutions provide remote lock and erase (also called wipe) operations similar to the remote lock and erase operations that Find My provides, but MDM solutions do not require Location Services to be enabled.

After a Mac receives a command for a remote lock or a remote erase, the Mac immediately restarts. Upon restart, the behavior varies by kind of Mac.

For a Mac with Apple silicon, Recovery Assistant displays the Activate Mac window, where you must select an administrator user whose password you know, then provide that user's password. After you successfully provide an administrator's password, Recovery Assistant displays the Activation Lock window, where you must provide the Apple ID that the Mac is linked to. After you provide the correct Apple ID credentials, Recovery Assistant displays the message, "Your Mac is activated." and a Restart button. If you don't know an administrator password, you can click the Recovery Assistant menu and choose Erase Mac. If you don't know the Apple ID credentials linked to the Mac, you can click the "Use Device Password" or "Forgot Apple ID or password" links for more options. See Reference 9.7, "Protect Your Mac with Activation Lock" for more details about Activation Lock. The administrator password and Apple ID password protect the contents of the Mac from unauthorized users. Without those credentials, an unauthorized user can't access any internal storage on the Mac.

For an Intel-based Mac, the remote lock function works even while the Mac is using a firmware password, which is covered in Reference 5.3. The Mac may display a lock icon, a field for the passcode, and a right arrow button, or it may display six fields (one for each digit of the PIN) with the message "Enter your system lock PIN code to unlock this Mac."

The passcode protects the contents of the Mac from unauthorized users. Without the correct passcode, an unauthorized user can't access any internal storage on the Mac. Also, without the correct passcode, an unauthorized user can't modify how the Mac starts up.

For the remote erase operation, upon restart, both a Mac with Apple silicon and an Intel-based Mac remove all user data. Additionally, a Mac that's protected with FileVault deletes the encryption keys needed to decrypt the startup disk. This is called an instant wipe, and it makes the data on your startup disk completely inaccessible. See Lesson 12 for more information about FileVault.

You can also log in to www.icloud.com/find to find Apple devices that have Find My turned on. You can use this site from another Mac or PC.

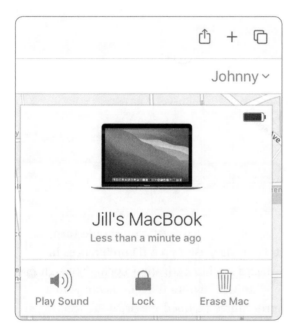

See "Find My User Guide" at support.apple.com/guide/findmy-mac for more information.

Reference 9.7
Protect Your Mac with Activation Lock

Activation Lock is designed to prevent an unauthorized person from using or selling your device. This section focuses on Activation Lock for Mac computers with the T2 chip.

When you set up Find My on your Mac, Activation Lock is turned on automatically if your Mac meets the following requirements:

▶ Your Mac must have macOS Catalina or macOS Big Sur.

▶ Your Mac must be a Mac with Apple silicon or be an Intel-based Mac with the T2 chip.

▶ Your Apple ID account must have two-factor authentication.

▶ If your Mac doesn't have Apple silicon, it must have the default Secure Boot setting of Full Security and the External Boot setting of "Disallow booting from external media." Reference 5.3 has more information about these settings.

You can use System Information to check the status of Activation Lock on your Mac. Open System Information, then select Hardware. If your Mac is eligible to have Activation Lock turned on, you'll see an Activation Lock Status field.

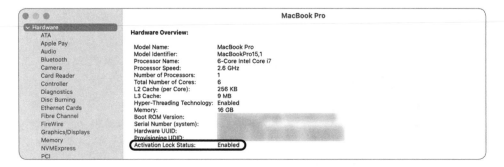

Before you send your Mac in for service, sell it, or give it away, you should turn off Activation Lock. If you have access to your Mac, use Apple ID preferences in System Preferences to turn off Find My Mac to disable Activation Lock, then sign out of iCloud. If you don't have access to your Mac, sign in to iCloud.com with a web browser and erase your Mac, using procedures outlined the previous section, Reference 9.6, "Use Find My."

If you set up a Mac that is protected by Activation Lock, you'll see the Activation Lock screen.

This could be your own Mac or a Mac you bought from someone else. On the Activation Lock screen, you can turn off Activation Lock by entering the correct Apple ID and password.

See Apple Support article HT208987, "About Activation Lock on your Mac," and Apple Support article HT201441, "How to Remove Activation Lock," for more information.

> **NOTE ▶** If your organization uses Apple School Manager or Apple Business Manager and has an MDM solution that supports Activation Lock escrow, you can use your MDM solution to turn Activation Lock on or off on your supervised Mac computers. See "Using Activation Lock for Apple devices" at support.apple.com/guide/mdm/apd593fdd1c9 for more information about Activation Lock.

Reference 9.8
Approve Legacy System Extensions

A kernel extension (kext) is a dynamically loaded bundle of executable code that runs in kernel space to perform low-level tasks. This guide generally refers to kernel extensions that are part of macOS as *kexts*, and third-party kernel extensions as *legacy system extensions*. Legacy system extensions use methods that aren't as secure or reliable as their replacements, System Extensions, covered in the next section.

In 2019 Apple notified app developers that macOS Catalina will be the last version of macOS to fully support legacy system extensions. Apple has been working with app developers to transition their apps from legacy system extensions to System Extensions.

> **WARNING ▶** If you use an app that requires a legacy system extension, contact the app developer to find out whether they plan to update the app to use a System Extension. If not, consider finding a different app that meets your needs.

Although installing a legacy system extension places the legacy system extension on the file system, the legacy system extension isn't active until it's approved to be loaded and the Mac is restarted.

If your Mac is enrolled in your organization's MDM solution, you might be able to use your MDM solution to allow approving legacy system extensions. You have the option of allowing standard users to initiate the restart from within Security & Privacy preferences that's required to load the legacy system extension.

If your Intel-based Mac is not enrolled in your organization's MDM solution, only some categories of legacy system extensions are allowed to be installed and loaded with administrator user approval.

If your Apple silicon-based Mac is not enrolled in your organization's MDM solution with Automated Device Enrollment, you can install legacy system extensions if all the conditions are met:

▶ Your volume for macOS has a Security Policy configured with Reduced Security mode (keep in mind that with Apple silicon-based Mac computers, there can be multiple volumes with macOS installed, and each volume has its own Security Policy configuration, as covered in Reference 5.3).

▶ For the Security Policy, the "Allow user management of kernel extensions from identified developers" checkbox must be selected.

▶ The legacy system extension must be notarized, which is covered in Reference 18.2, "App Security."

For more information, see Apple Support article HT210999, "About system extensions and macOS."

Reference 9.9
Approve System Extensions

For macOS Catalina and later, System Extensions replace the functionality of kexts. Developers can use System Extensions to create powerful apps that extend the functionality of macOS while preserving the reliability and stability of macOS. System Extensions are safer and easier to develop than kexts. Types of System Extensions include:

▶ Network Extensions can filter and reroute network traffic or connect to a virtual private network (VPN).

▶ Endpoint Security Extensions can intercept and monitor security-related events.

▶ Driver Extensions can control hardware devices and make their services available systemwide.

To install a System Extension, install the app that contains the System Extension. During the installation process, when an app attempts to load its System Extension, macOS displays a dialog that it blocked loading the System Extension.

Click Open Security Preferences to open the General pane in Security & Privacy preferences. macOS requires administrator user approval before loading a new System Extension. To load the new System Extension, click the lock, provide administrator credentials, then next to the System Extension information, click Allow.

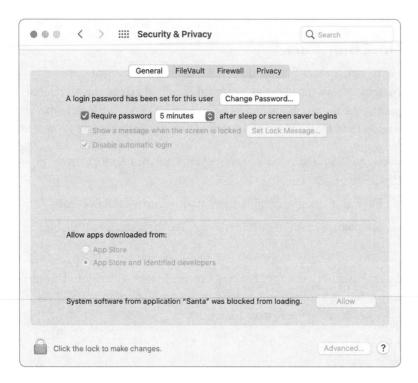

If macOS blocked more than one System Extension, click Allow to inspect the list of items that were blocked from loading. Select the checkbox for each System Extension you want to allow to load, then click OK.

macOS automatically loads and unloads approved System Extensions as needed.

To remove a System Extension, remove the app that contains the System Extension.

NOTE ▶ Your organization may be able to use your MDM solution to approve System Extensions, a topic that is outside the scope of this guide.

To see whether any System Extensions have been installed, you can use the systemextensionsctl command in Terminal with the list option.

In the following figure:

▶   The bottom portion of the General pane of Security & Privacy preferences displays a message that the Allow button is available to be clicked (administrator credentials were provided to unlock the lock).

▶ In Terminal, the systemextensionsctl list command reports that a System Extension is "activated waiting for user."

In the following figure, which continues the scenario of approving a System Extension:

▶ The bottom portion of the General pane of Security & Privacy preferences displays a message that the Allow button no longer appears, because the Allow button was clicked.

▶ After the Allow button was clicked, in Terminal, clearing the screen and running the systemextensionsctl list command again shows that the System Extension is "activated [and] enabled."

For more information about System Extensions, see developer.apple.com/system-extensions/.

Reference 9.10
Lock Your Screen

If you're logged in to your Mac and you need to leave its proximity, lock your screen so that no one can access your Mac in your absence. Click the Apple menu, then choose Lock Screen (or press Control-Command-Q).

macOS locks your screen immediately. No one can use your Mac without first authenticating as you.

In the Screen Saver pane in Desktop & Screen Saver preferences, you can click Hot Corners, click a menu for one of the corners, then choose Lock Screen. Then when you move the pointer to that corner of your screen, your screen locks.

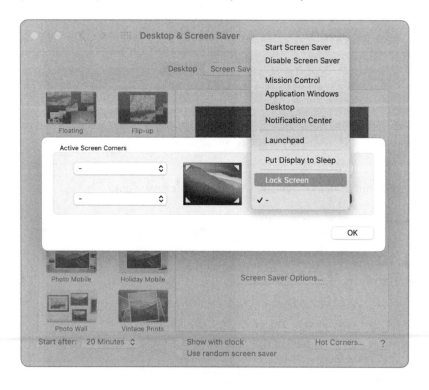

If your organization requires a Mac to display a lock screen message, see Apple Support article HT203580, "Display a message in the Mac login window."

Exercise 9.1
Manage Keychains

▶ **Prerequisites**

- ▶ You must have created the Johnny Appleseed account (Exercise 7.1, "Create a Standard User Account").

- ▶ You must have performed Exercise 8.1, "Restore a Deleted User Account."

By default, when you log in to your local account, your login keychain is automatically unlocked and remains unlocked until you log out. If you want more security, you can configure the login keychain to lock after a period of inactivity or when your Mac goes to sleep.

In this exercise, you explore keychain management techniques.

Configure the Keychain to Lock Automatically

1   Log in as Johnny Appleseed.

2   In the Finder, open the Utilities folder by choosing Go > Utilities or by pressing Shift-Command-U.

3   In the Utilities folder, open Keychain Access.

In the upper left of the app window you will notice that each keychain has a padlock icon indicating whether it is locked or unlocked. The icon for the login keychain indicates that it is unlocked.

4   Select the login Keychain, then from the menu bar, choose Edit > Change Settings for Keychain "login."

5 Select the "Lock after 5 minutes of inactivity" and "Lock when sleeping" checkboxes.

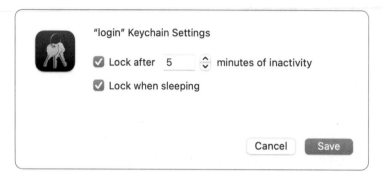

6 Click Save, then quit Keychain Access (Command-Q).

7 Open System Preferences, then select Security & Privacy.

8 If necessary, click General, then deselect the "Require password" checkbox.

WARNING ▶ macOS has default preferences to protect your computer from unauthorized access. In production, you should always consider requiring a password immediately if your Mac will be unattended.

9 At the prompt, enter Johnny Appleseed's password, then click OK.

This is a per-user preference setting, so administrator authorization isn't required.

10 In the confirmation dialog that appears, click Turn Off Screen Lock.

11 Close System Preferences.

12 If you are presented with a "Do you want to turn off iCloud Keychain and remove Safari passwords saved on this Mac?" dialog, click Turn Off & Remove Passwords.

For more information about the iCloud Keychain, see Reference 9.3, "Use iCloud Keychain."

13 Choose Apple menu > Sleep.

14 Press any key to wake the Mac.

15 Open Keychain Access.

The lock icon next to the login keychain appears locked (not open), indicating that the keychain is locked.

16 In Keychain Access, Control-click the login keychain, then select Unlock Keychain "login."

17 Enter Johnny's password, then click OK.

The lock opens and your keychain unlocks.

18 Quit Keychain Access.

Configure the Login Session to Lock

Instead of locking only the login keychain, you can configure the entire login session to lock on sleep or after a period of inactivity.

1 Open Security & Privacy preferences, then click General.

2 Select "Require password," then choose "immediately" from the menu.

3 At the prompt, enter Johnny Appleseed's password, then click OK.

4 Choose Apple menu > Sleep.

5 Press any key to wake the Mac.

You see an unlock screen similar to the login screen but with only Johnny's account shown.

6   Enter Johnny's password, then press Return.

Your session unlocks. When you entered the password, the keychain unlocked with the login session.

To simplify the rest of the exercises, you can relax these security measures.

WARNING ▶ macOS has default preferences to protect your computer from unauthorized access. In production, you should always consider requiring a password immediately if your Mac will be unattended.

7   Deselect the "Require password" checkbox in Security & Privacy preferences, then click Turn Off Screen Lock in the confirmation dialog.

8   Quit System Preferences.

9   Open Keychain Access, if necessary, select the login keychain, then from the menu bar choose Edit > Change Settings for Keychain "login."

10   If necessary, enter Johnny's password to unlock the keychain.

11   Deselect both "Lock after 5 minutes of inactivity" and "Lock when sleeping."

12   Click Save, then quit Keychain Access.

Store a Password in a Keychain

Your login keychain has a number of automatically created entries. In this section, you create an entry by asking macOS to remember a password in your keychain.

1   Open the StudentMaterials/Lesson9 folder. Remember that you created a shortcut to StudentMaterials in your Dock.

2   Open the file named "Johnny's private files.dmg."

This disk image is encrypted, so macOS asks you for the password to open it.

3   Select the "Remember password in my keychain" checkbox.

4   Type the password **private**, then click OK.

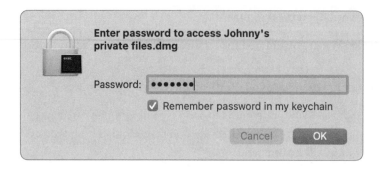

5 If necessary, enter Johnny's account password.

6 Select the disk image on your desktop, then press Command-E to eject it.

7 Open the disk image again.

Since the password is now stored in your keychain and the keychain is unlocked, the image opens without asking for your password.

8 Eject the disk image.

Retrieve a Password from a Keychain

Even though passwords are stored to make them available for apps, there may be times when a user needs to retrieve a stored password. For example, a user who wants to access their mail from Safari on a different Mac may want to retrieve their email password to do so. In this section, you use the keychain to retrieve a forgotten password.

1 Open Keychain Access from the Utilities folder.

You can reach this folder in the Finder by choosing Go > Utilities or by pressing Command-Shift-U.

2 Double-click the password entry named "Johnny's private files.dmg." If necessary, scroll down or use the search field at the upper-right corner of Keychain Access.

A window opens, displaying information about this password entry.

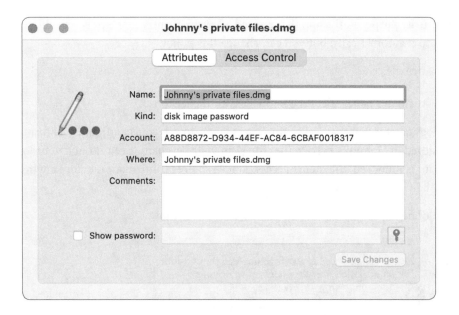

3 Click Access Control.

The Access Control pane displays information about which apps or processes are allowed to access the keychain entry. In this case, the diskimageshelper app can automatically access the password, but if any other app requests access, macOS asks the user for confirmation first.

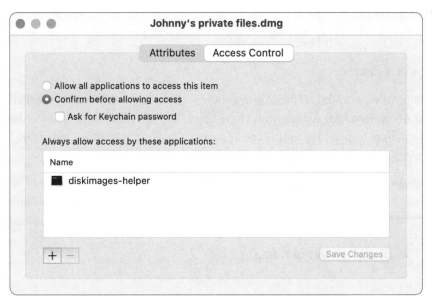

For security purposes, the app that created a keychain entry is the only one allowed access to it automatically, but you can change this policy.

4 Click Attributes.

5 In the Attributes pane, select the Show Password checkbox.

A dialog informs you that Keychain Access wants to use your confidential information, stored in "Johnny's private files.dmg," in your keychain. Even though your login keychain is unlocked, this item's access policy requires confirmation before anything other than diskimageshelper is allowed to access the password.

6 Enter Johnny's account password, then click Always Allow.

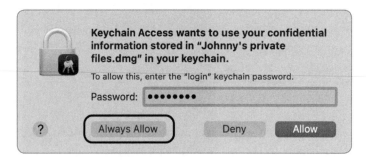

WARNING ► In production, allowing access only once ("Allow") is best practice to keep your computer secure.

The disk image password becomes visible.

7 Click Access Control.

Keychain Access is added to the "Always allow access" list for this item. If you had clicked Allow, Keychain Access would have been allowed access to the password but would not have been added to this access control list. Since it is added to the list, Keychain Access displays the password without asking for confirmation.

8 If Keychain Access doesn't appear in the Access Control tab, quit and reopen Keychain Access, then select the Access Control tab for "Johnny's private files.dmg" again.

9 Close the "Johnny's private files.dmg" window.

Move a Password to the System Keychain

Normally, resource passwords are stored in a login keychain and are accessible only by the user whose account is associated with that keychain. You can move resource passwords to the System keychain, making them accessible to all users. You may want to do this for a disk image that resides on a shared network volume or cloud storage location and you want to facilitate access for all users of the computer.

1   In the login keychain, find the "Johnny's private files.dmg" keychain item, then Control-click and select Copy "Johnny's private files.dmg."

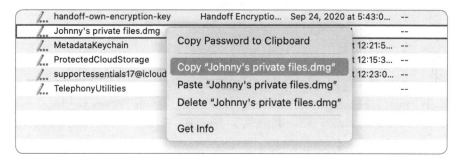

2   Select the System keychain, then Control-click in an area where secrets are not stored, and select Paste "Johnny's private files.dmg."

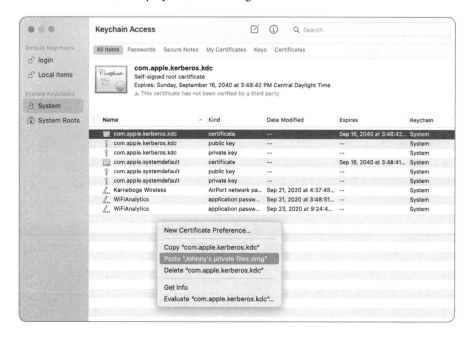

3 Authenticate as Local Administrator.

4 When you're asked to allow kcproxy to use the confidential information in "Johnny's private files.dmg," click Allow. If necessary, enter Johnny's account password.

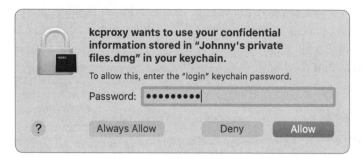

kcproxy is a process that Keychain Access uses to move entries into the System keychain.

Observe that "Johnny's private files.dmg" now exists in your System keychain, along with several automatically created items, and any Wi-Fi passwords stored on your Mac.

5 Select your login keychain, then find the "Johnny's private files.dmg" keychain item.

6 Control-click "Johnny's private files.dmg," then select Delete "Johnny's private files.dmg."

7 Confirm that you want to delete "Johnny's private files.dmg."

"Johnny's private files.dmg" now exists only in the System keychain. Though we deleted the item from Johnny's keychain, it is available to Johnny and all other users on the Mac.

8 Quit Keychain Access, then log out of the Johnny Appleseed account.

9   Log in as Emily Davidson.

Use the next two steps to open /Users/Shared/StudentMaterials/Lesson9/
Johnny's private files.dmg.

Emily's Finder preferences aren't customized to allow easy access outside her home
folder.

10   Choose Go > Computer (Shift-Command-C).

11   Open Macintosh HD > Users > Shared > StudentMaterials > Lesson9 > Johnny's private files.dmg.

The disk image opens. Because the keychain item access controls allow diskimageshelper
full access to the item for all users, you aren't asked to authenticate or allow access.

12   Eject the disk image, then log out of the Emily Davidson account.

Exercise 9.2
Allow Apps to Access Your Data

> **Prerequisite**
>
> ▶   You must have created the Johnny Appleseed account (Exercise 7.1, "Create a
> Standard User Account").

macOS Big Sur requires user approval before it allows apps to access certain types of user
data. You manage this in Security & Privacy preferences. In this exercise, you install an
app that requests access to your contacts.

Install an App

1   Log in as Johnny Appleseed.

2   Open the StudentMaterials/Lesson9 folder.

3   Open the file named Directory.dmg.

Directory is an app that must be installed in the Applications folder.

4   From the menu bar, choose Go > Applications (Shift-Command-A).

5   Drag and drop Directory from the disk image to your Applications folder.

6   At the "Finder wants to copy 'Directory'" prompt, authenticate as
    Local Administrator, then click OK.

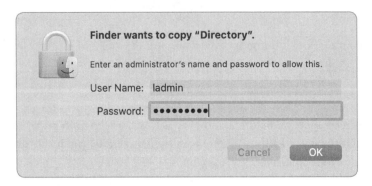

Directory is installed in your Applications folder.

7   Eject the disk image.

Approve an App

1 Open Directory, then at the quarantine prompt warning that Directory was downloaded from the internet, click Open (see "File Quarantine" in Reference 18.2, "App Security").

Directory

In Directory, the People pane contains a Request Contacts Access button. Many apps have different mechanisms for app approval, but if an app in macOS Big Sur wants data from another source, it must first obtain user consent.

2 Click the Request Contacts Access button in Directory.

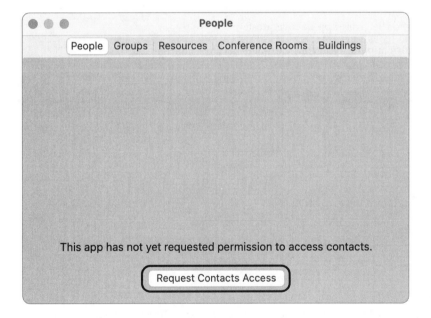

3 At the "'Directory' would like to access your contacts" prompt, click OK.

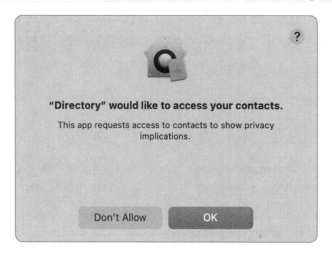

You approved the cross-app data request.

The Directory app tells you that Contacts access is authorized.

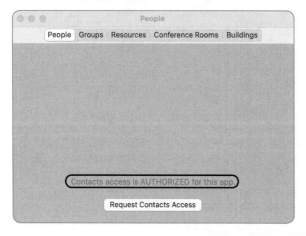

4 Open Security & Privacy preferences. Do not quit the Directory app.

5 Click Privacy.

Notice the different categories in the sidebar.

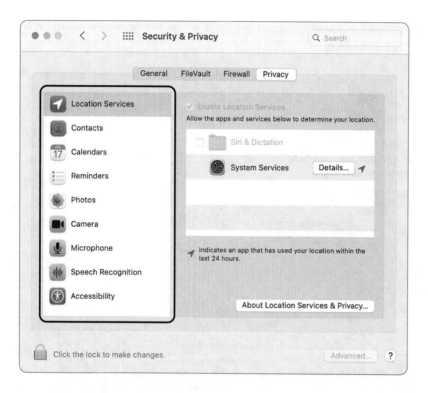

6   Select Contacts, then confirm that the checkbox for Directory is selected.

This indicates that Directory is approved for access to Contacts.

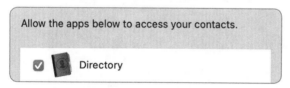

7   Deselect the checkbox next to Directory.

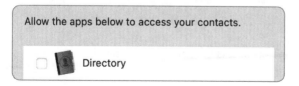

8   In the dialog telling you that Directory will have access to your contacts until it is quit, click Quit & Reopen.

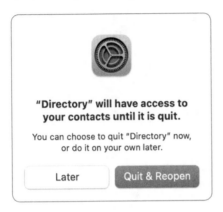

9   Switch to Directory.

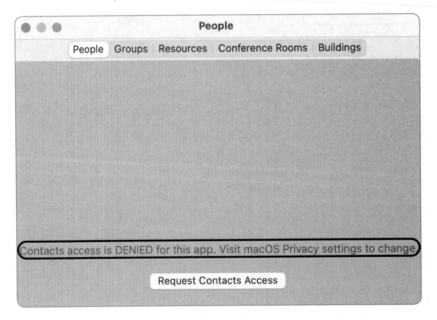

Directory now tells you that Contacts access is denied and directs you to "Visit macOS Privacy settings to change."

10 Quit Directory.

Lesson 10
Manage Password Changes

A password change is different from a password reset. You can change a password if you know it, but if you don't know it, you might be able to reset it. Changing and resetting passwords both result in a new password, but you should reset a password only if a user doesn't know their password.

In this lesson, you learn how to change and reset passwords. You also learn about the ramifications of modifying passwords.

GOALS

▶ Change known passwords

▶ Reset lost user passwords

Reference 10.1
Change Known Passwords

If you know your local computer account password but want to change it, you can do so from the General pane of Security & Privacy preferences, or you can select your user account in Users & Groups preferences. In either case, you click Change Password.

You must enter your old password once, followed by the new password twice. You enter the new password twice to confirm your entry.

If you enter a password that doesn't meet the password requirements, then place your pointer in the Verify field. macOS will then display information about the requirements. When you enter a password that meets the requirements, macOS displays a green status indicator next to the requirements. When FileVault is turned on, a blank password is no longer a choice when you change a password.

If your Mac has a mobile device management (MDM) configuration profile installed that configures a password policy, the most restrictive password settings are enforced.

Use Password Assistant

To pick a strong password, use Password Assistant, which gauges the strength of your passwords or creates strong passwords for you. Whenever you create or modify a password that grants access to a substantial resource, like an account or keychain password, you can use Password Assistant. It's available whenever a small key icon appears next to a password field, as illustrated in the previous screenshot showing the local account password change dialog.

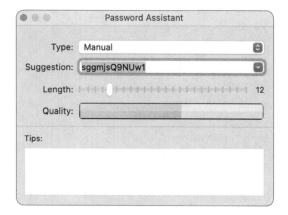

Reference 10.2
Reset Lost Passwords

macOS gives you multiple ways to reset a local user account password.

Reset the Password of Another User

If you have access to an administrator account on a Mac, you can reset other user account passwords from Users & Groups preferences. Authenticate as an administrator, select the user account for the password you want to change, then click Reset Password.

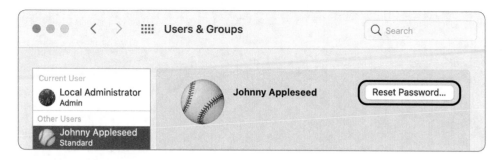

Enter and verify the new password. Optionally enter a password hint, then click Change Password.

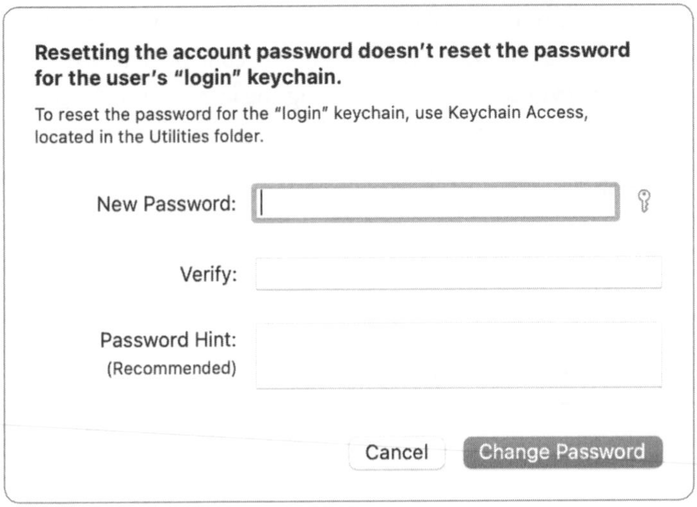

Resetting the account password doesn't reset the password for the user's "login" keychain.

To reset the password for the "login" keychain, use Keychain Access, located in the Utilities folder.

New Password: |

Verify:

Password Hint:
(Recommended)

Cancel   Change Password

When you log in to your Mac, if your login password doesn't match your login keychain password, macOS creates new empty keychain items for you and sets their new passwords to match your login password. See Exercise 10.3, "Observe Automatic Login Keychain Creation," for details.

Reset Your Login Password Using Your Apple ID or FileVault Recovery Key

You can reset your login password using your Apple ID or your FileVault personal recovery key in the following situations:

▶   When you set up your Mac and use Setup Assistant to create your computer account, first provide your Apple ID credentials. Then, on the "Create a Computer Account" screen, select "Allow my Apple ID to reset this password."

► When in Users & Groups preferences, click the lock and authenticate with administrator credentials, select a user, and if the option "Allow user to reset password using Apple ID" appears for that user account, select it.

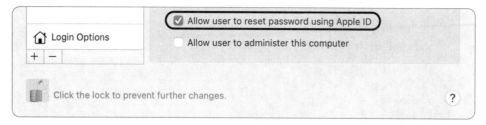

► When you turn on FileVault and select "Set up my iCloud account to reset my password" and still have access to your iCloud account; or select "Create a recovery key and do not use my iCloud account" and still have access to your recovery key. See Lesson 12, "Manage FileVault," for more details on FileVault.

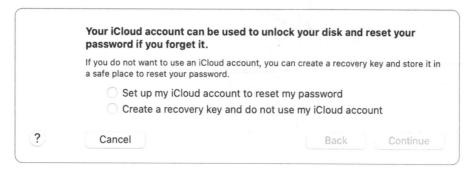

There are a few ways to start the process of resetting your password using your Apple ID or your FileVault recovery key, depending on how your Mac is configured. After you start the process, follow the onscreen prompts to provide the information your Mac requests (either your Apple ID and password or your FileVault recovery key) to reach the point where you can specify and verify a new password.

If you're not already at the login window, begin by logging out or turning your Mac on. At the login window, select a user account whose password you want to reset. The login window displays a question mark next to the Password field if any of the following is true:

- ▶ You can use your Apple ID and password to reset user account passwords.
- ▶ You can use your FileVault recovery key to reset user account passwords.
- ▶ Your user account has a password hint configured.

After you click the question mark, the login window displays your user account password hint if one is configured, along with additional options. These options can include one or more of the following, depending on how your Mac is configured:

- ▶ "reset it using your Recovery Key"
- ▶ "reset it using your Apple ID"
- ▶ "Restart and show password reset options"

If a question mark doesn't appear next to the Password field, you may be able to display more options by entering a wrong password for your user account three times.

After you click the arrow next to an option, follow the onscreen instructions. For example, if you turned on FileVault and have your FileVault Recovery Key, and click the option for "reset it using your Recovery Key," the screen will look like the following figure.

For some Intel-based Mac computers, an alternative to clicking the question mark next to the Password field is to wait up to 60 seconds until a message similar to this appears: "If you're having a problem entering your password, press and hold the power button on your Mac to shut it down. Then press it again to start up in the Recovery OS." Then follow those instructions.

Reset Passwords Using macOS Recovery

Recovery Assistant is available only from macOS Recovery. As covered in Reference 5.1, "Start Up from macOS Recovery," if your Mac has FileVault or Activation Lock turned on, then Recovery Assistant requires you to authenticate as an administrator user before you can access macOS Recovery.

After you start up from macOS Recovery, choose Utilities > Terminal, type **resetpassword**, and press Return. Recovery Assistant opens and provides methods for resetting the local user's account.

Recovery Assistant presents screens that vary based on the Mac computer's storage and configuration:

▸ Storage volume selection—If a Mac has more than one attached external storage device, you might have to select the system volume containing the account password that you want to reset.

▸ FileVault enabled volume—If the selected volume is protected with FileVault and you stored the recovery key with your iCloud account, enter the password for that iCloud account. If you did not store the recovery key with your iCloud account, then use your recovery key to unlock the volume in the login window (you might have to restart first, depending on how your Mac is configured).

▸ Local user selection—If there is more than one local user account on the selected system volume, you must select the account you want to reset the password for.

▸ Local user with associated Apple ID—If the selected local account is associated with an Apple ID, you may be able to reset the local account password by entering the password for the associated Apple ID.

▸ Local user without an associated Apple ID—If the selected local account isn't associated with an Apple ID, you can enter a new password for the local account.

See Exercise 10.1, "Reset Account Passwords in macOS Recovery," for more details.

Anyone with access to macOS Recovery can use Recovery Assistant to reset local account passwords. Consider requiring authentication to access the Mac from macOS Recovery by turning on FileVault or Activation Lock (covered in Reference 9.7, "Protect Your Mac with Activation Lock"). For Intel-based Mac computers, another option is to use a firmware password to restrict access to macOS Recovery.

For more information about changing or resetting a password, see Apple Support article HT202860, "Change or reset the password of a macOS user account."

After You Reset Your Password

When you log in after you reset your password, you might have to enter your Apple ID password again. This is because your newly created login keychain does not contain your Apple ID password. Learn more details in the next section.

After you reset your password and log in:

1   In the message that your Mac can't connect to iCloud or to Apple Media Services, click Apple ID Preferences.

2   Enter your Apple ID password and click Next.

3   If you use iCloud Keychain, then Apple ID preferences displays the prompt Update Apple ID Settings. Click Continue, click Continue, enter your Mac password, then click OK.

Reference 10.3
Manage User Keychains

Reference 9.1, "Password Security," introduced Keychain Access. This section covers a little bit more detail about using Keychain Access to manage user keychains. When a user's account password is reset (as opposed to changed), the user's existing login keychain and Local Items keychain (or iCloud keychain if iCloud Keychain is turned on) items are renamed, so they are effectively moved aside and no longer used. A new login keychain and a new Local Items keychain are created with the same password as the user's login password. The user isn't notified.

Manage Keychain Files

Use Keychain Access to manage keychain files. Open Keychain Access (you can use Launchpad or Spotlight). Choose File > New Keychain, and enter a six-character (or longer) password for the keychain to create a new local keychain file. The default location for new keychains is the Keychains folder inside your home folder > Library folder.

Select a keychain from the sidebar. Then choose Edit > Change Settings for Keychain to adjust keychain settings. A dialog appears where you can change automatic keychain locking settings for a selected keychain file.

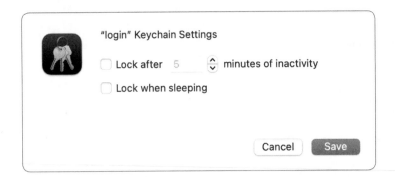

To change a keychain's password, select it from the list, then choose Edit > Change Password for Keychain. You must enter the keychain's current password, followed by a new password and verification.

To delete a keychain, select it from the sidebar and choose File > Delete Keychain. When the Delete Keychain dialog appears, click Delete References to ignore the keychain, or click Delete References & Files to erase the keychain files.

Avoid deleting the original login keychain files manually in the Finder. Don't delete the login keychain unless another keychain is available to take its place. A user should have access to at least one local keychain.

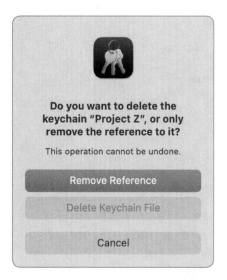

Move keychain items between keychains by dragging and dropping an item from one keychain to another. The exception to this is the Local Items/iCloud keychain, for which macOS manages the addition and removal of items.

Reset Keychain Files

If macOS is unable to open a keychain file or retrieve secrets from it, the keychain file may be corrupted. If so, you must replace or reset your keychain.

If you have a Time Machine backup, as covered in Lesson 17, "Manage Time Machine," you can manually replace a user's Keychains folder with earlier versions of the files. After you replace the keychain files, restart the Mac and log in as the user. Open Keychain Access to verify the presence of the recovered keychain files.

If the user's keychain files are corrupted and the user doesn't have a backup, you must reset the keychain items. In this case, reset the user's password or delete the contents of the user's Keychains folder and restart the Mac. Log in as the user. If the user's login or Local Items keychain is missing, or has a password that doesn't match the user's login password, macOS creates a new empty keychain for each affected keychain. Then macOS automatically creates new keychain items in appropriate keychains as necessary.

Keychain Access allows any user to reset their own keychains. Open Keychain Access > Preferences, and then click Reset Default Keychains.

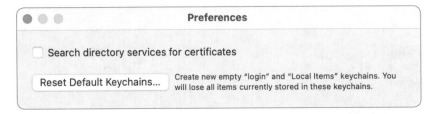

After you click Reset Default Keychains, macOS asks for your login password.

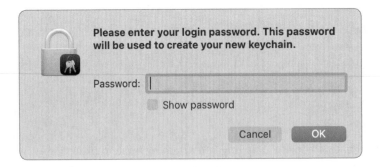

Enter your login password, then click OK. If the password you enter isn't the same as your login password, the next time you log in macOS creates new empty keychain items for you that match your login keychain. See Exercise 10.3 for details.

Reset iCloud Keychain

The iCloud Security Code gives you an additional way to add new devices, and it provides a last resort to recover your iCloud keychain if you lose all your devices. If you don't create an iCloud Security Code and you have disabled iCloud Keychain or your devices are lost, your iCloud keychain contents aren't accessible, and you must reset your iCloud keychain.

If your login keychain password is lost, so is your access to the local instance of the iCloud keychain. If you create a new login keychain, as recommended in the keychain update dialog, the local iCloud keychain is reset. This results in a new empty Local Items keychain, and the contents of iCloud Keychain remain in the cloud.

You can reenable iCloud Keychain to access your secrets, but iCloud Keychain will treat your Mac as if it were new. You are asked to authenticate with an Apple ID and to use either the iCloud Security Code or two-factor authentication to regain access to iCloud Keychain.

For more information about iCloud Keychain, see Apple Support article HT204085, "Set up iCloud Keychain."

Exercise 10.1
Reset Account Passwords in macOS Recovery

▶ Prerequisites

- ▶ You must have created the Local Administrator (Exercise 3.1, "Configure a Mac for Exercises") and Johnny Appleseed (Exercise 7.1, "Create a Standard User Account") accounts.

- ▶ You must have turned on FileVault (Exercise 3.2, "Configure System Preferences").

macOS provides several ways to reset lost account passwords. In this exercise, you use macOS Recovery to reset Johnny Appleseed's password.

Reset a User Password in macOS Recovery

1   Restart your Mac, then press and hold Command-R until the Apple logo appears.

2   If a language selection screen appears, select your preferred language, then click the right-arrow button to continue.

3   On the macOS Recovery screen, select Local Administrator, click Next, enter the password, then click Continue.

4   From the menu bar, choose Utilities > Terminal.

5   Enter the command **resetpassword**, then press Return.

The Recovery Assistant utility opens.

6   At the Reset Password screen, select "I forgot my password," then click Next.

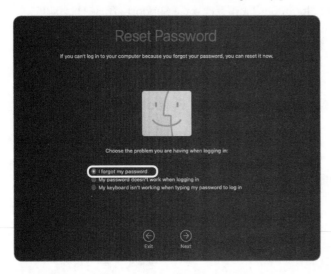

7   Enter the recovery key you recorded when you turned on FileVault in Exercise 3.2, "Configure System Preferences."

Because your startup volume is locked, you can't select a user to reset until the volume is unlocked.

8 Once your volume is unlocked, select the Johnny Appleseed user account (displayed as "johnny"), then click Next.

9 Type **password1** in both password fields. Leave the hint field blank.

10 Click Next.

11 When you are notified that your user account password is reset, click Exit.

12 Choose Restart from the Apple menu.

You just reset Johnny's password. Rather than confirming that the password is reset correctly, go on to the next exercise to try another method of resetting a password. Then use Exercise 10.3 to experience what happens when you log in after your password has been reset.

> **NOTE ▶** Johnny Appleseed's login keychain is no longer synchronized with his login password. You may perform Exercise 10.2, "Reset Account Passwords," next, followed by Exercise 10.3, "Observe Automatic Login Keychain Creation," or you may skip directly to Exercise 10.3. In any case, reset Johnny's keychain by performing Exercise 10.3 before going on to any other lesson.

Exercise 10.2
Reset Account Passwords

> ### Prerequisites
>
> ▸ You must have created the Local Administrator (Exercise 3.1, "Configure a Mac for Exercises") and Johnny Appleseed (Exercise 7.1, "Create a Standard User Account") accounts.
>
> ▸ You must have turned on FileVault (Exercise 3.2, "Configure System Preferences").

macOS provides several ways to reset lost account passwords. In this exercise, you reset Johnny Appleseed's password as an administrator.

Reset a User Password as an Administrator

1   Log in as Local Administrator.

2   Open System Preferences, then select Users & Groups.

3   Click the Lock icon, then authenticate as Local Administrator.

4   Select the Johnny Appleseed account.

5   Click Reset Password.

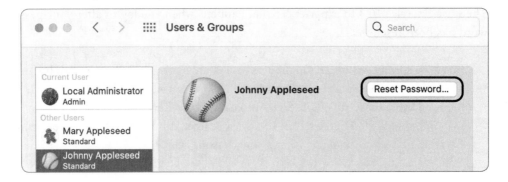

6   Click the small key icon next to the New Password field.

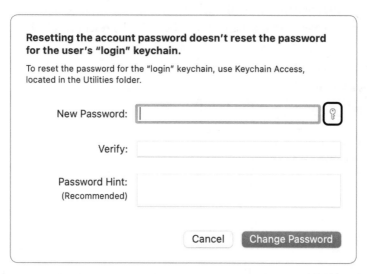

Resetting the account password doesn't reset the password for the user's "login" keychain.

To reset the password for the "login" keychain, use Keychain Access, located in the Utilities folder.

New Password:

Verify:

Password Hint:
(Recommended)

Cancel   Change Password

Password Assistant opens to help you choose a secure password. It rates the quality of the password (red, to indicate it's non-secure), suggests a more secure password (in the Suggestion field), and lists tips on how to avoid non-secure passwords.

7   Click the disclosure button next to the Suggestion field to show more suggested passwords.

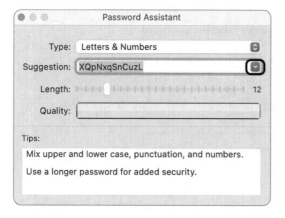

Password Assistant

Type: Letters & Numbers

Suggestion: XQpNxqSnCuzL

Length: ├─┼─┼─┼─┼─┼─┼─┼─┼─┼─┼─┼─┼─┼─┼─┤   12

Quality:

Tips:

Mix upper and lower case, punctuation, and numbers.

Use a longer password for added security.

8 Click one of the suggested passwords. The Quality bar expands and turns green to indicate a more secure password, and the selected password is copied into the Suggestion field and the New Password and Verify fields in the reset password dialog.

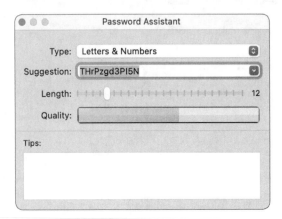

You don't need to memorize or record this password. You choose another password in the next step.

9 Close Password Assistant.

10 In the reset password dialog, enter **password2** in the New Password and Verify fields to replace the password you chose with Password Assistant.

11 Click Change Password.

12 Quit System Preferences, then log out as Local Administrator.

Exercise 10.3
Observe Automatic Login Keychain Creation

▶ **Prerequisites**

- ▶ You must have created the Local Administrator account (Exercise 3.1, "Configure a Mac for Exercises").

- ▶ You must have turned on FileVault (Exercise 3.2, "Configure System Preferences").

- ▶ You must have created the Johnny Appleseed account (Exercise 7.1, "Create a Standard User Account").

- ▶ You must have completed Exercise 10.1, "Reset Account Passwords in macOS Recovery," and Exercise 10.2, "Reset Account Passwords."

After Johnny's (or anyone's) account password is reset, without notification, macOS creates a new login keychain to keep the account password and login keychain password in sync. The login keychain that existed prior to the password reset is archived and is still encrypted with the old account password.

If Johnny remembers his old password, he can open the archived login keychain and copy the items he needs to the new login keychain. If he can't remember his password, he won't be able to recover the old login keychain contents.

In this exercise, assume that Johnny's account password was reset because he forgot his old password. He needs to abandon the old keychain after macOS automatically creates a new one.

Observe the Effects of a New Login Keychain

1 Log in as Johnny Appleseed (after the previous exercise, his password is **password2**).

Johnny's account password was reset, so macOS created a new login keychain for him when you logged in with Johnny Appleseed's account.

2 If a dialog appears indicating that your Mac can't connect to iCloud, click Apple ID Preferences.

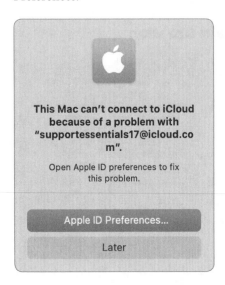

Since Johnny's keychain was reset automatically, his iCloud credentials are lost and you need to reenter them.

3 Enter the password for the Apple ID Johnny's account is linked to, then click Next.

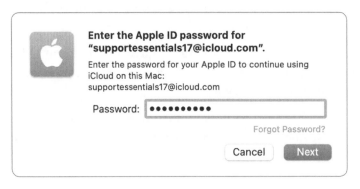

4   If two-factor authentication is enabled, you may be asked to verify the sign-in. Follow the prompts to finish authenticating.

5   Quit System Preferences.

Verify the New Login Keychain Creation

1   Open Keychain Access. If necessary, select your login keychain.

Keychain Access displays the status and contents of your login keychain. The login and Local Items keychains are unlocked because macOS set the password for each of these newly created keychains to be the same password as the login password.

The new keychain normally contains several entries, but it consists only of items that are automatically created in a new keychain plus those items relating to the Apple ID Johnny's account is linked to. The items that were in the old keychain are no longer available in this keychain.

2   Control-click the login keychain, then choose Change Settings for Keychain "login."

3   Select "Lock after 1 minutes of inactivity," then click Save.

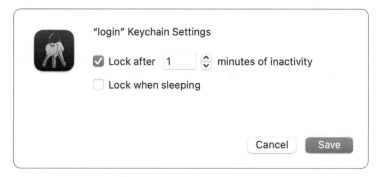

4   Quit Keychain Access, then wait one minute.

5   Open Keychain Access.

Observe that the login keychain is now locked.

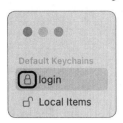

6   Control-click the login keychain, then choose Unlock Keychain "login" to unlock it.

You are asked for the keychain password.

7   Enter Johnny's current account password (**password2**), then click OK.

Since this is the new keychain password, it unlocks.

8   Quit Keychain Access.

Inspect and Import the Archived Login Keychain

1   In the Finder, navigate to ~/Library/Keychains by choosing Go > Go to Folder. In the Go to Folder dialog, type **~/Library/Keychains/**, then click Go.

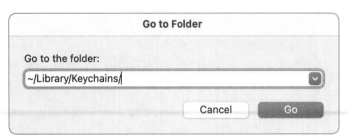

2   Find the item named login_renamed_1.keychain-db, then open it.

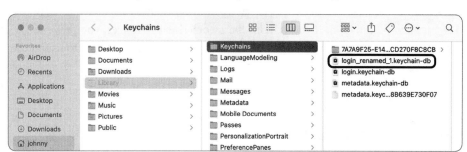

3   Keychain Access opens, and the archived keychain appears in the Keychains sidebar. Select login_renamed_1, then inspect its contents.

If Johnny remembered the password for this keychain, he could unlock it and drag items such as passwords and certificates that he needs into his new login keychain. Because the scenario is that Johnny doesn't know his old login keychain password, performing these actions is unnecessary.

4   Log out as Johnny Appleseed, then log back in as Johnny Appleseed.

5   If necessary, open Keychain Access.

If you are asked to enter your keychain password for the **assistantd** process, click Cancel. You can also use Command-period repeatedly until the prompts go away.

If you are asked to unlock the login_renamed_1 keychain, click Cancel.

6   In the Keychain Access sidebar, Control-click login_renamed_1, then choose "Delete Keychain login_renamed_1."

7   In the dialog, click Remove Reference.

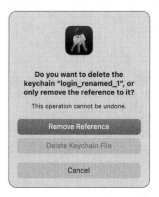

Deleting references leaves login_renamed_1.keychain.db inside the ~/Library/
Keychains folder. It remains there in case you need it again. If you remove the
archived keychain from the keychains list by deleting references, you prevent
macOS from asking you to unlock it if macOS finds a secret it wants to use in the
login_renamed_1 keychain.

8   Quit Keychain Access.

Change Johnny's Password

When you reset Johnny's account password, macOS created a new keychain. If a user with
a standard account changes their own password during their logged-in session, macOS
doesn't create a new keychain. To test this, change Johnny's password.

1   Open Users & Groups in System Preferences, then make sure the Johnny Appleseed
     account is selected.

2   Click Change Password.

     Unlike the Reset Password option you used earlier, this option has a field for the old
     password. macOS uses this old password to decrypt the login keychain and then re-
     encrypt it with the new password.

3   Enter the following:

     Old password: **password2**

     New Password and Verify: **Apple321!**

     Enter a password hint if you want.

4   Click Change Password.

5   The Confirm Mac Password notification may appear in the upper-right corner of
     your screen. Place your mouse over the notification, then click View.

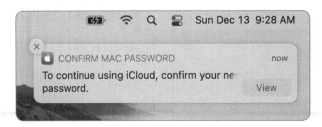

6 In Apple ID preferences, click Continue, then in the Confirm Mac Password dialog, click Continue.

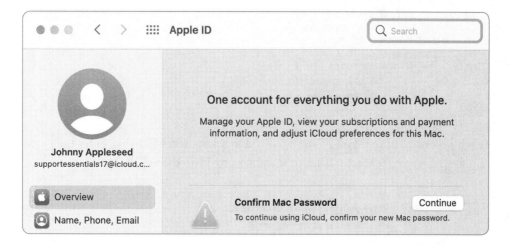

7 In the "Enter your Mac password" dialog, type the new password for Johnny's account (**Apple321!**).

When two-factor authentication is enabled, it is critical that your iCloud account knows about the correct local account password, since it is used to protect sensitive data in iCloud.

8 If necessary, in Apple ID preferences, click Continue, then in the Update Apple ID Settings dialog, click Continue.

9   If necessary, in the "Enter your password to set up iCloud" dialog, enter the password for the Apple ID account that your trainer provided, then click OK.

10   If you are asked to enter your keychain password for the assistantd process, click Cancel. You can also use Command-period repeatedly until the prompts go away.

11   Quit System Preferences.

Verify Synchronization

1   Log out as Johnny Appleseed, then log back in as Johnny Appleseed.

2   Open Keychain Access.

3   Observe that the login keychain is unlocked.

     As before, the login keychain is automatically unlocked, demonstrating that it is in sync with the account password.

4   Quit Keychain Access.

5   Log out as Johnny Appleseed.

File Systems

Manage File Systems and Storage

Apple File System (APFS) is the file system for Mac computers with macOS Catalina and macOS Big Sur.

In this lesson, you examine the storage technology used by macOS. You learn about storage hardware, such as flash disks, and logical storage concepts like partitions, containers, and volumes.

In this lesson, you use About This Mac, System Information, and Disk Utility to inspect, manage, and troubleshoot file-system components.

macOS Catalina introduced a read-only APFS System volume and a read-write APFS Data volume. These two volumes often appear as a single disk or volume to users, even though tools like Disk Utility reveal two separate volumes.

In this lesson you'll also learn about APFS snapshots, because macOS Big Sur adds another security-related change: rather than mounting the APFS System volume directly, macOS Big Sur makes an APFS snapshot of the APFS System volume, cryptographically signs it, and mounts the APFS snapshot. When you are running macOS Big Sur, you aren't directly using the APFS System volume—you're running from the signed snapshot of the APFS System volume.

GOALS

▶ Recognize and describe file systems supported by macOS

▶ Manage disks, containers, partitions, and volumes

▶ Troubleshoot and repair disk and volume issues

Reference 11.1
File Systems

Before you manage storage in macOS, you must understand the distinction between various terms that represent the various layers of abstraction that enable you to store a file on a storage device. One way to consider the layers of abstraction is to start from the bottom and work up; you store a file on a volume, a volume is inside a partition, and a partition is inside a storage device. Given that, the following sections consider the layers of abstraction from the top layer to the bottom layer: storage devices, partitions, then volumes. Along the way, you learn about APFS containers, APFS volume groups, and with new importance in macOS Big Sur, APFS snapshots.

Storage

Computer storage is the technology consisting of components that store data.

> **NOTE ▶** The term *disk* can refer to magnetic storage media such as a hard disk. *Disk* is also used more broadly to include other types of storage, such as flash storage and solid-state drives (SSDs). The terms *storage device* and *external storage device* can help differentiate if storage is internal to your Mac or connected to your Mac with an external cable. macOS uses terms that don't indicate the kind of storage media, like *startup disk*, *disk partition*, *disk image*, and *target disk mode* (available for Intel-based Mac computers).

Formatting is the process of applying logic to storage in the form of partitions, containers, and volumes.

Partitions

A partition is a logical space on a storage device. Every storage device has to have at least one partition before you can create a volume on the storage device.

How you partition a storage device depends on the file format it uses.

Each partition has a partition scheme that defines how the partition behaves. Mac supports three types of partition schemes:

▶ GUID Partition Map—This is the default partition scheme used by Mac computers. It is also the only partition scheme supported for Mac computers to use for a disk to start up from. The terms *GUID Partition Map* and *GUID Partition Table (GPT)* are used interchangeably.

▶ Apple Partition Map (APM)—This was the default partition scheme used by previous PowerPC-based Mac computers.

▶ Master Boot Record (MBR)—This is the default partition scheme used by most non-Mac computers, including Windows-compatible PCs. This partition scheme is commonly used by peripherals that use flash memory for storage.

Adding a new partition to a storage device, also called partitioning, divides the storage device into separate individual partitions. However, APFS gives you the flexibility to just create a new volume in the same partition instead of creating more partitions.

If you're partitioning your internal storage because you want to install Windows on Intel-based Mac computers, use Boot Camp Assistant. See the Boot Camp Assistant User Guide at support.apple.com/guide/bootcamp-assistant/ for more information.

Volumes

A volume is a storage area inside a partition. A volume must be formatted with a file system before you can store a file on it.

macOS supports many kinds of volume formats. The next section explores the various kinds of volumes macOS supports, followed by more details about APFS volumes.

Volume Formats

The volume format defines how the files and folders are saved. To maintain compatibility with other operating systems and provide advanced features for later-model Mac computers, macOS supports a variety of storage volume formats.

Volume formats supported as read/write in macOS include:

▶ APFS—When you upgrade to or install macOS Mojave or later on your Mac startup disk, it is automatically converted to APFS. APFS supports advanced features required by macOS, including Unicode filenames, rich metadata, POSIX (Portable Operating System Interface) permissions, access control lists, aliases, UNIX-style hard links and soft links, and a feature introduced in macOS Catalina, firm links.

▶ APFS (Encrypted)—This APFS format option adds full volume encryption. This technology supports FileVault system volume encryption. Lesson 12, "Manage FileVault," covers this topic in greater detail.

▶ APFS (Case-sensitive)—This APFS format option adds case sensitivity to APFS. In its default state, APFS is case-preserving but case-insensitive. For example, case-insensitive APFS won't recognize "Makefile" and "makefile" as different file-names. Case sensitivity is generally an issue only for volumes that need to support traditional UNIX clients, like those shared with the File Sharing service in Sharing preferences.

▶ APFS Case-sensitive, Encrypted)—This APFS format option adds case sensitivity and encryption to APFS.

▶ Mac OS Extended—The file system that came with macOS Sierra and earlier (also referred to as HFS Plus).

▶ Case-sensitive Mac OS Extended—This option adds case sensitivity to Mac OS Extended.

▶ Journaled or case-sensitive journaled Mac OS Extended—File-system journaling helps preserve volume structure integrity for Mac OS Extended volumes.

▶ Journaled and encrypted or case-sensitive, journaled, and encrypted Mac OS—This Mac OS Extended format option adds full volume encryption.

▶ File Allocation Table (FAT)—FAT is the legacy volume format used by Windows PCs and by many peripherals.

▶ Extended File Allocation Table (ExFAT)—Created specifically for large flash storage disks, ExFAT extends the legacy FAT architecture to support disks larger than 32 GB.

At least one volume format is supported as read-only in macOS:

▶ New Technology File System (NTFS)—Recent versions of Windows use this as their default native volume format. Boot Camp supports running Windows 10 or newer from an NTFS volume, but macOS can't write to or start up from it. Disk Utility doesn't support the creation of NTFS volumes.

APFS

APFS features enhanced data performance, security, and reliability and provides a foundation for future storage innovations. An advanced architecture optimized for today's massive storage technologies, APFS makes common operations such as copying files and folders instantaneous, helps protect data from power outages and system crashes, and keeps files safe and secure with native encryption. macOS also maintains complete read-and-write compatibility with previously formatted MacOS Extended drives and data and is designed to accommodate future advancements in storage technology.

Earlier parts of this lesson explained that a storage device contains at least one partition, which contains at least one volume. APFS has a couple of extra layers between partition and volume, which provide more flexibility.

APFS is a system of virtual volumes, in which an APFS *container* holds one or more APFS volumes.

APFS volumes share storage space within their container. For most purposes, you don't need to create multiple APFS volumes per container.

macOS Catalina introduced two new APFS volume roles:

▶ APFS System—for the operating system

▶ APFS Data—for user data

macOS Catalina also introduced the concept of the APFS volume group. An APFS volume group is a collection of APFS volumes in the same APFS container that are associated with one another.

The new APFS roles and the APFS volume group concepts enable macOS to separate operating system files from user files. The volumes are separated for security, backup, and software update. For the most part, the two volumes appear as a single volume. For example, when you open a new Finder window and choose Go > Computer, only one disk is displayed (named Macintosh HD by default).

macOS Big Sur introduces the concept of a signed system volume (SSV). The SSV adds cryptographic validation of the system volume. In macOS Big Sur, the kernel rejects any data in the SSV that doesn't have a valid cryptographic signature from Apple. This protection helps prevent anything, whether malicious or unintentional, from tampering with any code that's part of macOS.

MORE INFO ▸ You can find more information about SSV in the article "Protecting data at multiple layers," at developer.apple.com/news/?id=3xpv8r2m.

In macOS Big Sur, the SSV uses an APFS snapshot, which is a read-only copy of the base read-only APFS System volume. This makes updating macOS more reliable and safer. If you perform a macOS update and something prevents the update from completing, you can restore the old system version without reinstalling macOS.

For the most part, the separation of the SSV and the APFS Data volume is transparent. However, when you open Disk Utility and choose View > Show Only Volumes (the default setting), two volumes are displayed:

▸   The SSV, an APFS snapshot of the APFS System volume, displayed as Macintosh HD

▸   The APFS Data volume, which might be named Macintosh HD - Data, or just Data.

Your volumes may have different names.

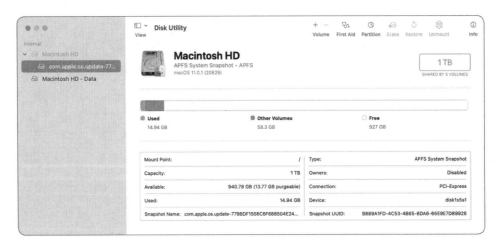

When you first open Disk Utility, the APFS snapshot is automatically selected. With the APFS snapshot selected, press Command-I to view more information about the volume. The mount point (where the APFS snapshot is mounted) is / just like in previous versions of macOS. But it is not writable.

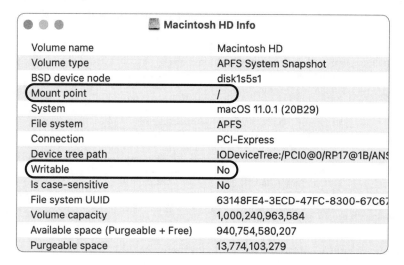

When you select your APFS Data volume, Disk Utility displays the disk with a special icon (it looks like a house), which indicates that this is the volume where macOS stores home folders. The mount point for this volume is /System/Volumes/Data.

To help macOS present an APFS volume group (that has an SSV and a Data volume) appear as a single volume, macOS Catalina introduced APFS firm links. Firm links allow forward and reverse traversal between parts of the two volumes.

The following figure from Terminal illustrates that the /System/Applications folder (from the read-only APFS System volume) contains most of the apps that come with macOS.

```
● ● ●                          johnny — -zsh — 80×14
johnny@Johnnys-MacBook-Pro ~ % ls /System/Applications
App Store.app           Image Capture.app      Preview.app
Automator.app           Launchpad.app          QuickTime Player.app
Books.app               Mail.app               Reminders.app
Calculator.app          Maps.app               Siri.app
Calendar.app            Messages.app           Stickies.app
Chess.app               Mission Control.app    Stocks.app
Contacts.app            Music.app              System Preferences.app
Dictionary.app          News.app               TV.app
FaceTime.app            Notes.app              TextEdit.app
FindMy.app              Photo Booth.app        Time Machine.app
Font Book.app           Photos.app             Utilities
Home.app                Podcasts.app           VoiceMemos.app
johnny@Johnnys-MacBook-Pro ~ % ▌
```

And the /System/Volumes/Data/Applications folder (from the writable APFS Data volume) has other apps, like Safari, apps from the App Store, and apps installed after they were downloaded from the developer.

```
● ● ●                          johnny — -zsh — 80×8
johnny@Johnnys-MacBook-Pro ~ % ls /System/Volumes/Data/Applications
Cisco Webex Meetings.app        Safari.app
GarageBand.app                  Utilities
Keynote.app                     Webex Teams.app
Numbers.app                     Xcode.app
Pages.app                       iMovie.app
Push Diagnostics.app
johnny@Johnnys-MacBook-Pro ~ % ▌
```

And in the Finder, when you choose Go > Applications, the Finder displays the combined contents of both volume's Applications folders.

For a Mac startup disk running macOS Big Sur, its APFS container has at least six volumes. All six APFS volumes share the space of the APFS container. The System volume and the Data volume appear as a single disk to the user. Here are the six APFS volumes:

▶ System volume—This read-only volume is named Macintosh HD on a new Mac that comes with macOS Big Sur and contains system files. It is not mounted.

▶ Signed System Volume Snapshot—This APFS snapshot of the System volume is mounted at /.

▶ Data volume—This read-and-write volume contains files that change, including those in the Users folder. This volume is often named Macintosh HD - Data. This guide uses the name Macintosh HD - Data for examples and illustration. However, the volume might be named Data, such as on a new Mac that comes with macOS Big Sur, or a Mac with Apple silicon that you restored with Apple Configurator 2.

▶ Preboot volume—This hidden volume contains data needed for booting each of the system volumes in the container. Only one Preboot volume per APFS container is allowed. The Preboot volume contains one folder per System volume in the container.

▶ Recovery volume—This hidden volume contains macOS Recovery. Only one Recovery volume per APFS container is allowed. The Recovery volume contains one folder per System volume in the container. When you start up from this volume, you are using recoveryOS.

▶ VM volume—The virtual memory (VM) volume is created for the first time after a Mac starts up.

The following figure illustrates the relationships between the various elements. It is not to scale.

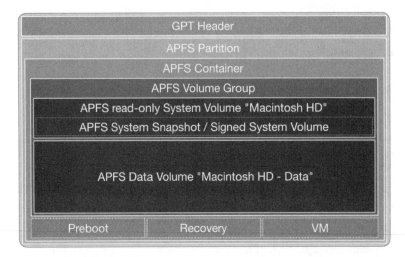

In addition to this APFS container, a Mac with Apple silicon includes a separate and hidden container called System Recovery. It contains a minimal macOS environment that you can use to reinstall macOS and macOS Recovery. The following figure is not to scale.

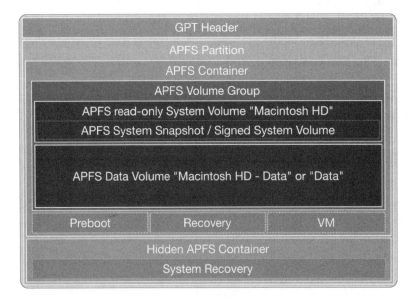

Tools like Disk Utility don't display information about hidden APFS volumes because they are automatically created and maintained, and you won't ever need to edit those volumes.

To obtain a list of APFS containers and volumes, open Terminal and enter the diskutil APFS list command. The information for your Mac may differ significantly from what is displayed in the following figure, but the volume names and mount points should be similar.

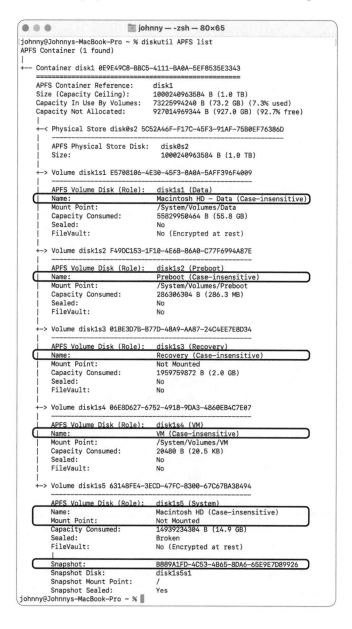

And to obtain information about the items in the APFS volume group, open Terminal and enter the diskutil APFS listVolumeGroups command.

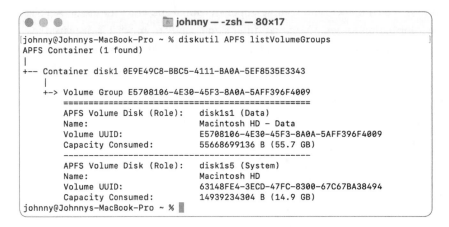

You can find out more about APFS in the following resources:

▶ "What's New in Apple File Systems," available at developer.apple.com/videos/play/ wwdc2019/710/

▶ The Apple Developer article "About Apple File System," at developer.apple.com/ documentation/foundation/file_system/about_apple_file_system

Add an APFS Volume

You can add an APFS volume to an existing APFS container with Disk Utility. Just select an existing APFS volume or APFS container, click Add Volume (+) in the toolbar, then enter a name for the new volume.

By default, APFS volumes don't have a fixed size, but share the space of the APFS container with other volumes in that container. But you can click Size Options to specify an

optional reserve size to ensure that amount of storage remains available for this new volume, no matter how much storage space other volumes use. And you can specify a quota size, which limits the total amount of space the volume can allocate and use.

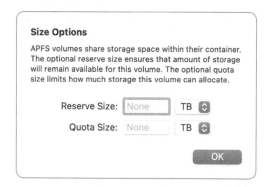

If you want to add a new APFS container, you have to first create a new partition; when you choose APFS as the format for the new partition, macOS automatically creates an APFS container in the new partition. Select a disk, container, or volume, then click Partition in the toolbar.

Disk Utility displays a dialog to inform you that adding and deleting APFS volumes is faster and simpler than editing a partition map. Place your pointer over the message and scroll to reveal the rest of the message. If you are sure that you want to add a partition, click Partition. Adding a new partition is not recommended and is outside the scope of this guide.

One use for creating a new volume is for software testing. If you are a member of the Apple Beta Software Program or the Software Customer Seeding program and you want to test a prerelease version of macOS without replacing your current system software, you can install the prerelease system software on a volume that you create for that purpose. See Apple Support article HT208891, "Installing macOS on a separate APFS volume," for more information.

APFS Compatibility

Storage devices formatted as Mac OS Extended can be read from and written to by Mac computers.

Storage devices formatted as APFS can be read from and written to by:

▶ Other Mac computers that started from a storage device formatted as APFS

▶ Mac computers that started from a storage device formatted as Mac OS Extended if you are using macOS High Sierra or newer

APFS and Boot Camp

Boot Camp, a utility that comes with your Intel-based Mac and lets you switch between macOS and Windows, doesn't read from or write to APFS-formatted volumes.

APFS and File Sharing

Volumes formatted as APFS can't offer share points over the network using Apple Filing Protocol (AFP).

APFS supports Server Message Block (SMB) and Network File System (NFS), with the option to enforce only SMB-encrypted share points.

Fusion Drive

Fusion Drive combines the performance of flash storage with the capacity of a hard drive.

Presented as a single volume on your Mac, Fusion Drive moves files that you use frequently to flash storage so that you can access them faster. Fusion Drive moves files that you don't use a lot to a high-capacity hard disk. As a result, you enjoy shorter startup times and—as the system learns how you work—you can open apps and files faster.

Reference 11.2
Mount, Unmount, and Eject Disks

When you mount a volume, your Mac establishes a logical connection to that volume. Users don't normally need to think about this because a Mac automatically mounts any connected volume. When you plug in a disk, the disk's volumes automatically appear in the Finder and Disk Utility. You need to enter a password to unlock encrypted volumes.

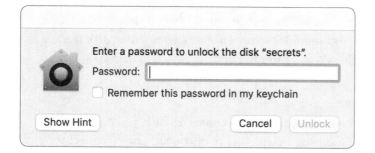

Ensuring that users properly unmount and eject volumes is critical to maintaining data integrity. The term *unmount* refers to the process of having the Mac cleanly disconnect from a disk's volumes, whereas the term *eject* refers to the process of having the Mac additionally disconnect electronically from the hardware disk or media. When you choose to eject a disk from the Finder, the Mac unmounts the volumes first and then ejects the disk.

Eject Disks or Volumes

There are several ways to unmount and eject a disk or volume from the Finder:

▶ In the Finder, select the disk or volume you want to unmount and eject, and choose File > Eject.

▶ In the Finder, drag the disk or volume icon to the Trash icon in the Dock. The Trash icon changes to an Eject icon, indicating the appropriate action.

▶ In the Finder sidebar, click the small Eject button next to the disk or volume you want to unmount and eject.

▶ In the Finder, select the disk or volume you want to unmount and eject, then press Command-E.

▶ In the Finder, select the disk or volume you want to unmount and eject, Control-click to reveal the shortcut menu, then choose Eject "*diskname*."

▶ In a Finder window, select the disk or volume you want to unmount and eject, click the Action button in the Finder window toolbar (it looks like a circle with three dots), and choose Eject "*diskname*".

When you use the Finder to unmount and eject a single volume that is part of a disk with several mounted volumes, macOS displays a warning dialog giving you the choice to unmount and eject all the volumes on the disk or just the one you originally selected. To eject all volumes of a disk, select one of the volumes in the Finder, then press Option-Command-E or press and hold the Option key and choose File > Eject *number of volumes* Volumes. You shouldn't experience problems with a disk if some volumes are mounted and others remain unmounted.

Remount Volumes

If you're using the Finder to remount a volume on a connected disk, you must first unmount and eject remaining volumes, then physically disconnect and reconnect the disk. Alternatively, you can open Disk Utility to manually mount and unmount volumes without physically disconnecting and reconnecting the disk.

In the following screenshot of Disk Utility, several volumes are shown. The "secrets" volume appears in dimmed text because it's physically connected to the Mac but isn't mounted. Other external volumes are mounted, so macOS displays an Eject button near each volume's name.

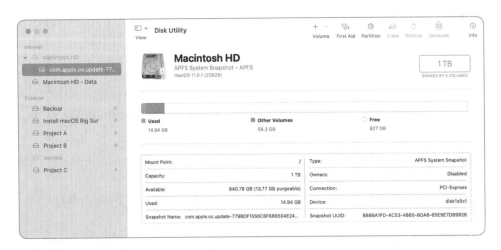

To mount an unmounted volume on a connected disk, select the volume's dimmed name and then click the Mount button in the toolbar. The volume immediately mounts and appears in the Finder, and its name is undimmed in Disk Utility.

Eject In-Use Volumes

If you remove a volume that contains a file that's still in use, you might corrupt data if an app or process tries to write to the file. The Finder won't allow you to eject a volume with in-use files, but it might try to help you eject the volume. If the app or process using the volume belongs to your account, the Finder displays the following dialog.

If this dialog appears, quit the app and try to eject the volume again.

If you don't own the app or process that is using the volume, the Finder asks if you want to attempt to eject the volume by force. To do so, you must click the Force Eject button twice.

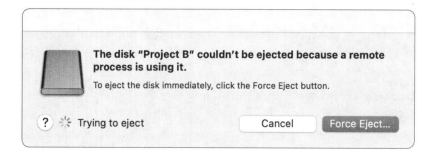

After you click Force Eject, the Finder tries to quit the app or process and eject the volume. If it succeeds, a dialog notifies you. If the volume still doesn't eject and the Finder doesn't tell you which app is still running, log out and log in again or restart your Mac.

When Terminal is open and your current working folder is on a volume—even if no process is active—you can't eject the volume.

> **NOTE ▶** You can use commands such as **fs_usage** or **lsof** in the command-line interface (CLI) to discover which process is using the volume. Consult the man page for those commands for more information.

Reference 11.3
Inspect File-System Components

If you plan to manage or troubleshoot the Mac file system, become familiar with its current configuration. You can access a graphical overview of the Mac storage from the Storage pane of the About This Mac window, which you can open from the Apple menu.

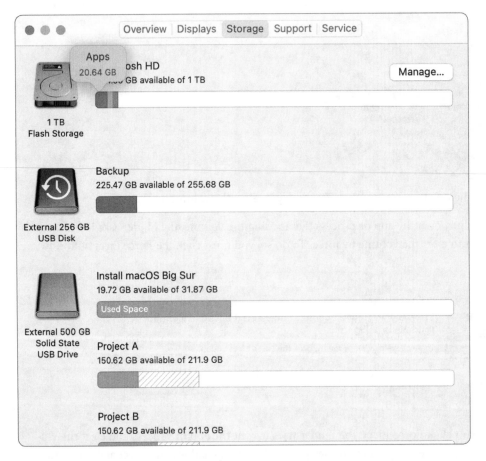

You can find out more about Purgeable items and storage optimization features (accessed with the Manage button in the About This Mac dialog) in Lesson 19, "Manage Files."

For a more detailed examination of the storage systems, use Disk Utility and System Information. These tools enable you to inspect the availability and status of storage hardware.

Examine Storage with Disk Utility

Use Disk Utility as your primary storage management tool in macOS. When you open Disk Utility, it scans the file system for attached devices and volumes.

By default, Disk Utility displays volumes. To view information about the physical disk, click View in the upper-left corner, then choose Show All Devices.

When you select Show All Devices, macOS lists items in this hierarchical order:

1. Storage hardware (disk)
2. APFS containers and non-APFS volumes in partitions in the disk
3. APFS volumes in APFS containers

When you select any item in Disk Utility, information about the item, including its utilization, formatting, and connection information, is displayed.

Select a disk name to view information about a physical disk. A disk's name is a combination of the manufacturer and model name. To identify a hardware failure, view a disk's S.M.A.R.T. (self-monitoring, analysis, and reporting technology) status. S.M.A.R.T. can determine whether a disk has an internal hardware failure. Many external disks don't support S.M.A.R.T.

Select an APFS container to view information about that container, such as information about its APFS volumes. The container name is automatically generated.

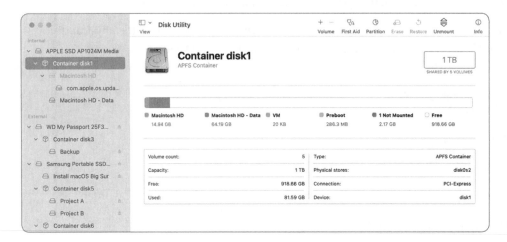

Select an APFS volume to view information about that volume. Volume names are set when the volume is formatted, but you can change them. The following figure illustrates that two APFS volumes, Project A and Project B, share space in the APFS container (which is labeled Container disk5). Disk Utility displays the amount of space that Project A uses, the amount of space that other volumes (in this case, Project B) use, and the amount of free space in the APFS container.

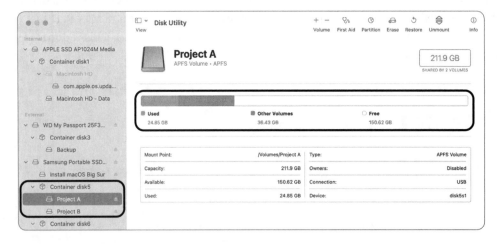

To gather detailed information about a disk or volume in Disk Utility, select the item from the column on the left and click the Info button in the toolbar.

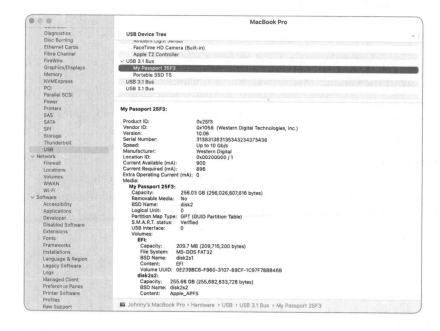

Project B Info

Volume name	Project B
Volume type	APFS Volume
BSD device node	disk5s2
Mount point	/Volumes/Project B
File system	APFS
Connection	USB
Device tree path	IODeviceTree:/PCI0@0/PEG1@1,1/UP
Writable	Yes
Is case-sensitive	No
File system UUID	1BF36EAA-34F0-487C-9E0E-6C1C1
Volume capacity	211,898,105,856
Available space (Purgeable + Free)	150,617,051,200
Purgeable space	1,118,272
Free space	150,615,932,928

Examine Storage with System Information

You may want to double-check a disk's status using System Information. For example, a disk might fail and won't appear in the Disk Utility list.

To inspect physical storage devices (disks), open System Information and select one of the storage interfaces. If a physical device doesn't appear in System Information, that means it's not available to your Mac in its current state and you should troubleshoot the disk hardware. Tighten loose connections. Replace bad cables and hardware (such as the disk enclosure).

The Storage section shows currently mounted volumes.

Reference 11.4
Manage File Systems

In the Finder, you can rename any volume without having to reformat or erase its content. Select the volume, press Return, edit the name, then press Return to stop editing the name. Or use any of these other methods:

► From the Finder sidebar, Control-click to rename it.

► In the Finder, Control-click the volume and choose Rename.

► In the Finder, select the volume, then choose File > Rename.

In this section, you explore how you can use Disk Utility to modify disks and volumes.

Format Unreadable Disks

Many new storage devices are formatted for Windows. For the most part, you can use Windows-formatted disks on the Mac without reformatting. If you want to install macOS on a disk, or you have a new disk that is completely blank, you have to erase and format (or initialize) the disk.

If you attach an unformatted or unreadable disk, macOS asks you to eject, ignore, or initialize. If you click Initialize, Disk Utility opens.

Erase a Disk or Volume

When you erase a disk, container, or volume in Disk Utility, the storage is formatted (initialized). When Show All Devices is selected, select the disk, container, or volume you want to erase and click Erase in the toolbar.

When you erase a disk, Disk Utility creates a new volume format and partition scheme. Disk Utility defaults to the APFS format and the GUID Partition Map scheme. To select a different format or scheme, first choose the scheme you want from the Scheme menu, then make a choice from the Format menu (the options on the Format menu change depending on what is chosen in the Scheme menu).

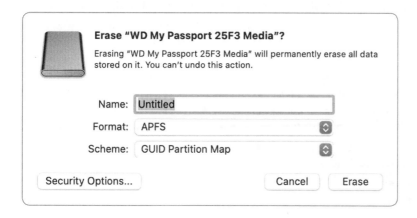

When you erase a volume (as opposed to a disk), Disk Utility creates a new volume format. If the volume you erase is an APFS volume, the Format menu offers APFS-related formats.

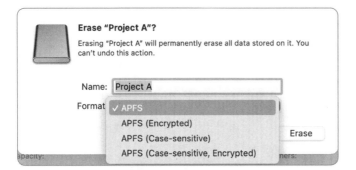

If you select an encrypted APFS volume format, a dialog appears that enables you to set the encrypted volume's password. If you lose the password, you won't be able to recover data from the encrypted volume.

If the volume you erase has a Mac OS Extended format, you have options for the new volume format.

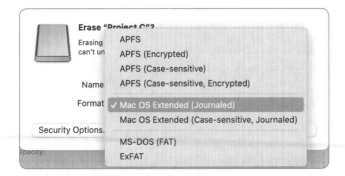

When you erase a selected volume, no other volumes on the disk are affected. Further, you can't change the disk partition scheme—that would affect all volumes on the disk.

When you erase and reformat storage, you destroy existing volume formatting (reformatting a disk erases its contents). The default Disk Utility erase process doesn't erase files from an unencrypted disk. Disk Utility creates new empty volumes by replacing the file and folder structures. The old data files remain on the disk, and you can recover them using third-party tools.

To prevent the erased files from being recovered from nonencrypted disks, when you erase a disk click Security Options, use the slider to choose how many times to write over the erased data, click OK, and click Erase.

> **NOTE ▶** Secure erase options are available in Disk Utility only for HDD (hard disk drive) and some flash storage.

The best way to prevent erased files from being recovered is to store files on encrypted storage devices only, because when you erase an encrypted storage device, you remove the key or keys that allow the files to be decrypted. For more security, consider doing the following:

▶ Turning on FileVault when you start using your Mac with SSD or all-flash storage

▶ Encrypting other storage devices before you start using them

Erase Files in Terminal

When you open Terminal (the macOS CLI) and enter the rm command to remove files, macOS marks the deleted files as free space and leaves the files intact until they are written over by another action. You can still access these files with third-party tools. If security is a concern, consider storing data on encrypted volumes.

Encrypt an External Disk

You can convert an existing APFS volume to an encrypted volume using the Finder. It's best to encrypt a volume before saving any sensitive data to it. To encrypt the APFS Data volume portion of your startup disk, turn on FileVault. Lesson 12 covers FileVault in greater detail.

To encrypt any other APFS volume in the Finder, Control-click the volume you want to encrypt, and from the shortcut menu choose Encrypt *volumename*, where *volumename* is the name of the volume you selected.

The Finder asks you to set a password and a password hint for the encrypted disk. You must set a password hint.

> **You must create a password. Finder will use this password to encrypt "Project B".**
>
> Warning: If you forget this password, you won't be able to retrieve any data from "Project B". This operation cannot be canceled.
>
> For help creating a good password, click the key.
>
> Encryption password: [   ] 🔑
>
> Verify password: [   ]
>
> Password hint: [Required   ]
>
> (?)   Cancel   Encrypt Disk

You can continue to use a disk while macOS encrypts its contents in the background. When you attempt to connect an encrypted disk, you're asked for the disk password, unless you store the password in your keychain. Using keychains is covered in Lesson 9, "Manage Security and Privacy."

Reference 11.5
Troubleshoot File Systems

Bad hardware and media cause most file-system failures.

First Steps

If you have a storage device (disk) with a problem, try these steps:

1   Verify hardware connectivity from your Mac to the problematic storage device.

2   If the problematic storage is an external storage device, use the methods described in Reference 11.3, "Inspect File-System Components," to verify storage hardware functionality.

3   If the problem involves the system disk, try to start up from macOS Recovery.

► Start your Mac in macOS Recovery (use the procedure covered in Lesson 5, "Use macOS Recovery.")

▶ From macOS Recovery, open Disk Utility to inspect and possibly repair the system disk.

▶ If the default macOS Recovery system doesn't work, use the methods detailed in Lesson 5.

If you think that a catastrophic hardware failure is the problem, there isn't anything you can do from a software perspective to repair the Mac. A commercial data recovery service may be able to recover your data.

If you're experiencing file-system issues but the storage hardware seems to function, you may be experiencing partial hardware failure or file-system corruption. In these cases, you can use the built-in utilities in macOS to repair the volumes or recover data.

Disk Utility First Aid

To access data on a disk, the file system must read the partition scheme and volume directory structure to find the appropriate bits that make up the requested item or items. The file system uses the partition scheme to define the space where volumes exist. It uses the volume directory structure to catalog where files and folders exist. Damage to the partition scheme or volume directory structure could cause serious problems, including data loss.

Before a disk is mounted, a Mac performs a quick consistency check to verify the disk's partition scheme and volume directory structure. The Mac also quickly scans the startup disk during startup. If the Mac is unable to mount a disk or its volumes, or you have problems accessing a disk's content, use Disk Utility First Aid to verify and repair the partition scheme or volume directory structures.

To use the First Aid feature in Disk Utility, verify that the disk you want to repair is attached to the Mac, then open Disk Utility. Select the disk or volume you want to inspect or repair from the column on the left, then click the First Aid button in the toolbar.

When you select a disk, you indicate that you want to repair its partition scheme. When you select a volume, you indicate that you want to repair its directory structure. Start with a disk's partition scheme, then move to its volumes to resolve problems.

First Aid might take a few minutes to complete because it runs until it finds no problems. During this time, Disk Utility shows a progress indicator and log entries in the history area. Click the Show Details disclosure triangle to obtain more detail in the history log.

If First Aid doesn't find any problems, a green checkmark appears. If First Aid finds problems, it describes them in bright red text in the log and attempts to repair them.

Target Disk Mode

Target disk mode enables you to share files from one Intel-based Mac computer to another Mac that's connected to it.

You can use the following ports for target disk mode:

- Thunderbolt 3 (USB-C) ⚡—Available on iMac Pro, iMac models from 2017, Mac mini (2018), MacBook Pro models from 2016 or later, MacBook Air (Retina, 13-inch, 2018) or later, and Mac Pro (2019)
- USB-C ψ—Available on MacBook models from 2015 or later
- Thunderbolt 2 ⚡

With target disk mode, one Mac appears as an external disk on the other Mac, enabling you to browse and copy files. Use target disk mode when you need high transfer speeds or if the display on one of your Mac computers isn't working and you need to get files from it.

MacBook (12-inch, Retina, Early 2015) or later supports USB target disk mode using the following USB-C cables to transfer data:

- USB 3.0 or USB 3.1 USB-C Cable (USB-C to USB-C)—Use this cable to share files between a Mac with a USB-C port and a MacBook with a USB-C port.
- USB 3.0 or USB 3.1 USB-A to USB-C Cable—Use this cable to share files between a Mac with USB-A port(s) and a MacBook with a USB-C port—for example, the mophie USB-A Cable with USB-C Connector.

You can use target disk mode to transfer data between Mac computers with Thunderbolt 3 and other Mac computers:

- To use target disk mode between a Mac with Thunderbolt 3 (USB-C) and another Mac computer's Thunderbolt 3 (USB-C) port, connect the two Mac computers with a Thunderbolt 3 (USB-C) cable such as the Apple Thunderbolt 3 (USB-C) Cable (www.apple.com/shop/product/MQ4H2AM/A/thunderbolt-3-usb).
- To use target disk mode between a Mac with Thunderbolt 3 and another Mac with Thunderbolt 2, connect a Thunderbolt 3 (USB-C) to Thunderbolt 2 Adapter to your Mac, then use a Thunderbolt 2 cable to connect the adapter to the other Mac.

Target disk mode doesn't support the following cables:

- Apple USB-C Charge Cable

- USB-A to USB-A cable
- Mini DisplayPort cable |▢|

For more information, see Apple Support article HT207443, "Adapters for the Thunderbolt 3 or USB-C port on your Mac or iPad Pro."

Because target disk mode is built into Intel-based Mac computers, you can use it even if the installed macOS volume is corrupted. Any user can enable target disk mode on a running Mac by clicking the Target Disk Mode button in Startup Disk preferences if it's available.

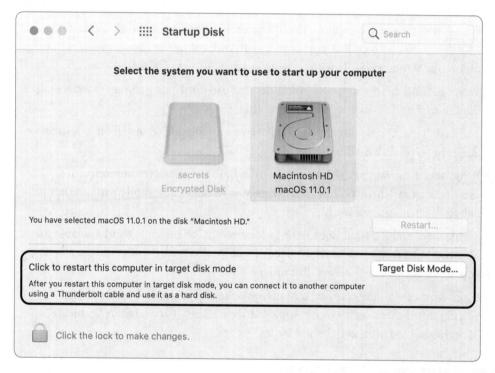

Alternatively, assuming your Intel-based Mac doesn't have a firmware password, any user can engage target disk mode during startup by pressing and holding the T key while turning on the Mac.

After target disk mode is engaged, USB or Thunderbolt symbols appear on the screen. Plug the targeted Mac into another Mac using an appropriate USB-C cable or a Thunderbolt cable.

After you connect an Intel-based Mac in target disk mode to your Mac, the internal storage of the Mac in target disk mode is connected to your Mac as if you had plugged in a normal external disk. You'll be asked to authenticate if the Intel-based Mac in target disk mode has FileVault turned on, and if the Intel-based Mac in target disk mode has the Apple T2 Security chip.

At this point, you can repair or migrate data from the mounted targeted Mac computer's internal volumes.

As useful as target disk mode is, be aware of these caveats:

▶   Mac computers with Apple silicon use Mac Sharing Mode instead of target disk mode.

▶   USB-A ports on Mac computers don't support starting in target disk mode. Older Mac computers with USB-A ports can mount disks of newer Mac computers in target disk mode through USB-C with an appropriate USB-C to USB-A adapter.

▶   Target disk mode isn't supported on disks that use third-party storage interfaces, like those found on PCI Express expansion cards.

▶   The Install macOS Big Sur app won't allow you to upgrade or install on a destination that is in target disk mode.

▶   If you set a firmware password on your Intel-based Mac, covered in Reference 5.3, "Secure Startup," then you can't start your Mac in target disk mode without first providing the firmware password.

▶   Secure Boot and External Boot settings (covered in Reference 5.3 and available for Mac computers with the Apple T2 Security Chip) do not prevent you from starting your Intel-based Mac in target disk mode.

▶   Some hardware failures prevent a Mac from entering target disk mode. If you suspect this is the case, try using Apple Hardware Test. It's covered in Lesson 28, "Troubleshoot Startup and System Issues."

Recover Data from a Nonstarting System

If your Intel-based Mac won't start up from its internal system disk, you can still recover data from the disk if it functions with target disk mode. Use this mode to access the internal system disk and transfer your data to another working Mac.

First, turn on or restart the problematic Intel-based Mac while pressing and holding the T key to engage target disk mode. Then connect the Mac to another, fully functioning Mac using an appropriate cable. If the volume in the problem Mac appears in the Finder, try to repair the disk and volumes with Disk Utility First Aid, as detailed earlier in this lesson.

If your Mac doesn't support, or can't engage, target disk mode, visit an Apple Authorized Service Provider.

You could also try to remove the disk from the troubled Mac and attach it to a fully functional Mac.

After you complete repairs, try one of these options to recover your data:

▶ Use the Finder to copy data from the problem Mac to an external storage device that is attached to the functioning Mac.

▶ Use Disk Utility on the functioning Mac to create a disk image archive of the problem Mac computer's system volume. Creating disk images is covered in Lesson 14, "Use Hidden Items, Shortcuts, and File Archives."

▶ Use Migration Assistant to transfer data to the functioning Mac as detailed in Lesson 8, "Manage User Home Folders."

▶ After you transfer the data, use Disk Utility to reformat macOS. Lesson 2, "Update, Upgrade, or Reinstall macOS," covers this topic in greater detail.

Depending on the amount of corruption to the problem system disk, you may not be able to use Disk Utility or Migration Assistant. If so, try to manually copy the data.

For more information, see the Disk Utility User Guide at support.apple.com/guide/disk-utility.

Exercise 11.1
View Disk and Volume Information

> **Prerequisite**
>
> ▶ You must have created the Local Administrator account (Exercise 3.1, "Configure a Mac for Exercises").

In this exercise, you view information that pertains to your Mac computer's internal storage. You'll see multiple ways to view information about the storage in your Mac. You'll also see the internal storage device and the volumes that the storage contains.

View Storage Information with About This Mac

1 Log in as Local Administrator.

2 Choose Apple menu > About This Mac.

3 Click Storage.

This pane shows the volumes that are mounted on your Mac. It also shows used and available space. Hover your pointer over the colored sections of the bar to see what type of content is on the volume.

NOTE ▶ It may take several minutes for System Information to analyze the content on your Mac.

4 Click Manage.

System Information opens and shows options for reducing storage use. Read Reference 19.5, "Optimize Local Storage," for more information.

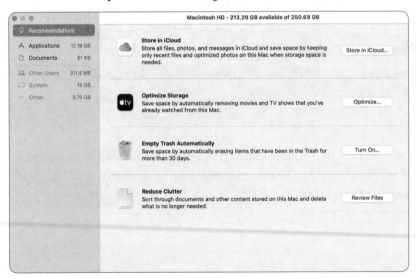

5   Click through the other items in the sidebar.

These items show details about different content. You're able to view the size of Other Users and System, but you are unable to view or alter the contents.

6   Quit System Information.

View Disk Information with Disk Utility

1   Choose Go > Utilities or press Shift-Command-U to navigate to the Utilities folder. Disk Utility is in this folder.

2   Open Disk Utility and make sure Show Only Volumes is chosen from the View menu on the toolbar.

In your day-to-day use of macOS Big Sur, you will notice a unified volume; however, in Disk Utility you will see two volumes.

You also notice an APFS System Snapshot, with the name starting with com.apple.os.update-*xxxxxx* (where xxxxxx is a 24 character-long unique identi-fier). This is the snapshot of the volume that your Mac is running from (typically Macintosh HD). For more information, see Reference 11.1, "File Systems."

3   In the sidebar, select your APFS System volume (named Macintosh HD in this exercise).

Observe that Macintosh HD is dimmed, and Disk Utility informs you that a System Snapshot is Mounted.

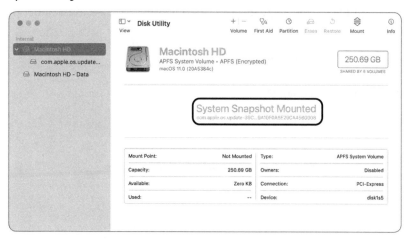

Disk Utility denotes with an icon which data each volume holds. Macintosh HD's snapshot holds operating system files (macOS icon). In this exercise, Macintosh HD - Data is the APFS Data volume that holds user data (house icon).

Macintosh HD
APFS System Snapshot · APFS (Encrypted)
macOS 11.0 (20A5384c)

Macintosh HD - Data
APFS Data Volume · APFS (Encrypted)
macOS 11.0 (20A5384c)

4   In the sidebar, select the volume snapshot that contains operating system files.

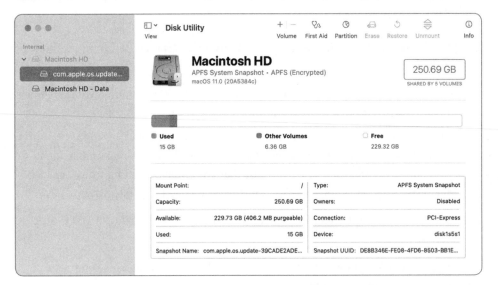

Information about the volume appears. The volume format is shown just under the volume name.

5   Check the amount of used space in the volume.

6   Click the Info button in the toolbar.

A window opens showing additional details about the volume. Notice that the volume type is an APFS System Snapshot. Scroll down to see all of the window contents.

🖥 Macintosh HD Info	
Volume name	Macintosh HD
Volume type	APFS System Snapshot
BSD device node	disk1s5s1
Mount point	/
System	macOS 11.0 (20A5384c)
File system	APFS (Encrypted)
Connection	PCI-Express
Device tree path	IODeviceTree:/PCI0@0/RP01@1C/AN;
Writable	No
Is case-sensitive	No
File system UUID	BE4440ED-DB49-4095-8625-6390
Volume capacity	250,685,575,168
Available space (Purgeable + Free)	229,719,056,870
Purgeable space	406,225,382

7   Close the Info window.

8   Repeat steps 3 through 6 for your volume that contains user data (in this exercise, Macintosh HD - Data).

9   In the toolbar, choose View > Show All Devices.

When you use this view, you see the storage device at the top, then the container, and finally any volumes that are in the container.

10 Select the entry for your internal storage device (generally the top item) in the sidebar.

Information about the device (including its total capacity and partition map type) appears near the bottom of the window.

11 Click the Info button in the toolbar.

The Media Info window opens. Because this window shows information about the entire disk, its contents are different from the volume Info window.

APPLE SSD AP0256N Media Info	
Volume type	Physical Device
BSD device node	disk0
Connection	PCI-Express
Device tree path	IODeviceTree:/PCI0@0/RP01@1C/AN!
Writable	No
Is case-sensitive	No
Volume capacity	251,000,193,024
Available space (Purgeable + Free)	0
Purgeable space	0
Free space	0
Used space	251,000,193,024
Owners enabled	No
Is encrypted	No
Can be verified	No

12 Close the Info window.

Exercise 11.2
Erase a Storage Device

> ### Prerequisites
>
> ▶ You must have created the Local Administrator account (Exercise 3.1, "Configure a Mac for Exercises").
>
> ▶ You must have an erasable external storage device, such as a flash disk.

In this exercise, you use Disk Utility to erase an external storage device using a new partition scheme. You use this device again in later exercises.

Use Disk Utility to Erase and Reformat a Device

Many external storage devices (for example, USB storage devices) are preformatted for Windows, using the Master Boot Record (MBR) partition scheme and the FAT32 volume format. For the best compatibility with macOS, reformat external storage devices to use the GUID Partition Map scheme and Mac OS Extended (Journaled) or the APFS volume format. Use the format that best meets your macOS backward compatibility needs.

1   If necessary, log in as Local Administrator.

2   Plug the external storage device into the appropriate port on your Mac.

    NOTE ▶ This exercise erases all information on the external disk. Don't perform this exercise with a disk that contains content you want to keep.

3   If necessary, open Disk Utility.

The Disk Utility sidebar lists internal and external storage devices separately.

4   In the sidebar, select the external storage device. Be sure to select the device, not the volume or volumes it contains.

5   In the toolbar, click Erase.

6   View the options in the Format and Scheme menus, choose GUID Partition Map from the Scheme menu, then choose APFS from the Format menu.

7   Name the disk **Backup**.

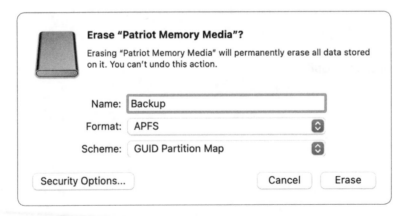

8   Click Erase.

9   Click the Show Details disclosure triangle to view the details.

When the details pane is open, the disclosure triangle's label changes to Hide Details.

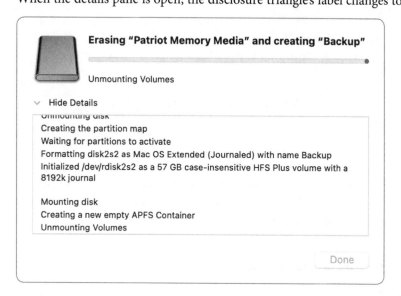

Erasing "Patriot Memory Media" and creating "Backup"

Unmounting Volumes

∨   Hide Details

Unmounting disk
Creating the partition map
Waiting for partitions to activate
Formatting disk2s2 as Mac OS Extended (Journaled) with name Backup
Initialized /dev/rdisk2s2 as a 57 GB case-insensitive HFS Plus volume with a 8192k journal

Mounting disk
Creating a new empty APFS Container
Unmounting Volumes

Done

10   When the reformatting is finished, click Done.

11   If a notification appears with a "Do you want to use the disk Backup to back up?" prompt, hover over it and click close (X).

12   Click the Eject button next to the new volume in the Disk Utility sidebar.

When the volume (in this case named Backup) ejects, the Finder no longer displays it on your desktop. It remains in the Disk Utility sidebar.

13   Unplug the external storage device from your Mac. This removes it from the Disk Utility sidebar.

14   Quit Disk Utility.

Exercise 11.3
Repair Volumes in Recovery Mode

> **Prerequisites**
>
> ▸ You must have created Local Administrator account (Exercise 3.1, "Configure a Mac for Exercises") and the Johnny Appleseed account (Exercise 7.1, "Create a Standard User Account").
>
> ▸ You must have enabled FileVault (Exercise 3.2, "Configure System Preferences").

In this exercise, you start your Mac in macOS Recovery and check its file structure. Use these techniques to repair a Mac that won't start up normally because of file-system damage. For more information, see Reference 11.5, "Troubleshoot File Systems."

Repair the Partition Table and Volume

1 Restart your Mac, then press and hold Command-R until the Apple logo appears.

2 If a language selection screen appears, select your preferred language, then click the right-arrow button to continue.

3 At the macOS Recovery screen, select Local Administrator, click Next, enter the password, then click Continue.

4 At the macOS Utilities screen, select Disk Utility, then click Continue.

5 In the toolbar, choose View > Show All Devices.

6 Select your Mac computer's internal storage device (generally the top entry in the sidebar).

7 Click the First Aid button in the toolbar.

8   In the confirmation dialog, click Run.

9   Click the Show Details disclosure triangle.

Disk Utility checks and, if necessary, repairs the volume(s).

10   When the process finishes, click Done.

11   Select the entry for the Macintosh HD volume, then click First Aid.

12   Click Run, then click the Show Details disclosure triangle.

13   When you are asked to enter a password to unlock the disk "Macintosh HD," select Local Administrator, then enter the password for the account.

Because Macintosh HD is encrypted, you need to unlock the disk before Disk Utility can check and repair it. Once unlocked, Disk Utility checks the file structure in the Macintosh HD volume and repairs it if necessary.

14   When the process finishes, click Done.

15   If you want to repeat this process, you can choose to check and, if necessary, repair the Macintosh HD - Data and Backup volumes.

16   Quit Disk Utility.

Lesson 12

Manage FileVault

In this lesson, you learn how FileVault protects data at rest and how to turn it on. You also learn how to recover a Mac protected with FileVault when all local users' passwords are lost.

Reference 12.1
FileVault Introduction

FileVault encrypts the built-in startup disk to protect your data.

> **NOTE ▶** When this reference mentions that FileVault encrypts your startup disk, that's a simplification, because in macOS Big Sur, the signed system volume (SSV) isn't encrypted, but it is cryptographically validated. Additionally, the SSV is read-only, doesn't contain any user data, and doesn't need to be encrypted. More precisely, FileVault encrypts the APFS Data volume portion of the built-in startup disk (by default named Macintosh HD - Data or Data).

If you use additional volumes, you should encrypt them too. Learn more about encrypting additional volumes in Lesson 11, "Manage File Systems and Storage."

FileVault on Mac Computers with Apple Silicon and Intel-based Mac Computers with the Apple T2 Security Chip

Mac computers with Apple silicon and Intel-based Mac computers with the Apple T2 Security Chip use their built-in hardware-accelerated Advanced Encryption Standard (AES) engine to encrypt data on the built-in storage for your Mac.

These Mac computers encrypt data by using 256-bit encryption keys that are tied to the chip's unique identifier. You'll need that specific chip to decrypt data stored on the built-in storage, and if the portion of the chip containing your encryption keys becomes damaged, you might need to restore the content of your built-in storage from a backup. This content includes apps, accounts, preferences, music, photos, movies, and files.

Always back up your content to a secure backup location so that you can restore it, if necessary. Go to Lesson 17, "Manage Time Machine," for more information on backing up your Mac.

If your Mac is a Mac with Apple silicon, or is an Intel-based Mac with the T2 chip, then the encrypted built-in storage in your Mac automatically mounts and decrypts when you turn on your Mac. You should turn on FileVault so that your Mac requires a password to decrypt your data.

FileVault on Intel-based Mac Computers without the T2 Chip

For Intel-based Mac computers without the T2 chip, FileVault encryption uses XTS-AES-128 encryption with a 256-bit key to help prevent unauthorized access to the information on your startup disk. FileVault performs the encryption at the file-system driver level of macOS. Most processes and apps run normally when the startup volume is encrypted.

For more details on FileVault encryption, go to the following pages:

- "Apple Platform Security," at support.apple.com/guide/security
- Apple Support article HT204837, "Use FileVault to encrypt the startup disk on your Mac"
- "Encrypt Mac data with FileVault," at support.apple.com/guide/mh11785
- "Volume encryption with FileVault in macOS," at support.apple.com/guide/security/sec4c6dc1b6e
- "Managing FileVault in macOS," at support.apple.com/guide/security/sec8447f5049

Login Window Behavior on a Mac with FileVault Turned On

When an Intel-based Mac starts up from an encrypted startup disk, it presents a login window, but macOS is not yet running. This login window displays all users that are enabled for FileVault. Select an account that is enabled for FileVault. Then enter your account password, which your Mac uses to unlock the protected system volume. After your Mac accesses the system volume, startup continues normally. And because you already authenticated to unlock encryption, you're logged directly in to your account.

Mac computers with Apple silicon have a unified login experience for a consistent look and feel regardless of FileVault status. Even if FileVault is turned on, a Mac computer with Apple silicon supports the following at the login window:

▶   Accelerated graphics

▶   Authentication with smart cards, including chip card interface device (CCID) and Personal Identity Verification (PIV) start cards

▶   VoiceOver for accessibility at the login window

▶   Displaying only fields for account name and password, or displaying all users that are enabled for FileVault

macOS Recovery Behavior on an Intel-based Mac with FileVault Turned On

When you attempt to start your Intel-based Mac in macOS Recovery and your Intel-based Mac has FileVault enabled, your Mac displays a window where you must select a user that you know the password for. Then you must provide the password for that user.

Reference 12.2
Turn On FileVault

As covered in Lesson 3, "Set Up and Configure macOS," if you provide your Apple ID during Setup Assistant, you are asked, "Would you like to use FileVault to encrypt the disk on your Mac?"

If you didn't turn on FileVault when asked by Setup Assistant, you can turn on FileVault at any time from Security & Privacy preferences. Click the lock button and authenticate as an administrator user, and then click Turn On FileVault.

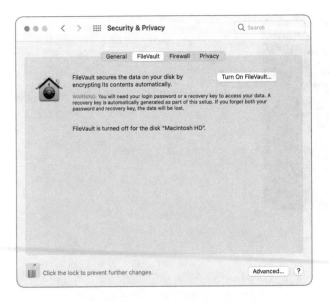

Configure FileVault Recovery

During FileVault setup, a dialog appears and offers you two ways to recover if the FileVault-enabled user passwords are lost.

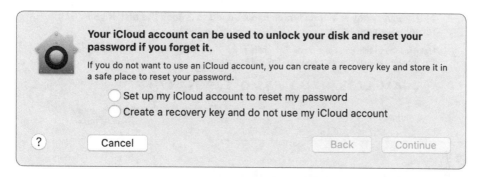

The first way to recover is to use your Apple ID to unlock the FileVault volume and reset your password. This generates a random FileVault recovery key and saves it to your iCloud account on Apple servers. Although your Mac doesn't display the recovery key, your Mac can retrieve the key from iCloud after you authenticate your Apple ID.

You must have internet access and sign in using an Apple ID for this to work.

You can configure only one user Apple ID for FileVault recovery. You can enable other users to log in to the FileVault-protected Mac, but they won't have access to the recovery key stored in iCloud.

A second way is to record the key that FileVault randomly generates. You must keep the key letters and numbers somewhere safe and not on your encrypted startup disk.

Use the key to unlock the FileVault-protected volume and reset a lost user password.

Make a copy of your recovery key and store it in a safe place. If you forget your password and lose your recovery key, you won't be able to access your startup disk. Apple can help you reset your password with your recovery key, but it can't provide your recovery key if you lose it.

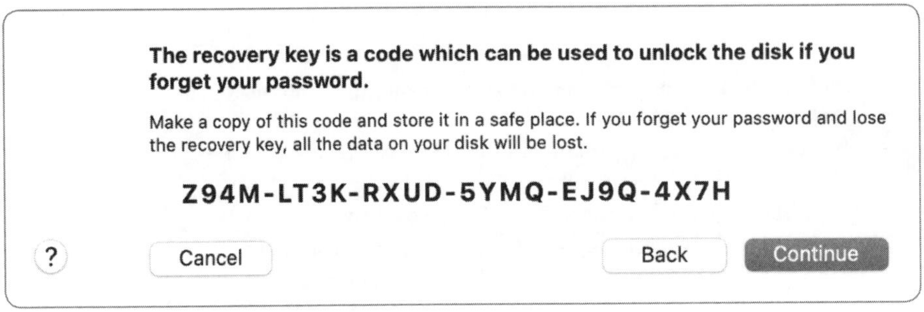

The recovery key is a code which can be used to unlock the disk if you forget your password.

Make a copy of this code and store it in a safe place. If you forget your password and lose the recovery key, all the data on your disk will be lost.

Z94M-LT3K-RXUD-5YMQ-EJ9Q-4X7H

(?)   Cancel   Back   Continue

Enable Additional Users for FileVault

If other users have accounts on your Mac, your Mac may display a message that users must type in their password before they can unlock the disk. For each user, click the Enable User button and enter the user's password. After you enable FileVault, when you create new user accounts, by default macOS creates them with the ability to unlock FileVault.

For more information about using Terminal to list, add, or remove users with the ability to unlock FileVault, and to obtain status about the current state of FileVault, consult the fdesetup man page.

Confirm FileVault Is On

After you turn on FileVault, the next time you restart your Mac the login window appears more quickly. Only FileVault-enabled users appear in the login window. After a FileVault-enabled user authenticates, startup continues until the user is automatically logged in to their account.

The Security & Privacy preferences FileVault pane displays the system volume encryption and estimated completion time. A Mac with Apple silicon or an Intel-based Mac with the T2 chip doesn't need to start the process of encrypting the startup disk contents; the startup disk is already encrypted. The following figure illustrates an encryption progress bar on an Intel-based Mac that does not have the T2 chip. For a Mac with Apple silicon or an Intel-based Mac with the T2 chip, no progress bar is displayed, as the process of turning on FileVault takes only a few moments.

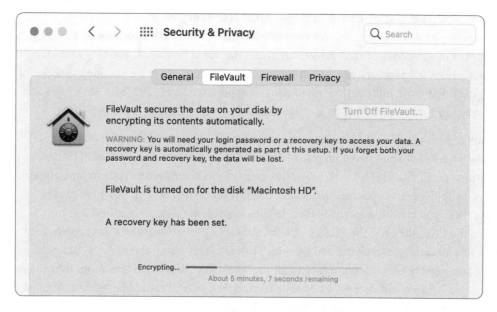

During encryption, you can close Security & Privacy preferences and use your Mac normally. No notification appears after encryption finishes.

To conserve battery power, portable Intel-based Mac computers that don't have the T2 chip might pause encryption when they aren't plugged in. Encryption continues after you connect the Mac to a power source.

You can turn off FileVault from Security & Privacy preferences. FileVault shows you the decryption progress. If you have a Mac with Apple silicon or an Intel-based Mac with the T2 chip, then your startup disk contents aren't decrypted when you turn FileVault off.

Use FileVault Recovery

If all FileVault-enabled account passwords are lost for a Mac protected with FileVault, you may still be able to unlock it. Go to Reference 10.2, "Reset Lost Passwords," for details on using your iCloud account or a FileVault recovery key to reset a local user account password and unlock your FileVault-encrypted system disk.

Recover a Lost FileVault Recovery Key

If you lose all FileVault-enabled account passwords and you are unable to access the FileVault recovery key, there is no way to recover the data on your startup volume.

Use an Institutional or Escrowed FileVault Recovery Key

You can use a FileVault institutional recovery key (IRK) to recover your users' FileVault-encrypted data when they can't remember their Mac login password. Your organization can set a FileVault recovery key, but the details about how to do it are outside the scope of this guide. For more information, go to Apple Support article HT202385, "Set a FileVault recovery key for computers in your organization."

If your organization's mobile device management (MDM) solution supports it, you can escrow a user's FileVault personal recovery key (PRK) when the user or the MDM solution turns on FileVault. This way, when the user returns their Mac to your organization without supplying their password, because FileVault is turned on and you have access to the PRK, you can still access the files on the data volume. Use your MDM solution to obtain the PRK, then use the PRK to change the user's password at the login screen; then you can access the data volume and the user's home folder. Using the PRK to change a user's password preserves the privacy of all the user's Keychain items. For more information, go to "Obtain and decrypt a personal recovery key with Profile Manager on Mac" at support.apple.com/guide/profile-manager/apda5f9c8c37.

Exercise 12.1
Restart a FileVault-Protected Mac

> **Prerequisites**

> ▸ You must have created the Local Administrator (Exercise 3.1, "Configure a Mac for Exercises") and Johnny Appleseed (Exercise 7.1, "Create a Standard User Account") accounts.

> ▸ You must have turned on FileVault (Exercise 3.2, "Configure System Preferences").

In Exercise 3.2, you turned on FileVault. In this exercise, you investigate how FileVault modifies the macOS startup process by requiring a user password.

Your Mac restarts and displays a FileVault access screen. This screen looks identical to the login screen, but macOS hasn't started yet. You must unlock the startup disk before your Mac can read system files.

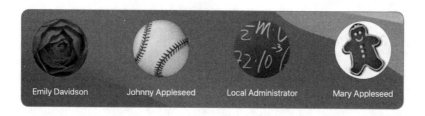

1 Restart your Mac.

2 On the FileVault access screen, click Johnny Appleseed.

3 Enter Johnny's password, then press Return.

As you have noticed throughout this guide, after restart you are presented with a FileVault access screen. After authentication, the macOS startup proceeds, and you are logged in as Johnny Appleseed. Since you authenticated as Johnny Appleseed at the FileVault access screen, macOS facilitates an automatic login for you.

4 Open Disk Utility, then select your current snapshot (starting with com.apple.os.update) from the sidebar.

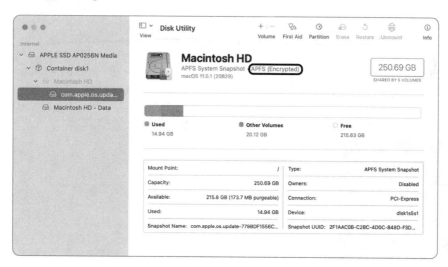

The format of the volume is APFS (Encrypted).

5 Quit Disk Utility.

Exercise 12.2
Use a FileVault Recovery Key

> **Prerequisites**
>
> ▸ You must have created the Local Administrator (Exercise 3.1, "Configure a Mac for Exercises") and Johnny Appleseed (Exercise 7.1, "Create a Standard User Account") accounts.
>
> ▸ You must have turned on FileVault (Exercise 3.2, "Configure System Preferences").

You can use the FileVault recovery key to reset user passwords at startup. In this exercise, you use the recovery key to reset Johnny Appleseed's password.

Reset Johnny Appleseed's Password

1   Restart your Mac.

2   At the FileVault access screen, click Johnny Appleseed.

3   Click the Help (?) button at the right of the Password field, or intentionally fail to authenticate with the correct password three times in rapid succession.

Your Mac displays an option to reset the password with a recovery key.

4   Click the arrow to start the reset process.

A Recovery Key field replaces the Password field.

5   Enter the recovery key you recorded earlier, then press Return.

The Recovery Key field will continue to shake and reset until you enter your recovery key correctly. If you are unable to enter your recovery key correctly, you can't perform the password reset portion of this exercise. In that case, click the left arrow, log in normally to an available account, and skip the rest of this exercise.

The Mac starts up. After the startup process finishes, a Reset Password dialog appears under the Johnny Appleseed account icon.

6   In the Reset Password dialog, type **vaultpw** in the "New password" and "Verify password" fields, then click Reset Password.

You are logged in to Johnny's account. Since his password was reset, Johnny's keychain was again archived, so saved items would have to follow the recovery method outlined in Lesson 10, "Manage Password Changes."

7   If you are asked to reenter the iCloud password, click Apple ID Preferences, then enter the password for your trainer-provided Apple ID.

Restore Johnny Appleseed's Original Password

To prepare for the remaining exercises, change the Johnny Appleseed password back.

1   Open Users & Groups in System Preferences.

2   Click Change Password.

3   Enter **vaultpw** as the old password, then enter the Johnny Appleseed account's original password (**Apple321!**) in the New Password and Verify fields.

4   Click Change Password.

Johnny's account password is now in sync with his login keychain password, as well as his Local Items/iCloud Keychain password.

5   If you receive a notification to confirm your Mac password, place your mouse over the notification, then click View.

6   If necessary, in Apple ID preferences, click Continue, then enter Johnny Appleseed's password (**Apple321!**).

This notification may take up to a few minutes to appear.

7   Quit System Preferences, then log out as Johnny Appleseed.

Manage Permissions and Sharing

You use file-system permissions to control macOS file and folder authorization. Used with user account identification and authorization, file-system permissions provide the Mac with a secure multiuser environment.

In this lesson, you learn how file-system ownership and permissions enable controlled access to local files and folders. You also explore macOS default permission settings that provide secure access to shared files. You then use the Finder to make ownership and permissions changes.

GOALS

► Describe file ownership and permissions

► Explore macOS default shared folders

► Securely manage file and folder access

Reference 13.1
File-System Permissions

macOS applies permission rules to every item on the system volume. The rules define file and folder access for standard, administrator, guest, and sharing users. Only users and processes with root account access can ignore file-system permission rules.

Inspect File-System Permissions

Any user can inspect file and folder permissions using the Finder Info window. There are several ways you can open the Finder Info window:

► Press Command-I.

► From the menu bar, choose File > Get Info.

► Control-click the selected item and choose Get Info from the shortcut menu.

► In a Finder window toolbar, click the Action menu (circle with three dots icon) and choose Get Info.

You can select multiple items to open multiple Info windows.

After you open an Info window, click the Sharing & Permissions disclosure triangle to inspect the item permissions. The permissions list is in two columns. The left column is a list of users or groups with access to this item. The right column shows the associated privilege assigned to each user or group. Modifying these settings is covered in Reference 13.3, "Manage Permissions."

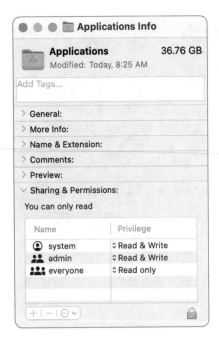

Permission Ownership

Every file and folder has owner, group, and "everyone" permission settings:

▶   Owner—By default, an item owner is the user who created the item or copied it to the Mac. Users usually own most of the items in their home folder. The root user usually owns system software items, including system resources and apps. In macOS, an administrator user can change item ownership and permissions regardless of who owns an item.

▶   Group—By default, the group permissions for an item are inherited from the folder it was created in. Most items belong to the staff (the primary group for local users), wheel (the primary group for the root system account), or admin groups. Group ownership enables users other than the owner access to an item. For instance, even though root owns the Applications folder, the group is set to admin so that administrator users can add and remove apps in this folder.

▸ Everyone—Use the "everyone" permission settings to define access for anyone who isn't the owner and who isn't part of the item's group. This means everyone else, including local, sharing, and guest users.

The items in the Sharing & Permissions pane of a file's Info window appear in the following order:

1. Owner—displayed with a single silhouette and the owner's name

2. Group—displayed with two silhouettes and the group's name

3. Everyone—displayed with the word "everyone"

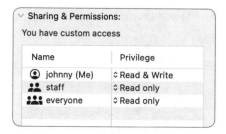

If the group permissions are set to No Access (as covered in the next section), macOS omits the group listing.

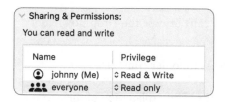

If a user or group doesn't exist—for example, because it was removed—then macOS displays a progress indicator (looks like a spinning gear) and the word "Fetching" for that user or group.

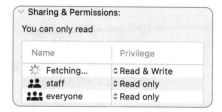

Standard Permissions

The standard file-system permissions structure of macOS is based on standard UNIX-style permissions. This system is also referred to as POSIX-style permissions (from Portable Operating System Interface). You can use POSIX-style permissions to define privilege rules separately at each ownership tier. The owner, the group, and everyone else have individually specified access to each file or folder. Because of the hierarchy inherent to the file system, where folders can reside inside other folders, you can create a complex file structure that allows varying levels of sharing and security.

Apple streamlined the Finder to enable the most common permissions. The full range of UNIX privilege combinations is available with Terminal.

File-level permissions options available in the Finder include:

▶ Read & Write—User or group members can open a file and save changes.

▶ Read Only—User or group members can open a file but can't save changes.

▶ No Access—User or group members have no access to a file.

Folder-level permissions options available in the Finder include:

▶ Read & Write—User or group members can browse and make changes to folder contents.

▶ Read Only—User or group members can browse folder contents but can't make changes.

▶ Write Only (Drop Box)—User or group members can't browse the Drop Box folder but can copy or move items to it.

▶ No Access—User or group members have no access to folder contents.

The Finder doesn't display the UNIX execute permission. The explanation of the execute permission in Terminal is outside the scope of this guide, but for the Finder, you need both read and execute permissions for a folder in order to open that folder in the Finder. Although the Finder doesn't show or allow changes to the UNIX execute permission, when you assign read permission for a folder, the Finder automatically also assigns execute permission for that folder.

Access Control Lists

Access control lists (ACLs) expand the standard UNIX permissions architecture to allow more file and folder access control. macOS adopted a style of ACLs similar to that available on Windows-based NTFS file systems and UNIX systems that support Network File System v4 (NFSv4). The ACL implementation is flexible but increases complexity by adding more than a dozen unique privilege and inheritance attribute types.

The macOS implementation of ACLs supports an essentially unlimited number of access control entries (ACEs). An ACE is a set of permissions defined for a specific user or group. An ACL consists of one or more ACEs. Any rules defined by an ACL are listed in the Sharing & Permissions table above the owner entry.

If an ACL rule applies to a user or group, this rule trumps standard UNIX permissions. Any users or groups that don't apply to a specific ACL are still bound by the standard permissions currently in place.

In the following figure, the folder has an ACL with one ACE that adds Read & Write permissions for the group ProjectZ and another ACE that adds Read & Write permissions for the user jane.

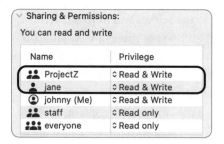

Permissions in a Hierarchical Context

Permissions don't exist in isolation; they're applied in a folder hierarchy. Your access to an item is based on an item's permissions in combination with the permissions of the folder in which it resides. Think of permissions as defining access to an item's content, not to the item itself. Remember the word "content" as you consider the following three examples.

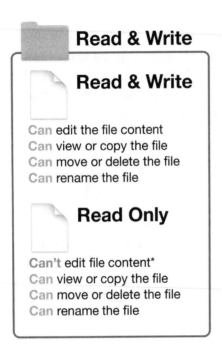

Example 1: You have both read and write permissions to the folder. You have full access to the first file, because your permissions here are read-and-write. You can view and copy the second file, but you can't make changes to the file content because your permissions are read-only. You can still move, delete, or rename the second file because you have read-and-write access to the folder contents. In this example, the second file isn't secure because you can make a copy of the original file, change the copied file's content, delete the original file, and replace it with the modified copy. This is how many apps save document changes in order to allow files to be edited.

NOTE ▸ The asterisk (*) in these examples indicates that editing behavior varies based on app design. For some apps, you might need read-and-write access to the file and the folder it's inside to save changes.

Read Only

Read & Write

Can edit the file content*
Can view or copy the file
Can't move or delete the file
Can't rename the file

Read Only

Can't edit the file content
Can view or copy the file
Can't move or delete the file
Can't rename the file

Example 2: You have read-only permission to the folder. You can edit the content of the first file because you have read-and-write access to it, but you can't move, delete, or rename it because you have read-only access to the folder contents. You can delete the file by erasing its contents. The second file is the only truly secure file, because you're allowed to view or copy it only. You can make changes to the contents of a copied file, but you can't replace the original.

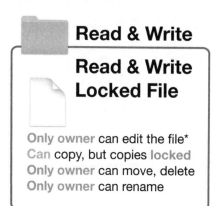

Read & Write

Read & Write
Locked File

Only owner can edit the file*
Can copy, but copies locked
Only owner can move, delete
Only owner can rename

Example 3: Your permissions are identical to the first document in the first example with one significant change. The owner of this file enabled the locked attribute, perhaps through the Versions document control feature. Even though you have read-and-write access to the example folder and file, the locked attribute prevents users who aren't the file owner from modifying, moving, deleting, or renaming it. In most apps, only the owner can change the file content or delete it. The owner can disable the locked attribute to return the file to normal permissions. You can make a copy of a locked file, but the copy is locked. You own the copy, so you can disable the locked attribute on the copy, but you can't delete the original locked file unless you're the owner.

Managing the Versions feature and the locked file attribute is detailed in Lesson 19, "Manage Files."

Reference 13.2
Examine Permissions for Sharing

The local file system is set up by default to provide a secure environment that enables users to share files.

Be sure to review Exercise 13.1, "Create Items with Default Permissions," and Exercise 13.2, "Test Permissions Changes," to illustrate the concepts in this section.

Use the Finder inspector window. This single floating window, which refreshes as you select items in the Finder, enables you to explore default permissions settings without opening multiple Finder Info windows.

Open the inspector from the Finder by pressing Option-Command-I, then click the disclosure triangle to reveal the Sharing & Permissions section.

Home Folder Permissions

Default home folder permissions protect user files and enable them to be shared. Users have read-and-write access to their home folder. The staff group and everyone else are allowed only read access.

Every local and guest user can access the first level of every other user's home folder. Guest users are allowed access to your Mac without a password. You can disable guest access in Users & Groups preferences.

Most user data is stored inside a subfolder in a user's home folder. Other users aren't allowed to access most of those subfolders.

Some subfolders in a user home folder are designed for sharing. The Public folder is readable by "everyone." A user can share files—without configuring permissions—by moving files into their Public folder. Other users are able to read the files, but they can't make changes to them.

By default, user-created files and folders at the root of a home folder have permissions similar to a Public folder. To secure new items at the root of a home folder, change the permissions, as outlined in Reference 13.3.

The Drop Box folder is in the Public folder. Drop Box folder permissions enable other users to copy files into it. But users can't see others' files in Drop Box. This enables users to discreetly transfer files to a specific user.

When items are created or copied, they are owned by the user who created or copied them. Because a Drop Box folder has a custom ACE, which ensures that the owner of a Drop Box folder has full access to all items in that drop box, normal ownership rules don't apply.

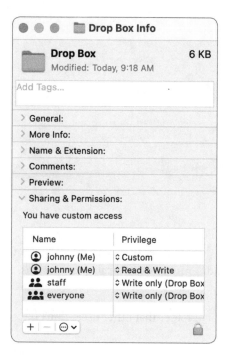

The Shared Folder

The /Users/Shared folder enables local users to read items in it and write items to it. This folder has a permissions setting (called a sticky bit) that prevents other users from deleting items they don't own. When one person copies a file to /Users/Shared, macOS adds the sticky bit to the file. Other users on the Mac can copy that file, but the sticky bit prevents other users from removing the file. /Users/Shared is the only place in macOS that uses the sticky bit. The sticky bit permissions setting doesn't appear in the Get Info window, but you can manage sticky bits in Terminal.

Secure New Items

New items are created with unrestricted read access. For example, when users create a new file or folder at the root of their home folder, by default other users can view the item contents. The same is true for new items created by administrators in local areas, such as the local Library and Applications folders.

The easiest way to secure new items is to store them in a folder that other users don't have access to.

To store items in a public area and modify the permissions to ensure that they are accessible only to the owner, you can change the item's permissions using the Finder or Terminal, covered in the next section.

Reference 13.3
Manage Permissions

The Finder hides full UNIX and ACL permission complexity by showing a simple view of item permissions. For most common permission settings, the Finder permissions interface provides the simplest way to manage permissions.

This section explores the permissions changes you can make to get full access to a deleted user's home folder.

Manage Permissions with the Finder

You can use the Sharing & Permissions section of the Info window to manage permissions. To do so, if you aren't the owner of the item you must click the Lock button in the lower-right corner of the Info window and authenticate as an administrator user.

macOS immediately applies the changes you make using the Info window. As long as you keep the Info window open, the Finder remembers the original permissions setting for an item. Use the Finder to test different permission configurations. You can revert to the original permissions setting before you close the Info window. To revert, click the Action menu (circle with three dots) at the bottom of the Info window and then choose "Revert changes."

Add a Permissions Entry

To add a new permissions entry for a user or group, click the Add (+) button in the lower-left corner of the Info window. A dialog appears that enables you to search for and select a user or group.

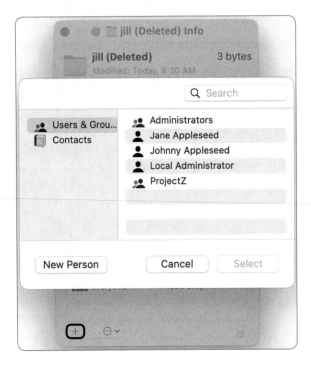

To create a new Sharing user, click the New Person button or select Contacts in the list on the left side of the dialog and select a contact. You must enter a new password for the new Sharing user. Details about creating Sharing user accounts and how to create additional groups are covered in Lesson 7, "Manage User Accounts."

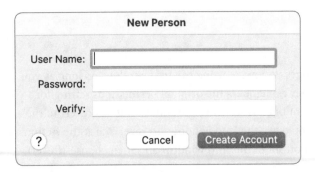

Change Ownership

Even though ACLs enable you to define multiple user permissions for an item, a file or folder can have only one owner. After you open an Info window, the bottom three entries in the permissions list are owner, group, and then everyone. If you own an item, you can change its privileges, but you can't change its ownership or group unless you authenticate as an administrator user. An administrator user can change ownership and privileges of any item, except items protected by System Integrity Protection (SIP).

To assign a new owner using the Finder Info window, you must first add the user as an additional permissions entry. After you add the user, click the lock in the lower-right corner, provide administrator credentials, select the user from the permissions list, and choose "Make *username* the owner" from the Action menu, where *username* is the selected user.

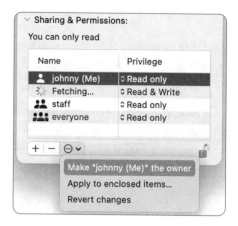

Modify a Permissions Entry

To assign different permissions to an entry, click a privilege and choose another access option for the user or group from the menu that appears.

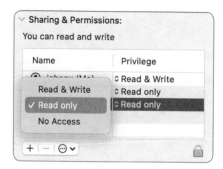

Remove a Permissions Entry

To remove an ACE, select the user or group from the permissions list and click the Remove (–) button in the lower-left corner of the Info window.

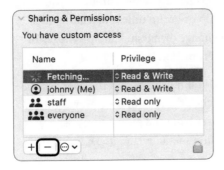

Propagate Folder Permissions

When you change permissions for a folder, you may want to propagate the same permissions to the items inside the folder. Click the lock, provide administrator credentials, and choose "Apply to enclosed items" from the Action menu to do so.

When you apply permissions to enclosed folder items, you apply all permission settings to all enclosed items (all enclosed folders and all enclosed files), not just the changes you recently made. Locked items inside the folder remain in their original state.

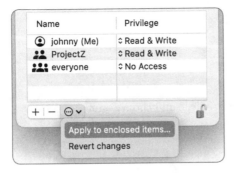

Permissions for External Storage Devices

External storage devices are useful for transferring files and folders from one Mac to another. But most Mac computers don't have the same user accounts, so when you move content from one Mac to another, macOS ignores ownership for files in volumes on external storage devices. This means local users have full access to the content of volumes in external storage devices. This includes volumes on the internal storage of an Intel-based Mac that's connected to your Mac with target disk mode (target disk mode is defined in Reference 11.5, "Troubleshoot File Systems"). If the other Intel-based Mac in target disk mode has FileVault turned on, or has a volume on its internal storage that's encrypted, you have to unlock the volume before you can access its contents.

To force macOS to recognize ownership on a volume, select it and then open the Info window. In the Sharing & Permissions section, click the Lock button in the lower-right corner and authenticate as an administrator user to unlock the Sharing & Permissions section. Deselect the "Ignore ownership on this volume" checkbox. The "Ignore ownership on this volume" option isn't displayed for the volume that your Mac starts up from.

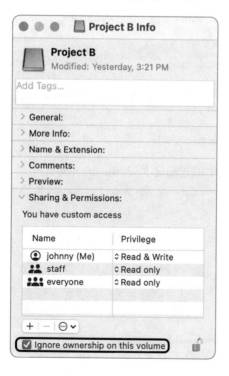

Exercise 13.1
Create Items with Default Permissions

> **Prerequisite**
>
> ▸ You must have created the Local Administrator (Exercise 3.1, "Configure a Mac for Exercises"), Johnny Appleseed (Exercise 7.1, "Create a Standard User Account"), and Emily Davidson (Exercise 8.1, "Restore a Deleted User Account") accounts.

In these exercises, you set permissions to control which users have access to files and folders.

Store Files and Folders in Johnny Appleseed's Home Folder

To see the effects of macOS default permissions, you create items while you're logged in as the user Johnny. You inspect the item permissions as well.

1   Log in as Johnny Appleseed.

2   Open TextEdit. There should be a shortcut to it in your Dock.

3   Click New Document (or, if necessary, press Command-N).

4   From the menu bar, choose File > Save (or press Command-S), name the new file **Secret Bonus List**, then save it to the desktop. Leave the File Format selection as Rich Text Document.

   In a Save dialog, you can use the shortcut Command-D to select the desktop.

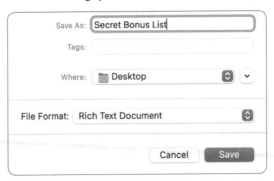

5 Click Save, then quit TextEdit.

6 In the Finder, choose Go > Home (or press Shift-Command-H) to navigate to your home folder.

7 Choose File > New Folder (or press Shift-Command-N) to create a new folder.

8 Name the new folder **Payroll Reports.**

9 Make sure the new Payroll Reports folder and the default user folders are in your home folder.

10 Drag the Secret Bonus List file from your desktop to the Payroll Reports folder.

As you will see, the root (top level) of your home folder isn't a good place to store confidential documents.

Examine Permissions as Another User

Now that Johnny Appleseed has created a test folder and file, experiment to learn what Emily Davidson can do with them.

1 Open Users & Groups preferences, then authenticate as Local Administrator.

2 From the sidebar, select Login Options.

3 Choose Icon from the "Show fast user switching menu as" menu.

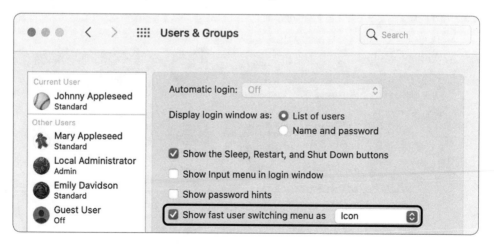

4 Use the fast user switching menu item (near the right side of the menu bar) to switch to Emily Davidson.

5 Authenticate as Emily Davidson.

Next, you'll navigate to Johnny Appleseed's home folder in the Finder. You haven't customized Emily's Finder preferences to show hard disks on the desktop.

6 Choose Go > Computer (or press Shift-Command-C), then open Macintosh HD > Users > Johnny.

Most of the folders in Johnny's home folder are displayed with a prohibitory badge to indicate that you aren't allowed to access them.

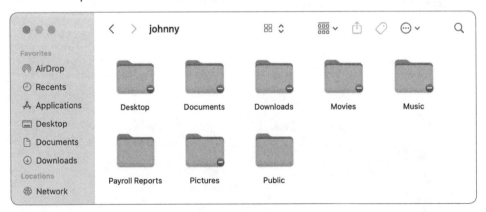

7   Press and hold the Option key while choosing File > Show Inspector (or press Option-Command-I).

The inspector follows your selection in the Finder, enabling you to inspect items quickly.

8   If necessary, click the disclosure triangle in the inspector window to expand the Sharing & Permissions section.

9   For each of the folders in Johnny's folder, click the folder, then watch what the inspector shows about permissions.

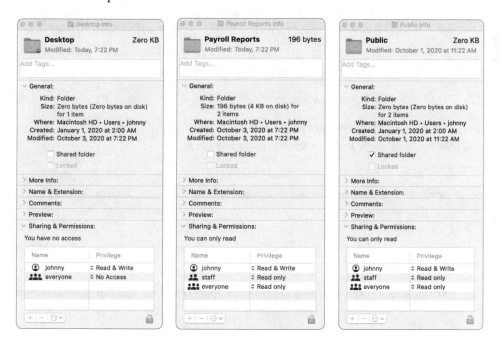

With the exception of Public, the folders that macOS creates in the home folder are protected from access by other users (the No Access permission). In this exercise, when you were logged in as Johnny Appleseed, and when you created the Payroll Reports folder, macOS associated the folder with the staff group and assigned read-only permissions to the staff group for that folder. macOS assigned "everyone" read-only access.

10 Click in the background of Johnny's home folder.

The inspector shows that staff and everyone are also allowed read-only access to the top level of Johnny's home folder.

11 Open the Payroll Reports folder.

The folder opens, and the Secret Bonus List file is displayed.

12 Select the Secret Bonus List file.

The inspector shows that staff and everyone have read-only access.

This result may be contrary to what is expected by users. Be sure to instruct your users to store their folders in appropriate places, based on the type of access they want to allow for other users. Although others can't add or remove items stored in the Payroll Reports folder, they can open and read the contents.

13 Open the Secret Bonus List file.

Since the file is readable by everyone but writable only by its owner, Johnny Appleseed, TextEdit shows that it is locked.

14 Try to enter some text into the file.

TextEdit asks if you would like to create a duplicate so that you can save your changes.

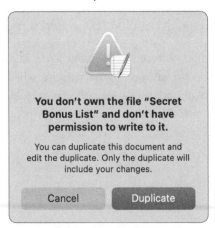

15 Click Duplicate.

A duplicate document named Untitled (Secret Bonus List copy) opens and allows you to enter text.

16 Save the duplicate document to your desktop (leave the name "Secret Bonus List copy").

17 Quit TextEdit.

18 In the Finder, navigate back to Johnny's home folder, then open Johnny's Public folder.

19 Select the Drop Box folder.

The inspector shows that staff and everyone have write-only access to this folder. Johnny has read and write access and a custom access control entry (ACE). "Custom" means that the ACE grants something other than normal read, write, or read/write access. In this case, it's an inheritable ACE that grants Johnny additional access to items moved to this folder.

20 Try to open Johnny's Drop Box folder.

The write-only permission doesn't allow you to open another user's Drop Box folder.

21 Try to copy the Secret Bonus List copy file from your desktop into Johnny Appleseed's Drop Box folder.

The Finder warns you that you won't be able to see the items you put into the Drop Box folder.

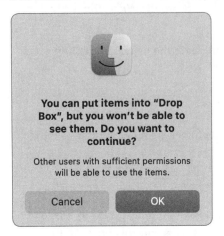

22 Click OK.

In the next exercise, you learn how to adjust the permissions on the Payroll Reports folder.

Exercise 13.2
Test Permissions Changes

> **Prerequisite**
>
> ▸ You must have performed Exercise 13.1, "Create Items with Default Permissions."

In this exercise, Johnny Appleseed changes the permissions on the Payroll Reports folder and tests the results from Emily Davidson's account.

Change Permissions as Johnny Appleseed

1 Open Users & Groups preferences, then authenticate as Local Administrator.

2 From the sidebar, select Login Options, then choose Icon from the "Show fast user switching" menu.

3   Switch back to Johnny Appleseed's account.

4   Select the Payroll Reports folder in Johnny's home folder, then from the menu bar, choose File > Get Info (Command-I).

5   Expand Sharing & Permissions.

6   Click the small lock button in the Info window, then authenticate as Local Administrator.

7   Select the group (staff), then click the Remove (–) button below the permissions list.

8   Change the privilege level for everyone to No Access.

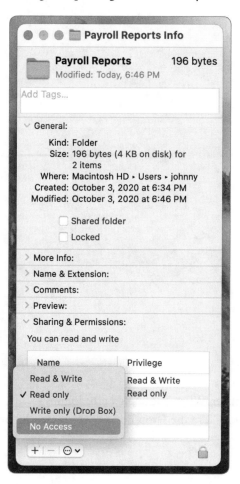

9 Close the Info window.

10 Navigate to Johnny's Drop Box folder (inside the Public folder).

11 Select the Secret Bonus List copy file that Emily placed in Johnny's Drop Box folder.

12 Choose File > Get Info. If necessary, expand the Sharing & Permissions section.

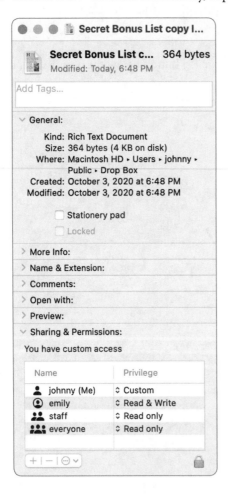

Since Emily created this file, she is its owner. When she copied it to Johnny's Drop Box folder, the inheritable custom ACE in the Drop Box folder granted Johnny full access to it.

13 Close the Info window.

14 Open the Secret Bonus List copy file, then edit its contents.

The inherited access control allows Johnny to edit the file, and the changes are saved automatically.

15 Quit TextEdit.

Test the New Permissions as Emily Davidson

1 Use fast user switching to switch back to Emily's account.

2 Try to open the Payroll Reports folder.

This time you can't open the folder because the new permissions don't grant you read access.

The folder "Payroll Reports" can't be opened because you don't have permission to see its contents.

OK

The default permissions didn't protect the Payroll Reports folder as Johnny intended, but after Johnny changed the permissions, the folder is protected from access by other users.

3 Click OK in the dialog.

4 Log out of Emily's account.

5 At the login window, switch to Johnny Appleseed.

6 Navigate back to Johnny's home folder (Go > Home or Shift-Command-H), then drag the Payroll Reports folder to the Trash.

7 From the Finder menu, choose Empty Trash.

8 In the dialog that appears, click Empty Trash.

Use Hidden Items, Shortcuts, and File Archives

macOS makes complex file-system structures simple. For example, the Finder displays just four folders at the root level of the system volume. Also, many items are shown in convenient locations but are stored elsewhere. And you can use the archiving technology built into macOS to combine multiple items into a compressed file.

In this lesson, you explore hiding, redirecting, and archiving items. You learn how to manage file-system aliases and links. You also open and create ZIP file format (.zip) archives and disk images.

Reference 14.1
Examine Hidden Items

The root level of the system volume contains resources that macOS processes require and that you probably won't ever need to examine. You can identify many of these resources because they have a period (.) at the beginning of the filename.

In macOS, you can hide files and folders in two ways. You can use the mv command in Terminal to add a period to the beginning of a filename or use the chflags command to enable an item's *hidden* file flag. Changing an item's file flag to *hidden* hides it only in the Finder. To prevent confusion, you can't use macOS to hide items using the Finder or the default apps.

GOALS

▶ Navigate to hidden files and folders

▶ Examine packages and bundles

▶ Manage aliases and links

▶ Create and open ZIP archives and disk images

Reveal Hidden Folders in the Finder

To reveal hidden items, go to the Library folder or open the Finder and select the Go menu.

The user Library folder includes important resources, but it's hidden in the Finder. Press and hold the Option key, then click the Go menu to reveal the Library menu item.

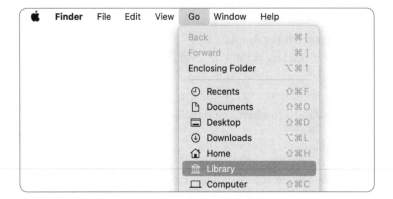

If you frequently access a user Library folder, you can make it always visible.

1   Open Finder preferences (Command-Comma).

2   Click Sidebar at the top of the Finder Preferences window.

3   Select the checkbox for your home folder.

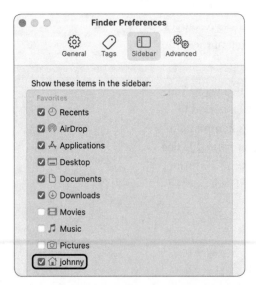

4   Close the Finder Preferences window.

5   Choose Go > Home.

6   In the Finder window toolbar, click the button to show items as icons, in columns, or in a gallery.

> **TIP** If the Finder window is narrow enough, the Finder displays a menu to change between showing items as icons, in a list, in columns, or in a gallery.

7   Choose View > Show View Options (Command-J).

8   In the View Options window, select the Show Library Folder checkbox.

To reveal all hidden items in the Finder, press Shift-Command-Period. Hidden items remain visible in the Finder until you use the keyboard shortcut again to return the items to their default hidden state.

If you show a user Library folder in the Finder, it also appears in the Go menu and has a keyboard shortcut (Shift-Command-L).

Go to Folder

You can leave hidden items hidden in the Finder and still navigate to a particular hidden folder. To examine the contents of hidden folders in the Finder, choose Go > Go to Folder, or press Shift-Command-G. This opens a dialog that enables you to enter an absolute path to any folder on the Mac.

In the Go to Folder dialog, use Tab key completion to enter file-system pathnames. Enter the first few letters of a pathname, then press Tab, and macOS attempts to complete the name. If multiple possibilities exist for what you entered, choose from the displayed list.

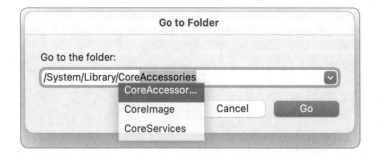

Click Go after you enter the pathname. The Finder reveals the folder in a window. For example, to navigate to /private, type **/p** and press Tab, then click Go or press Return.

You can also navigate to past destinations from the "Go to the folder" menu. Click the down-arrow button to the right of the text field to reveal past destinations.

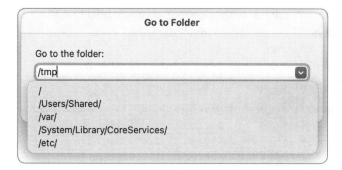

The folder /private is one example of a hidden folder. It contains resources that macOS requires.

Reference 14.2
Examine Packages

Although packages and bundles are sometimes referred to interchangeably, they represent distinct concepts:

▶ A *package* is any folder that the Finder presents to the user as if it were a single file.

▶ A *bundle* is a folder with a standardized hierarchical structure that holds executable code and the resources used by that code.

An item can be both a package and a bundle. It's a package because when you double-click it, the Finder does not show you its contents. It's a bundle because it's a folder that holds executable code and resources. Examples of items that are both a package and a bundle include the following:

▶ Optional plug-ins in /Library/Internet Plug-Ins

▶ Screen savers in /System/Library/Screen Savers

▶ Most apps

Some items are packages but not bundles, because they don't contain executable code. Examples of packages that are not bundles include the following:

▶ Photos Library—The Photos app keeps your pictures, videos, and other information in your Photos Library package, which is in your Pictures folder.

▶ Photo Booth Library—Photo Booth keeps its data in this package in your Pictures folder.

▶ Large Pages, Numbers, or Keynote documents.

If you're working in Pages, Numbers, or Keynote and you have created a file that is larger than 500 MB, saving it as a package helps the app you're using perform better. Go to Apple Support article HT202887, "Save documents as a package or a single file in Pages, Numbers, or Keynote," for more information.

Frameworks are bundles but not packages. This includes:

▶ The frameworks in /System/Library/Frameworks and /Library/Frameworks.

Frameworks contain shared resources that multiple apps can use simultaneously. macOS loads frameworks into memory as needed and shares the one copy of the resource among all apps whenever possible.

Because packages are folders, you can copy them as regular folders to another volume even if it isn't formatted as APFS or Mac OS Extended. The Finder recognizes the items as packages even when they are on a third-party volume.

View Package Contents

To access a package's contents in the Finder, Control-click the item you want to view and choose Show Package Contents from the shortcut menu. If you want to learn how to create or modify a bundle or package bundle, join the Apple Developer Program. You can find out more at developer.apple.com.

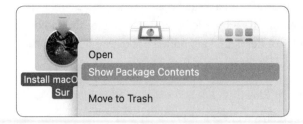

Installer Package Resources

An installer package contains a compressed archive of the software you want to install, as well as a few configuration files used by Installer. Other software bundles and packages contain resources for the app or software.

Software packages often include the following:

▶ Executable code for multiple platforms

▶ Document description files

▶ Media resources such as images and sounds

▶ User interface description files

▶ Text resources

▶ Resources localized for specific languages

▶ Private software libraries and frameworks

▶ Plug-ins or other software to expand capability

Reference 14.3
Use File-System Shortcuts

File-system shortcuts are files that refer to other files or folders. This enables you to have an item appear in multiple locations or with multiple names without having to create multiple copies of the item. Shortcuts in the Dock or in the Finder aren't file-system shortcuts. The Dock and the Finder save references to original items as part of their configuration files. File-system shortcuts are files that you can find anywhere on a volume.

About File-System Shortcuts

macOS uses four primary file-system shortcut types: aliases, symbolic links, hard links, and firm links. To help you compare these shortcut types, this section uses a 28.4 MB Pages document file named BigReport.pages for demonstration purposes. This file is referred to using each shortcut type. Throughout this section, the Info window in the Finder displays the differences for each shortcut type.

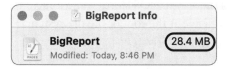

Aliases

You can create aliases using the Finder, but they aren't recognized by Terminal. Command-line tools can't follow alias references created in the Finder back to the original items.

Aliases are more resilient than other shortcut types. If the original item is replaced or moved, the alias is designed to never lose the original item.

The following screenshot shows the Finder Info window inspecting an alias pointing to BigReport.pages. The kind is reported as Alias and the file is much smaller than the 28.4 MB original. The Size field reports that the file is 940 bytes and uses 4 KB of disk space. The extra information in the alias is what allows macOS to keep track of the original item should it ever change location.

Symbolic Links

Symbolic links are pointers to the file-system path of the original item. In many cases, if you move the original item the symbolic link is broken. You can replace the original item with a file of the same name because the path remains the same.

You can create symbolic links only in Terminal, but the Finder follows symbolic links to an original item. An example of symbolic links is the way macOS stores some folders in the /private folder but also makes those folders available at the root of the file system using symbolic links. For example, /var is a symbolic link to /private/var.

The following screenshot shows the Finder Info window inspecting a symbolic link pointing to BigReport.pages. The kind is also reported as Alias, but the file is only 39 bytes. This illustrates a symbolic link saving a path to the original item. There is no Select New Original button. This indicates that you can't use the Finder to repair a symbolic link.

Hard Links

Hard links are references to an original item. A file has two parts: the bits on the physical storage device that make up the file content and a name that points to those bits. Every file has at least one hard link. If you create an additional hard link, you create another name that points to the same bits on the physical device.

If you remove an additional hard link, you don't delete the original item. If you delete the original item, you don't delete the data or additional hard links because the other hard links still point to the same bits on the device, which won't be freed until there are no links left to them. With aliases and symbolic links, deleting the original item leaves the shortcut pointing at nothing.

You can create hard links only in Terminal, but the Finder can follow them. To save space, Time Machine uses hard links to refer to items that haven't changed since the previous backup. macOS uses folder hard links for Time Machine. The man page for ln has more information about creating hard links and about creating symbolic links with the -s option.

Firm Links

Firm links help macOS display a single unified volume to the user and apps, even though macOS Big Sur separates the signed system volume (SSV) read-only APFS snapshot of the APFS System volume from the read-write APFS Data volume. Firm links allow forward and backward navigation between folders that straddle the SSV volume and the read-write APFS Data volume. These are transparent to the user. You cannot create or modify firm links. Go to Reference 11.1, "File Systems," for more information.

Create Aliases

To create an alias in the Finder, select the item you want to create an alias for and use one of the following methods:

- ▶ Choose File > Make Alias.

- ▶ Press Command-L.

- ▶ In a Finder window, choose Make Alias from the Action menu (the icon looks like a circle containing three dots).

- ▶ In the Finder, Control-click an item and choose Make Alias from the shortcut menu.

- ▶ Drag the original item while pressing and holding the Option and Command keys to drop the alias in another location. This method doesn't append the extension ".alias" to the filename of the new alias, but it updates the icon.

- ▶ Drag an app to the desktop. This gives you access to the app without the risk of accidentally removing it from its original installed location.

After you create an alias, you can rename it or move it. As long as the original item remains on the original volume—even if it's replaced or its name changes—the Finder can locate the alias. An alias file has a small curved arrow at the lower-left corner of the icon. Locate an alias target from the Finder by Control-clicking the alias and choosing Show Original from the shortcut menu, or by pressing Command-R.

Repair Aliases

Double-click a broken alias to repair it in the Finder. The Finder tells you if it can't locate the original for a broken alias. In the dialog, you can delete the broken alias, click Fix Alias to select a new original item, or click OK to dismiss the dialog.

You can also redirect an existing alias. Select the alias, open its Finder Info window, and in the General area, click the Select New Original button.

Both methods open a file browser dialog, where you can select a new original item for the alias.

Reference 14.4
Use File Archives

Unlike automated backup solutions, archiving is typically a manual process where you create compressed copies of data. Archive formats are efficient for storage and data transfer. In this section, you learn about ZIP archives and disk images.

File Archives

You can select files and folders to compress (or zip) into ZIP archives. This is an efficient way to archive small amounts of data. The ZIP archive format is widely compatible. Many operating systems include software to decompress ZIP archives back to their original state.

You can create disk images using Disk Utility. You can use disk images to archive an entire file system, including files, folders, and associated metadata, into a single file. You can compress, encrypt, or make read-only any disk image. You can also configure disk images with read/write permissions so that you can make changes.

Disk images you create with Disk Utility that use the .dmg filename extension can be accessed only by Mac computers. Other systems require third-party software to access Mac disk images.

Create ZIP Archives

By default, creating a ZIP archive in the Finder doesn't delete the original items, and expanding a ZIP archive doesn't delete the original archive.

To create a ZIP archive in the Finder, select the items you want to archive and compress in the Finder. Press and hold the Shift key to select contiguous lists of items, or press and hold the Command key to select noncontiguous items. With a single file selected in the Finder choose File > Compress *Item*, or Control-click the file and choose Compress *Item* from the shortcut menu, where *Item* is the name of the file. If multiple files are selected, the command is Compress.

The Finder may show a progress dialog with the estimated time required to complete the compression. You can cancel the archive by clicking the small x button on the far right. When the process finishes, you are left with a ZIP archive named either Archive.zip or *Item*.zip, where *Item* is the name of the item you chose to archive and compress.

After the archiving is complete, compare the original item size with the archive size using the Info or Inspector window in the Finder. Many media formats come compressed, so your results may vary when you again compress these file types.

Expand ZIP Archives

Expand a ZIP archive in the Finder by double-clicking the archive file. The Finder cannot list or extract individual items from a ZIP archive.

If you need more control over how ZIP archives are expanded, use Spotlight to open Archive Utility and choose Archive Utility > Preferences. These preferences enable you to adjust how ZIP archives are expanded and compressed. The preferences include options for handling original items after an archive transition.

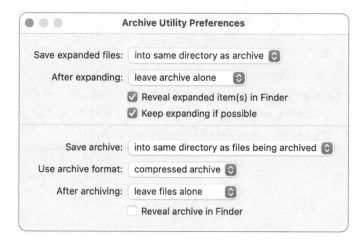

Mount Disk Images

Safari mounts downloaded disk images, but you can manually mount disk images from the Finder too. To access the contents of a disk image, double-click the disk image file in the Finder. Doing so mounts the volume inside the disk image file as if you had just connected an external storage device.

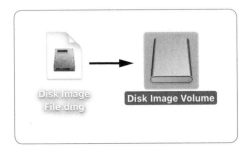

Even if the disk image file is on a remote file server, you can mount it as if it were a local volume. You can treat the mounted disk image volume as you would other storage devices by navigating through its hierarchy and selecting files and folders. If the disk image is read/write, you can add to the contents of the disk image by dragging items to the volume.

Create Empty Disk Images

To create an empty disk image, which you can fill with content over time, log in as an administrator user, open Disk Utility, and choose File > New Image > Blank Image.

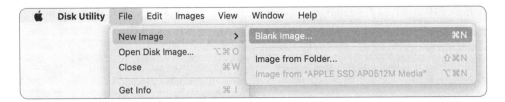

In the New Blank Image dialog, you can define the parameters for the new disk image. At the least, you need to select a name and destination for the disk image file. You should also enter a name for the volume inside the disk image. The disk image file and volume names don't have to match, but they should be similar so that you can recognize their relationship.

Disk image size is limited by the storage destination capacity. You can select the "sparse disk image" image format to create an image file that's only large enough to store items that are in the disk image volume. Empty space inside a disk image volume doesn't count as storage space.

After you define your disk image options, click Save to create the disk image. After macOS creates the new blank disk image, macOS mounts it. If you chose to create a sparse disk image, you can open Info windows in the Finder for the disk image file and the disk image volume to verify that the volume size is much larger than the image size. As you copy files to the volume, the disk image file grows.

You can change the format of a disk image with Disk Utility by choosing Images > Convert. This opens a dialog where you can select the image you want to change and save a copy of the image with new options.

Create Disk Image Archives

To create a disk image that contains copies of items, open Disk Utility and choose File > New Image > Image from Folder. This opens a file browser window in which you can select the folder you want to copy into a new disk image.

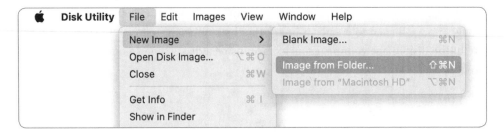

To create a disk image from the contents of an entire volume or disk, select the source from the Disk Utility window disks list and choose File > New Image > Image from *Source* (where *Source* is the name of the selected volume or disk).

After you select the disk image source, a Save dialog appears. At the least, you must select a name and destination for the resulting disk image file. The name of the volume inside the disk image is set to the name of the selected source. You can compress the disk image contents to save storage space. Also, you can enable encryption for the disk image. If you do, you must set a password and provide a hint for the resulting secure disk image. Be sure to use Keychain Access to save the password to a keychain for easy, secure access.

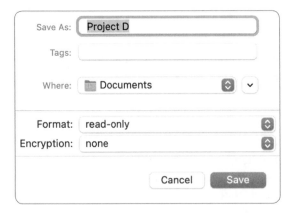

After you define your disk image options, click Save to create the disk image. Depending on the amount of data to be copied and the image format you choose, it can take seconds to hours for the disk image to copy. Disk Utility opens a progress dialog that lets you cancel the copy.

You can find out more information about Disk Utility in the Disk Utility User Guide at support.apple.com/guide/disk-utility/.

Exercise 14.1
Navigate Hidden Items

> **Prerequisite**
>
> ▸ You must have created the Johnny Appleseed account (Exercise 7.1, "Create a Standard User Account").

macOS hides portions of the folder structure to simplify the user experience and to prevent accidental damage that may be caused by a user. In this exercise, you explore some of the hidden folders in macOS.

Examine Your User Library Folder

1   Log in as Johnny Appleseed.

2   In the Finder, open your home folder. You can do this by choosing Go > Home (or pressing Shift-Command-H).

    No folder named Library appears.

3   In the Finder, open the Go menu. Don't choose anything yet.

4   Press and hold the Option key.

    As long as you hold down the Option key, a Library choice appears in the menu.

5   With the Option key held down, choose Library.

This opens the hidden Library folder in Johnny's home folder.

6   Choose View > as Columns (or click the Items button in the Finder toolbar and choose Column View from the menu).

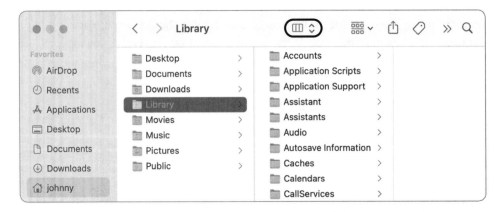

Johnny's user Library folder is shown in Johnny's home folder. It's dimmed to indicate that it's normally invisible.

7   Explore some subfolders in Johnny's user Library folder. You can navigate into them normally.

8   Close the Finder window that shows Johnny's user Library folder.

9   Press Shift-Command-H to open Johnny's home folder in a new Finder window.

The Library folder isn't shown.

10 Choose Go > Go to Folder (Shift-Command-G).

11 In the "Go to the folder" dialog, type **~/Li**, then press Tab.

The field completes the path to ~/Library/.

This is an example of how you navigate to a folder by its path.

12 Click Go.

Johnny's user Library folder appears in the Finder.

You could have reached this folder by entering the full path, **/Users/johnny/Library**, but the tilde (~) is an easier way to specify locations in your home folder.

Examine Hidden System Folders

1   Press Shift-Command-G to reopen the Go to Folder dialog.

2   This time, enter **/L**, then press Tab.

The field completes the path to /Library/. This path looks similar to the previous one, but because it doesn't start with a tilde, it specifies a different folder. When a path starts with a slash (/), it starts at the top level of the startup volume (sometimes called the root of the file system).

3   Click Go.

This time, the Finder opens the Library folder at the top of the startup volume. The next lesson discusses the various Library folders.

This Library folder isn't hidden, but you can use the same technique to reach any folder you know the path to, whether or not it is hidden.

4   Use the "Go to the folder" dialog to reach the /private/var/log/ folder. (You can type part of a name, then press Tab to complete it.)

The /private/var/log folder holds some of the system log files (there are more in /Library/Logs and ~/Library/Logs). Normally, you don't need to access these files in the Finder, so they are hidden from view unless you specifically navigate to them.

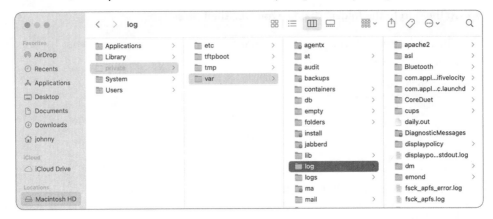

5   Use the "Go to the folder" dialog to reach the /var/log/ folder.

This takes you to /private/var/log because /var is a symbolic link to /private/var.

Data Management

Lesson 15

Manage System Resources

The macOS system files are streamlined and organized in a layout that is easy to manage and that provides strong security. This lesson focuses on the composition and organization of the files and folders that make up macOS.

As covered in Reference 11.1, "File Systems," macOS Big Sur uses a read-only signed system volume (SSV) to protect macOS system software. The read-write APFS Data volume is usually named Macintosh HD - Data or Data and is mounted at /System/Volumes/Data in a way that preserves the appearance of a single volume. macOS uses firm links so that when you use the Finder to open /Applications, for example, the Finder displays the contents of both /Applications (from the read-only snapshot of the APFS System volume) and /System/Volumes/Data (from the read-write APFS Data volume).

GOALS

▶ Explore and understand macOS file layout

▶ Discover common system files, their location, and their purpose

▶ Describe System Integrity Protection

▶ Manage font resources

Reference 15.1
macOS File Resources

If you open the root (beginning) of the file system from the Finder, the Finder displays four default visible folders: Applications, Library, System, and Users. If you use Terminal to examine the root of the file system, you'll discover more items.

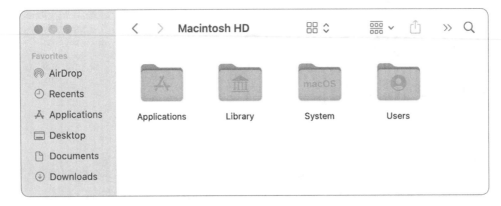

Here are descriptions of the default system root folders that the Finder displays:

▶ Applications—Often called the local Applications folder, this is the default location for apps available to local users. Only administrator users can make changes to the contents of this folder.

▶ Library—Often called the local Library folder, this is the default location for ancillary system and app resources available to users. Only administrator users can make changes to the contents of this folder.

▶ System—This folder contains resources required by macOS for primary functionality. With System Integrity Protection (SIP) enabled by default in macOS, no user or process can make changes to most of the content of the System folder. Details regarding SIP are covered later in this lesson.

▶ Users—This is the default location for local user home folders. Lesson 8, "Manage User Home Folders," covers this topic in greater detail.

Library Resources

macOS-specific system resources are stored in Library folders throughout the system volume. A system resource is a resource that is not a general-use app or a user file. The Library folder keeps user and system resources organized and separated from the items you use every day.

You should be familiar with these system resources:

▶ Application Support—This folder is in the user and local Library folders. Any ancillary data needed by an app might be in this folder. For example, it often contains help files or templates for an app.

▶ Containers and Group Containers—These folders contain resources for sandboxed apps. There is more information about these folders later in this section.

▶ Extensions—Legacy system extensions, previously called kernel extensions (kexts), these items are found only in the /Library and /System/Library folders. Legacy system extensions are low-level drivers that attach themselves to the kernel, or core, of the operating system. Legacy system extensions provide driver support for hardware, networking, and peripherals. Legacy system extensions load and unload automatically. Extensions are covered in greater detail in Lesson 26, "Troubleshoot Peripherals."

▶ Fonts—Fonts are files that describe typefaces used for both screen display and printing. Font management is covered later in this lesson.

▶ Frameworks—Frameworks are repositories of shared code used among different parts of the operating system or apps. Frameworks load and unload automatically. You can view your Mac computer's currently loaded frameworks with System Information.

▶ Keychains—Keychains are used to securely store sensitive information, including passwords, certificates, keys, Safari AutoFill information, and notes. Keychain technology is covered in Lesson 9, "Manage Security and Privacy."

▶ LaunchDaemons and LaunchAgents—These define processes that start with the launchd process. macOS uses many background processes that are started by launchd. LaunchAgents are used for processes that need to start up only when a user is logged in, whereas LaunchDaemons are used to start processes that always run in the background, even when no users are logged in. More about launchd can be found in Lesson 28, "Troubleshoot Startup and System Issues."

▶ Logs—Many system processes and apps record progress or error messages to log files. You can inspect log files using Console.

▶ PreferencePanes—PreferencePanes are used by System Preferences to provide interfaces for system configuration. Using System Preferences is covered in Lesson 3, "Set Up and Configure macOS."

▶ Preferences—Preferences are used to store system and app configuration settings. Every time you configure a setting for any app or system function, it is saved to a preference file. Because preferences play such a critical role in system functionality, troubleshooting preference files is covered separately in Lesson 20, "Manage and Troubleshoot Apps."

Resource Hierarchy

Library folders are in separate domains: user, local, network, and system (network domains are legacy and outside the scope of this guide). Segregating resources into domains provides increased administrative flexibility, resource security, and system reliability. Resource domains allow for administrative flexibility, because you can choose to allocate certain resources to all users or just specific users. Standard users can add resources to their own home folder only and cannot access other users' resources.

The system resource domains are, in order:

- ▶ User—Each user has their own Library folder in the home folder for resources. When resources are placed here, only the user has access to them. The user's Library folder is hidden by default to prevent users from accidentally making changes that could be detrimental. Many apps and processes continue to rely on this location for resources.

- ▶ Local—Both /Applications and /Library are part of the local resource domain. Any resources placed in these two folders are available to all local user accounts. By default, only administrator users can make changes to local resources.

- ▶ System—The system domain encompasses the items necessary to provide core system functionality. This includes an app folder located at /System/Library/CoreServices. Many hidden items at the root of the system volume also make up the system resource domain, but the only one the Finder displays is the /System/Library folder. With SIP enabled, no user or process can modify most of the /System folder.

With different domains containing resources, there may be multiple copies of similar resources available to the Mac and user. macOS handles this by searching for resources from the most specific (those in the user domain) to the least specific (those in the system domain). The following graphic represents the order in which resource contention is resolved from a user's home folder (1) to the System folder (3).

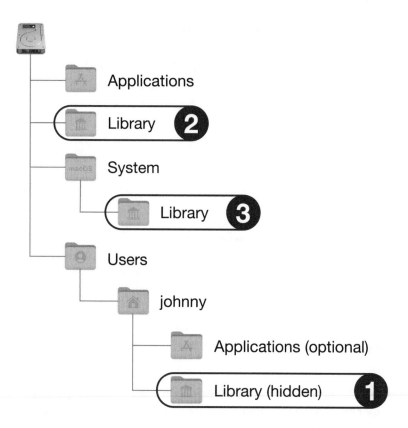

If multiple similar resources are discovered, macOS uses the resource most specific to the user. For example, if two versions of the font Times New Roman are found—one in the local Library and one in the user's Library—macOS uses the copy of the font in the user's Library.

App Sandbox Containers

App sandbox containers enhance running-app security. Sandboxed apps are allowed access only to the specific items they need to function. Most apps built into macOS and apps from the App Store are sandboxed apps.

Sandboxed apps can access special folders that are referred to as containers. macOS manages the content of these containers to ensure that an app isn't allowed access to other items in the file system. A user opening a document outside of an app container is the only way a sandboxed app is allowed access outside of its container.

App containers are in ~/Library/Containers. When a sandboxed app starts up the first time, macOS creates a container folder for the app if it doesn't exist already, named with its bundle identifier. The bundle identifier identifies an app by its creator and app title. For example, the container folder for News is ~/Library/Containers/com.apple.News. The Finder may display the container with the app's name and custom icon.

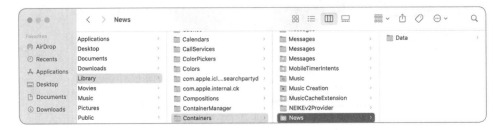

The root content of an app container is a hidden property list file (with the extension .plist) containing app information, a Data folder, and possibly an OldData folder. The Data folder is the app's current active container. Any OldData folder you find contains previously used app items. The content of the Data folder mostly mimics the user home folder, but with one key distinction: it contains only the items that the app is allowed to access.

Items created and managed by the sandboxed app are the only original items in the container Data folder. If a user enables iCloud Drive, you might also find a CloudKit folder for maintaining items stored in iCloud.

Items that originated from other apps or a user's file-opening action are represented as symbolic links that point to the original item outside of the container. macOS creates these symbolic links when the user opens an item in the sandboxed app. With external items represented in this way, an item can stay in its original location while also being accessible to a sandboxed app that can access only its own container.

App Group Containers

Although a user can allow sandboxed apps to access files beyond the app container, sandboxing prevents apps from doing this automatically. To facilitate sharing app resources automatically, developers of sandboxed apps can request that macOS create a shared app group container.

The ~/Library/Group Containers folder contains shared app containers. When a sandboxed app starts up the first time and requests access to share app resources, macOS creates a group container folder for the app, named with its bundle identifier.

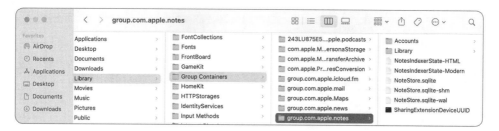

Unlike app sandbox containers that simulate an entire user home folder, app group containers hold only items to be shared between apps. Using Notes as an example, in the previous screenshot the Finder displays the NoteStore database and other files. In this instance, the Notes data is shared so that other apps can access user note entries. macOS controls access to this to ensure that only Apple-verified processes can access the user's Notes database.

Troubleshoot System Resources

You may experience an error message calling out an issue with a specific item, but you may also experience a situation where the item appears to be missing. macOS ignores a system resource if it determines that the resource is corrupted or missing. Replace the suspect or missing item with a working copy.

When troubleshooting system resources, remember the resource domain hierarchy. Using fonts as an example, you may load a version of a font in the local Library folder as required by your workflow to operate properly. In spite of this, a user may load another version of the same font in their home folder. In this case, the user might experience workflow problems even though it appears that they are using the correct font.

Logging in with another account is a quick way to determine whether the problem is in the user's home folder. You can also use System Information to list active system resources. System Information shows the file path of the loaded system resources, so you can spot resources that are loading from the user's Library.

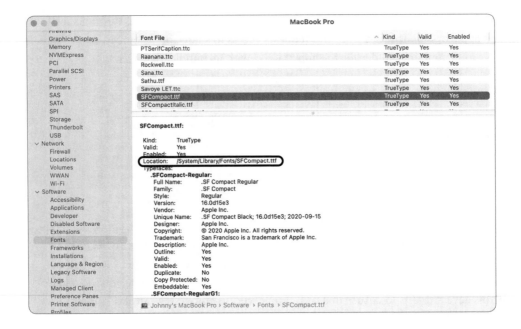

Reference 15.2
System Integrity Protection

In macOS Big Sur, one layer of protection is that the SSV is a read-only APFS snapshot of the read-only APFS System volume. System Integrity Protection (SIP) further protects your Mac by preventing potentially malicious software from modifying protected files and folders. SIP restricts the System Administrator account (the root user account) and limits the actions that the root user can perform on protected parts of the Mac operating system.

SIP includes protection for these parts of macOS that are already part of the read-only SSV mounted at /:

- ▶ /System
- ▶ /usr
- ▶ /bin
- ▶ /sbin

SIP also protects portions of macOS that are part of the read-write APFS Data volume mounted at /System/Volumes/Data:

- ▶ Apps that are preinstalled with macOS (including /System/Volumes/Data/Applications/Safari.app)
- ▶ /private/var/db/ConfigurationProfiles

Third-party apps and installers can continue to write to the following paths in the read-write volume:

- ▶ /Applications (/System/Volumes/Data/Applications)
- ▶ /Library
- ▶ /usr/local

SIP allows only processes that are signed by Apple with special entitlements to modify parts of your Mac that are protected by SIP. For instance, Apple software updates and Apple installers are allowed to write to system files. Apps that you download from the App Store already work with SIP.

SIP also helps ensure that only a user, and not malicious software, can change a startup disk .

If you upgrade from an earlier version of macOS, the installer might move an item aside if it conflicts with SIP.

Older peripheral and printer driver software may be impacted by SIP. If you discover that a third-party product is impeded by SIP, contact the developer to provide a version compatible with macOS Big Sur.

You can disable SIP by using the csrutil command when your Mac started from macOS Recovery; however, doing so greatly reduces the security of data on your Mac. The setting is saved to the Mac computer's firmware, so resetting the parameter RAM enables SIP again. It's also possible that a software update will reenable SIP.

If SIP is disabled, the root user has access to any file in the APFS Data volume that isn't protected by privacy protections, including third-party apps that run as the root user. Malicious software can obtain root-level access if a user enters an administrator name and password to install the software. This would allow the software to modify or overwrite any system file or app. It's best practice to keep SIP enabled at all times.

To prevent an unauthorized user from disabling SIP, you can secure how your Intel-based Mac starts up, including setting a computer firmware password to disallow starting from macOS Recovery, as detailed in Reference 5.3, "Secure Startup."

For more information about SIP, see Apple Support article HT204899, "About System Integrity Protection on your Mac."

Reference 15.3
Manage Font Resources

One way to experience the system resource domain hierarchy is by managing fonts. macOS has advanced font-management technology that enables a nearly unlimited number of fonts using nearly any font type, including bitmap, TrueType, OpenType, and all PostScript fonts.

Fonts are installed in the Font folders in the Library folders throughout macOS. A user can manually install fonts by dragging them into ~/Library/Fonts. Administrators can install fonts for all users by dragging them into /Library/Fonts. This flexible font system enables administrators to better control font use. For example, a font vendor licensing model may grant only specific access for an individual user.

And macOS includes fonts in /System/Library/Fonts. You can't modify the contents of that folder.

Install Fonts Using Font Book

macOS includes a font-management tool, Font Book, which automatically installs fonts for you. Font Book can also be used to organize fonts into more manageable collections, enable or disable fonts to simplify font lists, and resolve duplicate fonts. Exercise 15.1, "Manage Font Resources," has detailed instructions for managing fonts.

> **NOTE ▸** Third-party font-management tools interrupt Font Book and take over font management for macOS.

For a list of fonts included with macOS Big Sur, see Apple Support article HT211240, "Fonts included with macOS Big Sur," which includes lists of fonts in the following categories:

▶ Fonts included with macOS Big Sur—fonts installed and enabled automatically

▶ Fonts available for download in macOS Big Sur with Font Book—fonts that you can use Font Book to download and enable

▶ Fonts available for document support in macOS Big Sur—fonts that are available only in documents that already use the font, or in apps that request the font by name

Exercise 15.1
Manage Font Resources

▶ **Prerequisite**

> ▶ You must have created the Local Administrator (Exercise 3.1, "Configure a Mac for Exercises") and Johnny Appleseed (Exercise 7.1, "Create a Standard User Account") accounts.

In this exercise, you validate that when a font is in /Library/Fonts, it is available to all users. You also confirm that when a font is installed in a single user's Fonts folder, it is available only to that one user.

Add a Font

You can use Font Book to install a font that only one user of the Mac can use.

1   Verify that no users have fast user switching sessions active. If users other than Johnny are logged in, log them out.

2   If necessary, log in as Johnny Appleseed.

3   Open Font Book, which is in the /Applications folder.

4   Choose Font Book > Preferences (Command-Comma).

5   Ensure that Default Install Location is set to User.

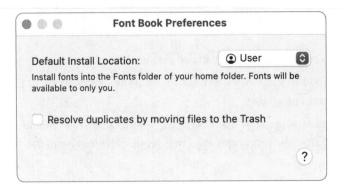

6   Close Font Book preferences.

7   Switch to the Finder, then open /Users/Shared/StudentMaterials/Lesson15.

8   Double-click the font OpenSans-Regular.ttf.

This opens OpenSans-Regular.ttf in Font Book, which shows a preview of the font and gives you the option to install it.

9   Click Install Font.

10 If necessary, select User in the sidebar.

Open Sans is the only font that's installed for Johnny's user account.

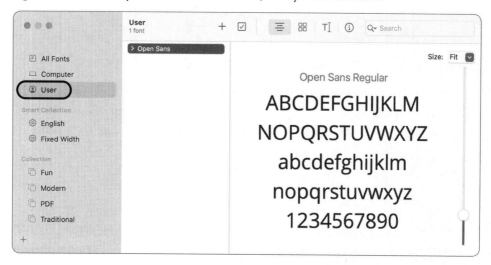

11 Select All Fonts from the sidebar, then scroll to find the instance of Open Sans.

Since this view shows all available fonts, including those installed for the current user and those installed for all Mac users, Open Sans appears in the list.

12 Control-click Open Sans, then choose Show in Finder from the shortcut menu.

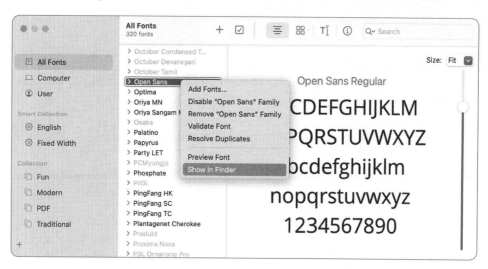

The Finder opens a window that displays the font file.

13 If necessary, widen the Finder window, then choose View > as Columns. You can also click the column view button in the toolbar or use the shortcut Command-3.

14 To verify your location, choose View > Show Path Bar.

The path bar at the bottom of the window shows that the font file is in the Fonts folder in Johnny's user library, previously referred to as ~/Library/Fonts, /Users/johnny/Library/Fonts, and Macintosh HD > Users > johnny > Library > Fonts. It's the only font installed there.

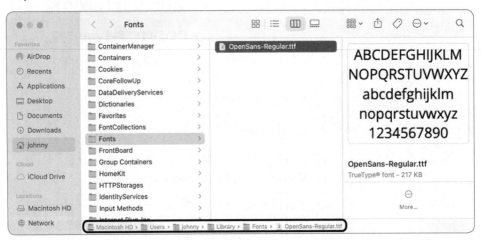

Confirm a Font Is Unavailable to Other Users

If you log in as a different user, even as an administrator, you don't have access to the fonts in Johnny's Fonts folder.

1   Use fast user switching to switch to the Local Administrator account.

2   Open Font Book, then look for the Open Sans font.

Open Sans doesn't appear in Font Book for the Local Administrator account. At this time, you could add Open Sans to this account, just as you added it to Johnny's account. You would have to copy the font file to a location that Local Administrator can access or install it to the location for all users, /Library/Fonts.

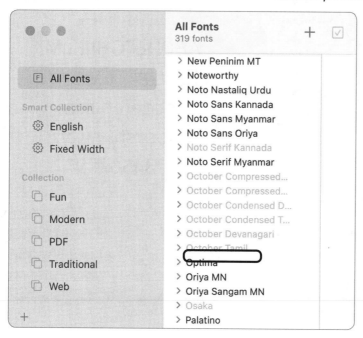

3   Quit Font Book.

4   Log out of Local Administrator.

Make a Font Available to Other Users

Move Open Sans to the Fonts folder for all users.

1   Log in as Johnny Appleseed, then if necessary, open Font Book.

2   Control-click Open Sans, and choose Remove "Open Sans" Family.

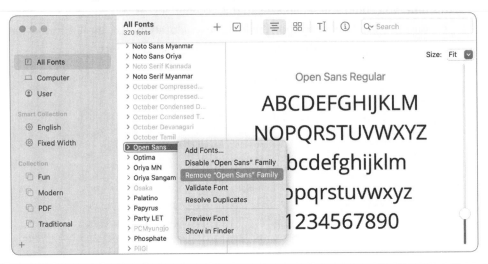

3   In the dialog that appears, click Remove.

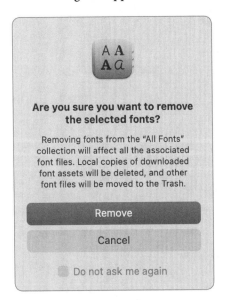

Open Sans is removed from Johnny's Fonts folder (/Users/johnny/Library/Fonts) and placed in the Trash.

4   Choose Font Book > Preferences (Command-Comma), then change Default Install Location to Computer.

5   Close Font Book preferences.

6   Switch to the Finder, then open /Users/Shared/StudentMaterials/Lesson15.

7   Double-click the font OpenSans-Regular.ttf.

8   Click Install Font.

9   Authenticate as Local Administrator.

10   Control-click Open Sans, then choose Show in Finder from the shortcut menu.

The Finder opens a window that displays the font file. Notice that in the path bar, Open Sans is now installed in /Library/Fonts, which makes it available to all users.

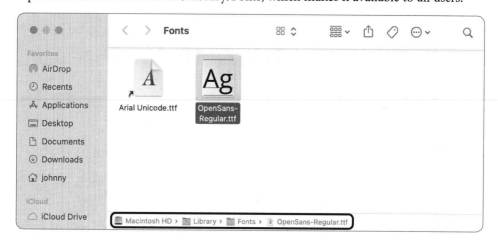

Disable a Font
Use Font Book to watch what happens when you disable a font.

1   Switch back to Font Book.

2   Locate Open Sans in the Font column.

3   Select Open Sans, then click the Disable button in the toolbar.

4   In the confirmation dialog, click Disable.

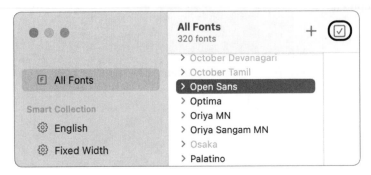

This disables the font. Confirm that the word Off appears next to the Open Sans font in Font Book.

5   In the Finder, navigate to the folder /Library/Fonts.

6   Observe that the font Open Sans is still in the folder.

Disabling a font in Font Book does not remove it from its installed location. Even though the font is disabled for use, Font Book shows a real-time display of the fonts in the macOS search path.

Validate Fonts

Since you changed your font configuration, you use Font Book to check your new setup.

1   In the Font Book window, select All Fonts in the sidebar, click any font in the Font column, then press Command-A to select all fonts.

2   Choose File > Validate Fonts.

Font Book reads and validates the font files, then checks for corruption.

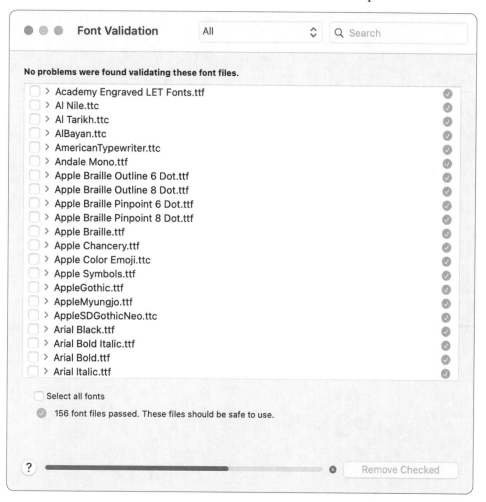

3   When the validation scan finishes, quit Font Book.

4   Log out as Johnny Appleseed.

Lesson 16

Use Metadata, Siri, and Spotlight

Metadata is information used to describe content. The most basic forms of file and folder metadata are names, paths, modification dates, and permissions. Metadata isn't part of an item's content; rather, it describes an item in the file system.

In this lesson you learn how macOS uses file metadata and how this metadata is stored in file systems. You learn how to take advantage of metadata by using the file-system tags feature. And you learn how to use Siri and Spotlight to search.

Reference 16.1
File-System Metadata

Forked file systems, such as Apple File System (APFS) and Mac OS Extended, enable data to appear as a single item in the file system. A file appears as a single item but is composed of two pieces: a data fork and a resource fork. This technology enables macOS to support file type identification in the data fork, whereas the extra information specific to macOS resides in the resource fork.

Some third-party file systems, like FAT, don't know how to store this additional data. The solution to this problem is addressed with the AppleDouble file format, covered later in this lesson.

File Flags and Extended Attributes

macOS also uses metadata in the form of file-system flags and extended attributes to implement system features. Examples of file-system flags include the hidden flag, covered in Lesson 14, "Use Hidden Items, Shortcuts, and File Archives," and the locked flag, covered in Lesson 19, "Manage Files."

Any process or app can add an arbitrary number of custom attributes to a file or folder. This enables developers to create new forms of metadata without having to modify the existing file system.

File-System Tags

Assign file-system tags to your files, then use those tags to search for or organize your files. File-system tags are stored as extended attributes. macOS uses extended attributes for several file features, including the Stationery Pad option, Hide Extension option, and comments. You can access these items from the Info window in the Finder. The following Info window screenshot shows a document featuring Red and Whitepaper file-system tags and a searchable text comment.

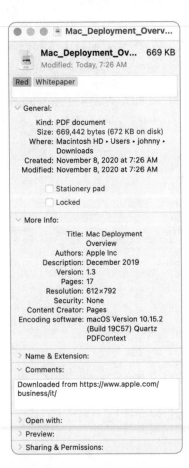

You can assign multiple tags to your files, and they can have custom user-defined tag colors and tag names. Any app that presents a Save dialog allows you to modify tags for documents. When you select tags for a document, type a new name in the Tags field to create a new tag.

To customize tags, open the Tags pane of the Finder preferences by choosing Finder > Preferences or by pressing Command-Comma and clicking Tags in the toolbar at the top of the window. From the Tags pane, create additional tags by clicking the Add (+) button, and you can remove existing tags by clicking the Remove (–) button. To rename a tag, click the tag name, and to change the color, click the tag color. Define which tags are shown in the Finder sidebar by selecting the tag checkbox, and you can set the tag order by dragging tag entries in the list. Below the tags sidebar list, you can define favorite tags so that they will appear in the Finder menus.

Stacks are useful for organizing your desktop by automatically gathering your files into related groups. In the Finder, from the View menu, choose Use Stacks, or just

Control-click anywhere in the desktop and choose Use Stacks. By default, macOS organizes stacks by kind. Here's an example of some files organized in stacks by kind.

macOS uses metadata to enable you to group your stacks by the following:

- ▶ Kind
- ▶ Date Last Opened
- ▶ Date Added
- ▶ Date Modified
- ▶ Date Created
- ▶ Tags

Here's an example of a desktop with stacks grouped by tags.

When stacks are organized by tag, files that don't have a tag get their own stack: "No Tags." A stack looks like a stack of files. You can place your pointer over a stack, then use two fingers on a trackpad or one finger on a Multi-Touch mouse to scroll through the contents. Click a stack to reveal its contents. You can have multiple stacks expanded at the same time. If you sort stacks by tags, each file that has multiple tags will appear in multiple stacks.

You can edit a file's tags in the Preview column, which is displayed when you view items in the Finder in columns or as a gallery. You can also choose View > Show Preview (or press Shift-Command-P) when you view items in the Finder as icons or in a list. When you select a file or multiple files, the Preview column also displays the quick actions available for the selection. Different kinds of files have different kinds of quick actions available. The following figure illustrates that quick actions are available for the selected document (Rotate Left, Create PDF, and More) while viewing items as a gallery.

macOS allows you to search for or organize your items by tag. In the Finder, you can find tags with Spotlight or in the sidebar. Using Spotlight is detailed later in this lesson.

AppleDouble File Format

File-system metadata compatibility with third-party file systems might be an issue. Only volumes formatted with the APFS or Mac OS Extended file system fully support resource forks, data forks, file flags, and extended attributes. Third-party software exists for Windows operating systems to enable them to access the extended metadata features of APFS and Mac OS Extended. More often, though, users take advantage of the compatibility software built into macOS to help other file systems work with these metadata items.

For almost anything other than APFS or Mac OS Extended volumes, including FAT volumes, older Xsan volumes, and older NFS shares, macOS stores metadata from the file system in a separate hidden data file. The data retains the original name, but the metadata is saved with a period and underscore (._) before the original name. This file is sometimes referred to as a dot-underscore file. This technique is called AppleDouble.

For example, if you copy a file that contains metadata and is named My Document.docx to a FAT32 volume, macOS automatically splits the file and writes it as two discrete pieces on the FAT32 volume. The file's internal data is written with the same name as the original, but the metadata is written to a file named ._My Document.docx, which remains hidden from the Finder. This works out well for most files, because Windows apps use only the contents of the data fork. But if you use Windows to edit and save a file like this to a FAT32 volume, the resource fork will not be preserved, so if you later open the file on your Mac, information might be missing. And if users on other operating systems display hidden files, they will encounter the dot-underscore files if they exist.

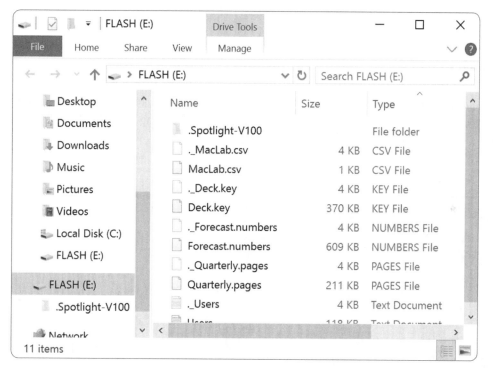

Windows systems default to automatically hiding dot-underscore files. In fact, to acquire the Windows screenshot shown here, we had to manually turn on visibility for Hidden Items. macOS includes a method for handling metadata on SMB network shares from NTFS volumes that doesn't require the AppleDouble format. The native file system for current Windows-based computers, NTFS, supports something similar to file forking, known as alternative data streams. The file system writes the metadata to the alternative data stream, so the file appears as a single item on both Windows and macOS.

Reference 16.2
Siri and Spotlight

For any query, Siri and Spotlight can go beyond file-system searches. Siri and Spotlight can find relevant information from inside local documents, app function results, and internet sources. If you enabled Siri, the Siri icon is in the upper-right corner of the screen, immediately to the left of the day and time (or just the time if you turned off displaying the day). From left to right, the following figure displays the Spotlight icon, the Control Center icon, the Siri icon, and the day and time.

Search with Siri

With Siri you can speak plain-language requests and macOS returns the results, often both in spoken word and as a visual representation. You can initiate a Siri request by clicking the Siri icon at the upper-right corner of the screen or by using the default Siri keyboard shortcut: press and hold Command-Space bar until the Siri window appears.

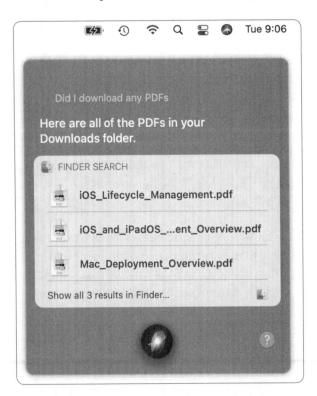

As you speak, Siri will translate your words to text and, more importantly, interpret your meaning. As the preceding screenshot illustrates, Siri interpreted "Did I download any PDFs" to mean "PDFs in your Downloads folder" and returned a Finder search. You can drag some types of Siri search results into an app or a window on your desktop. And you can double-click your words, modify your request, then press Return to make a new Siri request.

When you make a request with Siri, your Mac will send the translated text to Apple servers to interpret the meaning of your words. In a local file search, Siri leverages Spotlight to provide the file list results.

If you ask Siri to find a password, Siri opens Safari and then opens the Passwords pane in Safari preferences.

> **NOTE ▶** This guide primarily focuses on using Siri to search for local items, but Siri is capable of much more, like helping you find your iPhone. Find out what else you can ask by opening Siri, not asking anything, and waiting a few moments. For more information, see Apple Support article HT206993, "How to use Siri on your Mac."

Search with Hey Siri

Hey Siri enables you to access Siri hands-free. Just say "Hey Siri," then make your request. The following Mac computers support Hey Siri:

▶ MacBook Pro introduced in 2018 or later

▶ MacBook Air introduced in 2018 or later

▶ iMac Pro

▶ iMac introduced in 2020

Hey Siri can also access HomeKit and control your HomeKit-compatible devices.

For more information about devices that support Hey Siri, see Apple Support article HT209014, "Devices that support 'Hey Siri.'"

Search with Spotlight

Spotlight combines the search results list and search results preview into a window, called the Spotlight window, that appears on top of your other open windows. You can initiate a Spotlight search by clicking the Spotlight (magnifying glass) icon at the upper-right corner of the screen or by using the default Spotlight keyboard shortcut: Command-Space bar.

You can drag the top of the Spotlight window to move the Spotlight window around if you want.

Spotlight search is so fast that the results change in real time as you type in your search query. Spotlight also suggests variations of your search terms.

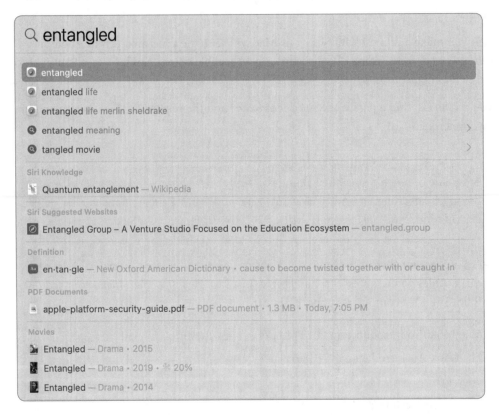

Use the pointer or the Up Arrow and Down Arrow keys to navigate the results list. Click an item to show a preview area in the right side of the Spotlight window. Or just press Tab. Both the results list and the preview area are scrollable to reveal more content.

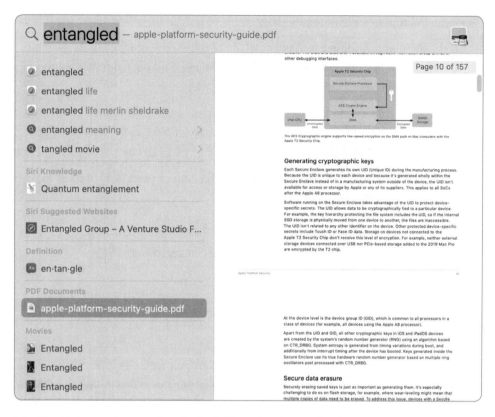

The Spotlight window works a little differently when it displays the preview area. To remove the preview area, remove the text of your search query.

You have lots of flexibility with the results. You can do the following:

▶ Open the first result: Press Return.

▶ Display a preview for the item: Click a file, folder, definition, song, movie, or other kind of item to display a preview for that item. Click it again to open it. Or click the Play button to play a song.

▶ See the results of a suggested search in Spotlight (indicated by a Spotlight icon): Click the item.

▶ See the results of a suggested search on the web (indicated by a Safari icon): Click the item.

▶ Open an item: Double-click an item, or select an item and then press Return.

▶ Show the location of a file in the Finder:

  ▶ If the Spotlight window doesn't display the preview area, use the Up Arrow and Down Arrow keys to select an item, then press and hold the Command key. The item's icon changes to the Finder icon.

  ▶ If the Spotlight window displays the preview area, press and hold the Command key to display the full path of the selected item at the bottom of preview area of the Spotlight window.

  ▶ While still holding the Command key, click the item or press Return to open the item's enclosing folder in the Finder.

▶ Copy an item: Drag a file to your desktop or a Finder window.

▶ Perform a search in your default web browser for your search terms: Press Command-B.

▶ Open a new web browser or Finder window with your search terms automatically entered in the Search field: Scroll to the bottom of the Spotlight window and select "Search the Web" or "Search in Finder."

See "Search with Spotlight on Mac" at support.apple.com/guide/mac-help/mchlp1008 and "Spotlight keyboard shortcuts on Mac" at support.apple.com/guide/mac-help/mh26783 in the macOS User Guide for more information.

Search with Look Up

In macOS Big Sur, to learn more about a word or phrase, Control-click it, then choose Look Up from the shortcut menu. Look Up casts a wide net for your search topic, returning results from the web, Music, and the App Store. It can also browse movie showtimes and nearby locations. The first time you use Look Up, macOS displays a dialog about the sources Look Up uses :

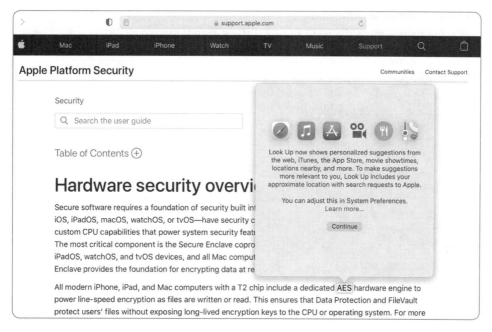

After you click Continue, you can scroll through the categories of Look Up results at the bottom of the Look Up window.

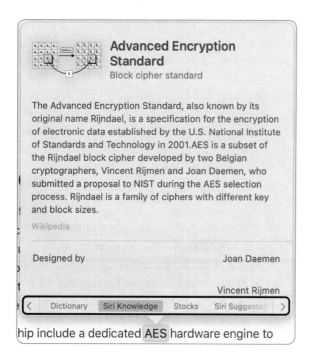

About Search Results

The following figure shows the results of a Spotlight search for "Apple M1 chip."

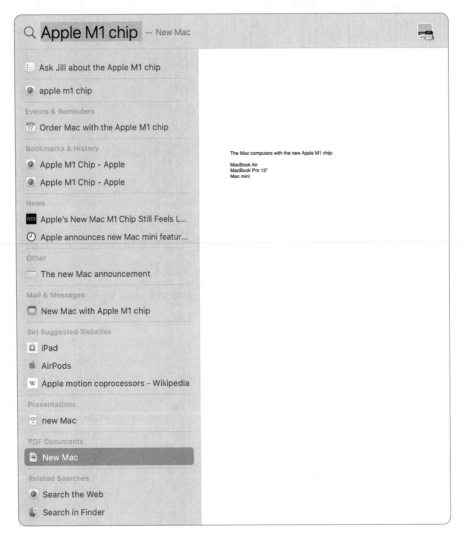

The results list contains results from reminders from Reminders, internet sources, events from Calendar, documents, notes from Notes, articles from News, and messages from Mail. Spotlight can also search inside app data sources. In the preceding Spotlight search result, the selected item being previewed is a PDF document. Note the Preview app icon in the upper-right corner of the Spotlight search window. The document's name doesn't contain the words "Apple M1 chip." Instead, Spotlight searched inside the text of the document.

Siri and Spotlight can also take advantage of an app's functions. For example, Siri and Spotlight can perform mathematical calculations and unit conversions (including market-based currency conversion) by integration with Calculator.

The metadata technologies covered previously in this lesson are also searchable with Siri and Spotlight, including filenames, file flags, modification dates, and file-system tags. Additionally, many files contain internal metadata used to describe the file's content. For example, many photo files contain information about camera settings as metadata embedded within the file. Siri and Spotlight can search through this document-specific metadata information as well.

In addition to local files, Spotlight (and by proxy Siri) can search through the contents of shared files from other Mac clients, Time Machine backups, and iCloud Drive.

Extending beyond local network services, Siri and Spotlight can search a variety of internet sources through Apple services known as Siri Suggestions. These Apple-hosted services use a combination of search history, location information, and user information to generate relevant search results from a wide variety of internet sources. An internet connection is required to take advantage of Siri Suggestions.

Spotlight Indexing

Spotlight (and by proxy Siri) is able to perform wide and deep searches of local items and shared files quickly because it works in the background to maintain highly optimized databases of indexed metadata for each attached local volume. When you first set up macOS, it creates these databases by indexing all the available local volumes. macOS also indexes new volumes when they are first attached.

A background process automatically updates the index databases on the fly as changes are made throughout the file system. As these indexes are kept current, Spotlight needs to search only the databases to return thorough results. Spotlight preemptively searches everything for you in the background, so you don't have to wait for the results when you need them.

Spotlight directly indexes Time Machine, but it doesn't index shared volumes from other computers. Spotlight can connect to indexes on shares hosted from other Mac operating systems.

In each external volume that you can write to, macOS keeps the Spotlight general index databases at the root level of the volume in a folder named .Spotlight-V100. For your startup volume, the folder is /private/var/db/Spotlight-V100. A few apps maintain their own databases separate from these general index databases. One example is Mail, which maintains its own optimized email database in each user's folder inside the ~/Library/Mail/V8/MailData folder.

If you are experiencing problems with local file searching, go to the end of the lesson to learn how to force Spotlight to rebuild the index databases with the privacy pane in Spotlight preferences. It's not recommended to manually modify the Spotlight index databases.

Spotlight Plug-ins

Spotlight can create indexes, and search—from an ever-growing variety of local metadata—using plug-in technologies. Each Spotlight plug-in examines specific types of files or databases. Many Spotlight plug-ins are included by default, but Apple and third-party developers can create additional plug-ins to expand Spotlight search capabilities.

You can use the included Spotlight plug-ins to:

▶ Search with basic file metadata, including name, file size, creation date, and modification date

▶ Search with media-specific metadata from picture, music, and video files, including timecode, creator information, and hardware capture information

▶ Search through the contents of a variety of file types, including text files; app databases; audio and video files; Photoshop files; PDF files; Pages, Numbers, and Keynote files; and Microsoft Office files

▶ Search through personal information like the contents in Contacts and Calendar

▶ Search for correspondence information such as the contents of Mail messages and Messages chat transcripts

▶ Search for relevant information like your favorites or web browser bookmarks and history

▶ Perform internet searches

Spotlight plug-ins are stored in various Library folders. The Apple built-in Spotlight plug-ins can be found in both /System/Library/Spotlight and /Library/Spotlight. Third-party plug-ins should always be installed in either /Library/Spotlight or ~/Library/Spotlight, depending on who needs access to them.

For a file, you can create custom metadata for Spotlight by entering Spotlight comments in the Info and Inspector windows from the Finder.

Search Security

To provide security on par with the rest of the file system, Spotlight indexes every item's permissions. Even though Spotlight indexes every item on a volume, it automatically filters search results to show only items that the current user has permissions to access. For example, you can't search the content of another user's Documents folder. All users can search through locally attached nonsystem volumes, including mounted disk images, even if another user attached the device.

Siri takes advantage of many Apple services and internet sources, but it always adheres to the Apple Privacy Policy. Apple takes user privacy very seriously and always attempts to keep a user's information as safe as possible while still providing advanced services. You can disable Spotlight and Look Up searches that require internet services in Spotlight preferences in the General pane by deselecting Siri Suggestions.

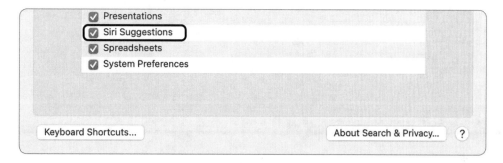

You can delete your Siri & Dictation history from Apple servers, as covered later in this lesson.

To learn more about the Apple Privacy Policy, see www.apple.com/privacy/.

Perform an Advanced Spotlight Search

The default Spotlight search provides quick search results, but as you've learned in this lesson, Spotlight has a powerful range of search features.

You can use the Finder to perform an advanced file-system search with any of the following methods:

- At the bottom of a Spotlight search list, click "Search in Finder."

- In a Finder window, enter a word or phrase in the Search field (in the upper-right corner).

- In the Finder, choose File > Find (or press Command-F).

NOTE ▸ If you use the last method in this list, the search window displays an attribute filter under the toolbar, set to "Kind is Any" by default. For the other two methods, you'll learn more about adding the attribute filter later in this section.

Select an item next to the word Search under the toolbar to limit the scope of the search.

If you haven't already done so, enter a word or phrase in the Search field in the upper-right corner. A menu appears with suggestions for search types, based on what you've entered. You can choose something from the menu or just press Return to include anything related to your search term.

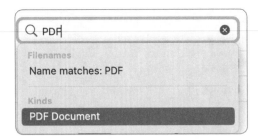

Select an item from the search results to display the path to the selected item at the bottom of the Finder window.

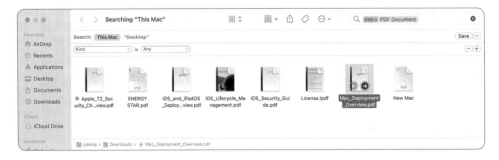

You can select an item and press the Space bar to open a preview of the selected item.

If the search attribute doesn't appear under the toolbar, click the small Add (+) button below the Search field; you can add as many search attributes as you need.

Refine your Spotlight search from the results in a Finder window. Click the first word in the search attribute (by default "Kind") to change the attribute.

After you add a new search attribute, click the first word in the search attribute to choose another type from the menu.

If the search attribute you're looking for isn't displayed, you can add other attributes that aren't enabled by default. To add search attributes, select any attribute and choose Other from the menu. The dialog that appears lets you add search attributes to the menu. Two especially useful search attributes for administrators are "File invisible" and "System files," neither of which is shown by default in any Spotlight search.

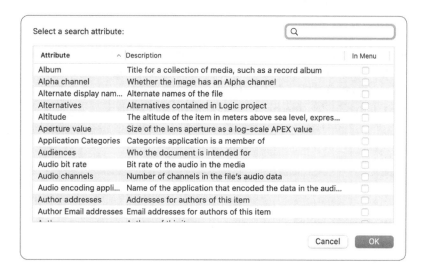

NOTE ► Take some time to explore the additional search attributes. Search attributes include specifying audio file tags, digital camera metadata, authorship information, contact information, and many other metadata types.

You can click the Save button on the right to save your search criteria as a Smart Folder.

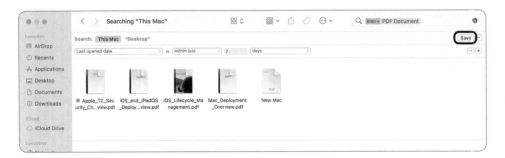

You can remove the suggested name for the Smart Folder, enter a descriptive name, then click Save. By default, the option to add the Smart Folder to the Finder sidebar is enabled.

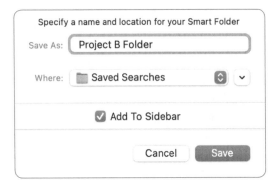

Smart Folders are like normal folders in that they can be given a unique name and placed anywhere you like, including the Finder sidebar. Smart Folders are special because their contents always match your search criteria no matter how the file system changes. The Recents and Tags items in the Finder sidebar are predefined Smart Folders.

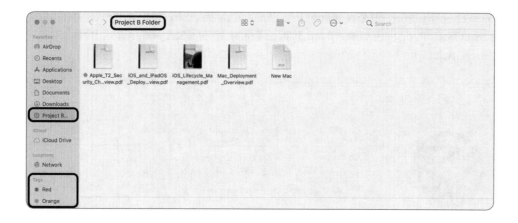

Manage Siri Preferences

When you use Siri, the words you say will be recorded and sent to Apple to process your requests. Your device will also send Apple other information, such as your name and nickname; the names, nicknames, and relationships (for example, "my dad") found in your contacts; song names in your collection; the names of your photo albums; and the names of apps installed on your device (collectively, your "User Data"). All of this data is used to help Siri understand you better and recognize what you say. It is not linked to other data that Apple may have from your use of other Apple services.

When you use Siri to search for your documents:

▶ The Siri request is sent to Apple, but the names and the content of your documents are not sent to Apple.

▶ The search for your documents is performed locally on the Mac.

If you have Location Services enabled, the location of your device at the time you make a request will also be sent to Apple to help Siri improve the accuracy of its response to your requests. You may choose to disable Location Services for Siri. To do so, open System Preferences on your Mac, click Security & Privacy, click the Privacy button, click Location Services, and deselect the checkbox for Siri & Dictation.

Siri requires an internet connection to query Apple services to interpret the meaning of your requests.

You may choose to turn off Siri at any time. You can disable Siri with Setup Assistant during a macOS setup or upgrade or from System Preferences > Siri preferences by deselecting Enable Ask Siri.

If you turn off Ask Siri and Dictation is turned on, or if you turn off Dictation and Ask Siri is turned on, this message appears: "The information that *the service you just turned off* uses to respond to your requests is also used for *the service that is still turned on* and will remain on Apple servers unless *the service that is still turned on* is also turned off."

In addition to enabling or disabling Siri, you can adjust several features from Siri preferences, including the following:

▶ You can select the language that Siri will be expected to understand and respond in. Siri supports over 40 languages and dialects.

▶ You can select the voice that Siri will use to speak responses. The choices in the Siri Voice menu are based on the selected language. You can also disable the voice feedback.

▶ You can use the Input pane in Sound preferences to select the microphone input that Siri will use to listen for your requests. The internal microphone on Apple portable computers is optimized for Siri input and often includes noise-cancellation technology. For desktop Mac computers lacking a microphone, or if you are in a particularly noisy environment, you can use a dedicated headset-style microphone.

▶ You can select the keyboard shortcut used to start a Siri request.

▶ You can click Delete Siri & Dictation History, then confirm that you want to remove Siri and Dictation interactions from Apple servers.

▶ You can click Siri Suggestions & Privacy to modify how Siri will learn from and use various apps to make suggestions. For each of the listed apps, you can deselect the "Learn from this App" checkbox to prevent Siri from learning from that app. Some apps in the list, like Messages in the following figure, offer an additional option that you can turn off or on: "Show Siri Suggestions in App."

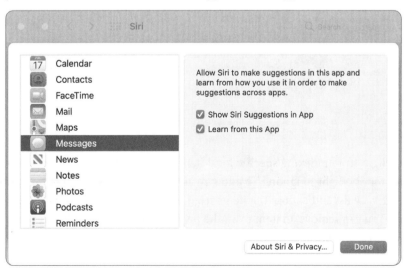

Manage Spotlight Preferences

From Spotlight preferences, any user can choose to disable specific categories so that they don't appear in Spotlight searches. For example, users can choose to disable Siri Suggestions if they don't want any search information sent over the internet. You can also prevent some volumes from being indexed by specifying those volumes in the privacy list. However, by default all new volumes are automatically indexed, so users must manually configure Spotlight to ignore a volume.

The Spotlight privacy list is a systemwide setting that remains the same across all user accounts, but users can change the privacy list.

Opening Spotlight preferences defaults to the Search Results pane, where you can disable specific categories from the search results. Deselect the checkboxes next to the categories you want to ignore. Individual users have their own separate Search Results settings.

To prevent Spotlight from indexing specific local items, click the Privacy button to reveal the list of items for Spotlight to ignore. To add new items, click the Add (+) button at the bottom of the privacy list and choose the items from a browser dialog, or drag items into the privacy list. You can remove an item from the privacy list by selecting it and then clicking the Remove (–) button at the bottom of the list.

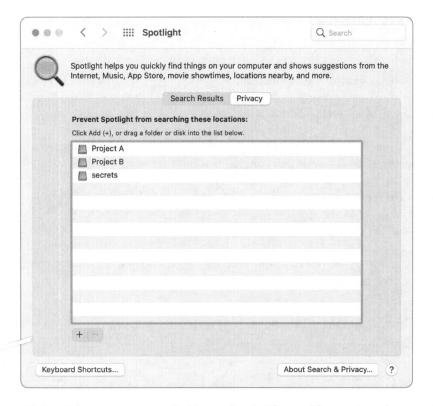

All Spotlight settings are applied immediately. If you add an entire volume to the privacy list, macOS deletes the Spotlight index database from that volume. In turn, removing a volume from the privacy list rebuilds the Spotlight index database on that volume. For more information, see Apple Support article HT201617, "Rebuild the Spotlight index on your Mac."

Exercise 16.1
Examine File Metadata

> ▶ **Prerequisite**
>
> ▶ You must have created the Johnny Appleseed account (Exercise 7.1, "Create a Standard User Account").

In this exercise, you examine file metadata in the Finder Info window and add custom metadata.

Use Tag and Comment Metadata

1   Log in as Johnny Appleseed.

2   Open Safari, then navigate to www.apple.com.

3   Choose File > Save As (or press Command-S).

4   In the Tags field, type **Apple Info**. The tag might complete automatically if a previous participant performed this exercise using the same iCloud account.

5   If necessary, in the menu that appears, click the "Create new tag 'Apple Info'" option.

6   Click elsewhere in the dialog to dismiss the tags or press the Tab key.

7   Ensure that the location (the Where menu) is set to Documents and the Format menu is set to Page Source, then click Save.

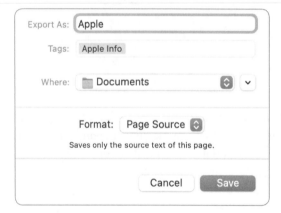

8   Quit Safari.

9   In the Finder, navigate to your Documents folder (choose Go > Documents, or press Shift-Command-O).

10 Select the HTML file, probably called "Apple.html," then choose File > Get Info (or press Command-I).

11 Expand the General, More Info, and Comments sections of the Info window.

The Info window in the Finder displays information about the file, for example:

▶ Basic metadata such as its size

▶ Information about where on the web it came from

▶ The tag you added when you saved it

You can also edit some metadata types in the Info window.

12 In the Comments section, type **The Apple Orchard**.

This field adds custom metadata to the file, enabling you to attach searchable comments and keywords. You use this comment later, in step 2 of "Use Spotlight to Search for Documents."

13 Close the Info window.

14 If necessary, widen the Finder window, then change the view of the Documents folder to list view (click the List View button in the toolbar, choose View > as List, or press Command-2).

15 Choose View > Show View Options (or press Command-J).

16 In the Show Columns section, select Comments and Tags.

Lesson 17

Manage Time Machine

In this lesson, you learn how Time Machine enables you to browse the backup history of a file system. You become familiar with how to configure Time Machine. And you explore ways to recover files from Time Machine backups.

Reference 17.1
About Time Machine

Every Mac includes Time Machine. Time Machine backs up all your personal files, including apps, music, photos, email, and documents, to an external storage device. If you accidentally delete or change files, or if you have to replace or erase the internal storage for your Mac, you can use Time Machine to recover your files.

Time Machine also performs local snapshots, which capture your content at a specific time when your external storage device for Time Machine isn't available. These backups and local snapshots mean that you can use Time Machine to restore files even when your external storage device isn't available. Time Machine keeps:

- Hourly backups for the past 24 hours
- Daily backups for the past month
- Weekly backups for all previous months
- Local snapshots as space permits

GOALS

- Describe Time Machine

- Configure Time Machine to back up files

- Restore files from a Time Machine backup

To make sure that you have storage space when you need it, when your external storage device becomes full, Time Machine deletes the oldest backups. And Time Machine stores local snapshots only on disks that have plenty of free space. When storage space gets low, Time Machine deletes the oldest snapshots. This is why the Finder, About This Mac, and Get Info don't include local snapshots in their calculations of available disk storage space.

You can turn off Time Machine and wait a few minutes for macOS to delete local snapshots. When you turn Time Machine back on, it remembers the previous external storage devices you were using.

Backups

Your initial backup might take a long time, depending on how many files Time Machine needs to back up. But you can use your Mac while Time Machine backs it up. Time Machine backs up only files that changed since the previous backup, so your subsequent backups complete faster than your first backup. See Apple Support article HT204412, "If a Time Machine backup takes longer than you expect," for more information.

After you set up Time Machine, it automatically makes hourly backups. Between backups, a background process, like the one Spotlight uses, tracks changes to the original file system. When the next scheduled backup occurs, Time Machine backs up only files that have changed. Time Machine then combines the new content with hard-link file-system pointers (which occupy nearly zero storage space) to the previous backup content and creates a simulated view of the entire file system at that point in time.

Time Machine doesn't back up the signed system volume (SSV), which includes macOS and the apps that come with macOS. Also, Time Machine ignores files that don't need to be backed up (ones that can be re-created after a restoration) to save space. Generally speaking, Time Machine ignores temporary files, Spotlight indexes, items in the Trash, and anything that can be considered a cache. Time Machine doesn't back up system log files. Software developers can also instruct Time Machine to ignore specific app data that doesn't need to be backed up. For example, apps for internet file storage providers, like Box or OneDrive, can instruct Time Machine to ignore files saved to a cloud service.

Some database files appear as large, single files to the file system. Using a database app, a user might edit only a few bytes in a large database file. Even so, Time Machine creates another copy of the entire file. This can fill your external storage device much more quickly than if the database was stored as many smaller files. Check with third-party database app developers, such as Claris International Inc., on their recommendations for backing up database files with Time Machine.

Even though Time Machine creates local snapshots, you should also periodically connect your external storage device—that's configured for Time Machine—to your Mac to back up your files to a location besides your internal disk. If anything happens to your Mac or its internal disk, you can use your external storage device to restore your entire system to another Mac or to a blank replacement disk on your Mac.

Time Machine works best if you use your external storage device only for Time Machine backups. In fact, if your external storage device for Time Machine backups is formatted with APFS, the Finder won't let you copy files directly to that external storage device.

If your external storage device for Time Machine isn't formatted with APFS, you can keep other files on that external storage device, but Time Machine won't back up those files, and there will be less space for Time Machine backups.

> **NOTE** ▶ After you create a Time Machine backup from a volume of macOS Big Sur, you can use that backup only on Mac computers with macOS Big Sur.

Local Snapshots

Time Machine saves local snapshots under four circumstances:

- ▶ When you start a Time Machine backup to an external storage device for the first time.

- ▶ Every hour after you turn on Time Machine.

  An hourly local snapshot is saved for 24 hours. macOS saves Time Machine local snapshots hourly, unless you deselect Back Up Automatically in Time Machine preferences.

- ▶ Until macOS needs to use the storage space that the local snapshots use.

  In this case, Time Machine saves a local snapshot of your last successful Time Machine backup.

- ▶ Before you install any macOS update, even if you don't turn on Time Machine.

For more information about local snapshots, see Apple Support article HT204015, "About Time Machine local snapshots," and the tmutil man page.

Reference 17.2
Configure Time Machine

Get one of these types of external storage devices:

▶ One that can connect to a USB or Thunderbolt port on your Mac

▶ On a Mac using macOS High Sierra (10.13) or later: a shared folder configured to be a Time Machine backup destination on your network over SMB

▶ A network-attached storage (NAS) device that supports Time Machine over SMB

Set Up Time Machine from an Alert

When you connect an external storage device (also called a disk) directly to your Mac, you may be asked if you want to use it to back up your Mac with Time Machine. To use the disk for Time Machine, move your pointer to the alert, click Options, then click "Set up."

After you click "Set up," Time Machine requires you to create a backup password to encrypt your backup disk. Use the dialog to set a password.

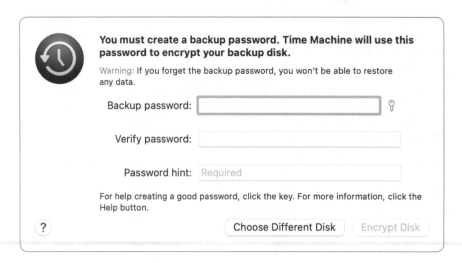

When you click "Set up" in the alert about using a disk for Time Machine and provide a password to encrypt your backup disk:

► You must provide a password and a password hint.

► Your backups will be accessible only to users with the password.

► macOS erases the external storage device and creates a new volume that's formatted as APFS (Encrypted, Case Sensitive).

► If the disk is named "Untitled" (regardless of case), then macOS names the volume "Backups of *Computer Name*," where *Computer Name* is the computer name of your Mac.

► macOS updates permissions for the volume so that only Time Machine can use the volume (you can't copy files to the volume in the Finder). In fact, the backups are not even visible for a Mac with an earlier version of macOS than macOS Big Sur.

► macOS assigns a Time Machine icon to the external storage device, as illustrated in the following figure.

If you access a locally attached Time Machine external storage device that's formatted as APFS (Apple File System), the backup files are in the root of the external storage device. Inside are folders named using the date and time of each backup.

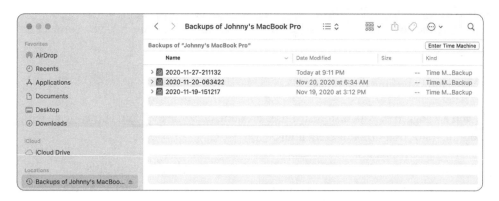

Inside each dated folder are folders representing each backed-up volume.

When you encrypt your Time Machine external storage device, macOS doesn't initially save the encryption password to your keychain. After you eject your encrypted Time Machine external storage device, the next time you connect it, macOS prompts you to enter the password and optionally save it to the keychain system for automatic retrieval.

If you have multiple external storage devices connected, you can choose which one to use.

Set Up Time Machine Manually

If Time Machine doesn't ask you to select an external storage device when you connect the external storage device to your Mac:

1   Open Time Machine preferences.

2   If you are logged in with a standard user account, click the lock and authenticate with administrator user account credentials.

3   Click Select Backup Disk or Select Disk, or "Add or Remove Backup Disk" (Time Machine preferences displays different options based on whether you have zero, one, or multiple external storage devices configured).

4   Select an external storage device from the list.

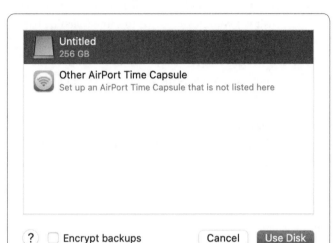

NOTE ▶ Apple recommends that you select "Encrypt backups," then enter a password to use for encryption. Go to the next section for more information about encryption.

5   Click Use Disk.

If the encryption checkbox is dimmed, hover your pointer over it to display an explanation of why. For example, the explanation might say that you must reformat or repartition the selected disk. If no explanation appears, the disk you selected doesn't support encryption.

If you connect your encrypted external storage device to another Mac with macOS Big Sur, you must enter the password on the other Mac to access the backed-up files.

If you don't encrypt your external storage device, then the first time you make a Time Machine backup macOS displays an alert that tells you that your external storage device isn't encrypted. You can click Settings, then configure your Time Machine external storage device to be encrypted.

What happens next after you click Use Disk depends on how the external storage device is configured.

When You Use a Blank Disk

If the external storage device doesn't have any files on it yet, then Time Machine erases the disk and creates a new APFS (Case-sensitive) volume dedicated to Time Machine back-ups, just as if you replied to an alert asking if you wanted to use the disk for Time Machine backups. If the disk is named "Untitled" (regardless of case), then macOS names the volume "Backups of *Computer Name*," where *Computer Name* is the computer name of your Mac.

When You Use an Existing Time Machine Disk Formatted as APFS

If the external storage device is already formatted with APFS and is being used as a Time Machine destination for another Mac, Time Machine preferences may display a red "i" badge next to the disk.

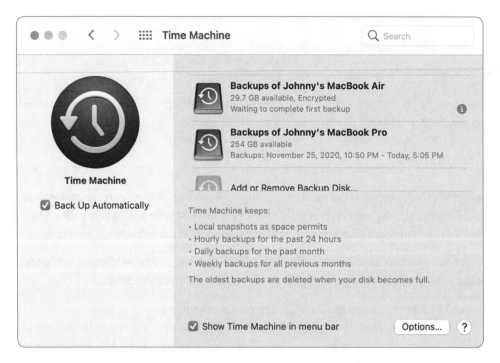

After you click the red "i," macOS displays a dialog with the options:

▶ Claim Existing Backups

▶ Start New Backup

▶ Decide Later

If you click Claim Existing Backups, you can't use the external storage device for backups on the other Mac.

If you click Start New Backup, you must provide a password and hint to secure the backup, then you can click Encrypt Disk. After you click Encrypt Disk, macOS creates a new APFS volume dedicated to Time Machine backups, and names the volume "Backups of *Computer Name*," where *Computer Name* is the computer name of your Mac. The following figure in Disk Utility illustrates that multiple Time Machine volumes can share the same APFS container on your external storage device, and they share the available space within the APFS container.

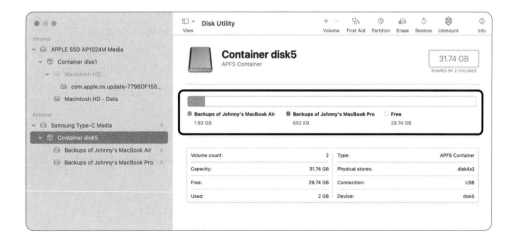

When You Use an Existing Time Machine Disk Formatted as Mac OS Extended

Prior to macOS Big Sur, the most common format for a Time Machine external storage device was Mac OS Extended (Journaled) (HFS Plus Journaled). Time Machine also supports all Mac OS Extended (Journaled) formats and Xsan formats for external storage devices that are attached to a USB or Thunderbolt port on your Mac.

If you access a locally attached Time Machine external storage device that's not formatted as APFS, the backup files are in the root of the external storage device in a folder named Backups.backupdb. This database folder contains more folders that have the name of each Mac that was backed up to the disk.

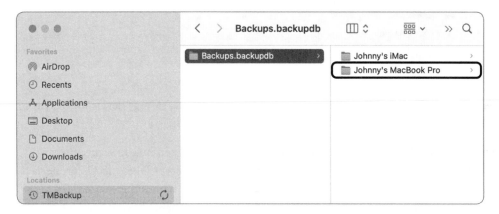

Inside each Mac folder are folders named using the date and time of each backup. Inside each dated folder are folders representing each backed-up volume.

When You Use a Disk That Isn't Blank or Supported

If you select an external storage device that's connected directly to your Mac and it isn't blank, or it doesn't use one of these supported format, then macOS Big Sur asks if you want to erase the volume so that it can be used for Time Machine. The dialog varies depending on the external storage device.

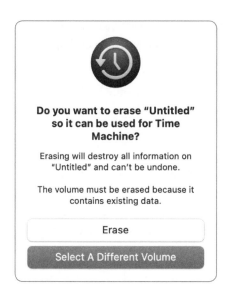

If you click Erase, macOS reformats the disk with the APFS (Case-sensitive) format.

NOTE ▶ Reformatting erases all files on the disk, so do it only if you no longer need the files or you have copied them to a different external storage device.

When You Use a Network Volume

If you select a network storage device, any existing backups are upgraded. These upgraded backups and new backups that you make with macOS Big Sur are compatible with macOS Big Sur only.

Inherit Backups

macOS Big Sur asks you if you want to inherit a backup under the following situations:

▶ You used Migration Assistant to transfer settings from an old Mac to a new Mac.

▶ You used Migration Assistant to transfer settings from a Time Machine backup on an old Mac to a new Mac.

▶ You cloned your startup volume, or physically moved the disk from one Mac to a new Mac.

▶ You had the main logic board of your Mac replaced.

If you still want to use the Time Machine backup on the old Mac, click Create New Backup. This preserves the backup history so that you can still use the Time Machine backup with the old Mac. And it starts a separate backup for your new Mac.

If you're replacing an old Mac and you won't try to use the Time Machine backup with the old Mac and want to preserve the backup history, click Inherit Backup.

Use Multiple Volumes

For additional backup security and convenience, you can repeat the steps from earlier in this lesson to add another external storage device. For example, you might connect your Mac to one external storage device at work and leave the external storage device at work. Then when you bring your Mac home, you might connect your Mac to a different external storage device and leave that external storage device at home.

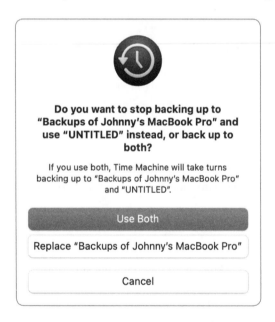

Configure Time Machine Preferences

You can use Time Machine preferences to do the following:

▶ Add or remove a backup disk.

▶ Verify the backup status.

▶ Manually configure backup options.

▶ Configure the option to show Time Machine in the menu bar.

▶ Configure the option to back up automatically.

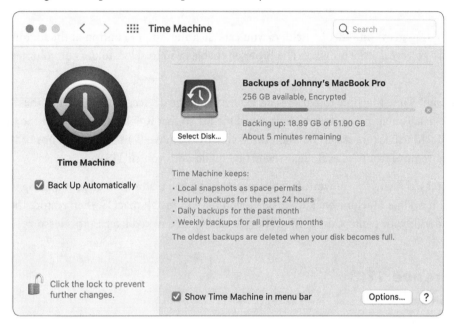

Manage Time Machine Options

Click the Options button at the bottom of Time Machine preferences to adjust backup settings.

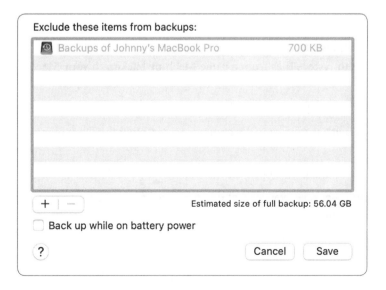

You can exclude items from a backup to reduce the backup space you'll need. Time Machine excludes Time Machine external storage devices from its backups. This prevents multiple external storage devices from backing up each other.

You can drag items into the list field, or you can click the Add (+) button at the bottom of the list to reveal a file browser. The browser enables you to select folders or volumes to exclude.

If you want Time Machine to back up an external storage device, remove it from the exclude list. To remove an item from the exclude list so that it will be included in the next Time Machine backup, select the item, then click the Remove (–) button. Backups of items that you remove from the exclude list won't be made until you click Save.

For increased security, you won't be able to perform a full restoration of your startup volume with a Time Machine backup. Instead, you have to install macOS, then restore the remainder of your content using Migration Assistant, as covered later in this lesson.

Reference 17.3
Restore Files

You can restore:

▶ Specific files with Time Machine

▶ User accounts and entire home folders with Migration Assistant

▶ Specific files with the Finder

Restore Files with Time Machine

Complete the following steps to restore files from a Time Machine backup to your Mac.

1   Open a window for the file that you want to restore. For example:

▶ To restore a file you deleted from your Documents folder, open the Documents folder.

▶ To restore an email, open Mail, then open the mailbox that the email message was in.

▶ If you're using an app that saves versions of documents as you work on them, you can open a document and use Time Machine to restore earlier versions of that document.

2   Connect your Time Machine external storage device to your Mac if it's available.

Otherwise, Time Machine uses your local snapshots.

If you back up to multiple external storage devices, you can switch them before you enter Time Machine. Press and hold the Option key, click the Time Machine menu item, then choose Browse Other Backup Disks. In the "Choose Time Machine Disk to Browse" window, select a disk, then click Use Selected Disk. Time Machine opens, and you can skip to step 4.

3   Open Time Machine with any of the following actions:

▶   Open Spotlight, type **Time Machine**, then press Return.

▶   Click the Time Machine menu, then choose Enter Time Machine.

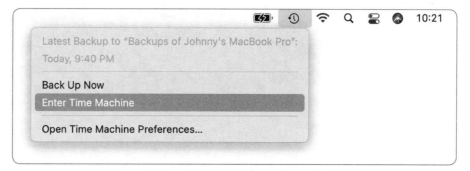

▶   Click the Time Machine menu, press the Option key, choose
Browse Other Backup Disks, select another backup disk from the list, then click
Use Selected Disk.

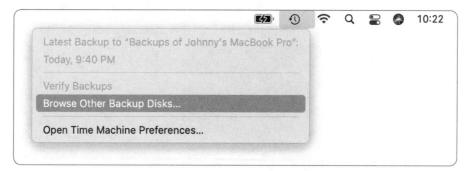

▶   Click Time Machine in the Dock if its icon is in the Dock.

The following figure shows Time Machine for the Documents folder.

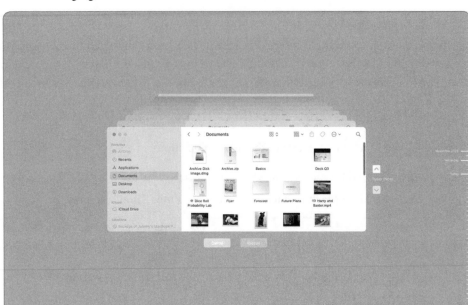

4   Find the files to restore:

▶   Use the timeline on the edge of the screen to display the files in your Time Machine backup as they were at that date and time.

▶   When you select a tick mark in the timeline, Time Machine displays files from that backup. You're browsing that backup. Time Machine displays the date and time of the backup and the tick mark in the timeline in red to indicate that you're browsing that backup.

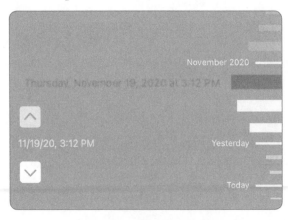

▶   A bright red tick mark is a backup that can be restored now, either from a local snapshot or from your external storage device. When your external storage device isn't available, only the local snapshots are bright red.

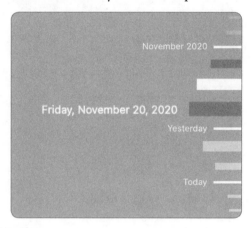

▶   A dimmed red tick mark is a backup that can be restored from your external storage device after it becomes available.

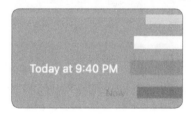

▶   Use the onscreen up and down arrows to jump to the last time the contents of the window changed. You can also use the Search field in a window to find a file, and move through time while focused on changes to that file.

5   Select a file and press the Space bar to preview it and make sure it's the one you want. You can select more than one file at a time, too.

6 Click Restore to restore your selection, or Control-click your selection for other options.

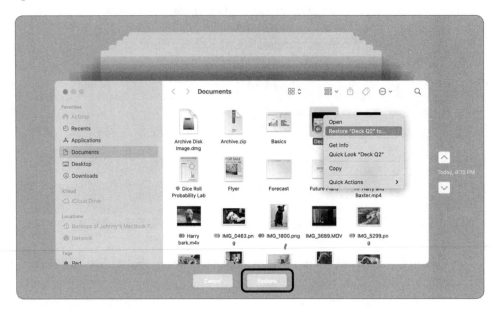

Restore with the Finder

If you experience problems using one of the other Time Machine restoration interfaces, you can browse the backup from the Finder. You don't need special software to browse through backup contents.

Remember the following when you access Time Machine backups from the Finder:

▶ You can only read the contents of a Time Machine backup, which has access control entries (ACEs) that deny write access.

▶ If you don't have file-system permissions to the backup folders, you have to change the ownership or permissions to open the folders in the Finder. You can find out more about changing permissions in Lesson 13, "Manage Permissions and Sharing."

If you access Time Machine over a network, you must manually connect to the Time Machine share first. Connecting to shares is covered in Lesson 24, "Manage Network Services." After you're connected, you must locate the Time Machine backup disk images. They're at the root of the Time Machine share and are most commonly named Backups. Each Mac computer's backup is saved as a separate sparse disk image file named with the Mac computer's sharing name.

Restore Files with Migration Assistant

You can restore a complete user home folder or other nonsystem files from a Time Machine backup using Migration Assistant.

1   When Migration Assistant opens—either when Setup Assistant runs on a new Mac, or on a new installation of Big Sur, or when you open it—choose to restore from a Time Machine backup.

Initial Setup Assistant is covered in Reference 3.1, "Configure a Mac with a New Installation of macOS Big Sur."

2   Select an external storage device and authenticate to access its content.

The remainder of the Migration Assistant process is like the standard migration process covered in Lesson 3, "Set Up and Configure macOS," for settings, or in Lesson 8, "Manage User Home Folders," for user-specific items.

For more information, see Apple Support article HT203981, "Restore your Mac from a backup," and "Change Time Machine preferences on Mac," in the macOS User Guide at support.apple.com/guide/mac-help/mh14037/.

Exercise 17.1
Configure Time Machine

> **Prerequisites**
>
>> You must have created the Local Administrator (Exercise 3.1, "Configure a Mac for Exercises") and Johnny Appleseed (Exercise 7.1, "Create a Standard User Account") accounts.
>
>> You must have an external storage device (USB flash drive or other media) to use for backups.

In this exercise, you configure Time Machine to back up your user home folders to your external storage device.

Configure Exclusions for Time Machine

By default, Time Machine backs up the user home folders, the /Library folder, and apps that did not come with macOS Big Sur. In this exercise, you configure Time Machine to back up only user files. In most cases, backing up only user files provides adequate protection because you can always reinstall macOS and apps. If you want to restore printers, network settings, and other systemwide elements, don't add any exclusions to the Time Machine exclusions list.

1   Log in as Johnny Appleseed.

2   Open System Preferences, then click Time Machine.

3   Click the lock button, then authenticate as Local Administrator.

4   Select the "Show Time Machine in menu bar" checkbox if it isn't selected.

5   Click the Options button to reveal a dialog that you can use to exclude folders from backups.

6   Click the Add (+) button at the bottom of the list.

7   Navigate to your startup volume (generally Macintosh HD), then select the Applications and Library folders.

    You can Command-click folders to add them to the selection.

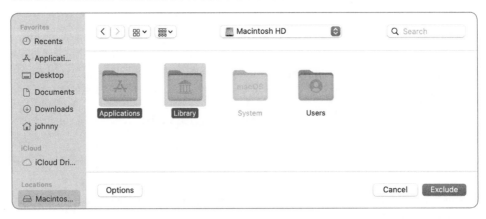

8   Click Exclude.

Your exclusion list now appears like the following figure. The option to back up while on battery power appears only on Mac portable computers.

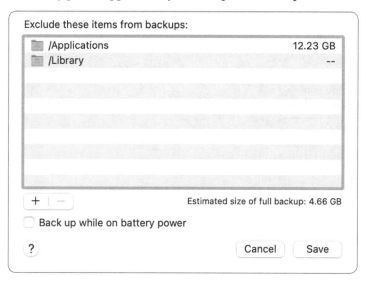

Exclude these items from backups:

/Applications	12.23 GB
/Library	--

Estimated size of full backup: 4.66 GB

☐ Back up while on battery power

?   Cancel   Save

NOTE ► For the purposes of this exercise, you keep the backup small. In a production environment, Apple recommends that you allow Time Machine to back up your entire Mac.

9   Click Save.

Select a Backup Volume

1   Connect your external storage device to your Mac.

2   If a dialog appears and asks if you want to use the disk to back up with Time Machine, click the close (X) button so that you can configure the backup manually.

3   If your external disk isn't currently named Backup, select it, choose File > Rename, then type **Backup** to rename the disk.

4   With Backup still selected, choose File > Get Info.

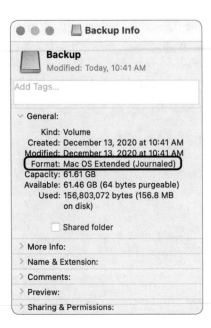

Observe that the format of the disk is either APFS or Mac OS Extended (Journaled), depending on the state of your media and its use case prior to this exercise.

5   In the Time Machine pane of System Preferences, select the Back Up Automatically checkbox.

A dialog appears with a choice of backup targets.

6   Select the external volume named Backup.

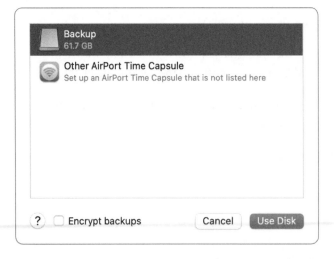

Note the "Encrypt backups" checkbox. When you select this checkbox, you encrypt the backup volume the same way you would encrypt it in the Finder. In production, you should encrypt all backups for security purposes. However, for the purpose of this exercise, leave the checkbox deselected.

7   Click Use Disk.

8   If you see a "Do you want to erase 'Backup' so it can be used for Time Machine?" prompt, click Erase.

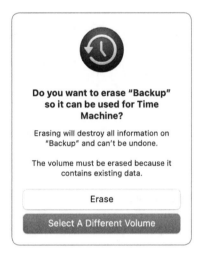

macOS displays a "preparing" message. The Backup volume unmounts, formats as APFS (Case-sensitive), then reappears. Time Machine starts backing up in two minutes. You don't have to wait for it before proceeding with the exercise.

9   Open Disk Utility, then in the sidebar, select Backup.

Confirm that the Backup volume is formatted as APFS (Case-sensitive).

10 Quit Disk Utility.

11 Quit System Preferences.

Perform Exercise 17.2, "Restore Using Time Machine," to test the backup.

Exercise 17.2
Restore Using Time Machine

> **Prerequisite**
>
> ▸ You must have performed Exercise 17.1, "Configure Time Machine."

In this exercise, you learn how to use Time Machine to recover lost files from the backup.

Wait for the Backup to Finish
Before testing the backup, make sure it is finished and up to date.

1 If necessary, log in as Johnny Appleseed.

2 Click the Time Machine menu bar item. If the menu indicates that the backup is still in progress, wait for it to finish.

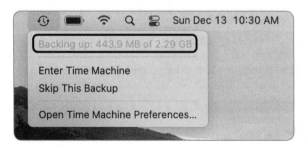

3 When you are notified that the backup is finished, move the mouse pointer over the notification. Click the X that appears in the upper-left corner to dismiss the notification.

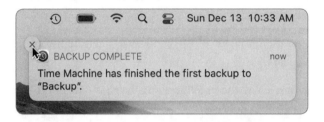

Delete Files

Use the following steps to delete files and folders from the StudentMaterials folder. In the next section you'll restore the deleted files and folders.

1 In the Finder, open /Users/Shared/StudentMaterials/Lesson17.

2 Move the "Archived announcements" folder to the Trash.

This folder contains the PretendCo company's old media information.

3 If necessary, authenticate as Local Administrator.

4 Choose Finder > Empty Trash. In the confirmation dialog, click Empty Trash.

5 Click the Time Machine status menu icon in the top-right corner of the menu bar, then choose Back Up Now to perform a second backup.

6 Close any Finder windows that are open.

Restore a File Using Time Machine

Search for an announcement about PretendCo's plans for solid-state encabulation device (SSED) development.

1 From the menu bar, choose Time Machine > Enter Time Machine.

Time Machine opens and shows successive snapshots of your files, with more recent snapshots in front of older ones, which appear to recede into the past.

2   Click the search (magnifying glass) icon in the top right of the window, then type
SSED plans.

No matching files appear, since the only match was in the folder you deleted and you
are viewing files as they exist now.

3   Use the up and down arrows on the right side of the window to navigate through time
until the file SSED plans.rtf appears.

You can also navigate through time using the timeline along the right side of the screen.

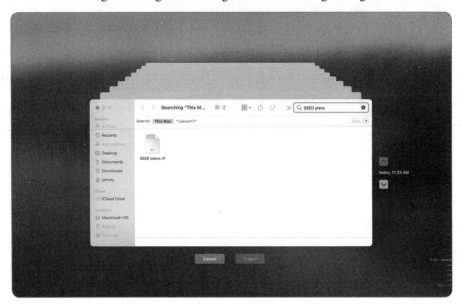

4   Select SSED plans.rtf, then press Command-Y or the Space bar.

A Quick Look preview opens. Quick Look is available in Time Machine so that you
can verify that you have the right file before you restore it.

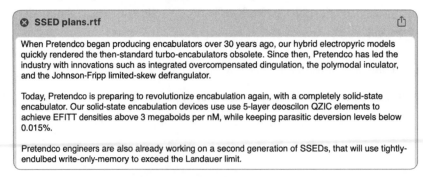

⊗ **SSED plans.rtf**

When Pretendco began producing encabulators over 30 years ago, our hybrid electropyric models
quickly rendered the then-standard turbo-encabulators obsolete. Since then, Pretendco has led the
industry with innovations such as integrated overcompensated dingulation, the polymodal inculator,
and the Johnson-Fripp limited-skew defrangulator.

Today, Pretendco is preparing to revolutionize encabulation again, with a completely solid-state
encabulator. Our solid-state encabulation devices use use 5-layer deoscilon QZIC elements to
achieve EFITT densities above 3 megaboids per nM, while keeping parasitic deversion levels below
0.015%.

Pretendco engineers are also already working on a second generation of SSEDs, that will use tightly-
endulbed write-only-memory to exceed the Landauer limit.

5   Press Command-Y, or the Space bar, to close Quick Look. For more information about Quick Look, see Reference 19.1, "Open Files."

6   With the file selected, click Restore.

Since the folder the file was in was deleted, Time Machine gives you the option to re-create the original enclosing folder or choose a new location for the restore.

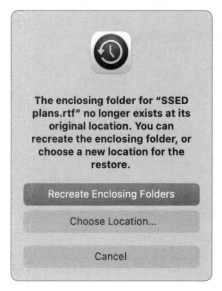

7   Click Choose Location. The Choose Folder dialog opens.

8   Navigate to your Documents folder by selecting it in the sidebar, then click Choose.

9   If necessary, authenticate as Local Administrator.

10 In the Finder, navigate to your Documents folder (choose Go > Documents, or press Shift-Command-O).

The restored SSED plans.rtf file is visible.

Restore Directly from Time Machine
Inspect the backup and copy files out of it to restore them.

1   In the Finder, open the volume you chose as your backup destination.

2 Locate the Backup volume that contains the SSED plans.rtf. In the example screen-shot, 2020-10-08-113341 contains the file.

3 Browse through these folders: */date and time of your backup*/Macintosh HD-Data/Users/Shared/StudentMaterials/Lesson17/Archived announcements/2010/04-April.

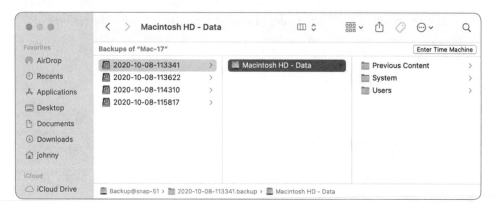

4 Drag a copy of SSED plans.rtf to your desktop.

5 If necessary, authenticate as Local Administrator.

6 Select the Backup volume on your desktop, Control-click, then choose Eject "Backup."

7 Unplug the external storage device from your Mac.

Apps and Processes

Lesson 18

Install Apps

It's easy for Mac users to find and install apps. In this lesson you install apps using the App Store and other installation methods. You also learn about Gatekeeper, the technology in macOS that's designed to ensure that only trusted software runs on your Mac.

Reference 18.1
The App Store

To find a wide variety of macOS and third-party apps, visit the App Store. To find an app, you can search for it by name, developer, type, or keyword, or you can browse the store. After you find the app you want, you can buy it using your Apple ID, or you can redeem a download code or a gift card.

Browse

To browse the App Store, open App Store in the Dock, select App Store in Launchpad, or choose App Store from the Apple menu.

The first time you open App Store, it displays information about what's new. Click the privacy icon or the "See how your data is managed" link to learn more about how your information is shared, or click Continue to use App Store.

<aside>
GOALS

▶ Install apps from the App Store

▶ Describe app support and identify security issues

▶ Install apps using software packages and drag-and-drop
</aside>

App Store initially displays the Discover tab. The Discover tab displays new and updated apps. Each week App Store editors feature new apps with in-depth stories. Check out a featured app's preview video to see how it works. The Discover tab also includes other features, such as perspectives from developers, top charts, and themed collections.

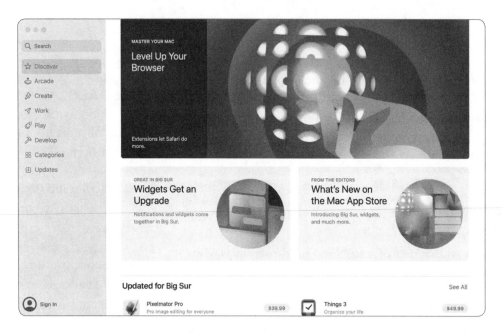

The App Store in macOS Big Sur includes Apple Arcade. With an Apple Arcade subscription, you can download and play a collection of new games from the App Store. Enjoy unlimited play on all your supported Apple devices. Apple Arcade is also available as part of Apple One, which bundles six Apple services into one subscription (Apple Music, Apple TV+, Apple Arcade, iCloud, Apple News+, Apple Fitness+). Apple Arcade isn't available in all countries or regions.

For each of the themed tabs—Arcade, Create, Work, Play, and Develop—App Store editors provide expert recommendations and tutorials.

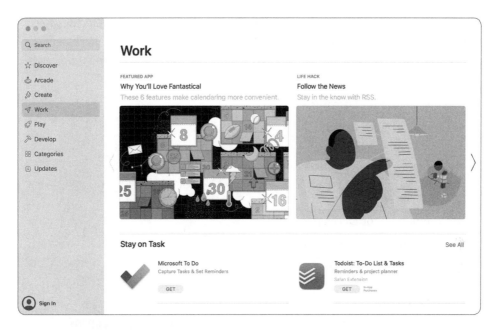

Scroll to the bottom of the Discover, Create, Work, Play, or Develop tabs to reach the Quick Links section.

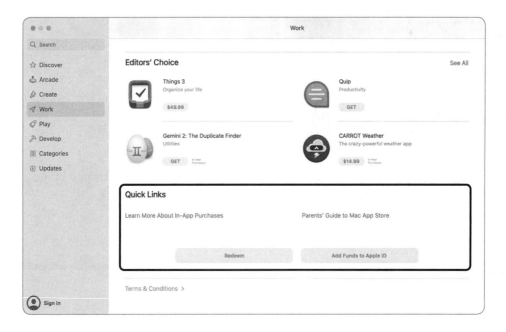

The Categories tab includes popular categories of apps. Each category includes an editor's choice, a suggested app to try, and top charts for that category.

You can use these keyboard shortcuts:

- ▶ Press Command-1 for Discover.

- ▶ Press Command-2 for Arcade.

- ▶ Press Command-3 for Create.

- ▶ Press Command-4 for Work.

- ▶ Press Command-5 for Play.

- ▶ Press Command-6 for Develop.

- ▶ Press Command-7 for Categories.

- ▶ Press Command-8 for Updates.

Search the App Store

If you enable Siri, you can use it to search for apps. Siri takes your request, opens App Store, and enters your request in the App Store Search field.

Or you can use the Search field at the top left of the App Store window. Enter part of the name of an app or developer, and the search returns a list of matching items.

Press the Return key or select an item to see a search results page. This gives you a more detailed view of the matching items.

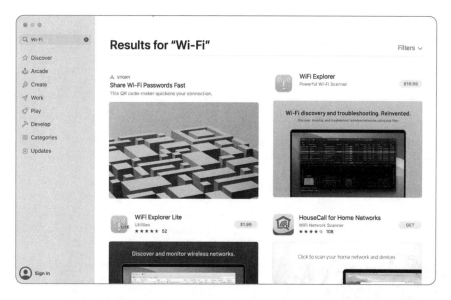

Click an app icon or name to open the details page. On the details page, you can learn more about the app, view screenshots of the app, and browse or write your own customer ratings and reviews. This page displays more developer and app information, including the version, download size, and system requirements.

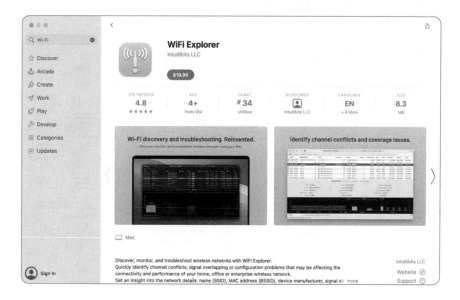

Click the share button (it looks like a box with an arrow pointing up) to copy or share a link to the app.

A free item displays the word "Get." A paid app displays a button with its price. If the button next to a purchased item says "Open," the item is already installed.

The following figure shows a paid app and a free app.

For a free app, click Get. The button changes to Install. Click Install to start installing the app.

If a button includes the price of an item, click the price. The button changes from the price to Buy App. Click Buy App to purchase the app.

To install an app that you already bought but that isn't currently installed on your Mac, click the Download button (it looks like a cloud with an arrow pointing down).

If your Mac has Apple silicon, you can install apps designed for iPhone and iPad. After you search for an app, click iPhone & iPad Apps.

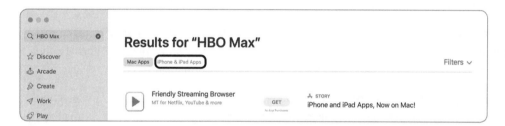

App Store displays results for iPhone and iPad apps. Most apps for iPhone and iPad are compatible with Mac computers with Apple silicon. Some apps aren't available because they use features available only on iPhone or iPad. A developer can opt out of making an app available for Mac.

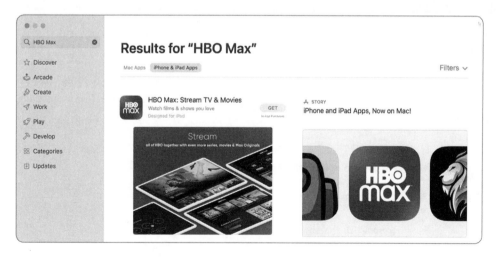

See the App Store story "iPhone and iPad Apps, Now on Mac!" at apps.apple.com/story/id1535100517 for more information. See Lesson 20, "Manage and Troubleshoot Apps," for more information about the kinds of apps you can run on your Mac.

Get an Apple ID

To download free apps from the App Store, you just need your Apple ID, a verified email address, and an internet connection. You'll also need a payment method if you want to buy something. See Apple Support article HT202631, "Payment methods that you can use with your Apple ID," for details about the forms of payment you can use. It's helpful to have a high-speed broadband connection, too. Any items you buy are associated with your Apple ID, and you can install them on any Mac you personally own or control. Using apps on multiple Mac computers is possible because Apple keeps track of the items you buy and install using your Apple ID.

If you don't have an Apple ID, you can create one in the App Store. If your primary email address is from a non-Apple source, you can use it to define an Apple ID. Alternatively, you can use a free iCloud account, which provides a free email address.

If your organization uses Apple School Manager (support.apple.com/guide/apple-school-manager/) or Apple Business Manager (support.apple.com/guide/apple-business-manager/), you can buy multiple app licenses for App Store items. The rest of this lesson focuses on buying apps outside the scope of Apple School Manager and Apple Business Manager.

You can update or reinstall any item you buy with your Apple ID. You'll receive a warning if you try to install an app from the App Store that replaces an earlier version of the same app that you bought outside the App Store.

To manage your App Store account, click the Sign In link at the lower-left corner of App Store, or choose Store > Sign In.

The App Store authentication dialog appears. If you're already logged in to iCloud, macOS enters your Apple ID, and you just have to enter your password. Otherwise, if you have an Apple ID, enter it.

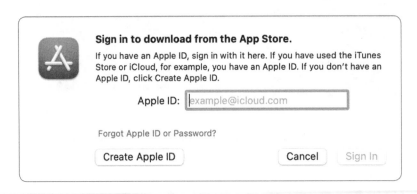

What happens next depends on the state of your Apple ID. If you click Sign In, you may proceed directly to install items, you may have to agree to updated Terms and Conditions, or you may have to verify or update your Apple ID information. If you don't have an Apple ID, or if you want to create a new one just for purchases, click Create Apple ID.

After you enter your name, email address, and password, you must enter a billing address. You might have to provide payment information. See Apple Support article HT201266, "Change, add, or remove Apple ID payment methods," for instructions on removing your payment information.

For more information about creating a new Apple ID that you can use for free items, see Apple Support articles HT204034, "Create or use an Apple ID without a payment method," and HT203905, "If you can't remove your last payment method or use no payment method with your Apple ID."

You'll receive an email from Apple asking you to verify your account. Click the link in the email to open a webpage where you can do so. After you verify your account, sign in to the App Store again to buy items.

If you have to verify or update your Apple ID information, you're asked to review your account. You must agree to the App Store Terms and Conditions and verify your Apple ID security details. You may also have to verify or update your billing information to continue with purchases.

When you are signed in, the App Store displays your Account page, and your name appears in the lower-left corner.

Apps Bundled with a New Mac

Five apps come preinstalled on new Mac computers that are treated a little differently than the other preinstalled apps. These apps include creativity apps (iMovie and GarageBand) and productivity apps (Pages, Keynote, and Numbers).

Unless installed by your organization's mobile device management (MDM) solution that works with Apple School Manager or Apple Business Manager, these apps:

▶ Aren't automatically installed when you erase a disk and reinstall macOS on a blank volume

▶ Are available in the App Store for free

▶ Require someone to adopt them (enter an Apple ID to associate the app license with that Apple ID) before you can install an update to them

When you adopt bundled apps, they are assigned to your Apple ID. macOS sends a unique hardware identifier from your Mac to Apple to verify eligibility.

After you own a license for an app, you can install the app on any other Mac as follows:

1   Sign in to the App Store.

2   Click your name in the lower-left corner to open your Account page.

3   Scroll to the Purchased section.

4   Click Download next to any purchased item.

You can also view your signed-in Apple ID and sign out of your account from the Store menu.

Visit the App Store User Guide at support.apple.com/guide/app-store for more details.

Manage Your Apple ID
If you want to make changes to your Apple ID:

1   Open the App Store.

2   Click the Account link in the lower-left corner of the App Store sidebar to open your Account page. You can also access your account by choosing Store > View My Account, or by pressing Command-0 (zero).

3   From the Account page, click View Information to manage settings, including your Apple ID, payment information, country or region setting, and Apple nickname.

Your Apple nickname is used to hide your personal identification in reviews you post in any of Apple's online stores.

If you, or an unauthorized user, make significant changes to your Apple ID, you'll receive an automated email letting you know changes were made.

Install

You don't have to be signed in to the App Store to browse, but you must be signed in to buy, install, or update an app. After you click Buy App or Install, if you haven't signed in yet, you will be asked to.

If you use more than one Mac, you can enable automatic downloads of purchased apps. You can set this option in the App Store preferences for every Mac that you configured with your Apple ID.

Use Screen Time preferences to set permissions remotely for kids.

Manage Family Sharing

As introduced in Reference 7.3, "Restrict Local User Access with Screen Time," Family Sharing makes it easy for up to six people in your family, without sharing accounts, to share Apple subscriptions and App Store purchases, an Apple Music family membership, and an iCloud storage plan.

When the family organizer turns on purchase sharing, you can pay for family purchases with the same credit card and approve kids' purchases right from a parent's device. Find out more at www.apple.com/family-sharing.

Manage Purchased Apps

To install an app that you or another member of your Family Sharing group has already purchased, open the App Store, sign in with your Apple ID, and then click your name in the sidebar. The Purchased section of your Account page shows all the items owned by the signed-in Apple ID, both installed and not installed on the Mac. If you're part of a Family Sharing group, you can also view another family member's purchases. To do so, click the name in "Purchased by *name*," and then choose another name in the menu.

Hover your pointer over an app to reveal an ellipsis button (…).

To temporarily hide a purchase, click the ellipsis button, then choose Hide Purchase. You can unhide purchases later from the Account Info page.

Update App Store Apps

The automatic software update mechanisms for macOS and the App Store, and notifications for available updates, are covered in detail in Reference 6.1, "Automatic Software Updates."

To install App Store updates manually, click the Updates tab in the App Store sidebar. Then you can do either of the following:

▶   Click Update next to an app that has an update available.

▶   In the upper-right corner of the Updates page, click Update All.

For more information about buying and downloading apps, see Apple Support article HT204266, "Download apps and games from the App Store on your Mac."

Reference 18.2
App Security

The safest place to get apps for your Mac is the App Store. Apple reviews each app in the App Store, and if there's ever a problem with an app, Apple can quickly remove it from the store and prevent an already-installed version from running.

The only apps in the App Store that might ask for administrator authorization after they are initially launched are those developed by Apple. For example, macOS Server and Xcode require administrator authorization because each app installs additional system services.

About Process Security

macOS includes several app security technologies that help protect you when you install third-party apps. For example, System Integrity Protection (SIP) is enabled by default, and processes can't access resources unless specifically allowed. Despite these security technologies, macOS allows systemwide privileges when needed. For example, Installer requires you to provide administrator authorization in order to install software that affects more than one user.

App Sandboxing

Even with the default process security mechanism in place, an app could still access many files owned by a user. This gives an app the potential to read your files and possibly gain unauthorized access to personal information.

macOS has support for full app and process sandboxing. With app sandboxing, apps are granted access only to the items they need. This is implemented in macOS through app sandbox containers, as covered in Lesson 15, "Manage System Resources."

Apple sandboxes any app or process built into macOS that could benefit from it. All apps available from the App Store must use app sandboxing.

Additionally, apps must be granted access to user information before they can access it, as covered in Lesson 9, "Manage Security and Privacy."

Code Signing

Code-signed apps and processes include a digital signature, which is used by macOS to verify the authenticity and integrity of the software code and resources. macOS verifies code at rest before you open it and as it's running as well. Even if some part of the app's or process's code is inappropriately changed while it's active, macOS can automatically quit it.

In addition to identifying changes to apps, code signing provides guaranteed app identification for other parts of macOS, including the keychain, the personal app firewall, Screen Time preferences, and app sandboxing.

macOS uses code signing to identify and trust newly installed items. All Apple software and apps from the App Store are code-signed.

Software developers who choose not to use the App Store can still take advantage of code signing. Developers can code-sign their installers and apps using an Apple-granted Developer ID. This way, code-signed apps installed from any origin can be trusted by macOS.

Notarization

macOS Mojave introduced software notarization—an indication that Apple performed a security check on software that was signed with a Developer ID and that no malicious software was found in the signed software.

With macOS Catalina and macOS Big Sur, macOS requires all new software (including apps, plug-ins, and installer packages) from outside the App Store to be signed with a Developer ID and notarized by Apple. To obtain notarization, third-party developers use the Apple notary service, an automated service that scans software for malicious content and checks for code-signing issues. If the notary service finds no issues, it generates a ticket, returns the ticket to the developer, and publishes the ticket online where Gatekeeper can find it.

For more information about code signing and notarization, see the article "Signing Your Apps for Gatekeeper" at developer.apple.com/developer-id/.

> **NOTE ▶** See the man page for the **spctl** command, specifically the **--assess** and **--verbose** options, to learn how to perform an assessment on items.

File Quarantine

macOS includes a file quarantine feature, which causes Gatekeeper to display information when you attempt to open an item downloaded from an external source such as the internet. Quarantined items include many file types, such as documents, scripts, and disk images. This lesson focuses primarily on quarantine as it relates to downloaded apps.

Quarantine starts only when an item is marked for quarantine by the quarantine-aware app that downloaded it. All apps built into macOS are quarantine aware, but not all third-party apps that can download apps are quarantine aware. Also, if you copy items to a Mac using any other method, they aren't marked for quarantine. For example, if you use the Finder to copy an app from an external storage device, you don't engage the quarantine service, so you won't see warnings about items that aren't notarized.

> **NOTE** ▶ If your organization uses an MDM solution or a third-party software distribution solution to distribute and install software, there is no requirement for software distributed this way to be signed and notarized.

When an item is marked for quarantine, macOS requires you to verify your intent to open the item or cancel if you have any suspicions about the safety of it.

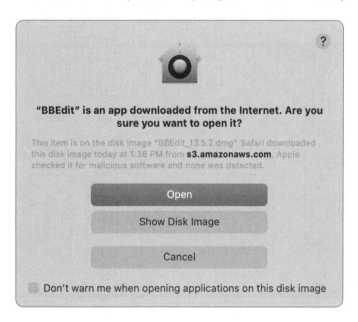

The first time you try to install or open an app that isn't signed by an identified developer, you see a warning that you cannot open the item because it is from an unidentified developer.

The first time you try to install or open an app that isn't signed by an identified developer and notarized by Apple, you see a warning that the app cannot be opened.

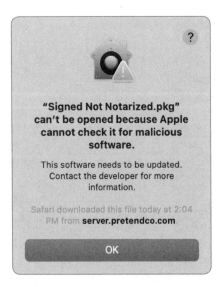

NOTE ▶ The warning icon for this dialog is slightly different than the warning icon for the dialog when an item isn't signed.

You can remove an item quarantine with the xattr command-line tool. Use this command to remove the quarantine on multiple items at once or in cases where the Finder can't remove the quarantine. To use this tool in Terminal, enter **xattr -dr com.apple.quarantine**, followed by the path of the item.

To find out more about Gatekeeper and safely opening apps, see Apple Support article HT202491, "Safely open apps on your Mac." This article includes the warning that "Running software that hasn't been signed and notarized may expose your computer and personal information to malware that can harm your Mac or compromise your privacy."

Malware Detection

Apple further secures macOS by maintaining a list of known malicious software. If you attempt to open any software on this list, macOS presents a warning dialog suggesting that you move the item to the Trash and report the malware to Apple to protect other users. The list of malicious software is automatically updated with the macOS Software Update.

To find out more about item quarantine, see Apple Support article HT201940, "About the 'Are you sure you want to open it?' alert (File Quarantine / Known Malware Detection) in OS X."

Configure "Allow apps downloaded from" Settings

macOS uses technology that leverages both code signing and file quarantine to protect your Mac from malicious apps. It does this by giving you the choice to allow downloaded apps from only trusted app sources.

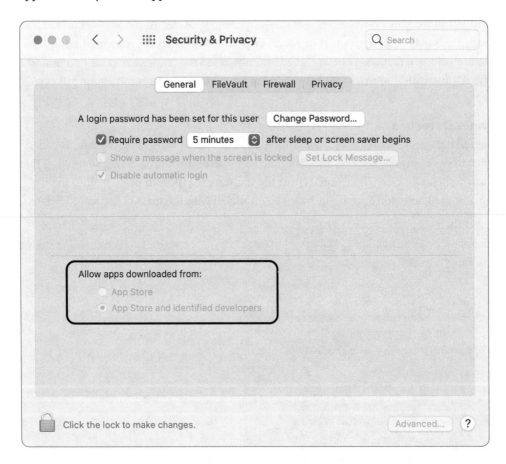

The "Allow apps downloaded from" setting has two options:

▶ App Store—Allow only apps from the App Store to open. Even when a version of the app is available from the App Store, if you download the app from somewhere else it will still be blocked.

> App Store and identified developers—The default option for macOS. If developers used their Apple-verified code-signing certificate to identify their app and notarized the app, the app is allowed to open, but macOS still presents the file quarantine dialog for downloaded items if quarantine is set.

Temporarily Bypass App Installation Settings

Even after you select an option for the "Allow apps downloaded from" setting, you can override it and allow untrusted apps with administrator credentials. In the Finder, Control-click the app file and then choose Open from the shortcut menu. A warning appears to verify your intent.

Click OK to open the app and clear the file quarantine (if you aren't logged in as an administrator, you must provide administrator credentials). However, doing this might not be enough for all unsigned apps, because some apps might automatically open other background or child apps. Examples include apps that also provide background software to facilitate hardware functionality.

These secondary apps may also trigger restrictions from running software. You won't be able to override these files from the Finder. In these cases, contact the software developer to ensure you have the latest macOS Big Sur–compatible version of the software.

You can also override an item blocked by macOS in the General pane of Security & Privacy preferences. Click Open Anyway.

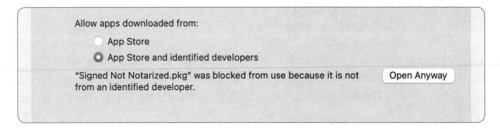

If you aren't logged in as an administrator, you must provide administrator credentials.

Reference 18.3
Install Apps Using Software Packages and Drag-and-Drop

In addition to using the App Store, you can install software using drag-and-drop installations or installation packages.

If a software developer creates a product that requires a folder that contains only a few items or even a single item, it's often deployed as a disk image that contains a drag-and-drop installation.

However, if a software developer creates a product that requires a set of items that must be installed in multiple specific locations throughout macOS, it's often deployed as an installation package.

Install with Drag-and-Drop

When you download software from the internet, it is often in an archive format or a disk image format.

In macOS, Safari downloads files by default to ~/Downloads. Safari by default unarchives ZIP files. You must open (or double-click) a downloaded disk image to make its contents available to you in the Finder.

You should move the new app to another location. The default location for apps available to all users is /Applications. Only administrator users can manually make changes to /Applications. However, users can place apps anywhere inside their own home folders.

To perform a drag-and-drop installation, drag the app to the /Applications folder or an alternative location. In the following example, the developer provided an alias to your Applications folder to make dragging and dropping easy.

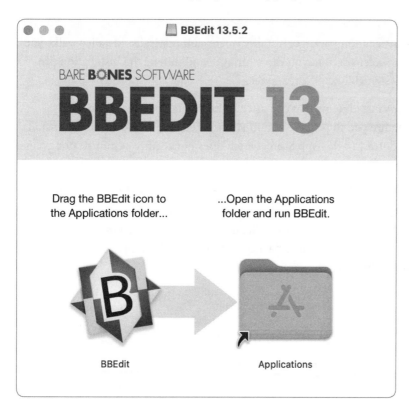

Drag-and-Drop App Security

Apps that a standard user is allowed to install and open can't interfere with other users on the Mac. However, poorly written or malicious software could potentially harm items in the user's home folder.

Installation Packages

Some developers distribute software installation packages (also called *packages*) that are ready for you to install when you open the package.

Teams_osx.pkg
97.4 MB

When you open an installation package, Installer opens automatically. Installer walks you through a few simple screens so that you can configure and initiate the installation process. Installer is in /System/Library/CoreServices.

Many third-party apps install items that can affect other users and macOS, so their installer packages require you to provide administrator credentials before you can install the apps. This is in contrast to the App Store, which does not require administrator access to install apps.

Installer supports signed packages. Signed packages contain code used to validate the authenticity and completeness of the software during installation. This makes it nearly impossible for unauthorized parties to insert illegitimate files in trusted installation packages. You can recognize a signed installer package by the small Lock button in the far right of the installer window title bar.

Clicking the Lock button displays details about the signed package, including its certificate status.

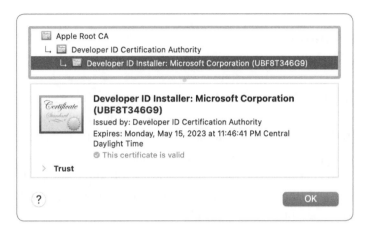

Use Other Installers

Some third-party installers use an installation method other than drag-and-drop or an installer package. If you have problems with a third-party installer, contact the developer.

Enable Software

When you install some third-party software, you might have to approve access to your Mac or approve the installation of system extensions. See Reference 9.5, "Manage User Privacy," Reference 9.8, "Approve Legacy System Extensions," and Reference 9.9, "Approve System Extensions," for more details.

Update Installed Software

You can keep your software updated in several ways:

- Apple software and App Store software—Software you get from the App Store, including Apple and third-party software, is updated by the App Store. See Lesson 6, "Update macOS," for more details.

- Automatically update third-party software—Automatic update mechanisms for third-party software vary. There is no standard method to determine whether an app has an automatic update capability. You can start by checking in common locations, including the app menu (the menu that appears with the app's name), the app's preferences window, or the app's Help menu. If the third-party item installed a preference pane, an automatic update mechanism might be there.

- Manually update third-party software—In some cases, you must manually install a newer app version.

Reference 18.4
Remove Installed Software

You can remove software in one of three ways:

▶ You can drag an app to the Trash. If the software item is a type of resource, like a preference pane or a font, locate the item in one of the Library folders and drag it to the Trash. Then empty the Trash. This method might leave some residual support files.

▶ You can remove App Store apps from Launchpad. In Launchpad, press and hold the Option key. A small x button appears next to apps installed from the App Store. Click the x button to remove an app. Using this method to remove some apps (GarageBand, for example) might leave residual support files behind.

▶ Some third-party developers distribute an uninstaller app with the original app installer. Use the third-party uninstaller app.

For more information see Apple Support article 202235, "How to delete apps on your Mac."

Exercise 18.1
Install an App from the App Store

> **Prerequisite**
>
> ▶ You must have created the Local Administrator (Exercise 3.1, "Configure a Mac for Exercises") and Johnny Appleseed (Exercise 7.1, "Create a Standard User Account") accounts.

In this exercise, you use the App Store app to buy, download, and install a free app on your Mac.

Sign In with an Apple ID to Use with the App Store

The way you configure Johnny Appleseed's account with an Apple ID for the App Store depends on whether you want to use the same Apple ID for iCloud and App Store purchases and what the Apple ID was used for in the past.

1 Log in as Johnny Appleseed.

2 From the Apple menu, choose App Store.

3 At the What's New on the App Store & Arcade screen, click "See how your data is managed" in order to review Apple's privacy policy, then click OK and click Continue.

4 Choose Store > Sign In or click the Sign In button in the lower-left corner of the App Store. Provide the same Apple ID that you have used in previous exercises, then click Sign In.

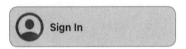

5 Provide your password, then click Sign In.

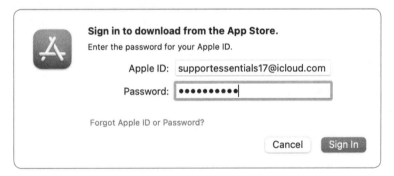

6 If two-factor authentication is enabled on your Mac, you may be asked for additional verification. Follow the prompts to finish authenticating.

Because you're signed in, the last item in the Store menu will display View My Account and your Apple ID. The lower-left corner of the App Store window will also display your name.

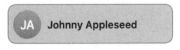

You should be signed in using the Apple ID you used for iCloud. Apple recommends using the same account for both iCloud and the App Store. For more information, see Apple Support article HT204053, "Sign in with your Apple ID."

7   In the menu bar, choose App Store > Preferences.

8   If "Automatically download apps purchased on other devices" is selected, deselect the checkbox.

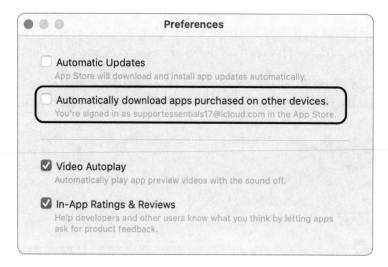

Select an App to Buy

1   Type **Apple Config** in the Search field (at the top left of the App Store window), and press Return.

The App Store might display more than one relevant app. Find a free app from Apple named Apple Configurator 2. Free apps show a Get button instead of a price (although if the app was previously acquired under this Apple ID, you see a Download button).

2   Click the free app's name.

The App Store displays more details about the app. You see a Get or a Download button.

3   Perform one of the following actions:

▶   If you see a Get button, click Get, and then click Install.

▶   If you see a Download button, click it to download the app.

If additional confirmation or configuration is required, a dialog appears and asks you to sign in to download the app.

4   If you are asked for additional information, follow the steps.

When the app starts to download, the progress is shown in the App Store.

Test the App

1 Open Launchpad.

If the app hasn't finished downloading, Apple Configurator 2 displays the progress of the download. When an app finishes downloading, you see its icon.

If the app has not been opened yet, you see a blue dot next to its name.

2 Click the icon for Apple Configurator 2 to open the app.

3 At the Apple Configurator 2 license agreement, review the terms, and if you agree to them, click Accept.

4 At the Apple Configurator 2 Welcome screen, click Get Started.

5 Quit the app.

Examine the App Store

1 In the App Store, choose Store > View My Account.

2 If the App Store notifies you that you have apps to adopt, do not accept them.

The App Store app lists the apps purchased with this Apple ID. If you used this Apple ID before, you might see additional apps that you purchased.

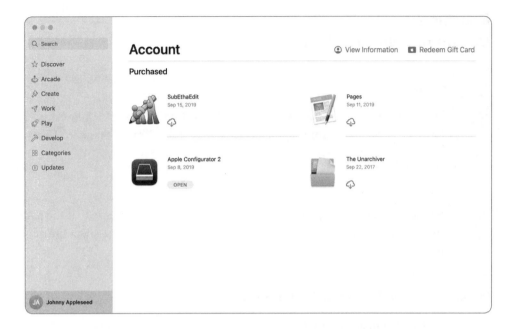

If you selected the option "Automatically download apps purchased on other Mac computers" in App Store preferences, additional apps would be downloaded and installed. Since this option is disabled, you see Download buttons that you use to install them manually.

The App Store terms and conditions limit the situations in which an app might be installed on several computers. Review www.apple.com/legal/internet-services/itunes/ for the current terms and conditions for using iTunes.

If other apps are listed, don't install them now.

3   In the App Store sidebar, click the Updates button.

The App Store displays updates available for apps installed on this Mac that were purchased from the App Store.

4   Quit App Store.

Exercise 18.2
Use an Installer Package

▶ **Prerequisite**

▶ You must have created the Local Administrator (Exercise 3.1, "Configure a Mac for Exercises") and Johnny Appleseed (Exercise 7.1, "Create a Standard User Account") accounts.

In this exercise, you install an app using an installer package. You observe that the package is signed by an identified developer, and you learn how to check the signature of an installer package.

Install an App with an Installer Package

1 If necessary, log in as Johnny Appleseed.

2 Open the StudentMaterials/Lesson18 folder.

3 Open Trust Me.dmg.

The image mounts showing the Trust Me package inside it.

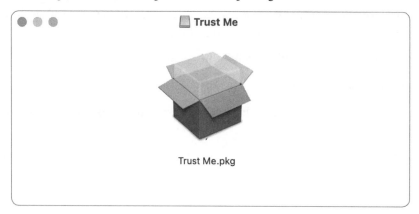

Trust Me.pkg

4 Open Trust Me.pkg.

The Installer opens and prepares to install the Trust Me app.

Because Gatekeeper did not activate, the Trust Me package is a signed package.

5   If you are asked to allow Installer to access files on a removable volume, click Don't Allow.

6   Open Terminal.

7   Type **pkgutil --check-signature "/Volumes/Trust Me/Trust Me.pkg"**, then press Return.

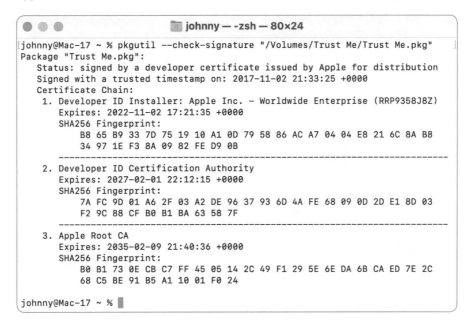

```
● ● ●                      johnny — -zsh — 80×24

[johnny@Mac-17 ~ % pkgutil --check-signature "/Volumes/Trust Me/Trust Me.pkg"  ]
Package "Trust Me.pkg":
   Status: signed by a developer certificate issued by Apple for distribution
   Signed with a trusted timestamp on: 2017-11-02 21:33:25 +0000
   Certificate Chain:
      1. Developer ID Installer: Apple Inc. - Worldwide Enterprise (RRP9358J8Z)
         Expires: 2022-11-02 17:21:35 +0000
         SHA256 Fingerprint:
             B8 65 B9 33 7D 75 19 10 A1 0D 79 58 86 AC A7 04 04 E8 21 6C 8A B8
             34 97 1E F3 8A 09 82 FE D9 0B
         ------------------------------------------------------------------------
      2. Developer ID Certification Authority
         Expires: 2027-02-01 22:12:15 +0000
         SHA256 Fingerprint:
             7A FC 9D 01 A6 2F 03 A2 DE 96 37 93 6D 4A FE 68 09 0D 2D E1 8D 03
             F2 9C 88 CF B0 B1 BA 63 58 7F
         ------------------------------------------------------------------------
      3. Apple Root CA
         Expires: 2035-02-09 21:40:36 +0000
         SHA256 Fingerprint:
             B0 B1 73 0E CB C7 FF 45 05 14 2C 49 F1 29 5E 6E DA 6B CA ED 7E 2C
             68 C5 BE 91 B5 A1 10 01 F0 24

johnny@Mac-17 ~ % ▊
```

8   Inspect the standard output (also called stdout) in the Terminal window.

The stdout tells you that the package is signed by a developer certificate issued by Apple for distribution and displays the certificate trust chain. In this case, the package was signed with Apple Inc. – Worldwide Enterprise's Developer ID Installer certificate, which was signed by the Developer ID Certification Authority (CA), which in turn was signed by the Apple Root CA.

Essentially, this means that the Apple Root CA vouches for the authenticity of the Developer ID Certification Authority, which vouches for the authenticity of Apple Inc. – Worldwide Enterprise's certificate, which vouches for the authenticity of the installer package.

This is the standard format of an Apple-issued Developer ID certificate.

9   Quit Terminal.

10   In the Installer app, choose File > Show Files.

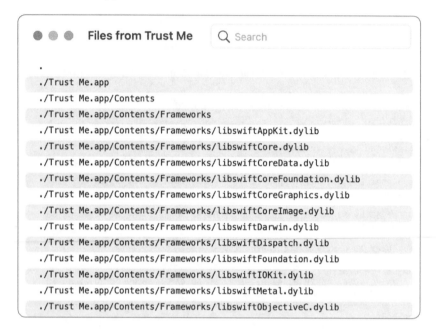

This shows what files the installer package contains. In this case, it is a folder named Trust Me containing Trust Me.app and the app package's files.

11   Close the files from the Trust Me window.

12   In the main Installer window, click Continue.

Some packages include additional items, such as readme information, license agreements, and choices of components to install. This is a simple package, so it proceeds to the Installation Type pane.

13   Click Install, then if necessary, authenticate as Local Administrator.

The installation completes quickly. The Installer then informs you that it was successful.

14   Click Close.

The Installer quits.

15 Eject the disk image.

16 In the Finder, navigate to the Applications folder.

The Trust Me app is installed.

17 Open Launchpad.

The new app is displayed with your other apps.

18 Open Trust Me.

Because this app was installed with a package (instead of downloaded directly from the internet), Gatekeeper doesn't activate, nor is a warning displayed. You see what happens with an untrusted app in the next exercise.

19 Quit Trust Me.

Unlike with the App Store, there is no standard update process for package-installed apps. Some apps manage their own updates; others require you to manually download, then install updates or manage them with a mobile device management (MDM) solution.

Exercise 18.3
Drag and Drop to Install an App

▶ **Prerequisite**

▶ You must have created the Local Administrator (Exercise 3.1, "Configure a Mac for Exercises") and Johnny Appleseed (Exercise 7.1, "Create a Standard User Account") accounts.

In this exercise, you drag and drop to install two apps. One app is signed and notarized, and the other app is neither signed nor notarized.

Obtain an App from the Internet

1 Navigate to www.barebones.com/products/bbedit/download.html, or double-click the Download BBEdit web location file from StudentMaterials > Lesson18.

2   Click the Download button next to Disk Image, then at the Safari prompt, click Allow.

Disk Image: (14.6 MB) (Download)

Although BBEdit is also available from the App Store, for the purposes of this exercise you are using the drag-and-drop installer.

3   Open the disk image from your Downloads folder. It includes installation instructions in the background image.

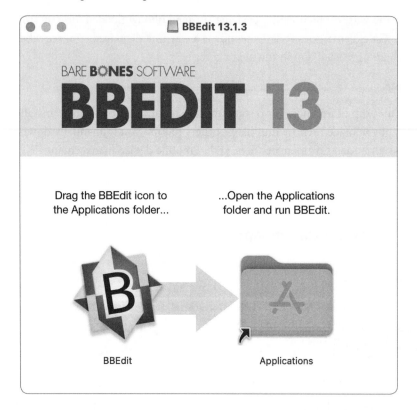

4   Drag the BBEdit icon to the Applications icon (which is an alias to /Applications).

macOS enables you to run apps no matter where they're stored, even if they aren't in /Applications. Running the copy of the app in the disk image you downloaded works, but it might cause odd behavior. Don't run the app in the disk image.

5   Authenticate as Local Administrator, then click OK.

The Finder copies BBEdit into the Applications folder.

6   Eject the disk image.

7   In the Finder, navigate to the Applications folder (Shift-Command-A).

8   Double-click BBEdit, then click Open at the prompt.

macOS applied a quarantine attribute to the BBEdit app when you downloaded the BBEdit app from a website. However, because it is signed and notarized, you are asked one time only. You will verify its signature and notarized state later on.

9   If you see a BBEdit Notification, hover over the notification, and click Close (X).

10   Quit BBEdit by choosing BBEdit > Quit BBEdit.

Obtain an App from Student Materials

1   If necessary, log in as Johnny Appleseed.

2   Open the StudentMaterials/Lesson18 folder.

3 Open Dead End.dmg.

This disk image contains an app that was previously downloaded from a website and still has the quarantine attribute applied, so macOS treats it as coming from an untrusted source.

Copy the App to /Applications

The Dead End app comes as a disk image with instructions in the background image.

1 Drag the Dead End icon onto the Applications icon.

2 Authenticate as Local Administrator, then click OK.

Don't open the Dead End app yet.

3 Eject the disk image.

Test Gatekeeper Security Settings

1 Open Security & Privacy preferences.

2 If necessary, click General.

3   Authenticate, then verify that the "Allow apps downloaded from" option is set to "App Store and identified developers."

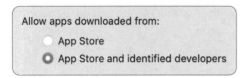

4   Quit System Preferences.

5   In the Finder, navigate to the Applications folder (Shift-Command-A).

6   Double-click Dead End.

Dead End contains metadata indicating that it is quarantined because it was downloaded from the internet. The first time you open it, Gatekeeper checks it against your allowed apps policy. Since the app isn't signed with a Developer ID, Gatekeeper doesn't allow it to open.

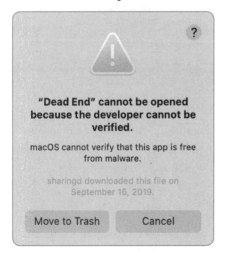

7   Click Cancel.

8   Control-click Dead End, then choose Open from the shortcut menu.

This time, Gatekeeper warns you about the app but gives you the option to bypass normal policy and open the app.

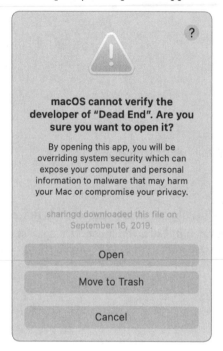

macOS cannot verify the developer of "Dead End". Are you sure you want to open it?

By opening this app, you will be overriding system security which can expose your computer and personal information to malware that may harm your Mac or compromise your privacy.

sharingd downloaded this file on September 16, 2019.

Open

Move to Trash

Cancel

9   Click Open.

WARNING ▶ By clicking Open, you are allowing macOS to execute code by an untrusted developer. This code could be dangerous for your Mac to run. In production, you should never run an app that is not signed by a trusted developer.

10 If necessary, authenticate as Local Administrator.

Because Johnny Appleseed is a standard user, he isn't allowed to open unsigned apps without an administrator's credentials unless they have been provided recently.

11 If necessary, click the Dead End icon in the Dock to bring it to the foreground.

Don't click "Download the internet." If you do, see Exercise 20.1, "Force Apps to Quit," for information on forcing apps to quit. This app isn't harmful, but it doesn't do anything useful.

12 Quit Dead End (choose File > Quit Dead End or press Command-Q).

13 Double-click Dead End to reopen it.

This time it opens without the warning. Since you opened it once, your Gatekeeper policy is modified to allow it to run normally.

14 Quit Dead End again.

Verify Signature and Notarization

1 Open Terminal.

2 Type the command **codesign -dv --verbose "/Applications/Dead End.app"**.

```
● ● ●                   🖥 johnny — -zsh — 80×24
[johnny@Mac-17 ~ % codesign -dv --verbose "/Applications/Dead End.app"
 /Applications/Dead End.app: code object is not signed at all
```

Because Dead End is not signed, you receive the message "code object is not signed at all." Although users with administrative privileges are able to bypass Gatekeeper today, this ability may not be present in future releases of macOS.

3 Type the command **codesign -dv --verbose /Applications/BBEdit.app**.

```
● ● ●                   🖥 johnny — -zsh — 80×24
[johnny@Mac-17 ~ % codesign -dv --verbose /Applications/BBEdit.app
 Executable=/Applications/BBEdit.app/Contents/MacOS/BBEdit
 Identifier=com.barebones.bbedit
 Format=app bundle with Mach-O thin (x86_64)
 CodeDirectory v=20500 size=113152 flags=0x10000(runtime) hashes=3527+5 location=
 embedded
 Signature size=8949
 Authority=Developer ID Application: Bare Bones Software, Inc. (W52GZAXT98)
 Authority=Developer ID Certification Authority
 Authority=Apple Root CA
 Timestamp=Jul 27, 2020 at 2:20:51 PM
 Info.plist entries=46
 TeamIdentifier=W52GZAXT98
 Runtime Version=10.15.0
 Sealed Resources version=2 rules=13 files=694
 Internal requirements count=1 size=212
```

Because BBEdit is signed by its developer, you receive output with details about the developer of the app and the issuer of the signing certificate.

4   Type the command
codesign --test-requirement="=notarized" --verify --verbose /Applications/BBEdit.app.

```
● ● ●                     📁 johnny — -zsh — 80×24
johnny@Mac-17 ~ % codesign --test-requirement="=notarized" --verify --verbose /A
pplications/BBEdit.app
/Applications/BBEdit.app: valid on disk
/Applications/BBEdit.app: satisfies its Designated Requirement
/Applications/BBEdit.app: explicit requirement satisfied
```

Because BBEdit meets notarization requirements required for future app development in macOS, you receive the message "explicit requirement satisfied."

5   Quit Terminal.

Exercise 18.4
Remove Apps

Prerequisite

▶   You must have performed Exercise 18.1, "Install an App from the App Store," and Exercise 18.2, "Use an Installer Package."

View Installed Apps

1   Option-click the Apple menu, then choose System Information.

System Information opens and displays the system report.

2   From the Software section of the sidebar, select Installations.

This part of the report shows software installed from the App Store and from packages. It shows Apple Configurator 2 and Trust Me. It doesn't show software installed in other ways. Because you installed BBEdit and Dead End by drag-and-drop, they do not appear.

3   Quit System Information.

Remove an App from Launchpad

1 Open Launchpad.

2 Press and hold Apple Configurator 2 (or the app you installed from the App Store) until an "X" appears in the top left of its icon and the other icons begin to jiggle.

In this mode, Launchpad enables you to drag app icons around to rearrange them. You can also use the delete (X) button to delete apps you bought from the App Store, like Apple Configurator 2.

3 Click the delete (X) button on Apple Configurator 2.

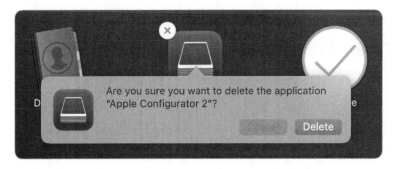

4 In the confirmation dialog that appears, click Delete.

5 If necessary, authenticate as Local Administrator.

Apple Configurator 2 is uninstalled from your Mac. Your preference file or files and user data still exist, so if you decide to reinstall the app, your settings are available.

6 Click twice in the background to exit Launchpad.

Reinstall an App from the App Store

1   Open the App Store.

2   Choose Store > View My Account.

Because you bought Apple Configurator 2, it's listed and available to download. Depending on the history of the Apple ID you're using, other apps might be listed.

 Apple Configurator 2
Sep 8, 2019

3   Click the Download button for Apple Configurator 2.

4   If necessary, enter your Apple ID's password to authenticate to the App Store.

The app is downloaded and reinstalled.

5   Wait for the download to finish, then quit the App Store.

Remove an App in the Finder

1   In the Finder, navigate to the Applications folder.

2   Select Apple Configurator 2, then drag it to the Trash.

3   If necessary, authenticate as Local Administrator.

4   Choose Finder > Empty Trash, then click Empty Trash in the confirmation dialog.

Apple Configurator 2 is uninstalled from your Mac.

5   Repeat steps 2 through 4 to uninstall BBEdit from your Mac.

Lesson 19
Manage Files

In this lesson you learn about tools that help you manage documents, beginning with Launch Services and continuing with Quick Look for previewing most document types. Then you learn about Auto Save, Versions, and document management in iCloud. You learn how macOS attempts to resume documents and apps. Finally, you learn how macOS can help you optimize storage to reclaim space on the volume that contains your home folder.

Reference 19.1
Open Files

In macOS, you double-click a file in the Finder or select a file in the Finder and choose File > Open to open it. When you do this, you also tell macOS to launch the appropriate app for the file. macOS uses Launch Services to do this. Launch Services uses a filename extension to know which app to open.

A filename extension is a string of characters preceded by a period (.) at the end of a filename. For example, filename.jpg is a file with a .jpg extension.

Joint Photographic Experts Group (JPEG) is a format for compressing many file types. Sometimes there can be more than one filename extension that indicates a file type. For example, a JPEG file can have the filename extension .jpg or .jpeg.

GOALS

▶ Use Launch Services and Quick Look to open files

▶ Describe how Launch Services uses the app database

▶ Preview files with Quick Look and the Preview pane

▶ Learn how to browse document versions and go back to an older version in apps that support Auto Save and Versions

▶ Open documents that were saved to iCloud

▶ Save documents to iCloud

▶ Optimize local storage to reclaim space on the system volume

By default, the Finder hides filename extensions. If you want the Finder to display a file's filename extension, select a file, choose File > Get Info, and click the disclosure triangle to display the Name & Extension information. In the following screenshot, the "Hide extension" option is deselected for the file, so its filename extension isn't hidden. The name that's displayed at the top of the Info window changes too.

You can choose Finder > Preferences, click the Advanced button, and select the checkbox next to "Show all filename extensions" for the Finder to display filename extensions for all documents.

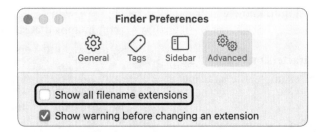

If you choose to show all filename extensions in the Finder, you override the individual file attribute that hides a filename extension.

If you leave the option "Show warning before changing an extension" selected in the Finder preferences, you'll get a warning before you try to make a filename extension change or remove a filename extension. This might prevent you from accidentally changing a file extension.

If you need to change the file type of an existing file, use an app to export the file as a different type. For example, in Pages you can use File > Export To and choose a different file type.

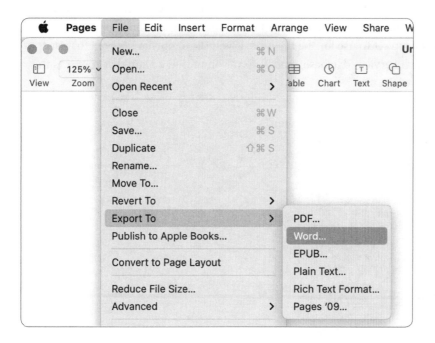

App Registration

When you try to open a file, Launch Services reads from a database of apps and file types to determine the correct app for the file type. When Launch Services finds a match, it caches it, so when you try to open the file again, Launch Services can quickly find the match. After you start up or log in, a background process scans for new apps and updates the database. The Finder and Installer track new apps and add their supported file types to the database.

If macOS displays a message that there is no app to open a file, you probably don't have the correct app for the file. Launch Services maps many common file types to Preview and TextEdit if the appropriate app is missing. For example, most Numbers or Microsoft Excel spreadsheets open in Preview and most Pages and Microsoft Word documents open in TextEdit.

With Quick Look you can preview many common file types, even without having the appropriate apps installed. This includes Pages, Keynote, Numbers, and Microsoft Office documents. Quick Look details are covered later in this lesson in the section "Preview Documents with Quick Look."

If Preview, or other apps, can't open a file, change Launch Services settings to force the files to open in an appropriate app, as outlined in the following section. Launch Services might not have an app set to use for the file type. If you try to open a file type that isn't stored in the Launch Services database, macOS asks you to find an app that supports the file in the App Store.

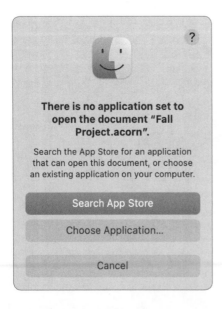

Manage Launch Services

If you prefer to open a file with an app different from that file type's default app, you can override the Launch Services default app settings for any file type. To override the default app settings for a file, use the Info or Inspector window in the Finder. Using the Info window is detailed in Lesson 13, "Manage Permissions and Sharing."

After you select the files for which you want to change Launch Services settings and open the Inspector, click the "Open with" disclosure triangle to reveal the default app selected by Launch Services. To change just the selected files' default app, select another app from the menu. This information is saved to the files' metadata and defines Launch Services settings only for the selected items.

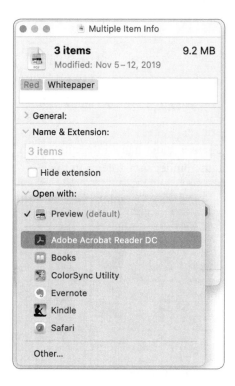

To change the default app for all files of the type of files selected, select the app you want to define as the default, and then click the Change All button.

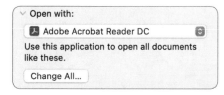

You can also modify Launch Services settings in the Finder. Control-click the selected files and then choose Open With from the shortcut menu. Press and hold the Option key to change the menu command to Always Open With.

This setting is saved per user, so one user's app preferences don't override another's. A user's custom Launch Services settings are saved inside that user's ~/Library/Preferences folder.

Preview Documents with the Finder Preview Pane

As a way of introducing the Finder Preview pane, this section first presents a little information about how the Finder displays your files.

By default, when you open a new Finder window, it opens a folder named Recents, which displays files you've recently opened. Also, by default, the Finder shows items in this folder as icons.

To change how the Finder displays items in the selected Finder window, you can click the View menu and choose any of the following (or use its shortcut keystroke):

▶ as Icons (Command-1)

▶ as List (Command-2)

▶ as Columns (Command-3)

▶ as Gallery (Command-4)

Or you can click the "Show items as icons," "Show items in a list," "Show items in columns," or "Show items in a gallery" button in the Finder toolbar.

> **NOTE ▸** If the Finder window is narrow enough, then the Finder displays the four buttons highlighted in the previous figure as a menu instead of as four separate buttons.

The Finder automatically displays the Preview pane when you show items in columns or in a gallery. The following figure illustrates the Preview pane when viewing items in a gallery:

You can use the Finder Preview pane to get more information about a selected file, including:

▸ A preview of the contents of a document or image

▸ A list of the metadata for the file (metadata is covered in detail in Reference 16.1, "File-System Metadata")

▸ Quick Actions buttons for the selected file if available

You can also show the Preview pane when viewing items in the Finder as icons or as a list by choosing View > Show Preview (or press Shift-Command-P). The following figure illustrates the Preview pane when viewing items as icons.

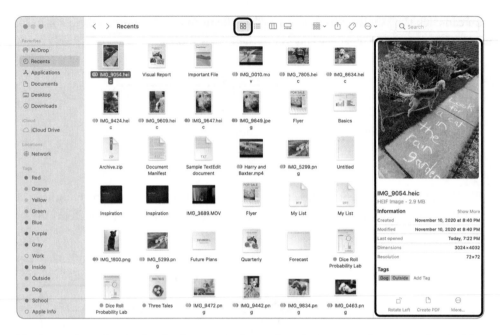

To change how the Finder displays a window, select an open window, then choose View > Show View Options (or press Command-J). The options vary depending on whether you're viewing the items in the window as icons, in a list, in columns, or in a gallery.

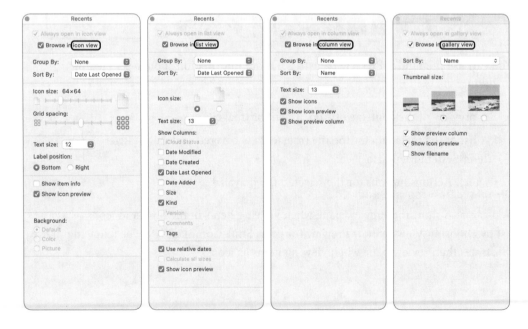

If the Finder displays the Preview pane, you can choose View > Show Preview Options to control whether the Preview pane shows Quick Actions and to select the metadata that the Preview pane shows for the type of file selected. The following figure displays a few kinds of file types.

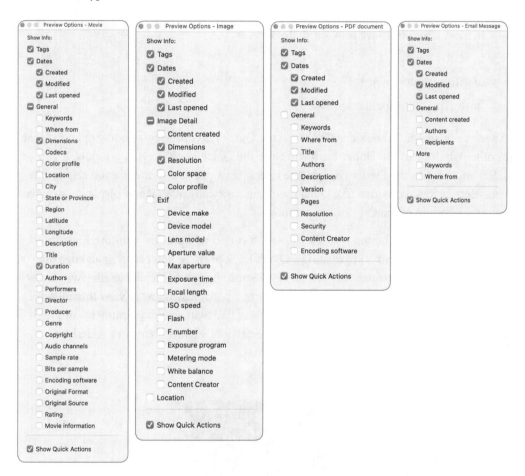

Preview Documents with Quick Look

Quick Look enables you to preview most file types without opening additional apps or when you don't have the appropriate apps installed.

You can open and close Quick Look previews by selecting a file and pressing the Space bar in the following contexts:

▶ In the Finder (you can also press Command-Y instead of the Space bar)

▶ In the Time Machine restore interface

▶ In most Open and Save browser dialogs

▶ In Mail

▶ In active printer queues

▶ In any app that supports Quick Look

After you open Quick Look, macOS keeps the Quick Look preview window open in front of other windows in the Finder until you close the Quick Look preview window. If you select another file, the Finder changes the Quick Look preview to the file you selected. If you select an audio or video file, Quick Look automatically plays it and displays a progress bar at the bottom of the Quick Look window.

The Quick Look close button is in the upper-left corner of a preview window. Press the Space bar (or Command-Y) to dismiss a Quick Look preview. You can drag an edge of a Quick Look window to resize it. Click the Full Screen button (which looks like twin arrows that point away from each other) at the top left of a preview window to view the full screen, then click the Exit Full Screen button (which looks like twin arrows pointing toward each other). Press Option-Command-Y to open one or more selected items in a slideshow.

Quick Look provides the Finder with the previews that the Finder displays when you view files on your desktop and when you view files in a Finder window.

Quick Look Plug-ins

Quick Look previews file types using plug-ins. Each Quick Look plug-in previews specific file types. Many Quick Look plug-ins are included in macOS by default. Apple and third-party developers create additional plug-ins to expand the Quick Look preview capabilities.

Included Quick Look plug-ins enable you to:

▶ Preview audio or video files that can be decoded by QuickTime.

▶ Preview graphics files, including photos taken with mobile phones and digital cameras, PDF files, EPS files, and standard graphics files.

▶ Preview productivity files, including standard text files, script files, and files you create with Pages, Numbers, Keynote, and Microsoft Office suites.

▶ Preview internet-centric files, including mailboxes, Messages transcripts, and web archives.

Quick Look plug-ins are stored in Library folders. Built-in Apple Quick Look plug-ins are in /System/Library/QuickLook/ and /Library/QuickLook/. Install third-party plug-ins in /Library/QuickLook/ or ~/Library/QuickLook/, depending on who must access them.

Quick Look Window

In the right portion of the title bar of the Quick Look window, you'll find other options for previewing a selected item. The options vary depending on the type of file you've selected and the app extensions installed on your Mac. See Reference 20.2, "Manage App Extensions," for more information on adding app extensions to the Share menu.

For many types of apps, the Quick Look window displays the "Open with *App*" button, where *App* is the name of the default app for the selected file. For ZIP files, instead of "Open with *App*," the button displays Uncompress. For a disk image file, the button displays Mount.

The Share button (the box with the up arrow) enables you to share a document. The list of options in the Share menu varies depending on the file type of the item you're previewing and the installed app extensions. Find out more about managing app extensions in Lesson 20, "Manage and Troubleshoot Apps."

If you've selected multiple files when you open Quick Look, use the arrow keys to navigate and preview the items adjacent to the original previewed item in the Finder. The Quick Look toolbar displays Back, Forward, and Show All buttons.

If the previewed file has multiple pages, you'll be able to scroll through the document. In some cases—Keynote presentations, for example—Quick Look shows a thumbnail preview of each slide, enabling you to scroll through the thumbnails.

To start a slideshow of files in the Finder, select the files, Control-click, press the Option key, then choose "Slideshow *number of selected files* Items."

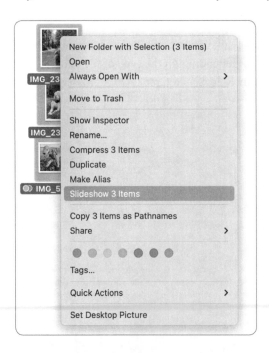

For some files, the Quick Look window also displays one or more Quick Actions, as in the following figure. Quick Actions are discussed in the next section.

Quick Actions

The Quick Actions feature enables you to perform tasks right from the Finder without opening another app. There are three ways to use Quick Actions in the Finder:

▶ Click the Quick Actions button that appears in the Quick Look window.

▶ Click the Quick Actions button that appears in the Preview pane.

▶ Control-click a file, then choose Quick Actions.

The list of actions available in Quick Actions depends on the kind of file or files you selected. The built-in Quick Actions include:

▶ Rotate an image or movie—Rotate Left is the default command, but you can press and hold the Option key to change it to Rotate Right.

▶ Mark up a document or image—After you choose Markup, the file opens in a Markup window. Learn more about the Markup window in the next section.

▶ Trim a movie or audio file—Choose Trim, then use the yellow handles in the trimming bar. Click Play to test your changes, then click Revert, or click Done to save your changes and close the window. After you click Done, macOS asks you to replace your original file, cancel, or save your changes in a new clip.

▶ Create a PDF—macOS creates a new PDF file from one or more selected files when you choose Create PDF. Enter a filename, or you can just leave the suggested name. Press Return or click somewhere else after entering the filename.

▶ Customize—Choose Customize to open the Extensions preferences in System Preferences. You can use Automator to create custom workflows for Quick Actions. Learn more about the Extensions preferences in Lesson 20.

Mark Up Files

Quick Look and Quick Actions enable you to mark up files without opening a separate app. If you're viewing a file in Quick Look or the Finder Preview pane, click the Markup tool (it looks like the tip of a marker). If you're using Quick Actions, choose Markup. The collection of tools offered by Markup depends on the type of file you're working on. The collection can include:

▶ Sketch—Sketch a shape with a single stroke. macOS replaces your stroke with a shape if it recognizes your stroke as a standard shape.

▶ Draw—Draw a shape with a single stroke. This tool appears only if you have a Force Touch trackpad. Use a firmer press to draw a heavier, darker line.

▶ Shapes—Click the Shape button, select a shape, then drag the shape where you want it. Use the blue handles to resize the shape. Use the green handles to change the shape. Select the Loupe tool to magnify an area. Select the Highlight tool, then use the blue handles to modify the highlighted area.

▶ Text—Enter text, then drag the text where you want it.

▶ Highlight Selection—Highlight selected text.

▶ Sign—Create a new signature with a trackpad or your Mac computer's built-in camera and select one of your signatures to insert it. Then you can drag and resize it.

▶ Shape Style—Change the thickness and type of lines in a shape, then add or remove a shadow to the lines in the shape.

▶ Border Color—Change the color of the lines in the shape.

▶ Fill Color—Change the color inside the shape.

▶ Text Style—Change the font, color, size, and characteristics of text.

▶ Rotate Right—Rotate to the right.

▶ Rotate Left—Rotate to the left.

- ▶ Crop —Drag the corner handles until only the area you want to keep is shown within the frame's border. You can also drag the frame to reposition it. When you're ready, click the Crop button.

When you're finished with your markup, click Done, or click Revert to discard your changes. After you click Done, you can't undo your changes.

Reference 19.2
Save Documents

macOS apps save files for you, and they can also maintain a version history of your files. In this section, you learn how Auto Save and Versions work together. These two features work with Locked and Resume to maintain the current state of your work environment even if you log out or restart your Mac.

About Auto Save and Versions

For apps that support Auto Save, after you save a file the first time the app doesn't ask you again if it should save changes. If you want to use the file in another app or share it with other users, you don't have to remember to save the latest version of the file. The file displayed in the Finder is the same as the file displayed in the app. The location where you first saved a file is always the latest version.

Apps that support Auto Save also support document versions. This provides an environment where macOS maintains a history of changes for any document. You can return a document to a previous state with a few clicks, or you can navigate to an earlier version of a document and copy elements to the latest version.

You can access a document version history using an interface similar to the Time Machine Restore interface. In each volume that you can write to, macOS saves the version histories in a hidden folder at the root of the volume containing the original document. The most recent version of a document is always saved to its original location, and you can copy or share it with other apps or users immediately after you make a change.

For information about how restore versions of Pages, Numbers, and Keynote documents, see Apple Support article HT205411, "Restore previous versions of iWork documents."

Apps that support macOS Auto Save and Versions are identified by the content of the File menu in the app. Apps that support Auto Save have the following commands in the File menu:

▶   Duplicate (instead of Save As)

▶   Rename

▶   Move To

Updated apps offer the File > Save command for saving a document the first time, but after you save a document, the behavior of this menu command changes to saving a version of the document. Most Apple-designed apps, including TextEdit, Preview, Pages, Numbers, and Keynote, support Auto Save and Versions.

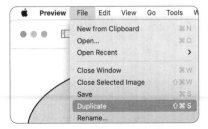

Automatically Save Document Changes

Saving documents to iCloud is covered in the next section of this lesson.

When you open a new document in an app that supports Auto Save, it's saved, even though you haven't set a location for it. Changes you make to the new document are saved, even if you have yet to manually save the document. The document is saved to the Versions history database on the system volume.

> **NOTE ▶** Some third-party apps include a feature that automatically saves documents periodically but doesn't use the Versions history database.

By default, if you choose to close a document window or an app with an open document, macOS asks you to save the document if you haven't saved the document yet. You can also choose File > Save or press Command-S. In the resulting Save dialog, you choose a name and location for the document. You can expand a minimized Save dialog to show a full file-system browser. Click the small arrow to the right of the folder name.

You can also click the document name in the title bar to save it. Doing so reveals a dialog similar to the Save dialog, except there are no Cancel and Save buttons.

When you enter a change in the dialog, it's saved after you click anywhere outside the title bar. You can return to the dialog to save changes to the document. For example, to rename a document enter a new name and then click elsewhere to dismiss the dialog.

Press and hold the Command key and click the document name in the title bar to reveal its path in the file system.

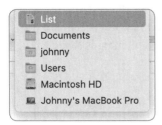

Auto-saves occur:

- ▶ When you make a change to a document
- ▶ When you close a document window
- ▶ When you close an app
- ▶ When you select the document in the Finder
- ▶ When you attempt to access the document from another app
- ▶ During pauses in your work
- ▶ Every five minutes as you work

As you make changes to a document, the app might display "Edited" in the document title bar. This is a visual cue to let you know macOS is saving changes. You can test this by making changes to a document and immediately using Quick Look to preview the document by selecting it in the Finder and pressing the Space bar. The Quick Look preview is identical to the open document in the app.

Save Duplicate Documents

To save a copy of a document, use Duplicate. With the document open, choose File > Duplicate (Shift-Command-S). A new window appears with a copy of the document. The filename in the title bar is highlighted, indicating that you can change the name of the duplicate document.

The Move To command in the File menu moves the original document to a new location without creating a new copy. Even though the document is moved, in most cases the version history is preserved.

The document is saved in the same folder as the original document. With Auto Save you never have to manually save this document again.

If you press and hold the Option key, the File > Duplicate menu option changes to File > Save As. You can also press Option-Shift-Command-S.

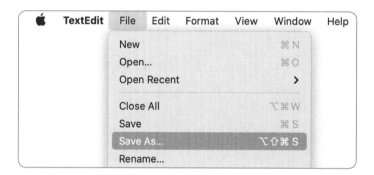

Choosing the Save As command is the same as choosing Duplicate, except that it presents the full Save dialog, enabling you to choose a different filename and location, and then it closes the original document. The new document replaces the original document in the active window. You have the option to also save the changes to the original document. This option is enabled by default, meaning that any changes made up to this point will also be saved to the original document. If you disable this option, you revert the original document to its previous state (before you made changes) and save a new document with the latest changes.

Explore Document Versions

With Versions, apps maintain a history of your changes. Whenever a document is saved, automatically or manually, a new document version is also saved. When you manually save by choosing File > Save or by pressing Command-S, macOS saves another version of the document in the version history.

If you're editing a document and have yet to trigger a manual or automatic save, you can revert to the previously saved state by choosing File > Revert To > Last Saved or File > Revert To > Last Opened. If a deeper version history is available, macOS enables you to browse the history of a document. To open the version history browser, choose File > Revert To > Browse All Versions.

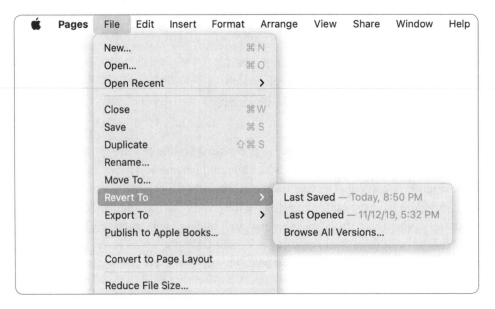

A document's version history isn't saved within the document. Instead, document history is stored on the volume where the original document is saved—specifically in the .DocumentRevisions-V100 folder. When you share the document by creating or sending a copy of the document, other users won't have access to the document version history.

Version history isn't always maintained on files being edited from a shared network volume. To ensure that a version history is maintained, you must copy the shared file to a local disk.

The Versions browser interface looks similar to Time Machine. If you have Time Machine turned on, as covered in Lesson 17, "Manage Time Machine," an app's version history can go much deeper by showing you versions that are also saved in the Time Machine backup.

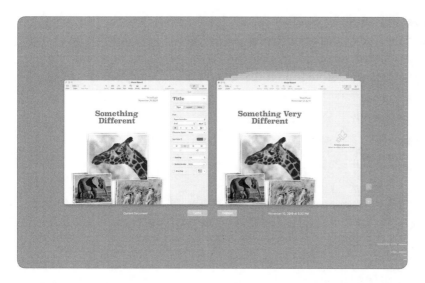

The current version of the document is displayed on the left, and the previous versions are displayed on the right. Navigate by clicking a previous version's title bar or by using the timeline to the right.

To restore a previous version, click Restore. If you want a specific section of a previous version copied to the latest version, make a selection inside the previous document, then copy and paste to the current document. When you finish making targeted edits, click Done to return to the standard app interface.

In the Versions browser, you can copy and paste using the Command-C and Command-V keyboard shortcuts or by Control-clicking to reveal a shortcut menu.

To delete a previous document version, in the Versions browser select the document name in the title bar to reveal a menu enabling you to choose Delete This Version.

Locked Files

macOS includes a file and folder attribute that trumps all write privileges and administrator user access. Users can choose to lock a file or folder that they own from the Finder Info window or any app that supports Auto Save.

Locking an item renders it unchangeable by any user except the item's owner. Even administrator users are prevented from making changes to another user's locked file in the Finder or with apps.

Locking a document prevents users—or, more appropriately, their apps—from accidentally auto-saving changes.

Manage File Locking with the Finder

Use the Finder and the Info or Inspector window to view and change a file's lock state. After an item is locked, no other users can modify, move, delete, or rename it in the Finder. Using the Info window to inspect files and folders is detailed in Lesson 13.

After the file is locked, the Finder prevents the owner from moving, renaming, or changing ownership and permissions for the locked item. If you as the owner try to move a locked item, the Finder defaults to making a copy. However, unlike other users, the owner can return the file to the normal state by disabling the locked attribute from the Info or Inspector window.

Another option in a file's Info window is "Stationery pad." In the Finder, when you open a file that's a "Stationery pad" the Finder makes a copy of the original, then opens the copy for you to edit.

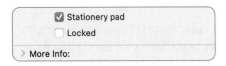

If you select both "Stationery pad" and Locked for a file you own, you must unlock the file before you can rename it.

Duplicating a locked document in the Finder results in another locked copy of the document. In macOS, apps that support Auto Save can create an unlocked duplicate of a locked file.

Manage File Locking with an App

Apps that support Auto Save also provide access to document locking. As long as you are the owner of a document, which is often the case if you created the document or are editing a copy of the document, you can manually lock it to prevent further changes. To manually lock a document in an app that supports Auto Save, select the document's filename in the title bar. A dialog appears where you can select the Locked checkbox.

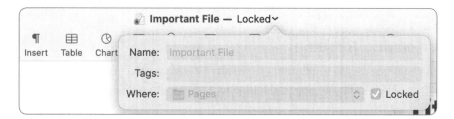

In the title bar, locked documents are labeled Locked and display a small lock icon. As long as you are the owner of a document, you can deselect the Locked checkbox to enable changes. You can also open a locked document that you own. A dialog appears that lets you select what you want to do with the file. You can duplicate the file and keep the previous version unchanged. You can unlock the file to edit it. And you can cancel and do neither.

If you aren't the owner of a locked document, you aren't allowed to unlock it—which means you aren't allowed to edit it. Also, as covered in Lesson 13, if you don't have write file permissions, you aren't allowed to edit a document. In both cases, the document's title bar displays "Locked."

You can treat a locked document as a template by duplicating the document and editing the copy. If you try to edit a locked, or otherwise unwritable, document, a prompt appears that enables you to duplicate the document.

You can manually duplicate a locked document. Choose File > Duplicate. After the app makes a copy, you can save the copy as you would a new document.

Reference 19.3
Manage Automatic Resume

Auto Save allows supported apps to maintain their current state even if you log out or quit the app. When an app quits, any open documents and the app state are saved.

macOS can quit apps that support Resume when resources, specifically memory, run low. macOS quits only apps that are idle (not in active use).

Manage Resuming After Logout

By default, macOS automatically resumes apps and windows after you log out. To prevent this, deselect the option "Reopen windows when logging back in" in the dialog that asks if you want to quit all apps and log out. Your selection remains active until you change it.

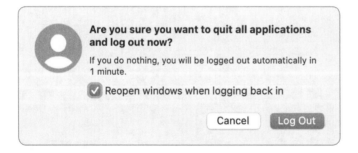

If "Reopen windows when logging back in" isn't selected, you can temporarily enable it by pressing and holding down the Option key when you log out.

Manage Resuming After Quit

By default, macOS closes associated open files and windows when you quit an app. In General preferences you can deselect "Close windows when quitting an app" to make macOS resume previously open files and windows when you open an app.

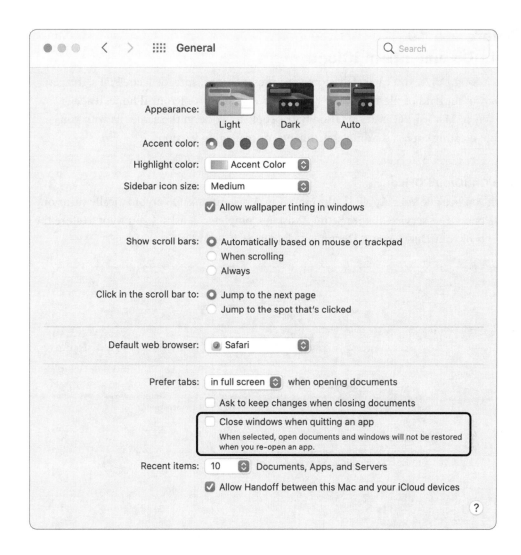

Disable Auto Save

Select "Ask to keep changes when closing documents" to disable the Auto Save feature for any app that supports it. Even if you disable the Auto Save feature, apps that support it still retain the rest of their document management behavior. For example, apps that support Auto Save offer a Duplicate menu option and automatically maintain a version history whenever you manually save documents.

Reference 19.4
Store Documents in iCloud

With iCloud Drive, you can safely store your presentations, spreadsheets, PDFs, images, and any other kind of file in iCloud. You can access them from your iPhone, iPad, iPod touch, Mac, or PC. You can also invite people to work on the same file with you—without creating copies, sending attachments, or managing versions.

Turn On iCloud Drive

When you provide your Apple ID during Setup Assistant, macOS automatically turns on the iCloud Drive service. Before Setup Assistant completes, it asks if you want to store the contents of your Desktop and Documents folders in iCloud Drive.

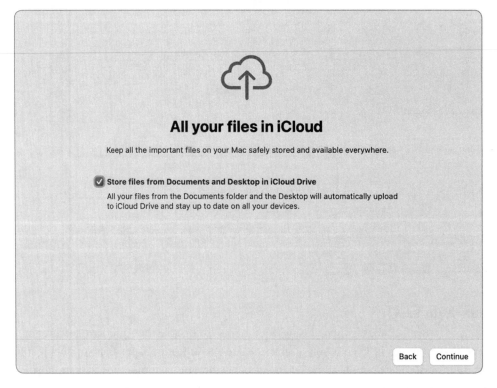

If you don't provide your Apple ID during Setup Assistant, you can turn on the iCloud Drive service later. In System Preferences, next to "Sign in to your Apple ID," click Sign In. Choose View > Show All Preferences, if necessary, to display this button.

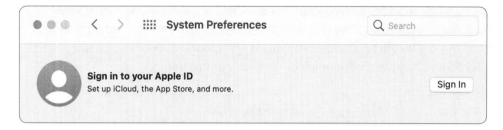

After you sign in with your Apple ID, click iCloud in the sidebar of Apple ID preferences, then confirm that iCloud Drive is selected.

Signing in with your iCloud account doesn't automatically save the contents of your Desktop and Documents folders to iCloud Drive. If iCloud Drive is turned on, you can click the Options button to configure supported app-specific iCloud Drive settings. Details about iCloud Drive options are covered later in this lesson.

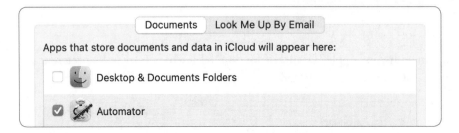

For more information, see Apple Support article HT201104, "iCloud Drive FAQ," and the iCloud website at www.apple.com/icloud/.

Use iCloud Drive

With iCloud Drive, iCloud storage appears as if it were an external storage device. All Finder file management features (move, copy, rename, folder creation, and more) work on files that you store in iCloud Drive.

A pie chart indicator immediately to the right of iCloud Drive in the Finder sidebar gives you the status of a file copy to iCloud Drive. If there is no pie chart icon, the copy is complete.

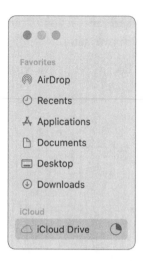

iCloud Drive also appears in Open and Save dialogs for any app. In iCloud Drive, you can create custom folder hierarchies and save documents inside any folder you choose. Apps can create folders in iCloud Drive with app-specific folders to facilitate document management. For example, for some apps like Pages, Numbers, and Keynote, when you create a new document and make any change to that document, the app automatically creates an app-specific folder in iCloud Drive before you save the document.

For example, the following screenshot shows the Open dialog for TextEdit. The menu at the top of the Open dialog contains a TextEdit-specific folder. The sidebar of the Open dialog contains an iCloud section with two items: a TextEdit-specific folder in iCloud Drive and the top level of iCloud Drive.

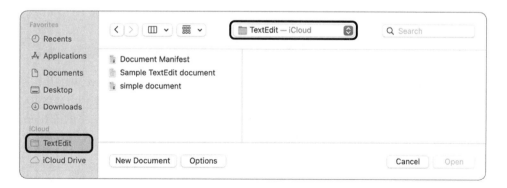

For apps that support iCloud Drive, the Save dialog offers an iCloud Library section in the menu. The following two screenshots show the iCloud Drive folder in two states.

In the first screenshot, the Finder window shows that iCloud Drive doesn't yet have a custom folder for Numbers. There's a blank Numbers file open.

The second screenshot illustrates that immediately after text was entered into the previously blank document, your Mac created a Numbers-specific folder. Numbers automatically saved the Untitled document in the new Numbers folder.

You can access custom folders and documents that were saved to iCloud Drive with the iCloud website (www.icloud.com), with the iCloud Drive app on iOS devices with iOS 10, and with the Files app on iOS devices with iOS 11 and newer or iPad OS devices. Further, you can share items in iCloud Drive with others, which enables collaborative document editing.

Store Desktop and Documents in iCloud Drive

You can save the contents of your Desktop and Documents folders to iCloud Drive.

To turn on or turn off saving Desktop and Documents in iCloud Drive, open Apple ID preferences, then select iCloud in the sidebar. Next to iCloud Drive, click Options, then select or deselect Desktop & Documents Folders.

When you turn on Desktop & Documents Folders in iCloud preferences for the first time per iCloud account, the Desktop and Documents folders from your home folder on that Mac are moved to iCloud Drive. Items in your Desktop folder still appear in the Finder and on your desktop background.

Accessing your Desktop and Documents folders in the Finder with the keyboard shortcuts (Shift-Command-D to open your Desktop folder and Shift-Command-O to open your Documents folder) and the Go menu work as before. Your Desktop and Documents folders appear in iCloud Drive and in the Finder sidebar under iCloud.

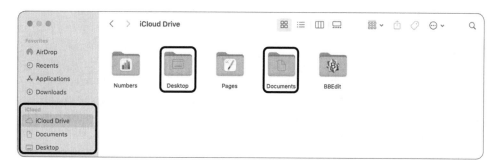

If you use the Finder to open your Desktop or Documents folder, then Option-click the name of the folder in the title bar, you can confirm that the folder is in your iCloud Drive folder.

When you use Terminal to find the location of your Desktop and Documents folders, they appear in their normal location at the root of your home folder, but the Finder doesn't display these folders at the root of your home folder.

An iCloud account can have only one set of Desktop and Documents folders in iCloud Drive. So the first Mac on which you turn on Desktop & Documents Folders (during Setup Assistant or in Apple ID preferences) defines the base contents in iCloud Drive.

When you enable Desktop & Documents Folders in iCloud on an additional Mac, and you have items in the Desktop folder or the Documents folder on the additional Mac, a message appears on the additional Mac that your existing items were moved to a new folder (or folders) in iCloud Drive.

Content from additional Mac computers is represented by new subfolders.

Make sure the initial upload to iCloud Drive is fully complete (wait until there is no pie chart status icon to the right of iCloud Drive in the Finder's sidebar) before you enable Desktop & Documents Folders in iCloud Drive on another Mac. This ensures that all items are available to all Mac computers with iCloud Drive.

In the following screenshot, another Mac, named Johnny's MacBook, was added as a second computer with Desktop & Documents Folders in iCloud preferences enabled for the account. This move was necessary so that the items already in the Desktop and Documents folders in iCloud Drive on the original Mac that turned on Desktop & Documents Folders in iCloud (Johnny's MacBook Pro) could replace the local Desktop and Documents folders on Johnny's MacBook. Now the contents from the Desktop and Documents folders on the original Mac and on Johnny's MacBook are available on both computers.

After you set up additional Mac computers, if you want to have a unified Desktop and Documents folder experience move the items out of the computer-named subfolders to the base folders. With iCloud Drive, changes made on one Mac automatically apply to other Mac computers with the same iCloud account. Reorganization of your Desktop and Documents folders on one Mac automatically applies to your configured Mac computers. If you move all items out of the computer-named subfolders, the folders can be deleted, leaving you with the content in one set of Desktop and Documents folders available to all your Mac computers with iCloud Drive.

You can find out more about using iCloud Drive by going to Apple Support article HT206985, "Add your Desktop and Documents files to iCloud Drive."

Remove Items from iCloud Drive

To remove an item from iCloud Drive, move it out of an iCloud Drive folder to the Trash or any other local file on your Mac. Moving something from iCloud Drive to a local folder on your Mac removes the item from iCloud and other Apple devices configured for iCloud Drive.

Because iCloud Drive items appear alongside locally stored items on your Mac, you might accidentally remove an item from iCloud Drive. macOS warns you when you move something out of iCloud Drive.

On the Advanced tab of the Finder preferences, you can configure whether macOS shows this warning.

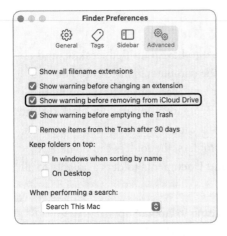

iCloud Drive Local Storage

With the exception of the Desktop and Documents folders, items saved in iCloud Drive are maintained locally in each user's ~/Library/Mobile Documents/ folder. It doesn't matter whether Desktop and Documents storage in iCloud Drive is enabled; those items are maintained locally in their normal locations, ~/Desktop and ~/Documents. Although you can reveal the Mobile Documents folder in the Finder, double-clicking this folder will redirect you to the root iCloud Drive view in the Finder.

App-specific folders, custom user folders, and all documents are visible in Terminal. Avoid using Terminal to modify content directly in the Mobile Documents folder. Any changes you make to the contents of the Mobile Documents folder are immediately saved to iCloud Drive.

Multiple devices on the same network that share an iCloud account transfer the data locally to improve performance. If you make changes to iCloud Drive while offline, macOS caches the changes and then silently pushes them the next moment an internet connection to the iCloud servers is available.

If you have multiple Apple devices on the same network that use iCloud Drive, consider using a Mac to provide the content caching service to cache iCloud content. This can reduce internet data usage and speed up downloads of iCloud content. See Reference 25.1, "Turn On Host-Sharing Services," for more information.

iCloud Drive Optimized Storage

iCloud Drive keeps older files and infrequently used files only in iCloud Drive. In iCloud Drive:

▶ Items that aren't downloaded locally to a Mac appear with an iCloud download icon (which looks like a cloud with an arrow).

▶ Items that are currently uploading or downloading appear with a pie chart status indicator or a cloud icon.

▶ In the Finder window sidebar, the iCloud Drive icon appears with a pie chart status indicator when items are currently downloading or uploading.

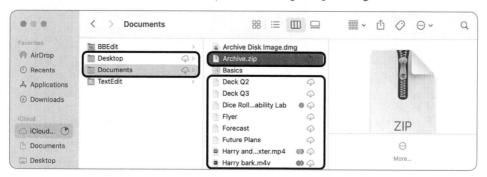

When you try to access items that aren't downloaded, they download to your Mac. This may take a few minutes if the items are large or your internet connection is slow. If you want to prevent iCloud Drive from optimizing storage, force it to save items locally too. In iCloud preferences, deselect Optimize Mac Storage at the bottom of the iCloud Drive options pane to make the change.

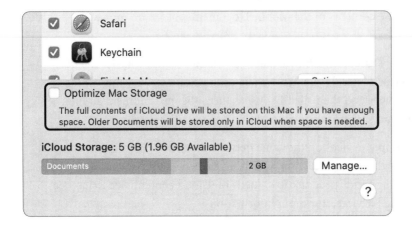

Turn Off iCloud Drive Features

By default, when you turn on iCloud Drive compatible apps save files to iCloud in a custom folder for that app. If you want to stop an app from saving content to a custom folder for that app in iCloud Drive, then in the iCloud Drive options pane, deselect the app.

This doesn't delete existing data in iCloud. It just hides the associated folder from the Finder.

You can also deselect Desktop & Documents Folders to stop content from being saved to them. If you do this, you won't remove already stored content from iCloud Drive or from other Apple devices.

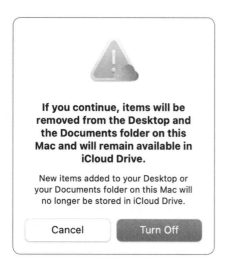

If you click Turn Off, you revert the iCloud Drive configuration for the Mac back to using local-only Desktop and Documents folders.

macOS displays a dialog that informs you can still access the Desktop and Documents folders in iCloud Drive.

If you click "Show in Finder," the Finder opens your iCloud Drive folder and selects your Desktop and Documents folders. In your iCloud Drive folder, you can open the Desktop or Documents folder and confirm that "Desktop — iCloud" or "Documents — iCloud" is displayed in the title bar.

In this case, your home folder on the local Mac will have new, empty Desktop and Documents folders. If you open one of these new folders at the root of your home folder, you can confirm that "Desktop — Local" or "Documents — Local" is displayed in the title bar.

No files or folders are removed, but you must move or copy items from iCloud Drive back to the local folders on your Mac if you want the items to be in your local Desktop folder or your local Documents folder. Moving something from iCloud Drive to another folder on your local Mac removes the item from iCloud Drive and configured Apple devices.

If you decide to completely turn off all iCloud Drive features, you can do so by deselecting the iCloud Drive checkbox in the iCloud preferences. Turning off iCloud Drive completely presents you with two options.

If you have Desktop & Documents Folders enabled, the dialog also notifies you that this affects your Desktop and Documents folders.

Neither option removes items from iCloud Drive or items from other Apple devices configured for it. Instead, clicking the "Remove from Mac" button removes iCloud Drive items only from the local Mac. Clicking the "Keep a Copy" button creates an iCloud Drive

(Archive) folder in your home folder on the local Mac. If you click "Keep a Copy" but you haven't yet finished downloading files from iCloud, a dialog appears with a progress bar and the message "iCloud Drive needs to finish updating before being turned off. Your documents will be downloaded and copied to a folder named 'iCloud Drive (Archive)' in your home folder on this Mac."

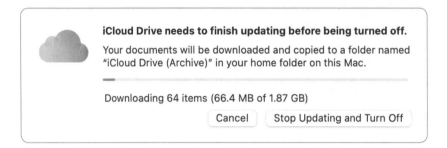

This local archive folder contains copies of items currently in your iCloud Drive.

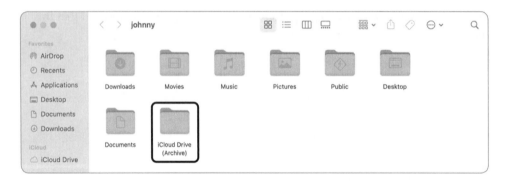

Reference 19.5
Optimize Local Storage

For a summary of how the storage space on your Mac is being used, choose About This Mac from the Apple menu, then click the Storage button. The Storage pane shows an overview of your free space and the space used by different categories of files, including apps, documents, and photos, for each disk. Each segment of the bar is an estimate of the storage space used by a category of files. Move your pointer over each segment for more detail.

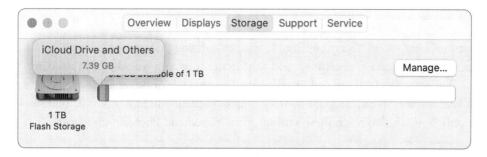

The calculations are based on storage optimization techniques that you can further inspect and implement by clicking the Manage button to open the Storage Management window. For more information, see Apple Support article HT206996, "How to free up storage space on your Mac."

System Information includes storage optimization features that are available in Storage Management. The Storage Management interface dynamically changes based on what features you enable. It may not appear on your Mac as it appears in this guide.

Storage Management opens with Recommendations, which offers suggestions to optimize storage on the volume that contains your home folder. You can also inspect and implement space-saving optimizations by selecting items from the list on the right of the Storage Management pane.

Recommendations offers various ways you can optimize storage:

▸ Store in iCloud—Click "Store in iCloud" to open a dialog that may vary based on your current iCloud Drive settings. You can choose what you would like to store in iCloud by selecting Desktop and Documents, Photos, and Messages. These selections can save considerable local space by relegating infrequently used items to iCloud storage only. You can also reach these settings from iCloud and Photos preferences.

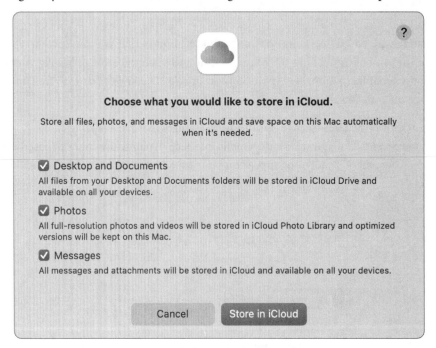

▸ Optimize Storage—Click Optimize to reveal a dialog that enables you to turn on the automatic removal of watched movies and TV shows. These settings can also be accessed from Apple TV preferences.

▸ Empty Trash Automatically—Click Turn On to enable the option for the Finder to automatically empty local items from the Trash if they were there for longer than 30 days.

▸ Reduce Clutter—Click Review Files to open the Documents view of the Storage Management window. From here you can view your largest and least used documents on the local Mac. You can delete items you no longer need by selecting an item and then clicking Delete in the lower-right corner of the window. Control-click a file to delete it or to open a Finder window for the file's parent folder.

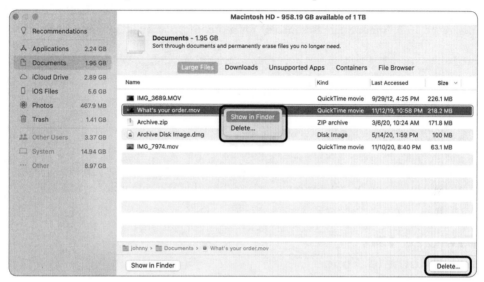

Click File Browser to browse your home folder, sorted by the folders that use the most storage. Select a file to display its preview.

A new category for the Storage Management window in macOS Big Sur is Containers, where you can browse app data containers and erase data you no longer need. We do not recommend that you erase app container data unless you understand what the data is. See Reference 15.1, "macOS File Resources," for more information about app containers.

In the Storage Management window, you can select a storage category in the far-left column to inspect, and potentially remove, large files that you might not need.

Exercise 19.1
Use Alternate Apps

> **Prerequisites**
>
> ▶ You must have performed Exercise 3.1, "Configure a Mac for Exercises."
>
> ▶ You must have created the Johnny Appleseed account (Exercise 7.1, "Create a Standard User Account").
>
> ▶ You must have signed in to the App Store (Exercise 18.1, "Install an App from the App Store").

In this exercise, you configure which apps open files when you make a one-time choice to use a different app and when you choose to change the default app that opens a file type. You also use Quick Look to inspect what's in a file.

Download an App

1 If necessary, log in as Johnny Appleseed.

2 Open App Store.

3   Enter **Pages** in the Search field (at the top left of the App Store window), then press Return. App Store displays Pages, then either a Get or a Download button.

4   Perform one of the following actions:

▶   If a Get button is displayed, click Get, then click Install.

▶   If a Download button is displayed, click it to download the app.

When the app starts to download, the progress is shown in App Store.

Don't open Pages.

View a File with Quick Look

1   In the Finder, open the StudentMaterials/Lesson19 folder.

2   Drag the file Pet Care Instructions to copy it to your desktop.

The file has no visible extension, although the icon may indicate its file type.

3   Select (single-click) the Pet Care Instructions file on your desktop.

4   Choose File > Quick Look "Pet Care Instructions" (or press Command-Y).

Quick Look displays a preview of how the file would appear if you opened it in its default app. You can open the file by clicking the "Open with *default app*" button in the upper-right corner of the preview, but for the purposes of this exercise, don't click the button. There are other ways to obtain a Quick Look preview of the file. You could select the file, then use the shortcut Command-Y; select the file, then press the Space bar; or Control-click the file, then choose Quick Look from the shortcut menu.

5   Press Command-Y or the Space bar to close the Quick Look window.

Choose an App to Open a File Once

1   Double-click Pet Care Instructions on your desktop.

The file opens in Pages. Confirm that Pages displays a rich view of the file.

2   In Pages, click Continue, then click View My Documents.

Even though Pages is now on this computer, not all Mac computers have Pages. You will see what to do if you need to open a file with a different app.

3   Choose Pages > Quit Pages to quit the app and close the file. Then, on your desktop, Control-click the file.

4   In the shortcut menu, hold the mouse pointer over the Open With choice.

A submenu opens that shows the apps that can open this document type.

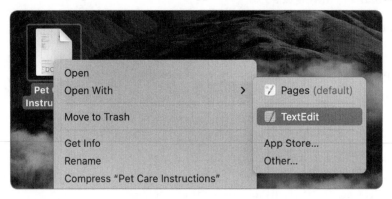

5   In the Open With submenu, choose TextEdit.

The file opens in TextEdit.

6   Compare how the file is displayed in TextEdit with how it was displayed in Pages.

Pages gives a richer view of the file, showing a background image and headings that TextEdit doesn't display. TextEdit lets you edit its content but does not show the same formatting or images. Depending on what you want to do with the file, you may prefer one over the other.

7   Close the file.

8   Double-click the file again.

The file opens in Pages because the Open With choice you made earlier wasn't a permanent setting.

9   Close the file.

Change the Default App for a File Type

1   In the Finder, select the Pet Care Instructions file.

2   Choose File menu > Get Info (or press Command-I).

3   If necessary, expand the General and Name & Extension sections of the Info window.

This is a Microsoft Word document, and it has a hidden .docx file extension.

4   Deselect "Hide extension." The extension is visible in the view of your desktop in the Finder.

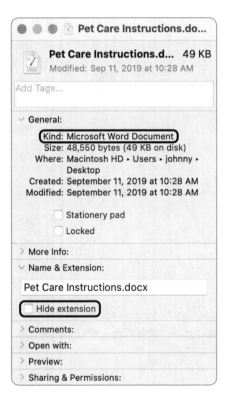

5   Expand the "Open with" section of the Info window, then choose TextEdit from its menu.

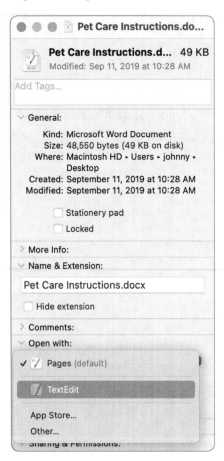

This menu shows the same possible apps as the Open With submenu in the Finder. When you choose an app from this menu without clicking Change All below the menu, you change the setting only for this file.

6   Click Change All.

7 In the confirmation dialog, click Continue.

You changed the default app for opening documents with the extension .docx in Johnny Appleseed's account.

8 Close the Info window.

9 Double-click the file on your desktop.

Confirm the file opens in TextEdit.

10 Quit TextEdit.

11 Move Pet Care Instructions.docx from your desktop to the Trash.

12 In the Finder, reopen the StudentMaterials/Lesson19 folder, then examine the original Pet Care Instructions file.

The filename extension isn't shown. When you used Get Info to show the extension of the copy on your desktop, it affected only that file.

13 Double-click the original Pet Care Instructions.

Pet Care Instructions opens in TextEdit because you used Change All in the Info window to apply the setting to all Microsoft Word documents.

14 Quit TextEdit.

Exercise 19.2
Practice Auto Save and Versions

▶ **Prerequisite**

▶ You must have created the Johnny Appleseed account (Exercise 7.1, "Create a Standard User Account").

In this exercise, you edit a file in TextEdit, save several versions, and revert to an earlier version.

Experiment with Auto Save

1 If necessary, log in as Johnny Appleseed.

2 Open System Preferences, then click General.

3 Ensure that "Ask to keep changes when closing documents" is unselected and "Close windows when quitting an app" is selected.

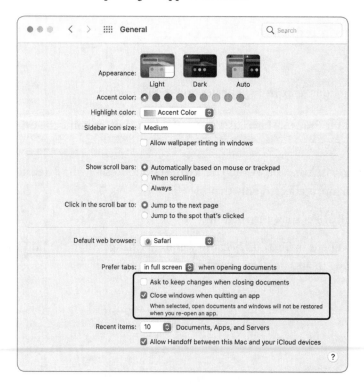

These are the default settings in macOS Big Sur. If you select "Ask to keep changes when closing documents," you turn off the Auto Save feature you're about to test. If you deselect "Close windows when quitting an app," you make apps remember open documents and windows when you quit and reopen an app.

4   Quit System Preferences.

5   If necessary, navigate to StudentMaterials/Lesson19.

6   Copy PretendCo Report.rtfd to your desktop, then open the copy.

7   Add some text to the file.

The window title bar indicates the file status as Edited.

8   Switch to the Finder, select your copy of the PretendCo Report file, then choose File > Get Info (or press Command-I).

Confirm that it was modified recently (your edits were saved automatically).

9   Close the Info window.

10 Switch to TextEdit, then add some more text to the file.

11 Select the file in the Finder, then choose File > Quick Look "PretendCo Report.rtfd."

The Quick Look view shows the text you added to the file.

12 Close the Quick Look window.

Work with Multiple Versions

1   Switch to TextEdit, then choose File > Save.

This save looks normal, but it saves a restorable version of the file.

TextEdit saves changes to a file during pauses in your work, and it saves a restorable version every five minutes.

2   Delete the graphic from the file.

3 Quit TextEdit.

You aren't asked to save changes; they were saved automatically.

4 Reopen the PretendCo Report file.

5 Choose File > Revert To > Previous Save.

The graphic is restored.

6 Add more text to the file, then choose File > Save.

7 Add more text, and examine the File > Revert To submenu.

It lists options to restore to the last-saved version, to restore to the last-opened version, and to browse all versions.

8 Choose File > Revert To > Browse All Versions.

TextEdit displays a full-screen version browser and shows the file state on the left and saved versions on the right. This view is similar to the Time Machine restore interface and shows versions from the Time Machine backups and restorable versions that TextEdit created.

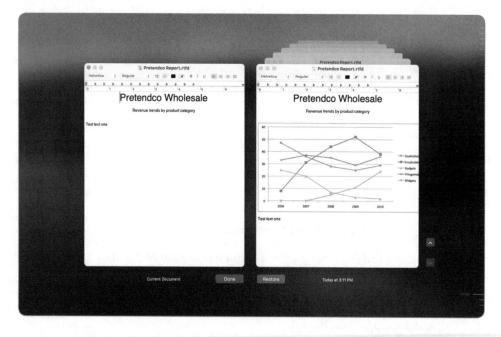

9   Experiment with the two windows. Click the arrows to the right of the stack or use the timeline on the right side of the screen to switch between saved versions. You can copy and paste content from old versions to the current file.

10 Click Done to exit the history browser.

11 Quit TextEdit.

Exercise 19.3
Manage Document Locking

> **Prerequisites**
>
> ▸   You must have created the Local Administrator (Exercise 3.1, "Configure a Mac for Exercises") and Johnny Appleseed (Exercise 7.1, "Create a Standard User Account") accounts.

In this exercise, you lock a document to prevent accidental changes.

Lock and Unlock a Document

1   If necessary, log in as Johnny Appleseed.

2   Select your copy of the PretendCo Report file, then choose File > Get Info.

3   In the General section of the Info window, select the Locked checkbox.

4   Close the Info window.

5   Open the file.

    The window title bar indicates the file is locked.

6   Attempt to add some text to the file.

A dialog appears telling you the file is locked, then gives you options for the locked file. Because you are the owner of the file, you can you can lock and unlock it in the Finder or in an app that supports Auto Save.

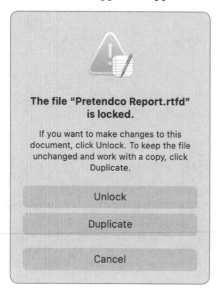

7   Click Unlock.

The lock is gone from the document icon on your desktop.

8   Add text to the file.

9   Click the filename in the title bar, then select the Locked checkbox.

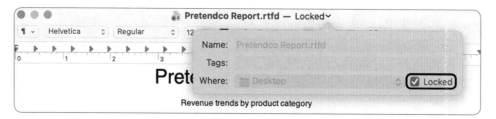

"Locked" reappears in the menu bar of the file.

10 Quit TextEdit.

Exercise 19.4
Store Documents in iCloud

> **Prerequisites**
>
> ▸ You must have created the Local Administrator (Exercise 3.1, "Configure a Mac for Exercises"), Johnny Appleseed (Exercise 7.1, "Create a Standard User Account"), and Emily Davidson (Exercise 8.1, "Restore a Deleted User Account") accounts.

You will store files in iCloud Drive. To simulate accessing the files from multiple Apple devices that are each signed in with the same Apple ID, you'll log in as a different user, signing in with the same Apple ID, as if this were a second Apple device. You'll confirm that you see the data in iCloud, then make a change to a document stored in iCloud. Then you'll log out, log in as the original user, and confirm that you can see the change you made from the simulated second Apple device.

Configure iCloud Drive

1   If necessary, log in as Johnny Appleseed.

2   Open System Preferences, then click Apple ID.

3   If Apple ID preferences require you to enter your password, click Enter Password, then authenticate.

4   If necessary, in the left sidebar, select iCloud.

5   If necessary, select the checkbox for Contacts.

6   If necessary, select the checkbox for iCloud Drive.

7   Quit System Preferences.

Save a Document to iCloud

1   From your desktop, open the PretendCo Report file.

2   Click the filename in the title bar.

3   If necessary, deselect Locked.

4   From the Where menu, choose iCloud Drive.

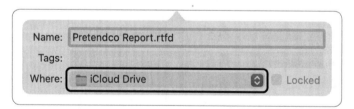

5   If a dialog appears and indicates that an item with the same name (PretendCo Report.rtfd) exists in the same folder, that means a previous student left this item in the iCloud account. Click Replace to replace the previous item with yours.

The document icon is no longer visible from your desktop.

6   Quit TextEdit.

7   In the Finder, navigate to StudentMaterials/Lesson19.

8 Open the file vCards.vcf.

Contacts opens, and a dialog opens asking you to confirm that you want to add the contacts.

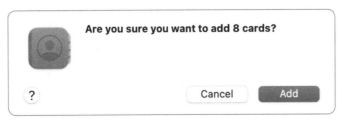

9 If the dialog indicates that some cards are duplicates, this might be because a previous student left them in the iCloud account. If this occurs, click Cancel, delete all the contacts besides yourself, then open the vCards.vcf file again.

10 Click Add.

You import eight vCards into Contacts, and they update automatically to iCloud.

11 Quit Contacts, then log out as Johnny Appleseed.

Open a Document from iCloud

Your files and contacts are stored in iCloud. They're available from any Mac account tied to the same iCloud account. Use the Emily Davidson account on your Mac to practice.

1 Log in to the Emily Davidson account (password: **Apple321!**).

2 Open System Preferences, then click Sign In next to "Sign in to your Apple ID."

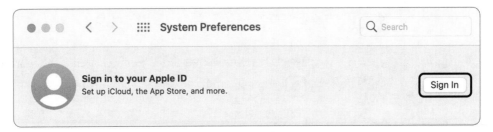

3 Enter the Apple ID you used with the Johnny Appleseed account, and click Next.

4   Enter the password for the Apple ID you used with the Johnny Appleseed account, then click Next.

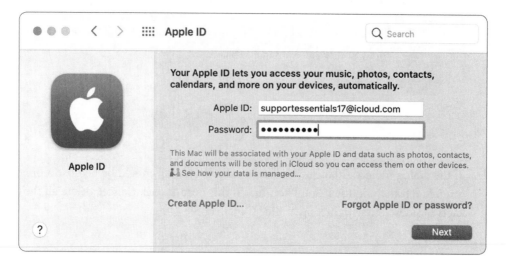

5   If your Apple ID has two-factor authentication turned on, you are asked to verify your identity. Follow the prompts to finish authenticating.

6   When you are asked to enter your Mac password to continue, type Emily's password, then click OK.

7   When your Mac displays the prompt "Allow Find My Mac to use the location of this Mac?" click Cancel.

8   Make sure that iCloud Drive and Contacts are selected.

9   Quit System Preferences.

10 In the Finder, choose Go > iCloud Drive (or press Shift-Command-I).

If PretendCo Report isn't downloaded to Emily's account, it has a cloud icon indicating that it's available from iCloud.

11 Double-click PretendCo Report.

The file downloads (if necessary), then opens in TextEdit.

12 Add text to the file.

Your edits are saved to iCloud and are available on other Mac computers that sign in to iCloud with the same Apple ID.

13 Quit TextEdit.

14 In the Finder, choose Go > Recents (or press Shift-Command-F).

PretendCo Report is listed. The Recents view shows both local documents and those in iCloud Drive.

15 In the Search field, enter **pretendco report**.

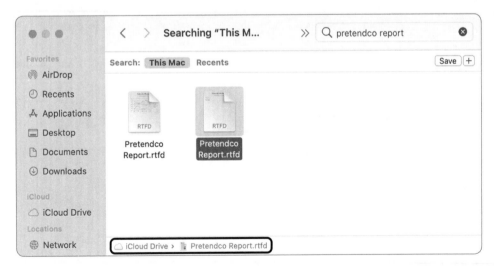

The Finder window displays two copies of PretendCo Report, since StudentMaterials is stored locally in /Users/Shared and also in iCloud Drive.

Use Contacts from iCloud

1   Open Contacts.

The contacts from the Johnny Appleseed account appear. You may have to wait for the contacts to update. If necessary, log out and back in as Emily Davidson.

2   Quit Contacts, then log out as Emily Davidson.

Verify Your Changes as Johnny Appleseed

1   Log back in as Johnny Appleseed.

2   In the Finder, choose Go > iCloud Drive (or press Shift-Command-I).

3   Open PretendCo Report.

4   Verify that the edit you made as Emily appears. You may have to wait for the file to update.

5   Quit TextEdit, then log out.

Lesson 20

Manage and Troubleshoot Apps

Your success in resolving issues with an app on your Mac depends on your experience with that app, your ability to gather relevant information about it, and your knowledge of macOS technologies. In this lesson, you learn about key elements of the macOS process architecture. You also learn to gather information about apps and processes. And you explore troubleshooting techniques that you can use for any type of app.

GOALS

- Describe and support app types
- Install Rosetta
- Manage app extensions and widgets in Notification Center
- Monitor and control processes and apps
- Explore app troubleshooting techniques

Reference 20.1
Apps and Processes

A *process* is any instance of executable code that is currently activated and addressed in system memory. In other words, a process is anything that is currently running or open. macOS handles processes efficiently, so even when a process is idle and probably consuming no processor resources, it's still active, because it has dedicated address space in system memory. The four general process types are apps, commands, daemons, and agents.

Process Types

An *app* is a process you run in the graphical interface.

A *command* is a process you run in the command-line interface (CLI). An exception is when you use the `open` command in the CLI to open an app in the graphical interface.

Processes that run on behalf of macOS are called *background* processes (or *daemons*) because they rarely have a user interface. Daemons usually launch during macOS startup and remain active the entire time a Mac is running. Most daemons run with root or systemwide access to all resources. Daemons are responsible for most automatic macOS features, such as detecting network changes and maintaining the Spotlight search metadata index.

An *agent* is a daemon that runs on behalf of a specific user. Agents are also daemons, or background processes. The primary difference is that agents run only when you're logged in. Agents are started automatically by macOS. Although apps and commands are also opened automatically, they aren't controlled by macOS the way agents are. Apps, commands, and agents are all part of the user's space because they are executed with the same access privileges the user has.

macOS Memory Management

The primary feature in macOS that keeps processes secure is *protected memory*. Processes are kept separate and secure in system memory. macOS manages memory allocation so that processes aren't allowed to interfere with one another's system memory space. In other words, an ill-behaved or crashed app doesn't normally affect other processes.

macOS automatically manages system memory for processes at their request. Although real system memory is limited by hardware, macOS dynamically allocates real and virtual memory when needed. So the only memory limitations in macOS are the size of installed RAM and the amount of free space you have on your startup disk.

macOS includes software-based memory compression that increases performance and reduces energy use. Instead of swapping memory out to internal storage when too many processes are active, macOS compresses the content used by less active processes to free up space for more active processes. This reduces traffic between active memory and the virtual memory swap files on the startup disk.

64-Bit Mode

macOS supports 64-bit mode exclusively. A process running in 64-bit mode can individually access more than 4 GB of system memory and can perform higher-precision computational functions much faster. All Mac computers compatible with macOS Big Sur feature 64-bit-capable processors and can take advantage of 64-bit system features.

Identify App Types

For an app that has not yet been updated for Apple silicon, the Get Info window in the Finder has "Kind" listed as "Application (Intel)." This kind of app is referred to as an Intel app.

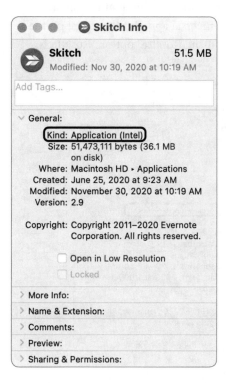

NOTE ▸ The "Open in Low Resolution" option prevents the use of high-resolution application graphic assets, which may not be compatible with older application plug-ins. For more information, see Apple Support article HT202471, "Using a Retina display."

Now developers can recompile their apps for a universal target: both a Mac with Apple silicon and an Intel-based Mac. The resulting app is called a Universal app.

NOTE ▸ Some documentation refers to current Universal apps as "Universal 2" apps, to distinguish them from the first Universal app type, which was used when Apple transitioned Mac computers from using PowerPC CPUs (central processing units) to using Intel CPUs.

The Get Info window for a Universal app displays Kind as "Application (Universal)." Universal apps run natively on both Mac computers with Apple silicon and Intel-based Mac computers. The following figures represent the Get Info window for the Mail app. The figure on the left is from a Mac with Apple silicon; the figure on the right is from an Intel-based Mac. Both reflect the fact that Mail is a Universal app. But the figure on the left, from the Mac with Apple silicon, has the "Open using Rosetta" option. Rosetta is covered in the next section.

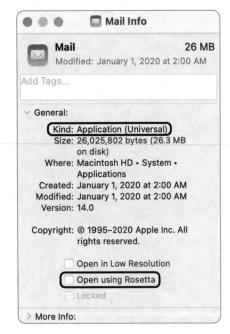 

In Reference 18.1, "The App Store," you learned that on a Mac with Apple silicon, you can use the App Store to install apps made for iPhone and iPad. The Get Info window for an app made for iPhone and iPad displays "Kind: Application (Apple silicon)."

You can use System Information to view the kinds of apps installed on your Mac. Open System Information, scroll to the Software section, then select Applications. You can click the Kind column to sort by kind.

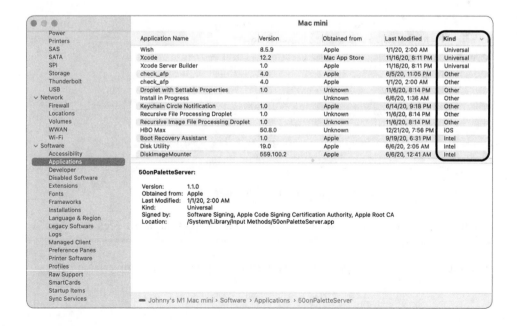

NOTE ▶ iOS and iPadOS apps appear as "Application (Apple Silicon)" in the Get Info window in the Finder, and as "iOS" in the Applications section of System Information.

There is more information about using System Information in Reference 20.3, "Monitor Apps and Processes."

Install Rosetta

Rosetta (technically Rosetta 2 to distinguish it from what Apple used in the transition of Mac from Power PC to Intel) is a translation process for Mac computers with Apple silicon. Rosetta enables a Mac with Apple silicon to use apps (and other kinds of code like plug-ins, add-ons, and extensions) that are built for Intel-based Mac computers and not updated for Apple silicon.

Rosetta runs only on Mac computers with Apple silicon. Rosetta works in the background and automatically translates code built for Intel. Mac computers with Apple silicon don't have Rosetta installed until you install it. You might not ever have to install Rosetta. If you run an app that needs Rosetta, macOS displays a dialog asking you to install it. You must be connected to the internet in order to successfully download and install Rosetta.

Here are some reasons you might have to install Rosetta:

▶ You want to use a package installer to install an Intel app that hasn't been recompiled to be a Universal app.

▶ You want to run an Intel app that hasn't been recompiled to be a Universal app.

▶ You want to use an email app, web browser, or other app with a plug-in, extension, or other add-on that hasn't yet been updated to support Apple silicon.

If you open a package and macOS detects that the code hasn't been updated for Apple silicon, the Installer app asks you to first install Rosetta.

The following figure shows the dialog that macOS displays when you open the installation package for a plug-in for Photoshop, a popular third-party graphics editor, and you haven't yet installed Rosetta.

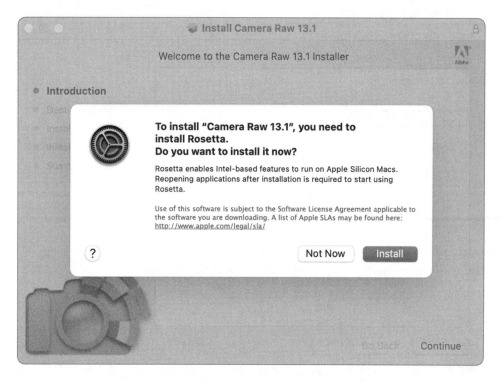

If an app that you run on a Mac with Apple silicon doesn't recognize a plug-in, extension, or other kind of add-on, quit the app, select the "Open using Rosetta" checkbox, then open the app again.

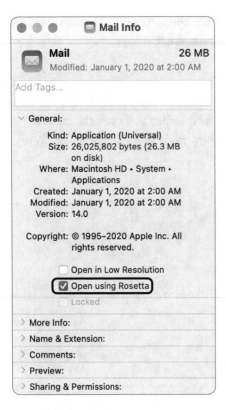

If you haven't installed Rosetta yet, opening the app with the "Open using Rosetta" option selected results in a dialog asking if you want to install Rosetta now.

After you install Rosetta once on a Mac, you don't have to ever install it again on that Mac. If you no longer have to use apps and other code that aren't updated for Apple silicon, don't worry about uninstalling Rosetta. If macOS won't use Rosetta if it doesn't need to, and having Rosetta available on your Mac won't affect the performance of your Mac.

For more information, see Apple Support article HT211861, "If you need to install Rosetta on your Mac."

Reference 20.2
Manage App Extensions

App extensions allow apps to use functionality and content from other apps. In this section you explore how to use app extensions.

App Extensions

App extensions provide a standard framework that allows apps from different developers to interact with one another—so much so that with app extensions one app's features appear as if they are built into another app.

As an example of app extensions, Preview includes markup features that you can use to manage pictures or PDF documents. This includes adding custom shapes, text, or your digital signature to documents. Click the Show Markup Toolbar button (pen tip icon) in the toolbar to access these features.

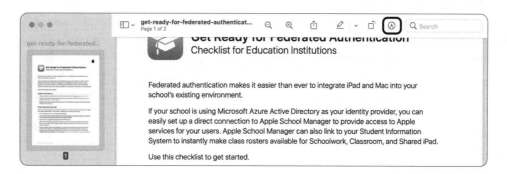

The Preview Markup toolbar appears.

The Preview Markup toolbar features are available as an app extension that can be used by other apps. In Mail, you can use markup features in an email that contains a picture or PDF document. When you send an email with an attachment, select the attachment, click Action (down-arrow button) at the top right of the document, then choose Markup to display markup features.

Manage App Extensions

Several app extensions are included in macOS. When you install an app that provides app extensions, you don't have to do anything extra, because installing an app automatically installs any app extension resources that are part of the app.

You can view installed app extensions and enable or disable their functionality from Extensions preferences. In Extensions preferences, select Added Extensions to view all extensions you've installed on your Mac. The following screenshot shows some extensions from apps in the App Store (Buffer, CloudApp, and Fantastical) and some from third-party installers (Acorn and Box).

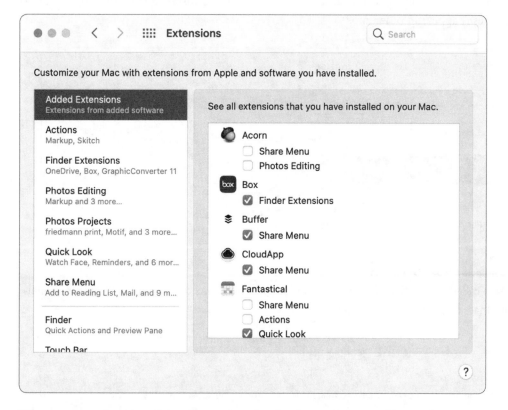

The next several sections cover the various kinds of extensions you can configure in Extensions preferences.

Configure Actions Extensions

Actions extensions enable you to edit or view content in one app, using the features of a second app without leaving the first app. For example, you can mark up images or PDF documents in Mail without leaving Mail. Deselect the checkbox next to an item to prevent that app extension from appearing in other apps. As an example, the checkbox next to the "Add to Fantastical" item is unselected (a third-party app installed from the App Store), so it doesn't appear in other apps.

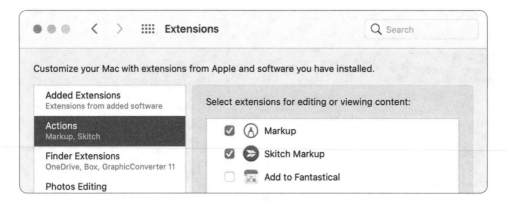

Configure Finder Extensions

Also called Finder Sync extensions, Finder app extensions can add file-system functionality that's displayed in the Finder.

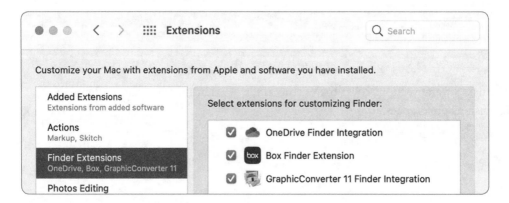

The following shows commands added to the Finder by the Box Finder extension after we signed in with the third-party file service Box.

Configure Photos Editing Extensions

Photos app extensions can add photo manipulation tools to Photos.

To use an app extension in Photos, open a photo in Edit mode, click the Extensions button , and choose an app.

You can also click the Extensions button and choose App Store to search for apps that offer Photo app extensions.

Configure Quick Look Extensions

Apps can include custom Quick Look extensions that enable Quick Look to give you a preview of additional kinds of files. You can deselect the checkbox for a third-party Quick Look extension to disable it. See Reference 19.1, "Open Files," for more information about Quick Look.

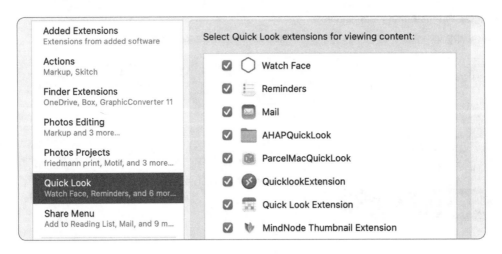

Configure Share Menu Extensions

Share Menu app extensions can add more options to the Share menu so that you can share content from one app with other apps.

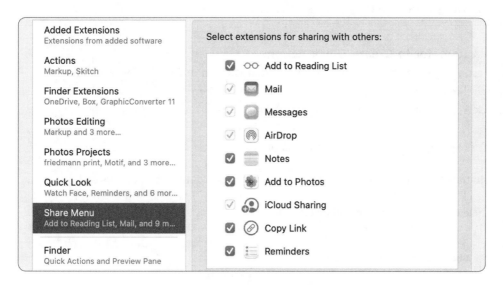

Configure Finder Quick Actions and Preview Pane Extensions

You can use these app extensions to perform Quick Actions on documents in the Finder and in the Finder's Preview pane. You can learn more about Quick Actions in Reference 19.1.

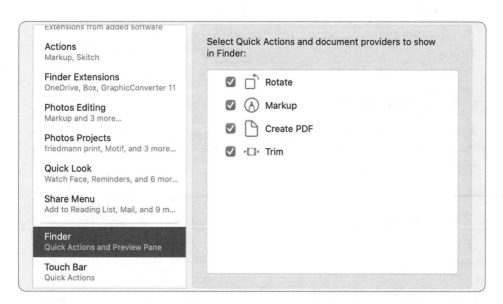

Configure Touch Bar Extensions

If your Mac has a Touch Bar, Extensions preferences has a Touch Bar entry. No Touch Bar extensions are included with a new installation of macOS Big Sur; when you install Touch Bar extensions, they will be listed here.

Use Automator to Create Quick Actions

You can use Automator to create workflows that you can make available in your Touch Bar and in Finder Quick Actions and in the Finder Preview pane. To create a Quick Action with Automator, use the following steps:

1   Use Spotlight Search to open Automator.

2   In the Open dialog, click New Document (or press Command-N or choose File > New).

3   Select Quick Action, then click Choose.

4   In the right side of the workflow, set "Workflow receives current" to "files or folders," then drag items from the Library on the left to the workflow on the right.

For more information about using Automator, choose Help > Automator Help.

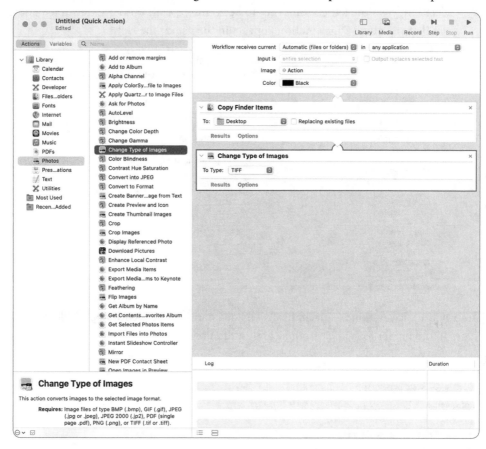

5   Choose File > Save (or press Command-S) to save the workflow.

6   Enter a name. This name will appear in Extensions preferences and in the Quick Actions menu.

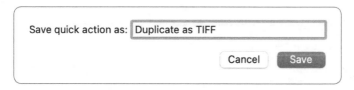

7   Click Save.

8   Open Extensions preferences.

9   Select Finder in the left column (not to be confused with Finder Extensions) and confirm that your new Quick Action appears in the list on the right.

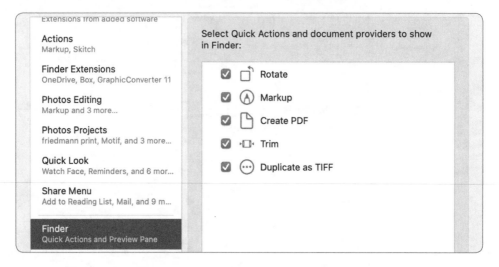

Your new Quick Action is automatically enabled and is available for applicable document types in the Finder for Quick Actions and in the Preview pane.

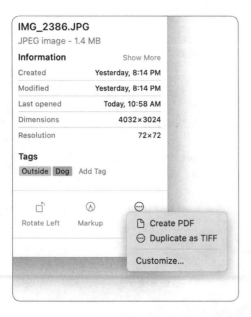

Manage Notification Center Widgets

App extensions can add functionality in the form of widgets that appear in the Notification Center. Notification Center in macOS Big Sur combines your alerts and your widgets. You can customize the information included in Notification Center. Click the date or time in the menu bar to access Notification Center—or from the right edge of your trackpad, swipe left with two fingers. The following figure displays an example of one notification and a default set of widgets.

NOTE ▶ To make many figures in this guide, we configured Dock & Menu Bar preferences to not display the date, just the time.

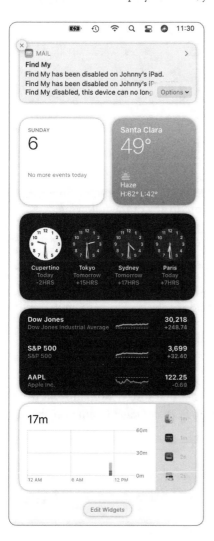

You can change how your Notification Center looks by doing any of the following:

▶ Reorder your widgets by dragging a widget to another location.

▶ Control-click a widget and choose a different size for the widget.

Like other app extensions, widgets in the Today view are included with the app that is providing the functionality or service. For example, the Calendar extension is built into Calendar.

You can manage widgets in the Today view by clicking the Edit Widgets button at the bottom center of Notification Center. Or Control-click a widget and choose Edit Widgets.

When you're managing your Notification Center, you can do any of the following:

▶ On the left side of the screen, select an app that offers widgets.

▶ Some widgets are available in more than one size. Select the size of a widget if you like.

▶ In the middle of the screen, click a widget to add it to the bottom of your existing Notification Center. Or drag a widget to the right side of the screen, placing it exactly where you want it to appear.

▶ On the right side of the screen, you can:

Drag a widget to change the order of widgets.

Click Remove (the minus icon in the upper-left corner of a widget) to remove it from your Notification Center view. After you click Remove, that widget is still available if you want to add it again later.

Drag a widget to the left to remove it.

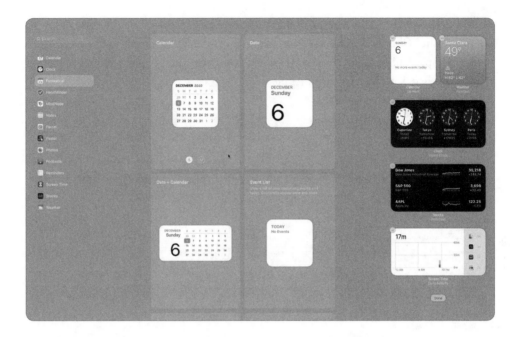

For more information about apps that offer extensions that include widgets for Notification Center, see the App Store story "Widgets Get an Upgrade," at apps.apple.com/us/story/id1531962992.

Reference 20.3
Monitor Apps and Processes

macOS provides several methods for identifying and managing apps and processes. You can use the Finder Info window to view basic app information, but you can find out a lot more about an app from System Information. To inspect an app or process as it's running on the Mac, use Activity Monitor.

Monitor Apps with System Information

If you want to gather information about all the apps on your Mac, use System Information. When you select the Applications category in System Information, the content of all available Application folders is scanned. This includes your home folder, /Applications, /Applications/Utilities, ~/Applications, /System/Library/, and any other Applications folders at the root of any mounted volumes.

From the apps list, select an entry to inspect more information about the app. The app's source, in the "Obtained from" column, is based on the code-signing certificate used to create the app. Unidentified apps don't have a code signature. Apps installed as part of macOS are listed as obtained from Apple.

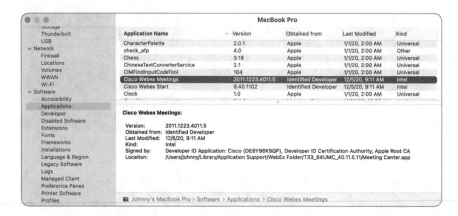

Monitor Processes with Activity Monitor

Activity Monitor is the primary app for monitoring running processes. If an app stops responding or is slow, check Activity Monitor. Also, check here if your Mac seems to be running slow. Activity Monitor helps you identify an app or background process that's using a significant percentage of macOS resources.

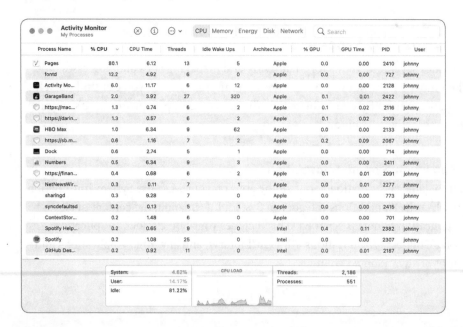

The main window of Activity Monitor presents a list of running processes and apps that belong to the current user. Below the process list you see macOS statistics. The default columns enable you to examine process statistics:

▶ Process Name—This is the name of the running process chosen by the developer who created it.

▶ % CPU—This number is the percentage of total processor (or CPU) capacity the process is consuming. The maximum percentage is 100 percent times the number of processor cores.

▶ CPU Time—This is the amount of time a process has been active since the last startup.

▶ Threads—This is the number of threads in the process. A process can be broken down into a number of thread operations. Multithreading helps increase a process's responsiveness by enabling it to perform multiple simultaneous tasks. Multithreading also increases performance, since each thread of a single process can run on a separate processor core.

▶ Idle Wake Ups—This is the number of times a process was woken up from a paused sleep state since the process was last started.

▶ Architecture—This is the type of architecture the process was compiled to support. The value for this column can be Apple or Intel. Activity Monitor displays Universal apps and apps for iPad and iPhone with "Apple" in the Architecture column.

▶ % GPU—Similar to % CPU, this number is the percentage of total GPU (graphic processing unit) capacity the process is consuming. The maximum percentage is 100 percent times the number of GPU cores.

▶ GPU Time—This is the amount of time a process has been active and using the GPU since the last startup.

▶ Process Identification (PID)—Each process has a unique identifier number. The numbers are assigned in sequence as processes are opened after macOS startup. The PIDs are recycled after 65,535 is reached.

▶ User—Each process is opened on behalf of a user. Each process has file-system access corresponding to the assigned user account.

An Intel-based Mac doesn't display the Architecture column.

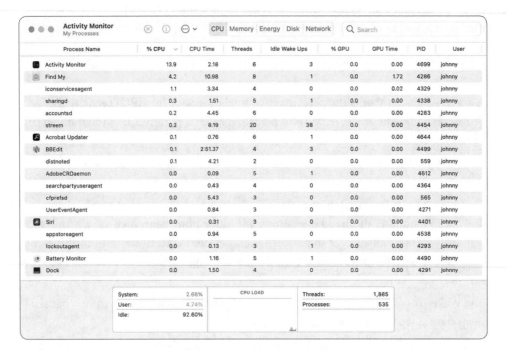

By default, Activity Monitor shows only processes running for the currently logged-in user. To increase your view of active processes, choose View > All Processes. You can also adjust the number of statistics shown in the columns and the update frequency from the View menu.

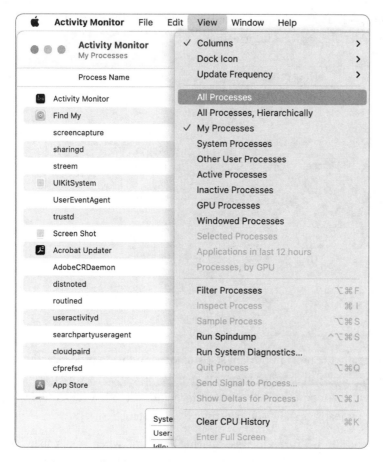

To narrow your view, use the Search field in the upper-right corner of the Activity Monitor window.

To sort the process list by column, click any column title. Click the column title again to toggle between ascending and descending sorts. By viewing all processes and then resorting the list by % CPU, you can determine whether a process is using excessive resources.

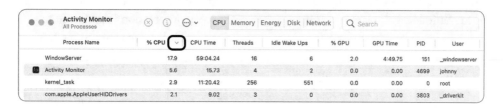

To further inspect a process, double-click its name in the Activity Monitor list. This reveals a window showing detailed process information.

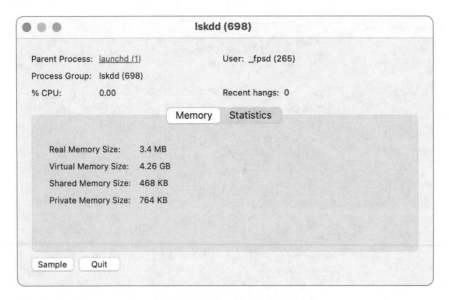

Although CPU use is generally the most important statistic for monitoring process activity, the Activity Monitor app can also monitor memory, energy, disk, and network use. Click through the buttons at the top of the Activity Monitor window to view the different categories. These monitoring features show you real-time macOS statistics.

As demonstrated in Reference 25.1, "Turn On Host-Sharing Services," when you enable Content Caching in the Sharing pane of System Preferences the Cache button appears at the top of the Activity Monitor window.

Hover your pointer over any statistic at the bottom of the Activity Monitor window to view a description of the statistic.

The Swap Used and Compressed statistics that appear when you click Memory provide a historical account, since the last macOS startup, of how much active process data was swapped out to local storage or compressed to save space. Compression is preferred to swapping because it's a higher-performance approach to making more room in memory.

MEMORY PRESSURE	Physical Memory:	16.00 GB		
	Memory Used:	8.84 GB	App Memory:	6.64 GB
	Cached Files:	7.14 GB	Wired Memory:	2.13 GB
			Compressed:	59.3 MB
	Swap Used:	0 bytes		

A low value for swap usage is acceptable, but a high value indicates that macOS doesn't have enough real memory to meet the user's app demands.

Use the Instruments app—installed as part of Xcode, a free integrated development environment (IDE) and developer tool found in the App Store—for a more detailed process view.

See the Instruments Help page at help.apple.com/instruments for more information about using Instruments.

See the Activity Monitor User Guide at support.apple.com/guide/activity-monitor for more information about using Activity Monitor.

Reference 20.4
Troubleshoot Apps

Each app provides unique features, and issues can manifest in unique ways, too. Fortunately, you can diagnose and fix these issues.

The actions you can take in the following list are in order from the least to the most invasive and time-consuming. These actions are also presented according to the likelihood of their success in resolving an issue, from most to least likely. Generally, when you troubleshoot apps, start with one of these actions:

▶ Restart the app—Often, if you restart an app you resolve the issue, or at least you get the app to respond.

▶ Open another known working document—If the known working document opens and works, you know that the problem document is corrupted and the cause of the issue. If you discover that the problem source is a corrupted document file, usually the best solution is to restore the document from an earlier backup, as covered in Lesson 17, "Manage Time Machine."

▶ Try another app—You can open many common document types with multiple Mac apps. Try opening the problem document in another app. If this works, save a new version of the document from the other app.

▶ Try another user account—Use this method to determine whether a user-specific resource file is the cause of the problem. If the app problem doesn't occur when you use another account, search for corrupted app caches, preferences, and resource files in the suspect user's Library folder. You can create a temporary account to test and then remove it, as covered in Lesson 7, "Manage User Accounts."

▶ Try disconnecting your Mac from the network temporarily if the app is waiting for a response from the internet—Use this method if an app can't continue until it receives information or a reply from an internet source.

▶ Check diagnostic reports and log files—This is the last information-gathering step before you replace items. Every time an app crashes, the macOS diagnostic reporting feature saves a diagnostic report of the crash. Use Console to inspect diagnostic reports.

▶ Replace preference files—Corrupted preference files are one of the most likely app resources to cause problems, because they change often and are required for apps to function.

▶ Replace app resources—Although corrupted app resources can cause problems, they are the least likely source of problems, since app resources are rarely changed.

▶ Delete cache files—To increase performance, many apps create cache folders in one or more of the following locations:

~/Library/Saved Application State

/Library/Caches/

~/Library/Caches/

~/Library/Containers/*bundleID*/Data/Library/Saved Application State/

~/Library/Containers/*bundleID*/Data/Library/Caches/

~/Library/Preferences/ByHost/

An app cache folder often matches the app's name. Although cache folders are not likely to be the app resource causing problems, you can delete them without affecting a user's information. After you delete an app's cache folder, the app creates a new one the next time you open it. To remove the various font caches, use safe boot, which clears font caches, as covered in Lesson 28, "Troubleshoot Startup and System Issues."

Force Quit Apps

It's easy to tell when an app becomes unresponsive—it stops reacting to your mouse clicks and the pointer often changes to a wait cursor (spinning pinwheel) and stays that way for a while.

Because the forward-most app controls the menu bar, it may seem as if the app locked you out of the Mac. If you move the wait cursor from the frozen app to another app or the desktop, usually the pointer returns to normal and you regain control of the Mac.

You can quit apps several ways:

▶ From the Force Quit Applications dialog—Choose Apple menu > Force Quit, or press Option-Command-Escape, to open the Force Quit Applications dialog. A frozen app appears with "(not responding)" next to its name. To force quit, select an app and click Force Quit.

▶ From the Dock—Use Control-click, or press and hold the app icon in the Dock, to display the app shortcut menu. If the Dock recognizes that the app is frozen, choose Force Quit from this menu. Otherwise, press and hold the Option key to change the Quit menu command to Force Quit.

▶ From Activity Monitor—Open Activity Monitor. If you're viewing the Cache pane, click one of the other buttons such as CPU in the toolbar. Then select the app you want to quit from the process list. Next, click the "X" (in the octagon icon at the far-left edge of the Activity Monitor toolbar), then click the Force Quit button. Activity Monitor is the only built-in app that lets administrator users quit or force quit other user processes or background system processes.

In Activity Monitor, webpages in Safari are shown as separate processes. That allows you to force quit individual pages in Safari.

Diagnostic Reports

The macOS diagnostic reporting feature displays a warning dialog that lets you know a problem occurred when an app quits unexpectedly (crashes) or stops functioning (hangs) and you have to force quit it.

In Security & Privacy preferences, in the Privacy pane, for Analytics & Improvements, the Share Mac Analytics option controls how macOS handles sharing diagnostic reporting with Apple for all users of the Mac. When you first set up your Mac, if you click Continue (instead of Customize Settings) in the Express Set Up screen of Setup Assistant, then the Share Mac Analytics and "Share with App Developers" options are turned on.

Diagnostic reporting creates log files that detail an app crash or hang.

If the Share Mac Analytics option is turned on, a warning dialog appears to inform you that the report will be sent to Apple automatically.

If you want, click the disclosure triangle next to Comments to open a text entry field. Type in a description of the circumstances that led to the problem that should be included in the report. Click Show Details to display more information about the problem.

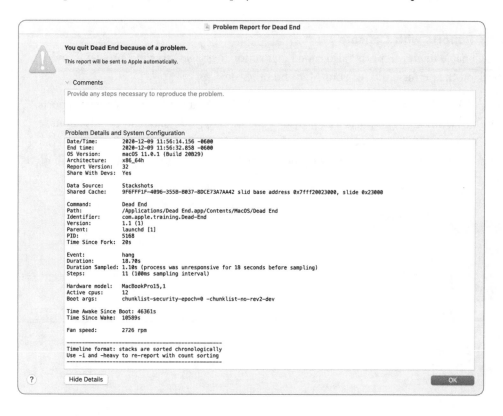

If the "Share Mac Analytics" option is turned off, a warning dialog appears to ask if you want to ignore the issue or share the report with Apple.

If you click Report, then the warning dialog illustrated previously appears to inform you that the report will be sent to Apple automatically. If you click Ignore, macOS doesn't send a report to Apple.

View Reports with Console

Use Console to view reports (also called logs or log messages) to solve problems and check on the performance of your Mac and other devices.

Your Mac and connected devices, like iPhone, iPad, and Apple Watch, generate reports. Console also compiles reports that provide general diagnostic data and details about macOS and apps. To preserve system performance, Console doesn't display streamed log messages until you click the link with the Play button and the phrase "Start streaming."

If you're not logged in as an administrator user, Console asks you to first provide administrator user credentials.

User reports are from apps used by the current user. System reports are from macOS components that affect all users. If you aren't logged in as an administrator user, you can view user reports, but you must provide an administrator name and password to view device and system reports. Some items in the Reports column contain additional multiple reports. Select an item in the Reports column to reveal its contents. To share a report with others, select the report and then click the Share button in the toolbar. If you hover the pointer over the report, Console displays the full path of the report. You can Control-click a report, then choose "Reveal in Finder" or "Move to Trash."

If you're logged in as an administrator user, you can view all reports. Here are report types you can view with Console:

▶ Devices—Reports about your Mac and about devices connected to your Mac. The Console sidebar has a separate section for device reports.

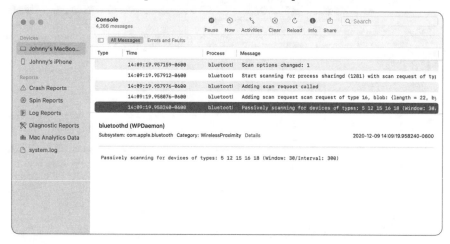

▶ Crash Reports and Spin Reports—More detailed diagnostic messages are created when processes crash or hang (become unresponsive). System reports are from macOS components that affect all users. These reports are saved to /Library/Logs/ DiagnosticReports. Crash report names have a *crash* filename extension. Spin report names have a *spin* filename extension.

▶ Log Reports—Reports with information about apps or processes that run. Log report names often have a filename extension of *its*, *log*, or *_log*.

▶ Diagnostic Reports—Reports about hardware resources or system response time. Diagnostic report names have a filename extension of *diag* or *dpsub*.

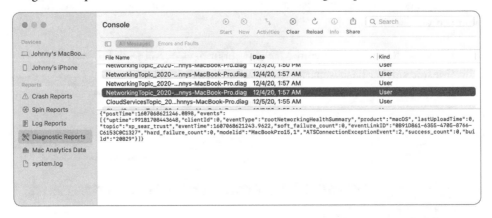

▶ Mac Analytics Data—Short diagnostic messages that show general use and problems are saved to /private/var/log/DiagnosticMessages. These processes can generate many diagnostic messages a day, and many of them are benign. The following two figures were made when an administrator account was logged in; most of the other figures in this lesson were made when a standard account was logged in.

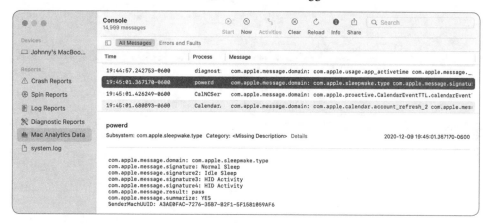

▶ system.log—Contains the contents of the legacy /private/var/log/system.log file. You can use Console to display this log only if you are logged in as an administrator. The following figure was made when an administrator account was logged in; most of the other figures in this lesson were made when a standard account was logged in.

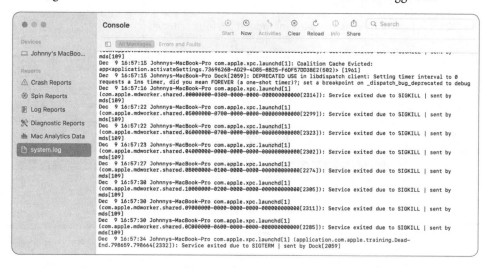

Diagnostic reports often indicate which files were being used by the app at the time. One of the reported files could be the source of the problem due to corruption.

View Activities

You can view log messages grouped by the activity they're associated with. Just click the Activities button in the toolbar. This helps you focus on specific log messages and allows for a more complete analysis.

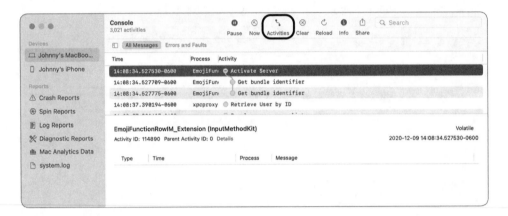

Search Logs and Activities

You can search for log messages and activities—for example, you can:

▶ Type a word or phrase to find log messages that match it.

▶ Show log messages from a certain process.

▶ Search for log messages that don't match certain criteria.

After you complete a search, you can save it to use again. Console displays buttons for your saved searches in the toolbar.

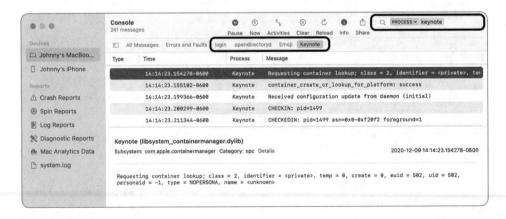

For more information about Console, including information about property shortcuts to use when searching, see the Console User Guide at support.apple.com/guide/console/.

Troubleshoot Preferences

Apps primarily access two types of often-changing files when they are in use: the documents for which the app handles viewing or editing, and the preference files that contain the app settings. From an administration perspective, preference files are often more important, because they might contain settings that are required for an app to work. For instance, an app serial number or registration information is often stored in a preference file.

You can find preferences in any Library folder, but most app preferences end up in the user's Library. App preferences are kept in user home folders because the local Library should be used only for systemwide preferences. This enables each user to have their own app settings that don't interfere with other users' settings. If you're troubleshooting a systemwide process, try to find its preferences in /Library.

Most app and systemwide preference files are saved as property list files. The naming scheme for a property list file usually positions the unique bundle identifier for the app first, followed by the file extension .plist. For example, the Finder preference file is com.apple.finder.plist. This naming scheme helps avoid confusion by identifying the software developer with the app.

Some apps are still not sandboxed, so they use the default preference folders for standard apps: ~/Library/Preferences or /Library/Preferences.

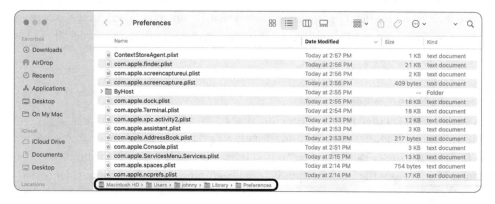

For sandboxed apps, the preference is located in the Containers or Group Containers folder. These folders are ~/Library/Containers/*bundleID*/Data/Library/Preferences and

~/Library/Group Containers/*bundleID*/Library/Preferences, where *bundleID* is the unique bundle identifier for the app.

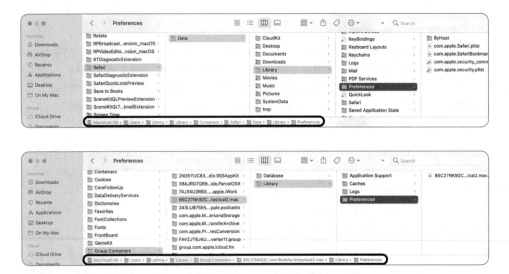

App preference files can contain both internal app configuration information and user-configured preferences. An app might frequently update information in its preference file, even if you haven't changed any preferences. It is the only file required by most apps that is regularly being rewritten, so it has the potential to become corrupted.

Many apps that use the Apple preference model, including third-party apps, recognize a corrupted preference file, ignore it, and create a new one. In contrast, some third-party apps use their own proprietary preference models that are not as resilient. In these cases, corrupted preferences typically result in an app that crashes frequently or that crashes during startup.

Resolve Corrupted Preferences

To isolate a corrupted preference, rename the suspect preference file. To do this, in the Finder add an identifier to the end of the suspect preference filename—something like .bad. To make the preference file easier to find later, put a tilde (~) at the beginning of the filename, which causes the Finder to put it at the beginning of the file listing when sorted alphabetically.

The preference architecture is maintained by a background process (cfprefsd). To improve performance, this process uses memory caching to store preference information. After you remove a potentially corrupted preference, restart this process to clear its cache. macOS restarts cfprefsd after you force it to quit. Be sure to force quit only the cfprefsd process owned by the appropriate user.

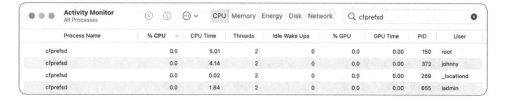

After you remove the preference file and restart the cfprefsd process, opening the app or process creates a new preference file based on the code's defaults. If this resolves the issue and doesn't remove irreplaceable settings, delete the old preference file. If it doesn't resolve the issue, move on to resource troubleshooting.

If you resolve the problem elsewhere, restore the previous settings with the following steps:

1   Delete the newer preference file.

2   Remove the temporary filename identifier you added to the original preference file.

3   Restart cfprefsd so that the app reloads its preference file.

The benefit of replacing the previous preference file is that you don't lose the settings or custom configuration saved in the file.

View and Edit Preference Files

While you are troubleshooting, verify settings by viewing the contents of the configuration property list file. The content of a property list file (ending in .plist) is formatted as plain-text Extensible Markup Language (XML) or binary code. Apps process binary-encoded files more efficiently than they process XML-encoded files. macOS automatically converts the format of property list files from XML to binary. You can inspect the binary files in one of two ways:

▶ In the Finder, select a property list file, then press the Space bar. This opens Quick Look so that you can preview the file contents.

```
⊗ ⊘ com.apple.Safari.plist                                                            ↥  Open with Xcode

<?xml version="1.0" encoding="UTF-8"?>
<!DOCTYPE plist PUBLIC "-//Apple//DTD PLIST 1.0//EN" "http://www.apple.com/DTDs/PropertyList-1.0.dtd">
<plist version="1.0">
<dict>
        <key>AutoplayPolicyWhitelistConfigurationUpdateDate</key>
        <date>2020-12-09T17:39:49Z</date>
        <key>AutoplayQuirksWhitelistConfigurationUpdateDate</key>
        <date>2020-12-09T17:39:49Z</date>
        <key>ClearBrowsingDataLastIntervalUsed</key>
        <string>today and yesterday</string>
        <key>DidAttemptToMigrateExtensionsPlistFromLegacyKeychain</key>
        <true/>
        <key>DidClearLegacySpotlightMetadataCaches</key>
        <true/>
        <key>DidMigrateNewBookmarkSheetToReadingListDefault</key>
        <true/>
        <key>DidMigrateResourcesToSandbox</key>
        <true/>
        <key>DidMigrateSecureDefaultsToUserDefaults</key>
        <true/>
        <key>DidMigrateStartPageDefaultSidebarVisibility</key>
        <true/>
        <key>DidMigrateToCoreSpotlightBasedHistorySearch</key>
        <true/>
        <key>DidMigrateToMoreRestrictiveFileURLPolicy</key>
        <true/>
        <key>DidMigrateWKViewContentPageGroupPreferences</key>
        <true/>
        <key>DidMigrateWebDriverAllowRemoteAutomation</key>
        <true/>
        <key>DidReportHistorySettings</key>
        <true/>
        <key>DidShowWhatsNewInSafari</key>
        <true/>
        <key>ExtensionsEnabled</key>
        <true/>
        <key>FaviconDatabaseDidEraseLegacyDatabase</key>
        <true/>
        <key>FrequentlyVisitedSitesCache</key>
        <array/>
        <key>HideStartPageFrecentsEmptyItemView</key>
        <true/>
        <key>HideStartPageSiriSuggestionsEmptyItemView</key>
        <true/>
        <key>HomePage</key>
        <string>https://www.apple.com/startpage/</string>
        <key>LastApplicationCacheMessageTraceTime</key>
        <real>628969381.03891802</real>
        <key>LastCloudHistoryConfigurationUpdateTime</key>
        <date>2020-12-09T17:38:47Z</date>
        <key>LastExtensionSelectedInPreferences</key>
        <string>5923738D-1BCE-4E69-A432-E594761AB821</string>
        <key>LastOSVersionSafariWasLaunchedOn</key>
        <string>11.0.1</string>
        <key>LastOpenedSubPaneInWebsitesPrefPane</key>
        <string>ReaderPreference</string>
        <key>LastSandboxFileExtensionMaintenanceDate</key>
        <date>2020-12-09T17:38:42Z</date>
        <key>LastSharedLinksMessageTraceTime</key>
        <real>628969677.09635496</real>
        <key>LocalFileRestrictionsEnabled</key>
        <true/>
```

▶ Use Terminal to run the command **plutil -convert xml1** *myfile.plist* (where *myfile.plist* is the name of the property list file you've selected) to convert the property list file from binary to XML, then use the less command to view its contents.

```
● ● ●        johnny — less ~/Library/Containers/com.apple.Safari/Data/Library/Preferences/com.apple.Safari.plist — 80×24
<?xml version="1.0" encoding="UTF-8"?>
<!DOCTYPE plist PUBLIC "-//Apple//DTD PLIST 1.0//EN" "http://www.apple.com/DTDs/
PropertyList-1.0.dtd">
<plist version="1.0">
<dict>
        <key>AutoplayPolicyWhitelistConfigurationUpdateDate</key>
        <date>2020-12-09T17:39:49Z</date>
        <key>AutoplayQuirksWhitelistConfigurationUpdateDate</key>
        <date>2020-12-09T17:39:49Z</date>
        <key>ClearBrowsingDataLastIntervalUsed</key>
        <string>today and yesterday</string>
        <key>DidAttemptToMigrateExtensionsPlistFromLegacyKeychain</key>
        <true/>
        <key>DidClearLegacySpotlightMetadataCaches</key>
        <true/>
        <key>DidMigrateNewBookmarkSheetToReadingListDefault</key>
        <true/>
        <key>DidMigrateResourcesToSandbox</key>
        <true/>
        <key>DidMigrateSecureDefaultsToUserDefaults</key>
        <true/>
        <key>DidMigrateStartPageDefaultSidebarVisibility</key>
        <true/>
ry/Containers/com.apple.Safari/Data/Library/Preferences/com.apple.Safari.plist
```

The XML format is relatively easy to analyze. It includes normal text interspersed with text tags that define the data structure for the information. You can view the XML code of plain text–formatted property list files using any text-reading app.

If you must edit a property list file, avoid using TextEdit, since it improperly formats any property list file that is saved as a binary. The most complete graphical app from Apple for editing property list files is Xcode. Xcode can decode binary property list files, and it enables you to view and edit any property list in an easy-to-read hierarchical format. You can get Xcode from the App Store.

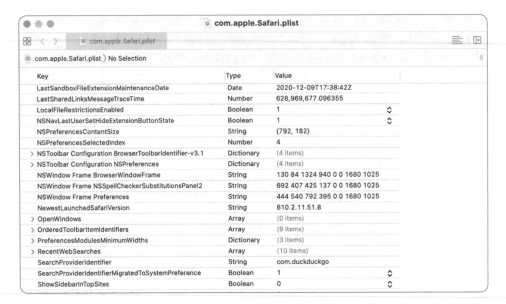

Avoid editing a property list file that is currently in use by a running app or process. The app or process might make a change to the file and save while you are editing it. If you must edit a property list that may be in use, first quit the app that uses the property list file, then stop the cfprefsd process.

Troubleshoot App Resources

Rarely, corrupted app software and associated nonpreference resources cause app problems, because these file types rarely change after the initial app installation. Many apps use other resources, such as fonts, plug-ins, and keychains, from the local and user Library folders and items in the Application Support folder. After you locate the problem resource, remove or replace the corrupted resource and restart the app.

Corrupted resources in the user's home folder Library affect only that user, whereas corrupted resources in the local Library affect all users. Use this fact to narrow your search when searching for a corrupted resource. App and diagnostic report logs, covered earlier in this lesson, may tell you which resources the app was attempting to access when it crashed. Those resources should be your primary suspects.

If the app exhibits problems with only one user, try to locate the resource at the root of the problem in the user's Library folder. Start with the usual suspects. If you find a resource that you think could be causing the problem, move that resource out of the user's Library folder and restart the app. Some apps store resources in ~/Documents.

If you've determined that the app issue is persistent across all user accounts, start by reinstalling or upgrading to the latest version of the app. You will probably find that a newer version of the app is available—one that likely includes bug fixes. At the very least, by reinstalling you replace any potentially corrupted files that are part of the standard app. If you continue to experience problems after reinstalling the app, search through the local Library resources to find and remove or replace the corrupted resource.

If you discover a large number of corrupted files, this may indicate a much more serious file-system or storage hardware issue. Troubleshooting these items is covered in Lesson 11, "Manage File Systems and Storage."

Exercise 20.1
Force Apps to Quit

> **Prerequisites**

> ► You must have created the Johnny Appleseed account (Exercise 7.1, "Create a Standard User Account").

> ► You must have installed the Dead End app (Exercise 18.3, "Drag and Drop to Install an App").

In this exercise, you learn to assess when an app is unresponsive. You see how you can use Force Quit and Activity Monitor to force unresponsive apps to quit. You also learn how to manage background processes that stop running.

Force an App to Quit in the Dock

1   Log in as Johnny Appleseed.

2   Open the Dead End app you installed in Exercise 18.3.

   The primary purpose of Dead End is to become unresponsive. It gives you an opportunity to practice different ways to force an app to quit.

   Dead End opens a window with a Download the Internet button.

3   Click Download the Internet.

Dead End becomes unresponsive. After a few seconds macOS may display the wait cursor (a colored pinwheel). The wait cursor appears when you hover your pointer over the Dead End window or, if Dead End is in the foreground, the menu bar.

4   Control-click the Dead End icon in the Dock, then choose Force Quit from the short-cut menu. Or you could click and hold the Dead End icon in the Dock and choose Force Quit from the shortcut menu.

Use the Force Quit Window

1   Open the Dead End app so that you can try another way to force an app to quit.

To open apps you used recently, click the Apple menu, then choose Recent Items. macOS keeps a list of the last 10 apps you opened.

2   Click Download the Internet.

3   Press Command-Option-Escape to open the Force Quit Applications window.

It takes about 15 seconds before Dead End is shown as "not responding."

4 Select Dead End, then click Force Quit.

5 In the confirmation dialog, click Force Quit.

6 If you are given the opportunity to send a report to Apple, click Ignore.

7 Close the Force Quit Applications window.

Practice Forcing an App to Quit with Activity Monitor

With Activity Monitor, you can force an app to quit, view running processes, gather information, then quit the processes.

1 Open Dead End.

2 Click Download the Internet.

3 Open Activity Monitor (from the Utilities folder).

Even though the wait cursor appears in Dead End, you can make the Finder active or use Launchpad. An unresponsive app normally won't affect the rest of macOS.

Activity Monitor displays a list of running processes. When you open this window, it shows processes that you recognize as apps. It also shows processes that run in the background and that don't have a graphical user interface.

4 If necessary, click the CPU tab above the process list.

5 If "% CPU" in the table header isn't selected, click it twice to get a top-down (most to least) list of processes in terms of their CPU usage. The arrow that appears next to "% CPU" should point down.

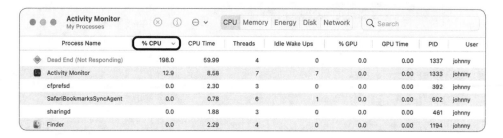

Process Name	% CPU	CPU Time	Threads	Idle Wake Ups	% GPU	GPU Time	PID	User
Dead End (Not Responding)	198.0	59.99	4	0	0.0	0.00	1337	johnny
Activity Monitor	12.9	8.58	7	7	0.0	0.00	1333	johnny
cfprefsd	0.0	2.30	3	0	0.0	0.00	392	johnny
SafariBookmarksSyncAgent	0.0	0.78	6	1	0.0	0.00	602	johnny
sharingd	0.0	1.88	3	0	0.0	0.00	461	johnny
Finder	0.0	2.29	4	0	0.0	0.00	1194	johnny

6   Look for the Dead End process by name. It should be at the top.

The name of an unresponsive app appears in red with a note saying the app is "Not Responding." As you look at the Dead End process, you see that the CPU usage is close to 200 percent. This demonstrates how an app can take over your CPU, even though the app isn't responding and seems to be doing nothing.

The % CPU statistic refers to the percentage of a CPU core being used. Current Mac computers have multiple cores and hyperthreading, so even "200%" CPU utilization isn't fully using the Mac computer's CPU power.

7   Choose Window > CPU Usage (or press Command-2).

This opens a window that displays how many processor cores your Mac has and how busy each one is.

This screenshot was taken on a Mac with two physical cores, but hyperthreading allows each of those cores to do two things at once, giving it four virtual cores. Therefore, 200 percent is only half of what it is capable of.

8   Select Dead End in the process list, then click the Quit Process button (its icon is an "X" in an octagon) on the toolbar.

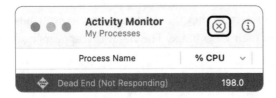

9   When asked to confirm, click Force Quit.

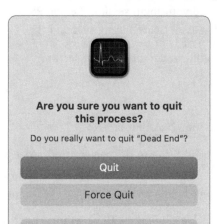

Quit is the default option in the dialog that appears. Because Dead End isn't respond-ing, it won't respond to a normal Quit command. You must use Force Quit to stop the process.

Dead End is not visible in the process list in the Activity Monitor window or in the Dock. After a few seconds, the CPU Usage window updates to show that utilization has decreased.

Unlike with the Dock and Force Quit Applications window, you can use Activity Monitor to force background processes to quit. Background processes are generally programs that start automatically. Normally, you won't have to manage them, but in a few cases forcing them to quit is useful.

10   Select Control Center in the process list. You can use the search field in the upper right of the window. The process ID (PID) number appears in a column to the right.

Control Center manages the menu bar items on the right side of the menu bar. If one of the menu bar items locks up, you may have to force Control Center to quit.

11   With Control Center selected, click the Stop button ("X"), then watch the right side of the menu bar as you click Force Quit.

The Time Machine menu bar item disappears and reappears. Examine your process list. Control Center is running but with a different process ID. The launchd process (a background process) detected that Control Center exited, then relaunched it. launchd starts, then monitors many background processes and restarts them if necessary.

You can't force quit all processes this way. For example, if you force WindowServer (a system process) to quit, you immediately end your login session. Lesson 28, "Troubleshoot Startup and System Issues," discusses launchd in more detail.

12 Clear the search field, then leave Activity Monitor open for the next section.

View System Processes and Use

1 From the Activity Monitor menu bar, choose View > All Processes.

You see processes appear in the process list. In addition to the background processes in your user session (sometimes called *agents*), macOS runs many background processes (sometimes called *daemons*) outside your login session.

2 At the top of the Activity Monitor window, click each of the CPU, Memory, Energy, Disk, and Network buttons in turn, then look at the information for each process and the statistics at the bottom of the window.

3 If you are continuing to Exercise 20.2, leave Activity Monitor open.

Exercise 20.2
Troubleshoot Preferences

> **Prerequisite**
>
> ▶ You must have created the Johnny Appleseed account (Exercise 7.1, "Create a Standard User Account").

Most app preferences are created and stored for users in their personal Library folder. This helps when you troubleshoot app issues. In this exercise, you learn how to set and restore a preference and then experience the effect of moving a preference file out of the ~/Library folder.

Create and Locate Preview Preferences

1 If necessary, log in as Johnny Appleseed.

2 Open Preview from the Applications folder.

3 If you are asked to open a file from iCloud, click Cancel.

4 Choose Preview > Preferences (or press Command-Comma) to open the Preview preferences window.

5 Select Images in the toolbar.

The default setting for "When opening files" is "Open groups of files in the same window."

6 Select "Open all files in one window."

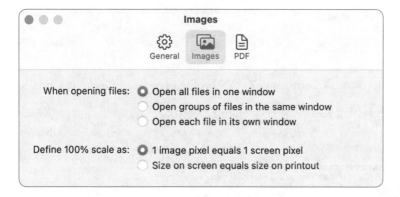

7 Close the Preferences window, then quit Preview.

8 Because the Finder normally hides the ~/Library folder, press and hold the Option key, then choose Go > Library to view the Library folder.

Preview is a sandboxed app, so its preference file isn't in the ~/Library/Preferences folder—it's in a sandbox container. See Reference 15.1, "macOS File Resources," for more details about sandbox containers.

9 In the ~/Library folder, open the Containers folder, then the Preview folder.

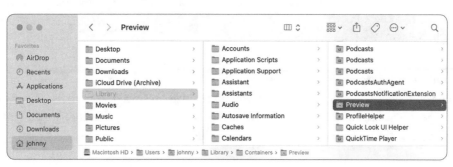

The Preview folder contains a Data subfolder, with a structure that mirrors your home folder. Most of its contents are aliases that point to what they represent.

10 Navigate to Data/Library/Preferences, then select the com.apple.Preview.plist file.

11 Use Quick Look (or press Command-Y) to view the preference file contents.

The preferences setting you made is listed in Extensible Markup Language (XML).

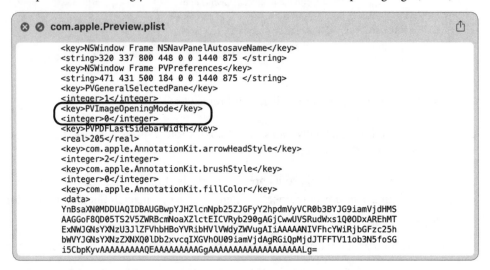

12 Close the Quick Look window.

Disable and Restore Preferences

When you move an app preferences file, you don't always reset its preferences. The preferences agent (`cfprefsd`) might cache old settings. To make sure the preferences reset, quit the program, quit the preferences agent, then move the file.

1   Open Activity Monitor.

2   From the Activity Monitor menu bar, choose View > My Processes.

3   If Preview is running, quit the app.

4   Sort the process list by process name or use the Search field to find cfprefsd.

    You see Johnny's cfprefsd processes running.

5   Select cfprefsd in the process list running as the user johnny, then click the Stop but-
    ton (the "X" in an octagon icon) in the toolbar.

6   In the confirmation dialog, click Quit.

    Because the process is responding normally, you don't have to use Force Quit.

    A new cfprefsd process starts when needed. This sometimes happens so quickly that
    you might not see it before it is no longer visible in the Activity Monitor list.

7   Switch to the Finder, then drag the com.apple.Preview.plist file to your desktop. Leave
    the Preferences folder open. A plist, or *property list*, file is an XML-based file that
    defines configuration settings, otherwise known as *preferences*, for an app.

8   Open Preview, then choose Preview > Preferences (or press Command-Comma).

9   Select Images from the toolbar.

    The setting for "When opening files" reset to its default of "Open groups of files in the
    same window."

10 Quit Preview.

11 Switch back to Activity Monitor, then quit cfprefsd.

12 In the Finder, move the com.apple.Preview.plist file from your desktop back to the
    Preferences folder.

13 When you are notified that a newer item named com.apple.Preview.plist already exists, click Replace.

14 Open Preview preferences.

This time your custom preference setting ("Open all files in one window") is restored.

15 Quit Preview.

Manage Corrupted Preferences

macOS has built-in features for handling corrupted preference files. In this exercise, you explore what happens when a preference file is corrupted.

1 Use Activity Monitor to quit cfprefsd.

2 In the Finder, Control-click the com.apple.Preview.plist file, then choose Open With > Other from the shortcut menu.

3 In the dialog, choose All Applications from the Enable menu, select TextEdit, then click Open.

Some plist files are stored in an XML or text format, which you can edit like other text documents. This plist file is stored in a binary format, so you see only part of the file contents.

4   Add some new text to the document.

5   Quit TextEdit.

Changes are saved automatically.

6   Try to view the file using Quick Look.

When you edit the file as if it were plain text, you damage its binary structure. As a result, Quick Look can't display its contents and shows a generic view.

7   Close the Quick Look window.

8   Reopen Preview, then open its preferences.

Because the preferences file is damaged, macOS reset it. The setting for "When opening files" reset to its default "Open groups of files in the same window."

9   Quit Preview, Activity Monitor, and other apps that are open.

10   Log out as Johnny Appleseed.

Exercise 20.3
Examine Logs

▶ **Prerequisites**

▸   You must have created the Local Administrator (Exercise 3.1, "Configure a Mac for Exercises") and Johnny Appleseed (Exercise 7.1, "Create a Standard User Account") accounts.

In this exercise, you use Console to view log files and then search them to determine whether your Mac is using the Content Caching service from another Mac on the network.

Generate Log Data

1   Log in as Local Administrator.

The log files you examine in this exercise are readable only by administrators.

2   Open Terminal.

3   Run the command **AssetCacheLocatorUtil**.

AssetCacheLocatorUtil discovers Mac computers running the content caching service. The command generates data, then prints it in the Terminal window (also called standard output, or stdout). Standard output sometimes refers to the standardized streams of data that are produced by command-line programs.

```
●  ●  ●                   ladmin — -zsh — 80×24
2020-10-14 18:11:37.950 AssetCacheLocatorUtil[1992:59807] Found 1 content cache
2020-10-14 18:11:37.950 AssetCacheLocatorUtil[1992:59807] Finding refreshed cont
ent caches supporting personal caching and import...
2020-10-14 18:11:37.952 AssetCacheLocatorUtil[1992:59807] Found 1 content cache
2020-10-14 18:11:37.952 AssetCacheLocatorUtil[1992:59807] Finding refreshed cont
ent caches supporting shared caching...
2020-10-14 18:11:37.953 AssetCacheLocatorUtil[1992:59807] Found 1 content cache
2020-10-14 18:11:37.953 AssetCacheLocatorUtil[1992:59807] 10.0.1.2:49396, rank 1
, not favored, healthy, guid 990051C7-B93B-4666-80DD-8FBE452F37C4, valid until 2
020-10-14 19:11:37; supports personal caching: yes, and import: yes, shared cach
ing: yes
2020-10-14 18:11:37.954 AssetCacheLocatorUtil[1992:59807] Determining refreshed
configured public IP address ranges...
2020-10-14 18:11:37.954 AssetCacheLocatorUtil[1992:59807] No public IP address r
anges are configured.
2020-10-14 18:11:37.954 AssetCacheLocatorUtil[1992:59807] Determining refreshed
favored server ranges...
2020-10-14 18:11:37.954 AssetCacheLocatorUtil[1992:59807] No favored server rang
es are configured.
2020-10-14 18:11:37.954 AssetCacheLocatorUtil[1992:59807] Testing all found cont
ent caches for reachability...
2020-10-14 18:11:37.964 AssetCacheLocatorUtil[1992:59807] This computer is able
to reach all of the above content caches.
ladmin@Mac-17 ~ %
```

If you are running this exercise on a network with a Mac running the Content Caching service, the results of the command should indicate that at least one content cache is available and being used by your Mac.

NOTE ► You may have to restart your Mac to discover a content cache if it was left on while you moved physical locations.

4   Leave Terminal open.

Use Console to View Logs

1   Open Console from the Utilities folder.

2   Select your Mac in the Devices section of the sidebar.

3   In the toolbar, click Start.

4   In the toolbar, make sure that Now is selected and Activities is unselected.

This view shows background events as they happen.

5   In Terminal, run **AssetCacheLocatorUtil** again.

6   Switch back to Console, and in the Search field, type **AssetCache**, then press the Return key.

You see the same messages that you saw in the Terminal window in an organized view. Details about the event are shown in the pane below the event list.

7   Select an event, then if necessary, select Info in the toolbar.

View some of the messages about the Content Caching service running on your network. You may see a message from AssetCacheLocatorUtil that identifies the content cache, its IP address and port, and what type of data is being cached.

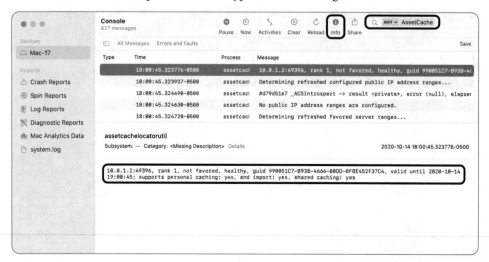

You might see a message from AssetCacheLocatorUtil that the Mac is able to reach all of the above content caches.

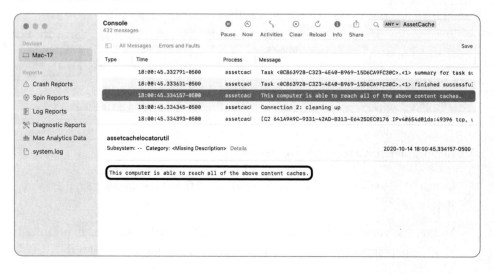

8   Quit Console, then log out as Local Administrator.

Network Configuration

Lesson 21

Manage Basic Network Settings

In this lesson, you learn about networking concepts and configure settings for Ethernet and Wi-Fi networks.

Reference 21.1
Network Terminology

There are three basic networking elements: the network interface, network protocols, and network service.

Data flows through the network interface. Network interfaces can be physical or virtual. The most common physical network interfaces are Ethernet and 802.11 wireless (called Wi-Fi). You can use virtual network interfaces to increase the functionality of the physical interface. For example, a virtual private network (VPN) uses the existing physical network interface to provide a secure connection without a dedicated physical interface.

A network protocol defines a set of standard rules used for data representation, signaling, authentication, or error detection across network interfaces. Protocols ensure that data is communicated properly. Specific protocols have a narrow focus, so often multiple protocols are combined or layered to provide a complete network solution. For example, the combined TCP/IP protocol suite provides addressing and end-to-end transport of data across the internet.

In Network preferences, "network service" describes a configuration assigned to a network interface. For example, you might see the Wi-Fi service listed. This represents the connection settings for the Wi-Fi network interface. macOS supports multiple network services, or connections, for each physical or virtual network interface.

> **NOTE ▶** A different definition of network service is used in Lesson 24, "Manage Network Services," and Lesson 25, "Manage Host Sharing and Personal Firewall." In those lessons, a network service is information provided on the network by a server for use by clients.

MAC Addresses

A media access control (MAC) address is used to identify a physical network interface on a local network. Each physical network interface has at least one MAC address associated with it.

Because the most common network interface is Ethernet, people often refer to MAC addresses as Ethernet addresses. Nearly every other network interface type also uses some type of MAC address for unique identification. This includes, but isn't limited to, Wi-Fi, Bluetooth, and Thunderbolt.

A MAC address is usually a 48-bit number represented by six groups of two-digit hexadecimal numbers separated by colons. For example, a typical MAC address looks like this: 00:1C:B3:D7:2F:99. The first three number groups make up the organizationally unique identifier (OUI), and the last three number groups identify the network device. You can use the first three number groups of a MAC address to identify who made the network device.

IP Addresses

An Internet Protocol (IP) address identifies each computer across the internet or a network. You need an IP address to communicate with Mac computers on local and remote networks. IP addresses, unlike MAC addresses, aren't permanently tied to a network interface. They are assigned to the network interface based on the local network they're connected to. This means that if you have a portable Mac, every new network you connect to probably requires a new IP address. You can assign multiple IP addresses to each network interface, but this approach is often only used for Mac computers that are providing network services.

IPv4 and IPv6 are the two standards for IP addresses. IPv4 is the most commonly used today. An IPv4 address is a 32-bit number represented by four groups of three-digit numbers, also known as octets, separated by periods. Each octet has a value between 0 and 255. For example, a typical IPv4 address would look something like this: 10.1.45.186. If you received an IP address that's a longer series of numbers and letters, divided by seven colons (for example, fa80:0000:0000:0123:0203:93ee:ef5b:44a0), then it's a different type of IP address, called IPv6.

Subnet Masks

A Mac uses the subnet mask to determine the IPv4 address range of the local network. Networks based on the IPv6 protocol don't require subnet masks. A subnet mask is similar to an IPv4 address in that it's a 32-bit number arranged in four groups of octets. The Mac applies the subnet mask to its own IP address to determine the local network address range. The nonzero bits in a subnet mask (typically 255) correspond to the portion of the IP address that determines which network the address is on. The zero bits correspond to the portion of the IP address that differs between hosts on the same network.

For example, assuming your Mac has an IP address of 10.1.5.3 and a commonly used subnet mask of 255.255.255.0, the local network is defined as hosts that have IP addresses ranging from 10.1.5.1 to 10.1.5.254.

Another way of writing the subnet mask is known as Classless Inter-Domain Routing (CIDR) notation. This is written as the IP address, a slash, and then the number of bits in the subnet mask. The previous subnet example would be 10.1.5.3/24.

Whenever a Mac attempts to communicate with another network device, it applies the subnet mask to the destination IP address of the other device to determine whether it's on the local network too. If so, the Mac attempts to directly access the other network device. If not, the other device is clearly on another network, and the Mac sends all communications bound for that other device to the router address.

Router Addresses

Routers manage connections between separate networks. They route network traffic between the networks they bridge. To reach a networked device beyond the local network, your Mac must be configured with the IP address of the router that connects the local network with another network or an internet service provider. Typically, a router address is at the beginning of the local address range, and it's always in the same subnet.

TCP

The Transmission Control Protocol (TCP) facilitates end-to-end data connectivity between two IP devices. TCP is the preferred transport mechanism for many internet services because it guarantees reliable and in-order data delivery.

Reference 21.2
Network Activity

You assign an IP address, a subnet mask, and a router address to configure a Mac to use TCP/IP-based networking on both local area networks (LANs) and wide area networks (WANs). Two network services are almost always involved in basic network functionality: Dynamic Host Configuration Protocol (DHCP) and the Domain Name System (DNS). These two services, combined with TCP/IP, characterize core network functionality that provides the foundation for nearly any network service.

LAN Traffic

Most LANs use some form of wired or wireless connection. After the network interface is established, you must configure TCP/IP networking, either manually or with DHCP. Then network communication can begin.

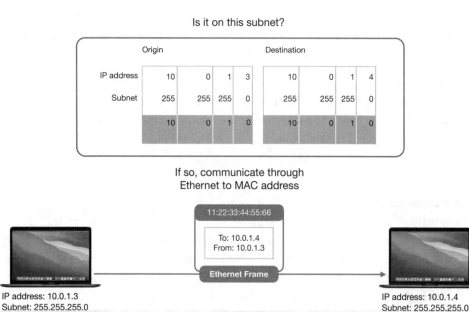

TCP/IP packets are encased inside Ethernet frames to travel across the local network. The TCP/IP packet includes the originating IP and destination IP addresses along with the data to be sent. The network device applies the subnet mask setting to determine whether the destination IP address is on the local network. If so, it consults its Address Resolution Protocol (ARP) table to see whether it knows the MAC address corresponding to the destination IP address. Each network host maintains and continuously updates an ARP table of known MAC addresses that correspond to IP addresses on the local network. If the MAC address is not listed yet, it broadcasts an ARP request to the local network asking the destination device to reply with its MAC address and adds the reply to its ARP table for next time. After the MAC address is determined, an outgoing Ethernet frame, encasing the TCP/IP packet, is sent using the destination MAC address.

WAN Traffic

When you send data over a WAN, it's sent through one or more network routers to reach the destination. You can use a router with network address translation (NAT). This enables you to use one real-world IP address as the external interface for your router, and internally you can use private IP addresses. Private IP address ranges are 10.0.0.0–10.255.255.255, 172.16.0.0–172.31.255.255, and 192.168.0.0–192.168.255.255.

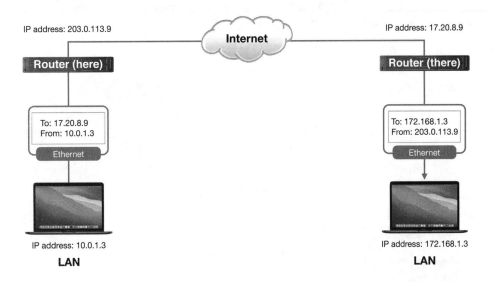

Transferring data across a WAN is similar to transferring data on a LAN. The first stop for the data destined for the WAN is at the network router on the local network. The network device prepares the packets as before by encasing the TCP/IP packets inside Ethernet frames. The subnet mask is applied to the destination IP address to determine whether the address is on the local network. In this case, the network device determines that the destination isn't on the local network, so it sends the data to the router. Because the router is on the local network, the transmission between the local network client and the router is identical to standard LAN traffic.

After the router receives the Ethernet-encased TCP/IP packets, it examines the destination IP address and uses a routing table to determine the next closest destination for this packet. This almost always involves sending the packet to another router closer to the destination. In fact, only the last router in the path sends the data to the destination network device.

In most cases, network data is transferred back and forth several times to establish a complete connection. Network routers handle thousands of data packets every second.

DNS

Even the simplest mobile phones feature a contact list so that users don't have to remember phone numbers. For TCP/IP networks, the Domain Name System (DNS) makes network addressing easier by enabling you to use a name instead of an IP address.

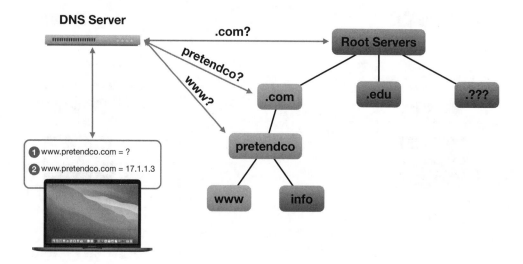

DNS is a worldwide network of domain servers that maintain human-friendly hostnames that are used to locate network IP addresses. Devices providing shared services, such as printers and server computers, are the most common devices to have DNS entries.

The top of the DNS naming hierarchy is the root, or " . " domain. The names that are part of the root domain are the familiar abbreviations at the end of nearly every internet resource.

When a local network device needs to resolve a DNS name into the corresponding IP address, it sends the name query to the IP address of a DNS server. The IP address for a DNS server is usually configured along with the other TCP/IP address information for the network device. The DNS server searches its local and cached name records first. If the requested name isn't found locally, the server queries other domain servers in the DNS hierarchy.

Bonjour is a name discovery service that uses a namespace similar to DNS. Bonjour is covered in Lesson 24.

DHCP

The Dynamic Host Configuration Protocol (DHCP) is used by most network clients to automatically acquire preliminary TCP/IP configuration. DHCP assigns IPv4 addressing.

A series of steps in the DHCP process ensures that two DHCP clients don't use the same DHCP configuration information. You can remember the following chain of events with the acronym DORA: Discover, Offer, Request, Acknowledgment:

▶ Discover—Your Mac broadcasts a DHCP DISCOVER message on the local subnet to look for DHCP servers.

▶ Offer—A DHCP server responds with an offer of configuration.

▶ Request—Your Mac requests the DHCP configuration information from the DHCP server.

▶ Acknowledgment—The DHCP server acknowledges that your Mac can use the DHCP configuration information.

The DHCP configuration information usually includes an IPv4 address, a subnet mask, a router, which DNS servers to use, and a DHCP lease time that defines how long the client can retain the address before it's given away.

If there's no DHCP reply, your Mac generates a random self-assigned address and checks the local network to make sure that no other network device is using that address. A self-assigned address always starts with 169.254, with a subnet mask of 255.255.0.0.

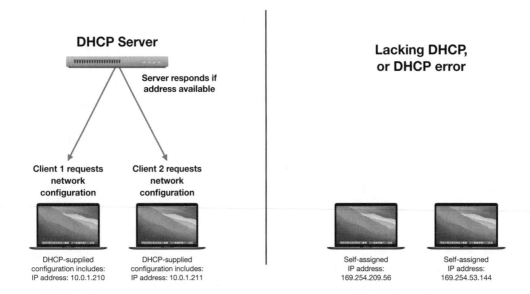

Reference 21.3
Configure Basic Network Settings

Use Network preferences to configure basic network settings. You must have an administrator user account to do so.

Configure Network Settings

You can configure your network address and settings in two ways:

▶ Automatically—Your Mac is assigned an address using DHCP.

▶ Manually—Your ISP or network administrator gives you an IP address, and you enter it in Network preferences.

Advanced network configuration techniques are covered in Lesson 22, "Manage Advanced Network Settings."

DHCP

If your Mac obtains valid network configuration from a DHCP server, any configured network interface is displayed with a green status indicator. Select the network interface to see the IPv4 address in the right side of the window.

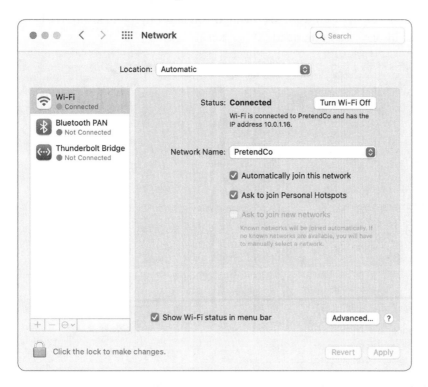

The following figure illustrates a scenario where the DHCP service isn't available. The network interface has a yellow status indicator, and the right side of the window displays a self-assigned IP address and the message that this Mac won't be able to connect to the internet.

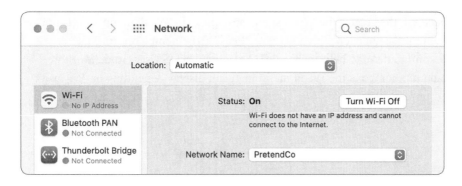

Select and Authenticate to Wi-Fi Networks

Wireless networking, or Wi-Fi, is also known by the technical specification 802.11. It allows easy network access for portable devices.

To join a Wi-Fi network, you can click the Wi-Fi status icon near the upper-right corner of the display and choose a network from the menu. If you haven't yet joined any Wi-Fi networks, your Mac displays a section titled "Other Networks."

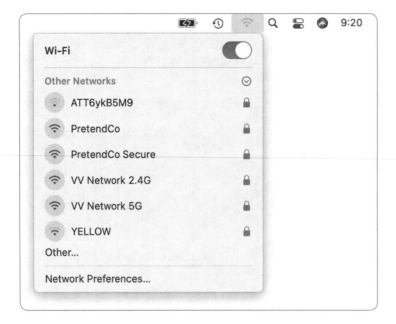

A service set identifier (SSID) identifies a Wi-Fi network name and associated configuration information. A Wi-Fi administrator sets the network name and configuration settings. macOS uses the information in the SSID configuration to establish Wi-Fi network communications.

The Wi-Fi menu icon itself displays the relative strength of a Wi-Fi network. The more black bars displayed, the greater the Wi-Fi signal strength. The Wi-Fi menu item is gray if Wi-Fi is on, but not associated with a network. See "Wi-Fi menu icons on Mac" at support.apple.com/guide/mac-help/mchlcedc581e in the macOS User Guide for more information about other icons the Wi-Fi menu item can display depending on Wi-Fi status and connection.

If you select an open wireless network, the Mac immediately connects to it, but if you select a secure wireless network, indicated by the lock icon, you have to enter the network password. When you select a secure network, macOS automatically negotiates the authentication type, and for many networks you need only enter a common shared Wi-Fi password.

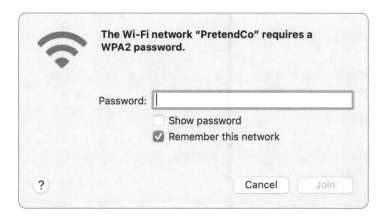

If you're signed in with your iCloud account, the dialog is slightly different. It shows that you can also access this Wi-Fi network by bringing your Mac near any iPhone, iPad, iPod touch, or Mac that is connected to this network and has you in its contacts. For information on how to configure a Mac to not share the password for a Wi-Fi network, see Reference 22.5, "Configure Advanced Network Settings."

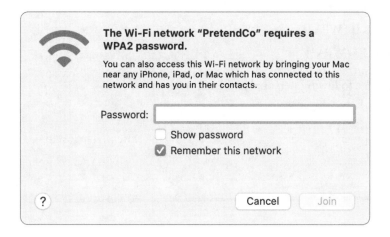

Here's an example of what your contact sees on an iPhone:

macOS supports the most common and modern Wi-Fi authentication standards, including the following:

► Wired Equivalent Privacy (WEP)

► Wi-Fi Protected Access (WPA)

► Wi-Fi Protected Access II (WPA2)

► Wi-Fi Protected Access 3 (WPA3)

This includes support for the following personal and enterprise forms:

► WPA/WPA2 Personal

► WPA2/WPA3 Personal

► WPA3 Personal

► Dynamic WEP

► WPA/WPA2 Enterprise

► WPA2 Enterprise

► WPA3 Enterprise

Essentially, WPA/WPA2 Personal and WPA2/WPA3 Personal use a common shared password for all users of the Wi-Fi network, whereas WPA/WPA2 Enterprise, WPA2 Enterprise, and WPA3 Enterprise include 802.1X authentication, which can allow for per-user password access to the Wi-Fi network. Dynamic WEP is outside the scope of this guide. WPA/WPA2 Enterprise, WPA2 Enterprise, and WPA3 Enterprise authentication are covered in the next section of this lesson.

If you join a WEP, WPA/WPA2 Personal, WPA2/WPA3 Personal, or WPA3 Personal Wi-Fi network, macOS automatically saves the passwords to the System keychain, which allows the Mac to automatically reconnect to the Wi-Fi network immediately after startup or waking up. The fact that the network password is saved to the System keychain enables all users to access the wireless network when they log in, without having to reenter the network password. Details of the Keychain system are covered in Lesson 9, "Manage Security and Privacy."

By default, macOS remembers Wi-Fi networks it previously joined. If you start up or wake your Mac, it attempts to locate and reconnect to any previously connected Wi-Fi networks. When you click the Wi-Fi status menu, macOS displays the Wi-Fi network you're currently using, marked by a blue Wi-Fi symbol next to it, as well as any Wi-Fi network in broadcast range that:

► This Mac has previously joined

► You have a valid keychain item for (unless the network doesn't require authentication)

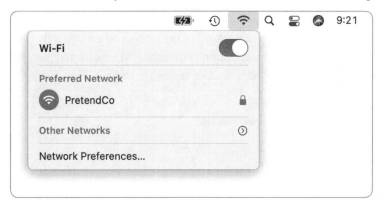

When you click the arrow next to Other Networks in the menu, macOS scans for advertised networks that are within range and displays them so that you can choose one.

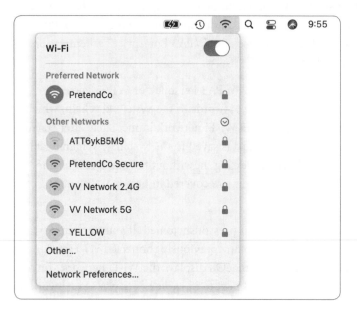

Authenticate to WPA Enterprise Networks

If you join and authenticate to a wireless network that uses WPA/WPA2 Enterprise, WPA2 Enterprise, or WPA3 Enterprise, authentication is handled with 802.1X.

When you use 802.1X, you must provide some kind of credentials to authenticate the connection. User name and password is a common credential, but some implementations allow you to provide a digital certificate for a user or computer instead.

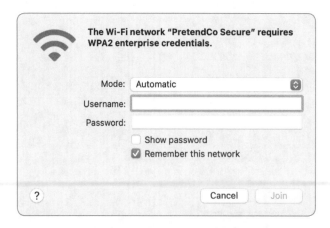

After you provide a user name and password, you may also be prompted with a server certificate verification dialog (if your Mac is not configured to trust the certificate).

Click Show Certificate to display information about the certificate.

You must click Continue and accept this certificate to continue and join the network.

You must also provide your password because doing so will add the wireless authentication server certificate to your login keychain.

After you join this type of network, Network preferences displays an 802.1X section for the network interface.

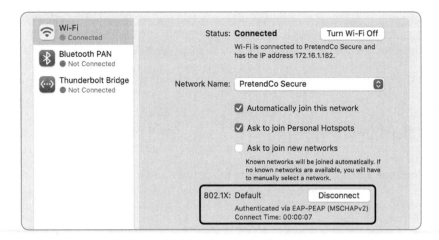

Reference 22.5 has more information about configuring 802.1X settings.

Join Hidden Wi-Fi Networks

In some cases, wireless networks may not advertise their availability. You can connect to these hidden wireless networks (also called closed networks) as long as you know their network name (or SSID) by clicking the Wi-Fi status menu, clicking the arrow next to Other Networks, and choosing Other at the bottom of the menu. In the dialog, you can enter all the appropriate information to join the hidden wireless network. For more information, see Apple Support article HT202068, "Recommended settings for Wi-Fi routers and access points."

Exercise 21.1
Connect to a Wi-Fi Network

▶ **Prerequisites**

▶ You must have created the Local Administrator (Exercise 3.1, "Configure a Mac for Exercises") and Johnny Appleseed (Exercise 7.1, "Create a Standard User Account") accounts.

▶ You must have access to an available Wi-Fi (wireless) network that you aren't already connected to. Wi-Fi and wireless are terms that are used interchangeably.

NOTE ▶ Even if you don't meet these prerequisites, reading the exercises will enhance your knowledge of the processes.

macOS makes joining a wireless network simple. In this exercise, you find and join a wireless network.

If your Mac has a mobile device management (MDM) configuration profile installed that configures a wireless network connection, the connection may happen automatically.

Verify Your Network Settings

1   Log in as Johnny Appleseed.

2   Open Network preferences.

3   Click the padlock, then authenticate as Local Administrator.

4   Select the Wi-Fi service from the sidebar.

If you don't have Wi-Fi service, you can't perform this exercise. However, reading this exercise will enhance your knowledge of the processes.

5   If necessary, click the Turn Wi-Fi On button.

6   If necessary, select "Show Wi-Fi status in menu bar."

7   Click Advanced.

8   Examine the options available in the Wi-Fi pane.

9   If you are currently connected to a Wi-Fi network, select it, then click the Remove (–) button to remove it from your Preferred Networks list.

Use the Preferred Networks list to control which networks a Mac joins automatically or manually. It includes an option to add networks to the list as your Mac joins them. You can also control whether administrator authorization is required to change certain configuration settings.

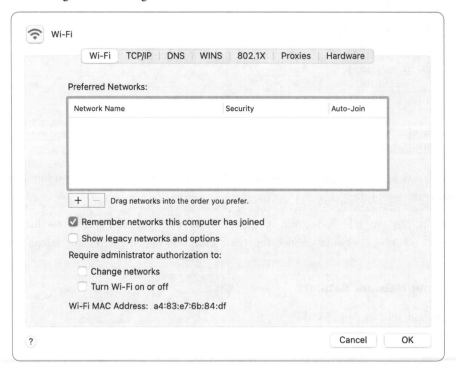

10 Click OK.

11 If you made changes, click Apply.

If you removed the Wi-Fi network you were connected to, your Mac disconnects.

12 Click the Wi-Fi status icon in the menu bar.

The menu lists visible networks in your area. Click the disclosure triangle next to Other Networks if necessary.

It may take a few seconds for your Mac to discover all local networks.

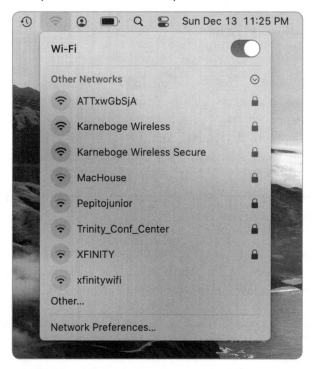

This list is also available in Network preferences, in the Network Name menu.

13 Choose the network you want to join from the Wi-Fi status menu. If you are in a classroom environment, your trainer will give you the name of the network to join.

If the wireless network is encrypted, you are asked for the network password. Selecting the "Remember this network" option allows your Mac to automatically reconnect to this network whenever it's available.

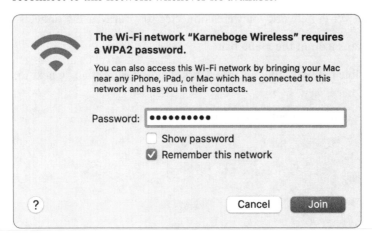

14 If necessary, enter the network password, then click Join.

Verify Your Connection

If macOS detects that the wireless network you joined is connected to a captive portal, it opens a window showing the portal sign-in page.

1 If a captive portal window appears, follow its instructions to get full network access. A captive portal may require you to agree to its terms of service, authenticate, watch an advertisement, or meet other requirements before it allows you full network access.

2 If you are not connected the Wi-Fi network you were connected to at the start of this lesson, reconnect to it.

3 In Network preferences, look at the status indicator immediately under the Wi-Fi service.

The status indicator is green if your Mac is connected to a network and has address information configured. If the indicator isn't green, you didn't successfully join the network and you might have to troubleshoot the connection.

4 Click the Wi-Fi status menu.

It shows bars to indicate the signal strength of the wireless network. If all the bars are dimmed, you aren't joined to a wireless network or are receiving a weak signal.

5 Option-click the Wi-Fi status menu.

The menu opens, then displays additional information about your connection, including the current wireless speed (Tx rate) and received signal strength indicator (RSSI: –50 is a strong signal and –100 is a weak one).

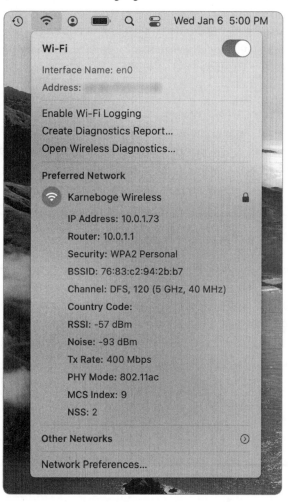

Exercise 21.2
Monitor Network Connectivity

▶ **Prerequisite**

▶ You must have created the Johnny Appleseed account (Exercise 7.1, "Create a Standard User Account").

In this exercise, you break your primary network connection and observe how Network preferences tracks the break. Network Status updates as network connectivity changes, so you can use it to troubleshoot connectivity issues.

Monitor Connectivity Using Network Preferences

In Network preferences, the Status field displays the status of configured network interfaces. User-initiated connections, such as virtual private networks (VPNs), are also listed. View the Network Status pane to verify active connections in order of priority.

1 If necessary, log in as Johnny Appleseed.

2 If necessary, open System Preferences, then click Network.

The status of your network connections is shown on the left side of the window. The green status indicators show which network services are active, and their order shows their priority. The service at the top of the list is your current primary service, and it's used for all internet connectivity. Record which service is currently the primary service.

If you don't have services with green status indicators, you don't have a network connection and you can't perform this exercise. However, reading this exercise will enhance your knowledge of the processes.

3 Select the current primary service.

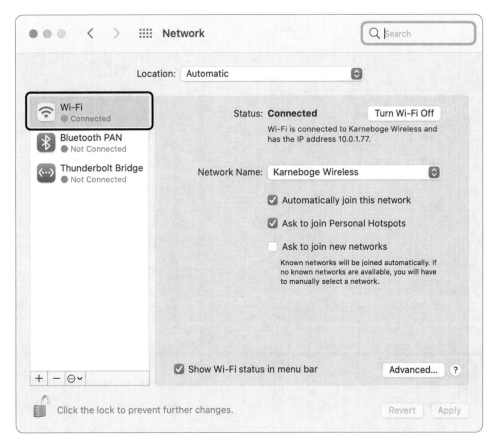

4 Watch the status indicators and service order as you turn off the connection for your primary network service. How you do this depends on what type of service it is:

▶ If it is an Ethernet service, unplug the Ethernet cable from your Mac.

▶ If it is a Wi-Fi service, click the Turn Wi-Fi Off button.

When the service is turned off, its status indicator turns red or yellow, and it drops down in the service order. If you have another active service, it becomes the new primary service.

The detailed view on the right changes to indicate the service is turned off.

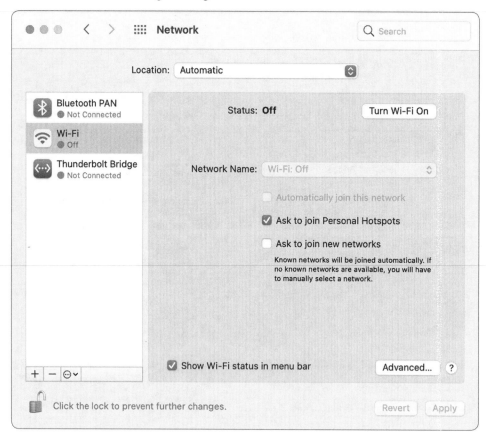

5   Watch the status indicators and service order as you turn the connection back on. How you do this also depends on what type of service it is:

▶   If it is an Ethernet service, plug the Ethernet cable back into your Mac.

▶   If it is a Wi-Fi service, click the Turn Wi-Fi On button and, if necessary, choose the network from the Network Name menu.

It may take a few seconds for the network connection to appear and the service to reconfigure itself. When the service becomes fully active, its status indicator turns green and the service rises to the top of the service list.

6   Quit System Preferences.

Lesson 22

Manage Advanced Network Settings

In this lesson, you learn about the macOS network configuration architecture and supported network interfaces and protocols. Then you explore advanced network configuration options.

Reference 22.1
Manage Network Locations

When you must manually configure your network settings, you can save network settings to network locations, then change between the locations. A network location contains network interface, service, and protocol settings, so you can configure unique network locations for different situations. For example, you can create one network location for home and a different one for work. Each location will contain the appropriate settings for that location's network state.

A network location can contain numerous active network service interfaces, which means you can define a single location with multiple network connections. macOS prioritizes multiple service interfaces based on a service order that you set ("TB Bridge" stands for "Thunderbolt Bridge," discussed later in this lesson).

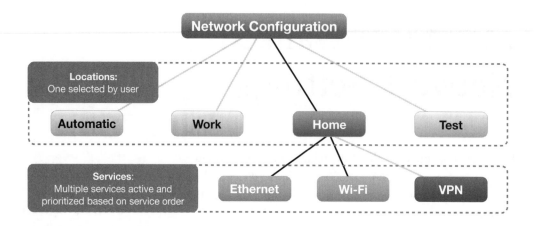

Configure Network Locations

The default network location in macOS is called Automatic.

To configure network locations:

1   Open System Preferences with Spotlight or by choosing Apple menu > System Preferences.

2   Click the Network icon.

3   If necessary, click the lock icon in the lower-left corner and authenticate as an administrator user to unlock Network preferences.

4   Choose Edit Locations from the Location menu to reveal the interface for editing network locations.

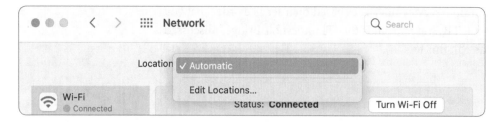

To add a new location with default settings, click the Add (+) button, then enter a new name for the location. Or you can duplicate an existing location by choosing its name from the Locations list, clicking the Action pop-up menu ☺, and choosing Duplicate Location from the menu. Double-click a location name to rename it.

After you make the location changes, click Done to return to Network preferences.

Network settings are different from other preferences in that when you modify settings, you must click Apply to activate the new settings. You can then prepare new network locations and services without disrupting the current network configuration.

Network preferences loads the newly created location but won't apply the location settings to macOS. To edit another location, choose it from the Location menu, and Network preferences loads it but won't apply it to macOS.

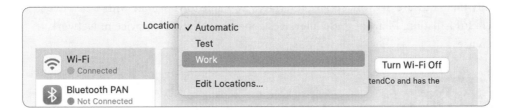

Select a Network Location

All users can change the network location by choosing Apple menu > Location > *location name*. This applies the selected network location. Changing locations might interrupt network connections. After you select a network location, it remains active until you select another location. Even if other users log in to the Mac or the Mac is restarted, the selected network location remains active. The Location menu option doesn't appear in the Apple menu until you create an additional network location.

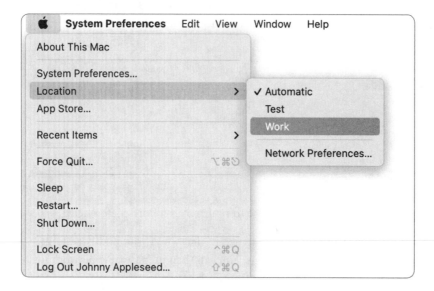

Reference 22.2
Network Interfaces and Protocols

Identify the hardware network service interfaces available to your Mac with System Information. Many of these interfaces appear as a network service in Network preferences.

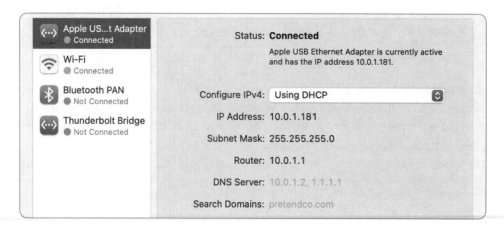

The newest hardware interface on Mac computers is Thunderbolt 4, a high-speed connection technology. Thunderbolt is flexible, allowing for a variety of adapters, such as the Thunderbolt-to-Gigabit Ethernet adapter.

> **NOTE ▶** You can learn more about Thunderbolt 4 and USB-4, which use the same port shape and style, in Reference 26.1, "Peripheral Technologies."

macOS includes built-in support for the following hardware network interfaces:

- ▶ Bluetooth—This relatively low-speed wireless interface is a short-range connectivity standard. Every Mac that includes Wi-Fi support also includes Bluetooth. macOS supports Bluetooth as a network bridge to some mobile phones and hotspots, like iPhone, that can provide internet connectivity through a cellular network.

- ▶ Ethernet—Ethernet is the family of IEEE 802.3 standards that define most modern wired local area networks (LANs).

- ▶ Thunderbolt Bridge—You can create small ad hoc networks using daisy-chained Thunderbolt cables.

- ▶ USB—Although USB is not technically a network connectivity standard, macOS supports a variety of USB adapters for Ethernet and adapters that provide internet access through cellular networks. Many modern phones feature a "tethering" service that provides internet access through a USB connection to the phone.

- ▶ Wi-Fi—Wi-Fi is the more common name for the family of IEEE 802.11 wireless standards, which have become the default implementation for most wireless LANs. Every currently shipping Mac supports Wi-Fi.

Cellular Internet Connections

Many devices and methods are available for providing cellular internet access. macOS supports use of cellular internet connections with:

- ▶ Bluetooth personal area network (PAN)—Many current cellular devices allow for internet connectivity by acting as a small router providing a PAN available through Bluetooth wireless. For example, an iPhone can provide internet access through Bluetooth PAN. As with any Bluetooth device, you must first pair your Mac with the mobile device, as covered in Lesson 26, "Troubleshoot Peripherals." After the two are paired, configuration should be automatic—the Mac should configure networking using DHCP hosted from the cellular device. You have to initiate the connection by clicking the Connect button in Network preferences or by choosing the device and clicking "Connect to Network" in the Bluetooth status menu.

▶ USB cellular network adapters—macOS supports many USB adapters and tethered phones that provide cellular internet access. iPhone is an example, and configuration on the Mac is automatic. If tethering is available on your mobile phone data plan, first connect your iPhone to your Mac with a USB cable; then on your iPhone turn on the Personal Hotspot feature. Third-party cellular internet devices vary, and many require the installation and configuration of third-party drivers.

▶ Wi-Fi PAN—Many cellular devices can act as a small Wi-Fi access point. On any iOS or iPadOS device that supports cellular connections, you can enable Personal Hotspot for Wi-Fi. Select the Wi-Fi network the iOS device is hosting and provide authentication, if necessary. You can take advantage of Handoff to automatically authenticate to an iOS device's personal hotspot service. This automatic authentication requires that Handoff be turned on and that you be signed in to iCloud on both devices. See Apple Support article HT209459, "Use Instant Hotspot to connect to your Personal Hotspot without entering a password," for more information.

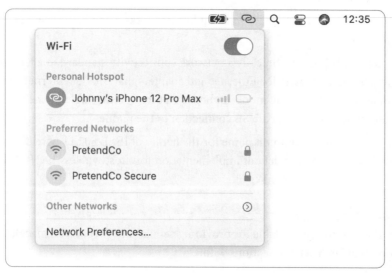

Virtual Network Services

A virtual network service is a logical network within a hardware network interface. A virtual network service provides another network interface by carving out a section of an established network connection.

Some virtual network services are used to increase security by encrypting data before it travels across an IP network, and others are used to segregate or aggregate network traffic across LAN connections. macOS includes client software that lets you connect to many common virtual network services and establish a virtual network service interface.

If necessary, you can define multiple separate virtual network service interfaces for each network location. Virtual network service interfaces are not always tied to a specific physical network interface; macOS attempts to seek out the most appropriate route when multiple active connections are available. Likewise, any virtual network service interface that is not destined for a LAN connection is always routed to the primary active network service interface.

Third-party virtualization tools, like Parallels Desktop and VMware Fusion, also use virtual network interfaces to provide networking for multiple simultaneous operating systems.

macOS includes built-in support for the following virtual network services:

▶ Point-to-Point Protocol over Ethernet (PPPoE)—This protocol is used by some service providers to directly connect your Mac to a modem providing a high-speed digital subscriber line (DSL) internet connection.

▶ Virtual private network (VPN)—VPNs are primarily used to create secure virtual connections to private LANs over the internet. Configuring VPN connections is detailed later in this lesson.

▶ Virtual local area network (VLAN)—The macOS VLAN implementation allows you to define separate independent LAN services on a single physical network interface.

▶ Link aggregate—Use this service to define a single virtual LAN service using multiple physical network interfaces. macOS uses the standard Link Aggregation Control Protocol (LACP), also known as IEEE 802.3ad.

▶ 6to4—This service transfers IPv6 packets across an IPv4 network. There is no enhanced security when using a 6to4 connection, but your Mac will appear to be directly connected to a remote IPv6 LAN.

Network Protocols

Each network service interface provides connectivity for standard networking protocols. Network preferences show primary protocol settings whenever you select a service from the services list, but many protocol configuration options are available only when you click the Advanced button.

macOS includes built-in support for the following network protocols (and others that are rarely used and not listed here):

▶ TCP/IP configured with DHCP—TCP/IP (Transmission Control Protocol/Internet Protocol) is the primary network protocol for LANs and WANs, and DHCP (Dynamic Host Configuration Protocol) is a network service that configures TCP/IP clients.

▶ TCP/IP configured manually—If you do not have DHCP service on your local network, or if you want to ensure that the TCP/IP settings never change, you can manually configure TCP/IP settings.

▶ DNS—DNS (Domain Name Service) provides hostnames for IP network devices. DNS settings are often configured alongside TCP/IP settings by either DHCP or manual configuration. macOS supports multiple DNS servers and search domains.

▶ Wireless Ethernet (Wi-Fi) protocol options—The wireless nature of Wi-Fi often requires additional configuration to facilitate network selection and authentication.

▶ Authenticated Ethernet with 802.1X—The 802.1X protocol is used to secure Ethernet networks (both wired and Wi-Fi) by allowing only properly authenticated network clients to join the LAN.

▶ Windows Internet Naming Service (WINS)— WINS is a protocol used on Windows-based networks to provide network identification and service discovery.

▶ IP proxies—Proxy servers act as intermediaries between a network client and a requested service and are used to enhance performance or provide an additional layer of security and content filtering.

▶ Ethernet hardware options—macOS supports both automatic and manual Ethernet hardware configuration, as covered later in this lesson.

Reference 22.3
Manage Network Service Interfaces

Typically, having multiple active network service interfaces means you also have multiple active IP addresses. macOS supports IP network multihoming to handle multiple IP addresses, and it supports multiple IP addresses for each physical network interface.

Using Multiple Simultaneous Interfaces

You can have an active wired Ethernet connection and an active Wi-Fi connection at the same time.

Suppose you have a work environment where you have one insecure network for general internet traffic and another network for secure internal transactions. With macOS, you can be on both of these networks at the same time. However, the first fully configured active service in the list is the primary network service interface.

In most cases the primary network service interface is used for all WAN connectivity, internet connectivity, and DNS hostname resolution. The exception to this is when the primary network interface doesn't have a router configuration. In this case, macOS treats the next fully configured active service as the primary network service interface.

When multiple IP addresses are available, macOS can communicate using any of those network service interfaces, but it will attempt to pick the most appropriate route for every network connection. A network client uses the subnet mask to determine whether an outgoing transmission is on the LAN. macOS takes this a step further by examining all active LANs when determining a destination for outgoing transmission.

Any network connections that are not destined for a LAN that your Mac is connected to are sent to the router address of the primary active network service interface. Any active network service interface with a valid TCP/IP setting is considered, but the primary active network service interface is automatically selected based on the network service order. You can manually configure the network service order, as outlined later in this lesson.

Using the previous example, in which you have a Mac active on both wired Ethernet and Wi-Fi, the default network service order prioritizes wired Ethernet over Wi-Fi. In this example, even though you have two active valid network service interfaces, the primary active network service interface is the wired Ethernet connection.

macOS features automatic source routing. This means that incoming connections to your Mac over a specific network service interface are always responded to on the same interface, regardless of the service order.

Inspect the Network Services List

When you open Network preferences, macOS identifies available network service interfaces. Even if a physical network interface isn't connected or properly configured, it creates a configuration for that interface, which shows up in the network services list. In Network preferences, each network interface is tied to one or more network services.

The network services list displays the status of all network interfaces and their configured services. Network services with a red indicator aren't connected. A yellow indicator shows services that are connected but not properly configured, as well as VPN services that are not connected. A green indicator shows connected and configured network services.

The active service at the top of this list is the primary network service interface as defined by the network service order. This list updates dynamically as new services become active or as active services become disconnected, so it's the first thing to check when you troubleshoot a network issue.

Manage Network Services

To manage network interfaces and their configured services:

1 Open and (if necessary) unlock Network preferences.

2 Make sure the network location you want to edit is chosen in the Location menu, or create a new network location.

3 To configure a specific network service, select it from the network services list.

The configuration area to the right of the list changes to reflect options available to the selected service.

4 Click Advanced to reveal all the advanced network protocol options available to the selected network service.

To create another configurable instance of a network interface, click the Add (+) button at the bottom of the network services list. This reveals a dialog that lets you choose a new interface instance from the Interface menu and then assign it a unique service name to identify it in the services list. Creating additional instances of a network service enables you to assign multiple IP addresses to a single network interface.

To make a service inactive, select it from the services list, click the Action pop-up menu ☺, and choose Make Service Inactive from the menu. A service that you make inactive doesn't activate, even if it's connected and properly configured. You can remove an existing network service by selecting its name from the services list, then clicking the

Remove (–) button at the bottom of the list. To remove a network service that was added by a configuration profile, you must remove the configuration profile.

Click the Action pop-up menu at the bottom of the network services list to reveal a menu with several management options. You can duplicate an existing network service by selecting its name from the services list, then choosing Duplicate Service from the menu. You can also rename an existing network service. To make a service inactive, select it from the services list, then choose Make Service Inactive from the menu. You can modify the active network service interface order by choosing Set Service Order from the menu.

In the Service Order dialog, you can drag network services into your preferred order for selection as the primary network interface. Click OK when you finish reordering. macOS reevaluates the active network service interfaces based on the new order.

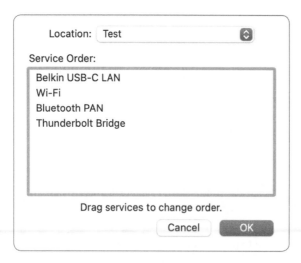

Reference 22.4
Configure VPN Settings

A VPN is an encrypted tunnel from your Mac to the network routing device providing the VPN service. After it's established, your Mac appears to have a direct connection to the LAN that the VPN device is sharing. So even if you're on a wireless internet connection thousands of miles away from your LAN, a VPN connection provides a virtual network interface as if your Mac were directly attached to that LAN. macOS supports three common VPN protocols:

▶ Layer 2 Tunneling Protocol over Internet Protocol Security (L2TP over IPSec)

▶ Cisco IPSec

▶ Internet Key Exchange version 2 (IKEv2)

Some VPN services require a third-party VPN client. Third-party VPN clients usually include a custom interface for managing the connection. Although Network preferences may display the virtual network interface provided by the third-party VPN client, it's usually not configurable from there.

Use a VPN Configuration Profile

To manage a VPN configuration, install a configuration profile. The administrator of a VPN system or mobile device management (MDM) solution can provide a configuration profile. After you install a configuration profile that contains VPN settings, the appropriate VPN settings should be configured for you.

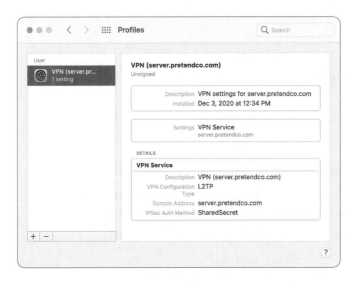

Manually Configure VPN Settings

Even with a VPN configuration profile, you might have to verify or further manage VPN connections from Network preferences. Or if the administrator of the VPN service is unable to provide a configuration profile, you must manually configure VPN services. To add a VPN interface, click the Add (+) button at the bottom of the network services list in Network preferences. This reveals a dialog where you can add a new network service interface.

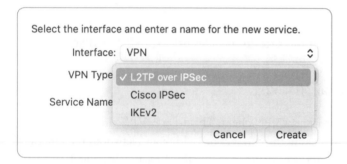

From the new network service interface dialog, you must choose the appropriate VPN protocol from the VPN Type menu.

> **NOTE ▸** After you click Create, if you later need to change the VPN type you can remove the service interface and create a new one with the right VPN type.

After you create the new VPN interface, select it from the network services list, and basic VPN configuration settings appear to the right. To configure VPN settings, first enter the VPN server address and, if you use user-based authentication, an account name.

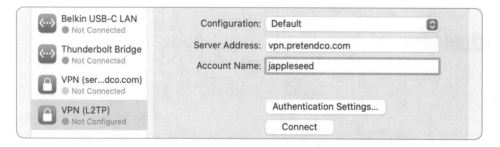

You must also define authentication methods by clicking the Authentication Settings button and specifying user and computer authentication settings. The VPN administrator can provide you with the appropriate authentication settings. If you select Password in the

User Authentication section and you do not enter the password, you're asked for the password when you connect. If you enter a VPN shared secret, macOS saves it to the System keychain.

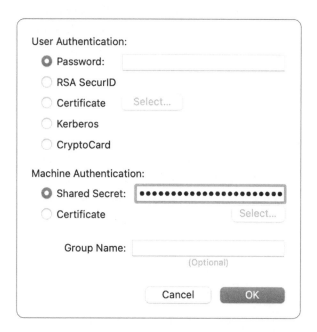

To configure advanced VPN settings, click the Advanced button in Network preferences. The options displayed in the Advanced Settings dialog depends on the type of VPN. For example, for an L2TP VPN interface, you can click Options or TCP/IP. The following figure illustrates the Options pane for an L2TP VPN interface with additional configuration options like "Send all traffic over VPN connection."

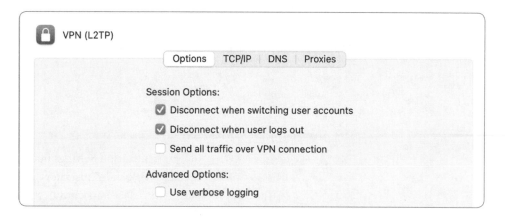

By default, active VPN connections do not move to the top of the network services list. macOS routes traffic to the VPN service only if the destination IP address is part of the LAN that the VPN service provides or if the VPN server supplies special routing information.

macOS also supports automatic VPN connections with certificate-based authentication and the VPN on Demand service. You can configure these VPN connections with configuration profiles.

Connect to a VPN

VPN connections aren't typically always-on connections. macOS supports automatic VPN connections with the VPN On Demand feature. You can manually connect and disconnect the VPN link from Network preferences. Select the "Show VPN status in menu bar" checkbox in Network preferences so that you can connect without opening Network preferences.

The VPN menu bar item enables you to select VPN configurations and connect, disconnect, and monitor VPN connections.

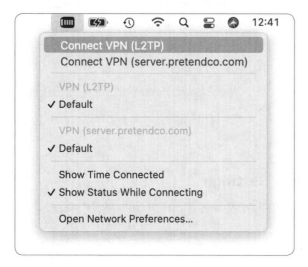

VPNs are often implemented in situations where user authentication is required, so for many, initiating a VPN connection opens an authentication dialog. Some VPN protocols require manual authentication every time a connection is established.

After the connection is authenticated and established, the VPN process automatically configures TCP/IP and DNS settings using the PPP protocol. By default, VPN interfaces are set at the bottom of the network service order, so they do not automatically become the primary network interface when activated. To override this behavior, select the "Send all traffic over VPN connection" option if it's available in Network preferences. You can also manually reorder the network service order.

When you troubleshoot VPN connections, you can use Console to inspect the connection log information in /private/var/log/system.log.

Reference 22.5
Configure Advanced Network Settings

The advanced network configuration techniques covered in this section are largely optional for many configurations.

Confirm DHCP-Supplied Settings

The default configuration for all Ethernet and Wi-Fi services is to automatically engage the DHCP process as soon as the interface becomes active. To verify TCP/IP and DNS settings for hardware or virtual Ethernet services when using the DHCP service, select the service from Network preferences.

IPv6 addressing information is automatically detected, too, if available. Automatic IPv6 configuration isn't provided by standard DHCP or PPP services.

Automatically configured DNS settings show as gray text, which indicates that you can override these settings by manually entering DNS information, as covered later in this section.

Network service interfaces that may require a manual connection process, like Wi-Fi, VPN, and PPPoE interfaces, automatically engage the DHCP or PPP process to acquire TCP/IP and DNS settings. To verify TCP/IP and DNS settings when using these interfaces, select the service from the services list and click Advanced in Network preferences. In the Advanced Settings dialog, you can click the TCP/IP or DNS button to inspect their respective settings. You can also verify network settings of any other interface this way.

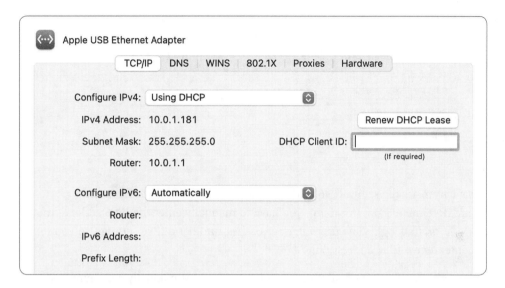

In some DHCP configurations, you must set a DHCP client ID. You can access this setting by clicking Advanced, then clicking the TCP/IP button.

Manually Configure TCP/IP

If you want to keep using DHCP but manually assign just the IP address, choose "Using DHCP with manual address" from the Configure IPv4 menu. You have to manually enter an IPv4 address for the Mac, but the rest of the TCP/IP settings remain configured by DHCP.

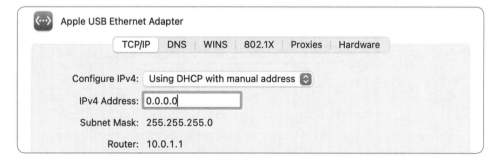

If you want to manually enter all TCP/IP settings, choose Manually from the Configure IPv4 menu. Enter the IPv4 address, the subnet mask, and the router address. The user interface caches the TCP/IP settings from the DHCP service, so you may have to enter a new IPv4 address only.

If you have to manually set up IPv6 settings as well, choose Manually from the Configure IPv6 menu. At a minimum you have to manually enter the IPv6 address, router address, and prefix length. The user interface caches automatic IPv6 settings, so you may have to enter a new IPv6 address only.

Whenever you choose to manually configure IPv4, you must manually configure DNS server settings. Click the DNS button to inspect the DNS settings. The user interface displays the DNS settings from the DHCP services, but these settings are no longer used when you switch from DHCP to a manual configuration.

Click the Add (+) button at the bottom of the DNS server list to add a new server, then enter the server's IP address. Entering a search domain is optional. Click the Add (+) button at the bottom of the Search Domains list, then enter the domain name. To edit an address, double-click its entry in the list. You can remove an entry by selecting it and clicking the Remove (–) button at the bottom of the list.

Enter the appropriate IP and DNS settings, click OK to dismiss the Advanced Settings dialog, and click Apply in Network preferences to save and activate the changes.

When you manually configure TCP/IP or DNS settings, test network connectivity to verify that you properly entered all information. Using standard apps to access network and internet resources is one basic test, but you could test more thoroughly using the included network diagnostic utilities, as covered in Lesson 23, "Troubleshoot Network Issues."

Manually Configure Wi-Fi

To manage advanced Wi-Fi options and connections:

1   Open and (if necessary) unlock Network preferences.

2   Select the Wi-Fi service from the services list.

3   Configure basic Wi-Fi settings from the Network Name menu, in much the same way that you would do it from the Wi-Fi status menu.

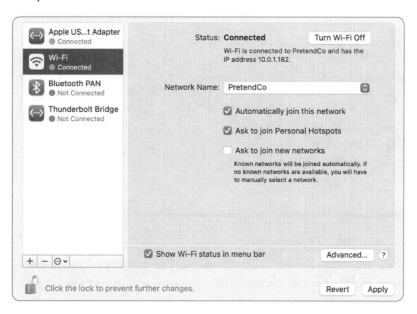

At this point you can enable non-administrator users to select Wi-Fi networks:

▶ When the "Ask to join new networks" checkbox is selected, macOS asks you to select another Wi-Fi network in the area when the Mac can't find a preconfigured wireless network.

▶ Selected by default, the "Show Wi-Fi status in menu bar" option allows any user to choose a wireless network from the Wi-Fi status menu.

Click the Advanced button to reveal the Advanced Settings dialog. If the Wi-Fi button at the top isn't already selected, click it to inspect the advanced Wi-Fi settings.

From the top half of the advanced Wi-Fi settings pane, you can manage a list of preferred wireless networks. By default, wireless networks that you previously joined appear here as well.

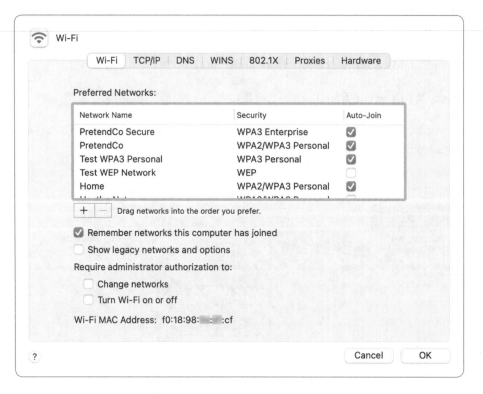

To add a new wireless network, click the Add (+) button at the bottom of the Preferred Networks list and either join a wireless network in range or manually enter the information for a hidden or not-currently-in-range network. To edit a network, double-click its entry in the list, or you can remove a network by selecting it and clicking the Remove (−) button at the bottom of the list.

Deselecting the Auto-Join option for a wireless network in the Preferred Networks list enables you to temporarily configure your Mac not to auto-join a particular wireless network while preserving the information about the network and its relative location in the Preferred Networks list.

> **NOTE ▶** One scenario where you might deselect Auto-Join for a Wi-Fi network is if you're using iCloud Keychain and want to have your iOS or iPadOS device use your Wi-Fi network but you want your Mac to use Ethernet rather than Wi-Fi. If you remove the Wi-Fi network from the Preferred Networks list on your Mac, your other devices won't automatically join that network. Instead, deselect Auto-Join for the network on your Mac, which preserves your ability to use AirDrop on your Mac and doesn't affect your iOS or iPadOS devices.

When you want to configure your Mac to automatically join a particular wireless network again, select the Auto-Join option for that network.

At the bottom of the advanced Wi-Fi settings pane, you have several settings that allow for more specific Wi-Fi administration options. You can restrict certain settings to only administrator users, including:

▶ Change networks

▶ Turn Wi-Fi on or off

To get even more control over your preferred networks, click Cancel here, then Option-click Advanced. This reveals the Advanced Settings dialog with two additional columns: Hidden and Shareable. Select the Hidden option for a network to have macOS consider it a hidden network. Deselect the Shareable option for a network to prevent anyone from sharing the password for that network.

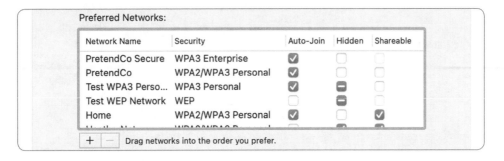

See "Change advanced Wi-Fi options on Mac" at support.apple.com/guide/mac-help/ mh11937 in the macOS User Guide for more information.

Configure 802.1X

The 802.1X protocol is used to secure both wired (Ethernet) and wireless (Wi-Fi) networks by allowing only properly authenticated network clients to join the network. Networks that require 802.1X don't allow traffic until the network client properly authenticates to the network.

To facilitate 802.1X authentication, macOS provides two methods for automatic configuration:

▸ Administrator-provided 802.1X configuration profile—You can install an 802.1X configuration profile by double-clicking a local copy of a profile or by using an MDM solution to install the profile.

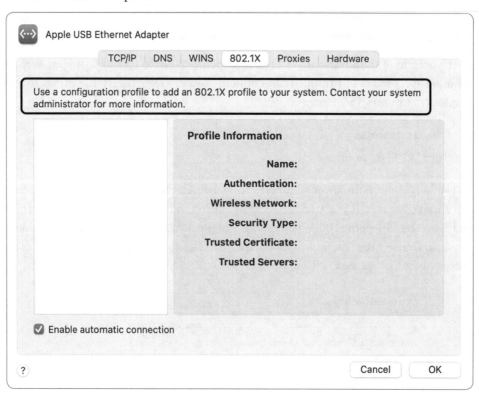

▶ User-selected network with 802.1X authentication—If you connect to an Ethernet network that uses 802.1X, or if you connect to a Wi-Fi network that uses 802.1X (including WPA/WPA2 Enterprise, WPA2 Enterprise, or WPA3 Enterprise authentication), macOS automatically configures 802.1X. You can verify the 802.1X configuration in Network preferences by selecting the network service, though you cannot modify the connection details in any way.

For network services that use Ethernet, the 802.1X pane includes the option "Enable automatic connection" that is turned on by default. If you deselect this option, your Mac will be able to connect to an Ethernet network that requires 802.1X only if an appropriate configuration profile for that 802.1X network is installed.

After the 802.1X connection is configured or the profile is installed, a Connect button appears in Network preferences for the appropriate network service.

Information about the 802.1X configuration appears in the 802.1X pane.

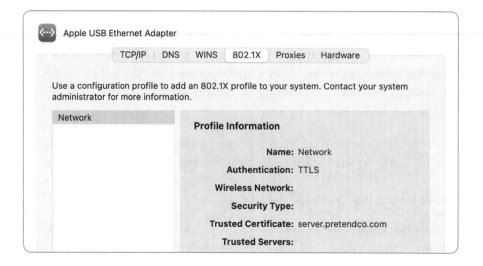

Configure WINS

Current Windows networks now use Dynamic DNS as a solution for network client discovery, but macOS still supports WINS to support legacy network configurations. To manually configure WINS settings:

1   Open and (if necessary) unlock Network preferences.

2   Select the network service you want to configure from the network services list.

3   Click Advanced.

4   In the Advanced Settings dialog, click the WINS button to inspect the WINS settings.

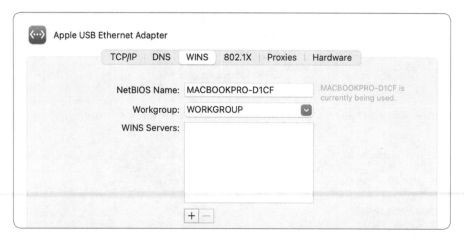

To enable WINS, enter at least one WINS server IP address. Click the Add (+) button at the bottom of the WINS server list to add a new server, then enter the server's IP address. If you configure multiple WINS servers, macOS attempts to access those resources in the order in which they appear in the list. To edit a server address, double-click its entry in the list, or you can remove a server by selecting it and clicking the Remove (–) button at the bottom of the list.

Configure Network Proxies

Proxy servers act as intermediaries between a network client and a requested service. Proxy servers are often used to enhance the performance of WAN or internet connections by caching recently requested data so that future connections appear faster to local network clients. Proxy servers are also implemented so that network administrators can limit network connections to unauthorized servers or resources, manage lists of approved resources, and configure the proxy servers to allow access to those resources only.

You might need to acquire specific proxy configuration instructions from a network administrator.

To enable and configure proxy settings:

1   Open and (if necessary) unlock Network preferences.

2   Select the network service you want to configure from the network services list.

3   Click Advanced.

4   Click the Proxies button at the top to inspect the proxy settings.

If you configure your proxy server settings automatically, select Auto Proxy Discovery to automatically discover proxy servers, or select Automatic Proxy Configuration if you're using a proxy auto-configuration (PAC) file. macOS Big Sur supports only HTTP and HTTPS URL schemes for PAC. This includes PAC URLs you configure manually or with a configuration profile. If you select Automatic Proxy Configuration, enter the address of the PAC file in the URL field. Check with your network administrator if you need more information.

If you configure your proxy settings manually, do the following:

▶   Select a proxy server, such as FTP Proxy, then type its address and port number in the fields on the right.

▶ Select the "Proxy server requires password" checkbox if the proxy server is protected by a password. Enter your account name and password in the Username and Password fields.

You can also choose to bypass proxy settings for specific computers on the internet (hosts) and segments of the internet (domains) by adding the address of the host or domain in the "Bypass proxy settings for these Hosts & Domains" field. This might be useful if you want to make sure you're receiving information directly from the host or domain and not information that's cached on the proxy server.

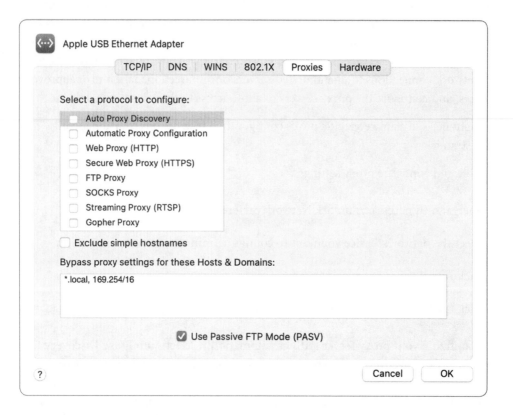

Manually Configure Ethernet

Ethernet connections establish connection settings automatically. macOS lets you manually configure Ethernet options. You probably should configure Ethernet options when you have Gigabit Ethernet switches and old or substandard wired infrastructure. In this case it's common for the Mac to attempt to automatically establish a gigabit connection but ultimately fail because the wired infrastructure doesn't support the high speeds. The most common symptom is that even with the Ethernet switch showing that the Mac has an active connection, Network preferences on the Mac shows Ethernet as disconnected.

To manually configure Ethernet settings:

1   Open and (if necessary) unlock Network preferences.

2   Select the Ethernet service you want to configure from the network services list.

3   Click Advanced.

4   Click the Hardware button at the top to inspect the current Ethernet hardware settings.

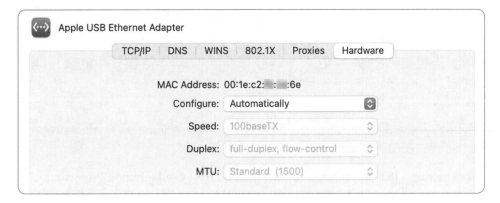

macOS caches the current automatically configured Ethernet settings, so you don't have to change the settings. macOS also populates the Speed, Duplex, and MTU options based on the network hardware in your Mac.

5   To manually configure Ethernet options, choose Manually from the Configure menu.

6   Make your custom selections from these menus.

7   Click OK to save the configuration changes.

After you manually configure your Ethernet settings, confirm that you have network connectivity as you expect. You can use the tools and techniques covered in Lesson 23.

Exercise 22.1
Configure Network Locations

NOTE ▶ Even if you don't meet these prerequisites, reading the exercises will enhance your knowledge of the processes.

Many networks that you connect to use Dynamic Host Configuration Protocol (DHCP). You configure your Mac to obtain an IP address through DHCP, then configure a location to switch to this configuration.

Examine Your DHCP-Supplied Configuration

1   Log in as Johnny Appleseed.

2   Open Network preferences.

3   Click the padlock, then authenticate as Local Administrator.

4   Select the primary network service.

5   In the right side of the Network preferences pane, confirm that you are connected to a Wi-Fi network with a valid IPv4 address.

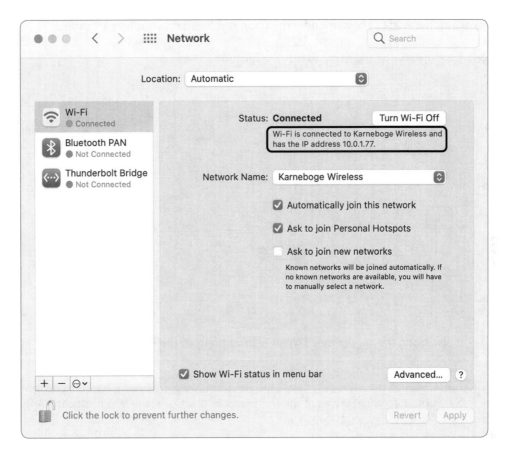

Your settings might vary from those shown in this screenshot, especially if you have different network services connected.

Create a DHCP-Based Network Location

1   From the Location menu, choose Edit Locations.

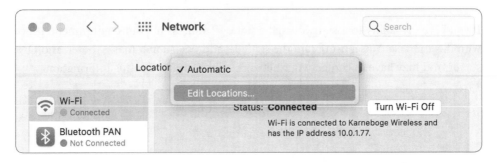

2   Click the Add (+) button under the Locations list to create a new location.

3   Type **Dynamic** as the name of the new location.

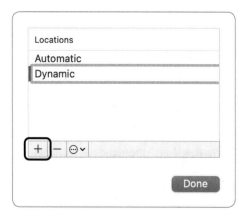

4   Click Done.

5   If necessary, choose the new Dynamic location from the Location menu.

6   Click Apply.

Network preferences is one of the few places in macOS where you must click Apply before your settings take effect.

macOS obtains an IP address from the DHCP server.

Create a Static Network Location

Some network configurations don't have a DHCP server, or there may be times when a DHCP server fails. In these instances, to establish and maintain proper network access you must configure your Mac with a static IP address.

In this exercise, you configure a new location called Static with a static IP address.

If you have the ability to assign yourself a static IP address in your environment, proceed with this exercise. You must obtain the static IP address, subnet mask, router, and DNS server. You may have to contact your network administrator for this information.

If you do not have the ability to assign yourself a static IP address, skip this portion and proceed to Exercise 22.2, "Advanced Wi-Fi Configuration."

1   From the Location menu, choose Edit Locations, then select the Dynamic location.

2   From the Action menu (with the ellipsis icon), choose Duplicate Location.

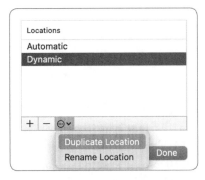

3   Name the new location **Static**, then click Done.

4   Use the Location menu to switch to the new Static location, if it's not already selected.

5   Click Apply.

6   Select the network service that's set up for these exercises from the service list on the left. It will be Ethernet or Wi-Fi.

7   Click Advanced.

8   If necessary, click TCP/IP.

9   From the Configure IPv4 menu, choose Manually.

10 In the IPv4 Address field, enter the IP address appropriate for your environment. You may have obtained this address from your network administrator.

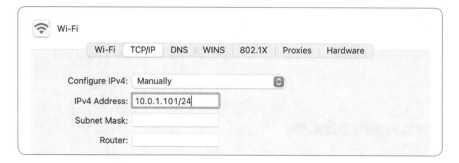

11 Press the Tab key.

In this example, the string "/24" at the end of the IP address is shorthand for the subnet mask 255.255.255.0 in CIDR (Classless Inter-Domain Routing) notation. The Subnet Mask field is filled in when you press the Tab key. macOS enters 10.0.1.1 as the Router address, which is correct for this network. You must obtain the correct router address for your network.

12 Click DNS.

13 Click the Add (+) button under the DNS Servers list, then enter the DNS server appropriate for your network.

14 Click the Add (+) button under the Search Domains list, then enter the search domain appropriate for your network.

Not all networks are configured with a search domain. A search domain is not required for correct functionality of these exercises.

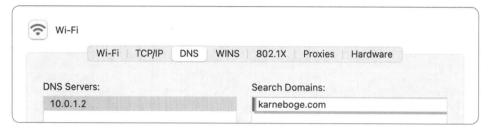

15 Click OK to dismiss the dialog.

16 Click Apply.

The status indicator for the service changes to green to indicate that it is connected and fully configured. The right side of the Network preferences pane contains information about the static IPV4 address your Mac uses.

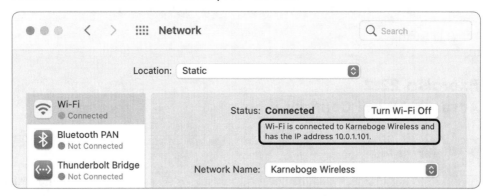

17 Quit System Preferences.

Test Internet Access

You've correctly configured your Mac to work on the network. You'll use Safari to test network access in this exercise. To make sure you're testing network connections rather than just loading pages from Safari caches, you'll empty the Safari caches first. Then you'll use Safari to verify that you can access the Apple website.

1 Open Safari.

2 Choose Safari > Preferences (or press Command-Comma).

3 Click Advanced in the preferences toolbar.

4 Select "Show Develop menu in menu bar," then close the preferences window.

5 Choose Develop > Empty Caches (or press Option-Command-E).

Normally, you wouldn't perform this action. You do here to ensure that the Apple website you load in the next step isn't cached.

6 In the Smart Search field, type **www.apple.com**, then press Return.

If Safari is trying to load a page from the internet, you don't have to wait for it to finish or time out. If everything is working, the Apple website appears.

If the Apple website doesn't load, there is something wrong with your network settings or connection. Troubleshoot before you proceed. First, verify your network settings match previous instructions. If they are correct, consult Lesson 23.

7   Quit Safari.

Exercise 22.2
Advanced Wi-Fi Configuration

▶ **Prerequisites**

  ▶ You must have created the Local Administrator (Exercise 3.1, "Configure a Mac for Exercises") and Johnny Appleseed (Exercise 7.1, "Create a Standard User Account") accounts.

  ▶ Your Mac must have a Wi-Fi interface, and you must have access to at least two Wi-Fi networks (at least one of which is visible).

In this exercise, you learn to use the Preferred Networks list to control how your Mac joins Wi-Fi networks.

Create a Wi-Fi-Only Location

1   If necessary, log in as Johnny Appleseed, open Network preferences, then authenticate as Local Administrator.

2   Note the currently selected location so that you can return to it at the end of the exercise.

3   From the Location menu, choose Edit Locations.

4   Click the Add (+) button under the Locations list to create a new location.

5 Type **Wi-Fi Only** as the name of the new location.

6 Click Done.

7 If necessary, choose the new Wi-Fi Only location from the Location menu.

8 Click Apply.

9 In the network services list, make the services other than Wi-Fi inactive. To do so, select each service, then from the Action menu choose Make Service Inactive.

When you are done, all services except Wi-Fi are listed as Inactive.

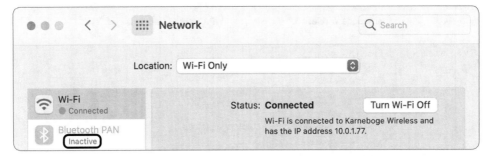

10 Click Apply.

11 Select the Wi-Fi service.

12 If necessary, click Turn Wi-Fi On.

13 If necessary, deselect "Ask to join new networks."

This prevents your Mac from suggesting networks to you when it can't find your preferred networks.

14 If necessary, select "Show Wi-Fi status in menu bar."

15 If your Mac hasn't joined a wireless network, join one by following the instructions in Exercise 21.1, "Connect to a Wi-Fi Network."

Clear the Preferred Networks List

1 Click Advanced.

2 Examine the Preferred Networks list.

This is the list of wireless networks that your Mac joins automatically when it's in range of them. If there is more than one in range, your Mac joins the one that is highest on the list, as long as you have selected Auto-Join.

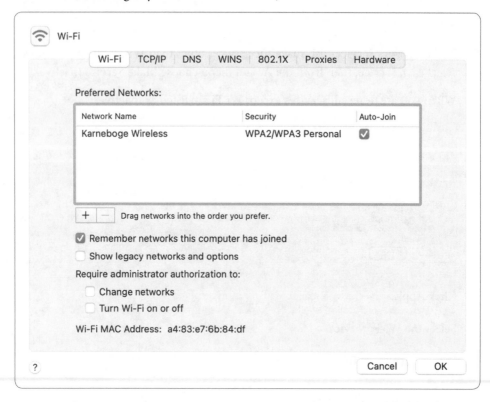

NOTE ▶ If you remove a wireless network from this list, you remove its password from your keychain. You must reenter the password the next time you join the wireless network. If you use iCloud Keychain, the same wireless network will be removed from other Apple devices that use the same iCloud account. If you do not know the password for the network you intend to remove, you can use Keychain Access to view its password and record it before you remove it from this list. See Reference 9.2, "Manage Secrets in Keychain," for the details of this process.

3   Select each entry, then click the Remove (–) button at the bottom of the list to clear it.

4   Make sure "Remember networks this computer has joined" is selected.

5   When the list is empty, click OK, then click Apply. If necessary, authenticate as Local Administrator. You may have to authenticate twice.

6   Click Turn Wi-Fi Off, then click Apply.

7   Wait 10 seconds, then click Turn Wi-Fi On.

The wireless interface turns on but doesn't connect to a network.

Add a Network to the Preferred List Manually

1   Click Advanced.

2   Click the Add (+) button under the Preferred Networks list.

3   Enter the network name and security information for another network you have access to.

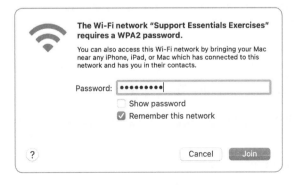

4   Click OK to add the entry.

5 Click OK to dismiss the advanced settings, then click Apply. If necessary, authenticate as Local Administrator.

Your Mac should join the wireless network. If it doesn't, there might be a problem with the manual entry, such as a typo in the name or password or an incorrect security mode. In this case, you could remove the wireless network from the list, then reenter it.

Add a Network to the Preferred List by Joining It

1 From the Network Name menu, choose another of the wireless networks you have access to.

2 Click Join.

3 If necessary, enter the network password to join it.

4 Click Advanced.

The network you joined is added to the top of the preferred list. This is because the "Remember networks this computer has joined" option is selected.

5 Click OK to dismiss the dialog.

Test the Preferred Networks Order

1 Click Turn Wi-Fi Off. Wait 10 seconds, then click Turn Wi-Fi On.

After a short delay, your Mac rejoins the network you just added.

2 Click Advanced.

3 Drag the current wireless network to the bottom of the list to change the Preferred Networks order.

4 Click OK, then click Apply.

5 Click Turn Wi-Fi Off. Wait 10 seconds, then click Turn Wi-Fi On.

This time, your Mac joins the network you added manually because it is first in the Preferred Networks list.

6 Switch back to the Static network location, then click Apply.

7 Quit System Preferences.

Lesson 23

Troubleshoot Network Issues

This lesson builds on the network topics covered in Lesson 21, "Manage Basic Network Settings," and Lesson 22, "Manage Advanced Network Settings." This lesson first covers general network troubleshooting and common network issues. Then, you learn how to use network troubleshooting tools and commands.

Reference 23.1
Troubleshoot General Network Issues

When you troubleshoot LAN and internet connection network issues, consider possible points of failure. Isolate the cause of the problem before you attempt generic resolutions.

GOALS

► Identify and resolve network configuration issues

► Verify network configuration with Network preferences

► Use command-line interface commands to aid in troubleshooting

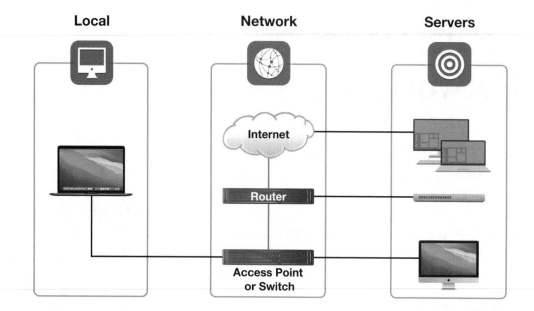

To help isolate network issues, you can categorize them into three general areas:

► Local issues—These are usually related to either improperly configured network settings or disconnected network connections.

► Network issues—Many possible points of failure could be involved. Become familiar with the physical topology of your network. Start by checking the devices that provide network access closest to your Mac. Something as simple as a bad Ethernet port on a network switch can cause problems. Start your investigation using the network diagnostic utilities included with macOS.

► Service issues—These issues are related to the network device or service you are trying to access. For example, the devices providing DHCP or DNS services could be temporarily down or improperly configured. You can often determine that the problem is with the service by testing other network services. If the other network services work, you're probably not dealing with network or local issues. Use diagnostic tools for testing service availability. Troubleshooting network services is also covered in Lesson 24, "Manage Network Services."

Use two main tools for diagnosing network issues in macOS: Network preferences and Terminal.

Verify Network Preferences Status

One of the diagnostic tools you should check first is Network preferences. Network preferences features a dynamically updating list that shows you the current status of any network interface. If a network connection isn't working, you first find out about it here.

Network status indicators are:

▶ Green—The connection is active and configured with TCP/IP settings. This doesn't guarantee that the service is using the proper TCP/IP settings.

▶ Yellow—The connection is active but the TCP/IP settings aren't properly configured. If you are experiencing problems with this service, double-check the network settings. If the settings appear sound, move on to the other diagnostic utilities.

▶ Red—This status usually indicates either improperly configured network settings or disconnected network interfaces. If this is an always-on interface, check for proper physical connectivity. If this is a virtual or Point-to-Point Protocol connection, double-check the settings and attempt to reconnect.

Common Network Issues

A good starting point for resolving network issues is to check for some common causes before hunting down more complex ones. This includes verifying Ethernet connectivity, Wi-Fi connectivity, DHCP services, and DNS services.

Ethernet Connectivity Issues

If you use an Ethernet connection, verify the physical connection to the Mac, and if possible, verify the entire Ethernet run back to the switch. If that's not possible, try swapping your local Ethernet cable or use a different Ethernet port. If you use an Ethernet adapter, try a different adapter.

Verify the Ethernet status from Network preferences. Also, keep an eye out for substandard Ethernet cabling or problematic switching hardware.

You may also find that although the Ethernet switch registers a link, Network preferences still shows the link as down. This issue may be resolved by manually setting a slower speed in the advanced hardware settings of Network preferences, as covered in Lesson 22.

MORE INFO ▶ Built-in network hardware for Intel-based Mac computers can some-times become unresponsive and may benefit from resetting the Mac computer's NVRAM or System Management Controller (SMC). For more information, see Apple Support article HT204063, "Reset NVRAM or PRAM on your Mac," and article HT201295, "How to reset the SMC of your Mac."

Wi-Fi Connectivity Issues

If you use Wi-Fi, start by verifying that you are connected to the correct SSID from the Wi-Fi status menu or Network preferences. Often, if the Mac detects a problem the Wi-Fi status menu shows an exclamation point (!) to indicate that there is a problem with the wireless network.

The Wi-Fi status menu can also serve as a diagnostic tool if you press and hold the Option key, then open the Wi-Fi status menu. This view shows connection statistics for the currently selected Wi-Fi network. Of particular note is the Tx Rate entry, which shows the current data rate for the selected Wi-Fi network. The Wi-Fi status menu is capable of other diagnostic tasks, including helping you quickly identify network issues and opening Wireless Diagnostics.

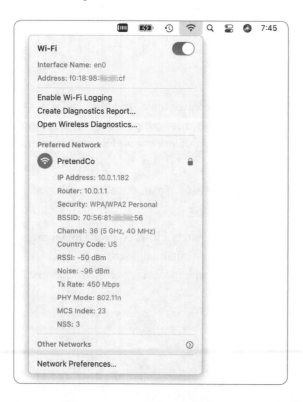

When you open Wireless Diagnostics, an assistant interface appears. Wireless Diagnostics creates and saves a diagnostic report archive about the Mac computer's wireless and network configuration. You must authenticate as an administrator user to create the report. The compressed archive is stored in /private/var/tmp. After Wireless Diagnostics completes the report, the Finder opens the folder that contains the compressed archive.

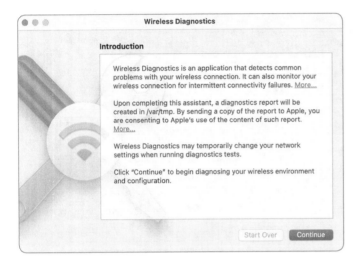

The Wireless Diagnostics archive contains relevant files that can you use to diagnose a connection issue. If the utility can't diagnose the problem, consult an experienced Wi-Fi administrator.

Open the Window menu to access additional advanced wireless network utilities in Wireless Diagnostics.

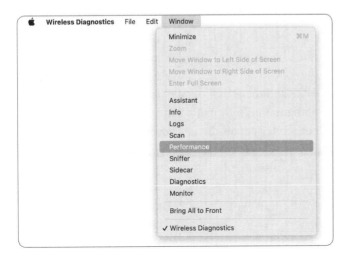

These utilities provide information that you can share with Wi-Fi vendors or support specialists to resolve Wi-Fi issues. For example, the Performance window provides a real-time view of the radio signal quality. With the Performance window open, you can physically move a Mac notebook computer around an area to identify wireless dead zones.

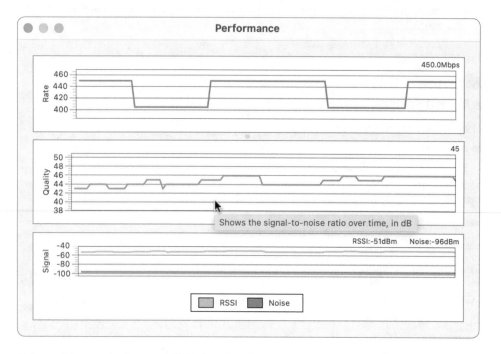

Sidecar Diagnostics is part of Wireless Diagnostics. You use it to gather information about wireless issues while you're using your iPad as a second display for your Mac with Sidecar.

For more information, see Apple Support article HT202663, "If your Mac doesn't connect to the Internet over Wi-Fi."

DHCP Service Issues

If you configure your Mac to use DHCP and the DHCP server runs out of available network addresses or doesn't provide configuration information to your Mac, your Mac might be able to communicate with other devices on the LAN even though it doesn't have access to WAN or internet resources. This is covered in Lesson 21, "Manage Basic Network Settings."

DNS Service Issues

Most network services require DNS services. If you have DNS service issues, verify the DNS server configuration in Network preferences. In most cases, the top listed network service interface is primary, and macOS uses it for DNS resolution. The exception is if the primary network service lacks a router configuration, in which case DNS resolution falls to the next fully configured network service interface.

Reference 23.2
Use Terminal to Troubleshoot Network Issues

macOS provides several network identification and diagnostic commands that you can access in Terminal. This includes, but isn't limited to, the following:

▶   **ifconfig** (interface configuration)—Inspect details regarding hardware network interfaces.

▶   **netstat** (network status)—View routing information and network statistics.

▶   **ping**—Test network connectivity and latency.

▶   **nslookup, dig, host**, and **dscacheutil**—Test DNS resolution.

▶   **traceroute**—Analyze how your network connections are routed to their destination.

▶   **nc** (netcat)—Check whether a network device has specific services available.

You can also open Terminal when you start your Mac from macOS Recovery (as covered in Lesson 5, "Use macOS Recovery") by choosing Utilities > Terminal. In macOS Recovery you can access the Wi-Fi status menu to use a different Wi-Fi network.

ifconfig

The ifconfig command enables you to view the detailed status of any network interface. Each network interface has a short UNIX-given name; for example, the default Wi-Fi interface for Mac portable computers is en0.

If you run ifconfig by itself, it returns the status of all network interfaces, even ones that aren't configured and that don't appear in Network preferences. The following figure displays only a portion of the result of running the command. en7 is the name of an Apple USB Ethernet Adapter that's connected to the MacBook Pro with a USB-C adapter. The name for a network interface may vary depending on the configuration of your Mac, including the other network interfaces you've configured for your Mac.

```
● ● ●                    johnny — -zsh — 80×24
          media: <unknown type>
          status: inactive
llw0: flags=8863<UP,BROADCAST,SMART,RUNNING,SIMPLEX,MULTICAST> mtu 1500
          options=400<CHANNEL_IO>
          ether fe:fc:bf:9c:6f:72
          inet6 fe80::fcfc:bfff:fe9c:6f72%llw0 prefixlen 64 scopeid 0x12
          nd6 options=201<PERFORMNUD,DAD>
          media: autoselect
          status: active
utun0: flags=8051<UP,POINTOPOINT,RUNNING,MULTICAST> mtu 1380
          inet6 fe80::678c:b05e:200c:23d4%utun0 prefixlen 64 scopeid 0x13
          nd6 options=201<PERFORMNUD,DAD>
utun1: flags=8051<UP,POINTOPOINT,RUNNING,MULTICAST> mtu 2000
          inet6 fe80::b90d:402b:388a:2e19%utun1 prefixlen 64 scopeid 0x14
          nd6 options=201<PERFORMNUD,DAD>
en7: flags=8863<UP,BROADCAST,SMART,RUNNING,SIMPLEX,MULTICAST> mtu 1500
          options=404<VLAN_MTU,CHANNEL_IO>
          ether 00:1e:c2:fb:ca:6e
          inet6 fe80::40d:fcd1:6c59:f021%en7 prefixlen 64 secured scopeid 0x15
          inet 10.0.1.181 netmask 0xffffff00 broadcast 10.0.1.255
          nd6 options=201<PERFORMNUD,DAD>
          media: autoselect (100baseTX <full-duplex,flow-control>)
          status: active
johnny@Johnnys-MacBook-Pro ~ % ▮
```

ifconfig is often run with the name of a single network interface. For example, the following figure illustrates running the command ifconfig en0, which returns information about the default Wi-Fi interface.

```
● ● ●                    johnny — -zsh — 80×10
[johnny@Johnnys-MacBook-Pro ~ % ifconfig en0                                   ]
en0: flags=8863<UP,BROADCAST,SMART,RUNNING,SIMPLEX,MULTICAST> mtu 1500
          options=400<CHANNEL_IO>
          ether f0:18:98:██:██:cf
          inet6 fe80::c4a:123b:d682:d6a9%en0 prefixlen 64 secured scopeid 0xf
          inet 10.0.1.182 netmask 0xffffff00 broadcast 10.0.1.255
          nd6 options=201<PERFORMNUD,DAD>
          media: autoselect
          status: active
johnny@Johnnys-MacBook-Pro ~ % ▮
```

The entire extent of the output of the command is outside the scope of this guide, but some of the key pieces of information include:

▸ **ether**—MAC address

▸ **inet6**—IPv6 address

▸ **inet**—IPv4 address

▸ **netmask**—Subnet mask

▸ **media**—Connection speed and characteristics

▸ **status**—Active or inactive

netstat

The netstat command enables you to view even more detailed status of any network interface. One example is netstat -di -I, followed by the interface name. The options include:

▶ **-di**—Show the number of dropped packets

▶ **-I (*name of interface*)**—Show information only about that specific interface

For example, the following figure illustrates running the command netstat -di -I en7, which returns information about a connected Apple USB Ethernet Adapter.

```
● ● ●                          🖥 johnny — -zsh — 92×24

[johnny@Johnnys-MacBook-Pro ~ % netstat -di -I en7                                            ]
Name      Mtu    Network        Address        Ipkts Ierrs    Opkts Oerrs  Coll Drop
en7       1500   <Link#21>      00:1e:c2:  :  :6e   1276    0      958    0      0   0
en7       1500   johnnys-mac fe80:15::40d:fcd1    1276    -      958    -      -   -
en7       1500   10.0.1/24      10.0.1.181     1276    -      958    -      -   -
johnny@Johnnys-MacBook-Pro ~ % ▌
```

The -I option provides a table with cumulative counts of network packets transferred, errors, and collisions. The -di option adds a count of dropped packets as well. Here are some of the values in the table:

▶ **Name**—Name of the interface

▶ **Address**—MAC address, IPv6 address, or IPv6 address; it's common to see each interface have three addresses listed

▶ **Ipkts**—Number of packets received by the interface

▶ **Ierrs**—Number of errors related to packets received by the interface

▶ **Opkts**—Number of packets sent by the interface

▶ **Oerrs**—Number of errors related to packets sent by the interface

▶ **Coll**—Number of collisions detected

▶ **Drop**—Number of dropped packets detected

You can also use netstat to analyze network transfer statistics. If you open an app like Safari to cause some network traffic, then run the netstat command again, you can verify that packets are being sent and received from this interface. In the following example, there were initially 1,276 received packets; Safari was then used to generate network traffic; then there were 16,100 received packets. It's safe to conclude that Safari used the en7 interface for network traffic.

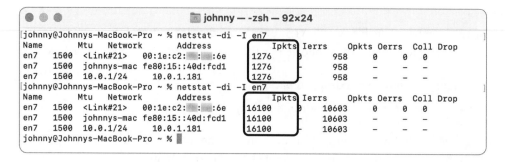

If the transfer statistics indicates activity but you still experience problems, the issue is probably a network or service problem and not the network interface. Or, if this interface is experiencing transfer errors, a local network hardware connectivity issue may be the root of your problem.

To resolve hardware network interface issues, check the physical connection. With wired networks, try different network ports or cabling to rule out physical connection issues. With wireless networks, double-check the Wi-Fi settings and the configuration of any wireless base stations. If the Mac network hardware isn't working, contact an Apple Authorized Service Provider.

ping

If your network settings are properly configured and the hardware network interface appears to be working correctly but you still experience network issues, test network connectivity using the ping command.

The word *ping* refers to several concepts:

► The name of a command

► A kind of network packet

► The act of using the ping command to send a ping packet

The ping command determines whether your Mac can successfully send and receive data to another network device. Your Mac sends a ping data packet to the destination IP address, and the other device returns the ping packet to indicate connectivity.

To use ping, type **ping**, then a space, then an IP address to a device on the LAN that should always be accessible, such as the network router; then press Return. Using a domain name assumes that your Mac is properly communicating with a DNS server, which might not be the case if you're troubleshooting connectivity issues.

If the ping command is successful, it returns the amount of time it took for the ping to travel to the network device and back. This round trip typically takes a few milliseconds. You can use the -c option (count) with a number of packets to send, or if you omit the -c option, the ping command will repeatedly send packets until you stop the ping command by pressing Control-C or Command-Period.

After you stop the ping command, the ping command returns how many packets ping transmitted, how many packets were received by the remote device, and a percentage of packet loss.

```
● ● ●                    johnny — -zsh — 80×12
[johnny@Johnnys-MacBook-Pro ~ % ping -c 5 10.0.1.1                            ]
PING 10.0.1.1 (10.0.1.1): 56 data bytes
64 bytes from 10.0.1.1: icmp_seq=0 ttl=255 time=2.484 ms
64 bytes from 10.0.1.1: icmp_seq=1 ttl=255 time=1.266 ms
64 bytes from 10.0.1.1: icmp_seq=2 ttl=255 time=1.392 ms
64 bytes from 10.0.1.1: icmp_seq=3 ttl=255 time=1.212 ms
64 bytes from 10.0.1.1: icmp_seq=4 ttl=255 time=1.271 ms

--- 10.0.1.1 ping statistics ---
5 packets transmitted, 5 packets received, 0.0% packet loss
round-trip min/avg/max/stddev = 1.212/1.525/2.484/0.483 ms
johnny@Johnnys-MacBook-Pro ~ % █
```

Some network administrators configure their firewalls to block pings or to set up their network devices not to respond to network pings.

After you establish successful pings to local devices, branch out to WAN or internet addresses. Using ping, you may find that everything works except for the one service you were looking for that prompted you to start troubleshooting the network.

Lookup

If you are able to successfully ping other network devices by their IP address but you can't connect to another device by its hostname, you likely have issues related to DNS. Several commands are available that let you test name resolution against your DNS server. This section covers the following commands, each listed here along with the description from the name section of its man page:

- ▶ **host**—DNS lookup utility
- ▶ **dig**—DNS lookup utility
- ▶ **nslookup**—Query internet name servers interactively
- ▶ **dscacheutil**—Gather information and statistics and initiate queries to the Directory Services cache

To verify DNS, use one of the commands in this section to query the hostname of a device or service in your local domain. If you can resolve local hostnames but not internet hostnames, your local DNS server is resolving local names but isn't properly connecting to the worldwide DNS network. If you don't have a local domain, use any internet hostname.

To start the network lookup process with the host command (DNS lookup utility), type **host**, a space, then an IP address or hostname; then press Return.

The following figure illustrates a successful forward lookup, which returns the IP address of the hostname you entered.

```
● ● ●                    🖿 johnny — -zsh — 80×24
[johnny@Johnnys-MacBook-Pro ~ % host server.pretendco.com
server.pretendco.com has address 10.0.1.2
server.pretendco.com mail is handled by 10 mail.pretendco.com.
johnny@Johnnys-MacBook-Pro ~ % █
```

The following figure illustrates a successful reverse lookup, which returns the hostname of the IP address you entered.

```
● ● ●                    🖿 johnny — -zsh — 80×24
[johnny@Johnnys-MacBook-Pro ~ % host 10.0.1.2
2.1.0.10.in-addr.arpa domain name pointer server.pretendco.com.
johnny@Johnnys-MacBook-Pro ~ % █
```

The nslookup command returns a bit more information, which might be useful for your troubleshooting. The following figure illustrates using nslookup for a forward lookup and then a reverse lookup.

```
● ● ●                    🖿 johnny — -zsh — 80×24
[johnny@Johnnys-MacBook-Pro ~ % nslookup server.pretendco.com
Server:         10.0.1.2
Address:        10.0.1.2#53

Name:   server.pretendco.com
Address: 10.0.1.2

[johnny@Johnnys-MacBook-Pro ~ % nslookup 10.0.1.2
Server:         10.0.1.2
Address:        10.0.1.2#53

2.1.0.10.in-addr.arpa    name = server.pretendco.com.

johnny@Johnnys-MacBook-Pro ~ % █
```

The dig command returns even more information. Use the **-x** option to perform a reverse lookup. The following figures illustrate using dig for forward and reverse lookups.

And finally, for this section, you can use the dscacheutil command for more advanced DNS troubleshooting.

NOTE ▶ Although the other commands in this section ignore the /private/etc/hosts file, which is outside the scope of this guide, dscacheutil consults the /private/etc/hosts file.

For a DNS lookup, use two dscacheutil options followed by the hostname or IP address you want to look up. Here are the two options, along with arguments you should use for a DNS lookup:

▶ **-q**—This is the type of query, like user, group, or host. For DNS lookups, use **-q host**.

▶ **-a**—This is the key to look up. For forward lookups, use **-a name**; for reverse lookups, use **-a ip_address**. And as a bonus, to use an IPv6 reverse lookup, use **-a ipv6_address**.

To perform a forward DNS lookup, type **dscacheutil**, a space, **-q host -a name**, a space, and the hostname; then press Return.

```
 ● ● ●                    🖼 johnny — -zsh — 80×24
[johnny@Johnnys-MacBook-Pro ~ % dscacheutil -q host -a name server.pretendco.com ]
name: server.pretendco.com
ip_address: 10.0.1.2

johnny@Johnnys-MacBook-Pro ~ %  ▌
```

To perform a reverse DNS lookup, type **dscacheutil**, a space, **-q host -a ip_address**, a space, and the IPv4 address; then press Return.

```
● ● ●                    🖥 johnny — -zsh — 80×24
johnny@Johnnys-MacBook-Pro ~ % dscacheutil -q host -a ip_address 10.0.1.2
name: server.pretendco.com
alias: 2.1.0.10.in-addr.arpa
ip_address: 10.0.1.2

johnny@Johnnys-MacBook-Pro ~ %
```

> **NOTE ▶** The man page for **dscacheutil** warns that the **-flushcache** option, which flushes the DNS cache but also the entire Directory Services cache, "should be used in extreme cases. Validation information is used within the cache along with other techniques to ensure the OS has valid information available to it."

If you are unable to successfully return lookups, it's possible that your Mac isn't connecting to the DNS server. Use the ping command to test for basic connectivity to the DNS server IP address.

traceroute

If you are able to connect to some network resources but not others, use traceroute to determine where the connection fails. WAN and internet connections often require the data to travel through many network routers to reach their destination. The traceroute command examines every network hop between routers by sending packets with low time-to-live (TTL) fields to determine where connections fail or slow down.

```
● ● ●              🖥 johnny — traceroute support.apple.com — 80×24
johnny@Johnnys-MacBook-Pro ~ % traceroute support.apple.com
traceroute to e2063.e9.akamaiedge.net (23.7.97.98), 64 hops max, 52 byte packets
 1  10.0.1.1 (10.0.1.1)  0.850 ms  0.389 ms  0.365 ms
 2  172.16.28.1 (172.16.28.1)  0.861 ms  0.606 ms  0.571 ms
 3  96.120.24.77 (96.120.24.77)  12.298 ms  10.358 ms  15.988 ms
 4  96.110.160.189 (96.110.160.189)  9.006 ms  9.814 ms  8.957 ms
 5  be-121-ar01.area4.il.chicago.comcast.net (69.139.203.169)  10.512 ms  10.618
ms  9.776 ms
 6  be-32231-cs03.350ecermak.il.ibone.comcast.net (96.110.40.57)  11.922 ms
    be-32211-cs01.350ecermak.il.ibone.comcast.net (96.110.40.49)  13.643 ms
    be-32241-cs04.350ecermak.il.ibone.comcast.net (96.110.40.61)  18.593 ms
 7  be-2111-pe11.350ecermak.il.ibone.comcast.net (96.110.33.194)  15.669 ms
    be-2311-pe11.350ecermak.il.ibone.comcast.net (96.110.33.202)  12.898 ms
    be-2411-pe11.350ecermak.il.ibone.comcast.net (96.110.33.206)  10.580 ms
 8  as16509-2-c.seattle.wa.ibone.comcast.net (50.242.148.94)  12.563 ms
    23.30.207.30 (23.30.207.30)  23.957 ms  14.337 ms
 9  * * ae2.r02.ord01.icn.netarch.akamai.com (23.203.151.40)  20.663 ms
10  ae2.r11.ord01.ien.netarch.akamai.com (23.207.231.37)  11.345 ms *
    ae2.r12.ord01.ien.netarch.akamai.com (23.207.231.41)  34.086 ms
11  ae20.r01.border101.ord01.fab.netarch.akamai.com (23.207.231.129)  12.504 ms
* *
12  * * *
13  * * *
14  * * *
```

To verify a network TCP/IP route, use traceroute followed by an IP address of a device on the LAN that should always be accessible, such as the network router. Using a domain name assumes that your Mac is properly communicating with a DNS server, which might not be the case if you're troubleshooting connectivity issues.

If traceroute is successful, it returns a list of routers required to complete the connection and the amount of time it took for the test packets to travel to each network router. It sends three probes at each distance, so three times are listed for each hop. The delay is typically measured in milliseconds; experiencing delay times of any longer than a full second is unusual. If traceroute doesn't get a reply from a particular router at all, it shows an asterisk rather than listing the router address, but this could be because the network equipment is configured not to respond to network requests.

Once you've established successful routes to local devices, you can branch out to WAN or internet addresses. Using the traceroute command, you may find that a specific network router is the cause of the problem.

For more information about any of the commands in this lesson, use the man page for the command.

Exercise 23.1
Troubleshoot Network Connectivity

▶ **Prerequisites**

▶ You must have created the Local Administrator (Exercise 3.1, "Configure a Mac for Exercises") and Johnny Appleseed (Exercise 7.1, "Create a Standard User Account") accounts.

▶ You must have created the Static Network location (Exercise 22.1, "Configure Network Locations").

NOTE ▶ Even if you don't meet these prerequisites, reading the exercises will enhance your knowledge of the processes.

In this exercise, you intentionally misconfigure your network settings. You then use the macOS built-in troubleshooting tools to view symptoms and isolate the problem.

Break Your Network Settings

1   Log in as Johnny Appleseed.

2   Open Network preferences, then authenticate as Local Administrator.

3   Record the currently selected location so that you can return to it at the end of the exercise.

4   From the Location menu, choose Edit Locations.

5   Select the Static location, then choose Duplicate Location from the Action menu below the location list.

6   Name the new location **Broken DNS**, then click Done.

7   If necessary, switch to the Broken DNS location.

8   Click Apply.

9   Select the primary network service (the one at the top of the left sidebar), then click Advanced.

10 Click DNS.

11 If there are entries in the DNS Servers list, record them so you can reenter them, then use the Remove (–) button to remove them.

12 Click the Add (+) button under the DNS Servers list, then add the server address **127.0.0.55**.

No DNS server is available at this address, which is in a block of addresses that do not legitimately appear on any network anywhere (with the exception of 127.0.0.1, which is the loopback address and outside the scope of this guide). As a result, 127.0.0.55 is an invalid address.

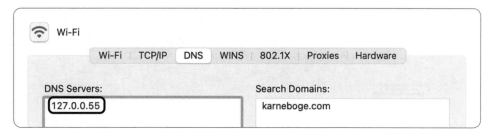

13 Click TCP/IP.

14 From the Configure IPv6 menu, choose "Link-local only."

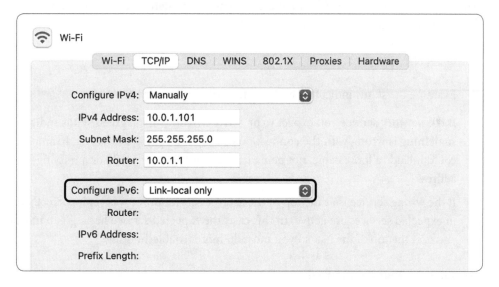

This prevents IPv6 from being an alternate internet connection.

15 Click OK, then click Apply.

Observe the Problem

1 Open Safari.

2 Type **www.apple.com** in the address bar, then press Return.

Safari attempts to load the webpage, but it doesn't get far because it's not able to reach anything. If you wait, it eventually gives up, then displays an error. Don't wait.

3 Quit Safari.

Check the Network Status in Network Preferences

When you have a network problem, one of the first things you should check is the network service status in Network preferences. Viewing the status lets you spot simple problems without performing detailed diagnostics.

1 Open Network preferences.

2 Examine the status indicators and the network services order.

If the network service you expect to be active isn't showing a green status indicator, something is wrong with the connection or a critical setting is missing. Examples could include a loose cable, not being joined to a Wi-Fi network, or a missing IP address.

If the wrong service is at the top of the list, the service order was set incorrectly or unexpected services are active. In this case, the expected service has a green indicator and is at the top of the list, so you must do more troubleshooting.

Use ping to Test Connectivity

In this section, you use the ping command. You can use ping to test network connectivity and DNS resolution.

1 Open Terminal.

Many of the macOS troubleshooting tools are available from the command-line interface.

2   In Terminal, type **ping -c 5**, followed by the domain name of the server you want to reach (**www.apple.com**).

The option -c 5 in the ping command indicates the number of ping requests to send to the host, which in this case is five.

```
● ● ●                        📁 johnny — -zsh — 80×24
johnny@Mac-17 ~ % ping -c 5 www.apple.com▮
```

3   Press Return.

After about 30 seconds, you receive a message telling you that ping couldn't resolve www.apple.com. The message indicates that ping wasn't able to use DNS to look up, or resolve, the name www.apple.com and match it to an IP address to send the ping to. In this case, you know that the name www.apple.com is valid because you have used it before, so this indicates that something is wrong with DNS.

```
● ● ●                        📁 johnny — -zsh — 80×24
[johnny@Mac-17 ~ % ping -c 5 www.apple.com                                      ]
ping: cannot resolve www.apple.com: Unknown host
johnny@Mac-17 ~ % ▮
```

Although this message gives you some information about the problem, it still doesn't tell you where the problem is. It can be hard to differentiate between a DNS problem and a complete network failure. If DNS resolution is the only thing failing, it can mimic a complete failure because almost all network access starts with (and depends on) a DNS lookup. If the network is completely disconnected, most attempts to use the network fail at the DNS step, so the only symptoms are DNS errors.

Try to reach a server by its numeric IP address to distinguish between a DNS-only problem and a complete network failure. This approach bypasses the usual DNS lookup and works even if DNS is broken.

4   At the prompt, type **ping -c 5 8.8.8.8**.

This is an easy-to-remember address of a public DNS server maintained by Google.

5   Press Return.

This time, ping reaches its destination successfully and shows statistics for its five test pings. This tells you that your basic network connectivity is OK and that it's likely only DNS isn't working.

```
● ● ●                    🖥 johnny — -zsh — 80×24
[johnny@Mac-17 ~ % ping -c 5 8.8.8.8
PING 8.8.8.8 (8.8.8.8): 56 data bytes
64 bytes from 8.8.8.8: icmp_seq=0 ttl=115 time=28.167 ms
64 bytes from 8.8.8.8: icmp_seq=1 ttl=115 time=31.345 ms
64 bytes from 8.8.8.8: icmp_seq=2 ttl=115 time=26.631 ms
64 bytes from 8.8.8.8: icmp_seq=3 ttl=115 time=31.086 ms
64 bytes from 8.8.8.8: icmp_seq=4 ttl=115 time=29.492 ms

--- 8.8.8.8 ping statistics ---
5 packets transmitted, 5 packets received, 0.0% packet loss
round-trip min/avg/max/stddev = 26.631/29.344/31.345/1.778 ms
johnny@Mac-17 ~ % ▊
```

Use the host Command to Test DNS

Even though the ping error message "cannot resolve" indicates a DNS problem, try the host command to discover whether it reveals a more specific error.

1   In Terminal, type **host www.apple.com**.

The host command is used for performing DNS lookups. You use it to convert names to IP addresses, and vice versa.

2   Press Return.

After about 30 seconds, you receive a message that the connection timed out and that no servers could be reached. This is the same result you got using the ping command.

```
● ● ●                    🖥 johnny — -zsh — 80×24
[johnny@Mac-17 ~ % host www.apple.com
;; connection timed out; no servers could be reached
johnny@Mac-17 ~ % ▊
```

Switch to Working Network Settings

1   From the Apple menu, choose Locations, then click the Static location.

Unlike the Broken DNS location, this location has valid settings, so your internet connectivity should be back to normal.

2   In Terminal, type **host www.apple.com** again.

```
● ● ●                    🔳 johnny — -zsh — 80×24
[johnny@Mac-17 ~ % host www.apple.com
www.apple.com is an alias for www.apple.com.edgekey.net.
www.apple.com.edgekey.net is an alias for www.apple.com.edgekey.net.globalredir.
akadns.net.
www.apple.com.edgekey.net.globalredir.akadns.net is an alias for e6858.dsce9.aka
maiedge.net.
e6858.dsce9.akamaiedge.net has address 23.202.195.131
e6858.dsce9.akamaiedge.net has IPv6 address 2001:559:19:5c94::1aca
e6858.dsce9.akamaiedge.net has IPv6 address 2001:559:19:5c93::1aca
e6858.dsce9.akamaiedge.net has IPv6 address 2001:559:19:5c8e::1aca
e6858.dsce9.akamaiedge.net has IPv6 address 2001:559:19:5c92::1aca
e6858.dsce9.akamaiedge.net has IPv6 address 2001:559:19:5c90::1aca
johnny@Mac-17 ~ % █
```

This time the host command reaches a DNS server and finds the IP address corresponding to the domain name www.apple.com.

The address displayed by host may differ from the address in the figure because the Apple website is hosted by a number of servers throughout the internet and uses DNS to direct you to a server near your network location for faster access.

If you knew the address the name should resolve to, you could verify that, but the fact that it resolved to an IP address at all is a good indication that DNS is working.

The stdout of the host command may also display both an IPv6 address and an IPv4 address, because network services in macOS Big Sur are configured to use IPv6 automatically.

3   Open Safari, then try browsing a website.

This time, Safari is able to load webpages from the internet.

Network Services

Manage Network Services

In this lesson, you learn about network services architecture. Then you're introduced to the key network service apps built into macOS. You learn how macOS accesses popular file-sharing services. Finally, you learn techniques for trouble-shooting network services.

Reference 24.1
Network Services

Shared network services are defined by client software (designed to access the service) and server software (designed to provide the service). The client and server software use network protocols and standards to communicate with each other.

By adhering to standards, software developers create unique yet compatible network client and server software, so you can choose the software tool that best fits your needs. For instance, you can use the built-in macOS Mail client created by Apple to access mail services provided by Apple, Microsoft, Google, Yahoo, and other service providers.

Network Services Software

Client software can be in the form of dedicated apps, as is the case with many internet services, like email and web browsing. Other client software is integrated into macOS (for example, file and print services). In either case, when you establish a network service connection, settings for

GOALS

► Describe how macOS accesses shared network services

► Configure built-in macOS network apps

► Browse and access network file services using the Finder

► Troubleshoot network shared service issues

services are saved to preference files on the local Mac. These client preferences often include resource locations and authentication information.

Server software provides access to the shared resource. Server-side settings include configuration options, protocol settings, and account information.

When you troubleshoot a network service, you must know the port numbers or ranges that a service uses. For instance, the standard TCP port for web traffic is port 80. Apple maintains a list of commonly used network services and their associated TCP or UDP ports at Apple Support article HT202944, "TCP and UDP ports used by Apple software products."

Network Service Identification

To access a network service, you must know the service's local network or internet location. Some network services feature dynamic service discovery, which enables you to locate a network service by browsing a list of available services. Or you must manually identify the service location with a network host address or name.

macOS can locate network services and appropriate network service resources. You can use Internet Account preferences to configure these services.

After you locate and connect to a network service, you must often prove your identity (authenticate) to the service provider. Successful *authentication* to a network service is usually the last step in establishing a connection to it. After you establish a connection, security technologies are normally in place to ensure that you're allowed to access only certain resources. This process is called *authorization*. Both of these fundamental network service concepts, authentication and authorization, are covered in this lesson and the next, Lesson 25, "Manage Host Sharing and Personal Firewall."

Dynamic Service Discovery

macOS supports dynamic network service discovery protocols to help you find the resources you need in situations like the following:

▸   You join a new network without knowing the exact names of all its available resources.

▸   The shared resource you need is hosted from another client computer that doesn't have a DNS hostname or the same IP address every time.

Dynamic network service discovery protocols enable you to browse local area network (LAN) and wide area network (WAN) resources without knowing specific service addresses. Some devices that provide network services advertise the availability of their services on the network. As available network resources change, or as you move your client to different networks, the service discovery protocols dynamically update the list of available services.

macOS uses dynamic network service discovery. For example, dynamic network service discovery enables you to browse for available network file shares with the Finder or to locate new network printers from Printers & Scanners preferences. Other network apps built into macOS use service discovery to locate shared resources, including Image Capture and Photos. Third-party network apps also use dynamic network service discovery.

The discovery protocol only helps you locate available services. After it provides your Mac with a list of available services, its job is done. When you connect to a discovered service, your Mac establishes a connection to the service using the service's protocol. For example, the Bonjour service discovery protocol can provide the Finder with a list of available screen-sharing systems, but when you select another Mac from this list, your Mac establishes a screen-sharing connection to the other Mac using the Virtual Network Computing (VNC) service, which uses the Remote Frame Buffer (RFB) protocol.

Bonjour

Bonjour is the Apple implementation of Zero Configuration Networking, or Zeroconf, a collection of standards drafts that provide automatic local network configuration, naming, and service discovery. Bonjour uses a broadcast discovery protocol known as multicast DNS (mDNS) on UDP port 5353.

Bonjour is the primary set of dynamic network service discovery protocols used by macOS native services and apps. Bonjour is based on TCP/IP standards, so it integrates well with other TCP/IP-based network services. macOS also includes support for Wide-Area Bonjour, which lets you browse WAN resources as well as LAN resources.

Local Bonjour requires no configuration. Wide-Area Bonjour requires that you configure your Mac to use a DNS server and search domain that supports the protocol. See support.apple.com/guide/deployment-reference-macos/apd0401947ff in the Deployment Reference for Mac for more information on Bonjour.

Server Message Block

Originally designed by Microsoft, Server Message Block (SMB) is the most common network service for sharing files and printers. SMB also includes a network discovery service that runs on UDP ports 137 and 138 and TCP ports 137 and 139. Most current operating systems that provide support for SMB sharing also support dynamic discovery with SMB.

Network Host Addressing

You can reach a network host by its IP address, but you can also use other technologies that give network hosts human-friendly network names. Network host identification methods include:

▶ IP address—An IP address can always be used to establish a network connection.

▶ DNS hostname—Your Mac has a hostname configured by one of two methods. Your Mac attempts to resolve its hostname by performing a DNS reverse lookup on its primary IP address. If your Mac can't resolve a hostname from the DNS server, it uses the Bonjour name instead.

▶ Computer name—Other Apple devices use this to identify your Mac for AirDrop peer-to-peer file sharing and for Finder browsing. The computer name is part of the Apple Bonjour implementation, and you set it in Sharing preferences.

▶ Bonjour name—Bonjour is the macOS primary dynamic network discovery protocol; in addition, Bonjour provides a convenient naming system for use on a local network. The Bonjour name is usually similar to the computer name, but it conforms to DNS naming standards and ends with .local. This allows the Bonjour name to be supported by other operating systems. When you use Sharing preferences to edit the Computer Name field and then click Edit, your Mac displays the updated Bonjour name, which is displayed in the Local Hostname field.

▶ NetBIOS name—This name is used for the legacy Windows dynamic network discovery protocols as part of the SMB service. This name is automatically generated based on the name that you set in Sharing preferences. You can verify it in the Network preferences by selecting an interface, clicking Advanced, clicking the WINS button, and inspecting the NetBIOS Name field.

Host network identification examples

Identifier	Example	Set by	Used by
IP Address	10.0.1.17	Network preferences	Any network host
DNS hostname	mac17.pretendco.com	Defined by DNS server	Any network host
Computer name	Mac 17	Sharing preferences	macOS Bonjour or AirDrop
Bonjour name	Mac-17.local	Sharing preferences	Bonjour hosts
SMB (NetBIOS) name	MACBOOKPRO-3C30	Network preferences	SMB hosts

Reference 24.2
Configure Network Service Apps

Services like email can work on a local level, but these services are also communicating across separate networks and between servers. macOS includes client apps that access different network services.

Although this guide focuses on the network client software built into macOS, many excellent third-party network clients are available for Mac. When you troubleshoot a network access problem, using an alternative network client is a good way to determine whether the issue is your primary client software or the service you're attempting to use.

Safari

The Hypertext Transfer Protocol (HTTP) handles web communication for Safari using TCP port 80. Secure web communication (HTTPS) encrypts HTTP over a Secure Sockets Layer (SSL) or, more recently, over a Transport Layer Security (TLS) connection that by default uses TCP port 443.

Generally, little additional network configuration is required to use web services. You must provide the web browser with the Uniform Resource Locator (URL) or web address of the resource to which you want to connect. Many web servers default to the most secure TLS communication even if you don't specify HTTPS in the URL. The only exception to not needing to configure anything to access web services is if you have to configure web proxies, as described in Lesson 22, "Manage Advanced Network Settings."

Internet Accounts Preferences

Internet Accounts preferences enable you to configure network service accounts. When you enter a network service account in Internet Accounts preferences, it configures appropriate network service apps built into macOS.

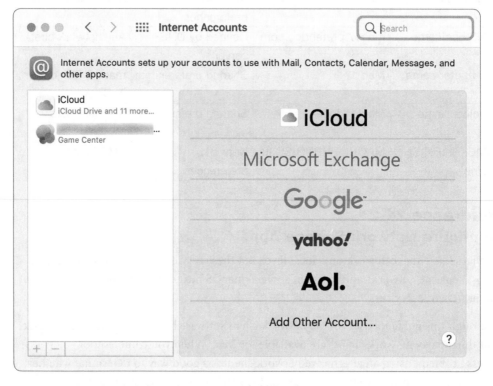

Through Internet Accounts preferences, you can configure macOS to use network service accounts for Apple iCloud, Microsoft Exchange, Google, Yahoo, and AOL. The Add Other Account option is covered later in this section.

> **NOTE ▶** For Microsoft Exchange support, macOS Big Sur requires Microsoft Office 365, Exchange 2016, Exchange 2013, or Exchange Server 2010. Installing the latest service packs from Microsoft for these services is recommended. For more information, see Apple Support article SP833, "macOS Big Sur - Technical Specifications."

Internet Accounts preferences also includes support for services popular in countries whose primary language isn't English. These services appear when you select the appropriate Language & Region preferences.

Each service type includes support for built-in macOS apps and services. When you sign in to a service that provides multiple features, like Microsoft Exchange, Google, or Yahoo, you configure multiple apps, such as Mail, Notes, Calendar, Reminders, and Contacts. iCloud provides support for even more features, including iCloud Drive, Photos, Safari, iCloud Keychain, Find My, and FaceTime.

Configure Network Service Accounts

Use Internet Accounts preferences to configure network service accounts. Click an included service provider to sign up. Your Mac displays a service sign-in dialog. Most services provide their own authentication dialogs.

If your Mac doesn't display the Internet Accounts list of services, click the small Add (+) button at the lower-left corner of the preferences pane.

If you sign in to a service that offers multiple features, after you authenticate you can enable those features. You can also return to Internet Accounts preferences to enable or disable a feature. From Internet Accounts, click the Details button to verify or reenter your account information.

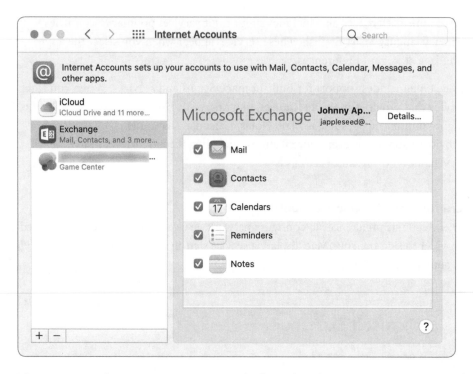

If you must configure an internet service that's not listed in Internet Accounts preferences, or you have to configure a local service provided by your organization, click Add Other Account at the bottom of the services list. Your Mac displays a dialog that lets you manually configure services for Mail, Calendar, Contacts, and Game Center. If you add a service this way, you'll probably have to define additional configuration information. This information should be provided to you by an administrator of the service.

Configure Mail

Mail supports standard email protocols and their encrypted counterparts, along with a variety of authentication standards. Mail also includes support for Microsoft Exchange–based services.

Configure Mail with the Internet Accounts pane of System Preferences. In Mail, choose Mail > Accounts to open Internet Accounts preferences. Or you can use a configuration profile to configure Mail.

Mail also includes its own account setup assistant that walks you through configuring mail account settings. The assistant starts automatically if you open Mail but haven't yet set up an account. Choose Mail > Add Account to start it.

When you select one of these default mail account types, the assistant attempts to automatically determine the appropriate mail protocol, as well as settings for security, and authentication. This automated configuration includes support for the Autodiscovery feature of Microsoft Exchange Server. When you set up a mail account here, macOS attempts to configure Notes, Calendar, Reminders, and Contacts, too.

If you want to configure Mail for an account type not listed in the defaults, select the Other Mail Account option. After you enter basic mail account information, the assistant attempts to determine the appropriate mail settings. If your mail service uses a nonstandard configuration or is unreachable, you might have to manually enter the mail service settings here. If necessary, work with the service administrator to obtain the appropriate configuration settings.

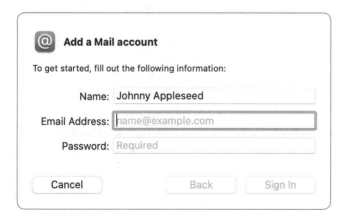

To adjust mail service settings, choose Mail > Preferences to access advanced options. When the Mail preferences window opens, click the Accounts button in the toolbar to view and manage Mail accounts.

Mail supports the following email services:

▶   Standard mailbox access protocols—The standard protocol used between mail clients and mail servers for receiving mail is either Post Office Protocol (POP) on TCP port 110 or Internet Message Access Protocol (IMAP) on TCP port 143. Both protocols can be encrypted with a TLS connection. By default, encrypted POP uses TCP port 995 and encrypted IMAP uses TCP port 993. iCloud defaults to secure IMAP.

▶   Standard mail-sending protocols—The standard protocol used for sending mail from clients to servers and from server to server is Simple Mail Transfer Protocol (SMTP) on TCP port 25. SMTP can be encrypted with a TLS connection on port 25, 465, or 587. The port used for secure SMTP varies by mail server function and administrator preference. iCloud defaults to secure SMTP.

▶   Exchange-based mail service—Mail communicates using the Exchange Web Services (EWS) protocol. EWS uses the standard ports for web traffic: TCP port 80 for standard transport and TCP port 443 for secure transport.

Configure Notes

When you add your internet accounts to Notes, you can keep your notes with you no matter which device you're using.

If you keep notes in iCloud, you can view and edit them there. Plus, you can add new notes and lock already-created ones. You can also add people so that you can collaborate with them. Within a note, you can apply paragraph styles, checklists, and most media types (such as tables, scanned documents, photos, video, freehand-drawn scribbles, and map locations).

Configure a New Notes Account

Ideally, you configure Notes with other services through iCloud or Internet Accounts preferences. In Notes, choose Notes > Accounts, which opens Internet Accounts preferences. You can use Internet Accounts preferences to configure Notes without configuring iCloud or Mail.

Configure Calendar and Reminders

Calendar integrates with Mail and Maps to help you plan your day. Although Calendar manages your calendar on your local Mac, it also integrates with network calendar services based on the EWS or CalDAV protocols. CalDAV, or Calendaring Extensions to WebDAV, extends WebDAV (Web Distributed Authoring and Versioning), which is an extension of HTTP.

Ideally, you configure Calendar with Mail through Internet Accounts preferences or a configuration profile. In Calendar, choose Calendar > Accounts. macOS redirects you to Internet Accounts preferences.

Calendar includes an account setup assistant, which walks you through configuring Calendar account settings. This assistant doesn't start when you open Calendar; choose Calendar > Add Account to start it.

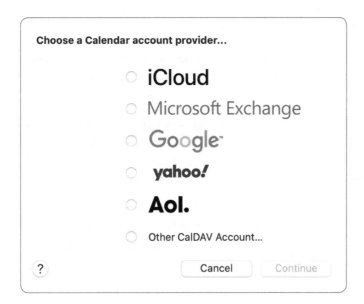

When you select one of the default calendar account types shown in the previous screenshot, the assistant attempts to determine the appropriate calendar service security and authentication settings. Calendar includes support for the Autodiscovery feature of Microsoft Exchange Server. When you set up a calendar account, macOS attempts to configure Mail, Notes, Reminders, and Contacts, too.

If you must configure Calendar for an account type not listed in the defaults, select the Other CalDAV Account option. After you enter your mail address and account password, the assistant attempts to determine the appropriate CalDAV settings. If your mail service uses a nonstandard configuration or is unreachable, you might have to manually enter the CalDAV service settings here. If necessary, work with the service administrator to obtain the appropriate configuration settings.

To edit Calendar service settings, from the Calendar menu choose Calendar Preferences. When Calendar preferences opens, click the Accounts button in the toolbar to view and manage calendar service accounts.

Reminders helps you to keep a personal to-do list. You can save Reminders to-do lists on all of your Apple devices when you configure Reminders for access to calendar services. This is because Reminders uses EWS or CalDAV network calendar services to save notes. Reminders creates to-do calendar events and manages these events.

You configure Reminders with other services through Internet Accounts preferences or with a configuration profile. Use Internet Accounts preferences to configure Reminders. You can configure Reminders without configuring Calendar—but you still need an EWS or CalDAV calendar service from a network service provider.

Calendar and Reminders support the following network calendar services:

▶ CalDAV collaborative calendaring—Calendar supports the CalDAV network calendar standard. This standard uses WebDAV as a transport mechanism on TCP port 8008 or 8443 for encrypted communication, but CalDAV adds the administrative processes required to facilitate calendar and scheduling collaboration. CalDAV is an open standard, so any vendor can create software that provides or connects to CalDAV services.

▶ Internet-based calendar services—Calendar and Reminders use internet-based calendar services, including iCloud, Yahoo, and Google calendar services. These services are based on CalDAV and use the encrypted HTTPS protocol over TCP port 443.

▶ Exchange-based calendaring service—Calendar includes support for this calendar service. The macOS Exchange integration relies on EWS, which uses TCP port 80 for standard transport and TCP port 443 for secure transport.

▶ Calendar web publishing and subscription—Calendar enables you to share your calendar information by publishing iCalendar files to WebDAV-enabled web servers. Because WebDAV is an extension to the HTTP protocol, it runs over TCP port 80, or TCP port 443 if encrypted. You can subscribe to iCalendar files, identified by the filename extension .ics, hosted on WebDAV servers; just provide Calendar with the URL of the iCalendar file.

▶ Calendar email invitation—Calendar is integrated with Mail to send and receive calendar invitations as iCalendar email attachments. The transport mechanism is whatever your primary mail account is configured to use. Although this method isn't a calendar standard, most popular mail and calendar clients can use it.

Configure Contacts

Contacts integrates with network contact services based on EWS, CardDAV (Card Distributed Authoring and Versioning), or LDAP (Lightweight Directory Access Protocol).

Ideally, you configure Contacts through Internet Accounts preferences or a configuration profile. Contacts also features an easy-to-use setup assistant for configuring specific contact or directory network service accounts. Choose Contacts > Add Account to start it.

Choose a Contacts account provider...

○ **iCloud**

○ Microsoft Exchange

○ Google™

○ yahoo!

○ **Aol.**

○ Other Contacts Account...

?   Cancel   Continue

When you select one of these default contacts account types, the assistant attempts to determine the appropriate account settings. This includes support for the Autodiscovery feature of Microsoft Exchange Server. When you set up a Contacts account here, macOS attempts to configure Mail, Notes, Calendar, and Reminders, too.

If you must configure Contacts for an account type not listed in the defaults, select the last option, Other Contacts Account. Contacts also supports CardDAV and LDAP account types. Choose the account type from the menu, and then provide the server and authentication information. If necessary, work with the service administrator to obtain the appropriate configuration settings.

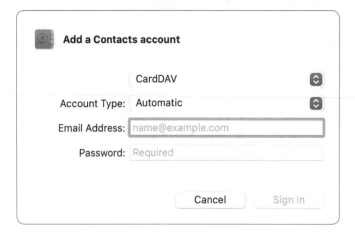

If you must make changes to contact service settings, choose Contacts > Preferences. When the Contacts preferences window opens, click the Accounts button in the toolbar to view and manage contact service accounts.

Contacts supports the following network contact services:

▶ CardDAV contacts service—Contacts supports a network contacts service standard known as CardDAV. This standard uses WebDAV as a transport mechanism on TCP port 8800 or 8843 for encrypted communication. CardDAV is an open standard, so any vendor can create software that provides or connects to CardDAV services.

▶ Internet-based contact services—Contacts can use a variety of internet-based contact services, including iCloud, Google, and Yahoo contact services. All of these services are based on CardDAV and use the encrypted HTTPS protocol over TCP port 443.

▶ Exchange-based contact service—Contacts includes support for this contact sharing service. The macOS Exchange integration relies on EWS, which uses TCP port 80 for standard transport and TCP port 443 for secure transport.

▶ Directory service contacts—Contacts can search contact databases using LDAP, the standard for network directory services, which uses TCP port 389 for standard transport and TCP port 636 for secure transport. You can configure Contacts for LDAP services either from its account setup assistant or through integration with the macOS systemwide directory service, in Users & Groups preferences.

Configure Messages

With Messages, you can text, add images and other files, start a video or audio call, share your screen, and more. Messages requires the push-based messaging service iMessage, which also enables you to communicate with iOS and iPadOS devices.

Ideally, Messages is configured for iMessage when you sign in to iCloud. If no account is configured when you open Messages, Messages opens its account setup assistant and walks you through configuring iMessage account settings. You can enter any valid Apple ID to configure iMessage.

Messages uses the iMessage service, which is unique to Apple. The iMessage protocol is facilitated by the Apple Push Notification service (APNs), which uses TCP port 5223, and falls back on Wi-Fi only to port 443. APNs is efficient for devices that rely on battery power and might lose network connectivity. This makes the iMessage service ideal for messaging with mobile Mac computers and iOS and iPadOS devices. Messages is limited to a single iMessage account per computer user account.

If you're signed in to the iMessage service using the same Apple ID on your Mac and an iPhone running iOS 8 or later, you can send and receive Short Message Service (SMS) messages with the iMessage protocol through an iPhone cellular connection. You must manually enable this feature on your iPhone in Settings > Messages before you can use SMS messaging on your Mac. For more information, see Apple Support article HT204681, "Use Continuity to connect your Mac, iPhone, iPad, iPod touch, and Apple Watch."

To edit Messages settings, choose Messages > Preferences. The General pane opens by default.

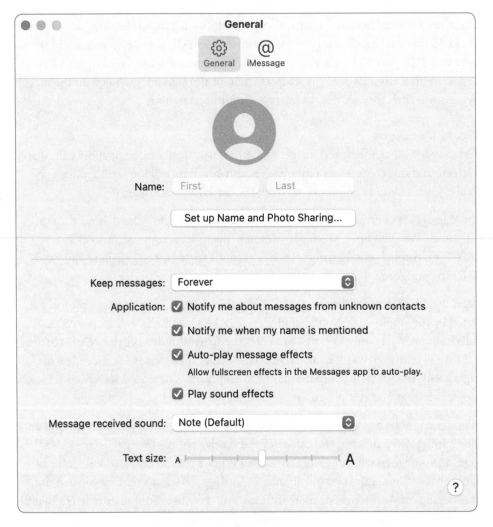

If you need to edit message service settings, click the iMessage button in the Messages preferences toolbar to edit your account settings or blocked numbers. To keep your entire message history updated and available on all your devices, select "Enable Messages in iCloud." For more information, see Apple Support article HT208532, "Use Messages in iCloud."

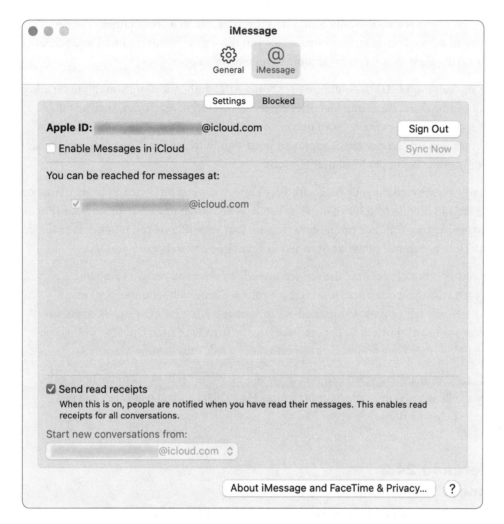

For more information about using Messages, see Apple Support article HT202549, "Use Messages with your Mac." If you're having trouble with the iMessage service, verify availability of APNs with Apple Support article HT202078, "If you use FaceTime and iMessage behind a firewall."

Configure FaceTime

FaceTime provides audio and video-conferencing abilities, including the ability to answer or call standard phone numbers with a compatible iPhone. Similar to the iMessage service, FaceTime is unique to Apple and uses APNs to start audio or video communications.

Ideally, FaceTime is automatically configured if you sign in to iCloud. Otherwise, FaceTime includes an account setup assistant that walks you through configuring FaceTime account settings. This assistant starts if no account is set when you open FaceTime.

Enter any valid Apple ID to configure FaceTime. After authentication, you might be asked to choose additional FaceTime identifiers that can be used to reach you, such as other email accounts or, if you have FaceTime on your iPhone, other mobile numbers. Unlike with other network service client apps, you must sign in to use FaceTime and you can sign in to only one account per local user account.

To handle phone calls on your Mac with FaceTime, you must be signed in to FaceTime on your Mac and iPhone with iOS 8 or later. You have to sign in to FaceTime on your iPhone first to enable FaceTime cell phone calls. Ensure that your iPhone cell number is enabled in FaceTime preferences on your Mac. Go to FaceTime preferences to do this.

After you sign in to FaceTime, the service is ready to send and receive FaceTime calls, even when you quit FaceTime. To turn off FaceTime calls, choose FaceTime > Turn FaceTime Off or press Command-K. To start receiving FaceTime calls again, use the same keyboard shortcut or choose FaceTime > Turn FaceTime On. Sign out of your account from FaceTime preferences to permanently halt calls to your Mac.

FaceTime uses many standard and non-reserved TCP and UDP ports to facilitate calls. Verify available ports in Apple Support article HT202078, "If you use FaceTime and iMessage behind a firewall."

Reference 24.3
Connect to File-Sharing Services

The Finder provides two ways to connect to a network file system:

▶ Browse shared resources in the Finder Network folder.

▶ Enter the server address of the server that provides the file service.

File-Sharing Services

Many protocols transfer files across networks and the internet. The most efficient are those that share file systems. Network file servers can make file systems available to your Mac across the network.

Client software built into the Finder can mount a network file service much as it would mount a locally connected storage volume. After a network file service is mounted to your Mac, you can read, write, and manipulate files and folders as if you were accessing a local file system.

Access privileges to network file services are defined by the same ownership and permissions architecture used by local file systems. Details on file systems, ownership, and permissions are covered in Lesson 13, "Manage Permissions and Sharing."

macOS provides built-in support for these network file service protocols:

▶ Server Message Block version 3 (SMB 3) on TCP ports 139 and 445—This is the default (and preferred) file-sharing protocol for OS X Yosemite 10.10 and later. Historically, the SMB protocol was mainly used by Windows systems, but many other platforms have adopted support for some version of this protocol. The SMB 3 implementation in macOS works with advanced SMB features such as end-to-end encryption (if enabled on the server), per-packet signatures and validation, Distributed File Service (DFS) architecture, resource compounding, large maximum transmission unit (MTU) support, and aggressive performance caching. macOS maintains backward compatibility with older SMB standards.

▶ Apple Filing Protocol (AFP) version 3 on TCP port 548 or encrypted over Secure Shell (SSH) on TCP port 22—This is the legacy Apple network file service. The current version of AFP is compatible with the features of the Mac OS Extended file system. Volumes formatted with Apple File System (APFS) can't be shared over AFP.

▶ Network File System (NFS) version 4, which may use many TCP or UDP ports— Used primarily by UNIX systems, NFS supports many advanced file-system features used by macOS.

▶ WebDAV on TCP port 80 (HTTP) or encrypted on TCP port 443 (HTTPS)— This protocol is an extension to the common HTTP service and provides read/write file services.

▶ File Transfer Protocol (FTP) on TCP ports 20 and 21 or encrypted on TCP port 989 and 990 (FTPS)—FTP is supported by nearly every computing platform. The Finder supports read capability for FTP or FTPS shares. FTPS (FTP-SSL) is different from SFTP (SSH File Transfer Protocol). FTPS uses SSL (or TLS) encryption on TCP port 990, and SFTP uses SSH encryption on TCP port 22. The Finder supports SFTP, and you can use Terminal to use FTPS and SFTP.

Browse File-Sharing Services

The Network folder displays a collection of dynamically discovered network file sharing services (also referred to as file services), screen-sharing services, and currently mounted file systems, including manually mounted ones. The Network folder constantly changes based on information gathered from the Bonjour network service discovery protocol, so you can browse screen-sharing services offered by other Mac computers and SMB and AFP file services.

You can go to the Network folder in two ways:

▶   Click Network in the Finder sidebar.

▶   Choose Go > Network (or press Shift-Command-K).

You can browse for dynamically discovered file services in the Network folder in these two locations:

▶   The Finder sidebar

    If Network doesn't appear in the Finder sidebar, choose Go > Network.

▶   The Open dialog of any app

Smaller networks might have only one level of network services. If you have a larger network that features multiple service discovery domains, they appear as subfolders inside the Network folder. Each subfolder is named by the domain it represents. Items inside the domain subfolders represent shared resources configured for that network area.

To browse for and connect to an SMB or AFP file service, double-click the icon for the file service in the Finder Network folder (or if you're showing the Network folder items in columns, just click the icon for the file service to select it).

NOTE ▸ The behavior of the Network folder varies slightly depending on whether you're viewing the Network folder items as icons, as a list, in a column, or in a gallery.

If you use the Finder to connect to a file service, and the service supports SMB and AFP, macOS defaults to using SMB. It uses the most secure version of SMB that the file service supports.

The first time you connect to a file service, your Mac might display a dialog that asks you to confirm that you are connecting to the server you expect. Your Mac might also display this dialog each time you connect.

Automatic File-Sharing Service Authentication

When you attempt to connect to a Mac that provides file-sharing services, your Mac attempts to authenticate using one of three methods:

▸ If you're using Kerberos single sign-on authentication, your Mac attempts to authenticate to the selected Mac using your Kerberos credentials.

▸ If you're using non-Kerberos authentication but you connected to the selected Mac before and chose to save the authentication information to your keychain, your Mac attempts to use the saved information.

▸ Your Mac attempts to authenticate as a guest user.

If your Mac authenticates to the selected Mac, the Finder shows you the account name it connected with (or Guest if it connected as a guest user) and lists the shared items available to this account.

After you make the connection, open a shared item to make it available (also known as *mounting* the shared item).

If you're viewing the Network folder items in columns, select a shared item to mount it. Otherwise, if you're viewing the Network folder items as icons or in a list you can mount a shared item with any of the following methods:

▶   Double-click the shared item.

▶   Select the shared item, then choose File > Open.

▶   Select the shared item, then press Command-O.

The Finder displays an eject button next to any shared item that is already mounted. If you're viewing the Network folder items in a list, shared items are displayed with Sharepoint in the Kind column.

Manual File-Sharing Service Authentication

If your Mac was unable to connect to the selected Mac, or if you want to authenticate with a different account, click the Connect As button to open an authentication dialog.

You can then authenticate to a sharing service using one of three methods:

▶ If Guest is available, select it to connect anonymously to the file service.

▶ Select Registered User to authenticate using a local or network account known by the computer providing the shared items. Optionally, you can select the checkbox that saves this authentication information to your login keychain.

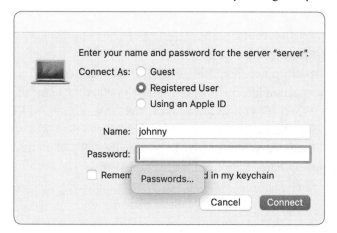

If the Passwords button appears, you can click Passwords, then enter your login password, select a saved password from your iCloud keychain or Local Items keychain, then click Fill to enter a saved password in the Password field.

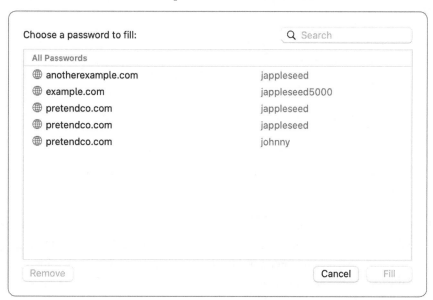

► If "Using an Apple ID" is an available option, select it to authenticate using an Apple ID. For this option to appear, your Mac and the Mac hosting the share must be running macOS (not Windows) and your local account must be associated with an Apple ID, as covered in Lesson 7, "Manage User Accounts."

Click the Connect button. Your Mac authenticates and shows you a new list of shared items that are available to the account.

Manually Connect to File-Sharing Services

Instead of browsing, you can specify a network identifier (URL) for a file service. You might also have to enter authentication information and choose or enter the name of a specific shared resource path. When you connect to an NFS, WebDAV (HTTP), or FTP service, you might have to specify the shared items or full path as part of the URL. When you connect to an SMB or AFP service, you don't have to provide the full path in the URL; you can authenticate and choose a shared item from the list of resources.

Manually Connect to SMB or AFP

To manually connect to an SMB or AFP file service from the Finder, choose Go > Connect to Server, or press Command-K, to open the Finder "Connect to Server" dialog. In the Server Address field, type **smb://** or **afp://**, followed by the server IP address, DNS hostname, computer name, or Bonjour name.

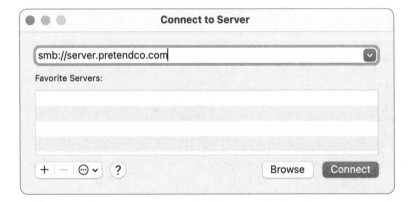

If you don't specify a protocol prefix, the "Connect to Server" dialog attempts to pick the appropriate file-sharing protocol. The default file-sharing protocol is SMB 3. Optionally, after the server address you can enter another slash and the name of a shared item. Doing so bypasses the dialog for selecting a file share.

If automatic file service authentication is available, you don't have to enter authentication information. Otherwise, a dialog appears requiring you to enter authentication information.

After you authenticate to a file service, if you have access to more than one shared folder, macOS displays the list of shared items that your account is allowed to access. Otherwise, the shared folder is automatically mounted.

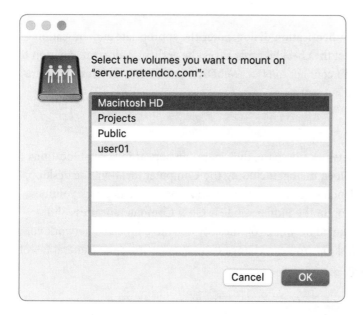

Select the shared item or items you want. Press and hold the Command key to select multiple shared items from the list. Then click OK.

Manually Connect to NFS, WebDAV, or FTP

To manually connect to an NFS, WebDAV, or FTP file service from the Finder, choose Go > Connect to Server, or press Command-K, to open the Finder "Connect to Server" dialog.

In the Server Address field, enter one of the following:

▶ **nfs://** followed by the server address, another slash, and then the absolute file path of the shared items.

▶ **https://** for WebDAV encrypted with SSL or TLS (or **http://** for unencrypted WebDAV), followed by the server address. Each WebDAV site has only one mountable share, but you can optionally enter another slash, then specify a folder inside the WebDAV share.

▶   **ftps://** for FTP encrypted with SSL or TLS (or **ftp://** for unencrypted), followed by the server address. FTP servers also have only one mountable root share, but you can optionally enter another slash, then specify a folder inside the FTP share.

Depending on the protocol settings, your Mac might display an authentication dialog. NFS connections never display an authentication dialog. The NFS protocol uses the local user that you're logged in as for authorization purposes or Kerberos single sign-on authentication.

If you are presented with an authentication dialog, enter the appropriate authentication information. You can also select the checkbox that saves the authentication information to your login keychain. When you connect to NFS, WebDAV, or FTP file services, the share mounts immediately after you authenticate.

Mounted Shares

After your Mac mounts the network file share, that share can appear in several locations from the Finder or any app's Open dialog, including the Computer location, the desktop, and the sidebar Shared list, depending on the configuration. Mounted network volumes appear at the Computer location in the Finder. Choose Go > Computer, or press Shift-Command-C, to view the mounted network volumes. By default, connected network volumes don't appear on your desktop. You can change this behavior from the General tab of the Finder Preferences dialog.

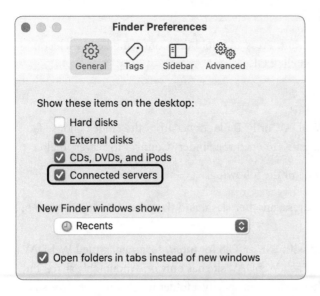

The "Connect to Server" dialog maintains a history of your past server connections. Click the menu to the right of the Server Address field to inspect the history.

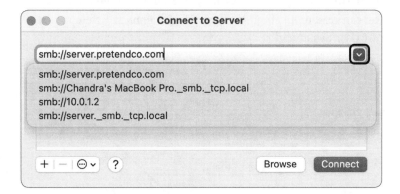

Click the Action pop-up menu ☺ and choose Clear Recent Servers to clear the past server connections history. Choose a server, then click Add (+) or Remove (–) to establish and maintain a favorite servers list.

Disconnect Mounted Shares

macOS treats mounted network volumes like locally attached volumes, so you should unmount and eject network volumes when you're done with them. Unmount and eject mounted network volumes from the Finder using the same techniques you would use on a locally connected volume, as covered in Lesson 11, "Manage File Systems and Storage."

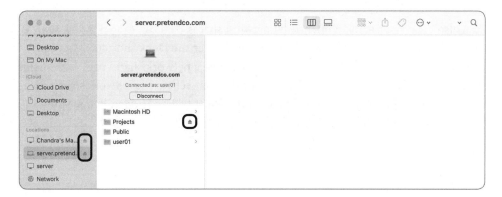

If a network change or problem disconnects your Mac from a mounted network share, your Mac tries to reconnect to the server hosting the shared items. If after several minutes your Mac can't reconnect to the server, macOS fully disconnects from the share and displays a dialog to let you know.

Automatically Connect to File Shares

You can configure automatic connections to network shared items. You can use a configuration profile or add a network share to your login items so that it mounts automatically when you log in. You can read more about managing login items in Reference 7.4, "Configure Login and Fast User Switching."

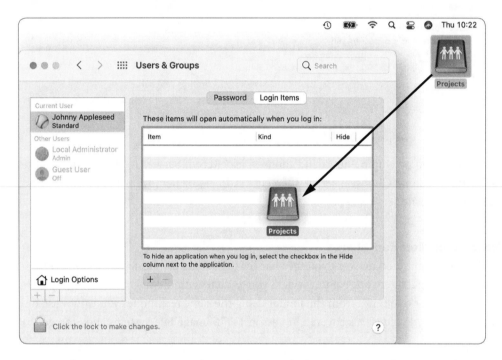

You can also create shortcuts to often-used network shares. You can drag network shares, or their enclosed items, to the right side of the Dock to create Dock shortcuts. You can also create aliases on your desktop that link to often-used network shares or specific items inside a network share. Either method automatically connects to the network share when you select an item. Creating aliases is covered in Lesson 14, "Use Hidden Items, Shortcuts, and File Archives."

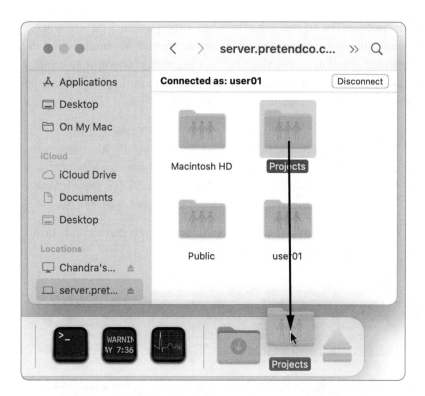

You can't drag items from the Finder sidebar to your login items or to the Dock. Instead, select the network share from the desktop or the Computer location in the Finder. From the Finder, choose Go > Computer to access the Computer location.

Reference 24.4
Troubleshoot Network Services

To troubleshoot a network issue, isolate the issue into one of three categories: local, network, or service. Most issues that involve failure to access network services probably fall under the service category. This means that you should probably focus most of your efforts on troubleshooting the service you're having issues with.

Before you troubleshoot a network service, check for general network issues. Verify that other network services work. Open Safari and navigate to local and internet websites to test general network connectivity.

Test other network services, or test connectivity from other computers on the same network. If you experience problems connecting to a file server but you can connect to web servers, your network configuration is probably fine, and you should concentrate on the file server. If you experience problems with one service, you probably don't have local or network issues. Focus your efforts on troubleshooting just that service.

If other network clients or services aren't working, your issue is likely related to local or network issues. Use Network preferences to double-check local network settings to ensure proper configuration. If other computers aren't working, you might have a widespread network issue that goes beyond troubleshooting the client Mac computers. For more information on general network troubleshooting, see Lesson 23, "Troubleshoot Network Issues."

If you experience problems with a service provided by Apple, you can check real-time Apple service status at www.apple.com/support/systemstatus.

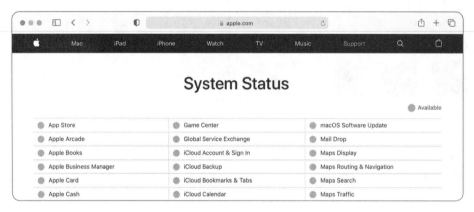

You can also check the status of developer-related Apple services, such as APNs, at developer.apple.com/system-status.

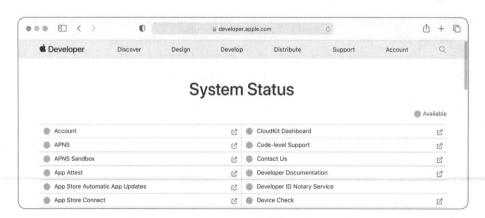

Use Terminal: ping and nc

You can use the nc (netcat) command to scan for open ports. A port scan gives you an idea about which ports are open and available to provide network services. With the nc command you can use the -z option to only scan for services on ports, without sending any data to the ports. A port scan can help you determine if any of the following conditions are true:

▶   If a port isn't open, meaning you can't connect to a port, your Mac won't be able to access a service at that port. For example, if you're trying to connect to port 80 for the HTTP service but port 80 isn't open, your Mac won't be able to access the HTTP service from that network device.

▶   If a network device offers a service but not on the port number that is standard for that service to use, you'll have trouble connecting to the service. For example, a network device might offer HTTP service on port 8080 instead of port 80.

If any of these conditions exist, then the issue is not with your Mac but with how the network service is configured or how the firewalls are configured between your Mac and the network service.

A port scan just tests whether a port is open; it doesn't test to discover whether a particular service is offered at the port.

To troubleshoot a network service, start with ping to confirm that you can connect to the computer or device that provides the service you're trying to connect to. Ping is covered in more detail in Reference 23.2, "Use Terminal to Troubleshoot Network Issues."

1   Open Terminal.

2   Enter **ping**, then press Space bar.

3   Enter the device network address or hostname.

4   Press Return.

If the ping is successful, press Control-C or Command-Period (.) to stop the ping command. Then continue with nc and the port scan.

To scan for a network service:

1   Type **nc**, then press Space bar.

2   Type **-z**, then press Space bar.

3   Enter the network address or hostname of the device that provides the service, then press Space bar.

4   Enter the starting port number, press the Minus key (–), then enter the ending port number.

5   Press Return.

```
● ● ●                    📑 johnny — -zsh — 80×11
[johnny@Johnnys-MacBook-Pro ~ % nc -z server.pretendco.com 1-1024        ]
Connection to server.pretendco.com port 22 [tcp/ssh] succeeded!
Connection to server.pretendco.com port 25 [tcp/smtp] succeeded!
Connection to server.pretendco.com port 53 [tcp/domain] succeeded!
Connection to server.pretendco.com port 80 [tcp/http] succeeded!
Connection to server.pretendco.com port 88 [tcp/kerberos] succeeded!
Connection to server.pretendco.com port 143 [tcp/imap] succeeded!
Connection to server.pretendco.com port 445 [tcp/microsoft-ds] succeeded!
Connection to server.pretendco.com port 587 [tcp/submission] succeeded!
Connection to server.pretendco.com port 993 [tcp/imaps] succeeded!
johnny@Johnnys-MacBook-Pro ~ % █
```

There are many TCP and UDP network ports. Scanning all of them is unnecessary and takes too much time. Even if you don't know the exact port number, most common ports are between 0 and 1024. Further, network administrators might view repeated network pings and broad port scans as a threat. Some network devices are configured not to respond to ping requests even when they're working properly. Avoid excessive network pings and scans (a broad port range) when you test others' servers.

Depending on the range you choose, the scan might take several minutes. The nc command lists discovered open ports with their associated network protocol. In addition, it displays each open port with the service name that's registered by the Internet Assigned Numbers Authority (www.iana.org) for that port number, regardless of the service that actually uses the port.

Troubleshoot Network Apps

To troubleshoot apps, you can troubleshoot general network services. You can also double-check app-specific configuration and preference settings. Users can inadvertently cause a problem when they change a setting.

Web Browsers

Some website designers might design a website to work with a browser other than Safari. These websites might not render properly in Safari.

To customize how Safari acts with various sites, choose Safari > Preferences (or press Command-Comma), then click Websites. In the General section, choose a category like Pop-up Windows, then in the right section of the pane, select a website and modify its setting.

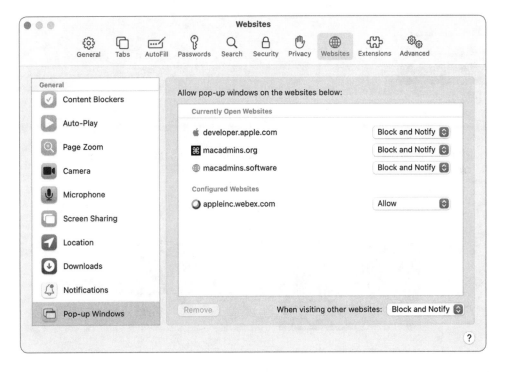

To customize the way your browser works, you can install Safari extensions. To verify the status of third-party Safari extensions, in Safari preferences click Extensions. You can turn each extension on or off.

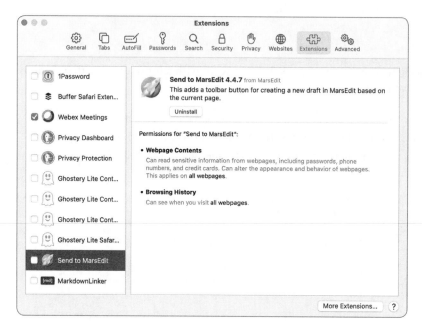

Click More Extensions to open the App Store and find more Safari extensions.

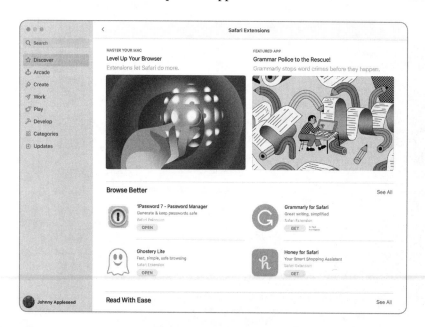

You might also try a third-party web browser.

To inspect problem webpages, open Safari preferences, click the Advanced button, and then select "Show Develop menu in menu bar."

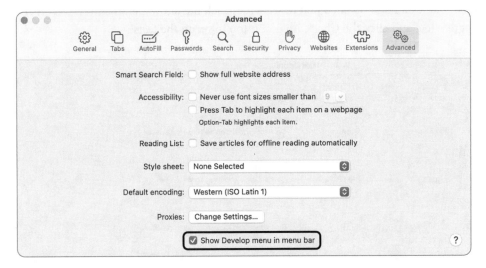

With this menu enabled, inspect the webpage details or try advanced troubleshooting, including emptying Safari caches and requesting the website with a different user agent.

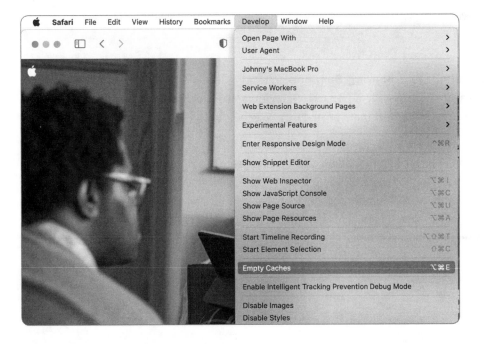

Mail

Mail includes a built-in account diagnostic tool, Mail Connection Doctor, that attempts to establish a connection with configured incoming and outgoing mail servers. Open Mail, then choose Window > Connection Doctor. If a problem is found, a suggested resolution is offered, but for a more detailed diagnostic view, click the Show Detail button to reveal the progress log, and click the Check Again button to rerun the tests.

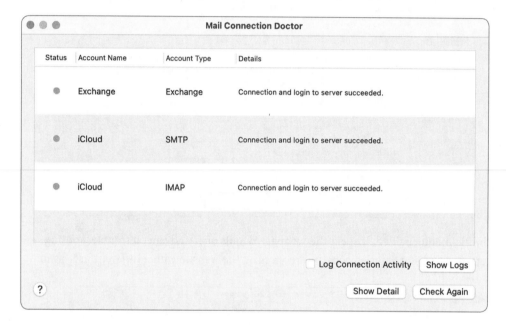

Troubleshoot File-Sharing Services

If you have problems with SMB services, try the steps in Apple Support article HT204021, "If you can't mount SMB share hosted by a Mac bound to Open Directory."

As covered in Lesson 16, "Use Metadata, Siri, and Spotlight," macOS uses separate metadata stores. The NFS and WebDAV file-sharing protocols don't support metadata of this type, so macOS splits these files into two separate files when writing to a mounted NFS or WebDAV volume. The Finder recognizes these split files and shows you only a single file. Users on other operating systems have two separate files displayed and might have trouble accessing the appropriate one.

Exercise 24.1
Use File-Sharing Services

NOTE ▶ Even if you don't meet these prerequisites, reading the exercises will enhance your knowledge of the processes.

In this exercise, you connect to a file server and copy files in both directions. You learn how to automatically mount shares and login, and manually connect to servers that may not advertise by a discovery protocol.

Connect to an SMB Share

In these steps you use the Finder sidebar to mount an SMB volume on the desktop.

1   If necessary, log in as Johnny Appleseed.

2   In the Finder, select Network in the Locations section of the sidebar, then double-click your file server.

Your Mac contacts your file server. Depending on the current permissions on the server, your Mac may log in as a guest.

If Network isn't shown, click your file server in the sidebar, then double-click your file server in the network view. In this exercise, a server named *files* is being used.

3   Click the Connect As button.

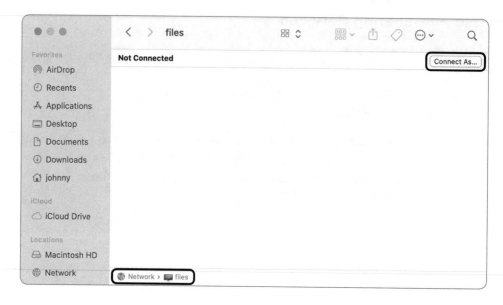

NOTE ▶ If the file server you are connecting to is a computer that has Screen Sharing turned on, you will also see a Share Screen button next to the Connect As button.

4   If the "You are attempting to connect to the server 'files'" dialog appears, click Connect.

5   When you're asked to authenticate, select Registered User, then enter the name and the password of the account with read/write access to the share.

6   Select "Remember this password in my keychain," then click Connect.

You are connected using the default file sharing protocol in macOS Big Sur, which is SMB. One share is visible, which in this exercise is called Support Essentials.

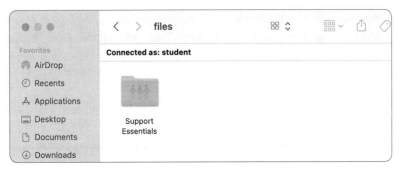

7   Copy any file or folder to your Mac by dragging it from the shared folder on your file server to your desktop.

As the file is being moved over your Desktop, a green plus indicator appears. Since you are dragging from one volume to another, this copies the file rather than moving it.

Copy Files to a Network Share

1   Open StudentMaterials/Lesson24 and locate a file named copy.rtf. Drag copy.rtf to your desktop while holding down the Option key. As in previous chapters, this copies the file.

2   Rename your copy of copy.rtf to **Student _nn_.rtf** (where _nn_ is the student number you assigned to yourself in Lesson 3, "Set Up and Configure macOS").

Press Return or click the filename, then wait a moment to rename it.

3   If necessary, connect to your file server and open the share.

Its icon appears on your desktop.

4   Drag the renamed file from your desktop to the shared folder on your file server.

Automatically Mount a Network Share

macOS provides ways for you to enable easy access to shared folders for users. This easy access allows users to be more productive. In this exercise, you configure your user preferences to mount a shared folder whenever you log in.

1   Open Users & Groups preferences.

2   With Johnny Appleseed selected in the user list, click the Login Items button.

You don't need to authenticate as an administrator to access your login items. They are a personal preference, so standard users can manage their login items.

3   Drag the shared folder icon from your desktop to the login items list.

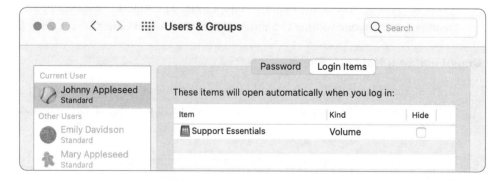

Anything in your login items list is opened every time you log in. It can include apps, documents, and folders. When you add a shared folder, you configure it to mount every time you log in. In this case, since you also saved the server account name and password to your keychain when you connected, the connection should be fully automatic.

4   Quit System Preferences.

5   Click the Eject button next to your file server icon in the Finder sidebar to disconnect from the server.

When you disconnect from the server, it automatically unmounts the shared folder you've been working in. You can also unmount them individually.

6   Log out, then log back in as Johnny Appleseed.

7   You see that the shared folder is mounted on the desktop. Because you chose to remember the password in the keychain, the share is mounted automatically.

8   Reopen Users & Groups preferences.

9   Click Login Items.

10 Select your shared folder from the login items list, then click the Remove (–) button under the list to remove it.

11 Quit System Preferences.

12 Disconnect from your file server.

Manually Connect to an SMB Share

1   In the Finder, choose Go > Connect to Server (or press Command-K).

2   In the Server Address field, enter the **smb://** prefix, followed by the IP address or fully qualified domain name (FQDN) of your file server. In this exercise, smb://files.karneboge.com is the FQDN.

3   Before you click Connect, click the Add (+) button at the bottom of the
       Favorite Servers list.

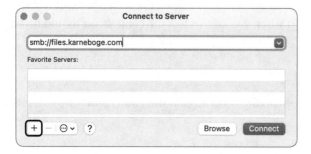

Clicking this button adds the server URL to your Favorite Servers list and is another
way to allow access to a shared folder.

4   Click Connect.

5   If necessary, click Connect at the "You are attempting to connect to the server" dialog.

6   If necessary, enter the name and the password off the account with read/write access
       to the share, then click Connect.

       If necessary, select the share you want to mount. Observe that the share is now
       mounted on the desktop.

7   Disconnect from your file server.

Manage Host Sharing and Personal Firewall

In this lesson, you focus on using macOS as both a network client and a shared resource for network and internet services. After an introduction to shared services, you delve into remotely controlling Mac computers with screen-sharing services. Then you learn how to use AirDrop—the easiest way to share files between Apple devices. You also learn how to secure access to shared resources from macOS using the built-in personal firewall. Finally, this lesson covers general troubleshooting methods to resolve issues that might arise when you attempt to share services from your Mac.

Reference 25.1
Turn On Host-Sharing Services

macOS includes an assortment of shared network services. These shared services vary in implementation and purpose, but you use them all to enable users to remotely access resources on your Mac. You can turn on and manage them from Sharing preferences. Standard users can make changes to Media Sharing and Bluetooth Sharing. For all other sharing services, standard users must click the lock in the lower-left corner of Sharing preferences and provide administrator credentials to make changes.

GOALS

- ▶ Examine and turn on host-sharing services built into macOS
- ▶ Examine and turn on Content Caching services built into macOS
- ▶ Use screen-sharing tools to access other network hosts
- ▶ Use AirDrop to share files
- ▶ Configure a personal firewall to secure shared services
- ▶ Troubleshoot sharing services

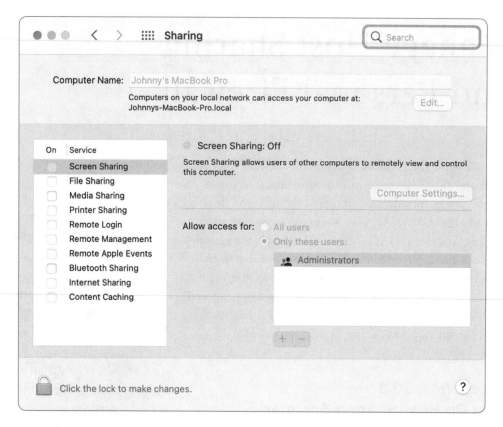

Remote users can't access services on your Mac if your Mac is in sleep mode. You can turn off your Mac computer's automatic sleep activation or turn on automatic waking for network access. To make these changes, for desktop Mac computers use Energy Saver preferences, and for notebook Mac computers use the Power Adapter pane of Battery preferences. Automatic wake on wired and wireless networks works on macOS if your network hardware supports it.

NOTE ▶ To prevent your Mac from going to sleep, select "Prevent computer from sleeping automatically when the display is off" in Energy Saver or Battery preferences, as covered in Reference 28.3, "Sleep Modes, Logout, and Shutdown." If your Mac doesn't have a display, you can use the **caffeinate** command in Terminal to keep your Mac awake.

You should recognize the security risk involved in providing a service that enables other users to control processes on your Mac. If you're providing a service that allows remote control and execution of software, it's possible for an unauthorized user to cause trouble. When you turn on these types of services, choose strong security settings. Use strong passwords and configure limited access to these services from Sharing preferences.

Configure Network Identification

You might be unable to control your Mac computer's IP address or DNS hostname, because the network administrator usually controls these settings. But as long as the Mac has properly configured TCP/IP settings, as outlined in Lesson 21, "Manage Basic Network Settings," your configuration is complete for these two identifiers. If your Mac has multiple IP addresses or DNS hostnames properly configured, it also accepts connections from those.

For dynamic network discovery protocols, though, your Mac uses network identification that can be set locally by an administrator. By default, your Mac automatically chooses a name based on either its DNS name or the name of the user created with Setup Assistant. However, at any time an administrator user can change the Mac computer's network identifier from the Sharing preferences. Just enter a name in the Computer Name field, and the system sets the name for each available discovery protocol.

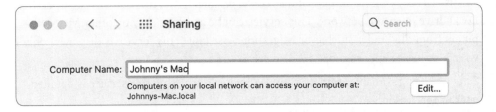

For example, if you enter the computer name **Johnny's Mac**, the Bonjour name is set to Johnnys-Mac.local. If the name you choose is already taken by another local device, the Mac automatically appends a number to the end of the name.

The local Bonjour service needs no additional configuration, but if you want to set a custom Bonjour name, click the Edit button below the Computer Name field to reveal the Local Hostname field. From this interface, you can also register your Mac computer's identification for Wide-Area Bonjour. Wide-Area Bonjour uses an intermediary service to facilitate Bonjour browsing to networks outside the computer's current subnet. If this service is available on your network, select the "Use dynamic global hostname" checkbox to reveal the Wide-Area Bonjour settings.

Use this name to reach this computer from machines on your
local subnet.

Local Hostname: | Johnnys-Mac .local |

☑ Use dynamic global hostname

Hostname: | |

User: | |

Password: | |

☐ Advertise services in this domain using Bonjour

(?)   [Cancel]   [OK]

Shared Services

The macOS sharing services include the following:

▸ DVD or CD Sharing (Remote Disc)—Enables you to share your Mac computer's optical disc (if it has a built-in optical disc drive, or an external drive such as a SuperDrive
   DVD drive) over the network. This service can be accessed only by other Mac computers from the Finder sidebar or Migration Assistant. This service is displayed only if
   your Mac has a supported optical disc drive.

▸ Screen Sharing—Enables remote control of your Mac. Using this service is detailed
   later in this lesson.

▸ File Sharing—Enables remote access to files on your Mac computer's file system. The
   "File Sharing" section after this list of shared services has more details.

▸ Media Sharing—Allows other devices on your home network to browse, play, or copy
   music, movies, photos, and more.

▸ Printer Sharing—Allows network access to printers that are configured on your Mac.
   Using this service is covered in Lesson 27, "Manage Printers and Scanners."

▸ Remote Login—Enables remote control of your Mac computer's command line with
   Secure Shell (SSH). Further, you can use SSH remote login to securely transfer files
   using Secure File Transfer Protocol (SFTP) or the secure copy command scp. With
   Remote Login enabled, the launchd control process listens for remote login service
   requests on TCP port 22 and starts the sshd background process as needed to handle
   any requests. By default, administrator user accounts are allowed to access the service.

WARNING ▶ Turning on the Remote Login service can reduce the security of your Mac. We recommend that you leave the Remote Login service turned off.

▶ Remote Management—Augments the Screen Sharing service to allow remote administration of your Mac with the Apple Remote Desktop (ARD) app. If your organization uses a mobile device management (MDM) solution and Apple School Manager or Apple Business Manager, you may be able to use scripting and a configuration profile to remotely turn on remote management for a Mac. See Apple Support article HT209161, "Use the kickstart command-line utility in macOS Mojave 10.14 and later," for more information.

▶ Remote Apple Events—Allows apps and AppleScripts on another Mac to communicate with apps and services on your Mac. This service is often used to facilitate automated AppleScript workflows between apps running on separate Mac computers. When this service is turned on, the launchd control process listens for remote Apple Events requests on TCP and UDP port 3031 and starts the AEServer background process as needed to handle any requests. By default, only administrator user accounts are allowed to access the service, but you can also select "All users" or click the Add (+) button, then select additional users or groups.

▶ Bluetooth Sharing—Allows access to your Mac with Bluetooth short-range wireless. Using this service is covered in Lesson 26, "Troubleshoot Peripherals."

▶ Internet Sharing—Allows your Mac to reshare a single network or internet connection with other network interfaces. For example, if your Mac had internet access through wired Ethernet and you didn't have a Wi-Fi router, you could turn on Internet Sharing for the Mac computer's Wi-Fi and turn it into a wireless access point for your other computers and devices. When you turn on the Internet Sharing service, the launchd process starts several background processes. The natd process performs the network address translation (NAT) service that allows multiple network clients to share a single network or internet connection. The bootpd process provides the DHCP automatic network configuration service for the network devices connected to your Mac. When a network device connects to your Mac computer's shared network connection, it automatically obtains an IP address, usually in the 10.0.2.X range. The named process provides DNS resolution for network devices connected to the internet with your Mac.

▶ Content Caching—Helps reduce internet bandwidth usage and speed up software installation and iCloud content sharing on Mac computers, iOS and iPadOS devices, and Apple TV. The "Content Caching" section that follows the "File Sharing" section has more information.

File Sharing

The default file sharing protocol uses the Server Message Block (SMB) protocol. When you turn on the File Sharing service, the launchd control process listens for SMB service requests on TCP port 445 and automatically starts the smbd process as necessary to handle any requests. By default, only standard and administrator users have access to file-sharing services, but you can modify access for other users as outlined in Lesson 13, "Manage Permissions and Sharing." Connecting to file-sharing services is covered in Lesson 24, "Manage Network Services." By default, each user's Public folder is shared when you turn on File Sharing.

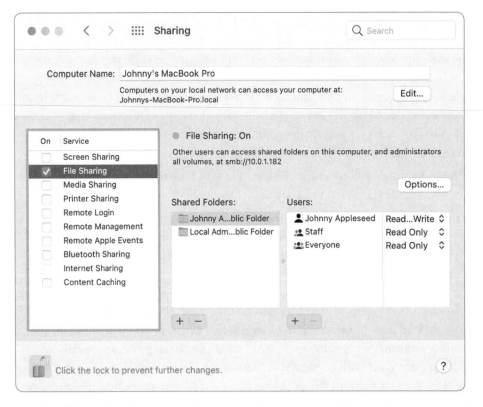

Near the Shared Folders field, click Add (+) to share another folder or select a shared folder, then click Remove (−) to stop sharing that folder. Sharing files with some Windows computers requires your Mac to store a user's passwords in a less secure manner. Click options to see a list of users on your Mac. Here you can select the checkbox for a user, then enter the password for the user so that your Mac can store the password in a way that enables the user to connect from Windows computers that require a less secure password to connect.

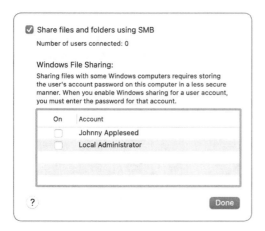

To share files with a user of some versions of Windows, select the On checkbox for the user, enter their password, then click OK. This stores the password in a less secure way on your Mac. When you are done sharing files with that user, deselect that user's On checkbox so that you can store that user's password in a more secure way on your Mac.

Content Caching

You can turn on and configure the content caching service in the Content Caching pane of Sharing preferences.

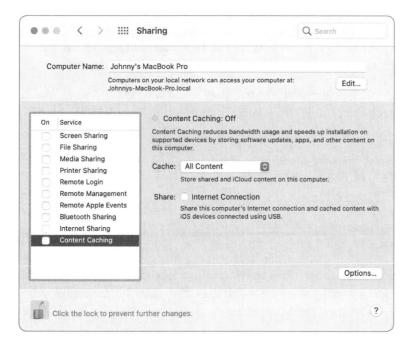

The content caching service speeds up downloading of software distributed by Apple and data that users store in iCloud by saving content that local devices have already downloaded. When you turn on content caching, your Mac displays a message that you can restart devices on your network for them to immediately start using your Mac computer's content cache.

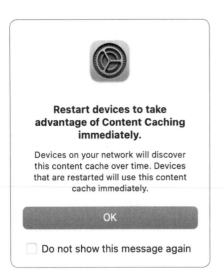

When you turn on content caching, the option to cache All Shared Content is turned on by default. You can click the Cache menu and choose:

▶ All Content—Store shared content, such as apps and software, and iCloud content, such as photos and documents

▶ Only Shared Content—Store only shared content, such as apps and software

▶ Only iCloud Content—Store only iCloud content, such as photos and documents

The Share Internet Connection option turns on *tethered caching* so that you can share your Mac computer's internet connection to iOS and iPadOS devices that are connected using USB. Doing so can save time, local Wi-Fi, and bandwidth when you're using a cart

or USB hub and updating several devices at once, compared to updating each device individually over Wi-Fi. Use the content caching service to install large apps while preparing devices for the beginning of a larger deployment, semester, or new school year.

NOTE ▶ When you select Share Internet Connection you also turn on Internet Sharing, and the checkbox for Internet Sharing in the Sharing preferences becomes unavailable.

Click the Options button to reveal how much storage content caching is currently using on your disk. Content caching uses the startup disk by default, but if your Mac has more than one disk, you can choose a different disk for content caching to use. Use the slider to change the amount of space content caching can use before it starts removing items to make room for newer items.

Option-click the Options button to reveal the advanced configurations. If you configure any advanced options, you no longer need to Option-click the Options button; it's displayed as Advanced Options automatically.

The buttons available include:

▶ Storage—Displays the configuration available when you click the Options button in Content Caching.

▶   Clients—Lets you configure which clients and networks you will provide content caching for.

On larger networks with multiple Mac computers that provide content caching, it is important to ensure that a content cache receives requests only from appropriate clients. Defining clients as "appropriate" means that you can choose to cache content for clients that use the same public IP address, the same local networks, networks that you specify, or networks that you specify in addition to clients that can't contact their preferred content cache. By default, the menu for "My local networks" is set to "use one public IP address," and the public IPv4 address is discovered automatically. If you click the menu for "My local networks" and choose "use custom public IP addresses," you must define at least one range of IPv4 addresses. This requires you to perform additional DNS configuration for your network; to assist with the additional DNS configuration, click the DNS Configuration button to generate an appropriate command to run or a DNS record to add, depending on what DNS service your network uses.

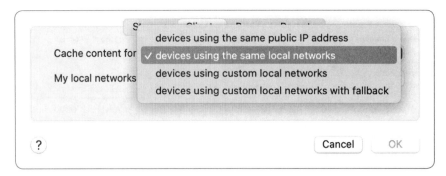

▶   Peers—Content caches on the same network are called *peers*, and they share content with one another.

Configure which other content caches to share content with (caches with the same public IP address, the same local networks, or networks that you specify).

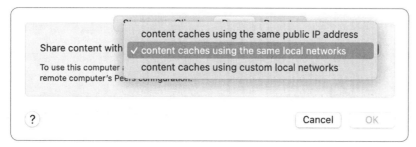

▶ Parents—You can arrange your content caches in a hierarchy. When you add the IPv4 addresses of other content caches here, they are considered parents to your Mac computer's content cache, and your Mac is a child. If you refer to a parent by its IPv4 address, you should configure the parent with a static IPv4 address. If you define multiple parents, open the menu for "Parent policy" to specify how your content cache chooses which parent to use.

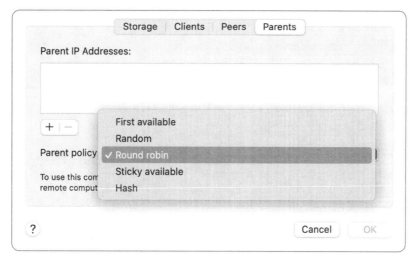

The content caching service writes log messages to the subsystem com.apple.AssetCache. You can use the log command in Terminal to inspect the logs, or you can use Console to inspect the logs.

▶ Inspect the logs in Terminal: Open Terminal, and then enter a log command; for example: **log show --predicate 'subsystem == "com.apple.AssetCache"'**.

▶ Inspect the logs in Console: Open Console, type **s:com.apple.AssetCache** in the search field, then press Return (**s:** is a shortcut for the search filter Subsystem; for more search filters, such as Process and Category, click the filter in the search field and choose from the menu that appears). Select an entry or hover your pointer over an entry for more details.

For Mac computers, use the AssetCacheLocatorUtil command in Terminal to return information about content caching services your Mac will use. Open Terminal, type the command **AssetCacheLocatorUtil**, then press Return.

After you turn on Content Caching in Sharing preferences, Activity Monitor automatically displays the Cache button in the Activity Monitor toolbar.

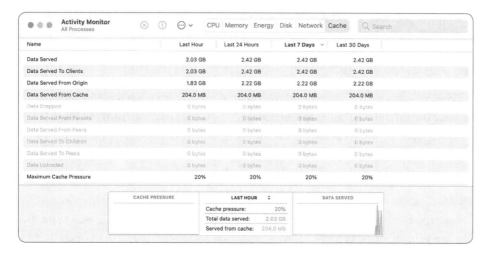

See "Change content caching preferences on Mac" at support.apple.com/guide/mac-help/mchleaf1e61d in the macOS User Guide for more information. See the Apple Support article HT204675, "Content types supported by content caching in macOS," for more information.

Reference 25.2
Control Remote Computers

You don't necessarily have to be in front of a Mac to administer and troubleshoot it. macOS includes built-in software that enables you to control a remote Mac and to display the contents of a remote Mac computer's screen on your Mac computer's screen.

Screen-Sharing Services

A standard installation of macOS includes only the client-side software for Remote Management. You can buy the administrative side of Remote Management, Apple Remote Desktop (ARD), used to control other Mac computers, from the Mac App Store.

Screen Sharing is a subset of Remote Management. When you turn on Remote Management, you also turn on Screen Sharing. After you turn on Remote Management, the checkbox for Screen Sharing becomes unavailable. If you select it, Screen Sharing displays "Screen Sharing is currently being controlled by the Remote Management service."

See the Apple Remote Desktop User Guide at support.apple.com/guide/remotedesktop/ for more information.

Apple screen-sharing services are based on a modified version of the Virtual Network Computing (VNC) protocol. It's modified to use optional encryption to enable you to view and control traffic. It also lets you copy files and clipboard content between Mac computers with Screen Sharing.

macOS allows you to access a virtual desktop on another Mac with Screen Sharing. You can have your own virtual login on another Mac, completely separate from the login currently being used by the local user. This feature is similar to fast user switching (covered in Lesson 7, "Manage User Accounts"), except the second user is remote with Screen Sharing and potentially using the Mac at the same time as the local user.

VNC is a cross-platform standard for remote control, so if configured properly, the macOS Screen Sharing service integrates well with other third-party VNC-based systems. Your Mac can control, or be controlled by, VNC-based software regardless of operating system or platform. For more details refer to "The Remote Framebuffer Protocol" at tools.ietf.org/html/rfc6143.

Turn On Screen Sharing

Before you can access a Mac remotely with Screen Sharing, the remote Mac must have the Screen Sharing service turned on. To turn on Screen Sharing for your Mac, open Sharing preferences, then select the Screen Sharing checkbox.

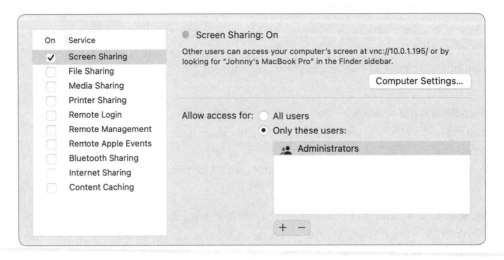

By default, only administrator user accounts are allowed to access the service, but you can adjust Screen Sharing access. Select the "All users" radio button or use the Add (+) and Remove (–) buttons at the bottom of the users list. When you add accounts, a dialog appears where you can select the users or groups to whom you want to grant Screen Sharing access.

You can allow a range of operating systems to access your Mac computer's Screen Sharing service by clicking the Computer Settings button. This displays a dialog where you can turn on guest and standard VNC screen-sharing access.

When you attempt to access your Mac computer's screen, the currently logged-in user must authorize the session. By default, only local authorized users and groups are permitted to use Screen Sharing. Select "Anyone may request permission to control screen" to enable anyone (from another Mac) to ask permission to share the screen. For this feature to work, you must remove any access restrictions for Screen Sharing by allowing access to all users.

Standard third-party VNC viewers can't authenticate using the secure methods used by the macOS Screen Sharing service. So if you select the "VNC viewers may control screen with password" checkbox, you must also set a specific password for VNC access. All standard VNC traffic is unencrypted. And standard VNC viewers can't use the Screen Sharing service's clipboard copy, file copy, or virtual desktop features.

Connect with Screen Sharing

You connect to and control another computer for Screen Sharing in the same way you connect to a shared file system. From the Finder, you connect to another Mac that has Screen Sharing, Remote Management, or VNC turned on. You can initiate the connection in two ways. The first way works only for Screen Sharing or Remote Management service hosts on the local network. In the Finder, choose Go > Network (or press Shift-Command-K), select a remote Mac, then click the Share Screen button.

The second way enables you to connect to and control hosts that provide Screen Sharing, Remote Management, or standard VNC services. In the Finder, choose Go > Connect to Server. In the "Connect to Server" dialog, type **vnc://** followed by the Mac IP address, DNS hostname, or Bonjour name, then click Connect.

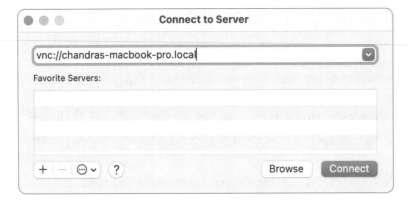

Regardless of the connection method, macOS opens Screen Sharing (which is in /System/Library/CoreServices/Applications/) and initiates a connection to the specified host. macOS displays a dialog that requires you to make an authentication choice. If you use Kerberos single sign-on or you saved your authentication information to a keychain, macOS authenticates for you and doesn't present the authentication dialog.

Otherwise, what happens next depends on how your Mac and the remote Mac are configured.

If no one is logged in to the remote Mac, your Mac displays an authentication dialog:

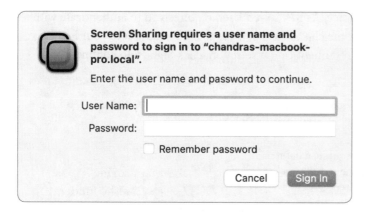

If someone else is logged in to the remote Mac, and the remote Mac has the "Anyone may request permission to control screen" option selected, then your Mac displays an authentication dialog with two options:

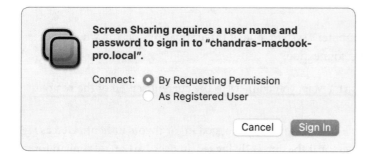

If you select By Requesting Permission and then click Sign In, a dialog that asks permission appears on the remote Mac.

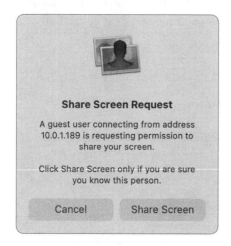

The second authentication choice, As Registered User, requires you to authenticate with a user account. You can select the checkbox that saves this information to your login keychain. After you make your authentication selection, click Sign In to continue.

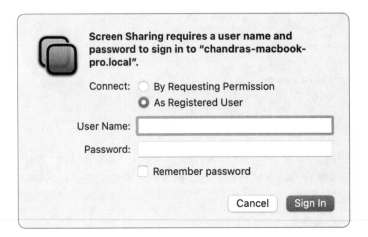

Depending on the remote computer's system, one of three situations occurs when Screen Sharing establishes the connection:

▶ If the remote computer isn't a Mac, you connect to the current screen of the remote computer.

▶ If the remote computer is a Mac and no one is logged in, or if you authenticated as the currently logged-in user, or if the currently logged-in user isn't an administrator, you connect to a login window screen of the remote Mac.

▶ If the remote computer is a Mac and you authenticated as a different user from the administrator who is currently logged in to the Mac, you are presented with a dialog that enables you to choose between asking permission or logging in as yourself to a virtual desktop.

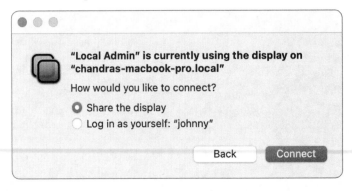

When presented with this Screen Sharing dialog, if you choose the option to ask for permission, the remote user is prompted with the Share Screen Request permission dialog.

The remote user's choice dictates whether you can connect. If you choose to log in as yourself, you are instantly connected to a new virtual screen that displays the login window. In this case, the other user doesn't know that you are remotely using their Mac, but the other user might notice if they search for your account name in Activity Monitor or notice your user account is unavailable to be modified in Users & Groups preferences. Additionally, if the other user logs out and the login window displays users, the user that you connected as is displayed with a checkmark. If the other user logs in again, the user you connected as has a checkmark in the Fast User Switching menu.

If you need to control another user's session without asking permission, you should turn on Remote Management instead of Screen Sharing. With Remote Management turned on, when you connect with Screen Sharing the remote user isn't asked for permission. You can use Remote Management with Apple Remote Desktop.

> **NOTE ▶** When you control or observe another user's session, the following message appears on the lock screen of the remote Mac: "Your screen is being observed."

Control Another Mac with Screen Sharing

After you connect to a remote Mac, a new window opens and shows the controlled Mac computer name and a live view of the controlled Mac computer screen or screens. When this window is active, keyboard entries and mouse movements are sent to the controlled Mac. For example, if you press Command-Q you quit the active app on the controlled Mac. To quit the Screen Sharing app, click the close (X) button in the upper-left corner of the window or choose Screen Sharing > Quit Screen Sharing. More options are available in the Screen Sharing toolbar.

The buttons in the toolbar show Screen Sharing features, including the option to share clipboard content between your Mac and the remote Mac. If the remote Mac is running macOS, you can drag and release files in the Finder between your Mac and the screen sharing window. Doing so opens a File Transfers dialog, where you can verify the transfer progress or cancel the file transfer.

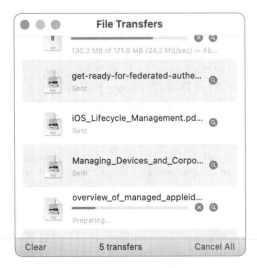

Choose Screen Sharing > Preferences (or press Command-Comma if no remote session is currrently open) to check Screen Sharing options. Use the preferences to adjust screen size and quality settings. If you experience slow performance, adjust the settings. Some network connections, such as crowded wireless or slow internet connections, are so slow that these settings might not help.

> **NOTE ▸** If the remote Mac is using more than one display, a Displays button also appears on the toolbar. Click it to open a menu that lets you choose which display or displays to view on your Mac.

Messages Screen Sharing

If iMessage is turned on for both Mac computers, you can use the Messages app to initiate a screen-sharing session and chat between the administrator Mac and the controlled Mac. Messages screen sharing also makes it easy to locate other Mac computers to control, because Messages resolves the location of remote computers based on your active chats using an iCloud account. Messages also supports reverse screen sharing—the administrator Mac can push its screen to display on another Mac for demonstration purposes.

Messages doesn't require a Mac to have Screen Sharing turned on in Sharing preferences. This is because Messages includes an authorization process for initiating a screen-sharing session with iCloud authentication and Messages. This requires that users on each Mac computer be signed in with an iCloud account both in iCloud preferences and with Messages. Details regarding signing in to Messages and iCloud are covered in Reference 24.2, "Configure Network Service Apps." The Messages User Guide article at support.apple.com/guide/messages/screen-sharing-icht11883 ("Share screens using Messages on Mac") has more information.

Control Another Mac with Messages

To initiate a Messages screen-sharing session, start an iMessage chat with the other user. Select the chat history of the other user in the main Messages window. After you select the user, click the Info button ⓘ in the top right of the main Messages window. This opens a dialog where you can click the Share button and choose "Invite to Share My Screen" or "Ask to Share Screen." Screen Sharing in Messages works in both directions.

The other Mac displays an authorization dialog that offers the choice to accept or decline your request to share screens. With Messages you can't force other users to share their screens. They can allow or deny your request.

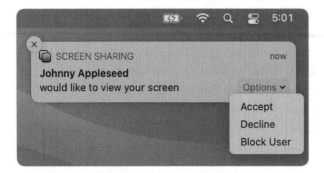

If the other user clicks the Accept button, they are asked to verify the screen-sharing session and select whether you can control or only observe their screen.

After the other user accepts the screen-sharing session, Screen Sharing initiates the connection.

If both Mac computers support voice chat, Messages starts a voice chat session. You might need to configure Audio/Video settings in Messages preferences for this feature to work.

If you are already communicating over audio using another communications method, you might want to click the Screen Sharing menu item and choose Mute Microphone.

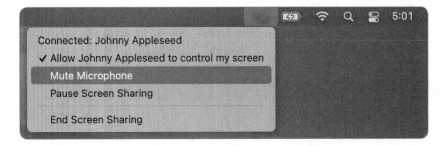

Messages leverages the same Screen Sharing app used by the system Screen Sharing service, as covered previously in this lesson. The only exception is that, by the other user's choice, you might not have control of the remote Mac. If the remote user selects "Observe my screen" instead of "Control my screen," or chooses "Allow <*your name* > to control my screen," then in the Screen Sharing toolbar, the binocular Control mode button is selected, indicating that you can observe but not control.

In this case, your Mac displays the pointer of the remote Mac, and your pointer turns into a magnifying glass.

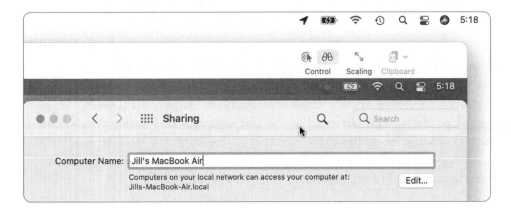

Clicking the shared screen has no effect, except that it shows a magnifying glass–style circle on the remote screen. This helps users identify something you are trying to assist them with.

Click the pointer Control mode button to request remote control of another Mac. This issues a notification prompt to the remote user so that they can agree (or not) to enable you to control their Mac.

The other user can select the Screen Sharing menu to manage features of the Messages screen-sharing session, including ending the session.

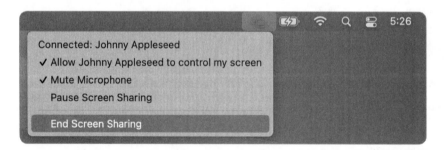

Turn On Screen Sharing with Automation and an MDM Solution

If your Mac is automatically enrolled with your MDM solution and has been added to Apple School Manager or Apple Business Manager, under certain conditions that are outside the scope of this guide, you can allow the Mac to be controlled with Screen Sharing by using a configuration profile with a Privacy Preferences Policy Control payload. You can use your MDM solution to send a command to your enrolled Mac to turn on Remote Desktop access (if MDM solution supports that command).

For more information, see the following Mobile Device Management Settings articles:

▸ "Privacy Preferences Policy Control MDM payload settings for Apple devices," at support.apple.com/guide/mdm/mdm38df53c2a.

▸ "Privacy Preferences Policy Control custom payload examples," at support.apple.com/guide/mdm/mdm9ddb7e0b5.

Reference 25.3
Share Files with AirDrop

macOS features a peer-to-peer Wi-Fi file-sharing service called AirDrop. It's the easiest way to share files between Apple devices that are in close proximity.

AirDrop uses Wi-Fi networking, but you don't need to be joined to a network to use AirDrop, because it creates a closed network between local Apple devices.

AirDrop requires no setup or configuration. It handles peer-to-peer file sharing, including discovery, easy authentication, and secure file transfer using Transport Layer Security (TLS) encryption.

AirDrop works only between Apple devices within local Wi-Fi and Bluetooth range. The range varies based on several factors, but it's generally limited to 30 feet. Also, with AirDrop you share only the items you specifically offer to share with another Mac, iOS, or iPadOS device, as opposed to sharing one or more folders with the File Sharing service in Sharing preferences. AirDrop is supported only on devices with the appropriate system software and wireless hardware. For more information, see Apple Support article HT204144, "How to use AirDrop on your iPhone, iPad, or iPod touch," and Apple Support article HT203106, "Use AirDrop on your Mac."

Send Items with AirDrop

To share files between Apple devices that support AirDrop, find other devices in the AirDrop discovery window. Click the AirDrop icon in the Finder sidebar or choose Go > AirDrop. Or you can press Shift-Command-R in the Finder. These methods open the AirDrop discovery interface in a Finder window, enabling you to share any item you can drag to the Finder window.

Alternatively, you can engage AirDrop to share a specific open document, or even a Safari page, by clicking the Share button (the box with an up-pointing arrow) if it's available in the document window or by choosing File > Share > AirDrop if it's available. Another option is to Control-click an item in the Finder and choose Share from the shortcut menu. Doing so opens the AirDrop discovery interface, but it shares the currently selected document too.

When the AirDrop discovery interface is open, macOS scans for other AirDrop devices within local wireless range. Other AirDrop devices appear as long as AirDrop is turned on and using a compatible discovery method.

After AirDrop finds the other device you want to transfer an item to, you have a couple of ways to send the item. If you are in the Finder, drag a file or folder on top of the icon representing the other device. If you are in a Share window, click the icon representing the other device. In either case, AirDrop notifies the other device that you would like to share something.

On the receiving device, a notification appears where you can accept (or decline) the incoming item. If the AirDrop window is open on the receiving Mac, you have three choices:

▸ Click the Accept button and the item is transferred to your Downloads folder.

▸ Click Accept & Open (or Open in Photos) to save to your Downloads folder and open the item.

▸ Click Decline to cancel the transfer and notify the other user in the AirDrop interface.

If you don't have the AirDrop window open on the receiving Mac, a notification appears in the upper-right corner. If you click Accept, you can choose Open (or Open in Photos) or Save to Downloads.

When you use AirDrop to send an item to another Mac computer, iOS device, or iPadOS device, if you're signed in to the same iCloud account on both devices the recipient device automatically accepts and downloads the item.

AirDrop Discovery

If your Mac can't discover another AirDrop device, that device may not have AirDrop turned on. If so, on the other Mac open the AirDrop window in the Finder to turn on AirDrop. AirDrop defaults to not being discoverable. This may limit your ability to discover other devices in the AirDrop discovery interface. To resolve this issue, on the other device you can set AirDrop discovery to allow everyone or to limit discovery to only users with matching information in your Contacts. To change AirDrop discoverability on macOS, click the words "Allow me to be discovered by" at the bottom of the AirDrop interface.

Reference 25.4
Manage the Personal Firewall

From a network services standpoint, your Mac is very secure, because, by default, no services are running that respond to external requests. Even after you provide shared services, your Mac responds only to services that are turned on.

You can configure services that could cause trouble if compromised—like File Sharing or Screen Sharing—to have limited access authorization. Still, users can open third-party apps or background services that could leave a Mac vulnerable to a network attack.

To maintain network security, leave sharing services off unless they're necessary. If you turn on sharing services, limit authorization access. And after you use them, turn them off.

Personal Firewall

Most people secure network services by configuring a network firewall. Doing so blocks unauthorized network service access. Most networks have a firewall to limit inbound traffic from an internet connection.

Most home routers are also network firewalls. Although network-level firewalls block unauthorized internet traffic to your network, they don't block traffic that originated from inside your network to your Mac. Also, if your Mac is mobile and is often joining new networks, odds are that every new network you join has different firewall rules.

To prevent unauthorized network services from allowing incoming connections to your Mac, turn on the built-in personal firewall. A personal firewall blocks unauthorized connections to your Mac no matter where they originated. The macOS firewall uses a single-click configuration that provides network service security, which works for most users.

A standard firewall uses rules based on service port numbers. Each service defaults to a standard port or set of ports. Some network services, like Messages, use a wide range of dynamic ports. If you manually configure a firewall, you have to make dozens of rules for every potential port a user may need.

To resolve this issue, the macOS firewall uses an adaptive technology that allows connections based on apps and service needs, without you having to know the specific ports they use. For example, you can authorize Messages to accept any incoming connection without configuring all the individual TCP and UDP ports used by Messages.

A personal firewall also leverages another built-in feature, code signing, to ensure that allowed apps and services aren't changed without your knowledge. Code signing enables Apple and third-party developers to provide a guarantee that their software wasn't tampered with. This level of verifiable trust enables you to configure the firewall in default mode with a single click, automatically allowing signed apps and services to receive incoming connections.

Because the personal firewall is fully dynamic, it opens only the necessary ports when the app or service is running. Using Messages as an example, the personal firewall allows incoming connections to the required ports only if Messages is running. If the app quits because the user logs out, the firewall closes the associated ports. Having the required ports open only when an app or service needs them provides an extra layer of security not found with traditional firewalls.

Turn On the Personal Firewall

To turn on and configure the macOS personal firewall, open Security & Privacy preferences, click the lock icon in the lower-left corner, and authenticate as an administrator user to unlock Security & Privacy preferences. Click the Firewall button, then click the Turn On Firewall button to turn on the default firewall rules. Once you do, this button changes to a Turn Off Firewall button.

The default firewall configuration allows incoming traffic for established connections (connections that were initiated from your Mac and are expecting a return) and signed software or turned-on services. This level of security is adequate for most users.

Configure the Personal Firewall

If you want to customize the firewall, you can reveal additional firewall configurations by clicking the Firewall Options button. From the firewall options window, a list of services currently allowed appears. Without any additional configuration, all services that are turned on in Sharing preferences automatically appear in the list of allowed services. Deselecting a shared service from Sharing preferences removes the service from the list of allowed services. The following figure illustrates the Firewall Options pane for a Mac that has the Screen Sharing service turned on.

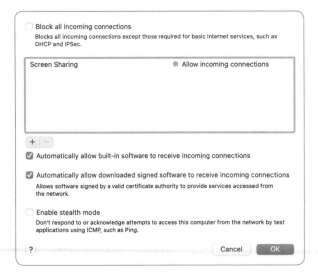

You can manually set which apps and services the firewall allows by deselecting the checkbox to automatically allow signed software. With this firewall choice, as you open new network apps for the first time or update existing network apps macOS displays a dialog where you can allow or deny the new network app. This dialog appears outside Security & Privacy preferences whenever a new network app requests incoming access.

If you click Allow and you're not logged in as an administrator, you need to provide administrator credentials in order to update the firewall settings.

If you are manually setting network app and service firewall access, you can return to the Advanced Firewall pane to review the list of items and either delete items from the list or specifically disallow certain items.

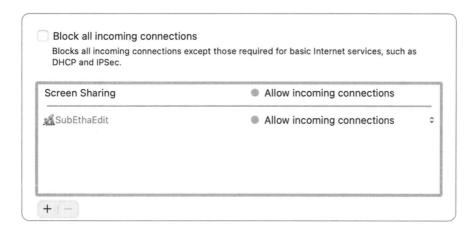

You can select the "Enable stealth mode" checkbox to prevent response or acknowledgment of a failed attempt to the requesting host. With this option selected, your Mac doesn't respond to unauthorized network connections, including network diagnostic protocols like ping, traceroute, and port scan. Your Mac still responds to other allowed services. This includes, by default, Bonjour, which announces your Mac computer's presence and prevents your Mac from being hidden on the network.

When you need more security, select the "Block all incoming connections" checkbox. Selecting this option automatically turns on stealth mode.

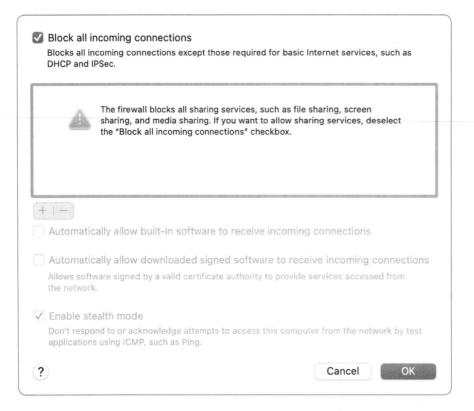

When you block all incoming connections, your Mac doesn't respond to incoming network connections except for those required for basic network services or established connections, such as those needed to browse the web or check email. This prevents shared services or apps hosted on your Mac from working remotely.

As with most System Preferences panes, you can click the Help button (question mark) for more information about the preference pane you have open.

Reference 25.5
Troubleshoot Shared Services

If you're providing a shared service from your Mac and others are having trouble reaching it, consider how established the service is to determine where to focus your efforts. For example, if your Mac was providing a shared service for a while but now a single client computer has trouble accessing the service, troubleshoot the client computer before troubleshooting your shared Mac.

Otherwise, if multiple clients can't access your shared Mac, you might have an issue with the sharing service. After ruling out other potential local client and network issues, assume that the problem is with the Mac providing shared services. If so, shared network service issues fall into two general categories: service communication and service access.

If you are unable to establish a connection to the shared service, this may signal a network service communication issue. If you are presented with an authentication dialog, the client and server are establishing a proper connection, and you should troubleshoot the issue as a service access issue. If authentication fails, or you can authenticate but you're not authorized to access the service, then you are experiencing a service access issue.

Troubleshoot Network Service Communication

If you are unable to establish a connection to the shared service, use these methods to troubleshoot a network service communication issue:

▶ Double-check the shared Mac network configuration—From Network preferences, make sure the Mac computer's network interfaces are active and configured with the appropriate TCP/IP settings. If a DNS server is providing a hostname for your shared Mac, use one of the commands in Terminal described in Reference 23.2, "Use Terminal to Troubleshoot Network Issues," to verify the hostname.

▶ Double-check the Mac computer's sharing service configuration—From the Sharing preferences, verify the Mac computer's sharing name and ensure that the appropriate services are turned on and configured.

▶ Double-check the Mac computer's firewall configuration—From Security & Privacy preferences, first temporarily stop the firewall to determine whether turning it off makes a difference. If you are able to establish a connection, adjust the list of allowed services and apps before you start the firewall again.

▶ Check for basic network connectivity to the shared Mac—First, turn off the firewall's stealth mode; then, from another Mac, use the ping command in Terminal (described in Reference 23.2) to check for basic connectivity to the shared Mac. If you can't ping the shared Mac, you're probably having a network-level issue that goes beyond service troubleshooting.

▶ Check for network service port connectivity to the shared Mac—First, turn off the firewall's stealth mode; then, from another Mac, use the nc command in Terminal (described in Reference 24.4, "Troubleshoot Network Services") to verify that the expected network service ports are accessible. If the shared Mac is configured properly, the appropriate network service ports should register as open. If there are network routers between the network clients and the shared Mac, a network administrator might have decided to block access to those ports.

Troubleshoot Network Service Access

Failure to authenticate or be granted authorization to a shared service is considered a network service access issue. Use the following methods to troubleshoot these access issues:

▶ Verify the local user account settings—When using local user accounts, make sure the correct authentication information is being used. Maybe the user isn't using the right information, and you may have to reset the account password. (Troubleshooting user account issues is covered in Lesson 7, "Manage User Accounts.") Also, some services don't allow the use of guest and sharing-only user accounts. Further, the VNC service uses password information that is not directly linked to a user account.

▶ Check directory service settings—If you use a network directory service in your environment, verify that the Mac is properly communicating with the directory service by checking its status in Directory Utility. Even if you're only trying to use local accounts, any directory service issues can cause authentication problems. Some services, like Remote Management, by default don't allow you to authenticate with accounts hosted from network directories.

▶ Check shared service access settings—Several authenticated sharing services enable you to configure access lists. Use Sharing preferences to verify that the appropriate user accounts are allowed to access the shared service.

Exercise 25.1
Use Host-Sharing Services

▶ **Prerequisites**

▷ You must have created the Local Administrator (Exercise 3.1, "Configure a Mac for Exercises") and Johnny Appleseed (Exercise 7.1, "Create a Standard User Account") accounts.

▷ You must have a primary Mac. Your primary Mac will be the Mac you have performed any exercises on thus far, including the prerequisites listed above.

▷ You must have a secondary Mac. Your secondary Mac must meet the above prerequisites, run macOS Big Sur, and be on the same network as your primary Mac. The secondary Mac must not be signed in with the same Apple ID used on the primary Mac , and it must have a different name from the primary Mac.

NOTE ▶ Even if you don't meet these prerequisites, reading the exercises will enhance your knowledge of the processes.

In this exercise, you use macOS Screen Sharing to control another Mac. You share the current user's session, and you use a virtual display to log in as a different user. Perform these steps on both your primary and secondary Mac.

Turn On Screen Sharing

1   On your secondary Mac, if the Local Administrator account is logged in (even as a background session), log it out.

2   If necessary, log in as Johnny Appleseed.

3   Open Sharing preferences.

4   Click the lock button, then authenticate as Local Administrator.

5 Make sure the Remote Management checkbox is selected. A dialog listing remote management options appears. If the dialog doesn't appear automatically, click the Options button.

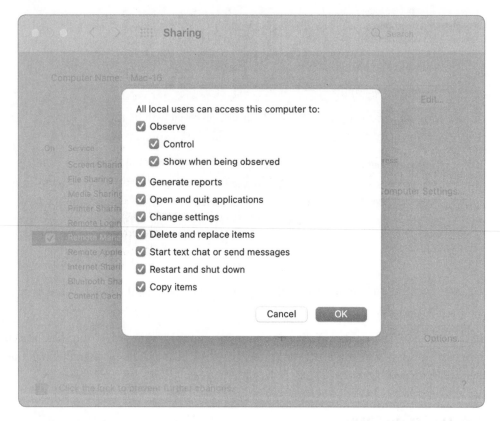

Although you use Screen Sharing, you configure the service using Remote Management (which is used for Apple Remote Desktop). Remote Management includes Screen Sharing. Notice that the checkbox for the Screen Sharing service is dimmed. This doesn't mean the service is unavailable. It means that it's being controlled by Remote Management.

6 Grant users all permissions. First, ensure that all options are selected. An easy way to do this is to Option-click one checkbox to select them all at once, then click OK to dismiss the dialog.

7 Ensure that "All users" is selected for "Allow access for."

8 Ensure that all other services are deselected in the Service column.

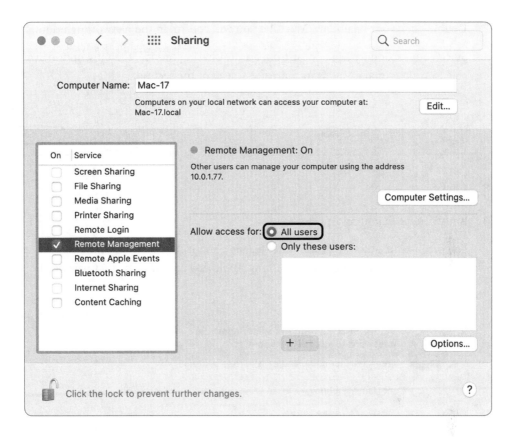

9 Quit System Preferences.

10 Repeat steps 1–9 on your secondary Mac.

Remotely Control Another Mac

In this section, you use Screen Sharing on your primary Mac to control your secondary Mac. Optionally, in a classroom environment, you may work with a partner and take turns controlling each other's Mac computers.

1 On your primary Mac, in the Finder, choose Go > Network (Shift-Command-K).

Your secondary Mac appears in the display of shared Mac computers on the local network. The display shows Mac computers that offer file sharing, screen sharing, or both.

2   Double-click your secondary Mac that you will control in the Network window.

Since your secondary Mac doesn't offer a file-sharing service, the only option available to your primary Mac is to share the screen of the secondary Mac.

3   Click Share Screen.

4   Authenticate as Johnny Appleseed.

You can use the account short name (**johnny**), and if the secondary Mac was set up with a different password for the Johnny Appleseed account, use that password.

5   Click Sign In.

Screen sharing begins, then a window opens, displaying a live, interactive view of the secondary Mac computer's desktop.

6   Open Desktop & Screensaver preferences on the secondary Mac.

7   Select a different desktop picture for the secondary Mac.

8   Press Command-Q.

This quits System Preferences on the secondary Mac. You can't use standard shortcuts to control screen sharing.

9   Click the Full Screen button in the title bar of the Screen Sharing window.

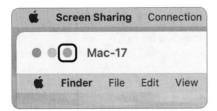

The window expands and fills your entire screen. In full-screen mode, your primary Mac computer's display is a virtual mirror of the secondary Mac computer's display.

10 Move your mouse to the top of the screen, then leave it there for a few seconds.

The Screen Sharing menu, window controls, and toolbar appear at the top of the screen. This enables you to exit full-screen mode or access the Screen Sharing toolbar.

11 Choose Screen Sharing > Quit Screen Sharing.

12 If you are working with a partner, switch roles, then have your partner repeat these steps.

Connect to a Virtual Display

When you connect to another Mac as a different user, you can work with a virtual display instead of sharing the local user's display. Because you connect to a virtual display, both the primary and secondary Mac computers can be used without interruption at the same time.

1   Ensure there are no remaining tasks to finish from the previous section.

2   Open the Network view (Shift-Command-K), then from your primary Mac, double-click the secondary Mac that you'll control.

3   Click Share Screen.

4   This time authenticate as Local Administrator (you can use the short name **ladmin**), then click Sign In.

Since you authenticated as a different user than is logged in to the secondary Mac, you are presented with the choice of sharing the current user's display or logging in as a different user with a virtual display.

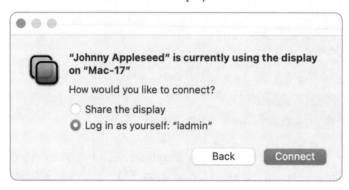

5   Select "Log in as yourself," then click Connect.

A screen-sharing window opens and displays a login screen for the secondary Mac. The orange checkmark next to Johnny Appleseed indicates that Johnny is logged in to the secondary Mac. Also, you see that the login window reports that your screen is being observed.

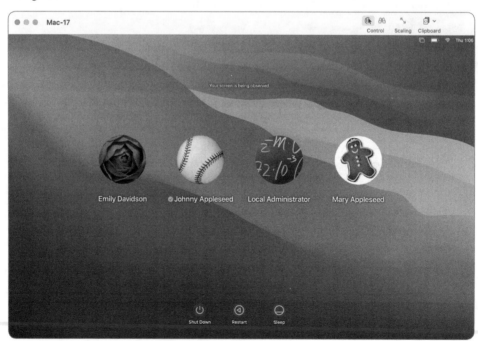

6 Log in to the secondary Mac as Local Administrator.

The virtual screen makes it easy to remotely manage users' Mac computers without disturbing the users. If a person was using the secondary Mac, they would not notice your interaction.

7 On the secondary Mac, open Users & Groups preferences.

If you use the Apple menu or the Dock, use the one contained in the screen-sharing window, not the one at the edge of your screen.

Observe that Johnny Appleseed has an orange checkmark next to his name, indicating that he is currently signed in.

8 Quit System Preferences on your secondary Mac.

9 Click the fast user switching menu on your secondary Mac.

The menu shows that Johnny Appleseed (the session you left logged in) and Local Administrator (you) are logged in to the secondary Mac. Your virtual display is treated as a fast user switching session.

10 In the Finder on the secondary Mac, choose Apple menu > Log Out Local Administrator, then click the Log Out button.

NOTE ▶ If you disconnect screen sharing without logging out first, you leave behind a fast user switching session.

11 Choose Screen Sharing > Quit Screen Sharing.

12 Depending on how you performed the exercise, do one of the following:

▶ If you are working with a partner, wait for them to finish before starting the next exercise.

▶ If you are working on your own, move back to your primary Mac for the first part of the next exercise.

Exercise 25.2
Configure a Personal Firewall

▶ **Prerequisites**

▶ You must have created the Local Administrator (Exercise 3.1, "Configure a Mac for Exercises") and Johnny Appleseed (Exercise 7.1, "Create a Standard User Account") accounts.

▶ You must have a primary Mac. Your primary Mac will be the Mac you have performed any exercises on thus far, including the prerequisites listed above.

▶ You must have a secondary Mac. Your secondary Mac must meet the above prerequisites, run macOS Big Sur, and be on the same network as your primary Mac.

NOTE ▶ Even if you don't meet these prerequisites, reading the exercises will enhance your knowledge of the processes.

In this exercise, you turn on the firewall and start a network-aware app, inspect the firewall log, configure the advanced stealth option, and observe that it blocks responses to network pings.

Turn On the Firewall

1 If necessary, on your primary Mac, log in as Johnny Appleseed.

2 Open Security & Privacy preferences.

3 Click the Firewall button.

4   Click the lock button, then authenticate as Local Administrator.

5   Click Turn On Firewall.

6   Click Firewall Options.

Remote Management and Screen Sharing are on the list as "Allow incoming connections." macOS assumes that if you turn on a service in the Sharing pane, you want users to be able to connect to it, so it allows those services through the firewall.

7   Deselect "Automatically allow built-in software to receive incoming connections" and "Automatically allow downloaded signed software to receive incoming connections."

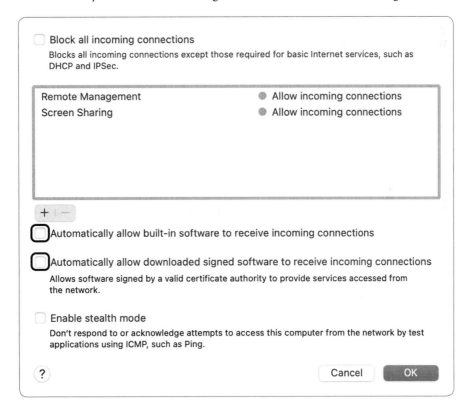

8   Click OK.

9   Leave System Preferences open.

NOTE ▸ With the firewall in this mode, you might receive alerts about system components that are attempting to accept incoming connections. Though it is generally safe to allow these connections through the firewall in a classroom environment, in a production environment it is best to identify a process before allowing it to connect.

10 Repeat steps 1–9 on your secondary Mac.

Test Firewall Settings

1 On your primary Mac, open Sharing preferences.

2 Turn on Media Sharing.

3 Select the checkbox "Share media with guests."

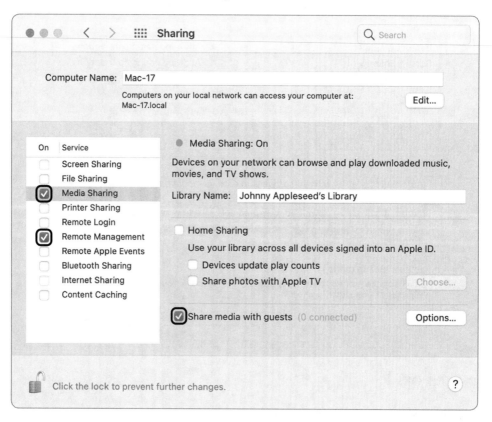

4 At the prompt to accept incoming network connections for the mediasharingd process, click Deny.

5 Navigate to Security & Privacy preferences.

6 Click the Firewall button, authenticate as Local Administrator, then choose Firewall Options.

Observe how the firewall is blocking incoming connections for the mediasharingd process. If you leave the firewall in this state, users of other Mac computers won't be able to connect to your Mac and access your media library.

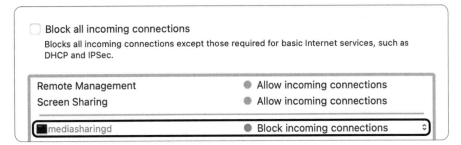

7   Next to mediasharingd, choose "Allow incoming connections" from the menu.

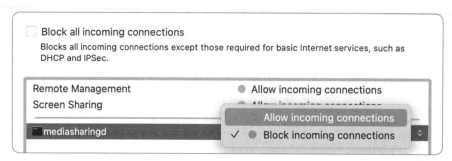

Since you have authenticated as an administrator, you can change the firewall policy for any process or app.

8   Click OK to dismiss the Firewall Options dialog.

9   Leave System Preferences open.

Test Stealth Mode

In this exercise, you use your primary and secondary Mac computers to observe the effects of stealth mode on the ping command.

1   On your primary Mac, in System Preferences, switch to the Sharing pane.

Your primary Mac computer's Bonjour name is displayed under Computer Name.

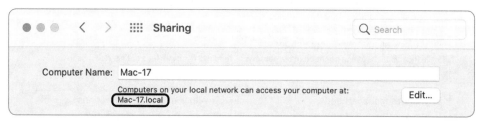

2   On your secondary Mac, open Sharing preferences, and take note of the Bonjour name.

3   Open Terminal on your primary Mac.

4 In Terminal, type **ping -c 5**, followed by the Bonjour name of your secondary Mac.

In this screenshot, the Bonjour name of the secondary Mac is **Mac-16.local**.

```
● ● ●                     🖥 johnny — -zsh — 80×24
Last login: Thu Nov 12 13:21:03 on console
johnny@Mac-17 ~ % ping -c 5 Mac-16.local▊
```

5 Press Return.

```
● ● ●                     🖥 johnny — -zsh — 80×24
Last login: Thu Nov 12 16:45:17 on ttys000
[johnny@Mac-17 ~ % ping -c 5 Mac-16.local
PING mac-16.local (10.0.1.74): 56 data bytes
64 bytes from 10.0.1.74: icmp_seq=0 ttl=64 time=32.210 ms
64 bytes from 10.0.1.74: icmp_seq=1 ttl=64 time=56.676 ms
64 bytes from 10.0.1.74: icmp_seq=2 ttl=64 time=78.375 ms
64 bytes from 10.0.1.74: icmp_seq=3 ttl=64 time=100.875 ms
64 bytes from 10.0.1.74: icmp_seq=4 ttl=64 time=20.209 ms

--- mac-16.local ping statistics ---
5 packets transmitted, 5 packets received, 0.0% packet loss
round-trip min/avg/max/stddev = 20.209/57.669/100.875/29.489 ms
johnny@Mac-17 ~ % ▊
```

The stdout of the ping command displays successful pings.

6 On your secondary Mac, Switch to Security & Privacy preferences, then click Firewall Options.

7 Select "Enable stealth mode," then click OK.

8 On your primary Mac, in Terminal, press the Up Arrow key, then press Return.

Pressing Up Arrow allows you to return to your previous typed command.

```
● ● ●                     🖥 johnny — -zsh — 80×24
Last login: Thu Nov 12 16:47:06 on ttys000
[johnny@Mac-17 ~ % ping -c 5 Mac-16.local
PING mac-16.local (10.0.1.74): 56 data bytes
Request timeout for icmp_seq 0
Request timeout for icmp_seq 1
Request timeout for icmp_seq 2
Request timeout for icmp_seq 3

--- mac-16.local ping statistics ---
5 packets transmitted, 0 packets received, 100.0% packet loss
johnny@Mac-17 ~ % ▊
```

You observe failed ping attempts. If you enable stealth mode, your Mac won't respond to ping requests. This increases security but could make it more difficult to troubleshoot.

9 On both your primary and secondary Mac computers, turn off the firewall, then quit all running apps.

System Management

Lesson 26

Troubleshoot Peripherals

macOS is compatible with most popular peripheral standards. At the start of this lesson, you learn how macOS supports different peripheral technologies. Then you learn how to manage and troubleshoot wired and wireless (Bluetooth) peripherals connected to macOS.

Reference 26.1
Peripheral Technologies

A *peripheral* is any device that you can connect to your Mac and that is controlled by that computer; a network device is shared over the network. This lesson shows you how to categorize peripherals by their connectivity type and device class. This information helps you manage and troubleshoot peripherals.

Peripheral Connectivity

To communicate with macOS, most peripherals use a *bus*. Bus connections are the most common peripheral connection types because they allow for different peripheral devices. Bus connections also allow multiple peripherals to connect to your Mac simultaneously.

Mac supports USB, Thunderbolt, and Bluetooth, and a few other buses that are outside the scope of this guide.

GOALS

▶ Manage peripheral connectivity

▶ Pair Bluetooth devices to your Mac

▶ Troubleshoot peripheral and driver issues

You can examine the status of each of these peripheral buses (and the items they are attached to) with System Information. In System Information, select a bus, then select a hardware interface to inspect its information.

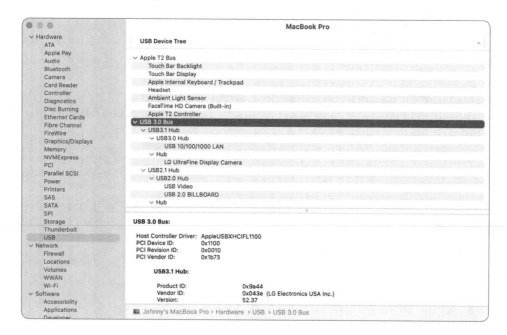

USB

USB is standard on every Mac. You can use System Information to verify what type of USB ports your Mac has, how fast these ports are, and what's currently connected to them.

USB is a highly expandable connection platform that allows for daisy-chained connections. You can connect one USB device to your Mac, then connect another USB device to the first, and so on. The USB specification allows for up to 127 simultaneous devices per host controller. Most Mac computers have at least two externally accessible USB host controllers.

USB Performance and Power Delivery

Several USB versions are currently supported by Apple on various Mac computer models:

▶ USB 4

▶ USB 3.1 Gen 2 (also known as USB 3.2 Gen 2)

▶ USB 3.1 Gen 1 (also known as USB 3.2 Gen 1 or USB 3)

▶ USB 2.0

▶ USB 1.1

Despite significant upgrades in performance, USB ports on Mac computers are backward compatible with USB 1.1 devices. Find out more about USB at the official USB Implementers Forum website: www.usb.org.

USB versions offer the following performance characteristics:

USB specification on Mac	Data transfer supported
USB 4	Up to 40 gigabits per second (Gbit/s)
USB 3.1 Gen 2	Up to 10 Gbit/s
USB 3.1 Gen 1	Up to 5 Gbit/s
USB 2.0	Up to 480 megabits per second (Mbit/s)
USB 1.1	Up to 1.5–12 Mbit/s

Mac computers provide different amounts of power to USB peripherals, depending on the model.

USB specification on Mac	Power delivery supported
USB 4	Up to 15W at 5V
USB 3.1 Gen 2	Up to 15W at 5V
USB 3.1 Gen 1	Up to 900mA at 5V
USB 2.0	Up to 500mA at 5V
USB 1.1	Up to 500mA at 5V

For more information, see Apple Support article HT204377, "If a Mac accessory needs more power or is using too much power."

USB Ports

USB-C describes the shape and style of a port on your computer and the connectors that you can plug into the port. USB-C ports look like this:

USB-C is a reversible connection that was developed by Intel and Apple.

You can use USB-C ports to do the following:

- Charge your notebook Mac.
- Charge your iPad Pro that has USB-C.
- Provide power.
- Transfer content between your Mac and a wide variety of other devices, such as storage devices.
- Connect video output such as HDMI, VGA, and DisplayPort (requires an adapter).
- Use an adapter to connect to other technologies, such as Ethernet.

This allows for radical simplification in ports. A variety of USB-C adapters are available that allow for simultaneous connection to multiple peripherals, a display, and battery charging. For Intel-based Mac computers, USB-C is the only version of USB that supports target disk mode.

Some Mac computers have USB-A ports (sometimes referred to as USB 3 ports), which look like this:

For more information, see Apple Support article HT201163, "About USB on Mac computers."

Different Mac Models Use USB-C Connections for Different Ports

The kinds of devices supported by a USB-C port on a Mac computer depend on the Mac model. This section covers three different kinds of USB-C ports:

- Thunderbolt / USB 4
- Thunderbolt 3 (USB-C)
- USB-C

At the time this guide goes to press, there are three Mac models that come with USB-C ports that support Thunderbolt 3 and USB 4 (referred to as "Thunderbolt / USB 4" ports):

▶ MacBook Pro (13-inch, M1, 2020)

▶ MacBook Air (M1, 2020)

▶ Mac mini (M1, 2020)

The Thunderbolt / USB 4 ports support Thunderbolt 4 accessories.

If your Intel-based Mac has one than one USB-C port, its USB-C ports support Thunderbolt 3 and USB-C. These ports are referred to as "Thunderbolt 3 (USB-C)."

Intel-based MacBook models introduced in 2015 or later have a single USB-C port. This USB-C port doesn't support Thunderbolt 3.

See Apple Support article HT201736, "Identify the ports on your Mac," for a complete list of current Mac models.

Thunderbolt

Originally designed by Intel, then later in collaboration with Apple, Thunderbolt represents the latest in peripheral connectivity. This standard folds PCI Express and DisplayPort data into a single connection and cable. Thunderbolt 3 adds USB compatibility and advanced power management.

With the appropriate adapters, a single Thunderbolt connection can provide access to any other networking, storage, peripheral, video, or audio connection. For example, a Thunderbolt display can provide not only a high-definition digital display but also a built-in camera, a microphone, audio speakers, USB ports, FireWire ports, Gigabit Ethernet ports, additional Thunderbolt ports for another peripheral, and even enough power to charge notebook Mac computers—all through a single Thunderbolt cable from the Mac to the display.

One Thunderbolt host computer connection supports a hub or daisy chain of up to six devices, with up to two of these devices high-resolution displays.

Only copper Thunderbolt cabling can deliver power, but it is limited to a maximum 3-meter length. Optical Thunderbolt cabling is available in lengths of up to 100 meters.

The latest Thunderbolt 3 standard uses the USB-C port.

Physically, the Thunderbolt 2, Thunderbolt, and Mini DisplayPort connectors have the same shape. All of these ports have the same shape, but they use different symbols on the cable and port. Thunderbolt 2, Thunderbolt, and Mini DisplayPort ports all look like this:

Mini DisplayPort devices and cables don't support the additional PCI Express data used by Thunderbolt, so items that support only Mini DisplayPort should be the last connection in a Thunderbolt daisy chain. You can identify items compatible with Thunderbolt by an icon that looks like a lightning bolt, whereas items compatible with only Mini DisplayPort feature an icon that looks like a flat-panel display.

Because Thunderbolt 3 uses the USB-C port, any Mac that includes Thunderbolt 3 can also accept USB-C devices without the need for adapters. Check the specifications for your Mac model to verify if it has Thunderbolt 3 (USB-C) ports. If it does, the Thunderbolt 3 (USB-C) ports support Thunderbolt 3 and USB 3.1 Gen 2. If your Mac has a USB-C port that doesn't support Thunderbolt 3, it supports USB 3.1 Gen 1.

USB-C devices and cables don't support the additional PCI Express data used by Thunderbolt. Items that support only USB-C should be the last connection in a Thunderbolt daisy chain.

Here are some of the differences between versions of Thunderbolt:

▶ Thunderbolt 3 provides two bidirectional 20 Gbit/s (20,000 Mbit/s) channels, providing a total of 40 Gbit/s outbound and 40 Gbit/s inbound. Thunderbolt 3 also features DisplayPort 1.2 signaling, which allows for 4K and 5K display resolutions. Thunderbolt 3 is fully backward compatible with USB-C (USB 3.1) signaling and power delivery.

▶ Thunderbolt 2 supports channel aggregation. A single peripheral can take advantage of the full 20 Gbit/s throughput.

▶ Thunderbolt provides two bidirectional 10 Gbit/s channels—this means a total of 20 Gbit/s outbound and 20 Gbit/s inbound. With this first version of Thunderbolt, these channels can't be combined to provide full bandwidth to a single peripheral. Thus, a single Thunderbolt peripheral has a maximum bandwidth of 10 Gbit/s, but you can use the full bandwidth when multiple peripherals are part of a single Thunderbolt chain. Thunderbolt also features DisplayPort 1.1 signaling, which allows for high-definition display resolutions. Copper Thunderbolt cabling also supplies up to 10 watts of power to connected devices, again providing more power than any previous external peripheral bus.

You can connect Intel-based Mac computers that support Thunderbolt 3 to an external graphics processor (eGPU) for additional graphics performance for pro apps, 3D gaming, virtual reality (VR) content creation, machine learning (ML) tasks, and more. See Apple Support article HT208544, "Use an external graphics processor with your Mac," for more information.

For more information on Thunderbolt 3, see the following Apple Support articles:

▶ HT202488, "About Apple Thunderbolt cables and adapters"

▶ HT206908, "Apple Thunderbolt 3 (USB-C) to Thunderbolt 2 Adapter requires Thunderbolt 3"

▶ HT207097, "Charge the MacBook Pro battery"

▶ HT207443, "Adapters for the Thunderbolt 3 or USB-C port on your Mac or iPad Pro"

▶ HT208368, "About the Apple Thunderbolt 3 (USB-C) Cable"

Bluetooth

Bluetooth is a wireless technology that makes short-range connections between devices (like your Mac and a mouse or keyboard).

Current Mac computers come with Bluetooth technology built in. You can check whether your computer supports Bluetooth:

▶ Look for the Bluetooth icon in the menu bar. If the Bluetooth icon is present, your computer has Bluetooth.

▶ Open System Preferences, then open Bluetooth preferences. If Bluetooth preferences lists options for enabling Bluetooth and making your device discoverable, Bluetooth is installed.

▶ In System Information, select Bluetooth from the Hardware section. If the Hardware section shows information, your Mac has Bluetooth installed.

For more information, see Apple Support article HT201171, "Using a Bluetooth mouse, keyboard, or trackpad with your Mac."

FireWire

FireWire is a high-speed, general-purpose peripheral connection originally developed by Apple. FireWire was ratified by the Institute of Electrical and Electronics Engineers (IEEE) as standard IEEE-1394 and was adopted as a standard interface for many digital video devices.

If your Mac supports Thunderbolt 3 (USB-C), Thunderbolt 2, or Thunderbolt, you can use an adapter or a combination of adapters to use a FireWire device:

▶ If your Mac has a Thunderbolt 3 (USB-C) port, use a Thunderbolt 3 (USB-C) to Thunderbolt 2 Adapter connected to an Apple Thunderbolt to Firewire Adapter.

▶ If your Mac has a Thunderbolt 2 or Thunderbolt port, use an Apple Thunderbolt to Firewire Adapter.

Reference 26.2
Manage Bluetooth Devices

Bluetooth wireless devices are associated with your Mac through a process called *pairing*. After you pair a device, your Mac automatically connects to it whenever it's in range.

If your iMac came with a wireless keyboard, mouse, or trackpad, they were pre-paired at the factory. Turn on the devices and your Mac should automatically connect to them when your computer starts up. If you bought the following Apple Bluetooth devices separately, you can use a Lightning to USB Cable or a USB-C to Lightning Cable to automatically pair them with your Mac:

▶ Magic Mouse 2

▶ Magic Keyboard

▶ Magic Keyboard with Numeric Keypad

▶ Magic Trackpad 2

For more information about how to set up an Apple wireless mouse, keyboard, or trackpad, see Apple Support article HT201178, "Set up your Apple wireless mouse, keyboard, and trackpad."

One way to configure Bluetooth devices is to use Bluetooth preferences. Open
System Preferences, then click Bluetooth. The on or off status is displayed in the left side
of the window. The right side of Bluetooth preferences contains the following:

▶   Bluetooth devices that are connected to your Mac

▶   Bluetooth devices that are not connected to your Mac but that have been connected
    before

▶   Bluetooth devices that you can attempt to connect to because they are in Discoverable
    Mode

You can select the checkbox "Show Bluetooth in menu bar" so that you can quickly verify
Bluetooth status and manage devices at any time.

The Bluetooth menu bar icon in the upper right of your display gives you information
about the status of Bluetooth and connected devices. Connected Bluetooth devices have
a solid blue icon. Click the slider to turn Bluetooth on or off. Some Bluetooth devices
have a disclosure triangle you can click to reveal more information and options for that

Bluetooth device. Click the icon to the left of a Bluetooth device to turn the connection to that Bluetooth device on or off. To manage Bluetooth preferences, choose Bluetooth Preferences.

You can also turn off and on Bluetooth from the Control Center. Click the Bluetooth icon in Control Center to turn Bluetooth off and on.

Pair a Bluetooth Device

Before you begin the pairing process, turn on Discoverable Mode on the Bluetooth device you're going to pair with your Mac. Each device is different, so you might have to consult the device user guide to turn on Discoverable Mode.

Continuity features use Bluetooth 4.0 or later, but traditional Bluetooth pairing isn't required. Instead, the Continuity features automatically connect as long as all devices are signed in to the same iCloud account. Find out more about Handoff from Apple Support article HT204681, "Use Continuity to connect your Mac, iPhone, iPad, iPod touch, and Apple Watch."

When Bluetooth preferences is open, it scans for any Bluetooth devices in range that are in Discoverable Mode.

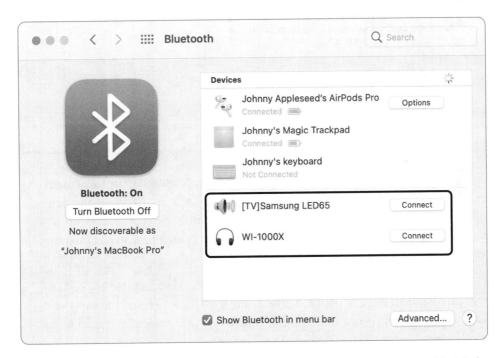

With Bluetooth preferences open, the Mac puts itself in Bluetooth Discoverable Mode. Discoverable Mode advertises your Mac as a Bluetooth resource to any device within range, which could invite unwanted attention to your Mac.

It may take several moments for the device name to appear. After it does, select it and click the Connect button. For some Bluetooth devices, you must enter a passcode to authorize pairing. Depending on the device, you will perform one of the following:

- ▶ Complete the pairing with little interaction by using an automatically generated passcode. This often happens with a device that has no method to verify the passcode.

- ▶ Enter a predefined passcode on your Mac, as specified in the device's user guide, and click Continue to authorize the pairing.

- ▶ Allow the Bluetooth Setup Assistant to create a random passcode, which you then enter or verify on the Bluetooth device to authorize the pairing. In this example, the passcode is generated automatically.

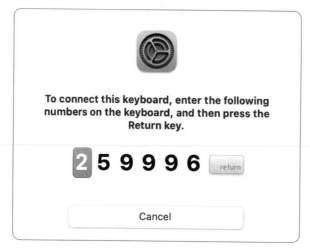

The Bluetooth Setup Assistant automatically detects the capabilities of your Bluetooth device and may present you with additional configuration screens. Continue through these screens until you complete the setup. When the pairing is complete, you can verify the pairing by reopening Bluetooth preferences. A device doesn't have to be currently connected to maintain pairing status with the Mac.

macOS saves Bluetooth input device pairings, like mice and keyboards, to NVRAM so that you can use them prior to macOS fully starting up. This is necessary to support FileVault and startup keyboard shortcuts (for Intel-based Mac computers) when using Bluetooth input devices.

Manage Bluetooth Settings

You can adjust settings such as the peripheral's name from Bluetooth preferences. To access all the Bluetooth management settings, open Bluetooth preferences from either the Apple menu > System Preferences or the Bluetooth status menu > Open Bluetooth preferences.

To manage a Bluetooth peripheral, select it from the list, then Control-click to open a shortcut menu. From this menu you can connect or disconnect a device, possibly rename a device, or remove a device pairing so your Mac will no longer attempt to connect to it. Some devices, such as iPhone, are named on the device and cannot be changed from Bluetooth preferences. You can also remove a device pairing from this list by clicking the small x button to the right.

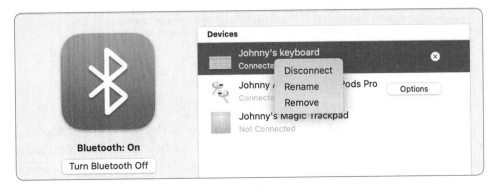

Bluetooth preferences displays an Options button for some devices, such as AirPods Pro. Click Options to reveal more options for that Bluetooth device.

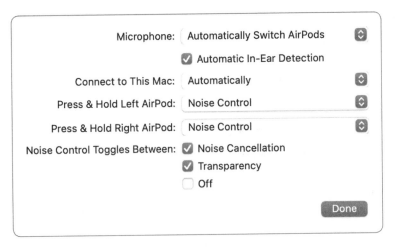

Click the Advanced button at the bottom of the Bluetooth preferences to reveal a dialog where you can adjust additional Bluetooth settings. These settings are especially useful for desktop Mac computers that use only wireless keyboards and mice.

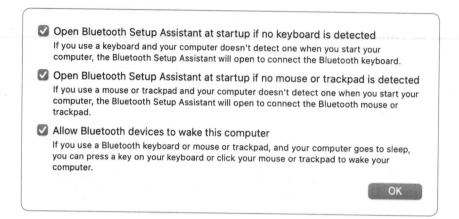

You'll find Bluetooth sharing settings in Shared preferences. Like other sharing services, Bluetooth sharing is off by default. Enable Bluetooth sharing as a last resort when traditional file-sharing methods aren't possible. Lesson 25, "Manage Host Sharing and Personal Firewall," discusses alternative file-sharing methods, including AirDrop wireless file sharing.

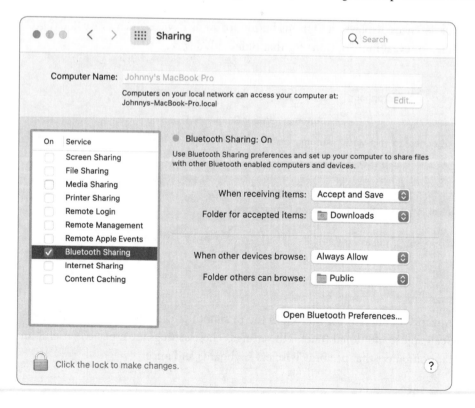

Reference 26.3
Troubleshoot Peripheral Issues

The first part of this section covers how macOS interacts with peripherals and how to iden-tify peripheral issues related to software. You also learn about general troubleshooting.

Peripheral Device Classes

Peripherals are divided into device classes based on their primary function. macOS includes built-in software drivers that allow your Mac to interact with peripherals from all device classes. Although these built-in drivers may provide basic support, many third-party devices require device-specific drivers for full functionality.

Device classes as defined in macOS include:

▶ Human input devices (HIDs)—Peripherals that allow you to directly enter informa-tion or control the Mac interface. Examples are keyboards, mice, trackpads, game controllers, tablets, and Braille interfaces.

▶ Storage devices—Internal disks, flash disks, and optical discs. Storage peripherals are covered in Lesson 11, "Manage File Systems and Storage."

▶ Video devices—These peripherals include video cameras and video converters con-nected with USB, Thunderbolt, or an expansion bus. macOS uses the QuickTime framework to support these video devices. This allows you to use QuickTime Player or any other compatible video app, such as iMovie or Final Cut Pro.

▶ Printers and scanners—Printers of all types; fax machines; and flatbed, negative, slide, document, and drum scanners. macOS uses the Image Capture framework to support scanners. This allows you to control scanners with Image Capture or any other com-patible third-party capture app, such as Adobe Photoshop. This topic is covered in Lesson 27, "Manage Printers and Scanners."

▶ Cameras—These peripherals include both directly connected cameras and camera storage cards. Many digital cameras, when connected to a computer, extend their internal storage to the computer. In this case, macOS accesses the camera's internal storage, or any directly attached camera storage cards, as it does any other storage device. An app like Photos then takes over to copy the picture files from the camera storage to the Mac. Some cameras support a tethered capture mode in which they are directly controlled by the Mac and send the captured picture data directly to the Mac. macOS uses the Image Capture framework to support this type of camera. This allows you to use Image Capture or another compatible third-party capture app.

▶ Audio devices—These peripherals include external audio interfaces connected with USB, Thunderbolt, or an expansion bus. macOS uses the Core Audio framework to support these audio devices. This allows you to use any compatible audio app, such as GarageBand or Logic Pro.

Peripheral Device Drivers

macOS is an intermediary between peripherals and apps. If an app supports a general device class, macOS handles all the technical details of communicating with each model of peripheral in that class.

Here's an example: for an app to receive input, it needs to receive information from the keyboard, mouse, trackpad, and the like, but it doesn't have to handle any details about how to interpret the electrical signals from that device, because that's handled by macOS. This separation of peripherals and apps by macOS enables you to use nearly any combination of the two with few incompatibilities.

macOS uses device drivers, which are specialized pieces of software, to allow peripherals to communicate with your Mac.

For some peripherals, macOS can use a generic driver, but for other peripherals, macOS must use a device driver created specifically for the peripheral. You install most device drivers using an installer utility that places the driver software in the appropriate resource folder on your Mac. macOS implements device drivers in one of four ways: System Extensions, legacy System Extensions, framework plug-ins, or apps.

When you add support for a new third-party peripheral that requires custom drivers, check the peripheral manufacturer's website to obtain the latest version of the driver software.

Device driver implementations in macOS include:

▶ System Extensions—System Extensions extend the functionality of your Mac. macOS loads and unloads System Extensions automatically as needed. Reference 9.9, "Approve System Extensions," has more information

▶ Legacy System Extensions—Previously referred to as third-party kernel extensions (kexts). Contact the device vendor to ask them for an updated System Extension or consider using a different device. See Apple Support article HT210999, "About system extensions and macOS," for more information.

▶ Framework plug-ins—This type of device driver adds support for a specific peripheral to an existing system framework. For example, support for additional scanners and digital cameras is facilitated through plug-ins to the Image Capture framework.

▶ Apps—In some cases a peripheral is best supported by an app written just for that peripheral.

Troubleshoot General Peripheral Issues

Use the following techniques for general peripheral troubleshooting:

▶ Check System Information first. Connected peripherals appear in System Information whether or not their software driver is functioning. So if a connected peripheral does not show up in System Information, then you are almost certainly experiencing a hardware failure. If a connected peripheral appears as normal in System Information, you are probably experiencing a software driver issue. In that case, use System Information to validate whether the expected kernel extensions are loaded.

▶ Unplug and then reconnect the peripheral. Doing so reinitializes the peripheral connection and forces macOS to reload any peripheral-specific drivers.

▶ Plug the peripheral into a different port or use a different cable. Doing so helps you rule out any bad hardware, including host ports, cables, and inoperable hubs.

▶ Unplug other devices on the same bus. Another device on the shared bus may be causing an issue.

▶ Resolve potential USB power issues. The USB interface can prove problematic if devices are trying to draw too much power. Try plugging the USB device directly into the Mac instead of a USB hub.

▶ Shut down the Mac, fully power down all peripherals, turn your peripherals on, then turn your Mac on. This troubleshooting technique reinitializes the peripheral connections and reloads the software drivers.

▶ Try the peripheral with another Mac. This helps you determine whether the issue is with your Mac or the peripheral. If the device doesn't work with other computers, your Mac is not the source of the issue.

▶ Use Software Update preferences to check for macOS updates.

▶ Use the App Store to check for app updates.

▶ Check for third-party app updates.

▶ Check the peripheral manufacturer's website for the latest driver updates.

▶ Check for peripheral software updates. Like software updates, firmware updates may also resolve peripheral issues.

Exercise 26.1
Examine Peripherals Using System Information

> **Prerequisites**
>
> ▸ You must have created the Johnny Appleseed account (Exercise 7.1, "Create a Standard User Account").
>
> ▸ You must have an external USB device. This device can include, but isn't limited to, flash media or a printer.

NOTE ▸ If you don't meet these prerequisites, reading the exercises will enhance your knowledge of the processes.

In Exercise 11.1, "View Disk and Volume Information," you used System Information to view information about your internal storage. In this exercise, you use System Information to identify devices on a bus.

Examine Internal Devices

There are several ways to open System Information. In an earlier exercise, you opened it by choosing Apple menu > About This Mac and then clicking System Report. In this exercise you open System Information a different way.

1   If necessary, log in as Johnny Appleseed.

2   Click the Apple menu.

3   Press and hold the Option key, then choose Apple menu > System Information.

   System Information opens and shows information grouped into Hardware, Network, and Software categories.

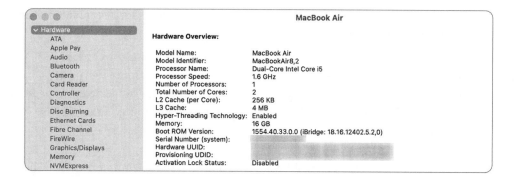

4   In the Hardware list on the left, click Graphics/Displays.

Information about your graphics processor is displayed.

5   In the Hardware list, click USB to inspect devices connected to the USB bus. (This is called the USB Device Tree.)

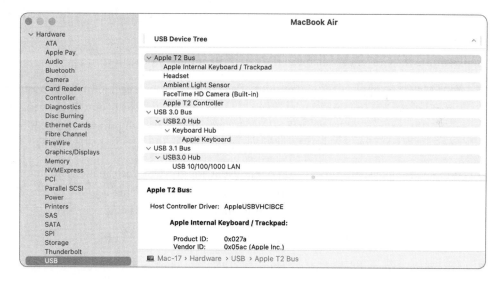

In this example, System Information indicates that there are three USB buses, all of which have devices connected to them. Several of the buses are internal to the Mac.

If a device is connected to a hub, it's listed beneath the hub and indented. This example shows a Keyboard Hub entry with an Apple Keyboard connected. Although the hub and keyboard are separate devices at the USB level, they are both parts of a single physical device: an Apple USB keyboard. Most USB keyboards contain a built-in hub.

6   Examine the USB report for your Mac and determine which devices are internal and which are external.

Examine External USB Devices

For this exercise, you must have at least one external USB device connected to your Mac. If no suitable USB device is available, quit System Information and skip this exercise. You may move on to Lesson 27.

1   If necessary, plug in the external USB device and refresh System Information. Choose File > Refresh Information (Command-R).

2   Select an external USB device in the USB report for your Mac.

Details about the device appear in the lower pane.

3   Examine the speed listed for the device.

The speed at which a USB device can run depends on its capability and the speeds of the port and intermediate hubs through which it is connected.

4   Examine the Current Available and Current Required information.

Your Mac can supply a certain amount of electricity through each of its USB ports. If too many devices are on the port, there may not be enough electricity. To prevent this, macOS keeps track of how much electricity is available at each point in the USB bus and disables devices if it calculates that not enough power is available for them.

5   While leaving System Information open displaying the USB information, unplug the device from your Mac (if it is a storage device, eject it first), plug it into a different USB port, and choose File > Refresh Information (Command-R).

System Information doesn't update the window unless you tell it to.

6   Locate the external device in the report to discover whether it changed places or if its statistics changed.

7   If you have an external hub, try plugging the device into a port and refresh the display in System Information again.

Determine whether enough power is available from the hub to run the device and whether its speed decreased because it's connected through a hub.

8   Quit System Information.

Lesson 27

Manage Printers and Scanners

In this lesson, you learn how macOS works with different print and scan technologies and how to manage and trouble-shoot printers and multifunctioning devices connected to your Mac.

Reference 27.1
Printing in macOS

macOS uses a combination of AirPrint and CUPS technologies to enable you to quickly set up printers.

AirPrint

AirPrint is an Apple technology that helps you find printers and then print full-quality output without downloading or installing printer drivers (software that allows computers to communicate with printers).

AirPrint is built into most popular printer models, which are listed in Apple Support article HT201311, "About AirPrint," updated regularly. If your printer was made in the last several years, it probably works with AirPrint.

If your printer isn't AirPrint-enabled, you can make sure it's compatible with macOS Big Sur by checking with the printer manufacturer.

GOALS

▶ Describe the technologies that enable macOS to print

▶ Configure macOS for printers and multifunctioning devices

▶ Manage and trouble-shoot print jobs

CUPS

macOS uses the open source CUPS printing system to manage local printing. CUPS uses the Internet Printing Protocol (IPP/2.1) standard to manage print tasks and PostScript Printer Description (PPD) files for printer drivers. PPD files can describe PostScript and non-PostScript printers.

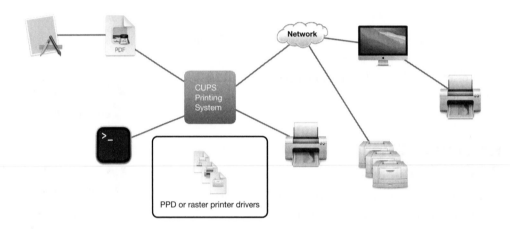

A print job starts when you print from an app or use a print command from Terminal. macOS generates a file called a spool file and places it in the /private/var/spool/cups/ folder.

The CUPS background process, cupsd, passes the spool file through filter processes known as the *print chain*. These processes convert the spool file to a format that is understood by the destination printer and communicate the information to the printer. To find out more about CUPS, see the official CUPS website at www.cups.org.

Printer Drivers

For printers that don't support AirPrint, you must associate an appropriate printer driver with the printer before you can use the printer.

Apple supplies printer drivers for most popular printer models, including Brother, Canon, Epson, Fuji-Xerox, HP, Lexmark, Ricoh, and Samsung.

New installations of macOS include only Apple and generic print drivers. macOS upgrade installations also install drivers for printers already in use by the Mac.

macOS also includes support for standard PostScript and Printer Command Language (PCL) printers.

Third-party printer drivers are installed to /Library/Printers/PPDs/Contents/Resources. This folder might contain other vendor folders that include ancillary printer driver resources.

After you add a printer configuration, a copy of the PPD with the name of the device is placed in the /private/etc/cups/ppd folder and two configuration files are modified:

▸ /private/etc/cups/printers.conf

▸ /Library/Preferences/org.cups.printers.plist

The first time you print or access a printer queue, macOS creates a printer queue app, with the name of the device, in ~/Library/Printers in the user's home folder.

Reference 27.2
Configure Printers and Scanners

The way you add and configure a printer on your Mac depends on the printer and how your Mac connects to it:

▸ AirPrint-enabled printers that are directly connected to your Mac—macOS automatically adds and configures them.

▸ AirPrint-enabled printers that are on your local network—You can add them with a little extra configuration.

▸ Printers that don't support AirPrint—You may have to choose the connection type, which printer driver to use, or even download and install a printer driver.

For best results when you add a new printer, enable the option "Automatically keep my Mac up to date" in Software Update preferences and add printers while you are logged in as an administrator user. Software Update is covered in Lesson 6, "Update macOS."

NOTE ► If you want a user to be able to add and remove printers without providing administrator credentials, make that user a member of the lpadmin group. The man page for *dseditgroup* has more information.

Configure a Directly Attached Printer

NOTE ► If you have an AirPrint-enabled printer, don't install software or drivers from the printer manufacturer. If you install printer software that you didn't get from Apple, your printer's software may not be updated automatically when you use Software Update.

Connect your AirPrint-enabled printer to your Mac with an appropriate cable. It doesn't matter what kind of user account you're logged in to your Mac with; macOS automatically configures the printer.

If your directly attached printer isn't AirPrint-enabled, contact the printer manufacturer for instructions on how to get and install printer drivers. Then connect the printer to your Mac.

However, if you have an older printer that doesn't support AirPrint driverless technology, be sure to log in as an administrator before you continue trying to configure the printer.

Your Mac might automatically install the driver software needed to use that device. For some older printers, your Mac displays a message asking you to download new software. In this case, be sure to click Install to download and install it.

If the "Automatically keep my Mac up to date" option is disabled in Software Update preferences, you can attach the printer to your Mac, then open Software Update to check for printer drivers. If printer drivers are available for the printer, Software Update installs printer drivers silently. You can close Software Update preferences and continue to configure the printer.

If a non-administrator user attaches a new printer for the first time, macOS won't configure the printer if the driver is missing. Also, if a printer driver for a directly attached printer is unavailable from Apple, then when you plug it in, macOS won't recognize the printer. In this case, you must manually acquire and install the printer driver with administrator credentials.

You can verify the printer was added by opening the Print dialog from any app (File > Print) or from Printers & Scanners preferences. In Printers & Scanners preferences, you can tell that a printer is locally connected if its location has the same name as the Computer Name (configured in Sharing preferences) for your Mac.

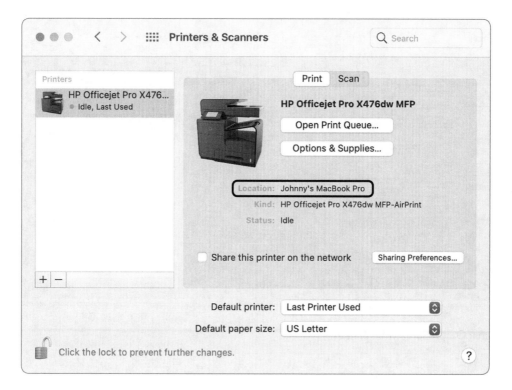

Configure a Local Network Printer

You must be logged in on your Mac with an administrator account to add a local network printer. If your Mac and printer are already connected to the same local network, the printer might be available to you without any setup. macOS can automatically discover standalone printers that support Bonjour (also known as mDNS), standalone printers that support AirPrint, and any printer shared from another Mac or AirPort wireless base station. If your network printer isn't AirPrint-enabled, use Software Update preferences to install available printer drivers.

One way to add and configure a network printer that your Mac discovers on your local network is with the following steps:

1   Open an app that enables you to print.

2   Choose File > Print.

3   Open the Printer menu, then in the Nearby Printers section of the menu, choose your printer.

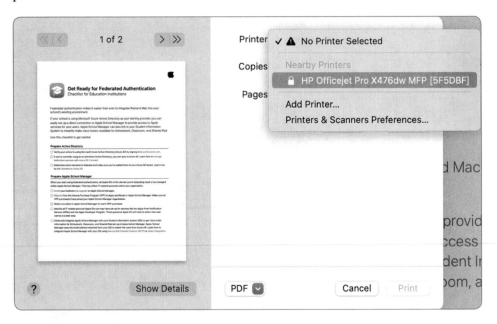

macOS prepares your printer.

4   Confirm that your printer is available in the Printer menu.

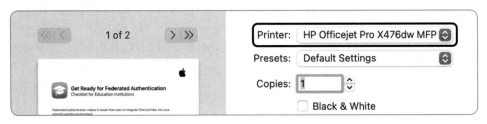

Manually Configure a Printer

If the network printer doesn't support automatic network discovery with Bonjour, you must configure it manually. Also, if a directly attached printer doesn't automatically configure, you can manually add it. Add a new printer or multifunctioning device in one of these ways:

▶ From any app, open a Print dialog by choosing File > Print. Next, from the Printer menu, choose Add Printer.

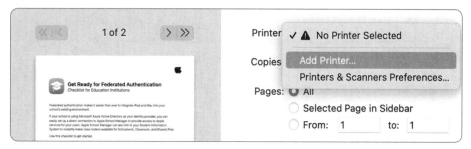

▶ Open System Preferences and click the Printers & Scanners icon. Click the Add (+) button at the bottom of the Printers list.

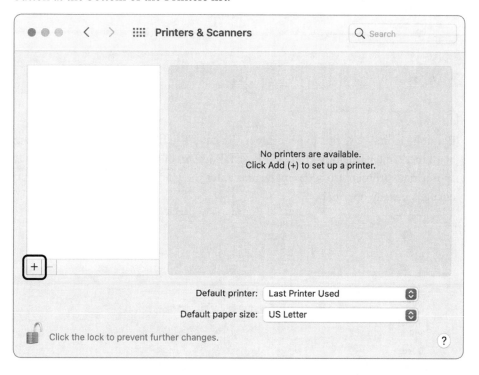

The Add Printer window features several panes for selecting a printer or multifunctioning device. Access these panes by clicking the following buttons in the toolbar:

▶ Default (printer icon)—Use the browser in this pane to find and select directly attached USB printers and network printers discovered using Bonjour, AirPrint, or network directory services.

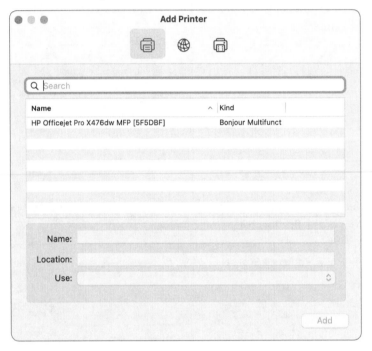

▶ IP (globe icon)—Use this pane to manually enter the IP address or DNS host name of a Line Printer Daemon (LPD), IPP, or HP JetDirect printer. You must choose the appropriate protocol from the menu and enter the printer's address. Entering a printer queue is usually optional.

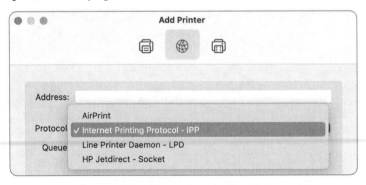

▶ Windows (printer icon)—Use this pane to select printers shared with the Server Message Block (SMB) printer sharing protocol. Double-click an SMB server and authenticate to access the server's shared printers. For more information, see "Use your Mac to print to a printer connected to a Windows computer," at support.apple.com/guide/mac-help/mchlp2437 in the macOS User Guide.

An advanced configuration option is also available if you want to manually enter the printer location, but you should do so only when macOS can't properly auto-locate a printer. The Advanced button is hidden by default. To reveal this button, Control-click in the Add Printer window toolbar. Then choose Customize Toolbar from the menu.

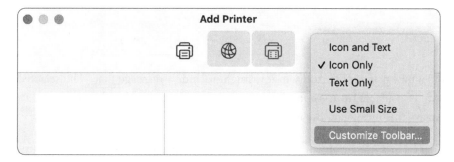

Drag the Advanced button to the toolbar, then click Done. You can click Advanced (the gear icon), then start configuring the printer by choosing the printer type.

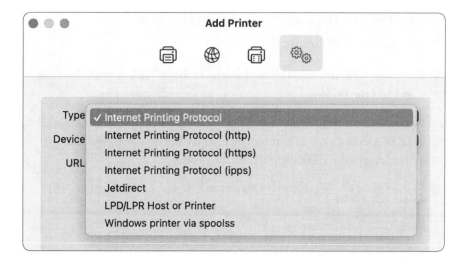

After you choose a printer or multifunctioning device from the top half of the new printer configuration dialog, macOS completes the bottom half for you using information it discovered, which includes selecting the appropriate printer driver if possible. The Name and Location fields are there to help you identify the device. Set those to anything you like.

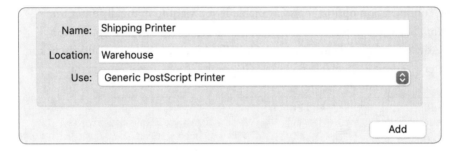

When you add a new printer, the Add window might include a message that "The selected printer software is available from Apple. Click Add to download it and add this printer." Your Mac displays this message if the following are true:

▶ You are logged in as an administrator user (or you are logged in as a standard account user who is a member of the lpadmin group).

▶ The option "Automatically keep my Mac up to date" is not selected in Software Update preferences.

▶ You add a printer that your Mac doesn't have the driver for already.

▶ Your Mac is connected to the internet.

If you meet all the conditions and your Mac displays the message, click Add to download the printer driver and add the printer.

If macOS doesn't ask you to download and add the printer driver (or you aren't connected to the internet), macOS selects a generic printer driver and displays a message that the printer driver may not let you use all the features of the printer.

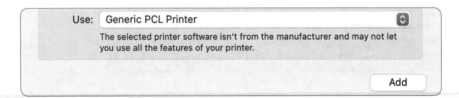

If Apple doesn't provide a suitable printer driver, you may be able to select a built-in printer driver. To select a printer driver, choose Select Software from the Use menu.

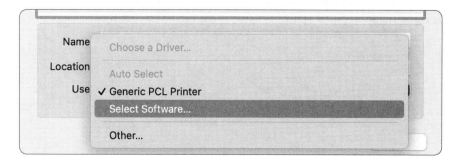

You can manually scroll through the list of installed printer drivers, but using the Filter field may be quicker. After you select an appropriate printer driver, click OK to use that driver. The following figure displays all of the default printer drivers that come with macOS Big Sur.

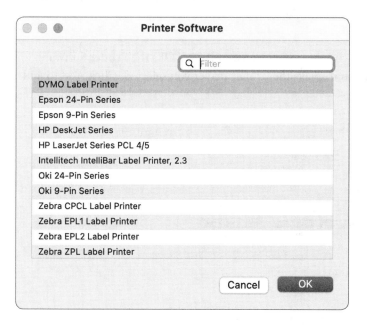

If your Mac doesn't already have an appropriate printer driver for your printer, you may be able to get a printer driver directly from the printer manufacturer. Try using Software Update to automatically install printer drivers before you try downloading printer drivers from the printer manufacturer.

If you already downloaded and installed any other printer drivers, the Printer Software window displays additional printer drivers. The following figure shows the Printer Software window on a Mac that has drivers installed from "HP Printer Drivers v5.1 for macOS" at support.apple.com/kb/DL1888 as an example.

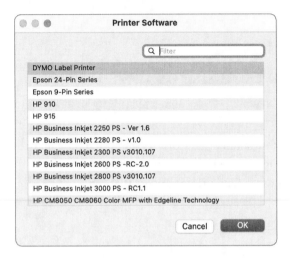

After you select the printer driver you want to use and click OK, the Printer Software window closes. The Use menu displays the printer driver you selected. Click Add to add the selected printer.

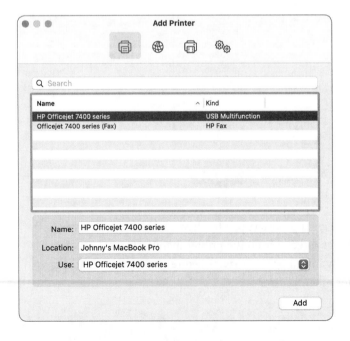

To select a printer driver that you downloaded directly from the printer manufacturer, choose Other from the Use menu; then in the open dialog, select the printer driver and click Open.

If no printer driver is available for your printer, you can use a built-in generic printer driver.

If you configure an LPD printer connection, you must manually specify the appropriate printer driver. This step can occur with HP JetDirect and SMB printer connections.

If you configure an IP printer, macOS displays an additional dialog where you can select special printer options. After you complete the printer configuration, open the Print dialog from any app, or from Printers & Scanners preferences, and verify that the printer is added.

In Printers & Scanners preferences, you can tell which printers are network printers if their location is shown as something different than your local Mac computer sharing name.

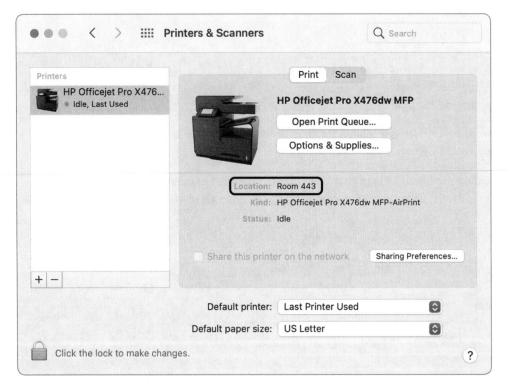

Some printer drivers include additional functionality. For example, the previous screenshot shows a multifunctioning device with a Scan tab, which indicates that macOS configured the scanning driver software. If your multifunctioning device doesn't include the Scan tab, try using Printers & Scanners preferences to remove the multifunctioning device, then add it again.

> **NOTE ▶** You can use Terminal to add printers, and in Apple Remote Desktop, you can choose Manage > Send UNIX Command to create printers on many Mac computers at the same time. The man pages for *lpadmin*, *cupsenable*, and *cupsaccept* have more information.

Modify an Existing Printer

You may have to edit a printer configuration after you set it up. Depending on the printer model, you may not be allowed to modify the print driver settings from Printers & Scanners preferences. In that case, to change a printer's selected driver you must delete the printer and add it again. From Printers & Scanners preferences, you can:

▶ Remove a printer configuration—Select the item you want to delete from the printer list, then click the Remove (–) button at the bottom of the list.

▶ Set printing defaults—From the two menus at the bottom of Printers & Scanners preferences, choose the default printer and paper size. Be careful when you set the default printer for Last Printer Used. You will have no permanent default printer and the default destination for print jobs might constantly change.

▶ Open a print queue—Select a printer from the list and click the Open Print Queue button. Details on print queues are covered later in this lesson.

▶ Edit an existing configuration and check supply levels—Select a printer from the list, then click the Options & Supplies button. In the resulting dialog, you can edit the printer configuration—including changing the printer name, changing the location, and if available, checking the printer supply levels—and open the printer hardware configuration utility.

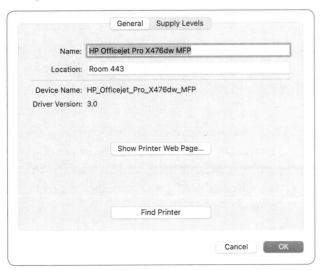

▶ Manage scanning—Select a multifunctioning device from the list and click the Scan
   button. From this interface, open the scanner image capture interface or enable local
   network scanner sharing.

Share Printers

Your Mac shared print service is made available with IPP printer sharing protocols. Although macOS and Windows are compatible with IPP, different versions of
Windows might require additional drivers for IPP. IPP supports automatic printer driver
configuration and installation for macOS, so when another Mac user connects to your
Mac shared print service, that user's Mac automatically selects, and downloads if necessary, the appropriate printer drivers.

The CUPS-shared print service also allows other network clients to locate your shared
printer configurations with Bonjour. Different versions of Windows might require additional drivers for Bonjour. Alternatively, network clients can enter your Mac computer's IP
address or DNS host name to access your Mac shared print service. Configuring your Mac
computer's identification for providing network services is covered in Lesson 25, "Manage
Host Sharing and Personal Firewall."

Users can't access shared print services on a Mac in sleep mode. But you can configure
your Mac to not sleep, or to wake from sleep when other users access those resources.
Use Energy Saver preferences (for desktop Mac computers) or Battery preferences (for
notebook Mac computers) to enable the appropriate option to wake for network access
(the option varies depending on the configuration of your Mac). See "Share your Mac
resources when it's in sleep," at support.apple.com/guide/mac-help/mh27905 in the
macOS User Guide, and see Reference 28.3, "Sleep Modes, Logout, and Shutdown," for
more information.

To share printers from your Mac, open Sharing preferences, then unlock if necessary.
Select the Printer Sharing checkbox to enable printer sharing. Selecting this checkbox configures cupsd (which is always running in the background) to listen for IPP print service
requests on TCP port 631.

By default, no printers are shared. To enable sharing for printer configurations, select
the checkboxes next to the printers you want to share. Optionally, you can limit who is
allowed to print to your shared printers. By default, all users are allowed access to your
shared printing devices. To limit access, select a shared device from the Printers list, then
click the Add (+) button at the bottom of the Users list.

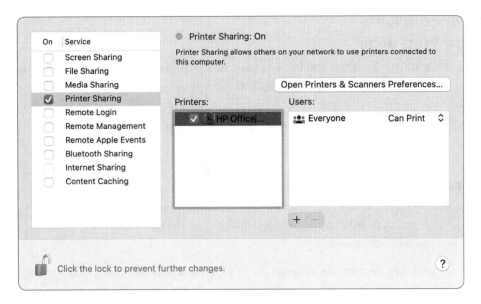

A dialog appears where you can select user or group accounts to whom you want to grant access to the printer. After you add an account, macOS automatically denies access to guest users by configuring No Access for Everyone in the Users list. Also, with limited printing access enabled, users have to authenticate to print to your shared printer.

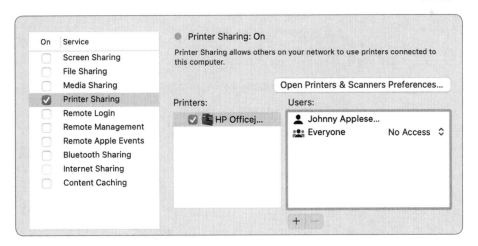

Share only printers that other Mac users can't otherwise discover. If you share a network printer that's already available on your network, other Mac users will discover that printer listed multiple times in the Nearby Printers list.

Reference 27.3
Manage Print Jobs

This unified Print dialog has two modes. The basic mode enables you to preview and start a print job using default settings, and the details mode lets you specify any page or print option and manage print setting presets. Some apps, especially graphic design and desktop publishing apps, use custom dialogs for printing that might look different from the standard Print dialog covered in this lesson.

Start a Print Job

To start a print job using default print settings, from an app choose File > Print (or press Command-P). Some apps bypass the Print dialog and send the print job to your default printer when you use Command-P.

When the Print dialog appears, depending on app support, it may slide out of the app's window title bar or it may also appear as its own dialog. Most apps show a print preview, and some might show the basic print options. The default printer and print preset are selected, but you choose the number of pages, copies, and duplex (two-sided) options, if available. Customizing printer presets is covered in the next section of this lesson.

When the print job is started, macOS automatically opens the print queue app associated with the destination printer. Although no window opens if the print job is successful, you can click the print queue in the Dock.

Configure Detailed Print Settings and Presets

To start a print job that uses custom print settings, from an app open the Print dialog. When you open the Print dialog, the default printer and print presets are selected, but you can choose other configured printers or presets from the associated menu.

Clicking the Show Details button expands the Print dialog to its full details mode. In the full details mode, you can click the Hide Details button to return to the basic Print dialog mode. The Print dialog also remembers which mode you last used for each app.

On the left side of the detailed Print dialog, you can page through a preview of the print job, much like the preview in the basic Print dialog. Changes you make to the page layout settings are instantly reflected in the preview. On the right side of the dialog, you can configure possible print settings for most apps. The top half features more detailed page setup and print settings.

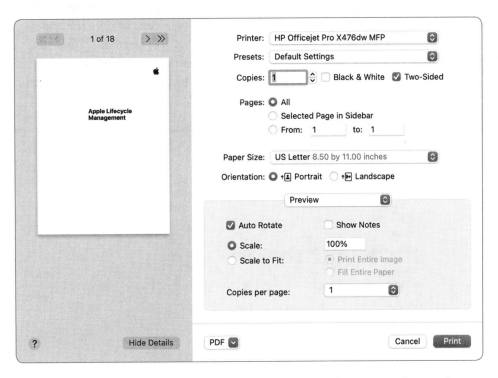

Settings on the bottom half vary depending on the app you're printing from and your printer driver. You can choose a category of print settings to modify from the menu that separates the print settings from top to bottom. The settings list and configuration options vary for different apps, printers, and printer drivers. The following figure displays the options available when printing a Keynote document.

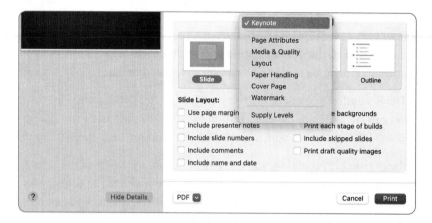

To save the current print settings as a preset, choose "Save Current Settings as Preset" from the Presets menu. Select whether you want this preset to apply to all printers or just the currently selected printer. By saving a preset, you make it accessible from the Presets menu in the details view of any Print dialog. The print presets are saved in ~/Library/Preferences/ in com.apple.print.custompresets.plist for presets that apply to all printers, and in com.apple.print.custompresets.forprinter.printername.plist for presets for a specific printer, so each user has their own custom print presets. Print presets apply to all apps.

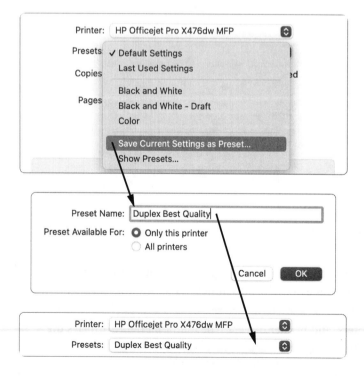

To manage existing print presets, open the print Presets dialog by choosing Show Presets from the Presets menu. In the print Presets dialog, select a preset to inspect its settings and values, and optionally use the Delete and Duplicate buttons at the bottom of the presets list. If you double-click a print preset, you can rename it. When you finish managing print presets, click OK to save the changes and return to the Print dialog.

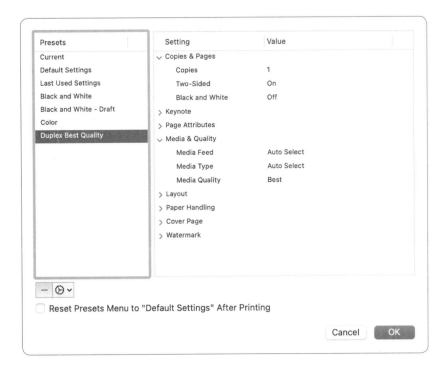

Create PDF Documents

macOS includes built-in Portable Document Format (PDF) architecture and editing tools, including tools to create PDF documents or perform basic editing. Any app that can print can also generate high-quality PDF documents. In any Print dialog, click the PDF button. A menu appears, which you can use to save a PDF to any location.

From the PDF menu, you can also choose a PDF workflow that accepts and processes PDF files. Some preset workflows are built in, but you can add your own PDF workflows by choosing Edit Menu from the PDF menu. Or, depending on who needs access to them, you can manually add PDF workflows to /Library/PDF Services or ~/Library/PDF Services. To create custom PDF workflows, use Automator to create a Print Plugin or use Script Editor.

You can also edit PDFs in Preview. Reference 20.2, "Manage App Extensions," has more information.

Manage Printer Queues

When a print job starts, the spool file is placed in /private/var/spool/cups, and CUPS takes over to process the file and send it to the printer. When you print from an app or the Finder, macOS opens a print queue app to manage the print job. If a job completes quickly, the file is in the print queue only for a few moments, and the print queue app quits when the print job is done.

If macOS detects an error with a printer, it stops all print jobs that are in the printer queue. You can still start print jobs, but they just back up in the queue.

To manage print job queues, access the printer queue app in one of the following ways:

▶ If a printer queue is open, click its icon in the Dock. In the following example screenshot, the printer queue's Dock icon shows a "1" in the red badge icon in the upper right of the icon, indicating that there is currently a job in the queue. Also, as indicated by the orange connection badge in the lower-left corner of the icon, this printer queue has network issues that are preventing the print job from completing.

▶ You can manually open a printer queue from Printers & Scanners preferences by double-clicking the device in the printer list or by selecting the device from the printer list and clicking the Open Print Queue button.

▶   You can also manually open a printer queue from the Finder by navigating to
~/Library/Printers and double-clicking a printer.

When the printer queue opens, it displays the printer status and queued print jobs.

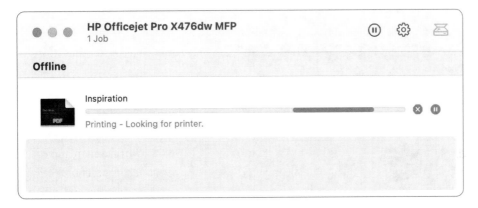

To pause or resume the jobs in the printer queue, click the Pause or Resume button (the
button toggles between the two modes) in the queue app toolbar. To hold or resume a
print job, select it from the job list and click the small Hold or Resume button to the right
of the print job progress bar (the button toggles between the two). To delete a job, select it
from the job list and click the small x button to the right of the print job progress bar.

You can select a job in the printer queue list, then press the Space bar to open
a Quick Look preview window for the print job. For a held job, choose Jobs >
Resume Job on Page, then specify a page number to resume printing on. You can reorder
print jobs in the printer queue by dragging the job you want to reorder in the list. You can
also drag jobs from one printer queue window to another.

Other features are available in the printer queue app toolbar. You can reconfigure the
printer by clicking the Settings button in the toolbar. Also, for a supported multifunctioning printer, you can click the Scanner button in the toolbar to open the Scanner interface.

You might want to leave often-used printer queues in the Dock for direct access.
Control-click the queue app's Dock icon and, from the shortcut menu, choose Options >
Keep in Dock. A benefit to having your printers in the Dock is that you can drag a docu-
ment on top of a printer icon to quickly print a single copy of the document.

You can also provide quick access to your printer queues by dragging the ~/Library/ Printers folder from the Finder to your Dock. Click this folder in your Dock to open a folder with your configured devices.

Reference 27.4
Troubleshoot Print Issues

You will probably experience more printing issues that are caused by hardware rather than software. The following is a series of general print system troubleshooting techniques:

▶ Check the printer queue app first. The printer queue lets you know if there is a printer connection issue. At the same time, verify that the queue isn't paused and that no jobs are on hold. Sometimes deleting old print jobs from the queue helps clear the problem.

▶ Double-check page and print settings. If the job is printing but doesn't print correctly, then double-check page and print settings using the Print dialog details mode.

▶ Review the PDF output of the app. The CUPS workflow is app > PDF > CUPS > printer. Verifying whether the PDF looks correct lets you know if the source of the problem is with the app or the printing system.

▶ Print from another app. If you suspect the app is the root of the problem, try printing from another app. You can also print a test page while in the printer queue app by choosing Printer > Print Test Page.

▶ If you have trouble adding a printer and finding an appropriate printer driver, try logging in as an administrator user before you add the printer.

▶ Check the printer hardware. Many printers have diagnostic screens or printed reports that help you identify a hardware issue. Many also have a software utility or a built-in webpage that reports errors. Click the Printer Setup button in the printer queue app toolbar to access these management interfaces. Double-check cables and connections. Lastly, contact the printer manufacturer to diagnose printer hardware issues.

▶ For directly connected printers, use the peripheral troubleshooting techniques outlined in Lesson 26, "Troubleshoot Peripherals."

▶ For network printers, use network troubleshooting techniques described in Lesson 23, "Troubleshoot Network Issues," and Lesson 24, "Manage Network Services."

▶ Delete and reconfigure printers. From Printers & Scanners preferences, delete and reconfigure a problem printer using the techniques described earlier in this lesson. Doing so resets the device drivers and queue.

▶ Reset the entire print system. Open Printers & Scanners preferences. If you're logged in with a standard user account, click the lock and provide administrator credentials. Control-click in the printers list and choose "Reset printing system" from the shortcut menu. Click Reset in the verification dialog. Following these steps clears configured devices, shared settings, custom presets, and queued print jobs.

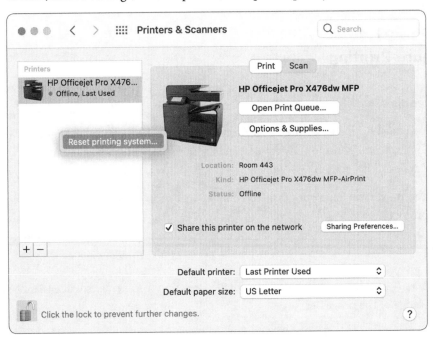

▶ For non-AirPrint printers, remove printer drivers by moving the contents of /Library/ Printers to another location.

▶ Review CUPS log files. Like other system services, CUPS writes important activity to log files. You can access the logs while in any printer queue app by choosing Printer > Error Log. This opens Console to the CUPS error_log report. While in Console, you can check the access_log and page_log reports. The error_log file may not exist if the CUPS service hasn't logged print errors. The files for these reports are in /private/var/log/cups.

▶ Reinstall or update printer drivers. You can use Software Update preferences to check for system and printer updates. You can also check the printer manufacturer's website for the latest printer driver updates. If you're using an AirPrint-enabled printer, you can check with the manufacturer to determine if there's an update for your printer model (as opposed to a printer driver update).

For advanced print system management and troubleshooting, go to the web interface to CUPS for your Mac at http://localhost:631 and follow the instructions.

See "Solve printing problems on Mac" at support.apple.com/guide/mac-help/mh14002 in the macOS User Guide for more information. Or in Printers & Scanners preferences, click the Help (question mark) button.

Exercise 27.1
Configure Printing

▶ **Prerequisites**

▶ You must have created the Local Administrator (Exercise 3.1, "Configure a Mac for Exercises") and Johnny Appleseed (Exercise 7.1, "Create a Standard User Account") accounts.

▶ You must have a network printer available that supports the Bonjour discovery protocol.

NOTE ▶ If you don't meet these prerequisites, reading the exercises will enhance your knowledge of the processes.

Configure a Bonjour Printer

In this exercise, you discover and configure a network printer through the Bonjour service discovery protocol.

1   If necessary, log in as Johnny Appleseed.

2   Open Printers & Scanners preferences.

3   If necessary, click the lock button, then authenticate as Local Administrator.

4   Click the Add (+) button under the printer list.

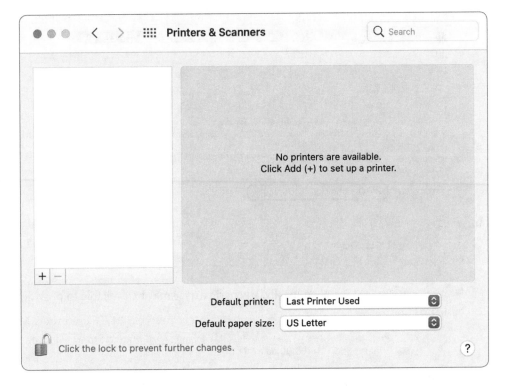

The Add Printer window opens and shows a list of nearby printers.

Depending on the local network environment, the contents of this list on your network may vary. See Reference 27.2, "Configure Printers and Scanners," for more information.

5   Select the printer you want to use in the list of available printers.

Depending on the type of printer, one of several things might happen:

▶ If a driver for the printer is installed on your Mac, is available from the Mac sharing the printer, or is available from the printer, it's selected and shown in the Use menu.

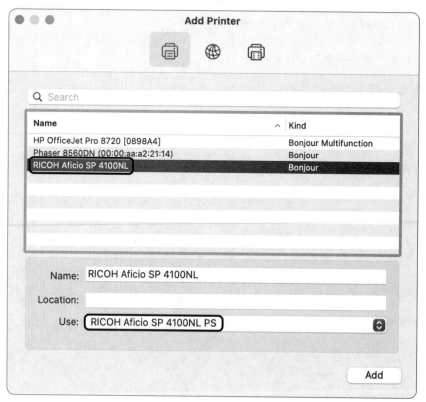

▶ If the driver isn't installed locally, a generic driver may be available to provide basic printing.

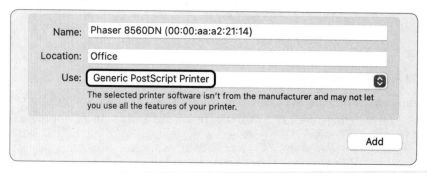

In this case, find and install a driver (probably from the printer manufacturer). Close the Add Printer window and try again after you find and install the appropriate driver.

▶   If the printer is AirPrint compatible, you are able to add it without having a printer-specific driver.

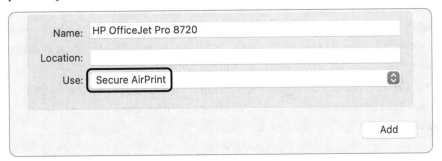

6   With the printer selected, click Add.

Your Mac fetches information about optional features from the printer (or the Mac sharing it), then completes the setup process. Your Mac is now configured to print to this printer.

7   When the new print queue is set up, select it and click the Open Print Queue button.

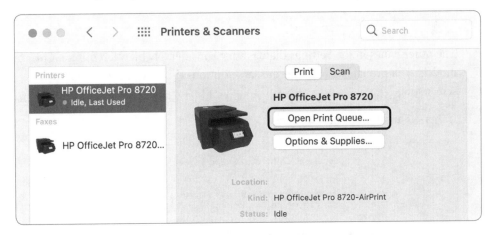

The window that appears lets you inspect and change settings for the print queue. Depending on the printer capabilities, options may include a Scanner button.

8   Click the Settings button.

A dialog opens that enables you to inspect and change information about the print queue configuration. These settings are also accessible from Printers & Scanners preferences when you click the Options & Supplies button.

Use the General pane to configure the name and location displayed for the printer. You may find it useful to name printers that would otherwise have their model name listed.

9   If appropriate, change the name and location to something more descriptive.

General	Supply Levels

Name:	Office Multifunction
Location:	Main Office
Device Name:	HP_OfficeJet_Pro_8720
Driver Version:	3.0

The other panes in the Settings dialogs vary considerably between different printer models. You probably won't find the same options that you see in the following screenshots.

10   If there is an Options button, click it.

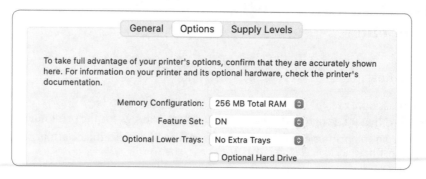

General	Options	Supply Levels

To take full advantage of your printer's options, confirm that they are accurately shown here. For information on your printer and its optional hardware, check the printer's documentation.

Memory Configuration:	256 MB Total RAM
Feature Set:	DN
Optional Lower Trays:	No Extra Trays
	☐ Optional Hard Drive

If this printer is shared from a Mac, the Mac controls what options are configured for the printer. If you are connecting to the printer directly, you can change the options.

11 If there is a Supply Levels button, click it.

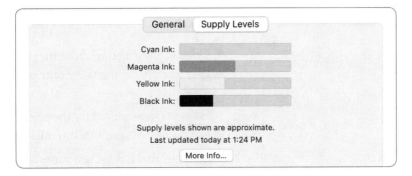

If you are connecting to the printer directly and the printer supports it, you can inspect the printer supply levels.

12 If there is a Utility button, click it.

If available, this Printers & Scanners pane gives you access to utilities supplied by this printer driver. The functions vary depending on the printer model. Some drivers include a separate utility program, which you can open from this pane.

13 Click OK to dismiss the Settings dialog.

14 Quit the printer queue.

The printer queue isn't an app, but it acts like one, including the Quit option under the "application" menu.

Exercise 27.2
Manage Printing

▶ **Prerequisites**

▶ You must have created the Johnny Appleseed account (Exercise 7.1, "Create a Standard User Account").

▶ You must have at least one print queue set up on your Mac from Exercise 27.1, "Configure Printing."

In this exercise, you explore the Print dialog, including saving print options as a preset, printing to PDF, and managing PDF workflows.

Print to a Printer

In this section, you print to one of the printers you just set up.

1 If necessary, log in as Johnny Appleseed.

2 Open TextEdit.

3 Click New Document (or, if necessary, press Command-N).

4 Type some text into the document, then save it to your desktop using a name of your choice.

5 In the TextEdit menu bar, choose File > Print (Command-P).

6 In the Print dialog, choose a printer from the Printer menu.

7 Click Show Details.

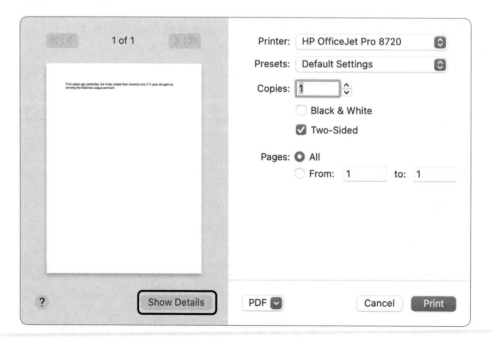

The Print dialog expands to show additional print settings.

8   Choose Layout from the configuration menu (initially set to TextEdit).

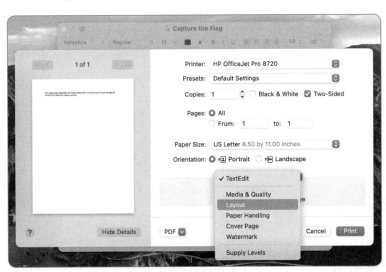

9   From the "Pages per Sheet" menu, choose 6.

10   From the Border menu, choose Single Thin Line.

As you change settings, the preview on the left shows the effects.

11   From the Presets menu, choose "Save Current Settings as Preset."

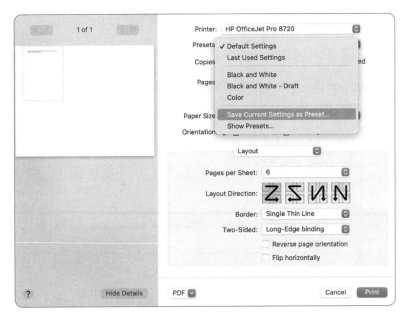

12 Name the preset **6-up with border**, make it available for all printers, then click OK.

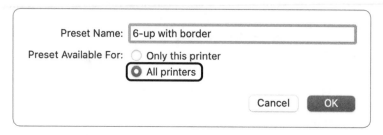

The print settings are available from the Presets menu whenever you print.

13 Use the Presets menu to switch between Default Settings and "6-up with border," then watch the effect on the print settings.

14 Click Print.

The print queue icon appears in your Dock and shows the number of jobs in the queue (1).

Manage a Print Queue

1 If possible, click the printer queue in your Dock before it becomes unavailable.

In the queue window, watch as the job is sent to the printer (or server), then is removed from the queue.

2   If the printer queue is no longer available in the Dock before you've had a chance to click it, open Printers & Scanners preferences, select the print queue on the left, then click Open Print Queue.

3   In the print queue window, click Pause.

4   Switch to TextEdit, then print the document again.

5   When you are warned that the printer has been paused, click "Add to Printer."

6   Switch to the print queue window. If your document isn't shown, quit the print queue, then reopen it from Printers & Scanners preferences. If the first document didn't successfully print, your document may be listed twice.

Your document is shown as "Ready to Print."

7   Preview the print job by double-clicking the document in the print queue or by pressing Command-Y or the Space bar.

8   Close the Quick Look window and click the Jobs menu.

This menu has options for holding, resuming, or deleting print jobs. Most of the options are also available in the print queue window.

9   Click the delete ("X") button to the right of the print job. If the queue contains two documents, delete both of them.

The job is no longer displayed in the print queue.

10   Quit the print queue.

Print to PDF

1   Switch to TextEdit, then press Command-P.

2   Click the PDF button near the bottom left of the Print dialog.

3   Choose "Open in Preview."

CUPS produces a PDF version of your document, then opens it in Preview. There are Cancel and Print buttons near the bottom right of the window.

4 Click Cancel.

This closes the document and quits Preview.

5 In TextEdit, press Command-P again.

6 From the PDF menu, choose "Save as PDF."

7 Save the PDF to your desktop.

8 Quit TextEdit.

Exercise 27.3
Troubleshoot Printing

▶ **Prerequisites**

▸ You must have created the Local Administrator (Exercise 3.1, "Configure a Mac for Exercises") and Johnny Appleseed (Exercise 7.1, "Create a Standard User Account") accounts.

▸ You must have at least one print queue set up on your Mac from Exercise 27.1, "Configure Printing."

To troubleshoot printing, you must know the print process. In this exercise, you examine print logs and reset the printing configuration.

Examine the CUPS Logs

You can examine system and user event logs in Console. In this exercise, you use Console to examine CUPS logs.

1 If necessary, log in as Johnny Appleseed.

2 Open Console.

3   Select Log Reports from the left column, then select access_log in the second column.

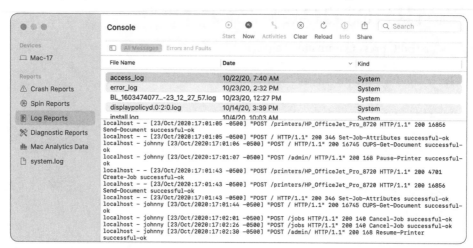

If you printed, entries appear in the access log. The page log may also contain entries for each job.

4   If the list includes page_log and error_log files, select them and examine their contents.

5   Quit Console.

Reset Printing

If you can't print to your printer and you've tried other solutions, you can restore the printing system to the macOS defaults. When you reset your printing system to the macOS defaults, you delete printers from your printer list as well as information about completed print jobs and printer presets.

1   Open Printers & Scanners preferences.

2   If necessary, click the lock button, then authenticate as Local Administrator.

3   Press and hold the Control key, then click in the printer list.

4   Choose "Reset printing system" from the menu that appears.

5   Click Reset when you're asked to confirm.

You can add your printers again when the process is complete.

6   Quit System Preferences.

Troubleshoot Startup and System Issues

This lesson focuses on the process that your Mac goes through from the moment you turn your Mac on until your Mac displays the Finder. You identify the essential files and processes required to successfully start up macOS. You also explore macOS sleep modes, logout, and shutdown. You then learn about startup shortcuts and diagnostic modes that work with macOS. Finally, you learn how to troubleshoot system initialization and user session issues.

Reference 28.1
System Initialization and Secure Boot

This section examines the main stages of the macOS startup procedure: *system initialization* (the processes required to start macOS) and *user sessions* (the processes required to prepare the user environment). When you start your Mac from macOS, different screens appear to show you the startup progress, including any issues that might keep your Mac from starting up. The startup cues discussed here are what you experience during a typical startup. Deviations are covered as you learn more.

It all starts when you turn on your Mac. You can press its power button. Some Mac notebooks also turn on in other ways—for example, when you open the lid, connect to a power adapter, or press a key or the trackpad. See "Log out, sleep, wake, restart, or shut down your Mac" at support. apple.com/guide/mac-help/mchlp2522 in the macOS User Guide for more information.

Components of system initialization covered in this guide include the following:

- Firmware—The Mac firmware tests and initializes hardware, and it locates and starts the booter.

- Booter—The booter loads the macOS kernel and essential hardware drivers into main memory and then allows the kernel to take over. During the booter stage, your Mac displays the Apple logo on the main display.

- Kernel—The kernel provides the macOS foundation and loads additional drivers and the core operating system. Your Mac displays a progress bar under the Apple logo on the main display when the kernel is loading.

- launchd—After the core operating system is loaded, it starts the first nonkernel process, launchd, which loads the rest of macOS. During this stage, your Mac displays a progress bar under the Apple logo on the main display. When this stage successfully completes, your Mac displays the login screen or the Finder, depending on whether FileVault is turned on or you are set to automatically log in.

Security Policy: Apple Silicon and Apple T2 Security Chip

If your Mac has Apple silicon, or your Intel-based Mac has the T2 chip, then by default it has a security policy to ensure that your hardware and software haven't been tampered with. With the default security policy, from the time you turn your Mac on, your Mac uses its hardware to verify every step of the boot process to ensure that the hardware and software haven't been tampered with. This way, you know your Mac is in a trustworthy state when it's started up.

Although Apple doesn't recommend changing the security policy, you can use the Startup Security Utility to inspect and modify the security policy. Using Startup Security Utility in macOS Recovery is covered in Reference 5.3, "Secure Startup."

> **NOTE ▶** As this guide went to press, in-depth details about the boot process for Mac computers with Apple silicon were not available. See "Boot process of Mac computers" at https://support.apple.com/guide/security/sec5d0fab7c6 for more information.

In the context of starting up, keep in mind that it's possible to install macOS on additional APFS volumes on the internal storage of your Mac. This way, you can switch between versions of macOS for testing, including beta versions of macOS. See Apple Support article HT208891, "Installing macOS on a separate APFS volume," for more information.

For Mac computers with Apple silicon, each version of macOS has its own security policy. This is in contrast to Intel-based Mac computers with the T2 chip, which have a security policy for the entire Mac.

For Mac computers with Apple silicon, when you start in macOS Recovery and open Startup Security Utility, you must select the system you want to use to set the security policy for, even if you have only one system.

> **NOTE** ▶ macOS Recovery displays each "system" with a disk icon and the version of macOS, where each system is actually an APFS volume group that consists of the read-only APFS System volume and the read-write APFS Data volume.

Here's an example of macOS 11.0.1 and macOS 11.1 installed on the same Mac with Apple silicon:

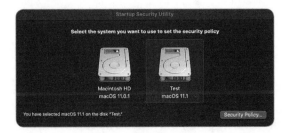

For Mac computers with Apple silicon, the default security policy for each instance of macOS is Full Security, which allows booting only software that was known to be the latest available at installation time (this is similar to the behavior for iOS and iPadOS). Apple recommends against changing the security policy.

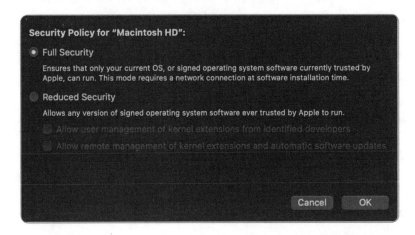

> **WARNING** ▶ Apple doesn't recommend setting the security policy to Reduced Security because it can reduce the security of your Mac. This guide mentions this configuration here to emphasize the importance of the default behavior of allowing your Mac to verify the hardware and software as part of the boot process.

By default, an Intel-based Mac with the T2 chip is configured with a security policy (labeled Secure Boot in the Startup Security Utility) of Full Security. Apple recommends that you not change this setting.

For an Intel-based Mac with the T2 chip, the security policy of No Security results in your Mac no longer evaluating the hardware and software as part of the boot process, and you can boot any system, even one that's been tampered with.

> **WARNING** ▶ Apple doesn't recommend setting the security policy to Medium Security or No Security because it can reduce the security of your Mac and result in data loss. This guide mentions this configuration here to emphasize the importance of the default behavior of allowing your Mac to verify the hardware and software as part of the boot process.

For Intel-based Mac computers without the T2 chip, the Unified Extensible Firmware Interface (UEFI) firmware loads the macOS booter from the file system without verifying that it hasn't been tampered with. And the macOS booter loads the kernel from the file system without verifying that it hasn't been tampered with. Because of this, you should use the following protections for Intel-based Mac computers without the T2 chip:

▶ Leave System Integrity Protection (SIP) enabled

▶ Turn on FileVault

▶ Configure a firmware password

See "Boot process of Mac computers without an Apple T2 Security Chip" at support.apple.com/guide/security/sec5d0fab7c6 for more information.

System Initialization: Firmware

Your Mac computer firmware, also called boot ROM (read-only memory), resides on flash memory chips built into the main computer board. The firmware has just enough software to test and initialize the hardware and locate and start the macOS booter.

> **NOTE ▶** Intel-based Mac computers have firmware based on Intel UEFI technology. In addition to supporting the Intel processor hardware, UEFI enables your Intel-based Mac to start up from macOS, Windows, or any other Intel-compatible operating system. Find out more at www.uefi.org.

Power-On Self-Test

One of the tasks your Mac firmware performs when it powers on is the power-on self-test (POST). The POST tests built-in hardware components such as processors, system memory, network interfaces, and peripheral interfaces. When your Mac passes the POST, the display should power on, and your Mac should play a startup tone. After a successful POST, the firmware locates the booter file.

Mac computers perform the POST only during a startup, not during a restart. If you're troubleshooting hardware issues, restarting isn't enough; you should shut down and then start up.

If your Mac fails the POST, the display remains blank or off and you may get hardware error codes. Depending on the age and model of your Mac, the error codes may be audible tones, a series of flashes from the external power-on light, or internal diagnostic lights illuminating. You may even encounter a combination of these things. Regardless of which error code you experience, it indicates that a hardware problem exists that macOS can't control. Visit Apple Support at support.apple.com to find your Mac error code, or take your Mac to an Apple Authorized Service Provider.

Booter Selection

By default, the firmware picks the system booter file that was last specified from Startup Disk preferences. For an Intel-based Mac computer, if you're using Boot Camp to run Windows, select the system booter in the Boot Camp control panel. The booter file location is saved in your Mac nonvolatile RAM (NVRAM) so that it persists across Mac restarts. If the booter file is found, the firmware starts the booter process and the Mac begins to start up; your Mac displays the Apple logo in the center of the main display.

If the firmware can't locate a booter file, your Mac displays a flashing folder icon with a question mark.

FileVault Unlock

If the system disk is protected with FileVault, only a FileVault-enabled user can log in at the login window.

Keep in mind some additional considerations for Intel-based Mac computers with FileVault. If the system disk is protected with FileVault, an Intel-based Mac can't access the macOS booter until you unlock the system disk.

For an Intel-based Mac with FileVault, a special UEFI booter presents you with an authentication unlock screen just a few seconds after POST. It looks similar to the standard macOS login window.

After you authenticate and unlock the encrypted system disk for an Intel-based Mac, the UEFI firmware is granted access to the system volume containing the macOS booter. Startup continues as usual, with one exception: because you authenticated to unlock the system disk, macOS logs in without you authenticating again at the login window. This login happens only once per startup and only if you unlocked the encrypted system disk.

Startup Shortcuts for Intel-based Mac Computers

For Intel-based Mac computers, your Mac firmware also supports keyboard shortcuts, which, when pressed and held during initial power-on, enable you to modify the startup process. Some of these shortcuts alter the booter selection, and others modify how macOS starts up.

Firmware Updates

Firmware consists of data or programs recorded onto computer chips. When your Mac is manufactured, its firmware is programmed to instruct your Mac how to perform tasks. The type of firmware installed in your Mac can be updated if your Mac requires a change.

Firmware updates are usually included in macOS updates. They are also included when you use the Install macOS Big Sur app. See Lesson 2, "Update, Upgrade, or Reinstall macOS," for more information.

System Initialization: Booter

The booter process is started by your Mac firmware and loads the macOS kernel and enough essential kernel extensions (kexts) that the kernel can take over the system and continue the startup process. For an Intel-based Mac, firmware also passes on special startup mode instructions for the booter to handle, such as entering startup shortcuts, as described in Reference 28.4, "Modify Startup." The booter is in /System/Library/CoreServices/boot.efi.

To expedite the startup process, the booter loads cached files when possible. These caches are located in /System/Library/Caches/com.apple.kext.caches. The files contain an optimized kernel and cached kexts that load more quickly than if the Mac had to load them from scratch. If macOS detects a problem or you start macOS in safe mode (detailed in Reference 28.4), these caches are discarded, and kernel loading takes longer.

> **NOTE ▶** This guide generally refers to third-party kernel extensions as legacy system extensions and kernel extensions that are part of macOS as kexts.

After the booter loads the kernel, it displays a small progress bar below the Apple icon. Some late-model Mac computers start up so fast you may not notice the progress bar before the next stage is indicated.

A spinning globe appears when your Intel-based Mac starts up from Internet recoveryOS. The globe icon is replaced by the standard progress bar after the kernel is loaded.

If your Intel-based Mac is unsuccessful in an attempt to start up from Internet recoveryOS, it displays a globe with an alert symbol.

If your selected startup disk isn't available or doesn't contain a Mac operating system, a flashing question mark replaces the Apple icon.

If the booter can't load the kernel, a prohibitory icon replaces the Apple icon.

System Initialization: Kernel

After the booter loads the kernel and essential kexts, the kernel takes over the startup process. The kernel loaded enough kexts to read the entire file system, allowing it to load additional kexts and start the core operating system.

For Mac computers with Apple silicon, and for Intel-based Mac computers that do not have FileVault turned on, a progress bar below the Apple icon indicates the kernel startup progress.

If your Intel-based Mac has FileVault turned on:

▶ The login window will be displayed before you see a progress bar (unless an update is being installed).

▶ The login window displays all FileVault-enabled users, regardless of how you've configured Login Options in Users & Groups preferences.

▶ After you select a user, enter the correct password, then click the right arrow, your Mac displays a progress bar below the name of the user who unlocked the startup disk and is logging in.

In most cases the kernel is loaded by the booter from cached files. The kernel is also on the system volume. This file is normally hidden from users in the graphical interface.

Finally, the kernel starts the launch daemon (launchd).

System Initialization: launchd

During system startup, the progress bar below the Apple logo indicates that the kernel has fully loaded and the launchd process is starting other items.

launchd is located at /sbin/launchd and has a process identification number of 1. The System Administrator (root) user is the owner of the launchd process, so it has read/write access to every file on the system (except those files protected by SIP and privacy controls). launchd is the first parent process that spawns other child processes, and those processes go on to spawn other child processes.

The first task for the launchd process is to start all other system processes. Then launchd replaces the Apple logo with the login window or the user's desktop background.

If you have a Mac with multiple displays, you might notice a brief flash coming from the secondary displays as they power on. This is a result of launchd starting the WindowServer process, which is responsible for drawing the macOS user interface, but it's still a good indication that the system startup process is progressing.

The launchd process expedites system initialization by starting multiple system processes simultaneously, whenever possible, and starting only essential system processes at startup. After startup, the launchd process starts and stops additional system processes as needed. By dynamically managing system processes, launchd keeps your Mac responsive and running as efficiently as possible.

launchd Items

As covered in Lesson 15, "Manage System Resources," launchd preference files control how various processes are configured. The two locations for these launchd preference files are:

▶ /System/Library/LaunchDaemons folder for system processes

▶ /Library/LaunchDaemons folder for third-party processes

Viewing the launchd Hierarchy

Each process has a parent (except the kernel_task process). Some processes have a single child process and others have multiple children processes. To better understand these relationships, use Activity Monitor. Choose View > All Processes, Hierarchically. Then select any process to inspect its parent and any children. Detailed information about using Activity Monitor is covered in Lesson 20, "Manage and Troubleshoot Apps." In the following figure, the kernel_task process is listed in the PID column as 0. It has one child process, launchd, which is PID 1.

Process Name	% CPU ⌄	CPU Time	Threads	Idle Wake Ups	Architecture	% GPU	GPU Time	PID	User
⌄ kernel_task	26.8	3:54.57	482	4172	Apple	0.0	0.00	0	root
⌄ launchd	0.8	13.90	8	0	Apple	0.0	0.00	1	root
⌄ 🎹 GarageBand	13.3	1:22.50	30	309	Apple	0.0	0.01	1600	johnny
com.apple.appkit.xpc.openAndS...	0.0	0.64	3	0	Apple	0.0	0.00	2070	johnny
QuickLookUIService (com.apple....	0.0	0.03	3	0	Apple	0.0	0.00	2071	johnny
PluginLibraryService	0.0	0.03	2	0	Apple	0.0	0.00	1607	johnny
MTLCompilerService	0.0	0.10	2	0	Apple	0.0	0.00	1605	johnny
com.apple.musicapps.MAConte...	0.0	0.71	2	0	Apple	0.0	0.00	1671	johnny
com.apple.audio.InfoHelper	0.0	0.02	3	0	Apple	0.0	0.00	1999	johnny
com.apple.audio.ComponentTag...	0.0	0.01	2	0	Apple	0.0	0.00	2001	johnny

System:	6.91%	CPU LOAD	Threads:	1,921
User:	11.38%		Processes:	473
Idle:	81.71%			

NOTE ▶ The previous figure has an Architecture column, which indicates that the screen shot was made on a Mac with Apple silicon. Activity Monitor does not display an Architecture column when you run it on an Intel-based Mac.

For more information about system initialization, see Apple Support article HT204156, "If your Mac doesn't start up all the way."

Reference 28.2
User Sessions

After enough system processes start, macOS begins the processes that manage a user session.

The three main user session stages are, in order:

▶ loginwindow—This is the process responsible for presenting the login screen and logging the user in. Successful completion of this stage results in initialization of the user environment, allowing user apps to run.

▶ launchd—The launchd process works in conjunction with the loginwindow process to initialize the user environment and start any user processes or apps.

▶ User environment—This is the "space" that users' processes and apps exist in when users are logged in. The user environment is maintained by the loginwindow and launchd processes.

User Session: Login Window

As soon as the system has started enough processes to present the login window, the launchd process starts loginwindow at /System/Library/CoreServices/loginwindow.app. loginwindow runs as a background process and a graphical interface app. It coordinates the login screen and, along with the opendirectoryd process, authenticates the user. After authentication, the loginwindow process, in conjunction with the launchd process, initializes the graphical user interface (GUI) environment. The loginwindow process continues to run in the background to maintain the user session.

Some of the settings for the login window are stored in this preference file: /Library/Preferences/com.apple.loginwindow.plist. As covered in Lesson 7, "Manage User Accounts," you can configure login window settings from Users & Groups preferences.

When no user is logged in, the loginwindow process is owned by the root user. After a user authenticates to log in, the loginwindow process switches ownership from the root user to the user who successfully authenticated. Then the loginwindow process sets up the GUI environment with help from the launchd process.

User Session: launchd

The moment a user is authenticated, the loginwindow and launchd processes work together to initialize the user's environment. If fast user switching is turned on, the launchd process starts additional processes to initialize and maintain each user's environment.

The loginwindow and launchd processes set up the graphical interface environment by:

▶ Retrieving the user account information from opendirectoryd and applying any account settings

▶ Configuring the mouse, keyboard, and system sound using the user's preferences

▶ Loading the user's computing environment: preferences, environment variables, devices and file permissions, and keychain access

▶ Opening the Finder, SystemUIServer (responsible for user interface elements like menu bar status icons on the right side of the menu bar), and Dock (also responsible for Launchpad and Mission Control, which gives you an overview of your open windows and thumbnails of your full-screen apps, all arranged in a unified view)

▶ Automatically opening the user's login items

▶ Automatically resuming any app that was open before the last logout, by default, in macOS

Launch agents can be started at any time as long as a user is logged in to macOS. Most launch agents are started during the initialization of the user environment, but they could also be started afterward or on a regular repeating basis. Launch agents provided by macOS are in /System/Library/LaunchAgents, whereas third-party launch agents should be located in either /Library/LaunchAgents or ~/Library/LaunchAgents.

The loginwindow process, with help from the launchd process, starts user login items at the end of the initialization of the user environment. As covered in Lesson 7, you configure a user login item list from Users & Groups preferences.

The User Environment

The loginwindow processes continue to run as long as a user is logged in to a session. The launchd process starts user processes and apps, and the user loginwindow process monitors and maintains a user session.

The user loginwindow process monitors the user session by:

▶ Managing logout, restart, and shutdown procedures

▶ Managing the Force Quit Applications window, which includes monitoring the currently active apps and responding to user requests to forcibly quit apps

While a user is logged in to the session, the launchd process restarts user apps, such as the Finder or the Dock, that should remain open. If the user's loginwindow process is ended, whether intentionally or unexpectedly, the user's apps and processes immediately quit without saving changes. If this happens, the launchd process restarts the loginwindow process as if the Mac had just started up.

Reference 28.3
Sleep Modes, Logout, and Shutdown

Processes are also required to pause or end a user session. Your Mac computer's sleep function doesn't quit open processes. If you log out, restart, or shut down the Mac, macOS attempts to quit open processes. You can manually issue a sleep, restart, shut down, or log out command from the Apple menu.

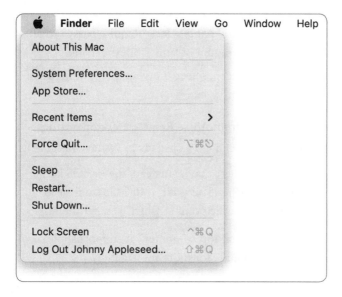

You can also quickly press and hold the power button on your Mac to put your Mac to sleep. If you press and hold the power button for more than a few seconds, you force the Mac to shut down. Shutting down your Mac might be useful if it's unresponsive. But don't shut your Mac down like this regularly, because doing so might cause data loss.

Other processes and apps can also initiate sleep, logout, or shutdown commands. For instance, the Installer and App Store apps and Software Update can request a restart when installation of new or updated software requires it.

You can configure your Mac to automatically perform certain commands related to startup, sleep, wake, and shutdown:

▶ For Mac mini computers, in Energy Saver preferences, use the "Turn display off after" slider and the "Prevent computer from sleeping automatically when the display is off" option. Additionally, for an Intel-based Mac mini computer, you can configure the "Put hard disks to sleep when possible" option.

▶ In Energy Saver preferences, click the Schedule button to set a schedule to start up or wake.

▶ In Energy Saver preferences, click the Schedule button, select the checkbox next to the menu, then choose Sleep, Restart, or Shut Down to set a schedule to sleep, restart, or shut down.

▶ In Security & Privacy preferences, in the General pane, select "Require password after sleep or screen saver begins," then choose an amount of time from the menu.

▶ In Security & Privacy preferences, click Advanced, select "Log out after _ minutes of inactivity," then enter the number of minutes.

You can manage many of these settings remotely from Apple Remote Desktop or from a mobile device management (MDM) solution.

The Mac sleep function doesn't quit active processes or apps. Instead, the macOS kernel pauses processes. This reduces the power used. When you wake your Mac from sleep mode, the kernel resumes processes and apps from the point at which you left them.

See "Change Energy Saver preferences on a Mac desktop computer" at support.apple.com/guide/mac-help/mchlp1168 in the macOS User Guide for more information.

See "Optimize energy settings for a Mac notebook" at support.apple.com/guide/mac-help/ mchlp1373 in the macOS User Guide for more information.

Other Sleep Modes

Mac computers that are compatible with macOS Big Sur support modes that use very little or no power:

► Some Mac notebook models support a deep sleep mode called *safe sleep.*

► Intel-based Mac models that start up from an internal flash or SSD storage device support a deep sleep mode called *standby mode.*

► When Mac computers go to sleep, they use less energy.

Safe Sleep

A Mac that supports safe sleep enters safe sleep if the battery becomes completely drained or if you leave your Mac idle for a long time. When your Mac enters safe sleep, the contents of system memory, including the state of apps and documents, are saved to your internal storage device, and your Mac powers off. To restart a Mac in safe sleep mode, you must press its power button. If you use a Mac notebook and its battery is low, connect the AC adapter first. When you restart a Mac from safe sleep mode, the booter process reloads the saved memory image from the system volume instead of proceeding with the normal startup process.

The booter process might indicate that the Mac is restarting from safe sleep mode by displaying the following:

► A light gray version of your Mac screen as it appeared when sleep was initiated

► A segmented progress indicator at the bottom of the main display

It should take a few moments to reload system memory. Then the kernel resumes processes and apps. If FileVault is turned on, your Mac displays the FileVault authentication unlock screen first; then the safe sleep wake process starts.

See "What is safe sleep on Mac?" at support.apple.com/guide/mac-help/ mh10328 in the macOS User Guide for more information.

Standby Mode

Intel-based Mac computers with flash storage that are compatible with macOS Big Sur enter a power-saving standby mode when they are asleep and completely idle for more than three hours. Completely idle means that macOS detects zero network or peripheral activity. When your Mac enters standby mode, the contents of system memory, including the state of apps and documents, are saved to your internal storage device. Then, your Mac removes power from some hardware systems such as RAM and USB buses. To enter standby mode, Intel-based Mac notebook computers must be running on battery power and disconnected from Ethernet, USB, Thunderbolt, SD cards, displays, Bluetooth, or any other external connections. To enter standby mode, Intel-based Mac desktop computers must have no external media mounted (such as USB or Thunderbolt storage devices or SD cards). Unlike with Mac computers in safe sleep, you don't need to restart a Mac computer in standby mode— you can wake it when you interact with the keyboard, trackpad, or mouse. While waking, your Mac might display a small, white, segmented progress bar at the bottom of the screen, similar to that of safe sleep mode, although in most cases, when a newer Mac wakes from standby it's so fast you may not notice.

Power Nap

Power Nap, available on Intel-based Mac computers with flash storage, lets some Mac computers stay up to date even while they're sleeping.

macOS Big Sur features advanced power management that's integrated with the Apple silicon chip. macOS automatically allocates tasks between parts of Apple silicon that are designed for performance and those that are designed for efficiency. One of the effects of this integration is that Power Nap isn't needed for Mac computers with Apple silicon.

When an Intel-based Mac goes to sleep, Power Nap activates periodically to update information. The information that's updated depends on whether your Mac is running on battery power or plugged into a power adapter. The Power Nap setting is in Energy Saver preferences (for Intel-based Mac desktop computers) or Battery preferences (for Intel-based Mac notebook computers). Select Enable Power Nap to turn Power Nap on or off.

The default setting varies:

▶ Intel-based Mac desktop computers that use flash storage (excluding Fusion Drive)—
   Power Nap is turned on by default.

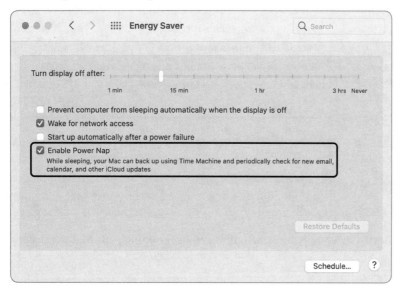

▶ Intel-based Mac notebook computers connected to a power adapter—Power Nap is
   turned on by default.

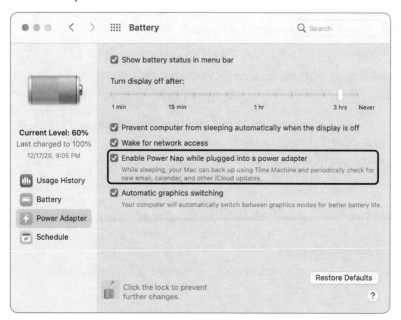

▶ Intel-based Mac notebook computers on battery and not connected to a power adapter—Power Nap is turned off by default.

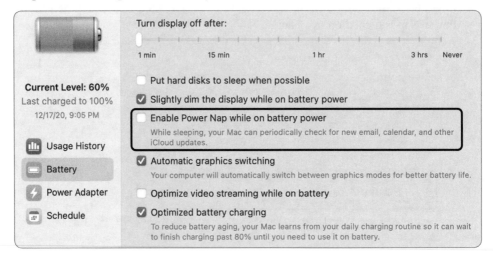

If your Mac supports Power Nap, these activities can occur while your Mac is asleep:

▶ Mail receives new messages.

▶ Contacts keep up to date with changes made on other devices.

▶ Calendar receives new invitations and calendar updates.

▶ Reminders keep up to date with changes made on other devices.

▶ Notes keep up to date with changes made on other devices.

▶ Documents stored in iCloud keep up to date with changes made on other devices.

▶ Photo Stream keeps up to date with changes made on other devices.

▶ Find My updates the location of the Mac so that you can find it while it's asleep.

▶ VPN On Demand continues working so that your corporate email updates securely. (Power Nap supports VPN connections that use a certificate to authenticate, not VPN connections that require entering a password.)

▶ An MDM solution can remotely lock and wipe your Mac.

These activities can occur while your Mac is asleep and plugged into a power outlet:

▶ Software updates download.

▶ App Store items (including software updates) download in the background.

▸ Time Machine performs backups.

▸ Spotlight performs indexing.

▸ User Guide and Help content (that appears in Help Viewer) updates.

▸ Wireless base stations can wake your Mac using Wake on Wireless.

Some Mac computers require firmware updates to support Power Nap. For more information about Power Nap and any required updates, see "What is Power Nap on Mac?" at support.apple.com/guide/mac-help/mh40773 in the macOS User Guide.

During Power Nap, your Mac plays no system sounds.

Intel-based Mac computers use Power Nap until the battery is drained. Power Nap resumes when you connect to AC power.

To increase battery life while using Power Nap, disconnect any USB or Thunderbolt devices that may draw power from the Mac.

When your Mac isn't connected to AC power, Power Nap communicates and transfers data for only a few minutes per Power Nap cycle. When your Mac is connected to AC power, communications and data transfers are continuous.

▸ Calendar, Contacts, Find My, iCloud documents, Mail, Notes, Photo Stream, and Reminders are checked every hour. To receive updates during Power Nap, Mail and Notes must be open before your Mac sleeps.

▸ Time Machine backups are attempted hourly until a successful backup is completed.

▸ Software Updates are checked daily.

▸ App Store downloads are checked once a week.

Logout

Users can log out whenever they want to end their user session, but they also have to log out to shut down or restart the Mac. When the currently logged-in user chooses to log out, the user's loginwindow process manages all logout functions with help from the launchd process.

After a user authorizes the logout, the loginwindow process issues a Quit Application Apple event to all apps. Apps that support Auto Save and Resume features can immediately save changes to any open documents and quit. Apps that don't support these features still respond to the Quit event, but they ask the user whether changes should be saved or processes terminated.

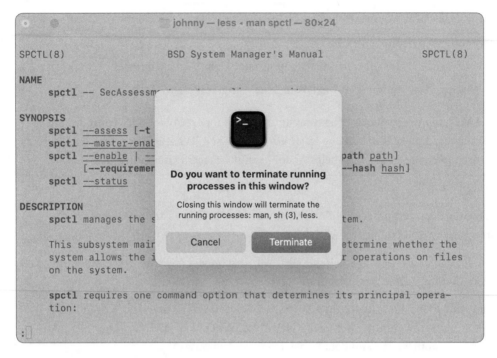

If the app fails to reply or quit, the logout process stops and loginwindow displays a message that explains why the Mac hasn't logged you out (because an app failed to quit).

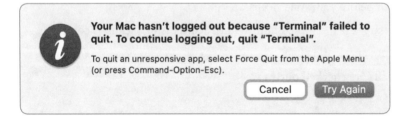

If the user's apps quit, the user's loginwindow process then forcibly quits background user processes. Finally, the user's loginwindow process closes the user's graphical interface session, runs any logout scripts, and records the logout to the main system.log file. If the user chooses only to log out, as opposed to shutting down or restarting, the user's loginwindow quits, the launchd process restarts a new loginwindow process owned by the root user, and the login screen appears.

If the user clicks Try Again and the app hasn't quit, the loginwindow process displays a message that an app interrupted logout.

"Terminal" interrupted logout.

To continue logging out, quit "Terminal".

Cancel   Try Again

Shutdown and Restart

When a logged-in user chooses to shut down or restart the Mac, the user's loginwindow process manages logout functions with help from the launchd process. First, the user's loginwindow process logs out the current user. If other users are logged in through fast user switching, loginwindow asks for administrator user authentication and, if it's granted, forcibly quits other user processes and apps, possibly losing user data.

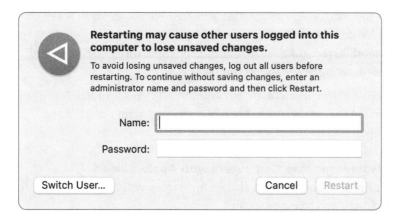

Restarting may cause other users logged into this computer to lose unsaved changes.

To avoid losing unsaved changes, log out all users before restarting. To continue without saving changes, enter an administrator name and password and then click Restart.

Name:

Password:

Switch User...   Cancel   Restart

After all user sessions are logged out, the user's loginwindow process tells the kernel to issue the quit command to remaining system processes. Processes like loginwindow should quit promptly, but the kernel must wait for processes that remain responsive while they are quitting. If system processes don't respond after a few seconds, the kernel forcibly quits them. After processes quit, the kernel stops the launchd process and shuts down the system. If a user chooses to restart the Mac, the firmware begins the macOS startup process again.

Reference 28.4
Modify Startup

This section covers how to modify the booter selection and how to modify the way macOS starts up. You can use these alternative startup and diagnostic modes to troubleshoot system issues.

There are several caveats to using startup shortcuts:

▶ If your Intel-based Mac has firmware password protection enabled, startup shortcuts are disabled until the user enters the Mac computer firmware password. Even after the user authenticates, the only startup shortcuts that work are shortcuts that access the Startup Manager or macOS Recovery. Using a firmware password is covered in Lesson 9, "Manage Security and Privacy."

▶ When you modify startup, Mac computers with FileVault turned on must still be authenticated and unlocked to proceed with system startup.

▶ Some hardware doesn't support startup shortcuts for Intel-based Mac computers, including some third-party keyboards and keyboards connected via certain USB hubs or a keyboard-video-mouse (KVM) switch. Also, although Bluetooth wireless keyboards should allow for startup shortcuts, they can be problematic—for example, if there are many Bluetooth keyboards nearby. You should have a wired USB keyboard and mouse for troubleshooting Mac desktop computers.

▶ Startup volumes selected with a shortcut are not saved in NVRAM for Intel-based Mac computers, so this setting doesn't persist between system restarts for Intel-based Mac computers.

Select an Alternate System for Mac Computers with Apple Silicon

For Mac computers with Apple silicon, you can change the startup system for one time, or change the startup system until you change it again.

To change the startup disk for a Mac with Apple silicon one time:

1   Shut down your Mac.

2   Press and hold the power button.

3   When your Mac displays the startup options window, release the power button (it should take 10 seconds).

4   Select your startup disk (with your pointer or with the Left Arrow and Right Arrow keys).

5 Click Continue or press Return.

To change the startup disk for a Mac with Apple silicon until you change the setting again:

1 Shut down your Mac.

2 Press and hold the power button.

3 When your Mac displays the startup options window, release the power button (it should take 10 seconds).

4 Select your startup disk (with your pointer or with the Left Arrow and Right Arrow keys).

5 Press and hold the Option key.

6 Click Always Use or press Return.

Select an Alternate System for Intel-based Mac Computers

For Intel-based Mac computers, you can use keyboard shortcuts to select another system, including:

▶ Option—Starts up into the Startup Manager, which enables you to select volumes containing a valid system from which to start up. This includes internal volumes, optical disc volumes, some external volumes, and, for Intel-based Mac computers that do not have the T2 chip, NetBoot images.

▶ Option-Command-R or Option-Shift-Command-R—These shortcuts force the Mac to start up from Internet recoveryOS, which in turn contacts Apple to download recoveryOS. See Apple Support article HT204904, "How to reinstall macOS," for more information about which version of macOS this installs (the possibilities include: the macOS that came with your Mac [or the closest version still available]; the latest macOS that was installed on your Mac; or the latest macOS that is compatible with your Mac). Lesson 5, "Use macOS Recovery," explores this topic in more detail.

▶ Command-R—Starts up to the local macOS Recovery, if available. If no local macOS Recovery is found, Intel-based Mac computers start up from Internet recoveryOS.

▶ D—Starts up to Apple Diagnostics if available. If no local resources are available, Mac computers will start up to Apple Diagnostics with an internet connection to Apple servers. See the next section for more information about Apple Diagnostics.

▶ Option-D—This shortcut forces startup Apple Diagnostics through an internet connection to Apple servers. See the next section for more information about Apple Diagnostics.

See Apple Support article HT201255, "Mac startup key combinations," for more information.

Use Apple Diagnostics

You can use Apple Diagnostics, formerly known as Apple Hardware Test, to check your Mac for hardware issues.

The way to start Apple Diagnostics depends on the kind of Mac you have.

For a Mac with Apple silicon:

1 Shut down your Mac if it's not already turned off.

2 Press and hold the power button as your Mac starts up (it should take 10 seconds).

3 When you see the startup options window, release the power button.

4 Press and hold Command-D on your keyboard.

5 Continue holding Command-D until your Mac restarts and opens Apple Diagnostics.

For an Intel-based Mac computer:

1   Shut down your Mac if it's not already turned off.

2   Turn on your Mac, then immediately press and hold the D key on your keyboard.

3   Release the D key when you see a progress bar or you're asked to choose a language.

   After you choose a language and click OK, read the information, then click "I agree."

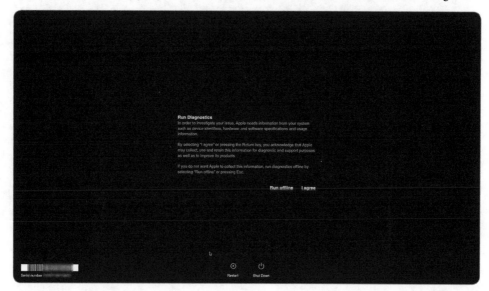

Wait while Apple Diagnostics runs. Your Mac displays a progress bar while Apple Diagnostics checks your Mac.

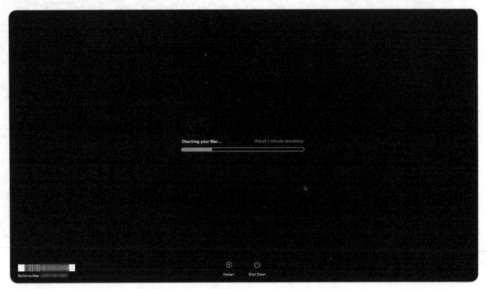

If Apple Diagnostics finds issues, it returns one or more reference codes. Otherwise, it displays "No issues found."

For a Mac with Apple silicon, you can click the "Get started" link to look up reference codes at Apple Support article HT203747, "Apple Diagnostics reference codes." For an Intel-based Mac, you can get more options by clicking the "Get started" link.

At this point, you can take any of the following actions:

▶   If "Run the test again" is displayed, click it (or press Command-R).

▶   Click Restart (or press R), then click Restart.

▶   Click Shut Down (or press S), then click Shut Down.

See Apple Support article HT202731, "Use Apple Diagnostics to test your Mac," for more information.

Use Safe Mode

Safe mode (sometimes called safe boot) is a way to start up your Mac so that it performs certain checks and prevents some software from automatically loading or opening. Starting your Mac in safe mode does the following:

▶   Verifies your startup disk and attempts to repair directory issues, if needed

▶   Loads only required system extensions

▶   Prevents login items from opening automatically

▶   Disables user-installed fonts

▶   Deletes font caches, the kernel cache, and other system cache files

The method to start your Mac varies.

For a Mac computer with Apple silicon:

1   Shut down your Mac.

2   Press and hold the power button.

3   When your Mac displays the startup options window, release the power button (it should take 10 seconds).

4   Select your startup disk (with your pointer or with the Left Arrow and Right Arrow keys).

5   Press and hold the Shift key.

6   Click "Continue in Safe Mode" or press Return.

7   Release the Shift key.

For an Intel-based Mac:

1   Turn on or restart your Mac, then immediately press and hold the Shift key.

2   When your Mac displays an Apple logo and a progress bar, or the login window, release the Shift key.

A Mac in safe mode shows the words Safe Boot in bright red text in the upper-right corner of the login screen.

On an Intel-based Mac, if FileVault is turned on, the first login window is displayed without the words Safe Boot in the upper-right corner. After you successfully authenticate at the first login window, the startup disk is unlocked and macOS starts in safe mode. Then your Mac displays a login window with the words Safe Boot in the upper-right corner.

After you log in, your Mac does not display Safe Boot in the menu bar until the screen locks or you log out.

You can also verify safe mode after login by opening System Information. The Software section of System Information lists Boot Mode as "Safe" instead of "Normal" when you're started in safe mode.

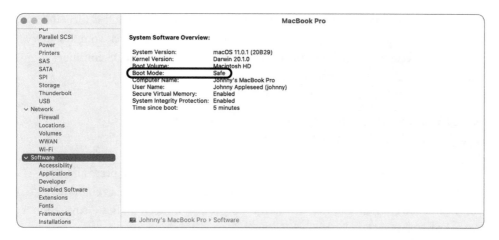

When your Mac is started in safe mode, it might take some time for your Mac to start up and for your graphics to load. Additionally, your Mac displays elements like the Dock, the menu bar, and windows without the transparency usually associated with macOS Big Sur.

For more information about safe boot, see Apple Support article HT201262, "How to use safe mode on your Mac."

Verbose Mode and Single-User Mode for Intel-based Mac Computers

Two other startup shortcuts for Intel-based Mac computers that modify the macOS default startup are:

▶ Command-V—Starts up macOS on an Intel-based Mac in verbose mode. In verbose mode, the system does not hide the startup progress from you. Instead, your Intel-based Mac displays a black background with white text showing details of the startup process.

▶ Command-S—Starts up macOS on an Intel-based Mac in single-user mode. When starting up in single-user mode, the system starts only core kernel and operating system functionality. You must be familiar with the command-line interface to use single-user mode. If your Mac has the T2 chip with Secure Boot set to Full Security or Medium Security, then pressing and holding the Command-S keys during startup results in verbose mode instead of single-user mode.

If you have a Mac with Apple silicon, or an Intel-based Mac that has the T2 chip, you can start from recoveryOS, then choose Utilities > Terminal instead of using single-user mode.

For verbose mode or single-user mode on an Intel-based Mac, if FileVault is turned on, you must provide a password at the first login window in order to unlock your system disk. After you successfully authenticate at the first login window, macOS continues to start in verbose mode or single-user mode.

Other Startup Shortcuts for Intel-based Mac Computers

Here are some other startup shortcuts for Intel-based Mac computers:

▶ T—For Mac computers with built-in USB-C or Thunderbolt ports, press and hold this key to start up your Mac in target disk mode, allowing other Mac computers to access the Mac computer's internal volume. Target disk mode details are covered in Lesson 11, "Manage File Systems and Storage."

▶ Option-Command-P-R—This shortcut resets NVRAM settings and restarts your Mac.

▶ Eject key, F12 key, mouse button, or trackpad button—These shortcuts eject any removable media.

Reference 28.5
Troubleshoot System Initialization

After you identify system initialization stages—and know which processes and files are responsible for each—you are on your way to diagnosing startup issues. The troubleshooting sections that follow are organized by each system initialization stage.

Safe mode can help you find and resolve issues. And for Intel-based Mac computers without the T2 chip, verbose mode and single-user mode can help you find and resolve issues as well. These three modes are initiated at the firmware stage but affect the remaining system initialization process.

Troubleshoot Firmware Issues

If your Mac can't reach the point where the Apple logo appears, you probably have a firmware issue. Determine whether this issue is related to the Mac hardware or system volume.

Intel-based Mac computers with hardware issues might benefit from a resetting the Mac computer's NVRAM or System Management Controller (SMC). For more information about resetting these items, see Apple Support article HT204063, "Reset NVRAM or PRAM on your Mac," and article HT201295, "How to reset the SMC of your Mac."

In very rare circumstances, such as a power failure during an upgrade of macOS, your Mac with Apple silicon or your Intel-based Mac with the T2 chip may become unresponsive. For a Mac with Apple silicon, you might need to revive the firmware. For an Intel-based Mac with the T2 chip, you might have to revive the firmware on the T2 chip.

See the following articles in the Apple Configurator 2 User Guide for more information:

▶ "Revive or restore a Mac with Apple silicon with Apple Configurator 2," at support. apple.com/guide/apple-configurator-2/apdd5f3c75ad

▶ "Revive or restore an Intel-based Mac with Apple Configurator 2," at support.apple. com/guide/apple-configurator-2/apdebea5be51

Hardware Issues

If your Mac doesn't make a startup tone, flash a power-on light, or display light on the screen when powering on, the Mac hardware may not have passed the POST. Additionally, if your Mac makes diagnostic tones or displays a series of power-on flashes, your Mac has a hardware issue. For more information about the startup tones, see Apple Support article HT202768, "If your Mac beeps during startup."

> **NOTE** ▶ Previous versions of macOS didn't play a sound on startup. If you'd like to turn off the startup sound, you can deselect the "Play sound on startup" option in Sound preferences. See Apple Support article HT211996, "Turn the Mac startup sound on or off," for more information.

Always check for simple things first. Is the Mac plugged into an electrical outlet? Are the keyboard and mouse working properly? A failure to pass the POST is usually indicative of a serious hardware issue. If this is the case, take your Mac to an Apple Store or Apple Authorized Service Provider.

System Volume Issues

If your Mac displays a flashing question mark folder icon, the firmware can't locate a valid system volume or booter file. The Mac main processor and components probably work correctly, and you might have a software issue.

If your Mac has Apple silicon, use the following procedure to locate system volumes:

1 Shut down your Mac.

2 Press and hold the power button.

3 When your Mac displays the startup options window, release the power button (it should take 10 seconds).

4   Select your startup disk (with your pointer or with the Left Arrow and Right Arrow keys).

5   Click Continue or press Return.

If your Mac is an Intel-based Mac, turn it off, then turn it on and hold the Option key during startup. Then use Startup Manager to locate system volumes.

To troubleshoot system volume issues:

▶   If the original system volume appears, select it to start up. If your Mac starts up from the system on the volume, open Startup Disk preferences to reset the volume as the startup disk. You can also try to define the startup disk when it's booted from another system volume, like macOS Recovery.

▶   If the original system volume appears but your Mac still can't find a valid system or booter, you may need to reinstall macOS on that volume. Back up important data from that volume before you make significant changes.

▶   If your original system volume doesn't appear, the issue is with that storage device. Start up from another system, like macOS Recovery, and use the storage troubleshooting techniques outlined in Lesson 11.

Troubleshoot Booter Issues

If your Mac displays a prohibitory icon, the kernel probably failed to load. To troubleshoot the booter:

▶   If you start up your Mac from a volume that contains an operating system the Mac never booted from, the prohibitory icon usually indicates that the version of macOS on the volume isn't compatible with your Mac hardware. This rare case occurs mainly when a new Mac is restored using an older system image. Reinstall macOS using macOS Recovery, which should install a version that works with your hardware.

▶   Start up the Mac in safe mode. The booter tries to verify and repair the startup volume. If repairs are needed, the Mac restarts before continuing. If this happens, start in safe mode again. The booter verifies the startup volume again, and if the volume appears to be working properly, the booter tries to load the kernel and essential kexts again. The booter judiciously and slowly loads the items and clears the kext and font caches. If successful, the booter passes the system to the kernel, which continues to safe-boot.

▶   If the booter can't find or load a valid kernel, reinstall macOS on that volume.

Troubleshoot Kernel Issues for Intel-based Mac Computers

If your Intel-based Mac displays the Apple logo startup screen and the Apple icon or progress bar but can't reach the login window or log in, then third-party legacy system extensions (also called third-party kernel extensions) or launchd probably failed to load. To troubleshoot the kernel for an Intel-based Mac:

▸ Start up the Intel-based Mac, and then press and hold the Shift key to initiate safe mode. This forces the kernel to ignore third-party legacy system extensions. If this is successful, the kernel starts launchd, which continues to start up in safe mode. If the kernel startup stage completes through safe mode, the issue might be a third-party legacy system extension. Start up in verbose mode to try to find the problem.

▸ Start up the Intel-based Mac, then press and hold Command-V to initiate verbose mode. The Mac shows you startup process details as a continuous string of text. If the text stops, the startup process has probably also stopped and you should examine the end of the text for troubleshooting clues. When you find a suspicious item, move it to a quarantine folder and restart the Mac without safe mode to determine if the problem was resolved. Accessing the Mac computer disk to locate and remove the item might not be possible if the Mac is crashing during startup. As covered in Lesson 11, you can start a Mac that's experiencing issues in target disk mode, then connect it to a second Mac. You can then use the second Mac to modify the contents of the storage device that is experiencing issues.

▸ If your problem Intel-based Mac successfully starts up in safe mode and you're still trying to find the issue, don't use safe mode and verbose mode at the same time. If startup succeeds, verbose mode is replaced by the standard startup interface, and you won't have time to find problems.

▸ If the kernel can't load during safe mode, or you are unable to locate and repair the problem, you may need to reinstall macOS on that volume.

Troubleshoot launchd Issues

If you can't get to the login screen or log in when the login screen appears, it's probably a launchd issue. If launchd isn't able to complete system initialization, the loginwindow process doesn't start. To troubleshoot launchd issues:

▸ Start up the Mac in safe mode. Safe mode forces launchd to ignore third-party fonts and launch daemons. If your startup in safe mode is successful, the launchd process starts the loginwindow process. At this point the Mac fully starts up and runs in safe mode. If you can complete system initialization with safe mode, the issue might be a third-party system initialization item. Start up in verbose mode to find it.

▶ For an Intel-based Mac, start up the Mac, then press and hold Command-V to initiate verbose mode. If the text stops scrolling down the screen, examine the end of the text; if you find a suspicious item, move it to another folder and then restart the Mac.

▶ You may be able to start up into the Finder in safe mode. If so, use the Finder to quarantine suspicious items.

▶ In safe mode, consider removing or renaming system cache and preference files, since they can be corrupted and cause startup issues. Remove /Library/Caches first. These files contain easily replaced information. Remove settings that are stored in the /Library/Preferences or /Library/Preferences/SystemConfiguration folders, but only if you can reconfigure them later. Or rename System Preferences files in these folders. After you move or rename these items, restart the Mac, and macOS replaces them with new versions.

▶ If starting up in safe mode continues to fail or you locate a suspicious system item you need to remove, start up the Intel-based Mac without the T2 chip, then press and hold Command-S to initiate single-user mode. Or if your Mac has Apple silicon, or your Intel-based Mac has the T2 chip, start up from recoveryOS, then open Terminal. Your Mac provides a minimal command-line interface that enables you to move suspicious files to a quarantine folder. If you want to modify files and folders in single-user mode, prepare the system volume. Enter **/sbin/fsck -fy** to verify and repair the startup volume. Repeat this command until there is a message stating that the disk appears to be OK. Then, enter **/sbin/mount -uw /** to mount the startup volume as a read-and-write file system. After you make your changes, exit single-user mode and enter the **exit** command to continue to start up the Mac. Shut down the Mac with the **shutdown -h now** command.

▶ If system initialization can't complete during startup in safe mode or you are unable to locate and repair the problem, reinstall macOS.

Reference 28.6
Troubleshoot User Sessions

If the loginwindow process can't initialize the user environment, the user can't control the interface. Your Mac might display the user's desktop background picture, but no apps load, including the Dock and the Finder. Or the user session starts, but the login screen reappears.

Safe Mode Login

Try safe mode login. At the login screen, press and hold the Shift key while you click the Log In button. Perform a safe mode login when you need to troubleshoot user issues, even if you didn't start up in safe mode. With safe mode enabled, the loginwindow process doesn't automatically open user-defined login items or apps that are set to resume. The launchd process doesn't start user-specific LaunchAgents. If safe mode login resolves your user session issue, adjust the user's Login Items list from Users & Groups preferences or adjust items in /Library/LaunchAgents or ~/Library/LaunchAgents.

Troubleshoot Logout and Shutdown

If you can't log out or shut down, it's probably because an app or process won't quit. If you can't log out, use Force Quit from the Apple menu. See Lesson 20 for more information.

If your Mac displays a blank screen after all your apps quit, the loginwindow process closed your user session and your Mac won't shut down. Give macOS a few moments to shut down. If a few moments pass and nothing happens, a system process isn't quitting. To force your Mac to shut down, press and hold the power button until the Mac powers off.

Exercise 28.1
Use Safe Mode

In this exercise, you start up your Mac in safe mode and identify visual startup cues.

Start Up in Safe Mode

When you use safe mode, macOS clears specific caches, carefully tests startup procedures, and limits automatically launched processes during each startup stage. Many nonessential system and third-party items are ignored. If your Mac fails to start up normally, safe mode is a noninvasive and effective choice to troubleshoot the startup.

1 Turn on your Mac, then log in to your Mac as Local Administrator.

2 Open Activity Monitor.

3 Choose View > All Processes.

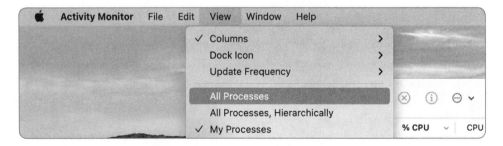

4 Record the number of processes shown at the bottom of the Activity Monitor window just to the right of the CPU Load graph.

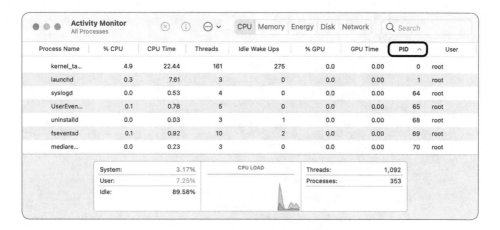

5   From the Apple menu, choose Restart. Press and hold the Shift key until your Mac displays the Apple logo on the screen. At the FileVault authentication screen, log in as Local Administrator to allow the Mac to start up.

After your Mac displays the FileVault authentication screen, you are past the startup process. At this point, any modifier keys you held down have been recognized, and you don't have to press and hold them again.

After your Mac starts up, you are presented with the login window, even if you have turned on automatic login. That's because safe mode disables automatic login, which is the default behavior when your Mac is protected with FileVault. Safe Boot appears in the menu bar.

6   Log in as Local Administrator. You notice that the Dock and menu bar lose transparency as safe mode disables nonessential drivers such as those for your graphics processor.

Safe mode disables automatic login, which is the default behavior when your Mac is protected with FileVault.

7   Open Activity Monitor, then record the number of processes running.

Because safe mode starts only essential processes for system operation, fewer processes run. For example, if you try to find Activity Monitor with Spotlight, you can't. Also, your screen may be redrawn unpredictably.

8   Close Activity Monitor, then restart your Mac.

Index